Fundamentals of

MULTINATIONAL FINANCE

Edition IV

The Prentice Hall Series in Finance

Adelman/Marks
Entrepreneurial Finance

Andersen
Global Derivatives: A Strategic Risk Management Perspective

Bekaert/Hodrick
International Financial Management

Berk/DeMarzo
Corporate Finance*

Berk/DeMarzo
Corporate Finance: The Core*

Berk/DeMarzo/Harford
Fundamentals of Corporate Finance*

Boakes
Reading and Understanding the Financial Times

Brooks
Financial Management: Core Concepts*

Copeland/Weston/Shastri
Financial Theory and Corporate Policy

Dorfman/Cather
Introduction to Risk Management and Insurance

Eiteman/Stonehill/Moffett
Multinational Business Finance

Fabozzi
Bond Markets: Analysis and Strategies

Fabozzi/Modigliani
Capital Markets: Institutions and Instruments

Fabozzi/Modigliani/Jones/Ferri
Foundations of Financial Markets and Institutions

Finkler
Financial Management for Public, Health, and Not-for-Profit Organizations

Frasca
Personal Finance

Gitman/Joehnk/Smart
Fundamentals of Investing*

Gitman/Zutter
Principles of Managerial Finance*

Gitman/Zutter
Principles of Managerial Finance—Brief Edition*

Goldsmith
Consumer Economics: Issues and Behaviors

Haugen
The Inefficient Stock Market: What Pays Off and Why

Haugen
The New Finance: Overreaction, Complexity, and Uniqueness

Holden
Excel Modeling in Corporate Finance

Holden
Excel Modeling in Investments

Hughes/MacDonald
International Banking: Text and Cases

Hull
Fundamentals of Futures and Options Markets

Hull
Options, Futures, and Other Derivatives

Hull
Risk Management and Financial Institutions

Keown
Personal Finance: Turning Money into Wealth*

Keown/Martin/Petty
Foundations of Finance: The Logic and Practice of Financial Management*

Kim/Nofsinger
Corporate Governance

Madura
Personal Finance*

Marthinsen
Risk Takers: Uses and Abuses of Financial Derivatives

McDonald
Derivatives Markets

McDonald
Fundamentals of Derivatives Markets

Mishkin/Eakins
Financial Markets and Institutions

Moffett/Stonehill/Eiteman
Fundamentals of Multinational Finance

Nofsinger
Psychology of Investing

Ormiston/Fraser
Understanding Financial Statements

Pennacchi
Theory of Asset Pricing

Rejda
Principles of Risk Management and Insurance

Seiler
Performing Financial Studies: A Methodological Cookbook

Shapiro
Capital Budgeting and Investment Analysis

Sharpe/Alexander/Bailey
Investments

Solnik/McLeavey
Global Investments

Stretcher/Michael
Cases in Financial Management

Titman/Keown/Martin
Financial Management: Principles and Applications*

Titman/Martin
Valuation: The Art and Science of Corporate Investment Decisions

Van Horne
Financial Management and Policy

Van Horne/Wachowicz
Fundamentals of Financial Management

Weston/Mitchel/Mulherin
Takeovers, Restructuring, and Corporate Governance

*denotes  myfinancelab titles   Log onto **www.myfinancelab.com** to learn more

Fundamentals of
MULTINATIONAL FINANCE

Edition IV

MICHAEL H. MOFFETT

Thunderbird School of Global Management

ARTHUR I. STONEHILL

Oregon State University and University of Hawaii at Manoa

DAVID K. EITEMAN

University of California, Los Angeles

Boston Columbus Indianapolis New York San Francisco Upper Saddle River
Amsterdam Cape Town Dubai London Madrid Milan Munich Paris Montreal Toronto
Delhi Mexico City Sao Paulo Sydney Hong Kong Seoul Singapore Taipei Tokyo

Editorial Director: Sally Yagan
Editor-in-Chief: Donna Battista
Acquisitions Editor: Tessa O'Brien
Editorial Project Manager: Amy Foley
Editorial Assistant: Elissa Senra-Sargent
Director of Marketing: Patrice Jones
Marketing Assistant: Ian Gold
Senior Managing Editor: Nancy H. Fenton
Senior Production Project Manager: Meredith Gertz
Production Coordinator: Alison Eusden
Permissions Project Supervisor: Michael Joyce
Permissions Editor: Tracy Metivier
Cover Designer: Jodi Notowitz
Senior Manufacturing Buyer: Carol Melville
Media Producer: Nicole Sackin
Image Manager/Image Asset Services: Rachel Youdelman
Copyeditor: Kathleen Cantwell, C4 Technologies
Proofreader: Holly McLean-Aldis
Indexer: Jack Lewis
Production Coordination and Text Design: Gillian Hall, The Aardvark Group
Composition and Art Creation: Laserwords, Ltd.

Credits and acknowledgments borrowed from other sources and reproduced, with permission, in this textbook appear on appropriate page within the text and as follows: Photo on part and chapter opening pages by Henk Badenhorst/iStockphoto. Photo on page 61 by G. Prentice/iStockphoto.

Many of the designations by manufacturers and sellers to distinguish their products are claimed as trademarks. Where those designations appear in this book, and the publisher was aware of a trademark claim, the designations have been printed in initial caps or all caps.

If you purchased this book within the United States or Canada you should be aware that it has been imported without the approval of the Publisher or the Author.

10 9 8 7 6 5 4 3 2 1

ISBN-10:   0-13-282991-6
ISBN-13:   978-0-13-282991-5

Preface

Fundamentals of Multinational Finance, Fourth Edition, is a major change from previous editions. It has been re-focused to the multitude of financial management challenges faced by the business leaders of tomorrow in multinational business—with three points of emphasis.

◆ **Organizations of all kinds.**   Multinational enterprises (MNEs) applies to organizations of all kinds—the publicly traded, the privately held, the state-run, the state-owned organizations—all forms that permeate global business today.

◆ **Emerging markets.**   Firms from all countries and all markets are looking to the economic drivers of the global economy today, the emerging markets. These country markets present a multitude of specific risks, opportunities, and challenges for business and multinational finance.

◆ **Financial leadership.**   The leaders of MNEs face numerous foreign exchange and political risks. These risks can be daunting but they also present opportunities for creating value if properly understood. These opportunities and risks are most effectively understood in the context of the global business itself, and the ability of management to integrate the strategic and financial challenges that business faces.

Audience

Fundamentals of Multinational Finance, Fourth Edition, is aimed at university-level courses in international financial management, international business finance, international finance, and similar titles. It can be used at either the undergraduate or graduate level as well as in executive education and corporate learning courses.

A prerequisite course or experience in corporate finance or financial management would be ideal. However, we review the basic finance concepts before we extend them to the multinational case. We also review the basic concepts of international economics and international business.

We recognize the fact that a large number of our potential adopters live outside of the United States and Canada. Therefore, we utilize a significant number of non-U.S. examples, Mini-Cases, and *Global Finance in Practice* examples seen in the business and news press (anecdotes and illustrations).

Organization

Fundamentals of Multinational Finance, Fourth Edition, has a number of new subjects, but is also shorter. This has been accomplished by integrating a number of previous topics along financial management threads. The book is in six parts, the parts unified by the common thread of the globalization process by which a firm moves from a domestic to a multinational business orientation.

◆ Part 1 introduces the global financial environment
◆ Part 2 explains foreign exchange theory and markets
◆ Part 3 analyzes foreign exchange rate exposure
◆ Part 4 explores the financing of the global firm
◆ Part 5 analyzes international investment decisions
◆ Part 6 examines special topics in international finance

The final section, Part 6, has been moved to the book's Web site at www.pearsonhighered.com/moffett. This allows us to provide you with a shorter physical text while still providing you access to selective topics which you may or may not wish to use.

New in the Fourth Edition

The theme for this Fourth Edition could be what some people call the *New Normal*. A world in which the developed or industrialized countries see slower growth, poorer job opportunities, and a growing insecurity over their competitiveness in the global marketplace.

The MNEs in this new world are not only dependent on the emerging markets for cheaper labor, raw materials, and outsourced manufacturing, but increasingly on those markets for sales and profits. These markets—whether they be labeled as BRICs (Brazil, Russia, India, China) or some other popular label—represent the majority of the earth's population and therefore consumers. We have pursued this growing theme throughout the book.

A short overview of the features in the Fourth Edition.

◆ We have worked to increase the clarity of principles and practices of the *fundamentals* of multinational finance—to accentuate the purpose behind the book's title
◆ We have integrated emerging market content throughout, highlighting both the promise and challenges of financial management in a global marketplace where the future likely rests with these countries and cultures
◆ Chapter 5 is an entirely new chapter detailing the global credit crisis of 2007–2009, including how the financial crisis spread like a contagion across the global financial markets
◆ 12 of the 19 Mini-Cases in the book are new, and the majority are inclusive of emerging market business, and we have tried to follow the same themes in the *Global Finance in Practice* boxes

In order to create a shorter, tighter text for today's more complex courses, we have merged and integrated a number of concepts and chapters.

◆ Chapters on currency derivatives—futures, options, and swaps—have been combined
◆ Chapters on transaction and translation exposures, the traditional accounting-based exposures in international finance, have been combined
◆ Chapters on the financial structures and capital sourcing strategies employed by multinational firms have been restructured and reorganized for a tighter presentation
◆ Three chapters that are the least utilized by adoptors according to user surveys—International Portfolio Theory and Diversification, Working Capital Management, and International Trade Finance—have been moved to the book's Web site at www.pearsonhighered.com/moffett to allow a shorter physical text but still provide full access to these subjects as the adoptors desire

A final note on style. International finance is a subject of sophistication, constant change, yet rich in history. We have tried to bridge the past and future with a mix of currency notations and symbols throughout the book, using both the increasingly common three-letter currency codes—USD, CNY, EUR—with the currency symbols of the past—$, ¥, £, €—which live on in modern media.

Pedagogical Tools

To make *Fundamentals of Multinational Finance,* Fourth Edition, as comprehensible as possible, we use a large number of proven pedagogical tools. Again, our efforts have been informed by the detailed reviews and suggestions of a panel of professors who are recognized individually for excellence in the field of international finance, particularly at the undergraduate level. Among these pedagogical tools are the following:

◆ A student-friendly writing style is utilized combined with a structured presentation of material, beginning with *learning objectives* for each chapter, and ending with a summarization of how those learning objectives were realized.

◆ A wealth of *illustrations and exhibits* provide a visual parallel to the concepts and content presented. The entire book utilizes a multi-color presentation that we believe provides a visual attractiveness, which contributes significantly to reader attention and retention.

◆ A running case on a hypothetical U.S.-based firm, *Trident Corporation*, provides a cohesive framework for the multifaceted globalization process, and is reinforced in several end-of-chapter problems.

◆ A *Mini-Case* at the end of each chapter illustrates the chapter (19 in all) content and extends it to the multinational financial business environment. And as noted, 12 of the 19 Mini-Cases in Fourth Edition are new.

◆ *Global Finance in Practice* boxes in every chapter illuminate the theory with accounts of actual business practices. These applications extend the concepts without adding to the length of the text itself.

◆ The power and resources of the *Internet* are leveraged throughout the text in a variety of applications. Every chapter has a number of end-of-chapter exercises requiring the use of the Internet, while a variety of Internet references are dispersed throughout the chapters in text and exhibits.

◆ A multitude of end-of-chapter questions and problems, which assess the students' understanding of the course material, are included. All end-of-chapter problems are solved using spreadsheet solutions. Selected end-of-chapter problem answers, indicated by an asterisk (*), are now included at the back of the book.

A Rich Array of Support Materials

A robust package of materials for both instructor and student accompanies the text to facilitate learning and to support teaching and testing.

◆ **Online Instructor's Manual.**   The Online Instructor's Manual, prepared by the authors, contains complete answers to all end-of-chapter questions, problems, and chapter Mini-Cases. All quantitative end-of-chapter problems are solved using spreadsheets, which are also available online.

◆ **Online Test Item File.**   The Online Test Item File, prepared by Curtis Bacon of the University of Southern Oregon, contains over 1,200 multiple-choice and short-essay questions. The multiple-choice questions are labeled by topic and by category—recognition, conceptual, and analytical types.

◆ **Computerized Test Bank.**   The Test Item File is also available in Pearson Education's TestGen Software. Fully networkable, it is available for Windows and Macintosh. TestGen's graphical interface enables instructors to view, edit and add questions; transfer questions to tests; and print different forms of tests. Search-and-sort features enable the instructor to locate questions quickly and arrange them in a preferred order. The TestGen plug-in allows the instructor to administer TestGen tests in CourseCompass QuizMaster, working with your school's computer network, automatically grades the exams, stores the results on a disk, and allows the instructor to view and print a variety of reports.

◆ **Online Mini-Case PowerPoint Presentations.**   A significant addition to the instructor's resources in this new Fourth Edition, each of the 24 Mini-Cases has a standalone PowerPoint presentation available online.

◆ **Online PowerPoint Presentation Slides.**   The extensive set of PowerPoint slides Center provides lecture outlines and selected graphics from the text for each chapter.

◆ **Study Guide.**   Prepared by Onur Arugaslan of Western Michigan University, the Study Guide enhances understanding and retention for concepts by providing detailed study outlines and helps students prepare for tests through a series of self-test questions, including true/false, multiple-choice, and short essay—all with answers.

◆ **Web Site.**   A dedicated Web site at www.pearsonhighered.com/moffett contains the Web exercises from the book with wired links, electronic flash cards of glossary terms, and selected solutions and spreadsheets for end-of-chapter problems. In addition, Part 6 of this book, "Topics in International Finance," now appears on the Web site.

All of the teaching resources are available online for download at the Instructor Resource Center at www.pearsonhighered.com/irc and on the catalog page for *Fundamentals of Multinational Finance.*

International Editions

Fundamentals of Multinational Finance and *Multinational Business Finance* have been used throughout the world to teach students of international finance. Our books are published in a number of foreign languages including Chinese, French, Spanish, Indonesian, Portuguese, and Ukrainian.

Acknowledgments

The authors are very thankful for the many detailed reviews of previous editions and suggestions from a number of colleagues. The final version of *Fundamentals of Multinational Finance,* Fourth Edition reflects most of the suggestions provided by these reviewers. The survey reviewers were anonymous, but the detailed reviewers were:

Cetin Ciner, *University of North Carolina, Wilmington*
Bento J. Lobo, *University of Tennessee, Chattanooga*
Robert Wyatt, *University of Northern Iowa*
Larry Wolken, *Texas A&M*
Ling He, *University of Central Arkansas*

Kristine Beck, *University of Wisconsin*
Tim Manuel, *University of Montana*
Amy Yueh-Fang Ho, *University of South Florida*

We would also like to thank all those with Pearson Education who have worked so diligently on this edition: Tessa O'Brien, Amy Foley, and Meredith Gertz. In addition, Gillian Hall, our outstanding project manager at The Aardvark Group, deserves much gratitude.

Finally, we would like to dedicate this book to our parents, Bennie Ruth and the late Hoy Moffett, the late Harold and Norma Stonehill, and the late Wilford and Sylvia Eiteman, who gave us the motivation to become academicians and authors. We thank our wives, Megan, Kari, and Keng-Fong, for their patience while we were preparing *Fundamentals of Multinational Finance,* Fourth Edition.

Glendale, Arizona	M.H.M.
Honolulu, Hawaii	A.I.S.
Pacific Palisades, California	D.K.E.

About the Authors

Michael H. Moffett. Michael H. Moffett is Continental Grain Professor in Finance at the Thunderbird School of Global Management, where he has been since 1994. He also has held teaching or research appointments at Oregon State University (1985–1993); the University of Michigan, Ann Arbor (1991–1993); the Brookings Institution, Washington, D.C.; the University of Hawaii at Manoa; the Aarhus School of Business (Denmark); the Helsinki School of Economics and Business Administration (Finland), the International Centre for Public Enterprises (Yugoslavia); and the University of Colorado, Boulder.

Professor Moffett received a B.A. (Economics) from the University of Texas at Austin (1977), an M.S. (Resource Economics) from Colorado State University (1979), an M.A. (Economics) from the University of Colorado, Boulder (1983), and Ph.D. (Economics) from the University of Colorado, Boulder (1985).

He has authored, co-authored, or contributed to a number of books, articles, and other publications. He has co-authored two books with Art Stonehill and David Eiteman, *Multinational Business Finance*, and this book, *Fundamentals of Multinational Finance*. His articles have appeared in the *Journal of Financial and Quantitative Analysis, Journal of Applied Corporate Finance, Journal of International Money and Finance, Journal of International Financial Management and Accounting, Contemporary Policy Issues, Brookings Discussion Papers in International Economics*, and others. He has contributed to a number of collected works including the *Handbook of Modern Finance*, the *International Accounting and Finance Handbook*, and the *Encyclopedia of International Business*. He is also co-author of two books in multinational business with Michael Czinkota and Ilkka Ronkainen, *International Business* (7th Edition) and *Global Business* (4th Edition), and *The Global Oil and Gas Industry: Strategy, Finance, and Management*, with Andrew Inkpen.

Arthur I. Stonehill. Arthur I. Stonehill is a Professor of Finance and International Business, Emeritus, at Oregon State University, where he taught for 24 years (1966-1990). During 1991–1997 he held a split appointment at the University of Hawaii at Manoa and Copenhagen Business School. From 1997 to 2001 he continued as a Visiting Professor at the University of Hawaii at Manoa He has also held teaching or research appointments at the University of California, Berkeley; Cranfield School of Management (U.K.); and the North European Management Institute (Norway). He was a former president of the

Academy of International Business, and was a western director of the Financial Management Association.

Professor Stonehill received a B.A. (History) from Yale University (1953); an M.B.A. from Harvard Business School (1957); and a Ph.D. in Business Administration from the University of California, Berkeley (1965). He was awarded honorary doctorates from the Aarhus School of Business (Denmark, 1989), the Copenhagen Business School (Denmark, 1992), and Lund University (Sweden, 1998).

He has authored or co-authored nine books and twenty-five other publications. His articles have appeared in *Financial Management, Journal of International Business Studies, California Management Review, Journal of Financial and Quantitative Analysis, Journal of International Financial Management and Accounting, International Business Review, European Management Journal, The Investment Analyst (U.K.), Nationaløkonomisk Tidskrift (Denmark), Sosialøkonomen (Norway), Journal of Financial Education*, and others.

David K. Eiteman. David K. Eiteman is Professor Emeritus of Finance at the John E. Anderson Graduate School of Management at UCLA. He has also held teaching or research appointments at the Hong Kong University of Science & Technology, Showa Academy of Music (Japan), the National University of Singapore, Dalian University (China), the Helsinki School of Economics and Business Administration (Finland), University of Hawaii at Manoa, University of Bradford (U.K.), Cranfield School of Management (U.K.), and IDEA (Argentina). He is a former president of the International Trade and Finance Association, Society for Economics and Management in China, and Western Finance Association.

Professor Eiteman received a B.B.A. (Business Administration) from the University of Michigan, Ann Arbor (1952); M.A. (Economics) from the University of California, Berkeley (1956); and a Ph.D. (Finance) from Northwestern University (1959).

He has authored or co-authored four books and twenty-nine other publications. His articles have appeared in *The Journal of Finance, The International Trade Journal, Financial Analysts Journal, Journal of World Business, Management International, Business Horizons, MSU Business Topics, Public Utilities Fortnightly*, and others.

Brief Contents

PART 1   Global Financial Environment   1

    Chapter 1   Current Multinational Challenges and the Global Economy   2

    Chapter 2   Financial Goals and Corporate Governance   28

    Chapter 3   The International Monetary System   59

    Chapter 4   The Balance of Payments   83

    Chapter 5   Current Multinational Financial Challenges: The Credit Crisis of 2007–2009   113

PART 2   Foreign Exchange Theory and Markets   145

    Chapter 6   The Foreign Exchange Market   146

    Chapter 7   International Parity Conditions   173

    Chapter 8   Foreign Currency Derivatives and Swaps   204

PART 3   Foreign Exchange Exposure   233

    Chapter 9   Foreign Exchange Rate Determination and Forecasting   234

    Chapter 10 Transaction and Translation Exposure   263

    Chapter 11 Operating Exposure   299

PART 4   Financing the Global Firm   323

    Chapter 12 The Global Cost and Availability of Capital   324

    Chapter 13 Sourcing Equity and Debt Globally   351

    Chapter 14 Multinational Tax Management   385

PART 5   Foreign Investment Decisions   407

    Chapter 15 Foreign Direct Investment and Political Risk   408

    Chapter 16 Multinational Capital Budgeting and Cross-Border Acquisitions   439

PART 6   Topics in International Finance

    Available online at www.pearsonhighered.com/moffett

    Answers to Selected End-of-Chapter Problems   A-1

    Glossary   G-1

    Index   I-1

Contents

PART I Global Financial Environment 1

Chapter 1 Current Multinational Challenges and the Global Economy 2
GLOBAL FINANCE IN PRACTICE Global Capital Markets: Entering a New Era 3
The Global Financial Marketplace 4
The Theory of Comparative Advantage 9
What Is Different about Global Financial Management? 12
Market Imperfections: A Rationale for the Existence of the Multinational Firm 13
GLOBAL FINANCE IN PRACTICE Corporate Responsibility and Corporate Sustainability 13
The Globalization Process 14
Summary of Learning Objectives 18
MINI-CASE Nine Dragons Paper—2009 18
Questions 26
Problems 26
Internet Exercises 27

Chapter 2 Financial Goals and Corporate Governance 28
Who Owns the Business? 28
GLOBAL FINANCE IN PRACTICE Family-Controlled Firms in France Outperform the Public Sector 30
What Is the Goal of Management? 31
Corporate Governance 36
GLOBAL FINANCE IN PRACTICE Is Good Governance Good Business Globally? 46
Summary of Learning Objectives 48
MINI-CASE Luxury Wars—LVMH vs. Hermès 49
Questions 54
Problems 55
Internet Exercises 57

Chapter 3 The International Monetary System 59
History of the International Monetary System 59
GLOBAL FINANCE IN PRACTICE Hammering Out an Agreement at Bretton Woods 61
Contemporary Currency Regimes 65
GLOBAL FINANCE IN PRACTICE Who Is Choosing What in the Trinity/Trilemma? 68
Emerging Markets and Regime Choices 69
The Birth of a European Currency: The Euro 72
Exchange Rate Regimes: What Lies Ahead? 75
Summary of Learning Objectives 76
MINI-CASE First Steps in the Globalization of the Yuan 77
Questions 80
Problems 81
Internet Exercises 82

Chapter 4   The Balance of Payments   83

Typical Balance of Payments Transactions   84
Fundamentals of Balance of Payments Accounting   85
The Accounts of the Balance of Payments   86
The Capital and Financial Accounts   89
GLOBAL FINANCE IN PRACTICE China's Twin Surpluses   93
GLOBAL FINANCE IN PRACTICE Official Foreign Exchange Reserves: The Rise of China   94
The Balance of Payments in Total   94
The Balance of Payments Interaction with Key Macroeconomic Variables   97
Trade Balances and Exchange Rates   99
Capital Mobility   102
Summary of Learning Objectives   104
MINI-CASE Global Remittances   105
Questions   109
Problems   110
Internet Exercises   112

Chapter 5   Current Multinational Financial Challenges: The Credit Crisis of 2007–2009   113

The Seeds of Crisis: Subprime Debt   114
The Transmission Mechanism: Securitization and Derivatives of Securitized Debt   117
The Fallout: The Crisis of 2007–2009   127
GLOBAL FINANCE IN PRACTICE Financial Fraud and Financial Recovery   134
The Remedy: Prescriptions for an Infected Global Financial Organism   134
GLOBAL FINANCE IN PRACTICE Refinancing Opportunities and the Credit Crisis   135
GLOBAL FINANCE IN PRACTICE Warren Buffett on the Credit Crisis   136
The Future   138
Summary of Learning Objectives   138
MINI-CASE Letting Go of Lehman Brothers   139
Questions   141
Problems   141
Internet Exercises   143

PART 2   Foreign Exchange Theory and Markets   145

Chapter 6   The Foreign Exchange Market   146

Geographical Extent of the Foreign Exchange Market   147
Functions of the Foreign Exchange Market   148
Market Participants   148
GLOBAL FINANCE IN PRACTICE The Foreign Exchange Dealer's Day   149
GLOBAL FINANCE IN PRACTICE My First Day of Foreign Exchange Trading   150
Transactions in the Interbank Market   151
Size of the Foreign Exchange Market   154
Foreign Exchange Rates and Quotations   156
Summary of Learning Objectives   165
MINI-CASE The Saga of the Venezuelan Bolivar Fuerte   166
Questions   168
Problems   168
Internet Exercises   171

Chapter 7   International Parity Conditions   173

Prices and Exchange Rates   174
GLOBAL FINANCE IN PRACTICE The Immiseration of the North Korean People—
The "Revaluation" of the NorthKorean Won   176
GLOBAL FINANCE IN PRACTICE Deviations from Purchasing Power Parity in the Twentieth Century   180
Interest Rates and Exchange Rates   181
Forward Rate as an Unbiased Predictor of the Future Spot Rate   189
Prices, Interest Rates, and Exchange Rates in Equilibrium   191
Summary of Learning Objectives   165
MINI-CASE Emerging Market Carry Trades   193
Questions   194
Problems   194
Internet Exercises   198
Appendix: An Algebraic Primer to International Parity Conditions   200
The Law of One Price   200
Purchasing Power Parity   200
Forward Rates   201
Covered Interest Arbitrage (CIA) and Interest Rate Parity (IRP)   201
Fisher Effect   202
International Fisher Effect   202

Chapter 8   Foreign Currency Derivatives and Swaps   204

Foreign Currency Futures   205
Currency Options   207
GLOBAL FINANCE IN PRACTICE The New Zealand Kiwi, Key, and Krieger   214
Option Pricing and Valuation   215
Interest Rate Risk   217
GLOBAL FINANCE IN PRACTICE A Fixed-Rate or Floating-Rate World?   218
Interest Rate Derivatives   219
Prudence in Practice   223
Summary of Learning Objectives   224
MINI-CASE McDonald's Corporation's British Pound Exposure   225
Questions   226
Problems   227
Internet Exercises   231

PART 3   Foreign Exchange Exposure   233

Chapter 9   Foreign Exchange Rate Determination and Forecasting   234

Exchange Rate Determination: The Theoretical Thread   236
Currency Market Intervention   240
GLOBAL FINANCE IN PRACTICE Rules of Thumb for Effective Intervention   242
Disequilibrium: Exchange Rates in Emerging Markets   243
GLOBAL FINANCE IN PRACTICE Was George Soros to Blame for the Asian Crisis?   246
Forecasting in Practice   251
GLOBAL FINANCE IN PRACTICE JPMorgan Chase Forecast of the Dollar/Euro   253
Summary of Learning Objectives   256
MINI-CASE The Japanese Yen Intervention of 2010   257
Questions   259
Problems   259
Internet Exercises   262

Chapter 10   Transaction and Translation Exposure   263

Types of Foreign Exchange Exposure   263
Why Hedge?   265
Trident's Transaction Exposure   269
GLOBAL FINANCE IN PRACTICE   The Credit Crisis and Option Volatilities in 2009   278
Translation Exposure   278
Trident Corporation's Translation Exposure   281
Managerial Implications   285
GLOBAL FINANCE IN PRACTICE   When Business Dictates Hedging Results   287
Summary of Learning Objectives   287
MINI-CASE   Banbury Impex (India)   289
Questions   293
Problems   293
Internet Exercises   298

Chapter 11   Operating Exposure   299

Trident Corporation: A Multinational's Operating Exposure   299
GLOBAL FINANCE IN PRACTICE   Do Fixed Exchange Rates Increase Corporate
   Currency Risk in Emerging Markets?   303
Measuring Operating Exposure   303
Strategic Management of Operating Exposure   308
Proactive Management of Operating Exposure   310
GLOBAL FINANCE IN PRACTICE   Key Challenges to Managing FX Risk   315
Summary of Learning Objectives   315
MINI-CASE   Toyota's European Operating Exposure   316
Questions   318
Problems   319
Internet Exercises   321

PART 4   Financing the Global Firm   323

Chapter 12   The Global Cost and Availability of Capital   324

Financial Globalization and Strategy   324
The Demand for Foreign Securities: The Role of International Portfolio Investors   333
GLOBAL FINANCE IN PRACTICE   Bang & Olufsen and Philips N.V.   337
The Cost of Capital for MNEs Compared to Domestic Firms   338
   Solving a Riddle: Is the Weighted Average Cost of Capital for MNEs Really Higher than for
Their Domestic Counterparts?   340
Summary of Learning Objectives   342
MINI-CASE   Novo Industri A/S (Novo)   342
Questions   346
Problems   347
Internet Exercises   349

Chapter 13   Sourcing Equity and Debt Globally   351

Designing a Strategy to Source Equity Globally   352
Optimal Financial Structure   353
Financial Structure of Foreign Subsidiaries   356
Foreign Equity Listing and Issuance   362
Effect of Cross-Listing and Equity Issuance on Share Price   364
Barriers to Cross-Listing and Selling Equity Abroad   366
Alternative Instruments to Source Equity in Global Markets   367
International Debt Markets   370
GLOBAL FINANCE IN PRACTICE   Pricing and Structure of a Syndicated Eurocredit   371

GLOBAL FINANCE IN PRACTICE Islamic Finance   375
Summary of Learning Objectives   375
MINI-CASE Petrobrás of Brazil and the Cost of Capital   377
Questions   380
Problems   381
Internet Exercises   383

Chapter 14   Multinational Tax Management   385

Tax Principles   386
Transfer Pricing   392
Tax-Haven Subsidiaries and International Offshore Financial Centers   396
GLOBAL FINANCE IN PRACTICE The Activities of Offshore Financial Centers   398
Summary of Learning Objectives   398
MINI-CASE The U.S. Corporate Income Tax Conundrum   399
Questions   403
Problems   404
Internet Exercises   406

PART 5   Foreign Investment Decisions   407

Chapter 15   Foreign Direct Investment and Political Risk   408

Sustaining and Transferring Competitive Advantage   409
Deciding Where to Invest   413
How to Invest Abroad: Modes of Foreign Involvement   414
Political Risk   418
GLOBAL FINANCE IN PRACTICE Apache Takes a Hit from Egyptian Protests   420
GLOBAL FINANCE IN PRACTICE Drugs, Public Policy, and the Death Penalty in 2011   430
Summary of Learning Objectives   433
MINI-CASE Corporate Competition from the Emerging Markets   435
Questions   436
Internet Exercises   438

Chapter 16   Multinational Capital Budgeting and Cross-Border Acquisitions   439

Complexities of Budgeting for a Foreign Project   440
Project versus Parent Valuation   441
Illustrative Case: Cemex Enters Indonesia   442
Real Option Analysis   454
Project Financing   455
Cross-Border Mergers and Acquisitions   456
GLOBAL FINANCE IN PRACTICE Statoil of Norway's Acquisition of Esso of Sweden   461
Summary of Learning Objectives   462
MINI-CASE Yanzhou (China) Bids for Felix Resources (Australia)   463
Questions   469
Problems   470
Internet Exercises   473

PART 6   Topics in International Finance
Available online at www.pearsonhighered.com/moffett

Answers to Selected End-of-Chapter Problems   A-1

Glossary   G-1

Index   I-1

PART

Global Financial Environment

CHAPTER 1

Current Multinational Challenges
the Global Economy

CHAPTER 2

Financial Goals and Corporate Governance

CHAPTER 3

The International Monetary System

CHAPTER 4

The Balance of Payments

CHAPTER 5

Current Multinational Financial Challenges
The Credit Crisis of 2007–2009

Current Multinational Challenges and the Global Economy

I define globalization as producing where it is most cost-effective, selling where it is most profitable, and sourcing capital where it is cheapest, without worrying about national boundaries.

—Narayana Murthy, President and CEO, Infosys.

LEARNING OBJECTIVES

◆ Examine the requirements for the creation of value.

◆ Consider the basic theory, *comparative advantage*, and its requirements for the explanation and justification for international trade and commerce.

◆ Discover what is different about international financial management.

◆ Detail which market imperfections give rise to the multinational enterprise.

◆ Consider how the globalization process moves a business from a purely domestic focus in its financial relationships and composition to one truly global in scope.

◆ Examine possible causes to the limitations to globalization in finance.

The subject of this book is the financial management of multinational enterprises (MNEs). MNEs are firms—for profit companies and not-for-profit organizations including NGOs— that have operations in more than one country, and conduct their business through foreign subsidiaries, branches, or joint ventures with host country firms.

MNEs are struggling to survive and prosper in a very different world than in the past. Today's MNEs depend not only on the emerging markets for cheaper labor, raw materials, and outsourced manufacturing, but also increasingly on those same emerging markets for sales and profits. These markets—whether they are emerging, less developed, developing, or BRICs (Brazil, Russia, India, and China)—represent the majority of the earth's population, and therefore, customers. And adding market complexity to this changing global landscape is the risky and challenging international macroeconomic environment, both from a long-term and short-term perspective, following the global financial crisis of 2007–2009. How to identify and navigate these risks is the focus of this book.

◆ The international monetary system, though dominated by floating exchange rates, possesses a multitude of managed and fixed exchange rates even today (see Chapter 3).

◆ Large fiscal deficits plague most of the major trading countries of the world, complicating fiscal and monetary policies, and ultimately, interest rates and exchange rates (see Chapter 4).

◆ Many countries experience continuing balance of payments imbalances, and in some cases, dangerously large deficits and surpluses, which will inevitably move exchange rates (see Chapter 4).

◆ Ownership, control, and governance changes radically across the world. The publicly traded company is not the dominant global business organization—the privately held or family-owned business may be the prevalent structure—and they act differently (see Chapter 2).

◆ Global capital markets that normally provide the means to lower a firm's cost of capital, and even more critically increase the availability of capital, have in many ways shrunk in size, openness, and accessibility by many of the world's organizations (see Chapters 1 and 5).

◆ Today's emerging markets are confronted with a new dilemma: the problem of being the recipients of too much global capital. Financial globalization has resulted in the flow of massive quantities of capital into many emerging markets in search of higher yields. The result has been the appreciation of many of the world's emerging market currencies, posing a problem for many export-oriented economies (see Chapters 6 and 9).

The Mini-Case at the end of this chapter, ***Nine Dragons Paper–2009***, highlights many of these MNE issues in emerging markets today. As described in *Global Finance in Practice 1.1*, the global credit crisis and its aftermath has damaged the world's largest banks and reduced the rate of economic growth worldwide, leading to higher rates of unemployment and putting critical pressures on government budgets from Greece to Ireland to Portugal to Mexico.

GLOBAL FINANCE IN PRACTICE   1.1

Global Capital Markets: Entering a New Era

The current financial crisis and worldwide recession have abruptly halted a nearly three-decade-long expansion of global capital markets. From 1980 through 2007, the world's financial assets—including equities, private and public debt, and bank deposits—nearly quadrupled in size relative to global GDP. Global capital flows similarly surged. This growth reflected numerous interrelated trends, including advances in information and communication technology, financial market liberalization, and innovations in financial products and services. The result was financial globalization.

But the upheaval in financial markets in late 2008 marked a break in this trend. The total value of the world's financial assets fell by $16 trillion to $178 trillion, the largest setback on record. Although equity markets have bounced back from their recent lows, they remain well below their peaks. Credit markets have healed somewhat but are still impaired.

Going forward, our research suggests that global capital markets are entering a new era in which the forces fueling growth have changed. For the past 30 years, most of the overall increase in financial depth—the ratio of assets to GDP—was driven by the rapid growth of equities and private debt in mature markets. Looking ahead, these asset classes in mature markets are likely to grow more slowly, more in line with GDP, while government debt will rise sharply. An increasing share of global asset growth will occur in emerging markets, where GDP is rising faster and all asset classes have abundant room to expand.

Source: Excerpted from "Global Capital Markets: Entering a New Era," McKinsey Global Institute, Charles Rosburgh, Susan Lund, Charles Atkins, Stanislas Belot, Wayne W. Hu, and Moira S. Pierce, McKinsey & Company, September 2009, p. 7.

The Global Financial Marketplace

Business—domestic, international, global—involves the interaction of individuals and individual organizations for the exchange of products, services, and capital through markets. The global capital markets are critical for the conduct of this exchange. The global financial crisis of 2008–2009 served as an illustration and a warning of how tightly integrated and fragile this marketplace can be.

Assets, Institutions, and Linkages

Exhibit 1.1 provides a map to the global capital markets. One way to characterize the global financial marketplace is through its *assets*, *institutions*, and *linkages*.

◆ **Assets.** The assets—the financial assets—which are at the heart of the global capital markets are the debt securities issued by governments (e.g., U.S. Treasury Bonds). These low-risk or risk-free assets then form the foundation for the creating, trading, and pricing of other financial assets like bank loans, corporate bonds, and equities (stock). In recent years, a number of additional securities have been created from the existing securities—derivatives, whose value is based on market value changes in the underlying securities. The health and security of the global financial system relies on the quality of these assets.

◆ **Institutions.** The institutions of global finance are the central banks, which create and control each country's money supply; the commercial banks, which take deposits and

---

EXHIBIT 1.1   Global Capital Markets

The global capital market is a collection of institutions (central banks, commercial banks, investment banks, not for profit financial institutions like the IMF and World Bank) and securities (bonds, mortgages, derivatives, loans, etc.), which are all linked via a global network — the *Interbank Market*. This interbank market, in which securities of all kinds are traded, is the critical pipeline system for the movement of capital.

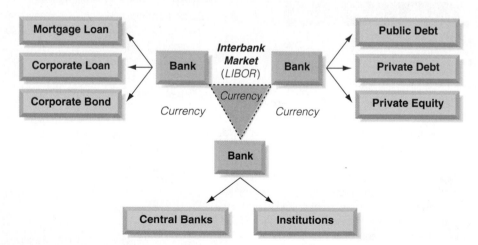

The exchange of securities — the movement of capital in the global financial system — must all take place through a vehicle — currency. The exchange of currencies is itself the largest of the financial markets. The interbank market, which must *pass-through* and exchange securities using currencies, bases all of its pricing through the single most widely quoted interest rate in the world — LIBOR (the London Interbank Offer Rate).

extend loans to businesses, both local and global; and the multitude of other financial institutions created to trade securities and derivatives. These institutions take many shapes and are subject to many different regulatory frameworks. The health and security of the global financial system relies on the stability of these financial institutions.

◆ **Linkages.** The links between the financial institutions, the actual fluid or medium for exchange, are the interbank networks using currency. The ready exchange of currencies in the global marketplace is the first and foremost necessary element for the conduct of financial trading, and the global currency markets are the largest markets in the world. The exchange of currencies, and the subsequent exchange of all other securities globally via currency, is the international interbank network. This network, whose primary price is the *London Interbank Offered Rate* (LIBOR), is the core component of the global financial system.

The movement of capital across borders and continents for the conduct of business has existed in many different forms for thousands of years. Yet, it is only within the past 50 years that these capital movements have started to move at the pace of an electron, either via a phone call or an email. And it is only within the past 20 years that this market has been able to reach the most distant corners of the earth at any moment of the day. This market has seen an explosion of innovative products and services in the past decade, some of which proved, as in the case of the 2008–2009 crisis, somewhat toxic to the touch.

The Market for Currencies

The price of any one country's currency in terms of another country's currency is called a foreign currency exchange rate. For example, the exchange rate between the U.S. dollar ($ or USD) and the European euro (€ or EUR) may be stated as "1.4565 dollar per euro" or simply abbreviated as $1.4565/€. This is the same exchange rate as when stated "EUR1.00 = USD1.4565." Since most international business activities require at least one of the two parties in a business transaction to either pay or receive payment in a currency which is different from their own, an understanding of exchange rates is critical to the conduct of global business.

A quick word about currency symbols. As noted, USD and EUR are often used as the symbols for the U.S. dollar and the European Union's euro. These are the computer symbols (ISO-4217 codes) used today on the world's digital networks. The field of international finance, however, has a rich history of using a variety of different symbols in the financial press, and a variety of different abbreviations are commonly used. For example, the British pound sterling may be £ (the pound symbol), GBP (Great Britain pound), STG (British pound sterling), ST£ (pound sterling), or UKL (United Kingdom pound). This book will also use the simpler common symbols—the $ (dollar), the € (euro), the ¥ (yen), the £ (pound)—but be warned and watchful when reading the business press!

Exchange Rate Quotations and Terminology. Exhibit 1.2 lists currency exchange rates for Thursday, January 6, 2011, as would be quoted in New York or London.The exchange rate listed is for a specific country's currency—for example, the Argentina peso against the U.S. dollar—Peso 3.9713/$, the European euro—Peso $5.1767/€, and the British pound—Peso 6.1473/£. The rate listed is termed a "mid-rate" because it is the middle or average of the rates at which currency traders buy currency (bid rate) and sell currency (offer rate).

The U.S. dollar has been the focal point of most currency trading since the 1940s. As a result, most of the world's currencies have been quoted against the dollar—Mexican pesos per dollar, Brazilian real per dollar, Hong Kong dollars per dollar, etc. This quotation convention is also followed against the world's major currencies as listed in

EXHIBIT 1.2 — Selected Global Currency Exchange Rates

January 6, 2011 Country	Currency	Symbol	Code	Currency to equal 1 Euro	Currency to equal 1 Dollar	Currency to equal 1 Pound
Argentina	peso	Ps	ARS	5.1767	3.9713	6.1473
Australia	dollar	A$	AUD	1.3106	1.0054	1.5564
Bahrain	dinar	—	BHD	0.4915	0.3770	0.5836
Bolivia	boliviano	Bs	BOB	9.1118	6.9900	10.8202
Brazil	real	R$	BRL	2.2047	1.6913	2.6181
Canada	dollar	C$	CAD	1.3000	0.9973	1.5437
Chile	peso	$	CLP	644.931	494.750	765.848
China	yuan	¥	CNY	8.6380	6.6265	10.2575
Colombia	peso	Col$	COP	2,533.35	1,866.20	2,688.78
Costa Rica	colon	₡	CRC	666.415	511.230	791.3600
Czech Republic	koruna	Kc	CZK	24.6050	18.8754	29.2182
Denmark	krone	Dkr	DKK	7.4508	5.7158	8.8477
Egypt	pound	£	EGP	7.5606	5.8000	8.9781
Euro Area	euro	€	EUR	—	0.7671	1.1875
Hong Kong	dollar	HK$	HKD	10.1335	7.7738	12.0334
Hungary	forint	Ft	HUF	276.2250	211.902	328.0140
India	rupee	Rs	INR	58.9791	45.2450	70.0370
Indonesia	rupiah	Rp	IDR	11,728.7	8,997.5	13,927.7
Iran	rial	—	IRR	13,498.3	10,355.0	16,029.0
Israel	shekel	Shk	ILS	4.6521	3.5688	5.5243
Japan	yen	¥	JPY	108.481	83.220	128.820
Kenya	shilling	KSh	KES	105.5220	80.950	125.307
Kuwait	dinar	—	KWD	0.3678	0.2821	0.4367
Malaysia	ringgit	RM	MYR	4.0039	3.0715	4.7545
Mexico	new peso	$	MXN	15.9481	12.2344	18.9383
New Zealand	dollar	NZ$	NZD	1.7243	1.3228	2.0476
Nigeria	naira	₦	NGN	198.726	152.450	235.985
Norway	krone	NKr	NOK	7.7635	5.9557	9.2191
Pakistan	rupee	Rs.	PKR	111.8190	85.7800	132.7830
Peru	new sol	S/.	PEN	3.6571	2.8055	4.3428
Phillippines	peso	₱	PHP	57.2487	43.9175	67.9821
Poland	zloty	—	PLN	3.8625	2.9631	4.5866
Romania	new leu	L	RON	4.2593	3.2675	5.0579
Russia	ruble	R	RUB	40.0353	30.7125	47.5414
Saudi Arabia	riyal	SR	SAR	4.8886	3.7502	5.8051
Singapore	dollar	S$	SGD	1.6872	1.2943	2.0035
South Africa	rand	R	ZAR	8.8665	6.8018	10.5289
South Korea	won	W	KRW	1,459.72	1,119.80	1,733.39
Sweden	krona	SKr	SEK	8.9427	6.8603	10.6194
Switzerland	franc	Fr.	CHF	1.2573	0.9645	1.4930
Taiwan	dollar	T$	TWD	38.1595	29.2735	45.3140
Thailand	baht	B	THB	39.4063	30.2300	46.7946
Tunisia	dinar	DT	TND	1.9027	1.4597	2.2595
Turkey	lira	YTL	TRY	2.0215	1.5508	2.4005
United Arab Emirates	dirham	—	AED	4.7878	3.6729	5.6855
United Kingdom	pound	£	GBP	0.8421	0.6460	—
Ukraine	hrywnja	—	UAH	10.3874	7.9685	12.3349
Uruguay	peso	$U	UYU	26.0059	19.9500	30.8816
United States	dollar	$	USD	1.3036	—	1.5480
Venezuela	bolivar fuerte	Bs	VEB	5.5983	4.2947	6.6479
Vietnam	dong	d	VND	25,416.0	19,497.5	30,181.2

Note that a number of different currencies use the same symbol (for example both China and Japan have traditionally used the ¥ symbol, yen or yuan, meaning round or circle). That is one of the reasons why most of the world's currency markets today use the three-digit currency code for clarity of quotation. All quotes are mid-rates, and are drawn from the *Financial Times,* January 6, 2011.

Exhibit 1.2. For example, the Japanese yen is commonly quoted as ¥83.2200/$, ¥108.481/€, and ¥128.820/£.

Quotation Conventions. Several of the world's major currency exchange rates, however, follow a specific quotation convention that is the result of tradition and history. The exchange rate between the U.S. dollar and the euro is always quoted as "dollars per euro" ($/€), $1.3036/€ as listed in Exhibit 1.2. Similarly, the exchange rate between the U.S. dollar and the British pound is always quoted as $/£, for example, the $1.5480/£ listed under "United States" in Exhibit 1.2. Many countries that are formerly members of the British Commonwealth will commonly be quoted against the dollar as U.S. dollars per currency (e.g., the Australian or Canadian dollars).

Eurocurrencies and LIBOR

One of the major linkages of global money and capital markets is the Eurocurrency market and its interest rate known as LIBOR. *Eurocurrencies* are domestic currencies of one country on deposit in a second country. Eurodollar time deposit maturities range from call money and overnight funds to longer periods. Certificates of deposit are usually for three months or more and in million-dollar increments. A Eurodollar deposit is not a demand deposit; it is not created on the bank's books by writing loans against required fractional reserves, and it cannot be transferred by a check drawn on the bank having the deposit. Eurodollar deposits are transferred by wire or cable transfer of an underlying balance held in a correspondent bank located within the United States. In most countries, a domestic analogy would be the transfer of deposits held in non-bank savings associations. These are transferred by having the association write its own check on a commercial bank.

Any convertible currency can exist in "Euro-" form. (Note that this use of "Euro-" should not be confused with the new common European currency called the *euro*.) The Eurocurrency market includes Eurosterling (British pounds deposited outside the United Kingdom); Euroeuros (euros on deposit outside the euro zone); Euroyen (Japanese yen deposited outside Japan) and Eurodollars. The exact size of the Eurocurrency market is difficult to measure because it varies with daily decisions made by depositors about where to hold readily transferable liquid funds, and particularly on whether to deposit dollars within or outside the United States.

Eurocurrency markets serve two valuable purposes: 1) Eurocurrency deposits are an efficient and convenient money market device for holding excess corporate liquidity; and 2) the Eurocurrency market is a major source of short-term bank loans to finance corporate working capital needs, including the financing of imports and exports.

Banks in which Eurocurrencies are deposited are called *Eurobanks*. A Eurobank is a financial intermediary that simultaneously bids for time deposits and makes loans in a currency other than that of the currency in which it is located. Eurobanks are major world banks that conduct a Eurocurrency business in addition to all other banking functions. Thus, the Eurocurrency operation that qualifies a bank for the name *Eurobank* is in fact a department of a large commercial bank, and the name springs from the performance of this function.

The modern Eurocurrency market was born shortly after World War II. Eastern European holders of dollars, including the various state trading banks of the Soviet Union, were afraid to deposit their dollar holdings in the United States because these deposits might be attached by U.S. residents with claims against communist governments. Therefore, Eastern European holders deposited their dollars in Western Europe, particularly with two Soviet banks: the Moscow Narodny Bank in London, and the Banque Commerciale pour l'Europe du Nord in Paris. These banks redeposited the funds in other

Western banks, especially in London. Additional dollar deposits were received from various central banks in Western Europe, which elected to hold part of their dollar reserves in this form to obtain a higher yield. Commercial banks also placed their dollar balances in the market because specific maturities could be negotiated in the Eurodollar market. Additional dollars came to the market from European insurance companies with a large volume of U.S. business. Such companies found it financially advantageous to keep their dollar reserves in the higher-yielding Eurodollar market. Various holders of international refugee funds also supplied funds.

Although the basic causes of the growth of the Eurocurrency market are economic efficiencies, many unique institutional events during the 1950s and 1960s helped its growth.

◆ In 1957, British monetary authorities responded to a weakening of the pound by imposing tight controls on U.K. bank lending in sterling to nonresidents of the United Kingdom. Encouraged by the Bank of England, U.K. banks turned to dollar lending as the only alternative that would allow them to maintain their leading position in world finance. For this they needed dollar deposits.

◆ Although New York was "home base" for the dollar and had a large domestic money and capital market, international trading in the dollar centered in London because of that city's expertise in international monetary matters and its proximity in time and distance to major customers.

◆ Additional support for a European-based dollar market came from the balance of payments difficulties of the United States during the 1960s, which temporarily segmented the U.S. domestic capital market from that of the rest of the world.

Ultimately, however, the Eurocurrency market continues to thrive because it is a large international money market relatively free from governmental regulation and interference.

Eurocurrency Interest Rates: LIBOR. In the eurocurrency market, the reference rate of interest is *LIBOR*—the London Interbank Offered Rate. LIBOR is now the most widely accepted rate of interest used in standardized quotations, loan agreements or financial derivatives valuations. LIBOR is officially defined by the *British Bankers Association* (BBA). For example, U.S. dollar LIBOR is the mean of 16 multinational banks' interbank offered rates as sampled by the BBA at 11 A.M. *London time in London*. Similarly, the BBA calculates the Japanese yen LIBOR, euro LIBOR, and other currency LIBOR rates at the same time in London from samples of banks.

The interbank interest rate is not, however, confined to London. Most major domestic financial centers construct their own interbank offered rates for local loan agreements. These rates include PIBOR (Paris Interbank Offered Rate), MIBOR (Madrid Interbank Offered Rate), SIBOR (Singapore Interbank Offered Rate), and FIBOR (Frankfurt Interbank Offered Rate), to name but a few.

The key factor attracting both depositors and borrowers to the Eurocurrency loan market is the narrow interest rate spread within that market. The difference between deposit and loan rates is often less than 1%. Interest spreads in the eurocurrency market are small for many reasons. Low lending rates exist because the eurocurrency market is a *wholesale* market, where deposits and loans are made in amounts of $500,000 or more on an unsecured basis. Borrowers are usually large corporations or government entities that qualify for low rates because of their credit standing and because the transaction size is large. In addition, overhead assigned to the eurocurrency operation by participating banks is small.

EXHIBIT 1.3   U.S. Dollar-Denominated Interest Rates

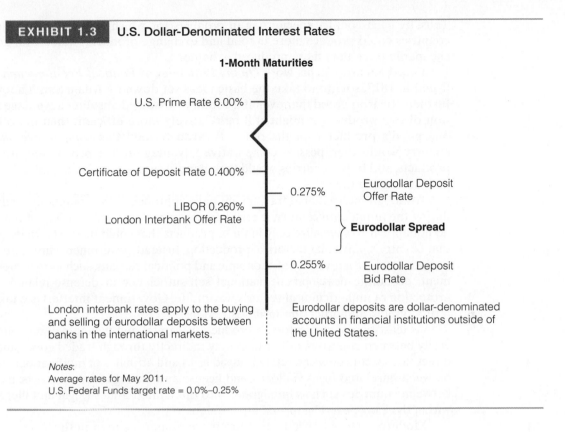

1-Month Maturities

U.S. Prime Rate 6.00%

Certificate of Deposit Rate 0.400%

0.275%   Eurodollar Deposit Offer Rate

LIBOR 0.260%
London Interbank Offer Rate

Eurodollar Spread

0.255%   Eurodollar Deposit Bid Rate

London interbank rates apply to the buying and selling of eurodollar deposits between banks in the international markets.

Eurodollar deposits are dollar-denominated accounts in financial institutions outside of the United States.

Notes:
Average rates for May 2011.
U.S. Federal Funds target rate = 0.0%–0.25%

Deposit rates are higher in the eurocurrency markets than in most domestic currency markets because the financial institutions offering eurocurrency activities are not subject to many of the regulations and reserve requirements imposed on traditional domestic banks and banking activities. With these costs removed, rates are subject to more competitive pressures, deposit rates are higher, and loan rates are lower. A second major area of cost avoided in the eurocurrency markets is the payment of deposit insurance fees (such as the Federal Deposit Insurance Corporation, FDIC, and assessments paid on deposits in the United States). Exhibit 1.3 illustrates how eurodollar deposit and loan rates, including dollar LIBOR and LIBID rates, compare with traditional domestic interest rates.

The Theory of Comparative Advantage

The *theory of comparative advantage* provides a basis for explaining and justifying international trade in a model world assumed to enjoy free trade, perfect competition, no uncertainty, costless information, and no government interference. The theory's origins lie in the work of Adam Smith, and particularly with his seminal book *The Wealth of Nations* published in 1776. Smith sought to explain why the division of labor in productive activities, and subsequently international trade of those goods, increased the quality of life for all citizens. Smith based his work on the concept of *absolute advantage*, where every country should specialize in the production of that good it was uniquely suited for. More would be produced for less.

Thus, by each country specializing in products for which it possessed absolute advantage, countries could produce more in total and exchange products—trade—for goods that were cheaper in price than those produced at home.

David Ricardo, in his work *On the Principles of Political Economy and Taxation* published in 1817, sought to take the basic ideas set down by Adam Smith a few logical steps further. Ricardo noted that even if a country possessed absolute advantage in the production of two products, it might still be relatively more efficient than the other country in one good's product than the other. Ricardo termed this *comparative advantage*. Each country would then possess comparative advantage in the production of one of the two products, and both countries would then benefit by specializing completely in one product and trading for the other.

Although international trade might have approached the comparative advantage model during the nineteenth century, it certainly does not today, for a variety of reasons. Countries do not appear to specialize only in those products that could be most efficiently produced by that country's particular factors of production. Instead, governments interfere with comparative advantage for a variety of economic and political reasons, such as to achieve full employment, economic development, national self-sufficiency in defense-related industries, and protection of an agricultural sector's way of life. Government interference takes the form of tariffs, quotas, and other non-tariff restrictions.

At least two of the factors of production, capital and technology, now flow directly and easily between countries, rather than only indirectly through traded goods and services. This direct flow occurs between related subsidiaries and affiliates of multinational firms, as well as between unrelated firms via loans, and license and management contracts. Even labor flows between countries such as immigrants into the United States (legal and illegal), immigrants within the European Union, and other unions.

Modern factors of production are more numerous than in this simple model. Factors considered in the location of production facilities worldwide include local and managerial skills, a dependable legal structure for settling contract disputes, research and development competence, educational levels of available workers, energy resources, consumer demand for brand name goods, mineral and raw material availability, access to capital, tax differentials, supporting infrastructure (roads, ports, and communication facilities), and possibly others.

Although the terms of trade are ultimately determined by supply and demand, the process by which the terms are set is different from that visualized in traditional trade theory. They are determined partly by administered pricing in oligopolistic markets.

Comparative advantage shifts over time as less developed countries become more developed and realize their latent opportunities. For example, over the past 150 years comparative advantage in producing cotton textiles has shifted from the United Kingdom to the United States, to Japan, to Hong Kong, to Taiwan, and to China. The classical model of comparative advantage also did not really address certain other issues such as the effect of uncertainty and information costs, the role of differentiated products in imperfectly competitive markets, and economies of scale.

Nevertheless, although the world is a long way from the classical trade model, the general principle of comparative advantage is still valid. The closer the world gets to true international specialization, the more world production and consumption can be increased, provided the problem of equitable distribution of the benefits can be solved to the satisfaction of consumers, producers, and political leaders. Complete specialization, however, remains an unrealistic limiting case, just as perfect competition is a limiting case in microeconomic theory.

Supply Chain Outsourcing: Comparative Advantage Today

Comparative advantage is still a relevant theory to explain why particular countries are most suitable for exports of goods and services that support the global supply chain of both MNEs and domestic firms. The comparative advantage of the twenty-first century, however, is one that is based more on services, and their cross border facilitation by telecommunications and the Internet. The source of a nation's comparative advantage, however, still is created from the mixture of its own labor skills, access to capital, and technology.

Many locations for supply chain outsourcing exist today. Exhibit 1.4 presents a geographical overview of this modern reincarnation of trade-based comparative advantage. To prove that these countries should specialize in the activities shown you would need to know how costly the same activities would be in the countries that are importing these services compared to their own other industries. Remember that it takes a *relative advantage* in costs, not just an *absolute advantage*, to create *comparative advantage*.

For example, India has developed a highly efficient and low-cost software industry. This industry supplies not only the creation of custom software, but also call centers for customer support, and other information technology services. The Indian software industry is composed of subsidiaries of MNEs and independent companies. If you own a Hewlett-Packard computer and call the customer support center number for help, you are likely to reach a call center in India. Answering your call will be a knowledgeable Indian software engineer or programmer who will "walk you through" your problem. India has a large number of well-educated, English-speaking technical experts who are paid only a fraction of the salary and overhead earned by their U.S. counterparts. The overcapacity and low cost of international telecommunication networks today further enhances the comparative advantage of an Indian location.

EXHIBIT 1.4   Global Outsourcing of Comparative Advantage

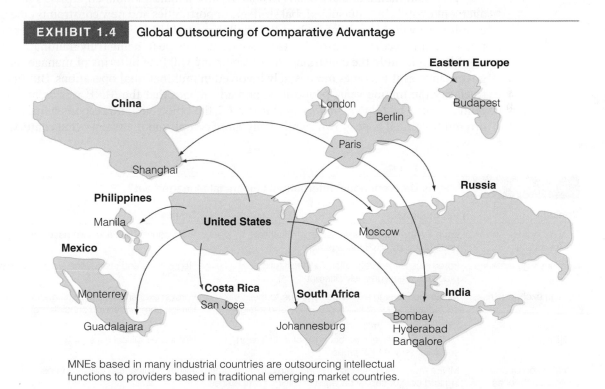

MNEs based in many industrial countries are outsourcing intellectual functions to providers based in traditional emerging market countries.

The extent of global outsourcing is already reaching out to every corner of the globe. From financial back-offices in Manila, to information technology engineers in Hungary, modern telecommunications now take business activities to labor rather than moving labor to the places of business.

What Is Different about Global Financial Management?

Exhibit 1.5 details some of the main differences between international and domestic financial management. These component differences include institutions, foreign exchange and political risks, and the modifications required of financial theory and financial instruments.

International financial management requires an understanding of cultural, historical, and institutional differences such as those affecting corporate governance. Although both domestic firms and MNEs are exposed to foreign exchange risks, MNEs alone face certain unique risks, such as political risks, that are not normally a threat to domestic operations.

MNEs also face other risks that can be classified as extensions of domestic finance theory. For example, the normal domestic approach to the cost of capital, sourcing debt and equity, capital budgeting, working capital management, taxation, and credit analysis needs to be modified to accommodate foreign complexities. Moreover, a number of financial instruments that are used in domestic financial management have been modified for use in international financial management. Examples are foreign currency options and futures, interest rate and currency swaps, and letters of credit.

The main theme of this book is to analyze how a multinational enterprise's financial management evolves as it pursues global strategic opportunities and new constraints emerge. In this chapter, we will take a brief look at the challenges and risks associated with Trident Corporation (Trident), a company evolving from domestic in scope to being truly multinational. The discussion will include the constraints that a company will face in terms of managerial goals and governance as it becomes increasingly involved in multinational operations. But first we need to clarify the unique value proposition and advantages that the MNE was created to exploit. And as noted by *Global Finance in Practice 1.2*, the objectives and responsibilities of the modern multinational have grown significantly more complex in the twenty-first century.

EXHIBIT 1.5	What Is Different about International Financial Management?	
Concept	**International**	**Domestic**
Culture, history, and institutions	Each foreign country is unique and not always understood by MNE management	Each country has a known base case
Corporate governance	Foreign countries' regulations and institutional practices are all uniquely different	Regulations and institutions are well known
Foreign exchange risk	MNEs face foreign exchange risks due to their subsidiaries, as well as import/export and foreign competitors	Foreign exchange risks from import/export and foreign competition (no subsidiaries)
Political risk	MNEs face political risks because of their foreign subsidiaries and high profile	Negligible political risks
Modification of domestic finance theories	MNEs must modify finance theories like capital budgeting and cost of capital because of foreign complexities	Traditional financial theory applies
Modification of domestic financial instruments	MNEs utilize modified financial instruments such as options, futures, swaps, and letters of credit	Limited use of financial instruments and derivatives because of fewer foreign exchange and political risks

GLOBAL FINANCE IN PRACTICE   1.2

Corporate Responsibility and Corporate Sustainability

Sustainable development is development that meets the needs of the present without compromising the ability of future generations to meet their own needs.
—*Brundtland Report*, 1987, p. 54.

What is the purpose of the corporation? It is increasingly accepted that the *purpose* of the corporation is to certainly create profits and value for its stakeholders, but the *responsibility* of the corporation is to do so in a way that inflicts no costs on society, including the environment. As a result of globalization, this growing responsibility and role of the corporation in society has added a level of complexity to the leadership challenges faced by the twenty-first century firm.

This developing debate has been somewhat hampered to date by conflicting terms and labels—*corporate goodness, corporate responsibility, corporate social responsibility* (CSR), *corporate philanthropy,* and *corporate sustainability,* to list but a few. Much of the confusion can be reduced by using a guiding principle—that *sustainability* is a goal, while *responsibility* is an obligation. It follows that the obligation of leadership in the modern multinational is to pursue profit, social development, and the environment, all along sustainable principles.

The term *sustainable* has evolved greatly within the context of global business in the past decade. A traditional primary objective of the family-owned business has been the "sustainability of the organization"—the long-term ability of the company to remain commercially viable and provide security and income for future generations. Although narrower in scope than the concept of environmental sustainability, there is a common core thread—the ability of a company, a culture, or even the earth, to survive and renew over time.

The Triple Bottom-Line

. . . balancing economic growth, social development, and environmental protection, so that future generations are not compromised by actions taken today.
—*2008 Sustainability Report,* ExxonMobil Corporation.

Nearly two decades ago a number of large corporations began to refine their publicly acknowledged corporate objective as "the pursuit of the triple bottom line." This triple bottom line—*profitability, social responsibility,* and *environmental sustainability*—was considered an enlightened development of modern capitalism. What some critics referred to as a softer and gentler form of market capitalism, was a growing acceptance on the part of the corporation for doing something more than generating a financial profit.

There have been a variety of theoretical rationalizations for this more expanded view of corporate responsibilities, one of which divides the arguments along two channels, the *economic channel* and the *moral channel.*

◆ The *economic channel* argues that by pursuing corporate sustainability objectives the corporation is actually still pursuing profitability, but is doing so with a more intelligent longer-term perspective—sometimes referred to as "enlightened self-interest." It has realized that a responsible organization must assure that its actions over time, whether or not required by law or markets, conducts its business in a way which does not reduce future choices.

◆ The *moral channel* argues that since the corporation has all the rights and responsibilities of a citizen, it also has the moral responsibility to act in the best interests of society and society's future, regardless of its impacts on profitability. This argument assumes that in some instances, doing the 'right thing' may have explicit costs, even to shareholders.

Our Commitment to corporate responsibility is unwavering, even during economic downturns. Taking a proactive, integrated approach to managing our impact on local communities and the environment not only benefits people and our planet, but is good for our business. Making corporate responsibility an integral part of Intel's strategy helps us mitigate risk, build strong relationships with our stakeholders, and expand our market opportunities.
—Letter from our CEO,
Intel 2008 Corporate Responsibility Report, p. 3.

Market Imperfections: A Rationale for the Existence of the Multinational Firm

MNEs strive to take advantage of imperfections in national markets for products, factors of production, and financial assets. Imperfections in the market for products translate into market opportunities for MNEs. Large international firms are better able to exploit such competitive factors as economies of scale, managerial and technological expertise, product differentiation, and financial strength than are their local competitors. In fact, MNEs thrive best in markets characterized by international oligopolistic competition, where these factors are particularly critical. In addition, once MNEs have established a physical presence abroad, they are in a better position than purely domestic firms to identify and implement market opportunities through their own internal information network.

Why Do Firms become Multinational?

Strategic motives drive the decision to invest abroad and become an MNE. These motives can be summarized under the following categories:

1. **Market seekers** produce in foreign markets either to satisfy local demand or to export to markets other than their home market. U.S. automobile firms manufacturing in Europe for local consumption are an example of market-seeking motivation.

2. **Raw material seekers** extract raw materials wherever they can be found, either for export or for further processing and sale in the country in which they are found—the host country. Firms in the oil, mining, plantation, and forest industries fall into this category.

3. **Production efficiency seekers** produce in countries where one or more of the factors of production are underpriced relative to their productivity. Labor-intensive production of electronic components in Taiwan, Malaysia, and Mexico is an example of this motivation.

4. **Knowledge seekers** operate in foreign countries to gain access to technology or managerial expertise. For example, German, Dutch, and Japanese firms have purchased U.S.-located electronics firms for their technology.

5. **Political safety seekers** acquire or establish new operations in countries that are considered unlikely to expropriate or interfere with private enterprise. For example, Hong Kong firms invested heavily in the United States, United Kingdom, Canada, and Australia in anticipation of the consequences of China's 1997 takeover of the British colony.

These five types of strategic considerations are not mutually exclusive. Forest products firms seeking wood fiber in Brazil, for example, may also find a large Brazilian market for a portion of their output.

In industries characterized by worldwide oligopolistic competition, each of the above strategic motives should be subdivided into *proactive* and *defensive* investments. Proactive investments are designed to enhance the growth and profitability of the firm itself. Defensive investments are designed to deny growth and profitability to the firm's competitors. Examples of the latter are investments that try to preempt a market before competitors can get established in it, or capture raw material sources and deny them to competitors.

The Globalization Process

Trident is a hypothetical U.S.-based firm that will be used as an illustrative example throughout the book to demonstrate the *globalization process*—the structural and managerial changes and challenges experienced by a firm as it moves its operations from domestic to global.

Global Transition I: Trident Moves from the Domestic Phase to the International Trade Phase

Trident is a young firm that manufactures and distributes an array of telecommunication devices. Its initial strategy is to develop a sustainable competitive advantage in the U.S. market. Like many other young firms, it is constrained by its small size, competitors, and lack of access to cheap and plentiful sources of capital. The top half of Exhibit 1.6 shows Trident in its early *domestic phase*. Trident sells its products in U.S. dollars to U.S. customers and buys its manufacturing and service inputs from U.S. suppliers, paying U.S. dollars. The creditworth of

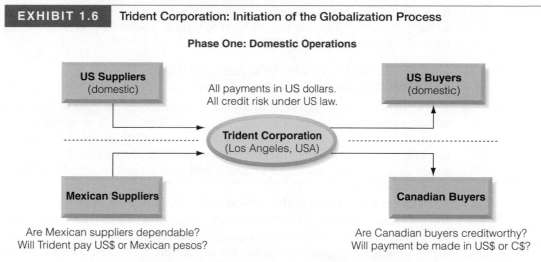

EXHIBIT 1.6   Trident Corporation: Initiation of the Globalization Process

Phase One: Domestic Operations

US Suppliers (domestic)

All payments in US dollars.
All credit risk under US law.

US Buyers (domestic)

Trident Corporation (Los Angeles, USA)

Mexican Suppliers

Canadian Buyers

Are Mexican suppliers dependable?
Will Trident pay US$ or Mexican pesos?

Are Canadian buyers creditworthy?
Will payment be made in US$ or C$?

Phase Two: Expansion into International Trade

all suppliers and buyers is established under domestic U.S. practices and procedures. A potential issue for Trident at this time is that although Trident is not international or global in its operations, some of its competitors, suppliers, or buyers may be. This is often the impetus to push a firm like Trident into the first transition of the globalization process, into international trade.

Trident was founded by James and Edgar Winston in Los Angeles in 1948 to make telecommunications equipment. The family-owned business expanded slowly but steadily over the following 40 years. The demands of continual technological investment in the 1980s, however, required that the firm raise additional equity capital in order to compete. This need led to its initial public offering (IPO) in 1988. As a U.S.-based publicly traded company on the New York Stock Exchange, Trident's management sought to *create value for its shareholders.*

As Trident became a visible and viable competitor in the U.S. market, strategic opportunities arose to expand the firm's market reach by exporting product and services to one or more foreign markets. The North American Free Trade Area (NAFTA) made trade with Mexico and Canada attractive. This second phase of the globalization process is shown in the lower-half of Exhibit 1.6. Trident responded to these globalization forces by importing inputs from Mexican suppliers and making export sales to Canadian buyers. We define this stage of the globalization process as the *International Trade Phase.*

Exporting and importing products and services increases the demands of financial management over and above the traditional requirements of the domestic-only business. First, direct *foreign exchange risks* are now borne by the firm. Trident may now need to quote prices in foreign currencies, accept payment in foreign currencies, or pay suppliers in foreign currencies. As the value of currencies change from minute to minute in the global marketplace, Trident will now experience significant risks from the changing values associated with these foreign currency payments and receipts.

Second, the evaluation of the credit quality of foreign buyers and sellers is now more important than ever. Reducing the possibility of non-payment for exports and non-delivery of imports becomes one of two main financial management tasks during the international trade phase. This *credit risk management* task is much more difficult in international business, as buyers and suppliers are new, subject to differing business practices and legal systems, and generally more challenging to assess.

Global Transition II: The International Trade Phase to the Multinational Phase

If Trident is successful in its international trade activities, the time will come when the globalization process will progress to the next phase. Trident will soon need to establish foreign sales and service affiliates. This step is often followed by establishing manufacturing operations abroad or by licensing foreign firms to produce and service Trident's products. The multitude of issues and activities associated with this second larger global transition is the real focus of this book.

Trident's continued globalization will require it to identify the sources of its competitive advantage, and with that knowledge, expand its intellectual capital and physical presence globally. A variety of strategic alternatives are available to Trident—the *foreign direct investment sequence*—as shown in Exhibit 1.7. These alternatives include the creation of foreign sales offices, the licensing of the company name and everything associated with it, and the manufacturing and distribution of its products to other firms in foreign markets. As Trident moves farther down and to the right in Exhibit 1.7, the degree of its physical presence in foreign markets increases. It may now own its own distribution and production facilities, and ultimately, may want to acquire other companies. Once Trident owns assets and enterprises in foreign countries it has entered the *multinational phase* of its globalization.

EXHIBIT 1.7   Trident's Foreign Direct Investment Sequence

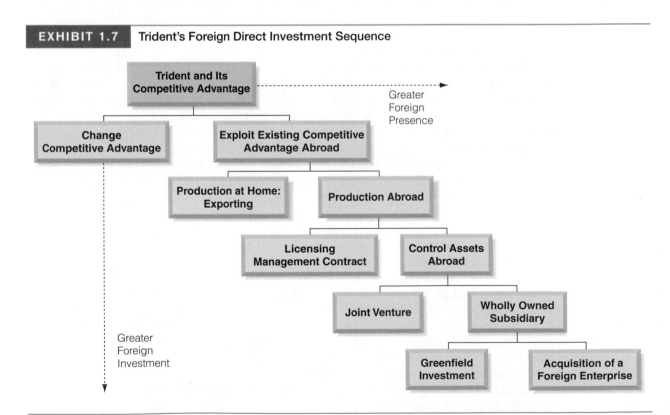

The Limits to Financial Globalization

The theories of international business and international finance introduced in this chapter have long argued that with an increasingly open and transparent global marketplace in which capital may flow freely, capital will increasingly flow and support countries and companies based on the *theory of comparative advantage*. Since the mid-twentieth century, this has indeed been the case as more and more countries have pursued more open and competitive markets. But the past decade has seen the growth of a new kind of limit or impediment to *financial globalization*: the growth in the influence and self-enrichment of organizational insiders.

One possible representation of this process can be seen in Exhibit 1.8. If influential insiders in corporations and sovereign states continue to pursue the increase in firm value, there will be a definite and continuing growth in financial globalization. But, if these same influential insiders pursue their own personal agendas, which may increase their personal power and influence or personal wealth, or both, then capital will not flow into these sovereign states and corporations. The result is the growth of financial inefficiency and the segmentation of globalization outcomes—creating winners and losers. As we will see throughout this book, this barrier to international finance may indeed be increasingly troublesome.

This growing dilemma is also something of a composite of what this book is about. The three fundamental elements—*financial theory*, *global business*, and *management beliefs and actions*—combine to present either the problem or the solution to the growing debate over the benefits of globalization to countries and cultures worldwide. The Mini-Case sets the stage for our debate and discussion. Are the controlling family members of this company creating value for themselves or their shareholders?

EXHIBIT 1.8   The Potential Limits of Financial Globalization

There is a growing debate over whether many of the insiders and rulers of organizations with enterprises globally are taking actions consistent with creating firm value or consistent with increasing their own personal stakes and power.

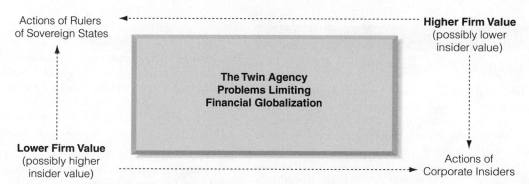

If these influential insiders are building personal wealth over that of the firm, it will indeed result in preventing the flow of capital across borders, currencies, and institutions to create a more open and integrated global financial community.

Source: Constructed by authors based on "The Limits of Financial Globalization," Rene M. Stulz, *Journal of Applied Corporate Finance*, Volume 19, Number 1, Winter 2007, pp. 8–15.

Summary of Learning Objectives

Examine the requirements for the creation of value

◆ The creation of value requires combining three critical elements: 1) an open marketplace; 2) high-quality strategic management; and 3) access to capital.

Consider the basic theory, comparative advantage, and its requirements for the explanation and justification for international trade and commerce

◆ The *theory of comparative advantage* provides a basis for explaining and justifying international trade in a model world assumed to enjoy free trade, perfect competition, no uncertainty, costless information, and no government interference.

Discover what is different about international financial management

◆ International financial management requires an understanding of cultural, historical, and institutional differences, such as those affecting corporate governance.

◆ Although both domestic firms and MNEs are exposed to foreign exchange risks, MNEs alone face certain unique risks, such as political risks, that are not normally a threat to domestic operations.

Detail which market imperfections give rise to the multinational enterprise

◆ MNEs strive to take advantage of imperfections in national markets for products, factors of production, and financial assets.

◆ Large international firms are better able to exploit such competitive factors as economies of scale, managerial and technological expertise, product differentiation, and financial strength than are their local competitors.

Consider how the globalization process moves a business from a purely domestic focus in its financial relationships and composition to one truly global in scope

◆ A firm may first enter into international trade transactions, then international contractual arrangements, such as sales offices and franchising, and ultimately the acquisition of foreign subsidiaries. At this final stage it truly becomes a multinational enterprise (MNE).

◆ The decision whether or not to invest abroad is driven by strategic motives, and may require the MNE to enter into global licensing agreements, joint ventures, cross-border acquisitions, or greenfield investments.

Examine possible causes to the limitations to globalization in finance

◆ If influential insiders in corporations and sovereign states pursue their own personal agendas which may increase their personal power, influence, or wealth, then capital will not flow into these sovereign states and corporations. This will, in turn, create limitations to globalization in finance.

MINI-CASE

Nine Dragons Paper—2009[1]

Rumors about this relatively secret company abound. Share prices fell below $1 in November. Following some action on the stock, and at the request of the Hong Kong stock market, the company had to issue a number of press releases denying rumors of acquisitions or other agreements. It also denied rumors that its Chinese mills had taken market-related downtime. Finally, a spokesman said the company had no "liquidity problems."

—"Five Companies to Watch," G. Rodden, M. Rushton, F. Willis, *PPI*, January 2009, p. 21.

"This time is really different. Large and small are all affected. In the past, the big waves would only wash away the sand and leave the rocks. Now the waves are so big, even some rocks are being washed away."

—Cheung Yan, Chairwoman of Nine Dragons Paper,"Wastepaper Queen: Letter from China," *New Yorker*, 30 March 2009, p. 8.

Incorporated in Hong Kong in 1995, Nine Dragons Paper (Holdings) Limited had become an international powerhouse in the paper industry. The company produced a portfolio of paper-board products used in consumer product packaging. The company had expanded rapidly, its capital expenditure growing at an average annual rate of 120% for the past five years.

But in January 2009, the company had been forced to issue a profit warning (Exhibit 1). Squeezed by market conditions and burdened by debt, Nine Dragons Paper (NDP), the largest paperboard manufacturer in Asia and second largest in the world, had seen its share price plummet. As the economic crisis of 2008 had bled into 2009, NDP's sales had fallen. Rumors had been buzzing since October that NDP was on the very edge of bankruptcy. Now, in April 2009, more than one analyst was asking "Will they go bust?"

The Wastepaper Queen

It is the largest of scaly animals, and it has the following nine characteristics. Its head is like a camel's, its horns like a deer's, its eyes like a hare's, its ears like a bull's, its neck like an iguana's, its belly like a frog's, its scales like those of a carp, its paws like a tiger's, and its claws like an eagle's. It has nine times nine scales, it being the extreme of a lucky number.

—www.ninedragonbaguazhang.com/dragons.htm.

Cheung Yan, or *Mrs. Cheung* as she preferred, was the visionary force behind NDP's success. Her empire was built from trash—discarded cardboard cartons to be precise. The cartons were collected in the United States and Europe, shipped to China, then pulped and remanufactured into paperboard. NDP customers then used the paperboard to package goods for shipment back to the United States and Europe, returning them to their origins.

Born in 1957, Mrs. Cheung came from a modest family background. She had started as an accountant for a Chinese trading company in Hong Kong, and then started her own company after her employer went under. Her company was a scrap paper dealer, purchasing scrap paper in Hong Kong and mainland China and selling it to Chinese paper manufacturers. Paper in China was of generally poor quality, made from bamboo stalk, rice stalk, and grass. The locally collected waste paper didn't meet the needs of paper manufacturers as a raw input. In Europe and the United States, however, paper was made from wood pulp, which produced a higher quality paper (United States companies use a higher percentage of pulp, while Chinese companies use more recovered paper). Realizing that by capturing the waste paper stream in the United States and Europe she could provide a higher quality product to her customers in China, Mrs. Cheung moved to the United States in 1990 to start another company, American Chung Nam Incorporated (ACN).

One of the first companies to export waste paper from the United States to China, ACN started by collecting waste paper from dumps, then expanded its network to include waste haulers and waste paper collectors. Mrs. Cheung negotiated favorable contracts with shipping companies whose ships were returning to China empty. ACN soon expanded abroad and became a leading exporter of recovered paper from Europe to China as well. By 2001, ACN had become the largest exporter, by volume, of freight from the United States. "In other words, nobody in America was shipping more of anything each year anywhere in the world."[2]

The Chinese economic miracle that began in the late 1990s rose through exports of consumer goods which needed a massive amount of packaging material. Within a few years, the demands for packaging far outgrew what

---

EXHIBIT 1 NPD's Profit Warning (14 January 2009)

NINE DRAGONS PAPER (HOLDINGS) LIMITED

(*Incorporated in Bermuda with limited liability*)
(Stock Code: 2689)

ANNOUNCEMENT

PROFIT WARNING

The Board wishes to inform the shareholders of the Company and potential investors that it is expected the Group will record a substantial reduction in its unaudited consolidated net profit arising from normal operations for the six months ended 31 December 2008 as compared to that for the corresponding period in 2007 due to the substantial decrease in the selling prices of the Group's products and the rising cost of raw materials.

Shareholders of the Company and potential investors are advised to exercise caution in dealing in shares of the Company.

---

[2]"Wastepaper Queen: Letter from China," *New Yorker*, 30 March 2009, p. 4.

domestic suppliers could provide. In 1995, Mrs. Cheung founded *Nine Dragons Paper Industries Company* in Dongguan, China. By 1998, the first papermaking machine was installed, a second in 2000, and a third in 2003. By 2008, NDP had 22 paperboard manufacturing machines at six locations in China and Vietnam. As illustrated by Exhibit 2, sales and profits soared.

NDP's Products

Containerboard is used for exactly what it sounds like: containing products in shipping between manufacturing and market. As illustrated in Exhibit 3, the containerboard value chain is a consumer-driven market, with consumer purchases of products driving the demand for packaging and containers and insulation worldwide. Companies like NDP purchase recovered pulp paper from a variety of raw material suppliers (e.g., American Chung Nam, ACN, Mrs. Cheung's own company), to manufacture containerboard. The containerboard is then sold to a variety of box manufacturers, most of which are located near the final customer, the consumer product companies.

NDP produced three different types of containerboard: *Linerboard* (47% of 2008 sales), *Corrugated Medium* (28% of sales), and *Corrugated Duplex* (23% of sales). Linerboard, light brown or white in color, is the flat exterior surface of boxes used to absorb external pressures during transport. Corrugated containerboard is the wavy fluted interior used to protect products in shipment. Corrugated Medium, also light brown in color, has a high stack strength and is lightweight, saving shippers significant shipping costs. Corrugated Duplex is glossy on one side, high in printability, and is used in packaging of electronics, cosmetics, and a variety of food and beverages. These three products made up 98% of sales in 2008, with pulp and specialty paper making up the final 2% of sales.

Expansion

"The market waits for no one. If I don't develop today, if I wait for a year, or two or three years, to develop, I will have nothing for the market, and I will miss the opportunity."
—Cheung Yan, Chairwoman of Nine Dragons Paper
"Wastepaper Queen: Letter from China," *New Yorker*,
30 March 2009, p. 2.

Since its founding in 1995, the company had continuously expanded production capacity. By 2008, NDP had three paperboard manufacturing plants in China: Dongguan, in Guangdong Province in the Pearl River Delta; Taicang, in Jiangsu Province in the Yangtze River Delta region; and Chongqing, in Sichuan Province in western China. All three were strategically located close to consumer goods manufacturers and shipping ports. NDP also had three other major investments in parallel with paperboard manufacturing, buying a specialty board producer in

---

EXHIBIT 2	NPD's Growing Sales and Profitability

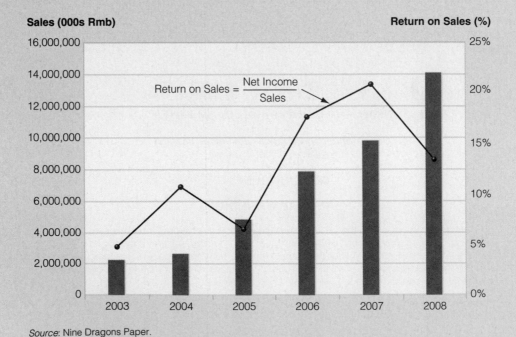

$$\text{Return on Sales} = \frac{\text{Net Income}}{\text{Sales}}$$

Source: Nine Dragons Paper.

EXHIBIT 3 Chinese Containerboard Value Chain

Nine Dragons Paper

Raw Material Suppliers	Containerboard Manufacturers	Box Manufacturers	Consumer Product Companies
• OCC (old corrugated cardboard) or recovered paper makes up 90% of volume	• Containerboard co's typically pass along cost changes due to highly fragmented box manufacturers	• Also able to pass along prices to customers as container costs make up a relatively small percentage of total product cost of final customer	• Highly cyclical with consumer spending
• Pulp paper about 10% of volume	• NDP & Lee & Man control roughly 25% of the total Chinese market	• Manufacturing needs to occur near customers due to high cost of transport of low value goods	• Market in China has been shifting to a domestic orientation as Chinese incomes and consumption patterns grow
• Input prices have been very volatile in recent years	• Sales mix has shifted to domestic market in recent years (78% domestic in 2008, only 49% in 2005)	• **Companies:**	• Chinese economy, domestic economy, recovered rapidly from the 2008 recession suffered by most nations globally
• NDP sources 60% of its OCC from American Chung Nam (ACN) owned by Mrs. Cheung	• **Companies:**	• Hop Fung supplies manufacturing sector in Hong Kong and the Pearl River Delta	
• Raw material costs make up 60% of cost of goods sold	• Shandong Huatai Paper Company Ltd.	• D&B Database returns 3892 paperboard box manufacturers (NAICS 32221) in China	
• Large quantities of water and electricity required in manufacture	• Kith Holdings Limited		
	• Samson Paper Holdings Limited		
	• Lee & Man Paper Manufacturing Limited		

Sichuan Province, a pulp manufacturer in Inner Mongolia, and a joint venture in a pulp manufacturer and paper mill in Binh Duong Province, Vietnam.

Even with NDP and competitor expansions, the demand for paperboard in China surpassed production. In 2005, Chinese manufacturers produced nearly 28 million tonnes of containerboard, yet consumption equaled 30 million tonnes. Domestic manufacturers had been narrowing the output gap, yet there was still an unmet need. Despite being the largest containerboard manufacturing country in the world, China remained a net importer. By 2008, NDP was the largest paperboard manufacturer in Asia.

Expansion came at a cost. A paper-making machine can cost anywhere from $100 to $200 million to purchase and set up, and then take up to two years before reaching optimal productivity. NDP operated its own electrical power plants, loading, and transportation services, had entered into several joint ventures to supply wood pulp, and held long-term agreements for waste paper supply. Though registered in Bermuda, corporate offices remained in Hong Kong.

Containerboard manufacturing is both energy intensive and water use intensive. To secure power supplies, NDP constructed coal-fired co-generation power plants to supply its plants in Dongguan, Taicang and Chongqing. With these plants, the cost of generating power was approximately one-third less than electricity purchased from the regional power grid.

The company owned and operated its own transportation infrastructure, including piers and unloading facilities, railway spurs, and truck fleets. The company received shipments of raw materials, including recovered paper, chemicals, and coal, at its own piers in Taicang and Chongqing, and at the Xinsha Port in Dongguan. These facilities took advantage of ocean and inland waterway transportation, reducing port loading and unloading charges and allowing the company to avoid transportation bottlenecks.

We only have a certain number of opportunities in our lifetime. Once you miss it, it's gone forever.
—Cheung Yan, Chairwoman of Nine Dragons Paper.

From the beginning, the company invested in the most advanced equipment available, importing papermaking machines from the U.S. and Italy. Each plant was constructed with multiple production lines, allowing flexible configuration. This allowed NDP to respond to changing customer demands, offering a diversified product portfolio with options including product types, sizes, grades, burst indices, stacking strengths, basis weights, and printability. NDP had become an innovation leader in the industry, with equipment utilization rates consistently averaging 94%, far surpassing the industry average.

Although now publicly traded, the family still controlled the business. Mrs. Cheung and her husband held 72% of the company's stock, with family members holding a number of the executive positions in the company: Mrs. Cheung was Chairman; her husband, Ming Chung Liu, was Chief Executive Officer; her brother Zhang Cheng Fei was a general manager; and her son, Lau Chun Shun, was an executive director.

Financing Expansion

Why are we in debt? she asked. . . . I took a high level of risk because that is the preparation for the future, so that we will be first in the market when things change.
—Cheung Yan, Chairwoman of Nine Dragons Paper "Wastepaper Queen: Letter from China," *New Yorker*, 30 March 2009, p. 2.

Although sometimes difficult, NDP had historically been able to fund its growing capital expenditures with a combination of operating cash flow and debt. But as the rate of expansion grew even faster, and the company's capital expenditures ballooned as illustrated by Exhibit 4, it became obvious that the company would need to restructure its financial base. Mrs. Cheung devised a second strategic plan.

Initial Public Offering. The first step was an initial public offering (IPO). In March 2006, NDP offered 25% of the company's equity, one billion shares, at an offer price of HK$3.40 per share. The official offering was oversubscribed as a result of intense investor interest. The company then exercised an over-allotment option through its joint underwriters, Merrill Lynch and BNP Paribas Peregrine, issuing an additional 150 million shares in a private placement to a select set of Hong Kong-based investors. The added shares raised an additional HK$490 million ($63.2 million) after fees, raising the total issuance to HK$3.9 billion ($504 million), representing 27.7% of the company's ownership.

NDP's shares (*HK:2689*) began trading on the Hong Kong stock exchange in March 2006 and within six months were a constituent stock of the Hang Seng Composite Index. Following the highly successful IPO, Mrs. Cheung was now the richest woman in China.

Raising Debt. The proceeds from the IPO allowed NDP to retire a large portion of its accumulated debt. But the respite from debt concerns was short-lived. As Mrs. Cheung increased the rate of asset growth, the company's debt once again began to grow. NDP once again generated a negative *free cash flow* (operating cash flow less capex as illustrated in Exhibit 4). In April 2008, NDP issued $300 million in senior unsecured notes, notes which Fitch

---

EXHIBIT 4   NDP's Capex and Operating Cash Flow

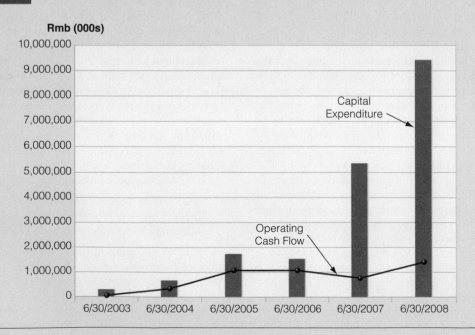

initially rated BBB-, the very edge of *investment grade*.[3] Fitch cited a multitude of factors in its rating: the current economy, raw material price increases, supply risk, and the company's aggressive capital expenditure program.

When global financial markets ground to a halt in September and October 2008 and the economic crisis spread around the globe, consumers stopped buying, Chinese exports slowed, and sales of containerboard plummeted. NDP's export orders declined 50%, sales revenue dropped, and the burden of debt grew noticeably heavier. Analysts became increasingly nervous. As price pressure from raw materials continued and NDP's margins fell, final customers started fighting higher containerboard and box prices. On October 13, Fitch downgraded NDP to BB+ NDP was now *speculative grade*, junk bond status.

NDP's Chinese New Year 2009

We understand that all NDP's banks have postponed for one year all earnings-based debt covenant ratios. We see this as a significant positive for shareholders as it should allow management enough time to restore confidence and restructure its Rmb14.7 bn in debt, of which half is due in two years.
— "Nine Dragons Paper," Morgan Stanley, January 29, 2009, p. 1.

Following new rumors of the company's possible bankruptcy, On December 29, 2008, NDP announced that it would delay Rmb1.5 billion in capital expenditure planned for the 2009 fiscal year. The company reassured analysts and shareholders alike that by late 2010 or early 2011 the paperboard markets would rebound. NDP also moved quickly to repurchase $16 million of its own notes and reported it would prepay $100 million of an existing $350 million syndicated loan and HK$720 million of a HK$2.3 billion credit line.

The debt restructuring had mixed results for NDP's outlook. The partial repayment on the two loan facilities convinced NDP's bankers to allow the debt covenants on the loan facilities to be relaxed for one year. In turn, NDP's costs under the loan facilities would reflect new higher spreads commensurate with its fallen credit rating. Its actions quelled the tempest somewhat, but not much, and not for long. NDP's share price, after recovering a bit in December 2008, started falling once again in January 2009, as shown in Exhibit 5. Two days later on January 15, NDP issued a *profit warning*, revising sales and profit forecasts downward (see Exhibit 1). The ratings agencies responded with another downgrade, Fitch pushing NDP's outstanding notes down to BB—. Rumors of the company's potential bankruptcy were widespread.

EXHIBIT 5   NDP's Share Price (ending April 30, 2009; weekly)

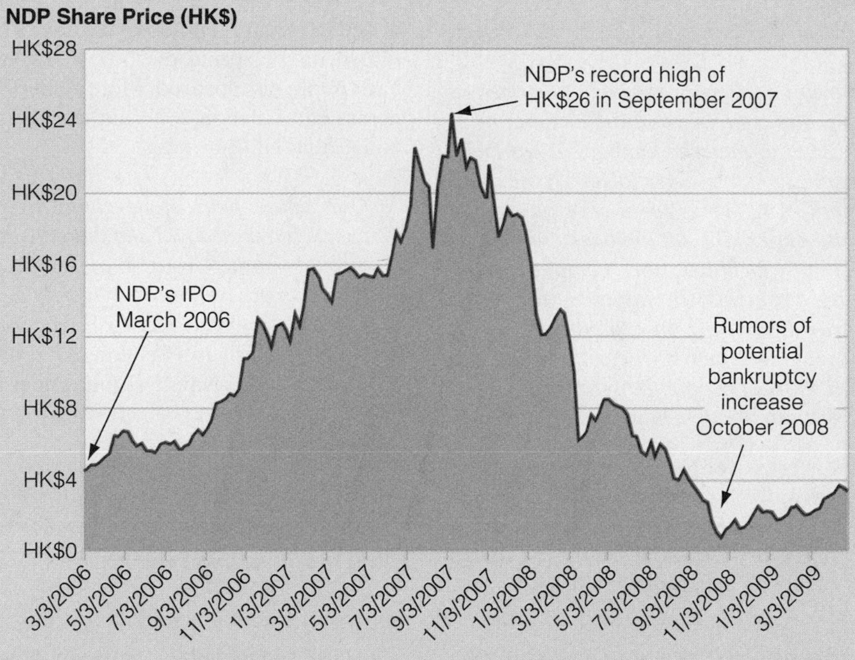

NDP Share Price (HK$)

---

[3]Fitch Ratings, market announcement, 14 April 2008.

By mid-February, many investment analysts were starting to reverse their recommendations on NDP shares. A few argued that the company's share price had over-reacted, and the company simply "had to be worth more" than what it was currently trading at. As more and more analysts endorsed the strategic and financial changes announced and implemented by management, the share price gradually rose. There were early signs that the Chinese economy was recovering from the recession quickly, margins were stabilizing, and that boded well for NDP's earnings and cash flows.

In mid-March, however, the analysts were stunned once again. In a briefing held by Mrs. Cheung, NDP announced it was re-instituting capex plans which had been shelved only three months before.

> *... we are concerned about the heavy reliance on bank borrowing in its current capital structure. Whilst the US$165 mn buyback of its senior notes and the relaxation of loan covenants in its syndicated term loans were positive catalysts for shareholders, in our view, we believe investors today are now asking what the company is doing to cut total debt, and at the meeting management failed to provide any new strategies.*
> —Morgan Stanley, March 18, 2009.

Estimates of earnings for the year would once again have to be revised downwards (as seen in the March 18, 2009 revision in Exhibit 6). The higher capital expenditures would now result in both higher depreciation charges and higher interest expenses for their funding.

Cash Flow Concerns

> *Nine Dragon's earnings are very sensitive to prices of both recycled paper and containerboard. Fluctuations in these prices could lead to material changes in earnings. With current net debt to equity close to 100%, the company relies on bank borrowings to finance part of its working capital and capex. Should the banks unexpectedly withdraw their facilities, the company may encounter liquidity problems. In addition, the company's earnings growth is based on expansion plans. If the company is unable to obtain sufficient funding, the expansion may fall short of the company's target.*
> —Morgan Stanley, January 29, 2009, p. 6.

The focus of analyst concerns over NDP's prospects was the impact of declining sales and margin on its ability to service its large debt burden. Morgan Stanley's frequent revision and reevaluation of NDP's key cash flow drivers and drains over the first quarter of 2009 is illustrated in Exhibit 5.

Key issues included:

◆ **Earnings**. NDP's primary source of ongoing cash flow was earnings, and as measured by EBITDA (Earnings before interest, taxes, depreciation and amortization), margins and earnings would be negatively impacted by the current paperboard market decline and higher input costs.

◆ **Interest Expenses**. Debt costs in the form of interest expenses were clearly rising rapidly as a result of continued high debt levels and the higher interest rates which followed from credit downgrades.

◆ **Capex**. NDP's massive asset expansion had brought about both its market dominance and its never-ending need for debt. Initially, management had announced postponement of capital expenditure plans in an attempt to calm bankruptcy fears.

◆ **Debt**. The debt-carrying capacity of NDP was the primary source of debate in the current recessionary environment. The company's debt/equity ratio, its *gearing*, was extremely high and potentially lethal in a recessionary environment amid a global financial crisis, with credit so tight that many banks had stopped answering the phone. Analysts agreed across the board that NDP needed to reduce debt—now.

The March announcement of higher capex, now revised upward to Rmb 4.45 bn, would result in both higher depreciation charges and higher interest expenses. It would again commit the company to a large negative free cash flow for the 2009 year, and would probably result in NDP carrying higher debt levels well into 2010 and 2011 while the world economic environment was predicted to remain fragile. As the global economic crisis continued in the spring of 2009, many of NDP's customers had simply disappeared. More than 670,000 Chinese businesses had failed in 2008, and early 2009 had been just as bad. Could NDP be next?

> *Our future path of development may remain thorny ahead, but armed with the shared confidence and courage throughout the Group to overcome and conquer, we are poised to act even more diligently and powerfully to prepare for the next global economic recovery ...*
> —"Chairlady's Statement," 2008/09 Interim Report, Nine Dragons Paper (Holdings) Limited.

CASE QUESTIONS

1. How does Mrs. Cheung think? What does she believe in when it comes to building her business?

2. How would you summarize the company's financial status? How does it reflect the business development goals and strategies employed by Mrs. Cheung?

3. Is NDP in trouble? How would your answer differ if you were an existing shareholder, a potential investor, or an analyst?

| EXHIBIT 6 | The Evolution of Earnings, Cash Flow, and Debt Analysis of Nine Dragons Paper |

Rmb (millions)	2007	2008	Maintain Sept 17, 2008 2009e	Downgrade Dec 16, 2008 2009e	Upgrade Jan 29, 2009 2009e	Downgrade Feb 19, 2009 2009e	Debt Concern Mar 18, 2009 2009e
INCOME							
Net sales	9,838	14,114	20,837	14,691	14,691	14,522	14,517
Cost of goods manufacturing	(7,201)	(11,341)	(16,849)	(12,886)	(12,779)	(12,482)	(12,468)
EBITDA	2,637	2,773	3,988	1,805	1,912	2,040	2,049
Percent of sales	26.8%	19.6%	19.1%	12.3%	13.0%	14.0%	14.1%
Depreciation & amoritization	(370)	(507)	(914)	(800)	(807)	(848)	(829)
EBIT	2,267	2,266	3,074	1,005	1,105	1,192	1,220
Percent of sales	23.0%	16.1%	14.8%	6.8%	7.5%	8.2%	8.4%
Interest	(105)	(102)	(795)	(887)	(887)	(556)	(480)
Pre-tax Profit (EBT)	2,162	2,164	2,279	118	218	636	740
Percent of sales	22.0%	15.3%	10.9%	0.8%	1.5%	4.4%	5.1%
CASH FLOW							
EBITDA	2,637	2,773	3,988	1,805	1,912	2,040	2,049
Less taxes paid	(93)	(263)	(296)	(15)	(28)	(44)	(22)
Less net financial	(272)	(102)	(814)	(918)	(918)	(588)	(1,057)
Less working capital	(1,517)	(1,012)	(1,202)	(691)	1,500	602	599
Operating Cash Flow	755	1,396	1,676	181	2,466	2,010	1,569
Capex	(5,345)	(9,601)	(2,950)	(1,500)	(1,700)	(2,800)	(4,450)
Acquisitions	(208)	(208)	(208)	(208)	—	—	—
Disposals & other	28	—	20	31	31	31	31
Investing Cash Flow	(5,525)	(9,809)	(3,138)	(1,677)	(1,669)	(2,769)	(4,419)
Equity raised	2,011	—	—	—	—	—	—
Debt raised	1,795	8,594	2,950	1,350	(1,000)	(500)	2,000
Dividends	(199)	(495)	(495)	(224)	(224)	(224)	(224)
Other	119	171	—	(452)	(12)	(17)	(17)
Financing Cash Flow	3,726	8,270	2,455	674	(1,236)	(741)	1,759
Net Changes in Cash	(1,044)	(143)	993	(822)	(439)	(1,500)	(1,091)
FREE CASH FLOW							
Operating Cash Flow	755	1,396	1,676	181	2,466	2,010	1,569
Less capex	(5,345)	(9,601)	(2,950)	(1,500)	(1,700)	(2,800)	(4,450)
Free Cash Flow (FCF)	(4,590)	(8,205)	(1,274)	(1,319)	766	(790)	(2,881)
CAPITAL STRUCTURE							
Payables	1,767	3,839	2,941	2,280	4,316	4,232	4,221
Borrowings	6,632	14,685	14,865	16,265	13,915	13,575	16,369
Other liabilities	328	544	39	91	532	527	527
Total Liabilities	8,727	19,068	17,845	18,636	18,763	18,334	21,117
Shareholders equity	11,513	13,272	14,426	13,090	13,178	14,419	13,706
Minority interest	123	274	243	334	334	334	334
Total Liabilities & Equity	20,363	32,614	32,514	32,060	32,275	33,087	35,157
Net Debt	5,007	13,396	13,458	15,858	13,124	13,845	16,231
Net Debt / Equity	43.5%	100.9%	93.3%	121.1%	99.6%	96.0%	118.4%
Interest Cover (EBITDA ×)	9.7	27.2	4.9	2.0	2.1	3.5	1.9
Gearing (Debt/Equity)	58%	111%	103%	124%	106%	94%	119%
Debt / EBITDA (5× or less)	2.51	5.30	3.73	9.01	7.28	6.65	7.99
EBIT / Interest (4× or more)	21.59	22.22	3.87	1.13	1.25	2.14	2.54

Source: Compiled by Authors from "Nine Dragons Paper," Morgan Stanley, September 17, 2008, December 16, 2008, January 29, 2009, February 10, 2009, February 19, 2009, and March 18, 2009.

Questions

1. **Globalization and the MNE.** The term globalization has become widely used in recent years. How would you define it?

2. **Assets, Institutions and Linkages.** Which assets play the most critical role in linking the major institutions that make up the global financial marketplace?

3. **Eurocurrencies and LIBOR.** Why have eurocurrencies and LIBOR remained the centerpiece of the global financial marketplace for so long?

4. **Theory of Comparative Advantage.** Define and explain the theory of comparative advantage.

5. **Limitations of Comparative Advantage.** Key to understanding most theories is what they say and what they don't. What are four or five key limitations to the theory of comparative advantage?

6. **Trident's Globalization.** After reading the chapter's description of Trident's globalization process, how would you explain the distinctions between international, multinational, and global companies.

7. **Trident, the MNE.** At what point in the globalization process did Trident become a multinational enterprise (MNE)?

8. **Trident's Advantages.** What are the main advantages that Trident gains by developing a multinational presence?

9. **Trident's Phases.** What are the main phases that Trident passed through as it evolved into a truly global firm? What are the advantages and disadvantages of each?

10. **Financial Globalization.** How do the motivations of individuals, both inside and outside the organization or business, define the limits of financial globalization?

Problems

Comparative Advantage

Problems 1–5 illustrate an example of trade induced by comparative advantage. They assume that China and France each have 1,000 production units. With one unit of production (a mix of land, labor, capital, and technology), China can produce either 10 containers of toys or 7 cases of wine. France can produce either 2 cases of toys or 7 cases of wine. Thus, a production unit in China is five times as efficient compared to France when producing toys, but equally efficient when producing wine. Assume at first that no trade takes place. China allocates 800 production units to building toys and 200 production units to producing wine. France allocates 200 production units to building toys and 800 production units to producing wine.

1. **Production and Consumption.** What is the production and consumption of China and France without trade?

2. **Specialization.** Assume complete specialization, where China produces only toys and France produces only wine. What would be the effect on total production?

3. **Trade at China's Domestic Price.** China's domestic price is 10 containers of toys equals 7 cases of wine. Assume China produces 10,000 containers of toys and exports 2,000 to France. Assume France produces 7,000 cases of wine and exports 1,400 cases to China. What happens to total production and consumption?

4. **Trade at France's Domestic Price.** France's domestic price is 2 containers of toys equals 7 cases of wine. Assume China produces 10,000 containers of toys and exports 400 containers to France. Assume France in turn produces 7,000 cases of wine and exports 1,400 cases to China. What happens to total production and consumption?

5. **Trade at Negotiated Mid-Price.** The mid-price for exchange between France and China can be calculated as follows:

Assumptions	Toys (containers/unit)	Wine (cases/unit)
China—output per unit of production input	10	7
France—output per unit of production input	2	7
China—total production inputs	1,000	
France—total production inputs	1,000	

What happens to total production and consumption?

Americo Industries—2010

Problems 6 through 10 are based on Americo Industries. Americo is a U.S.-based multinational manufacturing firm, with wholly owned subsidiaries in Brazil, Germany, and China, in addition to domestic operations in the United States. Americo is traded on the NASDAQ. Americo currently has 650,000 shares outstanding. The basic operating characteristics of the various business units is as follows:

Business Performance (000s, local currency)	U.S. Parent Company (US$)	Brazilian Subsidiary (reais, R$)	German Subsidiary (euros, €)	Chinese Subsidiary (yuan, ¥)
Earnings before taxes (EBT)	$4,500	R$6,250	€4,500	¥2,500
Corporate income tax rate	35%	25%	40%	30%
Average exchange rate for the period	—	R$1.80/$	€0.7018/$	¥7.750/$

6. **Americo Industries' Consolidate Earnings.** Americo must pay corporate income tax in each country in which it currently has operations.
   a. After deducting taxes in each country, what are Americo's consolidated earnings and consolidated earnings per share in U.S. dollars?
   b. What proportion of Americo's consolidated earnings arise from each individual country?
   c. What proportion of Americo's consolidated earnings arise from outside the United States?

7. **Americo's EPS Sensitivity to Exchange Rates (A).** Assume a major political crisis wracks Brazil, first affecting the value of the Brazilian reais and, subsequently, inducing an economic recession within the country. What would be the impact on Americo's consolidated EPS if the Brazilian reais were to fall in value to R$3.00/$, with all other earnings and exchange rates remaining the same?

8. **Americo's EPS Sensitivity to Exchange Rates (B).** Assume a major political crisis wracks Brazil, first affecting the value of the Brazilian reais and, subsequently, inducing an economic recession within the country. What would be the impact on Americo's consolidated EPS if, in addition to the fall in the value of the reais to R$3.00/$, earnings before taxes in Brazil fell as a result of the recession to R$5,8000,000?

9. **Americo's Earnings and the Fall of the Dollar.** The U.S. dollar has experienced significant swings in value against most of the world's currencies in recent years.
   a. What would be the impact on Americo's consolidated EPS if all foreign currencies were to appreciate 20% against the U.S. dollar?
   b. What would be the impact on Americo's consolidated EPS if all foreign currencies were to depreciate 20% against the U.S. dollar?

10. **Americo's Earnings and Global Taxation.** All MNEs attempt to minimize their global tax liabilities. Return to the original set of baseline assumptions and answer the following questions regarding Americo's global tax liabilities:
    a. What is the total amount—in U.S. dollars—which Americo is paying across its global business in corporate income taxes?
    b. What is Americo's *effective tax rate* (total taxes paid as a proportion of pre-tax profit)?

c. What would be the impact on Americo's EPS and global effective tax rate if Germany instituted a corporate tax reduction to 28%, and Americo's earnings before tax in Germany rose to € 5,000,000?

Internet Exercises

1. **International Capital Flows: Public and Private.** Major multinational organizations (some of which are listed below) attempt to track the relative movements and magnitudes of global capital investment. Using these Web pages and others you may find, prepare a two-page executive briefing on the question of whether capital generated in the industrialized countries is finding its way to the less developed and emerging markets. Is there some critical distinction between "less developed" and "emerging"?

The World Bank	www.worldbank.org
OECD	www.oecd.org
European Bank for Reconstruction and Development	www.ebrd.org

2. **External Debt.** The World Bank regularly compiles and analyzes the external debt of all countries globally. As part of their annual publication on World Development Indicators (WDI), they provide summaries of the long-term and short-term external debt obligations of selected countries online like that of Poland shown here. Go to their Web site and find the decomposition of external debt for Brazil, Mexico, and the Russian Federation.

The World Bank/data	www.worldbank.org/data

3. **World Economic Outlook.** The International Monetary Fund (IMF) regularly publishes its assessment of the prospects for the world economy. Choose a country of interest and use the IMF's current analysis to form your own expectations of its immediate economic prospects.

IMF Economic Outlook	www.imf.org/external/index.htm

4. ***Financial Times* Currency Global Macromaps.** The *Financial Times* provides a very helpful real-time global map of currency values and movements online. Use it to track the movements in currency.

Financial Times	http://markets.ft.com/ft/markets/currencies.asp

Financial Goals and Corporate Governance

Gerald L. Storch, CEO of Toys 'R' Us, says all CEOs share the same fundamental goals: enhance the value for the customer, maximize return to the shareholders, and develop a sustainable competitive advantage. "Largely, I believe that the differences are more subtle than what I've read in many articles. On a day-to-day basis, I do the same thing. I get to work every morning. I try to make the company better." — "Public vs. Private," *Forbes*, September 1, 2006.

LEARNING OBJECTIVES

◆ Examine how businesses can be owned, and how this impacts the separation between ownership and management—the agency problem.

◆ Evaluate the distinctions between the two major forms of management goals— shareholder wealth maximization versus stakeholder capitalism.

◆ Distinguish between the actual operational goals that may be pursued by management depending on whether the company is operated by owners or professional management.

◆ Analyze the goals and forms of corporate governance in use in the global marketplace today, and whether that attracts or deters cross-border investment.

◆ Examine how trends in corporate governance are altering the competitive landscape for multinational enterprises.

This chapter examines how cultural, legal, political, and institutional differences affect a firm's choice of financial goals and corporate governance. The chapter concludes with the Mini-Case, ***Luxury Wars—LVMH vs. Hermès***, the 2010 battle by Hermès of France to remain family controlled.

Who Owns the Business?

We begin our discussion of financial goals by asking two basic questions: 1) who owns the business? and 2) do the owners of the business manage the business themselves? Most companies are created by entrepreneurs who are either individuals or a small set of partners. In either case they may be members of a family. (Do not forget that even Microsoft started as the brain-child of two partners, Bill Gates and Paul Allen.) As shown in Exhibit 2.1, companies begin on the left-hand side as ownership version A, a 100% privately held business.

Over time, however, some firms choose to go public via an initial public offering, or IPO. Typically, only a relatively small percentage of the company is initially sold to the public, resulting in a company that may still be controlled by a small number of private investors, but who also have public shares outstanding, which are generating a market-based share price on a daily basis. This is ownership version B, as shown in Exhibit 2.1.

Whether the ownership structure ever actually moves from version B to C or D is very case specific. Some companies may sell more and more of their equity interests into the public marketplace, possibly eventually becoming totally publicly traded. Or the private owner or family may choose to retain a major share but does not have explicit control. Possibly, as has been the case in recent years, a firm that has reached ownership versions C or D may move back toward B or even A as the company becomes owned outright by a private owner. For example, in late 2005 a very large private firm, Koch Industries (U.S.), purchased all outstanding shares of Georgia-Pacific (U.S.), a very large publicly traded forest products company. Koch took Georgia-Pacific private.

An added consideration is that even when the firm's ownership is publicly traded, it may still be controlled by a single investor or a small group of investors, including major institutional investors. This means that the control of the company is much like the privately held company, and therefore reflects the interests and goals of the individual investor. And as shown in *Global Finance in Practice 2.1*, family-controlled firms all over the world, including France, may outperform publicly traded firms.

As discussed in the "Corporate Governance" section later in this chapter, something else of significance results from the initial sale of shares to the public: the firm becomes subject to many of the increased legal, regulatory, and reporting requirements in most countries surrounding the sale and trading of securities. In the United States, for example, going public

EXHIBIT 2.1   Who Owns the Business?

Who owns the business—whether it's privately held or publicly traded—has a significant impact on the relationship between ownership and operational ownership.

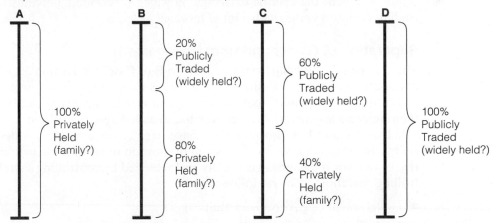

Although most businesses begin their lives as 100% privately held, often by a family, some firms go public gradually. Often selling only 20% equity interest publicly at first, some sell greater and greater equity interests to the public markets, possibly becoming 100% publicly traded.

Recently, however, many firms in the U.S. and U.K. markets have begun somewhat reversing the process, with private equity funds buying all outstanding shares, taking the firm private once more.

GLOBAL FINANCE IN PRACTICE   2.1

Family-Controlled Firms in France Outperform the Public Sector

Translation: "Why do family firms outperform the CAC 40 index?"

Among the major industrial countries, France has the highest number of family businesses (about 65% of the CAC 40 firms are family owned versus only about 24% in the U.K.). This includes Bouygues, Dassault, Michelin and Peugeot.

Over the 1990–2006 period, French family firms generated a 639% return to their owners, whereas the major French index, the CAC 40, returned only 292%. This family-owned firm dominance is attributed to three factors: 1) they focus on the long-term; 2) they stick to their core business; and 3) because the owners are closer to management, fewer conflicts arise between management and ownership (fewer agency problems in the terminology of Finance).

Source: Le Figaro, June 2007.

means the firm will now have to disclose a sizable degree of financial and operational detail, publish this information at least quarterly, comply with Securities and Exchange Commission (SEC) rules and regulations, and comply with all the specific operating and reporting requirements of the specific exchange on which it is traded. Obviously, the move to public trading of shares comes with a lot of luggage!

Separation of Ownership from Management

The change in ownership from version A to B or C or D in Exhibit 2.1 carries with it another major change—the possibility that the firm is managed by hired professionals, not owners. This raises the possibility that ownership and management may not be perfectly aligned in their business and financial objectives, the so-called *agency problem*.

The U.S. and U.K. stock markets have been characterized by widespread ownership of shares. Management owns only a small proportion of stock in their firms. In contrast, in the rest of the world ownership is usually characterized by controlling shareholders. Typical controlling shareholders are as follows:

◆ Government (e.g., privatized utilities)
◆ Institutions (e.g., banks in Germany)
◆ Family (e.g., in France and Asia)
◆ Consortiums (e.g., *keiretsus* in Japan and *chaebols* in South Korea)

Control is enhanced by ownership of shares with dual voting rights, interlocking directorates, staggered election of the board of directors, takeover safeguards, and other techniques not used in the Anglo-American markets. However, the recent emergence of huge equity funds and hedge funds in the United States and the United Kingdom has led to the privatization of some very prominent publicly traded firms.

What Is the Goal of Management?

As Trident becomes more deeply committed to multinational operations, a new constraint develops—one that springs from divergent worldwide opinions and practices as to just what the firms' overall goal should be from the perspective of top management, as well as the role of corporate governance.

> *What do investors want? First, of course, investors want performance: strong pre-dictable earnings and sustainable growth. Second, they want transparency, accountability, open communications and effective corporate governance. Companies that fail to move toward international standards in each of these areas will fail to attract and retain international capital.*
>
> —"The Brave New World of Corporate Governance," *LatinFinance*, May 2001.

An introductory course in finance is usually taught within the framework of maximizing shareholders' wealth as *the goal of management*. In fact, every business student memorizes the concept of *maximizing shareholder value* sometime during his or her college education. This rather rote memorization, however, has at least two major challenges: 1) it is not necessarily the accepted goal of management across countries to maximize the wealth of shareholders—other stakeholders may carry substantial weight and 2) it is extremely difficult to carry out. *Creating value* is—like so many lofty goals—much easier said than done.

Although the idea of maximizing shareholder wealth is probably realistic both in theory and in practice in the Anglo-American markets, it is not always exclusive elsewhere. Some basic differences in corporate and investor philosophies exist between the Anglo-American markets and those in the rest of the world. Therefore, one must realize that the so-called *universal truths* taught in basic finance courses are actually *culturally determined norms*.

Shareholder Wealth Maximization Model

The Anglo-American markets have a philosophy that a firm's objective should follow the *shareholder wealth maximization (SWM)* model. More specifically, the firm should strive to maximize the return to shareholders, as measured by the sum of capital gains and dividends, for a given level of risk. Alternatively, the firm should minimize the risk to shareholders for a given rate of return.

The SWM model assumes as a universal truth that the stock market is *efficient*. This means that the share price is always correct because it captures all the expectations of return and risk as perceived by investors. It quickly incorporates new information into the share price. Share prices, in turn, are deemed the best allocators of capital in the macro economy.

The SWM model also treats its definition of risk as a universal truth. Risk is defined as the added risk that the firm's shares bring to a diversified portfolio. The total operational risk of the firm can be eliminated through portfolio diversification by the investors. Therefore, this *unsystematic risk*, the risk of the individual security, should not be a prime concern for management unless it increases the prospect of bankruptcy. *Systematic risk*, the risk of the market in general, cannot be eliminated. This reflects risk that the share price will be a function of the stock market.

Agency Theory. The field of *agency theory* is the study of how shareholders can motivate management to accept the prescriptions of the SWM model.[1] For example, liberal use of stock options should encourage management to think like shareholders. Whether these inducements succeed is open to debate. However, if management deviates too much from SWM objectives of working to maximize the returns to the shareholders, then the board of directors should replace them. In cases where the board is too weak or ingrown to take this action, the discipline of the equity markets could do it through a takeover. This discipline is made possible by the one-share-one-vote rule that exists in most Anglo-American markets.

Long-Term versus Short-Term Value Maximization. During the 1990s, the economic boom and rising stock prices in the United States and abroad exposed a flaw in the SWM model, especially in the United States. Instead of seeking long-term value maximization, several large U.S. corporations sought short-term value maximization (e.g., the continuing debate about meeting the market's expected quarterly earnings). This strategy was partly motivated by the overly generous use of stock options to motivate top management. In order to maximize growth in short-term earnings and to meet inflated expectations by investors, firms such as Enron, Global Crossing, Health South, Adelphia, Tyco, Parmalat, and WorldCom undertook risky, deceptive, and sometimes dishonest practices for the recording of earnings and/or obfuscation of liabilities, which ultimately led to their demise. It also led to highly visible prosecutions of their CEOs, CFOs, accounting firms, legal advisers, and other related parties. This destructive short-term focus by both management and investors has been correctly labeled *impatient capitalism*. This point of debate is also sometimes referred to as the firm's *investment horizon* in reference to how long it takes the firm's actions, its investments and operations, to result in earnings.

In contrast to impatient capitalism is *patient capitalism*, which focuses on long-term shareholder wealth maximization. Legendary investor Warren Buffett, through his investment vehicle Berkshire Hathaway, represents one of the best of the patient capitalists. Buffett has become a multibillionaire by focusing his portfolio on mainstream firms that grow slowly but steadily with the economy such as Coca Cola. He was not lured into investing in the high growth but risky dot.coms of 2000 or the "high tech" sector that eventually imploded in 2001.

Stakeholder Capitalism Model

In the non–Anglo-American markets, controlling shareholders also strive to maximize long-term returns to equity. However, they are more constrained by powerful other stakeholders. In particular, labor unions are more powerful than in the Anglo-American markets. Governments interfere more in the marketplace to protect important stakeholder groups, such as local communities, the environment, and employment. Banks and other financial institutions are more important creditors than securities markets. This model has been labeled the stakeholder capitalism model (SCM).

Market Efficiency. The SCM model does not assume that equity markets are either efficient or inefficient. It does not really matter because the firm's financial goals are not exclusively shareholder-oriented since they are constrained by the other stakeholders. In any case, the SCM model assumes that long-term "loyal" shareholders, typically controlling shareholders, should influence corporate strategy rather than the transient portfolio investor.

---

[1]Michael Jensen and W. Meckling, "Theory of the Firm: Managerial Behavior, Agency Costs, and Ownership Structure," *Journal of Financial Economics*, No. 3, 1976, and Michael C. Jensen, "Agency Cost of Free Cash Flow, Corporate Finance and Takeovers," *American Economic Review*, 76, 1986, pp. 323–329.

Risk. The SCM model assumes that *total risk,* that is, operating and financial risk, does count. It is a specific-corporate objective to generate growing earnings and dividends over the long run with as much certainty as possible, given the firm's mission statement and goals. Risk is measured more by product market variability than by short-term variation in earnings and share price.

Single versus Multiple Goals. Although the SCM model typically avoids a flaw of the SWM model, namely impatient capital that is short-run oriented, it has its own flaw. Trying to meet the desires of multiple stakeholders leaves management without a clear signal about the trade-offs. Instead, management tries to influence the trade-offs through written and oral disclosures and complex compensation systems.

The Score Card. In contrast to the SCM model, the SWM model requires a single goal of value maximization with a well-defined score card. In the words of Michael Jensen:

> *Maximizing the total market value of the firm—that is, the sum of the market values of the equity, debt and any other contingent claims outstanding on the firm—is the objective function that will guide managers in making the optimal tradeoffs among multiple constituencies (or stakeholders). It tells the firm to spend an additional dollar of resources to satisfy the desires of each constituency as long as that constituency values the result at more than a dollar. In this case, the payoff to the firm from the investment of resources is at least a dollar (in terms of market value).[2]*

Although both models have their strengths and weaknesses, in recent years two trends have led to an increasing focus on the shareholder wealth form. First, as more of the non–Anglo-American markets have increasingly privatized their industries, the shareholder wealth focus is seemingly needed to attract international capital from outside investors, many of whom are from other countries. Second, and still quite controversial, many analysts believe that shareholder-based MNEs are increasingly dominating their global industry segments. Nothing attracts followers like success.

Operational Goals

It is one thing to say *maximize value*, but it is another to actually do it. The management objective of maximizing profit is not as simple as it sounds, because the measure of profit used by ownership/management differs between the privately held firm and the publicly traded firm. In other words, is management attempting to maximize current income, capital appreciation, or both?

The return to a shareholder in a publicly traded firm combines current income in the form of dividends and capital gains from the appreciation of share price:

$$\text{Shareholder return} = \frac{\text{Dividend}}{\text{Price}_1} + \frac{\text{Price}_2 - \text{Price}_1}{\text{Price}_1}$$

where the initial price, P_1, is equivalent to the initial investment by the shareholder, and P_2 is the price of the share at the end of period. The shareholder theoretically receives income from both components. For example, over the past 50 or 60 years in the U.S. marketplace, a diversified investor may have received a total average annual return of 14%, split roughly between dividends, 2%, and capital gains, 12%.

---

[2]Michael C. Jensen, "Value Maximization, Stakeholder Theory, and the Corporate Objective Function," *Journal of Applied Corporate Finance*, Fall 2001, Volume 14, No. 3, pp. 8–21, p. 12.

Management generally believes it has the most direct influence over the first component—the *dividend yield*. Management makes strategic and operational decisions that grow sales and generate profits. Then it distributes those profits to ownership in the form of dividends. *Capital gains*—the change in the share price as traded in the equity markets—is much more complex, and reflects many forces that are not in the direct control of management. Despite growing market share, profits, or any other traditional measure of business success, the market may not reward these actions directly with share price appreciation. Many top executives believe that stock markets move in mysterious ways and are not always consistent in their valuations.

A privately held firm has a much simpler shareholder return objective function: maximize current and sustainable income. The privately held firm does not have a share price (it does have a value, but this is not a definitive market-determined value in the way in which we believe markets work). It therefore simply focuses on generating current income, dividend income, to generate the returns to its ownership. If the privately held ownership is a family, the family may also place a great emphasis on the ability to sustain those earnings over time while maintaining a slower rate of growth, which can be managed by the family itself. It is therefore critical that ownership and ownership's specific financial interests be understood from the very start if we are to understand the strategic and financial goals and objectives of management.

The privately held firm may also be less aggressive (take fewer risks) than the publicly traded firm. Without a public share price, and therefore the ability of outside investors to speculate on the risks and returns associated with company business developments, the privately held firm may choose to take fewer risks. This may mean that it will not attempt to grow sales and profits as rapidly, and therefore may not require the capital (equity and debt) needed for rapid growth. Exhibit 2.2 provides a striking example of this lower leverage; private firms, according to McKinsey's survey analysis, have consistently used lower levels of financial leverage over the past decade. McKinsey also notes that according to their research,

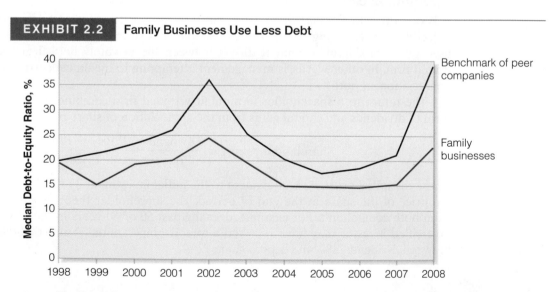

EXHIBIT 2.2   Family Businesses Use Less Debt

Source: "The Five Attributes of Enduring Family Businesses," Christian Caspar, Ana Karina Dias, and Heinz-Peter Elstrodt, *McKinsey Quarterly*, January 2010, p. 6.

the cost of debt is actually cheaper—the average yield spread on corporate bonds being 32 basis points lower for family-owned firms.[3]

Operational Goals for MNEs. The MNE must be guided by operational goals suitable for various levels of the firm. Even if the firm's goal is to maximize shareholder value, the manner in which investors value the firm is not always obvious to the firm's top management. Therefore, most firms hope to receive a favorable investor response to the achievement of operational goals that can be controlled by the way in which the firm performs, and then hope—if we can use that term—that the market will reward their results.

The MNE must determine the proper balance between three common operational financial objectives:

1. Maximization of consolidated after-tax income
2. Minimization of the firm's effective global tax burden
3. Correct positioning of the firm's income, cash flows, and available funds as to country and currency

These goals are frequently incompatible, in that the pursuit of one may result in a less desirable outcome in regard to another. Management must make decisions about the proper trade-offs between goals (which is why people rather than computers are employed as managers).

Consolidated Profits. The primary operational goal of the MNE is to *maximize consolidated profits, after-tax. Consolidated profits* are the profits of all the individual units of the firm originating in many different currencies expressed in the currency of the parent company. This is not to say that management is not striving to maximize the present value of all future cash flows. It is simply the case that most of the day-to-day decision making in global management is about current earnings. The leaders of the MNE, the management team who are developing and implementing the firm's strategy, must think far beyond current earnings.

For example, foreign subsidiaries have their own set of traditional financial statements: 1) a statement of income, summarizing the revenues and expenses experienced by the firm over the year; 2) a balance sheet, summarizing the assets employed in generating the unit's revenues, and the financing of those assets; and 3) a statement of cash flows, summarizing those activities of the firm that generate and then use cash flows over the year. These financial statements are expressed initially in the local currency of the unit for tax and reporting purposes to the local government, but they must be consolidated with the parent company's financial statements for reporting to shareholders.

Public/Private Hybrids. The global business environment is, as one analyst termed it, "a messy place," and the ownership of companies of all kinds, including MNEs, is not necessarily purely public or purely private. According to McKinsey's recent study of global businesses:[4]

> *One-third of all companies in the S&P 500 index and 40 percent of the 250 largest companies in France and Germany are defined as family businesses, meaning that a family owns a significant share and can influence important decisions, particularly the election of the chairman and CEO.*

---

[3]"The Five Attributes of Enduring Family Businesses," Christian Caspar, Ana Karina Dias, and Heinz-Peter Elstrodt, *McKinsey Quarterly*, January 2010, p. 6.

[4]"The Five Attributes of Enduring Family Businesses," Christian Caspar, Ana Karina Dias, and Heinz-Peter Elstrodt, *McKinsey Quarterly*, January 2010, p. 2.

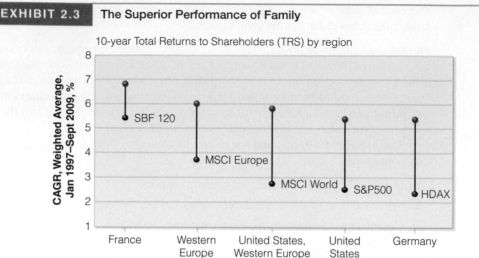

EXHIBIT 2.3   The Superior Performance of Family

10-year Total Returns to Shareholders (TRS) by region

● Family Businesses   ● Index

Source: "The Five Attributes of Enduring Family Businesses," Christian Caspar, Ana Karina Dias, and Heinz-Peter Elstrodt, McKinsey Quarterly, January 2010, p. 7.

In other words, the firm may be publicly traded, but a family still wields substantial power over the strategic and operational decisions within the firm. This, however, may prove to be a good thing. As illustrated in Exhibit 2.3, the financial performance of family-based businesses (as measured by total returns to shareholders) in five different regions of the globe were superior to their non-family publicly traded counterparts.

Why do family-influenced businesses seemingly outperform the truly independents? The answer appears to be the same as that noted by *Le Figaro* in *Global Finance in Practice 2.1*. According to Credit Suisse, there are three key catalysts for the performance of *stocks with significant family influence* (SSFI): 1) management with a longer term focus; 2) better alignment between management and shareholder interests; and 3) stronger focus on the core business of the firm.

Corporate Governance

Although the governance structure of any company, domestic, international, or multinational, is fundamental to its very existence, this subject has become the lightning rod of political and business debate in the past few years as failures in governance in a variety of forms has led to corporate fraud and failure. Abuses and failures in corporate governance have dominated global business news in recent years. Beginning with the accounting fraud and questionable ethics of business conduct at Enron culminating in its bankruptcy in the fall of 2001, failures in corporate governance have raised issues about the very ethics and culture of business conduct.

The Goal of Corporate Governance

The single overriding objective of corporate governance in the Anglo-American markets is the optimization over time of the returns to shareholders. In order to achieve this, good governance practices should focus the attention of the board of directors of the corporation on this objective by developing and implementing a strategy for the corporation, which ensures corporate growth and improvement in the value of the corporation's equity. At the same time, it should ensure an effective relationship with stakeholders.[5] One of the most widely accepted statements of good corporate governance practices are those established by the Organization for Economic Cooperation and Development (OECD):[6]

- ◆ **The rights of shareholders.** The corporate governance framework should protect shareholders' rights.

- ◆ **The equitable treatment of shareholders.** The corporate governance framework should ensure the equitable treatment of all shareholders, including minority and foreign shareholders. All shareholders should have the opportunity to obtain effective redress for violation of their rights.

- ◆ **The role of stakeholders in corporate governance.** The corporate governance framework should recognize the rights of stakeholders as established by law and encourage active cooperation between corporations and stakeholders in creating wealth, jobs, and the sustainability of financially sound enterprises.

- ◆ **Disclosure and transparency.** The corporate governance framework should ensure that timely and accurate disclosure is made on all material matters regarding the corporation, including the financial situation, performance, ownership, and governance of the company.

- ◆ **The responsibilities of the board.** The corporate governance framework should ensure the strategic guidance of the company, the effective monitoring of management by the board, and the board's accountability to the company and the shareholders.

These principles obviously focus on several key areas—shareholder rights and roles, disclosure and transparency, and the responsibilities of boards—which we will discuss in more detail.

The Structure of Corporate Governance

Our first challenge is to understand what people mean when they use the expression "corporate governance." Exhibit 2.4 provides an overview of the various parties and their responsibilities associated with the governance of the modern corporation. The modern corporation's actions and behaviors are directed and controlled by both *internal forces* and *external forces*.

The *internal forces*, the officers of the corporation (such as the chief executive officer or CEO) and the board of directors of the corporation (including the chairman of the board), are those directly responsible for determining both the strategic direction and the execution of the company's future. But they are not acting within a vacuum; they are subject to the constant prying eyes of the *external forces* in the marketplace who question the validity and soundness of their decisions and performance. These include the equity markets in which the shares are traded, the analysts who critique their investment prospects, the creditors and credit agencies who lend them money, the auditors and legal advisers who testify to the fairness and legality of their reporting, and the multitude of regulators who oversee their actions in order to protect the investment public.

---

[5]This definition of the corporate objective is based on that supported by the International Corporate Governance Network (ICGN), a nonprofit organization committed to improving corporate governance practices globally.

[6]"OECD Principles of Corporate Governance," The Organization for Economic Cooperation and Development, 1999, revised 2004.

EXHIBIT 2.4   The Structure of Corporate Governance

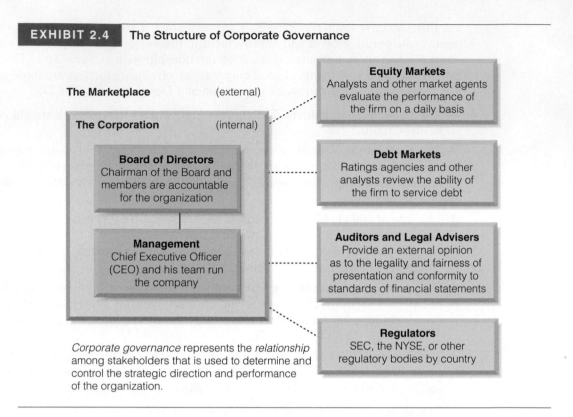

Corporate governance represents the *relationship* among stakeholders that is used to determine and control the strategic direction and performance of the organization.

The Board of Directors. The legal body that is accountable for the governance of the corporation is its board of directors. The board is composed of both employees of the organization (inside members) and senior and influential nonemployees (outside members). Areas of debate surrounding boards include the following: 1) the proper balance between inside and outside members; 2) the means by which board members are compensated for their service; and 3) the actual ability of a board to monitor and manage a corporation adequately when board members are spending sometimes less than five days a year in board activities. Outside members, often the current or retired chief executives of other major companies, may bring with them a healthy sense of distance and impartiality, which although refreshing, may also result in limited understanding of the true issues and events within the company.

Officers and Management. The senior officers of the corporation, the chief executive officer (CEO), the chief financial officer (CFO), and the chief operating officer (COO), are not only the most knowledgeable of the business, but also the creators and directors of its strategic and operational direction. The management of the firm is, according to theory, acting as a contractor—an *agent*—of shareholders to pursue value creation. They are positively motivated by salary, bonuses, and stock options or negatively motivated by the risk of losing their jobs. They may, however, have biases of self-enrichment or personal agendas, which the board and other corporate stakeholders are responsible for overseeing and policing. Interestingly, in more than 80% of the companies in the Fortune 500, the CEO is also the chairman of the board. This is, in the opinion of many, a conflict of interest and not in the best interests of the company and its shareholders.

Equity Markets. The publicly traded company, regardless of country of residence, is highly susceptible to the changing opinion of the marketplace. The equity markets themselves, whether they are the New York Stock Exchange/Euronext, London Stock Exchange, or

Mexico City Bolsa, should reflect the market's constant evaluation of the promise and performance of the individual company. The analysts are those self-described experts employed by the many investment banking firms who also trade in the client company shares. They are expected (sometimes naïvely) to evaluate the strategies, plans for execution of the strategies, and financial performance of the firms on a real-time basis. Analysts depend on the financial statements and other public disclosures of the firm for their information.

Debt Markets. Although the debt markets (banks and other financial institutions providing loans and various forms of securitized debt like corporate bonds), are not specifically interested in building shareholder value, they are indeed interested in the financial health of the company. Their interest, specifically, is in the company's ability to repay its debt in a timely and efficient manner. These markets, like the equity markets, must rely on the financial statements and other disclosures (public and private in this case) of the companies with which they work.

Auditors and Legal Advisers. Auditors and legal advisers are responsible for providing an external professional opinion as to the fairness, legality, and accuracy of corporate financial statements. In this process, they attempt to determine whether the firm's financial records and practices follow what in the United States is termed *generally accepted accounting principles* (*GAAP*) in regard to accounting procedures. But auditors and legal advisers are hired by the firms they are auditing, leading to a rather unique practice of policing their employers. The additional difficulty that has arisen in recent years is that the major accounting firms pursued the development of large consulting practices, often leading to a conflict of interest. An auditor not giving a clean bill of health to a client could not expect to gain many lucrative consulting contracts from that same firm in the near future.

Regulators. Publicly traded firms in the United States and elsewhere are subject to the regulatory oversight of both governmental organizations and non-governmental organizations. In the United States, the Securities and Exchange Commission (SEC) is a careful watchdog of the publicly traded equity markets, both of the behavior of the companies themselves in those markets and of the various investors participating in those markets. The SEC and other similar authorities outside of the United States require a regular and orderly disclosure process of corporate performance in order that all investors may evaluate the company's investment value with adequate, accurate, and fairly distributed information. This regulatory oversight is often focused on when and what information is released by the company, and to whom.

A publicly traded firm in the United States is also subject to the rules and regulations of the exchange upon which they are traded (New York Stock Exchange/Euronext, American Stock Exchange, and NASDAQ are the largest). These organizations, typically categorized as self-regulatory in nature, construct and enforce standards of conduct for both their member companies and themselves in the conduct of share trading.

Comparative Corporate Governance[7]

The origins of the need for a corporate governance process arise from the separation of ownership from management, and from the varying views by culture of who the stakeholders are and their significance. This assures that corporate governance practices will differ across countries, economies, and cultures. As described in Exhibit 2.5, though, the various corporate

---

[7]For a summary of comparative corporate governance see R. La Porta, F. Lopez-de-Silanes, and A. Schleifer, "Corporate Ownership Around the World," *Journal of Finance*, 54, 1999, pp. 471–517. See also A. Schleifer and R. Vishny, "A Survey of Corporate Governance," *Journal of Finance*, 52, 1997, pp. 737–783, and the Winter 2007 issue, Volume 19 Number 1, of the *Journal of Applied Corporate Finance*.

EXHIBIT 2.5	Comparative Corporate Governance Regimes	
Regime Basis	Characteristics	Examples
Market-based	Efficient equity markets; Dispersed ownership	United States, United Kingdom, Canada, Australia
Family-based	Management and ownership is combined; Family/majority and minority shareholders	Hong Kong, Indonesia, Malaysia, Singapore, Taiwan, France
Bank-based	Government influence in bank lending; Lack of transparency; Family control	Korea, Germany
Government affiliated	State ownership of enterprise; Lack of transparency; No minority influence	China, Russia

Source: Based on "Corporate Governance in Emerging Markets: An Asian Perspective," by J. Tsui and T. Shieh, in *International Finance and Accounting Handbook*, Third Edition, Frederick D.S. Choi, editor, Wiley, 2004, pp. 24.4–24.6.

governance regimes may be classified by regime. The regimes in turn reflect the evolution of business ownership and direction within the countries over time.

Market-based regimes, like that of the United States, Canada, and the United Kingdom, are characterized by relatively efficient capital markets in which the ownership of publicly traded companies is widely dispersed. *Family-based systems*, like those characterized in many of the emerging markets, Asian markets, and Latin American markets, not only started with strong concentrations of family ownership (as opposed to partnerships or small investment groups which are not family-based), but also have continued to be largely controlled by families even after going public. *Bank-based* and *government-based* regimes are those reflecting markets in which government ownership of property and industry has been the constant force over time, resulting in only marginal "public ownership" of enterprise, and even then, subject to significant restrictions on business practices.

These regimes are therefore a function of at least four major factors in the evolution of corporate governance principles and practices globally: 1) the financial market development; 2) the degree of separation between management and ownership; 3) the concept of disclosure and transparency; and 4) the historical development of the legal system.

Financial Market Development. The depth and breadth of capital markets is critical to the evolution of corporate governance practices. Country markets that have had relatively slow growth, as in the emerging markets, or have industrialized rapidly utilizing neighboring capital markets (as is the case of Western Europe), may not form large public equity market systems. Without significant public trading of ownership shares, high concentrations of ownership are preserved and few disciplined processes of governance are developed.

Separation of Management and Ownership. In countries and cultures in which the ownership of the firm has continued to be an integral part of management, agency issues and failures have been less problematic. In countries like the United States, in which ownership has become largely separated from management (and widely dispersed), aligning the goals of management and ownership is much more difficult.

Disclosure and Transparency. The extent of disclosure regarding the operations and financial results of a company vary dramatically across countries. Disclosure practices reflect a wide range of cultural and social forces, including the degree of ownership which is public, the degree to which government feels the need to protect investor's rights versus ownership rights, and the extent to which family-based and government-based business remains central to the culture. Transparency, a parallel concept to disclosure, reflects the visibility of decision making processes within the business organization.

Historical Development of the Legal System. Investor protection is typically better in countries in which *English common law* is the basis of the legal system, compared to the *codified civil law* that is typical in France and Germany (the so-called *Code Napoleon*). English common law is typically the basis of the legal systems in the United Kingdom and former colonies of the United Kingdom, including the United States and Canada. The Code Napoleon is typically the basis of the legal systems in former French colonies and the European countries that Napoleon once ruled, such as Belgium, Spain, and Italy. In countries with weak investor protection, controlling shareholder ownership is often a substitute for a lack of legal protection.

Note that we have not mentioned *ethics*. All of the principles and practices described so far have assumed that the individuals in roles of responsibility and leadership pursue them truly and fairly. That, however, has not always been the case.

Family Ownership and Corporate Governance

Although much of the discussion about corporate governance concentrates on the market-based regimes (see Exhibit 2.5), family-based regimes are arguably more common and more important worldwide, including the United States and Western Europe. For example, in a study of 5,232 corporations in 13 Western European countries, family-controlled firms represented 44% of the sample compared to 37% that were widely held.[8]

Recent research indicates that, as opposed to popular belief, family-owned firms in some highly developed economies typically outperform publicly owned firms. This is true not only in Western Europe but also in the United States. A recent study of firms included in the S&P500 found that families are present in fully one-third of the S&P500 and account for 18% of their outstanding equity. And, as opposed to popular opinion, family firms outperform nonfamily firms. (An added insight is that firms possessing a CEO from the family also perform better than those with outside-CEOs.) Interestingly, it seems that minority shareholders are actually better off according to this study when part of a family-influenced firm.[9]

Another study based on 120 Norwegian, founding family-controlled and nonfounding family-controlled firms, concluded that founding family control was associated with higher firm value. Furthermore, the impact of founding family directors on firm value is not affected by corporate governance conditions such as firm age, board independence, and number of share classes. The authors also found that the positive relation between founding family ownership and firm value is greater among older firms, firms with larger boards, and particularly when these firms have multiple classes of stock.[10] It is common for Norwegian firms and firms based in several other European countries to have dual classes of stock with differential voting rights.

---

[8]Mara Faccio and Larry H.P. Lang, "The Ultimate Ownership of Western European Corporations," *Journal of Financial Economics*, 65 (2002), p. 365. See also: Torben Pedersen and Steen Thomsen, "European Patterns of Corporate Ownership," *Journal of International Business Studies*, Vol. 28, No. 4, Fourth Quarter, 1997, pp. 759–778.

[9]Ronald C. Anderson and David M. Reeb, "Founding Family Ownership and Firm Performance from the S&P500," *The Journal of Finance*, June 2003, p. 1301.

[10]Chandra S. Mishra, Trond Randøy, and Jan Inge Jenssen, "The Effect of Founding Family Influence on Firm Value and Corporate Governance," *Journal of International Financial Management and Accounting*, Volume 12, Number 3, Autumn 2001, pp. 235–259.

Failures in Corporate Governance

Failures in corporate governance have become increasingly visible in recent years. The Enron scandal in the United States is well known. In addition to Enron, other firms that have revealed major accounting and disclosure failures, as well as executive looting, are World-Com, Parmalat, Global Crossing, Tyco, Adelphia, and HealthSouth.

In each case, prestigious auditing firms, such as Arthur Andersen, missed the violations or minimized them possibly because of lucrative consulting relationships or other conflicts of interest. Moreover, security analysts and banks urged investors to buy the shares and debt issues of these and other firms that they knew to be highly risky or even close to bankruptcy. Even more egregious, most of the top executives who were responsible for the mismanagement that destroyed their firms, walked away (initially) with huge gains on shares sold before the downfall, and even overly generous severance packages.

It appears that the day of reckoning has come. The first to fall (due to its involvement with Enron) was Arthur Andersen, one of the former "Big Five" U.S. accounting firms. However, many more legal actions against former executives are underway. Although the corruption scandals were first revealed in the United States, they have spread to Canada and the European Union countries.

Good Governance and Corporate Reputation

Does good corporate governance matter? This is actually a difficult question, and the realistic answer has been largely dependent on outcomes historically. For example, as long as Enron's share price continued to rise dramatically throughout the 1990s, questions over transparency, accounting propriety, and even financial facts were largely overlooked by all of the stakeholders of the corporation. Yet, eventually, the fraud, deceit, and failure of the multitude of corporate governance practices resulted in the bankruptcy of the firm. It not only destroyed the wealth of investors, but the careers, incomes, and savings of so many of its basic stakeholders—its own employees. Ultimately, *yes*, good governance does matter. A lot.

Good corporate governance is dependent on a variety of factors, one of which is the general governance reputation of the country of incorporation and registration. Exhibit 2.6 presents selected recent country rankings compiled by Governance Metrics International (GMI). Studies by many different organizations and academics, including GMI, have continued to show a number of important linkages between good governance (at both the country and corporate levels) and the cost of capital (lower), returns to shareholders (higher), and corporate profitability (higher). An added dimension of interest is the role of country governance as it may influence the country in which international investors may choose to invest. Early studies indicate that good governance does indeed attract international investor interest.

One way of signaling good governance to the investor markets is to adopt—and publicize—a fundamental set of governance policies and practices. Exhibit 2.7 presents four specific elements which make up what we believe is a growing consensus on good governance practices. Those practices—board composition, management compensation structure and oversight, corporate auditing practices, and public disclosure—are no longer elements of much debate. Although still influenced by country of incorporation, adoption of these basics will go a long ways toward improving a company's governance and reputation.

A third way to signal good corporate governance in non–Anglo-American firms is to elect one or more Anglo-American board members. This was shown to be true for a select

EXHIBIT 2.6 GMI's Country Governance Rankings 2010

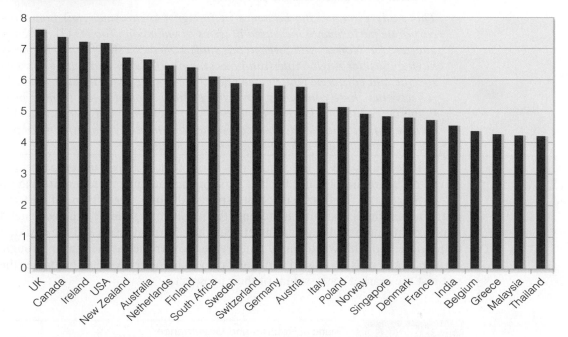

Source: Governance Metrics International, www.gmiratings.com. Top 24 rankings as of September 27, 2010.

EXHIBIT 2.7 The Growing Consensus on Good Corporate Governance

Although there are a multitude of different cultural and legal approaches used to corporate governance worldwide, there is also simultaneously a growing consensus on what constitutes good corporate governance. That consensus would include the following:

◆ **Composition of the Board of Directors.** The Board should have both internal and external members. More importantly, it should be staffed by individuals of true experience and knowledge of not only their own rules and responsibilities, but the nature and conduct of the corporate business.

◆ **Management Compensation.** A management compensation system which is both aligned with corporate performance (financial and otherwise), with significant oversight by the board and open disclosure to shareholders and investors.

◆ **Corporate Auditing.** Independent auditing of corporate financial results on a meaningful real-time basis. An audit process with oversight by a Board committee composed primarily of external members would be an additional significant improvement.

◆ **Public Reporting and Disclosure.** Timely public reporting of both financial and non-financial operating results which may be used by investors to assess the investment outlook. This should also include transparency and reporting around potentially significant liabilities.

The quality and credibility of all internal corporate practices on good governance, however, are still subject to the quality of a country's corporate law, its protection of both creditor and investor rights, including minority shareholders, and the country's ability to provide adequate and appropriate enforcement.

group of Scandinavian firms. A study by Oxelheim and Randøy of a database of Norwegian and Swedish firms concluded the following:[11]

> *This study examines the influence of foreign (Anglo-American) board membership on corporate performance measured in terms of valuation (Tobin's Q). Based on firms headquartered in Norway and Sweden this study indicates a significantly higher value for firms having outsider Anglo-American board member(s) after controlling for a variety of firm-specific and corporate governance related factors. We argue that the superior performance reflects that these companies have successfully broken away from a partly segmented domestic capital market by "importing," through their outsider Anglo-American board member(s), an Anglo-American corporate governance system offering improved monitoring opportunities and enhanced investor recognition.*

A follow-up study of the same firms found that CEO pay increased because of the perceived reduction in tolerance for bad performance and increased monitoring required.[12]

A fourth and final analysis focuses specifically on several financial performance metrics of the actual firms. Exhibit 2.8 presents the results of a series of studies which found that as equity rights increased the margin between the return on assets and the cost of capital for the firms increased. This would imply that greater governance as measured through equity rights contributes to or is correlated with higher financial returns of the companies themselves, and not just the market's assessment of their prospects.

EXHIBIT 2.8   **Financial Returns and Governance**

Greater equity rights translate into higher returns on investment relative to the cost of capital

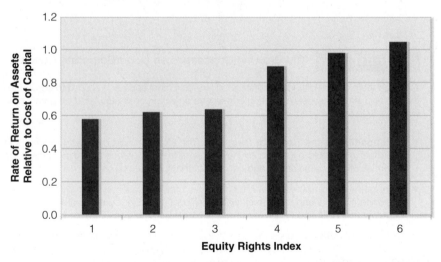

Source: "Corporate Governance and Development," Stijn Claessens, *Focus*, Global Corporate Governance Forum, Washington, DC, p. 18, Figure 7. The exhibit depicts the marginal rates of return on new investment adjusted for the cost of capital calculated using the Tobin's Q model. The index on equity rights is from La Porta, et al (1998), as Drawn from Gugler, Mueller, and Yurtoglu (2003).

---

[11]Lars Oxelheim and Trond Randøy, "The Impact of Foreign Board Membership on Firm Value," *Journal of Banking and Finance*, Volume 27, Number 12, 2003, pp. 2369–2392.

[12]Lars Oxelheim and Trond Randøy, "The Anglo-American Financial Influence on CEO Compensation in Non–Anglo-American Firms," *Journal of International Business Studies*, Volume 36, Number 4, July 2005, pp. 470–483.

Corporate Governance Reform

Within the United States and the United Kingdom, the main corporate governance problem is the one treated by agency theory: with widespread share ownership, how can a firm align management's interest with that of the shareholders? Since individual shareholders do not have the resources or the power to monitor management, the U.S. and U.K. markets rely on regulators to assist in the agency theory monitoring task. Outside the United States and the United Kingdom, large controlling shareholders (including Canada) are in the majority. They are able to monitor management in some ways better than regulators. However, controlling shareholders pose a different agency problem. How can minority shareholders be protected against the controlling shareholders?

In recent years, reform in the United States and Canada has been largely regulatory. Reform elsewhere has been largely adoption of principles rather than stricter legal regulations. The principles approach is softer, less costly, and less likely to conflict with other existing regulations.

Sarbanes-Oxley Act. The U.S. Congress passed the Sarbanes-Oxley Act (SOX) in July 2002. Named after its two primary congressional sponsors, SOX had four major requirements: 1) CEOs and CFOs of publicly traded firms must vouch for the veracity of the firm's published financial statements; 2) corporate boards must have audit and compensation committees drawn from independent (outside) directors; and 3) companies are prohibited from making loans to corporate officers and directors; and 4) companies must test their internal financial controls against fraud.

The first provision—the so-called *signature clause*, has already had significant impacts on the way in which companies prepare their financial statements. The provision was intended to instill a sense of responsibility and accountability in senior management (and therefore fewer explanations of "the auditors signed off on it"). The companies themselves have pushed the same procedure downward in their organizations, often requiring business unit managers and directors at lower levels to sign their financial statements. Severe penalties were enacted in case of non-compliance.

SOX has been much more expensive to implement than was originally expected during the debate in the U.S. Congress. Apart from the obvious costs of filling out more forms, many critics argue that too much time is consumed in meeting the new regulations, modifying internal controls to combat fraud, and restating past earnings, rather than running the operations of the firms. This cost may be disproportionately high for small firms that must meet the same regulatory requirements as large firms. In particular, auditing and legal fees have skyrocketed.

Everyone is afraid of following in the footsteps of Arthur Andersen that collapsed as a result of the Enron scandal. (The "Big Five" accounting firms became the "Big Four" overnight!) The net result may lead to more small but growing firms choosing to sell out to larger firms instead of going the initial public offering (IPO) route. Other firms may simply choose to stay private, feeling that the costs of public offerings outweigh the benefits. Moreover, many firms may become more risk averse. Lower level employees might pass all risky decisions up the line to a more central risk assessment level. Such an action would slow down decision making, and potentially, growth.

SOX has been quite controversial internationally. Its "one size fits all" style conflicts with a number of the corporate governance practices already in place in markets that view themselves as having better governance records than the United States. A foreign firm wishing to list or continue listing their shares on a U.S. exchange must comply with the law. Some companies, such as Porsche, withdrew plans for a U.S. listing specifically in opposition to SOX. Other companies, however, including many of the largest foreign companies traded on U.S. exchanges such as Unilever, Siemens, and ST Microelectronics, have stated their willingness to comply—if they can find acceptable compromises between U.S. law and the governance requirements and principles in their own countries. One example is Germany, where supervisory board audit committees must include employee representatives. But according to U.S. law, employees are not independent. Many of these listed firms have concluded that they need access to the U.S. capital market and therefore must comply, others have not. As *Global Finance in Practice 2.2* indicates, good governance is a global issue of considerable debate.

GLOBAL FINANCE IN PRACTICE   2.2

Is Good Governance Good Business Globally?

The term 'good governance' is, in many instances, a highly politically charged term. When talking to the press, many directors and executives argue that the pursuit of good governance practices is good for business globally. However, those same officials may also argue that stringent reporting and disclosure requirements, like those imposed by the U.S. under Sarbanes-Oxley, harm business competitiveness and growth and ultimately, the attractiveness of listing and trading their securities in the United States. In the end, the devil may indeed be in the detail.

A number of examples from around the world are helpful in understanding the complexity of finding common ground in "good" corporate governance.

◆ Siemens (Germany) has implemented a company-wide transformation program containing two significant mindset changes: seeing integrity and performance as not mutually exclusive (clean business always and everywhere), and defining corporate governance in a way that provides space for entrepreneurial behavior, focused on long-term sustainable value creation for all stakeholders. It believes that this will generate ever-greater transparency and higher-quality business and financial reporting.[1]

◆ Western governance practices are only now starting to take hold in the Gulf region of the Middle East. Sabic, the Saudi Basic Industries Corporation, is widely considered a leader in good governance practices in the region, is helping to promote board structures which separate audit, remuneration, and other director functions. The growing influence of the Gulf Cooperation Council Board Directors Institute, a nonprofit organization for the sharing of governance practices in the Gulf, has been instrumental in promoting transparency and disclosure.[2]

◆ Neeraj Bhargava, CEO of WNS Global Services, an India-based outsourcing firm, has adamantly argued that the stringent demands of Western governance practices like those of Sarbanes-Oxley have helped both investors and clients "view our organization as a trusted, well-run and compliant company." In a global marketplace in which it is ever-harder to raise capital critical for corporate growth and development, Bhargava argues that listing in the United States and therefore complying with U.S. corporate governance requirements has gained his firm credibility, global visibility, shareholder value, and liquidity. According to Bhargava "Sarbanes-Oxley compliance [has] benefits: Business processes are better defined, vetted by experts and made more efficient."[3]

◆ One size may not fit all, however. Culture has an enormous impact on business conduct, and many countries are finding their own way without necessarily following U.S. or European practices. For example, a number of Japanese leaders note that the Japanese corporate governance system differs from the Western system, but has evolved while preserving Japanese culture and history. They argue that cultural background and history should not be ignored when developing and implementing global standards, regulations, and oversight.

◆ Concerns over "governance shopping," however, continue. In January 2011, the U.S. Securities and Exchange Commission noted growing concerns over Chinese firms that were choosing to list in the United States rather than at home, frequently using a "network of professionals" who were facilitating the listing with questionable financial reports.[4] This is partly aided by the continuing evidence that listing in the United States provides a share premium from the umbrella of perceived U.S. good governance.[5]

[1]"Good Governance and Sustainability Fundamental for Improved Business Reporting," International Federation of Accountants, *Project on Business Reporting*, June 2010.

[2]"Making Good Governance Good Business in the Gulf," *Arabic Knowledge@Wharton*, April 6, 2010; "Building Better Boards: A Review of Board Effectiveness in the Gulf," GCC Board Directors Institute, 2009.

[3]"Good Governance Is Good Business," Neeraj Bhargava, *Wall Street Journal*, August 28, 2006.

[4]"U.S. Gets Tough on China Listings," Isabella Steger, *Wall Street Journal*, December 22, 2010.

[5]"Has New York Become Less Competitive in Global Markets? Evaluating Foreign Listing Choices over Time," Craig Doidge, George Andrew Karolyi, and Rene M. Stulz, National Bureau of Economic Research (NBER); European Corporate Governance Institute (ECGI), July 2007.

Board Structure and Compensation. Many critics have argued for the United States to move more toward structural reforms more consistent with European standards (e.g., prohibiting CEOs from also being chairmen). Although this is increasingly common, there is no regulatory or other legal requirement to force the issue. Secondly, and more radically, would be to move toward the two-tiered structure of countries like Germany, in which there is a supervisory board (largely outsiders, and typically large—Siemens has 18 members) and a management board (predominantly insiders, and small—Siemens has eight members).

Although SOX addresses the agency theory problem of transparency, it does not address the agency theory problem of aligning the goals of boards and managers with the interests of shareholders. In the past, the United States was characterized by compensation schemes to reward directors and management with a combination of an annual stipend or salary with significant stock options. However, when stock options go *underwater* (become essentially valueless because they are so far out-of-the-money), it does not cost the recipient anything directly, only the loss of a potential future benefit. Indeed, some firms simply rewrite the options so that they have higher values immediately. It now appears that many firms are changing their compensation schemes to replace options with *restricted stock*. Restricted stock cannot be sold publicly for some specified period of time. If the price of the firm's shares falls, the recipient has actually lost money and is normally not recompensated by receiving more restricted shares.

Transparency, Accounting, and Auditing. The concept of *transparency* is also one which has been raised in a variety of different markets and contexts. Transparency is a rather common term used to describe the degree to which an investor—either existing or potential—can discern the true activities and value drivers of a company from the disclosures and financial results reported. For example, Enron was often considered a "black box" when it came to what the actual operational and financial results and risks were for its multitude of business lines. The consensus of corporate governance experts is that all firms, globally, should work toward increasing the transparency of the firm's risk-return profile.

The accounting process itself has now come under debate. The U.S. system is characterized as strictly rule based, rather than conceptually based, as is common in Western Europe. Many critics of U.S. corporate governance practices point to this as a fundamental flaw, in which clever accountants find ways to follow the rules, yet not meet the underlying purpose for which the rules were intended. An extension of the accounting process debate is that of the role and remuneration associated with auditing. This is the process of using third parties, paid by the firm, to vet their reporting practices as being consistent with generally accepted accounting principles. As the collapse of Arthur Andersen following the Enron debacle illustrated, serious questions remain as to the validity of this current practice.

Minority Shareholder Rights. Finally, the issue of minority shareholder rights continues to rage in many of the world's largest markets. Many of the emerging markets are still characterized by the family-based corporate governance regime, where the family remains in control even after the firm has gone public. But what of the interests and voices of the other shareholders? How are their interests preserved in organizations where families or controlling investors make all true decisions, including the boards?

Poor performance of management usually requires changes to management, ownership, or both. Exhibit 2.9 illustrates some of the alternative paths available to shareholders when they are dissatisfied with firm performance. Depending on the culture and accepted practices, it is not unusual for many investors to—for an extended time—remain quietly disgruntled regarding share price performance. If more active in response, they may sell their shares. It is the third and fourth responses, shareholder activist responses, in which management hears a much louder dissatisfied shareholder voice.

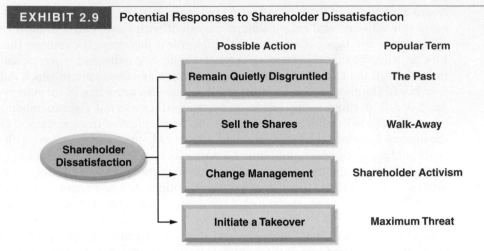

EXHIBIT 2.9   Potential Responses to Shareholder Dissatisfaction

What counts is that the management of a publicly quoted company, and its board of directors, know that the company can become the subject of a hostile takeover bid if they fail to perform. The growth of equity and hedge funds in the United States and elsewhere in recent years has strengthened this threat as leveraged buyouts are once again common.

Summary of Learning Objectives

Examine how businesses can be owned, and how this impacts the separation between ownership and management—the agency problem

◆ Most companies are created by entrepreneurs who are either individuals, partners, or members of a family.

◆ Over time, some firms may choose to go public via an initial public offering (IPO).

◆ The U.S. and U.K. stock markets are characterized by widespread ownership of shares. In the rest of the world, ownership is usually characterized by controlling shareholders. Typical controlling shareholders are government, institutions, family, and consortiums.

◆ When a firm becomes widely owned typically it is managed by hired professionals. Professional managers' interests may not be perfectly aligned with the interests of owners, thus creating an *agency problem*.

Evaluate the distinctions between the two major forms of management goals—shareholder wealth maximization versus stakeholder capitalism

◆ The Anglo-American markets have a philosophy that a firm's objective should follow the *shareholder wealth maximization* (SWM) model. More specifically, the firm should strive to maximize the return to shareholders, as measured by the sum of capital gains and dividends, for a given level of risk.

◆ In the non–Anglo-American markets, controlling shareholders also strive to maximize long-term returns to equity. However, they are more constrained by powerful other stakeholders. In particular, labor unions are more powerful than in the Anglo-American markets. Governments interfere more in the marketplace to protect important stakeholder groups, such as local communities, the environment, and employment. Banks and other financial institutions are more important creditors than securities markets. This model is known as the stakeholder capitalism model (SCM).

Distinguish between the actual operational goals that may be pursued by management depending on whether the company is operated by owners or professional management

◆ The return to a shareholder in a publicly traded firm combines current income in the form of dividends and capital gains from the appreciation of share price.

◆ A privately held firm tries to maximize current and sustainable income; since it has no share price, it does not use time or resources in attempting to influence the market's opinion of its business.

◆ The MNE must determine for itself the proper balance between three common operational objectives: maximization of consolidated after-tax income; minimization of the firm's effective global tax burden; and correct positioning of the firm's income, cash flows, and available funds as to country and currency.

Analyze the goals and forms of corporate governance in use in the global marketplace today, and whether that attracts or deters cross-border investment

◆ The relationship among stakeholders used to determine and control the strategic direction and performance of an organization is termed corporate governance.

◆ Dimensions of corporate governance include agency theory; composition and control of boards of directors; and cultural, historical and institutional variables.

◆ As MNEs become more dependent on global capital markets for financing they may need to modify their policies of corporate governance. A trend exists for firms resident in non–Anglo-American markets to move toward being more "shareholder friendly."

Simultaneously, firms from the Anglo-American markets may be moving toward being more "stakeholder friendly."

Examine how trends in corporate governance are altering the competitive landscape for multinational enterprises

◆ A number of initiatives in governance practices in the United States, the United Kingdom, and the European Union, including board structure and compensation, transparency, auditing, and minority shareholder rights, are spreading to a number of today's major emerging markets.

◆ These governance practices are seen by some, in some countries and cultures, as overly intrusive and occasionally are viewed as damaging to the competitive capability of the firm. The result is an increasing reluctance to go public in selective markets.

MINI-CASE

Luxury Wars—LVMH vs. Hermès[1]

The basic rule is to be there at the right moment, at the right place, to seize a promising opportunity in an environment guaranteeing sufficient longer-term growth.
   —Bernard Arnault, Chairman and CEO, LVMH.

Patrick Thomas focused intently on not letting his hands shake as he quietly closed the phone. He had been riding his bicycle in rural Auvergne, in south-central France, when his cell phone had buzzed. He took a long deep breath, closed his eyes and tried to think. He had spent most of his professional life working at Hermès International, SA and had assumed the position of CEO in 2006 after the retirement of Gean-Louis Dumas. The first non-family CEO to run the company was now facing the biggest threat to the family controlled company in its 173-year history.

The LVMH Position
The man on the other end of the phone had been none other than Bernard Arnault, Chairman and CEO of LVMH (Moët Hennessy Louis Vuitton), the world's largest luxury brand company, and the richest man in France. Arnault was calling to inform him that LVMH would be announcing in two hours that they had acquired a 17.1% interest in Hermès. Thomas had simply not believed

Arnault for the first few minutes, thinking it impossible that they could have gained control of that significant a stake without him knowing about it. Arnault assured him it was no joke and that he looked forward to participating in the company's continued success as a shareholder before repeating again that the press release would be made in two hours (Exhibit 1). Thomas snapped out of his stupor and snatched up the phone; he needed to call Hermès' Executive Chairman, Bertrand Puech, and begin assessing the potential threat, if it was indeed a threat.

Hermès International. Hermès International, SA is a multibillion dollar French company that makes and sells luxury goods across a number of different product categories including women and men's apparel, watches, leather goods, jewelry and perfume. Thierry Hermès, who was known for making the best saddles and harnesses in Paris, founded the company in 1837. The company's reputation soared as it began to provide its high-end products to nobility throughout Europe, North Africa, Russia, Asia and The Americas. As the years wore on, the company began to expand its product line to include the finest leather bags and the most luxurious silk scarves on the market, all while passing the company down through generations and maintaining family control.

Despite going public in 1993, roughly 60 direct descendants of Thierry Hermès, comprising the 5th and 6th generations, still controlled approximately 73% of the company.

EXHIBIT 1	LVMH becomes A Shareholder of Hermès International

LVMH Moët Hennessy Louis Vuitton, the world's leading luxury products group, announces that it holds 15 016 000 shares of Hermès International, representing 14.2% of the share capital of the company. The objective of LVMH is to be a long-term shareholder of Hermès and to contribute to the preservation of the family and French attributes which are at the heart of the global success of this iconic brand.

LVMH fully supports the strategy implemented by the founding family and the management team, who have made the brand one of the jewels of the luxury industry. LVMH has no intention of launching a tender offer, taking control of Hermès nor seeking Board representation. LVMH holds derivative instruments over 3 001 246 Hermès International shares and intends to request their conversion.

LVMH would then hold a total of 18 017 246 Hermès International shares, or 17.1% of its capital. The total cost of this shareholding would, in this case, be €1.45 billion.

Source: Press Release, October 23, 2010, LVMH.com.

In 2006, the job of CEO had been passed, for the first time, to a nonfamily member, Patrick Thomas.

Bernard Arnault

Arnault is a shrewd man. He has reviewed his portfolio and sees what he is missing—a company that still produces true luxury—and he is going after it.

—Anonymous luxury brand CEO speaking on the LVMH announcement.

Bernard Arnault had made a very profitable career out of his penchant for taking over vulnerable family-owned businesses (earning him the colorful nickname of "the wolf in cashmere"). Originally born in Roubaix, France, to an upper class family, Arnault excelled as a student and graduated from France's prestigious engineering school, Ecole Polytechnique, before working as an engineer and taking over his family's construction business. When the French government began looking for someone to acquire the bankrupt company, Boussac (and its luxury line, Christian Dior), Arnault promptly bought the company. It proved the first step in building what would eventually become the luxury titan, LVMH, and propel Arnault to the title of France's wealthiest man.

From that point on, Arnault began assembling what his competitors referred to as "the evil empire," by preying on susceptible family-owned companies with premium names. His takeover of Louis Vuitton was said to have gotten so personal and vicious that, after the last board meeting, the Vuitton family packed their belongings and left the building in tears. In addition to Louis Vuitton, Arnault had spent the last three decades forcibly adding such family-owned luxury brands as Krug (champagne), Pucci (fashion), Chateau d'Yquem (vineyard), and Celine (fashion), among others.

Arnault had nothing but success in his takeover attempts until 1999, when his attempted takeover of Gucci was stymied by Francois Pinault, whose company PPR served as the white knight for Gucci and effectively stole the deal out from under Arnault. It marked the one time in LVMH's history that it had failed in a takeover bid. It remained a bitter memory for Arnault.

Autorité des Marchés Financiers (AMF). Arnault's announcement of LVMH's ownership stake in Hermès came as a shock to both the fashion industry and the family shareholders of Hermès. Exhibit 2 is Hermès public response to LVMH's initiative. The French stock market regulator, the Autorité des Marchés Financiers (AMF), required any investor gaining a 5% or greater stake in a publicly traded company to publicly file their ownership percentage as well as a document of intent. But no such notice had been filed, and Patrick Thomas was livid.

In the days following the October 23 press release, LVMH confirmed through additional announcements that the company had complied with all current rules and regulations in the transactions, and that it would file all the necessary documentation within the allotted time. The AMF announced that it would be opening up a formal investigation of LVMH's acquisition of the Hermès stock, but this was little consolation to Thomas and the Hermès family, since even if the AMF found LVMH in violation, the only penalty would be a loss of voting rights for two years.

Equity Swaps. In the days following LVMH's announcement, new reports and evidence came to light documenting how the company had attained such a large ownership position under the radar of the Hermès family, company management, and industry analysts. The culprit was *equity swaps*.

Equity Swaps are derivative contracts whereby two parties enter into a contract to swap future cash flows at a preset date. The cash flows are referred to as "legs" of the swap. In most equity swaps, one leg is tied to a floating rate like LIBOR (the *floating leg*), and the other leg is tied to the performance of a stock or stock index (the *equity leg*). It is also possible for an equity swap to have two equity legs. Under current French law a company must acknowledge when they attain a 5% or more equity stake in another

EXHIBIT 2	Hermès Response via Press Release: October 24, 2010

Hermès has been informed that LVMH has acquired a 17% stake in the Company. In 1993, the shareholders of Hermès International, all descendants from Emile Hermès, decided to enlist the Company on the Paris stock exchange. This decision was made with two objectives in mind:

◆ support the long term development of the Company
◆ make shares easier to trade for the shareholders.

Over the last 10 years, the Hermès group has delivered an average annual growth rate of 10% of its net result and currently holds a very strong financial position with over M€ 700 of free cash. Today, Hermès Family shareholders have a strong majority control of nearly $3/4$ of the shares. They are fully united around a common business vision. Their long term control of Hermès International is guaranteed by its financial status as limited partnership by shares and the family shareholders have confirmed that they are not contemplating any significant selling of shares. The public listing of shares, allows investors who want to become minority shareholders to do so. As a Family Company Hermès has treated and will always treat its shareholders with utmost respect.

The Executive Management,
Sunday October 24th, 2010

Source: Hermes.com.

---

company, or the rights to purchase a 5% or more stake via derivatives like equity swaps.

However, equity swaps can be structured in such a way that only their value is tied to the equity instrument; at close-out the contract may be settled in cash, not shares. Using this structure, the swap holder is not required to file with the AMF, since they will never actually own the stock.

The LVMH Purchase. It was widely known that Arnault had long coveted Hermès as a brand. In fact, Mr. Arnault had previously owned 15% of Hermès when he first took over LVMH in the 1990s. At the time, Mr. Arnault had his hands full with reorganizing and redirecting LVMH after his takeover of the company, so he agreed to sell the shares to then Hermès CEO Jean-Louis Dumas when he wanted to take the company public.

But things had changed for LVMH and Arnault since 1990. Mr. Arnault had grown his company to the largest luxury conglomerate in the world, with over $55 billion in annual sales. He accomplished this through organic growth of brands and strategic purchases. Known for his patience and shrewd business acumen, when he saw an opportunity to target a long coveted prize, he took advantage.

The attack on Hermès shares was one of Arnault's most closely kept secrets, with only three people in his empire aware of the equity swap contracts. Arnault began making his move in 2008 when three blocks of Hermès shares—totaling 12.8 million shares—were quietly placed on the market by three separate French banks. The origins of these shares are still unknown, but with such a large number of shares in question, many suspected they had come from Hermès family members.

It is believed that Arnault was contacted by the banks and was given 24 hours to decide whether he would like to purchase them or not. At the time, Arnault was hesitant to take such a large ownership stake in Hermès, particularly one requiring registration with the AMF. Arnault and the banks then developed the strategy whereby he would hold rights to the shares via equity swaps, but only as long as he put up the cash. At contract maturity, LVMH would realize the profit/loss on any movement in the share price. As part of the agreement with the banks, however, LVMH would have the *option* to take the shares instead. Had the contracts required share settlement, under French law LVMH would have to acknowledge its potential equity position in Hermès publicly.

The design of these contracts prevented LVMH from actually holding the shares until October 2010, when they publicly announced their ownership stake in Hermès. During the period the swap contracts were in-place, Hermès share price floated between €60 and €102. This explained how LVMH was able to acquire its shares in Hermès at an average price of €80 per share, nearly a 54% discount on the closing price of €176.2 on Friday, October 22.

LVMH could have actually held its swap contracts longer and postponed settlement and therefore disclosure, but the rapid rise in Hermès share price over the previous months forced the decision last year (which many analysts attributed to market speculations of an LVMH takeover plot). If LVMH had postponed settlement, it would have had to account for €2 billion in paper profit, or more, earned on the contracts when publishing their year-end accounts in February 2011.

The Battle Goes Public

Although the original press release by LVMH made it very clear that the company had no greater designs on controlling Hermès, Hermès management did not believe it, and moved quickly. After a quick conference call amongst Hermès leadership, Patrick Thomas and Puech gave an uncharacteristic interview with *Le Figaro* on October 27.

> *It's clear his [Mr. Arnault] intention is to take over the company and the family will resist that.*

—Patrick Thomas, CEO Hermès,
Le Figaro, October 27, 2010.

> *We would like to convince him [Mr. Arnault] that this is not the right way to operate and that it's not friendly. If he entered in a friendly way, then we would like him to leave in a friendly way.*

—Mr. Puech, Executive Chairman of Emile Hermés SARL, *Le Figaro*, October 27, 2010.

Arnault wasted no time in responding in an interview given to the same newspaper the following day:

> *I do not see how the head of a listed company can be qualified to ask a shareholder to sell his shares. On the contrary he is supposed to defend the interests of all shareholders.*

—Bernard Arnault, CEO LVMH,
Le Figaro, October 28, 2010.

Pierre Godé, Vice President LVMH. On November 10, after much speculation regarding LVMH's intent, Pierre Godé, an LVMH Vice President, gave an interview with *Les Echos* newspaper (itself owned by LVMH) to discuss how and why the transactions took place the way they did, as well as to dispel media speculation about a potential hostile takeover attempt from LVMH. In the interview, Godé was questioned about why LVMH chose to purchase the equity swap contracts against Hermès in the first place, and why LVMH chose to close those contracts in Hermès shares rather than in cash.

Godé confided that LVMH had begun looking at Hermès in 2007 when the financial crisis started and the stock exchange began to fall. LVMH was looking for financial investments in the luxury industry—as that is where their expertise lies—and took the position that Hermès would weather the financial crisis better than other potential investments. It was for this reason alone that LVMH chose to purchase equity swaps with Hermès shares as the equity leg.

Godé argued that equity swaps with cash payment and settlement were trendy at that time, and virtually every bank offered this derivative. Even though LVMH already had just under a 5% stake of Hermès stock at the time the derivatives were being set up, Godé stated that LVMH never even considered the possibility of closing out the swaps in shares. For one thing, it was something they couldn't do contractually (according to Godé), nor did LVMH want to ask the banks for equity settlements. But by 2010, the situation had changed, prompting LVMH to reassess their Hermès equity swap contracts. The contracts themselves were running out,

and LVMH had a premium of nearly €1 billion on them. According to Godé, the banks that had covered their contracts with LVMH were now tempted to sell the shares, which represented 12% of Hermès' capital.

Godé explained that the selling of the shares in and of itself did not concern LVMH. What they did worry about however, was where the shares might end up. Godé stressed that at that time there were rumors that a "powerful group from another industry," and Chinese investment funds were interested in the Hermès shares. LVMH management felt the rising share price of Hermès lent support to these rumors. Additionally, the market had been improving and LVMH had the financial means to be able to pay for the contracts and settle in shares. As a result, LVMH spoke with the banks to assess their position, and after several weeks of talks LVMH reached an agreement with them in October for part of the shares.

At this time "the Board had to choose between receiving a considerable amount on the equity swaps or take a minority participation in this promising group but where our power would be very limited as the family controlled everything. There was an intense debate and finally the Board chose to have share payments." Godé completed the interview by stating that LVMH was surprised by the strong negative response from Hermès, especially considering that LVMH had owned a 15% stake in the company in the early 1990s.

Evolution of Hermès International and Its Control. Hermès was structured as a Société en Commandite, the French version of a limited partnership in the United States. In the case of Hermès, this structure concentrates power in the hands of a ruling committee which is controlled by the family.

In addition to the Société en Commandite structure of the company, former Hermès CEO Jean-Louis Dumas established a partner company, Hermès SARL, in 1989. This company represented the interests of family shareholders (only direct Hermès descendants could be owners), and was the sole authority to appoint management and set company strategy. This unusual structure allowed the Hermès family the ability to retain decision making power even if only one family member were to remain a shareholder. The structure had been adopted as protection against a hostile takeover after Dumas saw the way Bernard Arnault had dealt with the Vuitton family when he acquired their company.

In a further attempt to placate family members and minimize family infighting, Dumas listed 25% of Hermès SA on the French stock market in 1993. This was done to provide family members with a means to value their stake in the company as well as partially cash-out if they felt their family dividends were not enough (several family members were known to live large, and Dumas feared their lifestyles may exceed their means). Dumas believed—at least at that time—that his two-tier structure would insulate Hermès from a potential hostile takeover.

EXHIBIT 3	Hermès Family Confirms Its Long-Term Commitment

Creation of a holding company owning over 50% of Hermès International's share capital

Paris, 5 December 2010—Following a meeting on 3 December 2010, members of the Hermès family reasserted their unity and their confidence in the solidity of their current control of Hermès International, partly via the Emile Hermès family company, sole general partner responsible for determining the company's strategy and management, and via its shareholding.

The family has decided to confirm its long-term unity by creating a family holding company separate from Emile Hermès SARL, which will hold the shares transferred by family members representing over 50% of Hermès International's share capital. The family's commitment to create this majority holding company is irrevocable. The new family-owned company will benefit from preferential rights to shares still directly owned by the family.

This internal reclassification of shares will not impact the family's stake in Hermès International or the powers of the general partner. The plan will be submitted to the Autorité des Marchés Financiers for definitive approval before it is implemented.

Source: *Press Release*, December 5, 2010, Hermes.com.

However, analysts were now speculating that Hermès SARL may only provide protection through the 6th generation, and that with just a 0.1% stake in the company being worth approximately €18 million at current market prices, there was reason to fear some family members "defecting." This concern was made all the more real when it became known through AMF filings that Laurent Mommeja, brother to Hermès supervisory board member Renaud fe, sold €1.8 million worth of shares on October 25, at a share price of €189 per share.

After considerable debate, the Hermès family decided to consolidate their shares into a trust in the form of a holding company that would insure that their 73% ownership stake would always vote as one voice and ultimately secure the family's continued control of the company (Exhibit 3).

On December 21, LVMH announced that it had raised its total stake in Hermès to 20.21%, and had filed all required documents with AMF once passing the 20% threshold. LVMH also reiterated that it had no intention of taking control of Hermès or making a public offer for its shares. Under French law, once LVMH reached one-third share ownership it would have to make a public tender for all remaining shares. Hermès share price, as illustrated in Exhibit 4, continued to calm—at least for the moment—following the extended fight for corporate control.

EXHIBIT 4	Hermès International Share Price (July–Dec 2010)

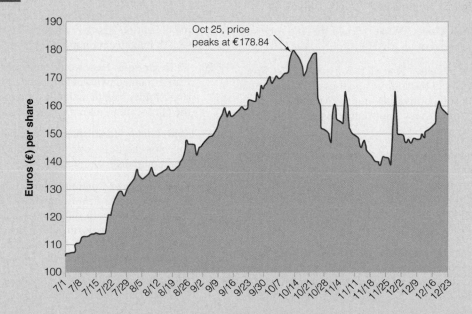

1. Hermès International was a family-owned business for many years. Why did it then list its shares on a public market? What risks and rewards come from a public listing?

2. Bernard Arnault and LVMH acquired a large position in Hermès shares without anyone knowing. How did they do it and how did they avoid the French regulations requiring disclosure of such positions?

3. The Hermès family defended themselves by forming a holding company of their family shares. How will this work and how long do you think it will last?

Questions

1. **Ownership of the Business.** How does ownership alter the goals and governance of a business?

2. **Separation of Ownership and Management.** Why is this separation so critical to the understanding of how businesses are structured and led?

3. **Corporate Goals: Shareholder Wealth Maximization.** Explain the assumptions and objectives of the shareholder wealth maximization model.

4. **Corporate Goals: Stakeholder Wealth Maximization.** Explain the assumptions and objectives of the stakeholder wealth maximization model.

5. **Corporate Governance.** Define the following terms:
   a. Corporate governance
   b. The market for corporate control
   c. Agency theory
   d. Cronyism
   e. Stakeholder capitalism

6. **Operational Goals.** What should be the primary operational goal of an MNE?

7. **Knowledge Assets.** "Knowledge assets" are a firm's intangible assets, the sources and uses of its intellectual talent—its competitive advantage. What are some of the most important "knowledge assets" that create shareholder value?

8. **Labor Unions.** In Germany and Scandinavia, among others, labor unions have representation on boards of directors or supervisory boards. How might such union representation be viewed under the shareholder wealth maximization model compared to the corporate wealth maximization model?

9. **Interlocking Directorates.** In an interlocking directorate, members of the board of directors of one firm also sit on the board of directors of other firms. How would interlocking directorates be viewed by the shareholder wealth maximization model compared to the corporate wealth maximization model?

10. **Leveraged Buyouts.** A leveraged buyout is a financial strategy in which a group of investors gain voting control of a firm and then liquidate its assets in order to repay the loans used to purchase the firm's shares. How would leveraged buyouts be viewed by the shareholder wealth maximization model compared to the corporate wealth maximization model?

11. **High Leverage.** How would a high degree of leverage (debt/assets) be viewed by the shareholder wealth maximization model compared to the corporate wealth maximization model?

12. **Conglomerates.** Conglomerates are firms that have diversified into unrelated fields. How would a policy of conglomeration be viewed by the shareholder wealth maximization model compared to the corporate wealth maximization model?

13. **Risk.** How is risk defined in the shareholder wealth maximization model compared to the corporate wealth maximization model?

14. **Stock Options.** How would stock options granted to a firm's management and employees be viewed by the shareholder wealth maximization model compared to the corporate wealth maximization model?

15. **Shareholder Dissatisfaction.** What alternative actions can shareholders take if they are dissatisfied with their company?

16. **Dual Classes of Common Stock.** In many countries, it is common for a firm to have two or more classes of common stock with differential voting rights. In the United States, the norm is for a firm to have one class of common stock with one-share-one-vote. What are the advantages and disadvantages of each system?

17. **Emerging Markets Corporate Governance Failures.** It has been claimed that failures in corporate governance

have hampered the growth and profitability of some prominent firms located in emerging markets. What are some typical causes of these failures in corporate governance?

18. **Emerging Markets Corporate Governance Improvements.** In recent years emerging market MNEs have improved their corporate governance policies and become more shareholder-friendly. What do you think is driving this phenomenon?

19. **Developed Markets Corporate Governance Failures.** What have been the main causes of recent corporate governance failures in the United States and Europe?

20. **Family Ownership.** What are the key differences in the goals and motivations of family business ownership as opposed to the widely held publicly traded business?

21. **Value of Good Governance.** Do markets appear to be willing to pay for good governance?

22. **Corporate Governance Reform.** What are the primary principles behind corporate governance reform today? In your opinion are these culturally specific?

Problems

Use the following formula for shareholder returns to answer questions 1 through 4, where P_t is the share price at time t, and D_t is the dividend paid at time t.

$$\text{Shareholder return} = \frac{P_2 - P_1 + D_2}{P_1} = \frac{P_2 - P_1}{P_1} + \frac{D_2}{P_1}$$

1. **Emaline Returns.** If the share price of Emaline, a New Orleans-based shipping firm, rises from $12 to $15 over a one-year period, what is the rate of return to the shareholder if the following:
   a. The company paid no dividends
   b. The company paid a dividend of $1 per share
   c. The company paid the dividend and the total return to the shareholder is separated into the dividend yield and the capital gain

2. **Carty's Choices.** Brian Carty, a prominent investor, is evaluating investment alternatives. If he believes an individual equity will rise in price from $59 to $71 in the coming one-year period, and the share is expected to pay a dividend of $1.75 per share, and he expects at least a 15% rate of return on an investment of this type, should he invest in this particular equity?

3. **Vaniteux's Returns (A).** Spencer Grant is a New York-based investor. He has been closely following his investment in 100 shares of Vaniteux, a French firm that went public in February 2010. When he purchased his 100 shares, at €17.25 per share, the euro was trading at $1.360/€. Currently, the share is trading at €28.33 per share, and the dollar has fallen to $1.4170/€.
   a. If Spencer sells his shares today, what percentage change in the share price would he receive?
   b. What is the percentage change in the value of euro versus the dollar over this same period?
   c. What would be the total return Spencer would earn on his shares if he sold them at these rates?

4. **Vaniteux's Returns (B).** Spencer Grant chooses not to sell his shares at the time described in problem 3. He waits, expecting the share price to rise further after the announcement of quarterly earnings. His expectations are correct; the share price rises to €31.14 per share after the announcement. He now wishes to recalculate his returns. The current spot exchange rate is $1.3110/€.

5. **Vaniteux's Returns (C).** Using the same prices and exchange rates as in problem 4, Vaniteux (B), what would be the total return on the Vaniteux investment by Laurent Vuagnoux, a Paris-based investor?

6. **Microsoft's Dividend.** In January 2003, Microsoft announced that it would begin paying a dividend of $0.16 per share. Given the following share prices for Microsoft stock in the recent past, how would a constant dividend of $0.16 per share per year have changed the company's return to its shareholders over this period?

First Trading Day	Closing Share Price	First Trading Day	Closing Share Price
1998 (Jan 2)	$131.13	2001 (Jan 2)	$43.38
1999 (Jan 4)	$141.00	2002 (Jan 2)	$67.04
2000 (Jan 3)	$116.56	2003 (Jan 2)	$53.72

7. **Fashion Acquisitions.** During the 1960s, many conglomerates were created by a firm enjoying a high price/earnings ratio (P/E). They then used their highly-valued stock to acquire other firms that had lower P/E ratios, usually in unrelated domestic industries. These conglomerates went out of fashion during the 1980s when they lost their high P/E ratios, thus making it more difficult to find other firms with lower P/E ratios to acquire.

Company	P/E ratio	Number of shares	Market value per share	Earnings	EPS	Total market value
ModoUnico	20	10,000,000	$20.00	$10,000,000	$1.00	$200,000,000
Modern American	40	10,000,000	$40.00	$10,000,000	$1.00	$400,000,000

During the 1990s, the same acquisition strategy was possible for firms located in countries where high P/E ratios were common compared to firms in other countries where low P/E ratios were common. Consider the hypothetical firms in the pharmaceutical industry shown in the table at the table above.

Modern American wants to acquire ModoUnico. It offers 5,500,000 shares of Modern American, with a current market value of $220,000,000 and a 10% premium on ModoUnico's shares, for all of ModoUnico's shares.

8. **Corporate Governance: Overstating Earnings.** A number of firms, especially in the United States, have had to lower their previously reported earnings due to accounting errors or fraud. Assume that Modern American (problem 7) had to lower its earnings to $5,000,000 from the previously reported $10,000,000. What might be its new market value prior to the acquisition? Could it still do the acquisition?

9. **Bertrand Manufacturing (A).** Dual classes of common stock are common in a number of countries. Assume that Bertrand Manufacturing has the following capital structure at book value. The A-shares each have ten votes and the B-shares each have one vote per share.

Bertrand Manufacturing	Local Currency (millions)
Long-term debt	200
Retained earnings	300
Paid-in common stock: 1 million A-shares	100
Paid-in common stock: 4 million B-shares	400
Total long-term capital	1,000

10. **Bertrand Manufacturing (B).** Assuming all of the same debt and equity values for Bertrand Manufacturing in problem 9, with the sole exception that both A-shares and B-shares have the same voting rights, one vote per share.
    a. What proportion of the total long-term capital has been raised by A-shares?
    b. What proportion of voting rights is represented by A-shares?
    c. What proportion of the dividends should the A-shares receive?

11. **Kingdom Enterprises (A): European Sales.** Kingdom Enterprises is a Hong Kong-based exporter of consumer electronics and files all of its financial statements in Hong Kong dollars (HK$). The company's European sales director, Phillipp Bosse, has been criticized for his performance. He disagrees, arguing that sales in Europe have grown steadily in recent years. Who is correct?

	2008	2009	2010
Total net sales, HK$	171,275	187,500	244,900
Percent of total sales from Europe	48%	44%	39%
Total European sales, HK$	_____	_____	_____
Average exchange rate, HK$/€	11.5	11.7	10.3
Total European sales, euros (€)	_____	_____	_____
Growth rate of European sales	_____	_____	_____

12. **Kingdom Enterprises (B): Japanese Yen Debt.** Kingdom Enterprises of Hong Kong borrowed Japanese yen under a long-term loan agreement several years ago. The company's new CFO believes, however, that what was originally thought to have been relatively "cheap debt" is no longer true. What do you think?

	2008	2009	2010
Annual yen payments on debt agreement (¥)	12,000,000	12,000,000	12,000,000
Average exchange rate, ¥/HK$	12.3	12.1	11.4
Annual yen debt service, HK$	_____	_____	_____

13. **Chinese Sourcing and the Yuan.** Harrison Equipment of Denver, Colorado, purchases all of its hydraulic tubing from manufacturers in mainland

China. The company has recently completed a corporate-wide initiative in six sigma/lean manufacturing. Completed oil field hydraulic system costs were reduced 4% over a one-year period, from $880,000 to $844,800. The company is now worried that all of the hydraulic tubing that goes into the systems (making up 20% of their total costs) will be hit by the potential revaluation of the Chinese yuan—if some in Washington get their way. How would a 12% revaluation of the yuan against the dollar impact total system costs?

14. **Mattel's Global Performance.** Mattel (U.S.) achieved significant sales growth in its major international regions between 2001 and 2004. In its filings with the United States Security and Exchange Commission (SEC), it reported both the amount of regional sales and what percentage change in regional sales occurred as a result of exchange rate changes.
   a. What was the percentage change in sales, in U.S. dollars, by region?
   b. What were the percentage change in sales by region net of currency change impacts?
   c. What relative impact did currency changes have on the level and growth of Mattel's consolidated sales between 2001 and 2004?

Internet Exercises

1. **Multinational Firms and Global Assets/Income.** The differences across MNEs is striking. Using a sample of firms such as the following, pull from their individual Web pages the proportions of their incomes which are earned outside their country of incorporation. (Note how Nestlé calls itself a "transnational company.")

Walt Disney	disney.go.com
Nestlé S.A.	www.nestle.com
Intel	www.intel.com
Mitsubishi Motors	www.mitsubishi.com
Nokia	www.nokia.com
Royal Dutch/Shell	www.shell.com

Also note the way in which international business is now conducted via the Internet. Several home pages of the above sites allow the user to choose the language of the presentation viewed.

2. **Corporate Governance.** There is no hotter topic in business today than corporate governance. Use the following sites to view recent research, current events and news items, and other information

Mattel's Global Sales

	Mattel's Global Sales			
(thousands of US$)	2001 Sales ($)	2002 Sales ($)	2003 Sales ($)	2004 Sales ($)
Europe	$ 933,450	$ 1,126,177	$ 1,356,131	$ 1,410,525
Latin America	471,301	466,349	462,167	524,481
Canada	155,791	161,469	185,831	197,655
Asia Pacific	119,749	136,944	171,580	203,575
Total International	$ 1,680,291	$ 1,890,939	$ 2,175,709	$ 2,336,236
United States	3,392,284	3,422,405	3,203,814	3,209,862
Sales Adjustments	(384,651)	(428,004)	(419,423)	(443,312)
Total Net Sales	$ 4,687,924	$ 4,885,340	$ 4,960,100	$ 5,102,786

	Impact of Change in Currency Rates		
Region	2001–2002	2002–2003	2003–2004
Europe	7.0%	15.0%	8.0%
Latin America	−9.0%	−6.0%	−2.0%
Canada	0.0%	11.0%	5.0%
Asia Pacific	3.0%	13.0%	6.0%

Source: Mattel, Annual Report, 2002, 2003, 2004.

related to the relationships between a business and its stakeholders.

Corporate Governance Net   www.corpgov.net

3. **Fortune Global 500.** *Fortune* magazine is relatively famous for its listing of the Fortune 500 firms in the global marketplace. Use Fortune's Web site to find the most recent listing of the global firms in this distinguished club.

Fortune   www.fortune.com/fortune

4. **Financial Times.** The *Financial Times*, based in London—the global center of international finance—has a Web site with a wealth of information. After going to the home page, go to the Markets Data & Tools page, and examine the recent stock market activity around the globe. Note the similarity in movement on a daily basis among the world's major equity markets.

Financial Times   www.ft.com

The International Monetary System

The price of every thing rises and falls from time to time and place to place; and with every such change the purchasing power of money changes so far as that thing goes. —Alfred Marshall.

LEARNING OBJECTIVES

◆ Learn how the international monetary system has evolved from the days of the gold standard to today's eclectic currency arrangement.

◆ Analyze the characteristics of an ideal currency.

◆ Explain the currency regime choices faced by emerging market countries.

◆ Examine how the euro, a single currency for the European Union, was created.

This chapter begins with a brief history of the international monetary system from the days of the classical gold standard to the present time. The next section describes contemporary currency regimes, fixed versus flexible exchange rates, and the attributes of the ideal currency. The next section analyzes emerging markets and regime choices, including currency boards and dollarization. The following section describes the birth of the euro and the path toward monetary unification, including the expansion of the European Union on May 1, 2004. The final section analyzes the trade-offs between exchange rate regimes based on rules, discretion, cooperation, and independence. The chapter concludes with the Mini-Case, *First Steps in the Globalization of the Yuan*, which details the evolution of the Chinese yuan from a purely domestic to an increasingly global currency.

History of the International Monetary System

Over the ages currencies have been defined in terms of gold and other items of value, and the international monetary system has been subject to a variety of international agreements. A review of these systems provides a useful perspective against which to understand today's system and to evaluate weaknesses and proposed changes in the present system.

The Gold Standard, 1876–1913

Since the days of the pharaohs (about 3000 B.C.), gold has served as a medium of exchange and a store of value. The Greeks and Romans used gold coins and passed on this tradition through the mercantile era to the nineteenth century. The great increase in trade during the free-trade period of the late nineteenth century led to a need for a more formalized system for settling international trade balances. One country after another set a par value for its currency in terms of gold and then tried to adhere to the so-called rules of the game.

This later came to be known as the classical gold standard. The gold standard as an international monetary system gained acceptance in Western Europe in the 1870s. The United States was something of a latecomer to the system, not officially adopting the standard until 1879.

Under the gold standard, the "rules of the game" were clear and simple. Each country set the rate at which its currency unit (paper or coin) could be converted to a weight of gold. The United States, for example, declared the dollar to be convertible to gold at a rate of $20.67 per ounce (a rate in effect until the beginning of World War I). The British pound was pegged at £ 4.2474 per ounce of gold. As long as both currencies were freely convertible into gold, the dollar/pound exchange rate was

$$\frac{\$20.67/\text{ounce of gold}}{£4.2474/\text{ounce of gold}} = \$4.8665/£$$

Because the government of each country on the gold standard agreed to buy or sell gold on demand with anyone at its own fixed parity rate, the value of each individual currency in terms of gold, and therefore exchange rates between currencies, was fixed. Maintaining adequate reserves of gold to back its currency's value was very important for a country under this system. The system also had the effect of implicitly limiting the rate at which any individual country could expand its money supply. Any growth in the amount of money was limited to the rate at which official authorities could acquire additional gold.

The gold standard worked adequately until the outbreak of World War I interrupted trade flows and the free movement of gold. This event caused the main trading nations to suspend operation of the gold standard.

The Interwar Years and World War II, 1914–1944

During World War I and the early 1920s, currencies were allowed to fluctuate over fairly wide ranges in terms of gold and in relation to each other. Theoretically, supply and demand for a country's exports and imports caused moderate changes in an exchange rate about a central equilibrium value. This was the same function that gold had performed under the previous gold standard. Unfortunately, such flexible exchange rates did not work in an equilibrating manner. On the contrary: international speculators sold the weak currencies short, causing them to fall further in value than warranted by real economic factors. *Selling short* is a speculation technique in which an individual speculator sells an asset such as a currency to another party for delivery at a future date. The speculator, however, does not yet own the asset, and expects the price of the asset to fall by the date when the asset must be purchased in the open market by the speculator for delivery.

The reverse happened with strong currencies. Fluctuations in currency values could not be offset by the relatively illiquid forward exchange market except at exorbitant cost. The net result was that the volume of world trade did not grow in the 1920s in proportion to world gross domestic product but instead declined to a very low level with the advent of the Great Depression in the 1930s.

The United States adopted a modified gold standard in 1934 when the U.S. dollar was devalued to $35 per ounce of gold from the $20.67 per ounce price in effect prior to World War I. Contrary to previous practice, the U.S. Treasury traded gold only with foreign central banks, not private citizens. From 1934 to the end of World War II, exchange rates were theoretically determined by each currency's value in terms of gold. During World War II and its chaotic aftermath, however, many of the main trading currencies lost their convertibility into other currencies. The dollar was the only major trading currency that continued to be convertible.

Bretton Woods and the International Monetary Fund, 1944

As World War II drew to a close in 1944, the Allied Powers met at Bretton Woods, New Hampshire, to create a new postwar international monetary system. The Bretton Woods Agreement established a U.S. dollar-based international monetary system and provided for two new institutions: the International Monetary Fund and the World Bank. The International Monetary Fund (IMF) aids countries with balance of payments and exchange rate problems. The International Bank for Reconstruction and Development (World Bank) helped fund postwar reconstruction and since then has supported general economic development. *Global Finance in Practice 3.1* provides some insight into the debates at Bretton Woods.

GLOBAL FINANCE IN PRACTICE 3.1

Hammering Out an Agreement at Bretton Woods

The governments of the Allied powers knew that the devastating impacts of World War II would require swift and decisive policies. Therefore, a full year before the end of the war, representatives of all 45 allied nations met in the summer of 1944 (July 1–22) at Bretton Woods, New Hampshire, for the United Nations Monetary and Financial Conference. Their purpose was to plan the postwar international monetary system. It was a difficult process, and the final synthesis of viewpoints was shaded by pragmatism and significant doubt.

Although the conference was attended by 45 nations, the leading policy makers at Bretton Woods were the British and the Americans. The British delegation was led by Lord John Maynard Keynes, termed "Britain's economic heavyweight." The British argued for a postwar system that would be decidedly more flexible than the various gold standards used before the war. Keynes argued, as he had after World War I, that attempts to tie currency values to gold would create pressures for deflation (a general fall in the level of prices in a country) in many of the war-ravaged economies. And these economies were faced with enormous re-industrialization needs that would likely cause inflation, not deflation.

The American delegation was led by the director of the U.S. Treasury's monetary research department, Harry D. White, and the U.S. Secretary of the Treasury, Henry Morgenthau, Jr. The Americans argued for stability (fixed exchange rates) but not a return to the gold standard itself. In fact, although the United States at that time held most of the gold of the Allied powers, the U.S. delegates argued that currencies should be fixed in parities, but redemption of the gold should occur only between official authorities (central banks of governments).

On the more pragmatic side, all parties agreed that a postwar system would be stable and sustainable only if there was sufficient credit available for countries to defend their

Mount Washington Hotel, Bretton Woods, New Hampshire

currencies in the event of payment imbalances, which they knew to be inevitable in a reconstructing world order.

The conference divided into three commissions for weeks of negotiation. One commission, led by U.S. Treasury Secretary Morgenthau, was charged with the organization of a fund of capital to be used for exchange rate stabilization. A second commission, chaired by Lord Keynes, was charged with the organization of a second "bank" whose purpose would be for long-term reconstruction and development. A third commission was to hammer out details such as what role silver would have in any new system.

After weeks of meetings the participants came to a three-part agreement—the *Bretton Woods Agreement*. The plan called for: 1) fixed exchange rates, termed an "adjustable peg" among members; 2) a fund of gold and constituent currencies available to members for stabilization of their respective currencies, called the *International Monetary Fund* (IMF); and 3) a bank for financing long-term development projects (eventually known as the *World Bank*). One proposal resulting from the meetings, which was not ratified by the United States, was the establishment of an international trade organization to promote free trade. That would take many years and conferences to come.

The IMF was the key institution in the new international monetary system, and it has remained so to the present. The IMF was established to render temporary assistance to member countries trying to defend their currencies against cyclical, seasonal, or random occurrences. It also assists countries having structural trade problems if they promise to take adequate steps to correct their problems. If persistent deficits occur, however, the IMF cannot save a country from eventual devaluation. In recent years, it has attempted to help countries facing financial crises. It has provided massive loans as well as advice to Russia and other former Russian republics, Brazil, Indonesia, and South Korea, to name but a few.

Under the original provisions of the Bretton Woods Agreement, all countries fixed the value of their currencies in terms of gold but were not required to exchange their currencies for gold. Only the dollar remained convertible into gold (at $35 per ounce). Therefore, each country established its exchange rate vis-à-vis the dollar, and then calculated the gold par value of its currency to create the desired dollar exchange rate. Participating countries agreed to try to maintain the value of their currencies within 1% (later expanded to 2.25%) of par by buying or selling foreign exchange or gold as needed. Devaluation was not to be used as a competitive trade policy, but if a currency became too weak to defend, a devaluation of up to 10% was allowed without formal approval by the IMF. Larger devaluations required IMF approval. This became known as the *gold-exchange standard*.

The Special Drawing Right (SDR) is an international reserve asset created by the IMF to supplement existing foreign exchange reserves. It serves as a unit of account for the IMF and other international and regional organizations, and is also the base against which some countries peg the exchange rate for their currencies.

Defined initially in terms of a fixed quantity of gold, the SDR has been redefined several times. It is currently the weighted average of four major currencies: the U.S. dollar, the euro, the Japanese yen, and the British pound. The weights are updated every five years by the IMF. Individual countries hold SDRs in the form of deposits in the IMF. These holdings are part of each country's international monetary reserves, along with official holdings of gold, foreign exchange, and its reserve position at the IMF. Members may settle transactions among themselves by transferring SDRs.

Fixed Exchange Rates, 1945–1973

The currency arrangement negotiated at Bretton Woods and monitored by the IMF worked fairly well during the post–World War II period of reconstruction and rapid growth in world trade. However, widely diverging national monetary and fiscal policies, differential rates of inflation, and various unexpected external shocks eventually resulted in the system's demise. The U.S. dollar was the main reserve currency held by central banks and was the key to the web of exchange rate values. Unfortunately, the United States ran persistent and growing deficits in its balance of payments. A heavy capital outflow of dollars was required to finance these deficits and to meet the growing demand for dollars from investors and businesses. Eventually, the heavy overhang of dollars held by foreigners resulted in a lack of confidence in the ability of the United States to meet its commitment to convert dollars to gold.

This lack of confidence forced President Richard Nixon to suspend official purchases or sales of gold by the U.S. Treasury on August 15, 1971, after the United States suffered outflows of roughly one-third of its official gold reserves in the first seven months of the year. Exchange rates of most of the leading trading countries were allowed to float in relation to the dollar and thus indirectly in relation to gold. By the end of 1971, most of the major trading currencies had appreciated vis-à-vis the dollar. This change was—in effect—a devaluation of the dollar.

A year and a half later, the U.S. dollar once again came under attack, thereby forcing a second devaluation on February 12, 1973; this time by 10% to $42.22 per ounce of gold. By late February 1973, a fixed-rate system no longer appeared feasible given the speculative flows of currencies. The major foreign exchange markets were actually closed for several weeks in March 1973. When they reopened, most currencies were allowed to float to levels determined by market forces. Par values were left unchanged. The dollar floated downward an average of another 10% by June 1973.

An Eclectic Currency Arrangement, 1973–Present

Since March 1973, exchange rates have become much more volatile and less predictable than they were during the "fixed" exchange rate period, when changes occurred infrequently. Exhibit 3.1 illustrates the wide swings exhibited by the IMF's nominal exchange rate index of the U.S. dollar since 1957. Clearly, volatility has increased for this currency measure since 1973.

Exhibit 3.2 summarizes the key events and external shocks that have affected currency values since March 1973. The most important shocks in recent years have been the European Monetary System (EMS) restructuring in 1992 and 1993; the emerging market currency crises, including that of Mexico in 1994, Thailand (and a number of other Asian currencies) in 1997, Russia in 1998, and Brazil in 1999; the introduction of the euro in 1999; the economic crisis in Turkey in 2001; and the currency crises and changes in Argentina and Venezuela in 2002.

EXHIBIT 3.1   The IMF's Nominal Exchange Rate Index of the Dollar

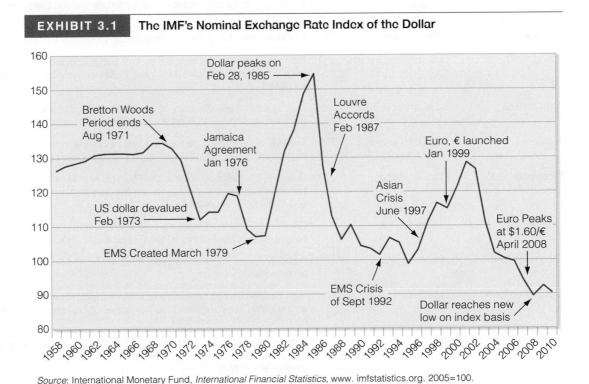

Source: International Monetary Fund, *International Financial Statistics*, www. imfstatistics.org. 2005=100.

EXHIBIT 3.2	World Currency Events, 1971–2010	
Date	**Event**	**Impact**
August 1971	Dollar floated	Nixon closes the U.S. gold window, suspending purchases or sales of gold by U.S. Treasury; temporary imposition of 10% import surcharge
December 1971	Smithsonian Agreement	Group of Ten reaches compromise whereby the US$ is devalued to $38/oz. of gold; most other major currencies are appreciated versus US$
February 1973	U.S. dollar devalued	Devaluation pressure increases on US$, forcing further devaluation to $42.22/oz. of gold
February–March 1973	Currency markets in crisis	Fixed exchange rates no longer considered defensible; speculative pressures force closure of international foreign exchange markets for nearly two weeks; markets reopen on floating rates for major industrial currencies
June 1973	U.S. dollar depreciation	Floating rates continue to drive the now freely floating US$ down by about 10% by June
Fall 1973–1974	OPEC oil embargo	Organization of Petroleum Exporting Countries (OPEC) impose oil embargo, eventually quadrupling the world price of oil; because world oil prices are stated in US$, value of US$ recovers some former strength
January 1976	Jamaica Agreement	IMF meeting in Jamaica results in the "legalization" of the floating exchange rate system already in effect; gold is demonetized as a reserve asset
1977–1978	U.S. inflation rate rises	Carter administration reduces unemployment at the expense of inflation increases; rising U.S. inflation causes continued depreciation of the US$
March 1979	EMS created	The European Monetary System (EMS) is created, establishing a cooperative exchange rate system for participating members of the European Economic Community (EEC)
Summer 1979	OPEC raises prices	OPEC nations raise price of oil again
Spring 1980	U.S. dollar begins rise	Worldwide inflation and early signs of recession coupled with real interest differential advantages for dollar-denominated assets contribute to increased demand for dollars
August 1982	Latin American debt crisis	Mexico informs U.S. Treasury on Friday 13, 1982, that it will be unable to make debt service payments; Brazil and Argentina follow within months
February 1985	U.S. dollar peaks	The U.S. dollar peaks against most major industrial currencies, hitting record highs against the deutsche mark and other European currencies
September 1985	Plaza Agreement	Group of Ten members meet at the Plaza Hotel in New York City to sign an international cooperative agreement to control the volatility of world currency markets and to establish target zones
February 1987	Louvre Accords	Group of Six members state they will "intensify" economic policy coordination to promote growth and reduce external imbalances
December 1991	Maastricht Treaty	European Union concludes a treaty to replace all individual currencies with a single currency—the euro
September 1992	EMS crisis	High German interest rates induce massive capital flows into deutsche mark-denominated assets, causing the withdrawal of the Italian lira and British pound from the EMS's common float
July 31, 1993	EMS realignment	EMS adjusts allowable deviation band to ±15% for all member countries (except the Dutch guilder); U.S. dollar continues to weaken; Japanese yen reaches ¥ 100.25/$

(continued)

EXHIBIT 3.2	World Currency Events, 1971–2010	
Date	**Event**	**Impact**
1994	EMI founded	European Monetary Institute (EMI), the predecessor to the European Central Bank, is founded in Frankfurt, Germany
December 1994	Peso collapse	Mexican peso suffers major devaluation as a result of increasing pressure on the managed devaluation policy; peso falls from Ps3.46/$ to Ps5.50/$ within days; the peso's collapse results in a fall in most major Latin American exchanges in a contagion process—the "tequila effect"
August 1995	Yen peaks	Japanese yen reaches an all-time high versus the U.S. dollar of ¥79/$; yen slowly depreciates over the following two-year period, rising to over ¥130/$
June 1997	Asian crisis	The Thai baht is devalued in July, followed soon after by the Indonesian rupiah, Korean won, Malaysian ringgit, and Philippine peso; following the initial exchange rate devaluations, the Asian economy plummets into recession
August 1998	Russian crisis	On Monday, August 17, the Russian Central Bank devalues the ruble by 34%; the ruble continues to deteriorate in the following days, sending the already weak Russian economy into recession
January 1, 1999	Euro launched	Official launch date for the euro, the single European currency; 11 European Union member states elect to participate in the system, which irrevocably locks their individual currencies rates among them
January 1999	Brazilian reais crisis	The reais, initially devalued 8.3% by the Brazilian government on January 12, is allowed to float against the world's currencies
January 1, 2002	Euro coinage	Euro coins and notes are introduced in parallel with home currencies; national currencies are phased out during the six-month period beginning January 1
January 8, 2002	Argentine peso crisis	The Argentine peso, its value fixed to the U.S. dollar at 1:1 since 1991 through a currency board, is devalued to Ps1.4/$, then floated
February 13, 2002	Venezuelan bolivar floated	The Venezuelan bolivar, fixed to the dollar since 1996, is floated as a result of increasing economic crisis
February 14, 2004	Venezuelan bolivar devalued	Venezuela devalues the bolivar by 17% versus the U.S. dollar, in an attempt to deal with its growing fiscal deficit
May 1, 2004	EU enlargement	Ten more countries join the European Union, thereby enlarging it to 25 members; in the future, when they qualify, most of these countries are expected to adopt the euro
July 21, 2005	Yuan reform	The Chinese government and the People's Bank of China abandon the peg of the Chinese yuan (renminbi) to the U.S. dollar, announcing that it will be instantly revalued from Yuan8.28/$ to Yuan8.11/$, and reform the exchange rate regime to a managed float in the future; Malaysia announces a similar change to its exchange rate regime
April 2008	Euro peaks	The euro peaks in strength against the U.S. dollar at $1.60/€. In the following months the euro falls substantially, hitting $1.25/€ by late 2008
December 2010	Dollar weakness	The U.S. dollar, on an index basis across multiple currencies, hits a record low

Contemporary Currency Regimes

Today, the international monetary system is composed of national currencies, artificial currencies (such as the SDR), and one entirely new currency (euro) that replaced the 11 national European Union currencies on January 1, 1999. All of these currencies are linked to one another via a "smorgasbord" of currency regimes.

IMF's Exchange Rate Regime Classifications

The IMF classifies all exchange rate regimes into eight specific categories. The eight categories span the spectrum of exchange rate regimes from rigidly fixed to independently floating.

1. **Exchange arrangements with no separate legal tender.** The currency of another country circulates as the sole legal tender or the member belongs to a monetary or currency union in which the same legal tender is shared by the members of the union.

2. **Currency board arrangements.** A monetary regime based on an implicit legislative commitment to exchange domestic currency for a specified foreign currency at a fixed exchange rate, combined with restrictions on the issuing authority to ensure the fulfillment of its legal obligation.

3. **Other conventional fixed peg arrangements.** The country pegs its currency (formally or *de facto*) at a fixed rate to a major currency or a basket of currencies (a *composite*), where the exchange rate fluctuates within a narrow margin or at most ±1% around a central rate.

4. **Pegged exchange rates within horizontal bands.** The value of the currency is maintained within margins of fluctuation around a formal or *de facto* fixed peg that are wider than ±1% around a central rate.

5. **Crawling pegs.** The currency is adjusted periodically in small amounts at a fixed, preannounced rate or in response to changes in selective quantitative indicators.

6. **Exchange rates within crawling pegs.** The currency is maintained within certain fluctuation margins around a central rate that is adjusted periodically at a fixed preannounced rate or in response to changes in selective quantitative indicators.

7. **Managed floating with no preannounced path for the exchange rate.** The monetary authority influences the movements of the exchange rate through active intervention in the foreign exchange market without specifying, or precommitting to, a preannounced path for the exchange rate.

8. **Independent floating.** The exchange rate is market-determined, with any foreign exchange intervention aimed at moderating the rate of change and preventing undue fluctuations in the exchange rate, rather than establishing a level for it.

The most prominent example of a rigidly fixed system is the euro area, in which the euro is the single currency for its member countries. However, the euro itself is an independently floating currency against all other currencies. Other examples of rigidly fixed exchange regimes include Ecuador and Panama, which use the U.S. dollar as their official currency; the Central African Franc (CFA) zone, in which countries such as Mali, Niger, Senegal, Cameroon, and Chad among others use a single common currency (the franc, tied to the euro) and the Eastern Caribbean Currency Union (ECCU), whose members use a single common currency (the Eastern Caribbean dollar).

At the other extreme are countries with independently floating currencies. These include many of the most developed countries, such as Japan, the United States, the United Kingdom, Canada, Australia, New Zealand, Sweden, and Switzerland. However, this category also includes a number of unwilling participants—emerging market countries that tried to maintain fixed rates but were forced by the marketplace to let them float. Among these are Korea, the Philippines, Brazil, Indonesia, Mexico, and Thailand.

It is important to note that only the last two categories, including 80 of the 186 countries covered, are actually "floating" to any real degree. Although the contemporary international monetary system is typically referred to as a "floating regime," it is clearly not the case for the majority of the world's nations.

Fixed versus Flexible Exchange Rates

A nation's choice as to which currency regime to follow reflects national priorities about all facets of the economy, including inflation, unemployment, interest rate levels, trade balances, and economic growth. The choice between fixed and flexible rates may change over time as priorities change.

At the risk of over generalizing, the following points partly explain why countries pursue certain exchange rate regimes. They are based on the premise that, other things being equal, countries would prefer fixed exchange rates.

◆ Fixed rates provide stability in international prices for the conduct of trade. Stable prices aid in the growth of international trade and lessen risks for all businesses.

◆ Fixed exchange rates are inherently anti-inflationary, requiring the country to follow restrictive monetary and fiscal policies. This restrictiveness, however, can often be a burden to a country wishing to pursue policies that alleviate continuing internal economic problems, such as high unemployment or slow economic growth.

Fixed exchange rate regimes necessitate that central banks maintain large quantities of international reserves (hard currencies and gold) for use in the occasional defense of the fixed rate. As international currency markets have grown rapidly in size and volume, increasing reserve holdings has become a significant burden to many nations.

Fixed rates, once in place, may be maintained at levels that are inconsistent with economic fundamentals. As the structure of a nation's economy changes, and as its trade relationships and balances evolve, the exchange rate itself should change. Flexible exchange rates allow this to happen gradually and efficiently, but fixed rates must be changed administratively—usually too late, too highly publicized, and at too large a onetime cost to the nation's economic health.

Attributes of the "Ideal" Currency

If the ideal currency existed in today's world, it would possess three attributes (illustrated in Exhibit 3.3), often referred to as the "impossible trinity":

1. **Exchange rate stability.** The value of the currency would be fixed in relationship to other major currencies, so traders and investors could be relatively certain of the foreign exchange value of each currency in the present and into the near future.

2. **Full financial integration.** Complete freedom of monetary flows would be allowed, so traders and investors could willingly and easily move funds from one country and currency to another in response to perceived economic opportunities or risks.

3. **Monetary independence.** Domestic monetary and interest rate policies would be set by each individual country to pursue desired national economic policies, especially as they might relate to limiting inflation, combating recessions, and fostering prosperity and full employment.

These qualities are termed "the impossible trinity" (or the "trilemma of international finance") because a country must give up one of the three goals described by the sides of the triangle: monetary independence, exchange rate stability, or full financial integration. The forces of economics do not allow the simultaneous achievement of all three. For example, a country with a pure float exchange rate regime can have monetary independence and a high degree of financial integration with the outside capital markets, but the result must be a loss of exchange rate stability (the case of the United States). Similarly, a country that maintains very tight controls over the inflow and outflow of capital will retain its monetary independence and a stable exchange rate, but at the loss of being integrated with global financial and capital markets (the case of Malaysia in the 1998–2002 period).

EXHIBIT 3.3   The Impossible Trinity

All countries must implicitly decide which of the Trinity Elements they wish to pursue, and therefore which element they must give up (you can't have all three).

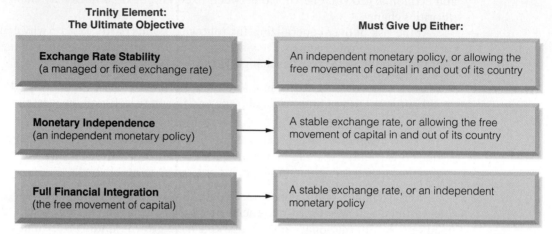

Trinity Element: The Ultimate Objective	Must Give Up Either:
Exchange Rate Stability (a managed or fixed exchange rate)	An independent monetary policy, or allowing the free movement of capital in and out of its country
Monetary Independence (an independent monetary policy)	A stable exchange rate, or allowing the free movement of capital in and out of its country
Full Financial Integration (the free movement of capital)	A stable exchange rate, or an independent monetary policy

In recent years, with the increasing deregulation of capital markets and capital controls around the globe, more countries are opting to pursue *Full Financial Integration*. The results are as theory would predict: more currency volatility and less independence in the conduct of monetary policy.

As shown in Exhibit 3.3, the consensus of many experts is that the force of increased capital mobility has been pushing more and more countries toward full financial integration in an attempt to stimulate their domestic economies and feed the capital appetites of their own MNEs. As a result, their currency regimes are being "cornered" into being either purely floating (like the United States) or integrated with other countries in monetary unions (like the European Union). *Global Finance in Practice 3.2* drives this debate home.

GLOBAL FINANCE IN PRACTICE   3.2

Who Is Choosing What in the Trinity/Trilemma?

The global recession of 2009/2010 sparked much debate over the value of currencies—in some cases invoking what one academic termed "currency wars." With most of the non-Chinese world suffering very slow economic growth, and under heavy pressure to stimulate their economies and alleviate high unemployment rates, there have been more and more arguments and efforts for a weak or undervalued currency. Although that sounds logical, the "impossible trinity" makes it very clear that each economy must choose its own medicine. Here is what many argue are the choices of three of the major global economic players:

	Choice #1	Choice #2	Therefore . . .
United States	Independent monetary policy	Free movement of capital	Currency value floats
China	Independent monetary policy	Fixed value of currency	Restricted movement of capital
Europe (EU)	Free movement of capital	Fixed rate of currency exchange between countries	'Integrated monetary policy'

The choices made by the EU are clearly the more complex. As a combination of different sovereign states, the EU has pursued integration of a common currency, the euro, and free movement of labor and capital. The result, according to the impossible trinity, is that it has had to give up an independent monetary policy. Although many may argue this, the recent fiscal deficits and near-collapses of government debt issuances in Greece, Portugal, and Ireland for example, may provide strong arguments for belief in the trinity.

Emerging Markets and Regime Choices

The 1997–2005 period saw increasing pressures on emerging market countries to choose among more extreme types of exchange rate regimes. The increased capital mobility pressures noted in the previous section have driven a number of countries to choose between either a free-floating exchange rate (as in Turkey in 2002) or the opposite extreme, a fixed-rate regime—such as a *currency board* (as in Argentina throughout the 1990s and detailed in the following section) or even *dollarization* (as in Ecuador in 2000).

Currency Boards

A *currency board* exists when a country's central bank commits to back its monetary base—its money supply—entirely with foreign reserves at all times. This commitment means that a unit of domestic currency cannot be introduced into the economy without an additional unit of foreign exchange reserves being obtained first. Eight countries, including the Hong Kong territory, utilize currency boards as a means of fixing their exchange rates.

Argentina. In 1991, Argentina moved from its previous managed exchange rate of the Argentine peso to a currency board structure. The currency board structure fixed the Argentine peso's value to the U.S. dollar on a one-to-one basis. The Argentine government preserved the fixed rate of exchange by requiring that every peso issued through the Argentine banking system be backed by either gold or U.S. dollars held on account in banks in Argentina. This 100% reserve system made the monetary policy of Argentina dependent on the country's ability to obtain U.S. dollars through trade or investment. Only after Argentina had earned these dollars through trade could its money supply be expanded. This requirement eliminated the possibility of the nation's money supply growing too rapidly and causing inflation.

An additional feature of the Argentine currency board system was the ability of all Argentines and foreigners to hold dollar-denominated accounts in Argentine banks. These accounts were in actuality *Eurodollar accounts*—dollar-denominated deposits in non-U.S. banks. These accounts provided savers and investors with the ability to choose whether or not to hold pesos.

From the very beginning, however, there was substantial doubt in the market that the Argentine government could maintain the fixed exchange rate. Argentine banks regularly paid slightly higher interest rates on peso-denominated accounts than on dollar-denominated accounts. This interest differential represented the market's assessment of the risk inherent in the Argentine financial system. Depositors were rewarded for accepting risk—for keeping their money in peso-denominated accounts. This was an explicit signal by the marketplace that there was a perceived possibility that what was then "fixed" would not always be so.

The market proved to be correct. In January 2002, after months of economic and political turmoil and nearly three years of economic recession, the Argentine currency board was ended. The peso was first devalued from Peso1.00/$ to Peso1.40/$, then floated completely. It fell in value dramatically within days. The Argentine decade-long experiment with a rigidly fixed exchange rate was over. The devaluation followed months of turmoil, including continuing bank holidays and riots in the streets of Buenos Aires. The Argentina crisis is presented in detail in Chapter 7.

Dollarization

Several countries have suffered currency devaluation for many years, primarily as a result of inflation, and have taken steps toward dollarization. Dollarization is the use of the U.S. dollar as the official currency of the country. Panama has used the dollar as its official currency since 1907. Ecuador, after suffering a severe banking and inflationary crisis in 1998 and 1999, adopted the U.S. dollar as its official currency in January 2000. One of the primary attributes of dollarization was summarized well by *BusinessWeek* in a December 11, 2000, article entitled "The Dollar Club":

> *One attraction of dollarization is that sound monetary and exchange-rate policies no longer depend on the intelligence and discipline of domestic policymakers. Their monetary policy becomes essentially the one followed by the U.S., and the exchange rate is fixed forever.*

The arguments for dollarization follow logically from the previous discussion of the impossible trinity. A country that dollarizes removes any currency volatility (against the dollar) and would theoretically eliminate the possibility of future currency crises. Additional benefits are expectations of greater economic integration with the United States and other dollar-based markets, both product and financial. This last point has led many to argue in favor of regional dollarization, in which several countries that are highly economically integrated may benefit significantly from dollarizing together.

Three major arguments exist against dollarization. The first is the loss of sovereignty over monetary policy. This is, however, the point of dollarization. Second, the country loses the power of *seignorage*, the ability to profit from its ability to print its own money. Third, the central bank of the country, because it no longer has the ability to create money within its economic and financial system, can no longer serve the role of lender of last resort. This role carries with it the ability to provide liquidity to save financial institutions that may be on the brink of failure during times of financial crisis.

Ecuador. Ecuador officially completed the replacement of the Ecuadorian sucre with the U.S. dollar as legal tender on September 9, 2000. This step made Ecuador the largest national adopter of the U.S. dollar, and in many ways set it up as a test case of dollarization for other emerging market countries to watch closely. As shown in Exhibit 3.4, this was the last stage of a massive depreciation of the sucre in a brief two-year period.

During 1999, Ecuador suffered a rising rate of inflation and a falling level of economic output. In March 1999, the Ecuadorian banking sector was hit with a series of devastating

---

EXHIBIT 3.4   The Ecuadorian Sucre/U.S. Dollar Exchange Rate, November 1998–March 2000

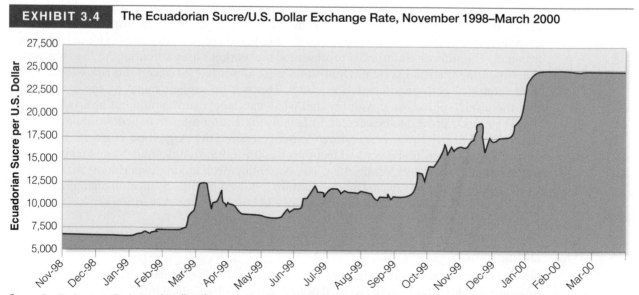

Source: Pacific Currency Exchange, http://pacific.commerce.ubc.ca/xr © 2001 by Prof. Werner Antweiler, University of British Columbia, Vancouver, BC, Canada.

"bank runs," financial panics in which all depositors attempted to withdraw all of their funds simultaneously. Although there were severe problems in the Ecuadorian banking system, the truth was that even the healthiest financial institution would fail under the strain of this financial drain. Ecuador's president at that time, Jamil Mahuad, immediately froze all deposits (this was termed a bank holiday in the United States in the 1930s, in which banks closed their doors). The Ecuadorian sucre, which in January 1999 was trading at roughly Sucre7,400/$, plummeted in early March to Sucre12,500/$. Ecuador defaulted on more than $13.6 billion in foreign debt in 1999 alone. President Mahuad moved quickly to propose dollarization to save the failing Ecuadorian economy.

By January 2000, when the next president took office (after a rather complicated military coup and subsequent withdrawal), the sucre had fallen in value to Sucre25,000/$. The new president, Gustavo Naboa, continued the dollarization initiative. Although unsupported by the U.S. government and the IMF, Ecuador completed its replacement of its own currency with the dollar over the next nine months.

The results of dollarization in Ecuador are still unknown. Ecuadorian residents immediately returned over $600 million into the banking system, money that they had withheld from the banks in fear of bank failure. This added capital infusion, along with new IMF loans and economic restructurings, allowed the country to close 2000 with a small economic gain of 1%. Inflation, however, remained high, closing the year at over 91% (up from 66% in 1999). Clearly, dollarization alone did not eliminate inflationary forces. Ecuador continues to struggle to find both economic and political balance with its new currency regime.

There is no doubt that for many emerging markets, a currency board, dollarization, and free-floating exchange rate regimes are all extremes. In fact, many experts feel that the global financial marketplace will drive more and more emerging market nations toward one of these extremes. As shown in Exhibit 3.5, there is a distinct lack of middle ground between

EXHIBIT 3.5   The Currency Regime Choices for Emerging Markets

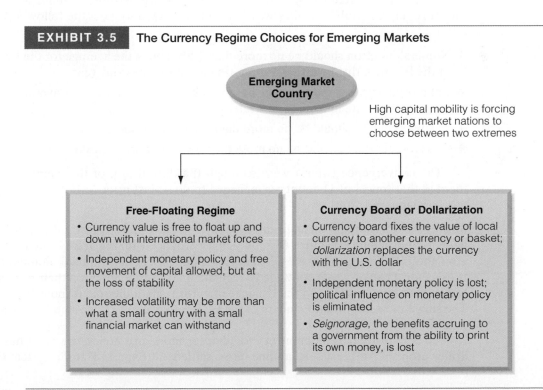

rigidly fixed and free-floating extremes. In anecdotal support of this argument, a poll of the general population in Mexico in 1999 indicated that 9 out of 10 people would prefer dollarization over a floating-rate peso. Clearly, there are many in the emerging markets of the world who have little faith in their leadership and institutions to implement an effective exchange rate policy.

The Birth of a European Currency: The Euro

The original 15 members of the European Union (EU) are also members of the European Monetary System (EMS). This group has tried to form an island of fixed exchange rates among themselves in a sea of major floating currencies. Members of the EMS rely heavily on trade with each other, so they perceive that the day-to-day benefits of fixed exchange rates between them are great. Nevertheless, the EMS has undergone a number of major changes since its inception in 1979, including major crises and reorganizations in 1992 and 1993, and conversion of 11 members to the euro on January 1, 1999 (Greece joined in 2001).

The Maastricht Treaty

In December 1991, the members of the EU met at Maastricht, the Netherlands, and concluded a treaty that changed Europe's currency future.

Timetable. The Maastricht Treaty specified a timetable and a plan to replace all individual ECU currencies with a single currency called the euro. Other steps were adopted that would lead to a full European Economic and Monetary Union (EMU).

Convergence Criteria. To prepare for the EMU, the Maastricht Treaty called for the integration and coordination of the member countries' monetary and fiscal policies. The EMU would be implemented by a process called convergence. Before becoming a full member of the EMU, each member country was originally expected to meet the following convergence criteria:

◆ Nominal inflation should be no more than 1.5% above the average for the three members of the EU with the lowest inflation rates during the previous year.

◆ Long-term interest rates should be no more than 2% above the average for the three members with the lowest interest rates.

◆ The fiscal deficit should be no more than 3% of gross domestic product.

◆ Government debt should be no more than 60% of gross domestic product.

The convergence criteria were so tough that few, if any, of the members could satisfy them at that time, but 11 countries managed to do so just prior to 1999. Greece adopted the euro on January 1, 2001.

Strong Central Bank. A strong central bank, called the European Central Bank (ECB), has been established in Frankfurt, Germany, in accordance with the Treaty. The bank is modeled after the U.S. Federal Reserve System. This independent central bank dominates the countries' central banks, which continue to regulate banks resident within their borders; all financial market intervention and the issuance of euros remain the sole responsibility of the ECB. The single most important mandate of the ECB is to promote price stability within the European Union.

As part of its development of cross-border monetary policy, the ECB has formed the Transeuropean Automated Real-time Gross settlement Express Transfer system (TARGET).

TARGET is the mechanism by which the ECB will settle all cross-border payments in the conduct of EU banking business and regulation. It will allow the ECB to conduct monetary policy and other intrabanking system capital movements quickly and without cost.

Why Monetary Unification?

According to the EU, EMU is a single-currency area within the EU single market, now known informally as the *euro zone*, in which people, goods, services, and capital are supposed to move without restrictions. Beginning with the Treaty of Rome in 1957 and continuing with the Single European Act of 1987, the Maastricht Treaty of 1991–1992, and the Treaty of Amsterdam of 1997, a core set of European countries worked steadily toward integrating their individual countries into one larger, more efficient, domestic market. Even after the launch of the 1992 Single Europe program, however, a number of barriers to true openness remained. The use of different currencies required both consumers and companies to treat the individual markets separately. Currency risk of cross-border commerce still persisted. The creation of a single currency is designed to move beyond these vestiges of separated markets.

The official abbreviation of the euro, EUR, has been registered with the International Standards Organization (letter abbreviations are needed for computer-based worldwide trading). This is similar to the three-letter computer symbols used for the U.S. dollar, USD, and the British pound sterling, GBP. The official symbol of the euro is €. According to the EU, the € symbol was inspired by the Greek letter *epsilon* (ε), simultaneously referring to Greece's ancient role as the source of European civilization and recalling the first letter of the word *Europe*.

The Launch of the Euro

On January 4, 1999, 11 member states of the EU initiated the EMU. They established a single currency, the euro, which replaced the individual currencies of the participating member states. The 11 countries were Austria, Belgium, Finland, France, Germany, Ireland, Italy, Luxembourg, the Netherlands, Portugal, and Spain. The United Kingdom, Sweden, and Denmark chose to maintain their individual currencies. Greece did not qualify for EMU but joined the Euro group in 2001. On December 31, 1998, the final fixed rates between the 11 participating currencies and the euro were put into place. On January 4, 1999, the euro was officially launched. Although it was the result of a long-term and methodical program for the alignment of all political and economic forces in the EU, the launch of the euro was only the first of many steps to come. The impacts of the euro on the economic environment and on society in general within the participating countries have been and will continue to be dramatic. It is only now becoming apparent what some of the impacts might be.

The euro affects markets in three ways: 1) countries within the euro zone enjoy cheaper transaction costs; 2) currency risks and costs related to exchange rate uncertainty are reduced; and 3) all consumers and businesses both inside and outside the euro zone enjoy price transparency and increased price-based competition.

Achieving Monetary Unification

If the euro is to be a successful replacement for the currencies of the participating EU states, it must have a solid economic foundation. The primary driver of a currency's value is its ability to maintain its purchasing power (money is worth what money can buy). The single largest threat to maintaining purchasing power is inflation. So, job one for the EU since the beginning has been to construct an economic system that would work to prevent inflationary forces from undermining the euro.

Fiscal Policy and Monetary Policy. Monetary policy for the EMU is conducted by the ECB, which has one responsibility: to safeguard the stability of the euro. Following the basic structures that were used in the establishment of the Federal Reserve System in the United States and the Bundesbank in Germany, the ECB is free of political pressures that have historically caused monetary authorities to yield to employment pressures by inflating economies. The ECB's independence allows it to focus simply on the stability of the currency without falling victim to this historical trap.

Fixing the Value of the Euro. The December 31, 1998, fixing of the rates of exchange between national currencies and the euro were permanent fixes for these currencies. The United Kingdom has been skeptical of increasing EU infringement on its sovereignty, and has opted not to participate. Sweden, which has failed to see significant benefits from EU membership (although it is one of the newest members), has also been skeptical of EMU participation. Denmark, like the United Kingdom and Sweden, has a strong political element that is highly nationalistic, and so far has opted not to participate. Norway has twice voted down membership in the EU and thus does not participate in the euro system.

On January 4, 1999, the euro began trading on world currency markets. Its introduction was a smooth one. The euro's value slid steadily following its introduction, however, primarily as a result of the robustness of the U.S. economy and U.S. dollar, and continuing sluggish economic sectors in the EMU countries. Exhibit 3.6 illustrates the euro's value since its introduction in January 1999. After declining in value against the U.S. dollar over 1999 and 2000, the euro traded in a relatively narrow band throughout 2001. Beginning in early 2002, however, the euro started a strong and steady rise in value versus the dollar.

EXHIBIT 3.6   The U.S. Dollar/Euro Spot Exchange Rate, 1999–2010

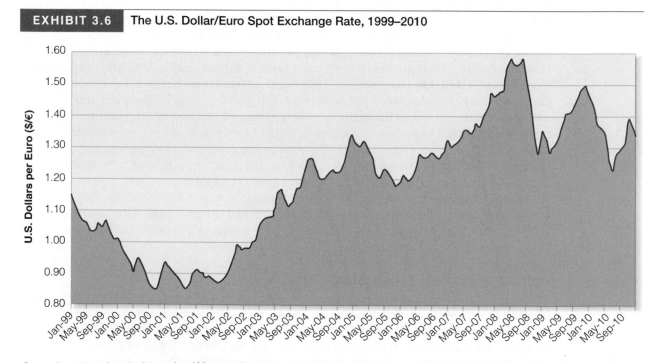

Source: Data drawn from the International Monetary Fund's *International Financial Statistics*, imf.org, monthly average rate.

Causes of the Dollar Decline. Since the introduction of the euro, the United States has experienced severe balance of payments deficits on the current account (explained in Chapter 4). The biggest bilateral deficits were with China and Japan. However, in order to protect their export competitiveness, both China and Japan followed macroeconomic policies that would maintain relatively fixed rates of exchange between their currencies and the U.S. dollar. In order to accomplish this result, both China and Japan had to intervene in the foreign exchange market by buying massive amounts of U.S. dollars while selling corresponding amounts of their own currencies, the Chinese yuan, and the Japanese yen. These purchases showed up as capital inflows into the United States. However, as the United States has continued to maintain historically low interest rates—both to stimulate the domestic economy and to promote liquidity in the financial system following the subprime mortgage failures in 2007–2009—some critics wonder whether China and Japan will continue to hold such large quantities of U.S. dollars.

Furthermore, several Asian and Middle Eastern governments are beginning to create so-called sovereign wealth funds to use their accumulating U.S. dollar balances. Sovereign wealth funds are government owned and funded investment funds that are either acquiring or taking a significant interest in private companies and major foreign banks in the United States and other Western countries. They are the subject of growing concern as foreign nations invest within other countries.

Expansion of the European Union and the Euro. The use of the euro has continued to expand since its introduction in 1999. As of January 2011, the euro was the official currency for 17 of the 27 member countries in the European Union, as well as five other countries (Montenegro, Andorra, Monaco, San Marino, and the Vatican) which may eventually join the EU. The 17 countries that currently use the euro—the so-called *eurozone*—include Austria, Belgium, Cyprus, Estonia, Finland, France, Germany, Greece, Ireland, Italy, Luxembourg, Malta, the Netherlands, Portugal, Slovakia, Slovenia and Spain. Although all members of the EU are expected eventually to replace their currencies with the euro, recent years have seen growing debates and continual postponements by new members in moving toward full euro adoption.

The Euro and Growth. Prior to the introduction of the euro, opponents thought political and economic conditions were unfavorable for a common currency. Most of the countries that eventually adopted the euro, such as Germany, France, and Italy, lacked the flexible labor markets they would need to compensate for losing individual (country-level) control over monetary policy as a tool to promote growth. Since the individual members of the EU cannot devalue their currencies, they would need to rely mainly on coordinated fiscal policies to stimulate growth. It is probably impossible to conduct a centralized monetary policy that fits all member countries, as illustrated by the impossible trinity discussed earlier. Some members are growing and some are not. Unemployment has been fairly high in some members but lower in others.

Exchange Rate Regimes: What Lies Ahead?

All exchange rate regimes must deal with the trade-off between *rules* and *discretion*, as well as between *cooperation* and *independence*. Exhibit 3.7 illustrates the trade-offs between exchange rate regimes based on rules, discretion, cooperation, and independence.

◆ Vertically, different exchange rate arrangements may dictate whether a country's government has strict intervention requirements—*rules*—or whether it may choose whether, when, and to what degree to intervene in the foreign exchange markets—*discretion*.

EXHIBIT 3.7   The Trade-offs between Exchange Rate Regimes

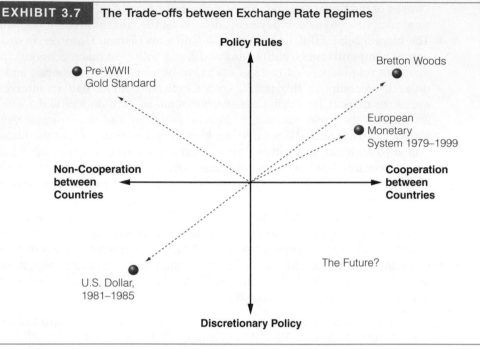

- Horizontally, the trade-off for countries participating in a specific system is between consulting and acting in unison with other countries—*cooperation*—or operating as a member of the system, but acting on their own—*independence*.

  Regime structures like the gold standard required no cooperative policies among countries, only the assurance that all would abide by the "rules of the game." Under the gold standard in effect prior to World War II, this assurance translated into the willingness of governments to buy or sell gold at parity rates on demand. The Bretton Woods Agreement, the system in place between 1944 and 1973, required more in the way of cooperation, in that gold was no longer the "rule," and countries were required to cooperate to a higher degree to maintain the dollar-based system. Exchange rate systems, like the European Monetary System's fixed exchange rate band system used from 1979 to 1999, were hybrids of these cooperative and rule regimes.

  The present international monetary system is characterized by no rules, with varying degrees of cooperation. Although there is no present solution to the continuing debate over what form a new international monetary system should take, many believe that it could succeed only if it combines cooperation among nations with individual discretion to pursue domestic social, economic, and financial goals.

Summary of Learning Objectives

Learn how the international monetary system has evolved from the days of the gold standard to today's eclectic currency arrangement

- Under the gold standard (1876–1913), the "rules of the game" were that each country set the rate at which its currency unit could be converted to a weight of gold.

- During the inter-war years (1914–1944) currencies were allowed to fluctuate over fairly wide ranges in terms of gold and each other. Supply and demand forces determined exchange rate values.

- The Bretton Woods Agreement (1944) established a U.S. dollar-based international monetary system.

Under the original provisions of the Bretton Woods Agreement, all countries fixed their the value of their currencies in terms of gold but were not required to exchange their currencies for gold. Only the dollar remained convertible into gold ($35 per ounce).

◆ A variety of economic forces led to the suspension of the convertibility of the dollar into gold in August 1971. Exchange rates of most of the leading trading countries were then allowed to float in relation to the dollar and thus indirectly in relation to gold. After a series of continuing crises in 1972 and 1973, the U.S. dollar and the other leading currencies of the world have floated in value since that time.

Analyze the characteristics of an ideal currency

◆ If the ideal currency existed in today's world, it would possess three attributes: a fixed value, convertibility, and independent monetary policy.

Explain the currency regime choices faced by emerging market countries

◆ Emerging market countries must often choose between two extreme exchange rate regimes, either a free-floating regime or an extremely fixed regime such as a *currency board* or *dollarization*.

Examine how the euro, a single currency for the European Union, was created

◆ The members of the European Union are also members of the European Monetary System (EMS). This group has tried to form an island of fixed exchange rates among themselves in a sea of major floating currencies. Members of the EMS rely heavily on trade with each other, so the day-to-day benefits of fixed exchange rates between them are perceived to be great.

◆ The euro affects markets in three ways: 1) countries within the euro zone enjoy cheaper transaction costs; 2) currency risks and costs related to exchange rate uncertainty are reduced; and 3) all consumers and businesses both inside and outside the euro zone enjoy price transparency and increase price-based competition.

MINI-CASE

First Steps in the Globalization of the Yuan[1]

The Chinese renminbi (RMB) or yuan (CNY) is evolving.[2] Trading in the RMB is closely controlled by the People's Republic of China (PRC), the Chinese government, with all trading inside China between the RMB and foreign currencies, primarily the U.S. dollar, being conducted only according to Chinese regulations. Its value, as illustrated in Exhibit 1, has been carefully controlled. Although it has been allowed to revalue gradually against the dollar over time, most indicators and analysts believe it to be grossly undervalued.

The degree to which trading in the yuan has been stunted can be seen through trade transactions. Of the $1.2 trillion in exports made by China in 2009, it is estimated that less than 1% were denominated in RMB. A Chinese exporter is typically paid in U.S. dollars, and has historically not been allowed to keep the dollar proceeds in any bank account. Exporters are required to exchange all foreign currencies for RMB at the official exchange rate set by the PRC. All hard-currency earnings from massive Chinese exports are therefore turned over to the Chinese government. The result has been a gross accumulation of foreign currency ($2,500 billion at end-of-year 2010) not seen in global business history.[3]

Inevitably, the currency of an economy of the size and scope of China's will result in more and more of its currency leaving China. Although it has restricted the flow of yuan out of China for many years, ultimately more and more will find its way beyond the reach of the onshore authorities. Once out of the reach of Chinese authorities, the yuan will be traded freely without government intervention. China knows this all too well, and has therefore adopted a gradual policy of developing the trading in the yuan—but through its own onshore offshore market, Hong Kong.

[2]The People's Republic of China officially recognizes the terms *renminbi* (RMB) and *yuan* (CNY) as names of its official currency. Formally, the term yuan is used in reference to the unit of account, while the physical currency itself is termed the renminbi. This Mini-Case will follow that usage, using RMB to refer to the currency of China and CNY and other forms to reflect its trading in different markets.

[3]"Offshore Trading in Yuan Takes Off," *The Wall Street Journal*, December 13, 2010.

EXHIBIT 1   The Gradual Revaluation of the RMB (1994–2010)

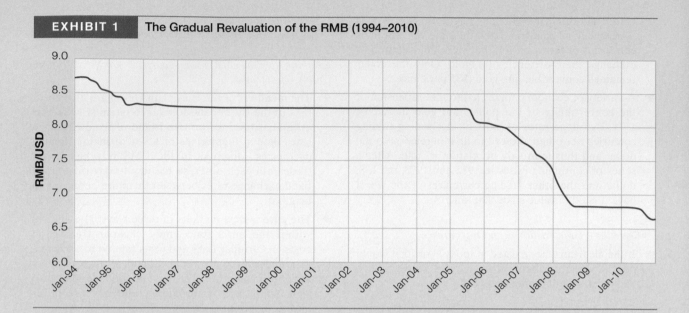

Offshore (Hong Kong) Trading

Hong Kong is a product of the "one country two systems" development of the PRC. Although a possession of the PRC, Hong Kong (as well as Macau) has been allowed to continue to operate and develop along its traditional free-market ways, but for currency purposes, Hong Kong was offshore. Hong Kong's own currency, the Hong Kong dollar (HKD), has long floated in value against the world's currencies.

But Hong Kong has a preferred access to yuan under PRC rules. Beginning in January 2004, Hong Kong residents were allowed to hold RMB in cash and bank deposits. They were allowed to obtain these balances through limited trading; daily transfers were limited to RMB 20,000 (roughly $2,400 at the exchange rate of RMB 8.27/USD at the time). Although this did allow a legal conduit for the movement of RMB out of the onshore market, its volume was so small it was inconsequential. This currency, however small in volume, is now referred to as CNH (as shown in Exhibit 2), Hong Kong-based trading in RMB.[4] It has been the basis for some limited financial product development, but has been significantly lacking in trading volume, liquidity, and depth. Still, over the following five years, the CNH market grew to about $9 billion in value.[5]

This has not, however, sated the thirst for RMB by a multitude of different traders outside of mainland China. As a result, a market has grown over the past decade for CNY-NDFs, non-deliverable forwards (NDFs) based on the officially cited value of the CNY by the Chinese government. These are forward contracts whose value is determined by the PRC-posted exchange value of the CNY, but are non-deliverable, meaning they are settled in a currency like the dollar or euro, not the CNY itself (because that would take access to physical volumes or deposits of RMB).

Chinese Deregulation 2010

The flow of RMB into the Hong Kong market, however, boomed in 2010 as a result of a series of regulatory changes by the PRC. In July 2010, the PRC began allowing unlimited exchange and flow of RMB into Hong Kong for trade-related transactions—payments for imports denominated in Chinese RMB. It is now expected that the CNH market will rise to more than $45 billion in value by the end of 2010, an enormous growth from the $9 billion in value at the start of 2010.

The Question of Backflow

The challenge to the growth of the Hong Kong offshore market is what to do with the growing balances of RMB. Although the RMB may flow from the onshore Chinese mainland into Hong Kong for import purchases, the receivers of the RMB will recycle these flows into the Hong Kong market upon receipt as the currency has no real trading use outside of Hong Kong or China as a whole. According to a variety of Hong Kong-based currency analysts, unless the holders of these RMB balances in Hong Kong

---

[4]CNY is the official ISO code for the Chinese currency. Although CNH is in increasingly common usage, it is not at this time an officially recognized code.

[5]*FX Pulse*, Morgan Stanley, December 2, 2010, p.12.

EXHIBIT 2   **Evolution of Trading in the Chinese Renminbi**

Chinese *yuan* (unit of account) and *renminbi* (physical currency)

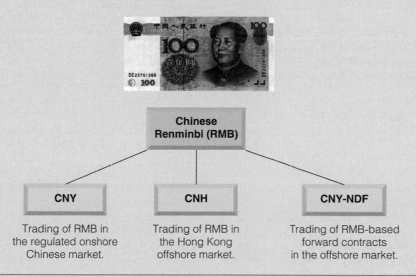

can gain access to the onshore market—mainland China—the market will still be limited in its growth potential.

Mr. Charles Li, Chief Executive of HKEx (Hong Kong Exchanges and Clearing Limited), had a unique way of explaining why the accumulating RMB in Hong Kong needs greater backflow ability to China (followed by Morgan Stanley's graphical depiction of the fish process in Exhibit 3):[6]

EXHIBIT 3   **Necessary Medium for the Growth of the RMB**

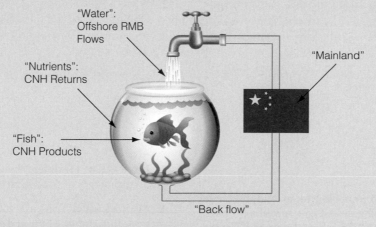

Source: *FX Pulse,* Morgan Stanley. December 2, 2010, p. 14.

[6]"Six Questions Regarding the Internationalisation of the Renminbi," HKEx Chief Executive Charles Li, 21 September 2010.

To understand the different challenges in these three stages, the following analogy might be of some help. If we see RMB flows as water and RMB products as fish, the logic will be clear. Fish do not exist where there is no water and they cannot survive if the water is stagnant. Without nutrients in the water, fish don't grow. The nutrients, representing returns on RMB products, can only come from the home market. That's why the offshore RMB must be allowed to flow back, at least at the initial stage.

As Mr. Li (and Morgan Stanley) make so vividly clear, for the RMB market in Hong Kong to grow and sustain it needs the ability to return to the Chinese mainland freely to have a "purpose"—to gain returns from RMB-based trading and commercial purposes. The RMB can only be used in China, and China's State Administration of Foreign Exchange (SAFE) must approve all transfers of RMB into the country on a case-by-case basis, even from Hong Kong.

Breadth and Depth of RMB Trading

Although the quotation of CNH deposit rates are listed on the counters of most Hong Kong banks today, side-by-side with U.S. dollar and Hong Kong dollar rates, there will continue to be a limited demand for these funds by the institutions themselves in the near future unless the PRC allows greater backflow into the onshore market.

The offshore Hong Kong market took a highly visible step forward in August 2010 with the launch of an RMB-denominated corporate bond issue for McDonald's Corporation (US):[7]

19 August 2010, Hong Kong—Standard Chartered Bank (Hong Kong) Limited proudly announces the launch of a RMB corporate bond for the Bank's Multinational Corporate Client McDonald's Corporation. It is the first ever RMB bond launched for a foreign Multi-national Corporate in the Hong Kong debt capital market signifying the commencement of a new funding channel for international companies to raise working capital for their China operations. It is also a significant contribution to the development of the off-shore RMB debt capital market in Hong Kong. The RMB 200 million 3% notes due September 2013, was targeted at institutional investors.

The bonds—colloquially termed *Panda Bonds* or *the Dim Sum Bond Market*—was the first issue denominated in RMB by a nonfinancial non-Chinese firm in the global market. Although small in size, roughly $30 million, the issue was something of a sign of what the future might hold for multinational enterprises operating in the world's second largest economy: the ability to both operate and fund their business growth in Chinese RMB. The McDonald's issuance was followed in November 2010 by a larger $150 million RMB-bond by Caterpillar Corporation (U.S.), and in January 2011 by a CNY 500 million ($75.9 million) issuance by the World Bank.[8]

Many experts today believe it may take a full generation or more, 20 or 30 years, for 20% to 30% of Chinese imports to be denominated in RMB, and the RMB to become a truly global currency. The growth of the offshore market in Hong Kong represents only the first step on that journey—but an important one for the RMB and for Hong Kong.

CASE QUESTIONS

1. How does the Chinese government limit the use of the Chinese currency, the RMB, on the global currency markets?

2. What are the differences between the RMB, the CNY, the CNH, and the CNY-NDF?

3. Why was the McDonald's bond issue so significant?

---

[7]"Standard Chartered Launches RMB Corporate Bond in Hong Kong for McDonald's Corporation," Press Release, Standard Chartered, August 19, 2010, Hong Kong.

[8]"World Bank Issues Yuan Bond," *The Wall Street Journal*, January 5, 2011.

Questions

1. **The Gold Standard and the Money Supply.** Under the gold standard all national governments promised to follow the "rules of the game." This meant defending a fixed exchange rate. What did this promise imply about a country's money supply?

2. **Causes of Devaluation.** If a country follows a fixed exchange rate regime, what macroeconomic variables could cause the fixed exchange rate to be devalued?

3. **Fixed versus Flexible.** What are the advantages and disadvantages of fixed exchange rates?

4. **The Impossible Trinity.** Explain what is meant by the term *Impossible Trinity* and why it is true.

5. **Currency Board or Dollarization.** Fixed exchange rate regimes are sometimes implemented through a *currency board* (Hong Kong) or *dollarization* (Ecuador). What is the difference between the two approaches?

6. **Emerging Market Regimes.** High capital mobility is forcing emerging market nations to choose between free-floating regimes and currency board or dollarization regimes. What are the main outcomes of each of these regimes from the perspective of emerging market nations?

7. **Argentine Currency Board.** How did the Argentine currency board function from 1991 to January 2002 and why did it collapse?

8. **The Euro.** On January 4, 1999, 11 member states of the European Union initiated the European Monetary Union (EMU) and established a single currency, the *euro*, which replaced the individual currencies of participating member states. Describe three of the main ways that the euro affects the members of the EMU.

9. **Mavericks.** The United Kingdom, Denmark, and Sweden have chosen not to adopt the *euro* but rather maintain their individual currencies. What are the motivations of each of these countries that are also members of the European Union?

10. **International Monetary Fund (IMF).** The IMF was established by the Bretton Woods Agreement (1944). What were its original objectives?

11. **Special Drawing Rights.** What are *Special Drawing Rights*?

12. **Exchange Rate Regime Classifications.** The IMF classifies all exchange rate regimes into eight specific categories that are summarized in this chapter. Under which exchange rate regime would you classify the following countries?
    a. France
    b. The United States
    c. Japan
    d. Thailand

13. **The Ideal Currency.** What are the attributes of the ideal currency?

14. **Bretton Woods Failure.** Why did the fixed exchange rate regime of 1945–1973 eventually fail?

15. **Euro Expansion.** With so many new countries joining the European Union in 2004, when will they officially move to the euro—if ever?

Problems

1. **Gilded Question.** Before World War I, $20.67 was needed to buy one ounce of gold. If, at the same time one ounce of gold could be purchased in France for FF410.00, what was the exchange rate between French francs and U.S. dollars?

2. **Worth Its Weight in Gold.** Under the gold standard, the price of an ounce of gold in U.S. dollars was $20.67, while the price of that same ounce in British pounds was £3.7683. What would be the exchange rate between the dollar and the pound if the U.S. dollar price had been $42.00 per ounce?

3. **DuBois and Keller.** Chantal DuBois lives in Brussels. She can buy a U.S. dollar for €0.7600. Christopher Keller, living in New York City, can buy a euro for $1.3200. What is the foreign exchange rate between the dollar and the euro?

4. **Mexican Peso Changes.** In December 1994, the government of Mexico officially changed the value of the Mexican peso from 3.2 pesos per dollar to 5.5 pesos per dollar. What was the percentage change in its value? Was this a depreciation, devaluation, appreciation, or revaluation? Explain.

5. **Amazing Incorporated.** The spot rate for Mexican pesos is Ps12.42/$. If U.S.-based company Amazing Inc. buys Ps500,000 spot from its bank on Monday, how much must Amazing Inc. pay and on what date?

6. **Loonie Parity.** If the price of former Chairman of the U.S. Federal Reserve Alan Greenspan's memoir, "The Age of Turbulence," is listed on Amazon.ca as C$26.33, but costs just US$23.10 on Amazon.com, what exchange rate does that imply between the two currencies?

7. **Hong Kong Dollar and the Chinese Yuan.** The Hong Kong dollar has long been pegged to the U.S. dollar at HK$7.80/$. When the Chinese yuan was revalued in July 2005 against the U.S. dollar from Yuan8.28/$ to Yuan8.11/$, how did the value of the Hong Kong dollar change against the yuan?

8. **Ranbaxy (India) in Brazil.** Ranbaxy, an India-based pharmaceutical firm, has continuing problems with its cholesterol reduction product's price in one of its rapidly growing markets, Brazil. All product is produced in India, with costs and pricing initially stated in Indian rupees (Rps), but converted to Brazilian reais (R$) for distribution and sale in Brazil. In 2009, the unit volume was priced at Rps21,900, with a Brazilian reais price set at R$895. But in 2010, the reais appreciated in value versus the rupee, averaging Rps26.15/R$. In order to preserve the reais price and product profit margin in rupees, what should the new rupee price be set at?

9. **Toyota Exports to the United Kingdom.** Toyota manufactures most of the vehicles it sells in the United Kingdom in Japan. The base platform for the

Toyota Tundra truck line is ¥1,650,000. The spot rate of the Japanese yen against the British pound has recently moved from ¥ 197/£ to ¥ 190/£. How does this change the price of the Tundra to Toyota's British subsidiary in British pounds?

10. **Vietnamese Coffee Coyote.** Many people were surprised when Vietnam became the second largest coffee producing country in the world in recent years, second only to Brazil. The Vietnamese dong, VND or d, is managed against the U.S. dollar but is not widely traded. If you were a traveling coffee buyer for the wholesale market (a "coyote" by industry terminology), which of the following currency rates and exchange commission fees would be in your best interest if traveling to Vietnam on a buying trip?

11. **Chinese Yuan Revaluation.** Many experts believe that the Chinese currency should not only be revalued against the U.S. dollar as it was in July 2005, but also be revalued by 20% or 30%. What would be the new exchange rate value if the yuan was revalued an additional 20% or 30% from its initial post-revaluation rate of Yuan 8.11/$?

12. **Middle East Exports.** Oriol Díez Miguel S.R.L., a manufacturer of heavy duty machine tools near Barcelona, ships an order to a buyer in Jordan. The purchase price is €425,000. Jordan imposes a 13% import duty on all products purchased from the European Union. The Jordanian importer then re-exports the product to a Saudi Arabian importer, but only after imposing their own resale fee of 28%. Given the following spot exchange rates on April 11, 2010, what is the total cost to the Saudi Arabian importer in Saudi Arabian riyal, and what is the U.S. dollar equivalent of that price?

13. **Chunnel Choices.** The Channel Tunnel or "Chunnel" passes underneath the English Channel between Great Britain and France, a land-link between the Continent and the British Isles. One side is therefore an economy of British pounds, the other euros. If you were to check the Chunnel's rail ticket Internet rates you would find that they would be denominated in U.S. dollars (USD). For example, a first class round trip fare for a single adult from London to Paris via the Chunnel through RailEurope may cost USD170.00. This currency neutrality, however, means that customers on both ends of the Chunnel pay differing rates in their home currencies from day to day. What is the British pound and euro denominated prices for the USD170.00 round trip fare in local currency if purchased on the following dates at the accompanying spot rates drawn from the *Financial Times*?

Date of Spot Rate	British Pound Spot Rate (£/$)	Euro Spot Rate (€/$)
Monday	0.5702	0.8304
Tuesday	0.5712	0.8293
Wednesday	0.5756	0.8340

Internet Exercises

1. **International Monetary Fund's Special Drawing Rights.** The Special Drawing Right (SDR) is a composite index of six key participant currencies. Use the IMF's Web site to find the current weights and valuation of the SDR.

International Monetary Fund   www.imf.org/external/np/tre/sdr/basket.htm

2. **Capital Controls.** One of the key "sides" of the Impossibility Trinity discussed in the chapter is the degree of capital mobility into and out of a country. Use the International Finance subsection of Yahoo! to determine the current state of capital movement freedom for the following countries: Chile, China, Malaysia, Taiwan, and Russia.

Yahoo!   biz.yahoo.com/ifc/

3. **Malaysian Currency Controls.** The institution of currency controls by the Malaysian government in the aftermath of the Asian currency crisis is a classic response by government to unstable currency conditions. Use the following Web site to increase your knowledge of how currency controls work.

EconEdLink   www.econedlink.org/lessons/index.cfm?lesson=EM25

4. **Personal Transfers.** As anyone who has traveled internationally learns, the exchange rates available to private retail customers are not always as attractive as those accessed by companies. The OzForex Web site possesses a section on "customer rates" which illustrates the difference. Use the site to calculate what the percentage difference between Australian dollar/U.S. dollar spot exchange rates are for retail customers versus interbank rates.

OzForex   www.ozforex.com/cgi-bin/spotrates_transfers.asp

5. **Exchange Rate History.** Use the Pacific Exchange Rate database and plot capability to track the British pound's, the U.S. dollar's, and the Japanese yen's value changes against each other over the past 15 years.

Pacific Exchange Rate Service   fx.sauder.ubc.ca

The Balance of Payments

The sort of dependence that results from exchange, i.e., from commercial transactions, is a reciprocal dependence. We cannot be dependent upon a foreigner without his being dependent on us. Now, this is what constitutes the very essence of society. To sever natural interrelations is not to make oneself independent, but to isolate oneself completely. —Frederic Bastiat.

LEARNING OBJECTIVES

◆ Learn how nations measure their own levels of international economic activity, and how that creates the balance of payments.

◆ Examine the economic relationships underlying the two basic subcomponents of the balance of payments—the current account and financial account balances.

◆ Consider the financial dimensions of international economic activity, and how they differ between merchandise and services trade.

◆ Identify balance of payment activities by nations in the pursuit of domestic and global economic and political policies.

◆ Examine how exchange rate changes and volatility influence trade balances over time.

◆ Evaluate the history of capital mobility, and the conditions that lead in times of crisis to capital flight.

International business transactions occur in many different forms over the course of a year. The measurement of all international economic transactions between the residents of a country and foreign residents is called the *balance of payments* (BOP). This chapter provides a type of navigational map to the understanding of balance of payments and the multitude of economic, political, and business issues which it involves. The chapter concludes with the Mini-Case, ***Global Remittances***, a subject of significant controversy globally.

The official terminology used throughout this chapter is that of the IMF. Because the IMF is the primary source of similar statistics for balance of payments and economic performance by nations worldwide, its language is more general than other terminology such as that employed by the U.S. Department of Commerce. Government policymakers need such measures of economic activity in order to evaluate the general competitiveness of domestic industry, to set exchange rate or interest rate policies or goals, and for many other purposes. MNEs use various BOP measures to gauge the growth and health of specific types of trade or financial transactions by country and regions of the world against the home country.

Home-country and host-country BOP data are important to business managers, investors, consumers, and government officials because the data influences and is influenced by other key macroeconomic variables such as gross domestic product, employment levels, price levels, exchange rates, and interest rates. Monetary and fiscal policy must take the BOP into account at the national level. Business managers and investors need BOP data to anticipate changes in host-country economic policies that might be driven by BOP events. BOP data is also important for the following reasons:

◆ The BOP is an important indicator of pressure on a country's foreign exchange rate, and thus of the potential for a firm trading with or investing in that country to experience foreign exchange gains or losses. Changes in the BOP may predict the imposition or removal of foreign exchange controls.

◆ Changes in a country's BOP may signal the imposition or removal of controls over payment of dividends and interest, license fees, royalty fees, or other cash disbursements to foreign firms or investors.

◆ The BOP helps to forecast a country's market potential, especially in the short run. A country experiencing a serious trade deficit is not as likely to expand imports as it would be if running a surplus. It may, however, welcome investments that increase its exports.

Typical Balance of Payments Transactions

International transactions take many forms. Each of the following examples is an international economic transaction that is counted and captured in the U.S. balance of payments:

◆ Honda U.S. is the U.S. distributor of automobiles manufactured in Japan by its parent company, Honda of Japan.

◆ A U.S.-based firm, Fluor Corporation, manages the construction of a major water treatment facility in Bangkok, Thailand.

◆ The U.S. subsidiary of a French firm, Saint Gobain, pays profits (dividends) back to its parent firm in Paris.

◆ An American tourist purchases a small Lapponia necklace in Finland.

◆ The U.S. government finances the purchase of military equipment for its NATO (North Atlantic Treaty Organization) military ally, Norway.

◆ A Mexican lawyer purchases a U.S. corporate bond through an investment broker in Cleveland.

This is a small sample of the hundreds of thousands of international transactions that occur each year. The balance of payments provides a systematic method for classifying these transactions. One rule of thumb always aids the understanding of BOP accounting: "Follow the cash flow."

The BOP is composed of a number of subaccounts that are watched quite closely by groups as diverse as investment bankers, farmers, politicians, and corporate executives. These groups track and analyze the major subaccounts, the *current account*, the *capital account*, and the *financial account*, continually. Exhibit 4.1 provides an overview of these major subaccounts of the BOP.

EXHIBIT 4.1   Generic Balance of Payments

A. Current Account

   1. Net exports/imports of goods (balance of trade)

   2. Net exports/imports of services

   3. Net income (investment income from direct and portfolio investment plus employee compensation)

   4. Net transfers (sums sent home by migrants and permanent workers abroad, gifts, grants, and pensions)

      A (1–4) = Current Account Balance

B. Capital Account

   Capital transfers related to the purchase and sale of fixed assets such as real estate

C. Financial Account

   1. Net foreign direct investment

   2. Net portfolio investment

   3. Other financial items

      A + B + C = Basic Balance

D. Net Errors and Omissions

   Missing data such as illegal transfers

      A + B + C + D = Overall Balance

E. Reserves and Related Items

   Changes in official monetary reserves including gold, foreign exchange, and IMF position

---

Fundamentals of Balance of Payments Accounting

The BOP must balance. If it does not, something has not been counted or has been counted improperly. Therefore, it is incorrect to state that the BOP is in disequilibrium. It cannot be. The supply and demand for a country's currency may be imbalanced, but supply and demand are not the same thing as the BOP. A subaccount of the BOP, such as the merchandise trade balance, may be imbalanced, but the entire BOP of a single country is always balanced.

There are three main elements of the actual process of measuring international economic activity: 1) identifying what is and is not an international economic transaction; 2) understanding how the flow of goods, services, assets, and money creates debits and credits to the overall BOP; and 3) understanding the bookkeeping procedures for BOP accounting.

Defining International Economic Transactions

Identifying international transactions is ordinarily not difficult. The export of merchandise—goods such as trucks, machinery, computers, telecommunications equipment and so forth—is obviously an international transaction. Imports such as French wine, Japanese cameras, and German automobiles are also clearly international transactions. But this merchandise trade is only a portion of the thousands of different international transactions that occur in the United States and other countries each year.

Many other international transactions are not so obvious. The purchase of a glass figure in Venice, Italy, by a U.S. tourist is classified as a U.S. merchandise import. In fact, all expenditures made by U.S. tourists around the globe for services (e.g., restaurants and hotels), but not for goods, are recorded in the U.S. balance of payments as imports of travel services in the current account. The purchase of a U.S. Treasury bill by a foreign resident is an international financial transaction and is duly recorded in the financial account of the U.S. balance of payments.

The BOP as a Flow Statement

The BOP is often misunderstood because many people infer from its name that it is a balance sheet, whereas in fact it is a *cash flow statement*. By recording all international transactions over a period of time such as a year, the BOP tracks the continuing flows of purchases and payments between a country and all other countries. It does not add up the value of all assets and liabilities of a country on a specific date like a balance sheet does for an individual firm.

Two types of business transactions dominate the balance of payments:

1. **Exchange of real assets.** The exchange of goods (e.g., automobiles, computers, watches, and textiles) and services (e.g., banking, consulting, and travel services) for other goods and services (barter) or for money

2. **Exchange of financial assets.** The exchange of financial claims (e.g., stocks, bonds, loans, and purchases or sales of companies) for other financial claims or money

Although assets can be identified as real or financial, it is often easier simply to think of all assets as goods that can be bought and sold. The purchase of a hand-woven area rug in a shop in Bangkok by a U.S. tourist is not all that different from a Wall Street banker buying a British government bond for investment purposes.

BOP Accounting

The measurement of all international transactions in and out of a country over a year is a daunting task. Mistakes, errors, and statistical discrepancies will occur. The primary problem is that double-entry bookkeeping is employed in theory, but not in practice. Individual purchase and sale transactions should—in theory—result in financing entries in the balance of payments that match. In reality, the entries are recorded independently. Current, financial, and capital account entries are recorded independently of one another, not together as double-entry bookkeeping would prescribe. Thus, there will be serious discrepancies (to use a nice term for it) between debits and credits.

The Accounts of the Balance of Payments

The balance of payments is composed of three primary subaccounts: the current account, the financial account, and the capital account. In addition, the *official reserves account* tracks government currency transactions, and a fifth statistical subaccount, the *net errors and omissions account*, is produced to preserve the balance in the BOP. The international economic relationships between countries, however, continue to evolve, as the recent revision of the major accounts within the BOP discussed in the following sections indicates.

The Current Account

The *current account* includes all international economic transactions with income or payment flows occurring within the year, the *current* period. The current account consists of four subcategories:

1. **Goods trade.** The export and import of goods is known as the goods trade. Merchandise trade is the oldest and most traditional form of international economic activity. Although many countries depend on imports of goods (as they should, according to the theory of comparative advantage), they also normally work to preserve either a balance of goods trade or even a surplus.

2. **Services trade.** The export and import of services is known as the services trade. Common international services are financial services provided by banks to foreign importers and exporters, travel services of airlines, and construction services of domestic firms in other countries. For the major industrial countries, this subaccount has shown the fastest growth in the past decade.

3. **Income.** This is predominantly *current income* associated with investments that were made in previous periods. If a U.S. firm created a subsidiary in South Korea to produce metal parts in a previous year, the proportion of net income that is paid back to the parent company in the current year (the dividend) constitutes current investment income. Additionally, wages and salaries paid to nonresident workers are also included in this category.

4. **Current transfers.** The financial settlements associated with the change in ownership of real resources or financial items are called current transfers. Any transfer between countries that is one-way—a gift or grant—is termed a *current transfer*. For example, funds provided by the U.S. government to aid in the development of a less-developed nation would be a current transfer. Transfers associated with the transfer of fixed assets are included in a separate account, the *capital account*.

All countries possess some amount of trade, most of which is merchandise. Many smaller and less-developed countries have little in the way of service trade, or items that fall under the income or transfers subaccounts.

The *current account* is typically dominated by the first component described, the export and import of merchandise. For this reason, the *balance of trade* (BOT), which is so widely quoted in the business press in most countries, refers to the balance of exports and imports of goods trade only. If the country is a larger industrialized country, however, the BOT is somewhat misleading, in that service trade is not included.

Exhibit 4.2 summarizes the current account and its components for the United States for the 2002–2009 period. As illustrated, the U.S. goods trade balance has been consistently negative, but has been partially offset by the continuing surplus in services trade balance.

Goods Trade

Exhibit 4.3 places the current account values of Exhibit 4.2 in perspective over time by dividing the current account into its two major components: 1) *goods trade* and 2) *services trade and investment income*. The first and most striking message is the magnitude of the goods

EXHIBIT 4.2	The United States Current Account, 2002–2009 (billions of U.S. dollars)							
	2002	**2003**	**2004**	**2005**	**2006**	**2007**	**2008**	**2009**
Goods exports	686	717	811	898	1020	1164	1309	1073
Goods imports	−1167	−1264	−1477	−1682	−1863	−1985	−2141	−1577
Goods trade balance (BOT)	−481	−548	−666	−783	−844	−820	−832	−504
Services trade credits	289	301	350	385	432	484	530	498
Services trade debits	−231	−250	−291	−314	−349	−366	−397	−369
Services trade balance	58	51	58	72	83	118	133	129
Income receipts	281	320	414	535	682	830	797	588
Income payments	−254	−275	−347	−463	−634	−730	−645	−467
Income balance	27	45	67	72	48	100	152	121
Current transfers, credits	12	15	20	19	26	24	24	21
Current transfers, debits	−77	−87	−105	−109	−117	−140	−146	−146
Net transfers	−65	−72	−84	−90	−91	−116	−122	−125
Current Account Balance	−461	−523	−625	−729	−804	−718	−669	−378

Source: Derived from *International Financial Statistics*, IMF.org, December 2010.

EXHIBIT 4.3   U.S. Trade Balances on Goods and Services, 1985–2009 (billions of U.S. dollars)

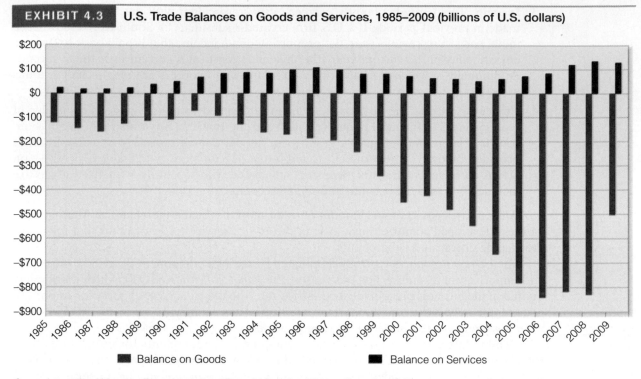

Balance on Goods   Balance on Services

Source: International Monetary Fund, *International Financial Statistics*, IMF.org, December 2010.

trade deficit in the period shown (a continuation of a position created in the early 1980s). The balance on services and income, although not large in comparison to net goods trade, has with few exceptions run a surplus over the past two decades.

The deficits in the BOT of the past decade have been an area of considerable concern for the United States, in both the public and private sectors. Merchandise trade is the original core of international trade. The manufacturing of goods was the basis of the industrial revolution and the focus of the theory of comparative advantage in international trade. Manufacturing is traditionally the sector of the economy that employs most of a country's workers. The goods trade deficit of the 1980s saw the decline of traditional heavy industries in the United States, industries that through history employed many U.S. workers. Declines in the BOT in areas such as steel, automobiles, automotive parts, textiles, and shoe manufacturing caused massive economic and social disruption.

Understanding merchandise import and export performance is much like understanding the market for any single product. The demand factors that drive both are income, the economic growth rate of the buyer, and price of the product in the eyes of the consumer after passing through an exchange rate. For example, U.S. merchandise imports reflect the income level of U.S. consumers and growth of industry. As income rises, so does the demand for imports.

Exports follow the same principles, but in the reverse. U.S. manufacturing exports depend not on the incomes of U.S. residents, but on the incomes of buyers of U.S. products in all other countries around the world. When these economies are growing, the demand for U.S. products rises.

The service component of the U.S. current account is a mystery to many. As illustrated in Exhibits 4.2 and 4.3, the United States has consistently achieved a surplus in services trade income. The major categories of services include travel and passenger fares; transportation services; expenditures by U.S. students abroad and foreign students pursuing studies in the United States; telecommunications services; and financial services.

The Capital and Financial Accounts

The capital and financial accounts of the balance of payments measure all international economic transactions of financial assets.

◆ **The capital account.** The capital account is made up of transfers of financial assets and the acquisition and disposal of nonproduced/nonfinancial assets. This account has been introduced as a separate component in the IMF's balance of payments only recently. The magnitude of capital transactions covered is relatively minor, and we will include it in principle in all of the following discussion of the financial account.

◆ **The financial account.** The financial account consists of three components: *direct investment*, *portfolio investment*, and *other asset investment*. Financial assets can be classified in a number of different ways, including by the length of the life of the asset (its maturity) and the nature of the ownership (public or private). The financial account, however, uses a third method, the degree of control over assets or operations, as in *portfolio investment*, where the investor has no control, or *direct investment*, where the investor exerts some explicit degree of control over the assets.

Direct Investment. This investment measure is the net balance of capital dispersed from and into the United States for the purpose of exerting control over assets. If a U.S. firm builds a new automotive parts facility in another country or actually purchases a company in another country, this is a *direct investment* in the U.S. balance of payments accounts. When the capital flows out of the United States, it enters the balance of payments as a negative cash flow. If, however, a foreign firm purchases a firm in the United States, it is a capital inflow and enters the balance of payments positively. Whenever 10% or more of the voting shares in a U.S. company are held by foreign investors, the company is classified as the U.S. affiliate of a foreign company, and as a *foreign direct investment*. Similarly, if U.S. investors hold 10% or more of the control in a company outside the United States, that company is considered the foreign affiliate of a U.S. company.

The 1980s boom in foreign investment into the United States, or foreign resident purchases of assets in the United States, was extremely controversial. The source of concern over foreign investment in any country, including the United States, focuses on two topics: control and profit. Some countries place restrictions on what foreigners may own in their country. This rule is based on the premise that domestic land, assets, and industry in general should be owned by residents of the country. On the other hand, the United States has traditionally had few restrictions on what foreign residents or firms can own or control; most restrictions remaining today relate to national security concerns. Unlike the case in the traditional debates over whether international trade should be free, there is no consensus that international investment should necessarily be free. This question is still very much a domestic political concern first, and an international economic issue second.

The second major source of concern over foreign direct investment is who receives the profits from the enterprise. Foreign companies owning firms in the United States will ultimately profit from the activities of the firms, or put another way, from the efforts of

U.S. workers. In spite of evidence that indicates foreign firms in the United States reinvest most of their profits in their U.S. businesses (in fact, at a higher rate than domestic firms), the debate on possible profit drains has continued. Regardless of the actual choices made, workers of any nation feel that the profits of their work should remain in their own hands. Once again, this is in many ways a political and emotional concern more than an economic one.

The choice of words used to describe foreign investment can also influence public opinion. If these massive capital inflows are described as "capital investments from all over the world showing their faith in the future of U.S. industry," the net capital surplus is represented as decidedly positive. If, however, the net capital surplus is described as resulting in "the United States being the world's largest debtor nation," the negative connotation is obvious. Both are essentially spins on the economic principles at work.

Capital, whether short-term or long-term, flows to where the investor believes it can earn the greatest return for the level of risk. And although in an accounting sense this is "international debt," when the majority of the capital inflow is in the form of direct investment, a long-term commitment to jobs, production, services, technological, and other competitive investments, the impact on the competitiveness of industry located within the United States is increased. When the "net debtor" label is applied to equity investment, it is misleading, in that it invites comparison with large debt crisis conditions suffered by many countries in the past.

Portfolio Investment. This is net balance of capital that flows in and out of the United States but does not reach the 10% ownership threshold of direct investment. If a U.S. resident purchases shares in a Japanese firm but does not attain the 10% threshold, we define the purchase as a *portfolio investment* (and in this case an outflow of capital). The purchase or sale of debt securities (like U.S. Treasury bills) across borders is also classified as portfolio investment, because debt securities by definition do not provide the buyer with ownership or control.

Portfolio investment is capital invested in activities that are purely profit-motivated (return), rather than ones made to control or manage the investment. Purchases of debt securities, bonds, interest-bearing bank accounts, and the like are intended only to earn a return. They provide no vote or control over the party issuing the debt. Purchases of debt issued by the U.S. government (U.S. Treasury bills, notes, and bonds) by foreign investors constitutes *net portfolio investment* in the United States. It is worth noting that most U.S. debt purchased by foreigners is U.S. dollar-denominated—denominated in the currency of the issuing country. Most foreign debt issued by countries such as Russia, Mexico, Brazil, and Southeast Asian countries is also U.S. dollar-denominated—in this case, the currency of a foreign country. The foreign country must earn dollars to repay its foreign-held debt. The United States need not earn any foreign currency to repay its foreign debt.

As illustrated in Exhibit 4.4, portfolio investment has shown much more volatile behavior than net foreign direct investment has over the past decade. Many U.S. debt securities, such as U.S. Treasury securities and corporate bonds, were in high demand in the late 1980s, while surging emerging markets in both debt and equities caused a reversal in direction in the 1990s. The motivating forces for portfolio investment flows are always the same—return and risk. This fact, however, does not make the flows any more predictable.

Other Investment Assets/Liabilities. This final category consists of various short-term and long-term trade credits, cross-border loans from all types of financial institutions, currency deposits and bank deposits, and other accounts receivable and payable related to cross-border trade.

Exhibit 4.5 shows the major subcategories of the U.S. financial account balance from 1985 to 2009: direct investment, portfolio investment, and other long-term and short-term capital investment.

EXHIBIT 4.4	The United States Financial Account and Components, 2002–2009 (billions of U.S. dollars)							
	2002	**2003**	**2004**	**2005**	**2006**	**2007**	**2008**	**2009**
Direct Investment								
Direct investment abroad	−154	−150	−316	−36	−245	−414	−351	−269
Direct investment in the US	84	64	146	113	243	271	328	135
Net direct Investment	−70	−86	−170	76	−2	−143	−23	−134
Portfolio Investment								
Assets, net	−49	−123	−177	−258	−499	−391	286	−393
Liabilities, net	428	550	867	832	1127	1157	520	367
Net portfolio investment	379	427	690	575	628	766	806	−27
Financial Derivatives, net					30	6	−33	51
Other Investment								
Other investment assets	−88	−54	−510	−267	−544	−671	226	574
Other investment liabilities	283	244	520	303	695	680	−394	−196
Net other investment	195	190	10	36	151	9	−167	378
Net Financial Account Balance	504	532	530	687	807	638	583	268

Source: Derived from *International Financial Statistics*, IMF.org, December 2010.

EXHIBIT 4.5	The United States Financial Account, 1985–2009 (billions of U.S. dollars)

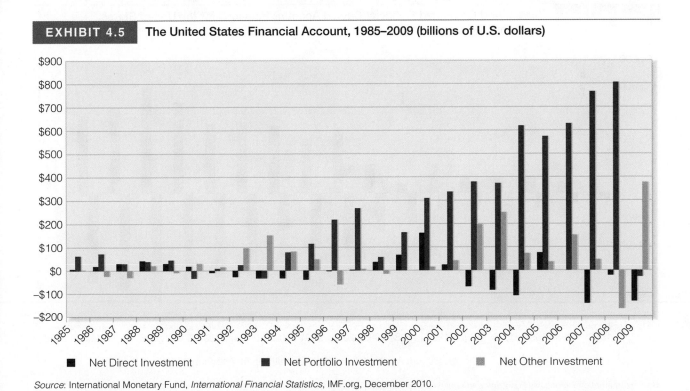

Source: International Monetary Fund, *International Financial Statistics*, IMF.org, December 2010.

Current and Financial Account Balance Relationships

Exhibit 4.6 illustrates the current and financial account balances for the United States over recent years. The exhibit shows one of the basic economic and accounting relationships of the balance of payments: *the inverse relation between the current and financial accounts*. This inverse relationship is not accidental. The methodology of the balance of payments, double-entry bookkeeping in theory, requires that the current and financial accounts be offsetting, *unless* the country's exchange rate is being highly manipulated or controlled by governmental authorities. *Global Finance in Practice 4.1* describes one very high profile case in which government policy has thwarted economics—the twin surpluses of China. Countries experiencing large current account deficits "finance" these purchases through equally large surpluses in the financial account, and vice versa.

Net Errors and Omissions. As previously noted, because current and financial account entries are collected and recorded separately, errors or statistical discrepancies will occur. The *net errors and omissions account* ensures that the BOP actually balances.

Official Reserves Account. The Official Reserves Account is the total reserves held by official monetary authorities within a country. These reserves are normally composed of the major currencies used in international trade and financial transactions (so-called "hard currencies" like the U.S. dollar, European euro, and Japanese yen; gold; and special drawing rights, SDRs).

The significance of official reserves depends generally on whether a country is operating under a *fixed exchange rate* regime or a *floating exchange rate* system. If a country's currency is fixed, the government of the country officially declares that the currency is convertible into a fixed amount of some other currency. For example, the Chinese yuan was fixed to the

---

EXHIBIT 4.6   Current and Combined Financial/Capital Account Balances for the United States, 1992–2009 (billions of U.S. dollars)

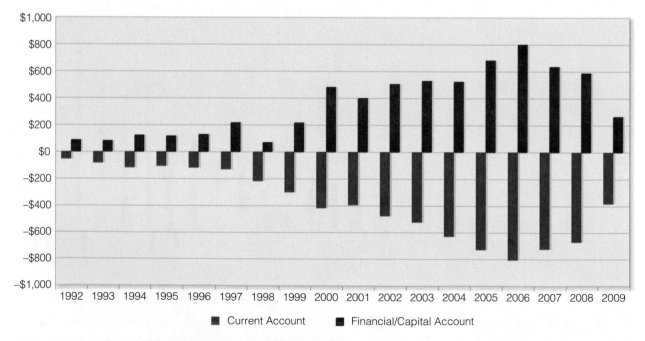

- ■ Current Account   ■ Financial/Capital Account

Source: International Monetary Fund, *International Financial Statistics*, IMF.org, December 2010.

GLOBAL FINANCE IN PRACTICE **4.1**

China's Twin Surpluses

Exhibit A illustrates the current and financial account balances for China over recent years. China's surpluses in both the current and financial accounts—termed the *Double Surplus* in the business press, is highly unusual. Ordinarily, for example, in the cases of the United States, Germany, and Great Britain, a country will demonstrate an inverse relationship between the two accounts. This inverse relationship is not accidental, and typically illustrates that most large, mature, industrial countries "finance" their current account deficits through equally large surpluses in the financial account. For some countries like Japan, it is the inverse; a current account surplus is matched against a financial account deficit.

China, however, has experienced a massive current account surplus and a marginal financial account surplus simultaneously. This is highly unusual, and an indicator of just how exceptional the growth of the Chinese economy is. Although current account surpluses of this magnitude would ordinarily always create a financial account deficit, the positive prospects of the Chinese economy have drawn such massive capital inflows into China in recent years, that the financial account too is in surplus. It will be interesting to watch how these balances perform in the coming years.

EXHIBIT A China's Twin Surplus, 1998–2009 (billions of U.S. Dollars)

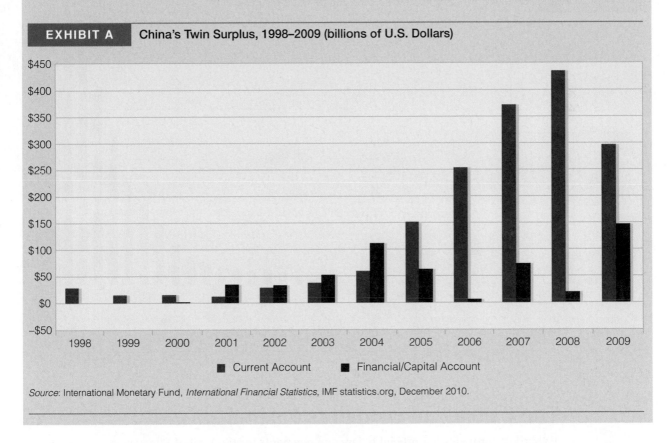

Source: International Monetary Fund, *International Financial Statistics*, IMF statistics.org, December 2010.

U.S. dollar for many years. It was the Chinese government's responsibility to maintain this fixed rate, also called *parity rate*. If for some reason there was an excess supply of Chinese yuan on the currency market, to prevent the value of the yuan from falling, the Chinese government would have to support the yuan's value by purchasing yuan on the open market (by spending its hard currency reserves, its official reserves) until the excess supply was eliminated. Under a floating rate system, the Chinese government possesses no such responsibility and the role of official reserves is diminished. But as discussed in *Global Finance in Practice 4.2*, the Chinese government's foreign exchange reserves are now the largest in the world, and if need be, it probably possesses sufficient reserves to manage the yuan's value for years to come.

GLOBAL FINANCE IN PRACTICE   4.2

Official Foreign Exchange Reserves: The Rise of China

The rise of the Chinese economy has been accompanied by a rise in its current account surplus, and subsequently, its accumulation of foreign exchange reserves. As illustrated in Exhibit A, China's foreign exchange reserves increased by a factor of 10 from 2001 to 2010—from $200 billion to nearly $2,500 billion. There is no real precedent for this build-up in foreign exchange reserves in global financial history. These reserves allow the Chinese government to manage the value of the Chinese *yuan* (also referred to as the *renminbi*) and its impact on Chinese competitiveness in the world economy. The magnitude of these reserves will allow the Chinese government to maintain a relatively stable managed fixed rate of the yuan against other major currencies like the U.S. dollar as long as it chooses.

EXHIBIT A   China's Foreign Exchange Reserves (billions of U.S. dollars)

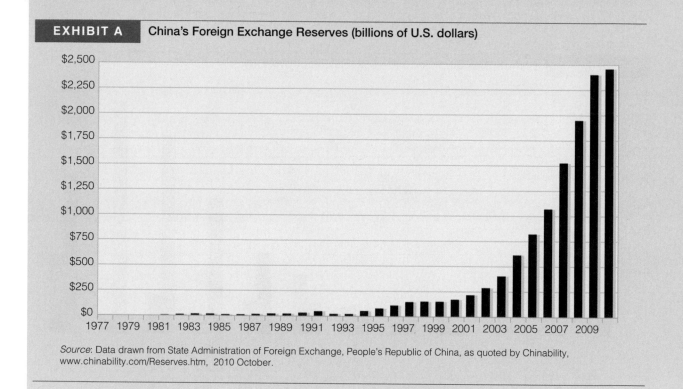

Source: Data drawn from State Administration of Foreign Exchange, People's Republic of China, as quoted by Chinability, www.chinability.com/Reserves.htm, 2010 October.

The Balance of Payments in Total

Exhibit 4.7 provides the official balance of payments for the United States as presented by the IMF, which collects these statistics for more than 160 different countries around the globe. Now that the individual accounts and the relationships among the accounts have been discussed, Exhibit 4.7 provides a comprehensive overview of how the individual accounts are combined to create some of the most useful summary measures for multinational business managers.

The current account (line A in Exhibit 4.7), the capital account (line B), and the financial account (line C) combine to form the *basic balance (Total, Groups A through C)*. This balance is one of the most frequently used summary measures of the BOP. It describes the international economic activity of the nation, which is determined by market forces, not by government decisions (such as currency market intervention). The U.S. *basic balance* totaled a

The sheer size and magnitude of China's official reserves (excluding gold) is illustrated by Exhibit B, which shows the 20 largest countries in terms of their reserve holdings in 2009. China's reserves are more than double those of the second largest country reserves, those of Japan. Note that only 8 countries even have reserves that exceed $130 billion. The United States, with roughly $130 billion in reserves, pales in comparison to the growing caches of the booming Asian economies.

There have been a variety of suggestions made as to what China could do with its growing reserves. Most of the proposals—stockpiling oil or other commodities for example—would only result in pushing up the price of these other critical global commodities, while not really stopping the accumulation of official reserves. The only real solution to this "problem," if it is a problem, is to reduce the Chinese current account surplus or allow the yuan to float to a stronger value. Both solutions, however, are not in-line with China's current political plan.

EXHIBIT B   Rising Reserves in Asia (billions of U.S. dollars, 2009)

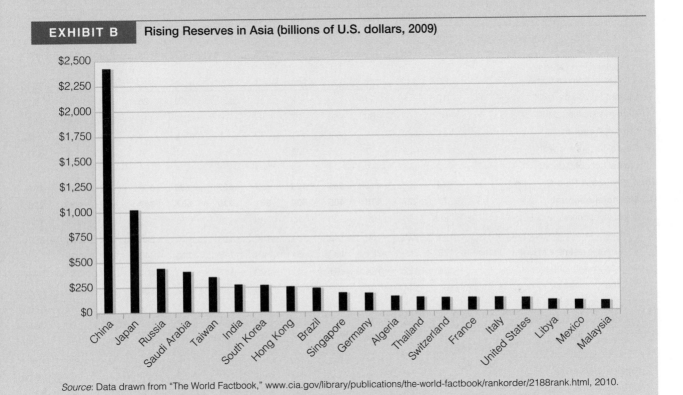

Source: Data drawn from "The World Factbook," www.cia.gov/library/publications/the-world-factbook/rankorder/2188rank.html, 2010.

deficit of $110 billion in 2009. A second frequently used measure, the *overall balance*, also called the *official settlements balance* (*Total, Groups A through D* in Exhibit 4.7), was at a surplus of $52 billion in 2009.

The meaning of the BOP has changed over the past 40 years. As long as most of the major industrial countries were still operating under fixed exchange rates, the interpretation of the BOP was relatively straightforward:

◆ A surplus in the BOP implied that the demand for the country's currency exceeded the supply and that the government should allow the currency value to increase—in value—or intervene and accumulate additional foreign currency reserves in the official reserves account. This intervention would occur as the government sold its own currency in exchange for other currencies, thus building up its stores of hard currencies.

EXHIBIT 4.7   The United States Balance of Payments, Analytic Presentation, 1998–2009 (billions of U.S. dollars)

	1998	1999	2000	2001	2002	2003	2004	2005	2006	2007	2008	2009
A. Current Account	−213	−300	−417	−385	−461	−523	−625	−729	−804	−718	−669	−378
Goods: exports fob	672	686	775	722	686	717	811	898	1020	1164	1309	1073
Goods: imports fob	−917	−1030	−1227	−1148	−1167	−1264	−1477	−1682	−1863	−1985	−2141	−1577
Balance on Goods	−245	−344	−452	−426	−481	−548	−666	−783	−844	−820	−832	−504
Services: credit	261	280	296	283	289	301	350	385	432	484	530	498
Services: debit	−181	−199	−224	−222	−231	−250	−291	−314	−349	−366	−397	−369
Balance on Goods and Services	−165	−263	−380	−365	−424	−497	−608	−712	−760	−702	−699	−375
Income: credit	262	294	351	291	281	320	414	535	682	830	797	588
Income: debit	−258	−280	−330	−259	−254	−275	−347	−463	−634	−730	−645	−467
Balance on Goods, Services and Income	−160	−249	−359	−333	−396	−452	−541	−639	−712	−603	−547	−254
Current transfers: credit	10	9	11	9	12	15	20	19	26	24	24	21
Current transfers: debit	−63	−59	−69	−60	−77	−87	−105	−109	−117	−140	−146	−146
B. Capital Account	−1	−5	−1	−1	−1	−3	−2	−4	−4	0	6	0
Capital account: credit	1	1	1	1	1	1	1	1	1	0	6	0
Capital account: debit	−2	−6	−2	−2	−2	−4	−3	−5	−5	0	0	0
Total, Groups A Plus B	−214	−305	−418	−386	−463	−527	−627	−733	−807	−718	−663	−379
C. Financial Account	77	227	478	405	504	532	530	687	807	638	583	268
Direct investment	36	65	162	25	−70	−86	−170	76	−2	−143	−23	−134
Direct investment abroad	−143	−225	−159	−142	−154	−150	−316	−36	−245	−414	−351	−269
Direct investment in United States	179	289	321	167	84	64	146	113	243	271	328	135
Portfolio investment assets	−130	−122	−128	−91	−49	−123	−177	−258	−499	−391	286	−393
Equity securities	−101	−114	−107	−109	−17	−118	−85	−187	−137	−148	39	−63
Debt securities	−29	−8	−21	18	−32	−5	−93	−71	−362	−243	247	−330
Portfolio investment liabilities	188	286	437	428	428	550	867	832	1127	1157	520	367
Equity securities	42	112	194	121	54	34	62	89	145	276	126	161
Debt securities	146	173	243	307	374	516	806	743	981	881	394	206
Financial derivatives, net	0	0	0	0	0	0	0	0	30	6	−33	51
Other investment assets	−74	−166	−273	−145	−88	−54	−510	−267	−544	−671	226	574
Monetary authorities	0	0	0	0	0	0	0	0	0	−24	−530	543
General government	0	3	−1	0	0	1	2	6	5	2	0	−2
Banks	−36	−71	−133	−136	−38	−26	−359	−151	−343	−500	308	−196
Other sectors	−38	−98	−139	−9	−50	−29	−153	−121	−207	−148	448	229
Other investment liabilities	57	165	280	187	283	244	520	303	695	680	−394	−196
Monetary authorities	7	25	−11	35	70	11	13	8	2	−11	29	60
General government	−3	−1	−2	−2	0	−1	0	0	3	5	9	10
Banks	30	67	123	88	118	136	347	232	344	468	−354	−248
Other sectors	23	74	171	66	96	98	160	62	346	217	−78	−18
Total, Groups A Through C	−138	−77	60	19	41	5	−98	−46	−1	−79	−80	−110
D. Net Errors and Omissions	144	69	−59	−14	−38	−6	95	32	−2	80	85	163
Total, Groups A Through D	7	−9	0.31	4.88	3.71	−1.33	−2.80	−14.10	−2	0	5	52
E. Reserves and Related Items	−7	9	0	−5	−4	2	3	14	2	0	−5	−52

Source: International Monetary Fund, *International Financial Statistics*. IMF.org. September 2009.
Note: Totals may not match original source due to rounding.

◆ A deficit in the BOP implied an excess supply of the country's currency on world markets, and the government would then either *devalue* the currency or expend its official reserves to support its value.

The transition to floating exchange rate regimes in the 1970s (described in Chapter 3) changed the focus from the total BOP to its various subaccounts like the current and financial account balances. These subaccounts are the indicators of economic activities and currency repercussions to come.

The Balance of Payments Interaction with Key Macroeconomic Variables

A nation's balance of payments interacts with nearly all of its key macroeconomic variables. *Interacts* means that the balance of payments affects and is affected by such key macroeconomic factors as the following:

◆ Gross domestic product (GDP)

◆ Exchange rate

◆ Interest rates

◆ Inflation rates

The BOP and GDP

In a static (accounting) sense, a nation's GDP can be represented by the following equation:

$$GDP = C + I + G + X - M$$

C = consumption spending
I = capital investment spending
G = government spending
X = exports of goods and services
M = imports of goods and services
$X - M$ = the balance on current account (when including current income and transfers)

Thus, a positive current account balance (surplus) contributes directly to increasing the measure of GDP, but a negative current account balance (deficit) decreases GDP.

In a dynamic (cash flow) sense, an increase or decrease in GDP contributes to the current account deficit or surplus. As GDP grows, so does disposable income and capital investment. Increased disposable income leads to more consumption, a portion of which is supplied by more imports. Increased consumption eventually leads to more capital investment.

Growth in GDP also should eventually lead to higher rates of employment. However, some of that theoretical increase in employment may be blunted by foreign sourcing (that is, the purchase of goods and services from other enterprises located in other countries).

Supply chain management has increasingly focused on cost reduction through imports from less costly (lower wages) foreign locations. These imports can be from foreign-owned firms or from foreign subsidiaries of the parent firm. In the latter case, foreign subsidiaries tend to buy components and intellectual property from their parent firms, thus increasing exports. Although outsourcing has always been a factor in determining where to locate or procure manufactured goods and commodities, as mentioned in Chapter 1, during the past decade, an increasing amount of high-tech goods and services have been sourced from abroad. Foreign sourcing from the United States and Western Europe has been to countries such as India (software and call centers), China, Eastern Europe, Mexico, and the Philippines. This pattern has caused a loss of some white-collar jobs in the United States and Western Europe and a corresponding increase elsewhere.

The BOP and Exchange Rates

A country's BOP can have a significant impact on the level of its exchange rate and vice versa, depending on that country's exchange rate regime. The relationship between the BOP and exchange rates can be illustrated by using a simplified equation that summarizes BOP data:

Current account balance	Capital account balance	Financial account balance	Reserve balance	Balance of payments
$(X-M)$ +	$(CI-CO)$ +	$(FI-FO)$ +	FXB =	BOP

$$X = \text{exports of goods and services}$$
$$M = \text{imports of goods and services}$$
$$CI = \text{capital inflows}$$
$$CO = \text{capital outflows}$$
$$FI = \text{financial inflows}$$
$$FO = \text{financial outflows}$$
$$FXB = \text{official monetary reserves such as foreign exchange and gold}$$

The effect of an imbalance in the BOP of a country works somewhat differently depending on whether that country has fixed exchange rates, floating exchange rates, or a managed exchange rate system.

Fixed Exchange Rate Countries. Under a fixed exchange rate system, the government bears the responsibility to ensure that the BOP is near zero. If the sum of the current and capital accounts do not approximate zero, the government is expected to intervene in the foreign exchange market by buying or selling official foreign exchange reserves. If the sum of the first two accounts is greater than zero, a surplus demand for the domestic currency exists in the world. To preserve the fixed exchange rate, the government must then intervene in the foreign exchange market and sell domestic currency for foreign currencies or gold so as to bring the BOP back near zero.

If the sum of the current and capital accounts is negative, an excess supply of the domestic currency exists in world markets. Then the government must intervene by buying the domestic currency with its reserves of foreign currencies and gold. It is obviously important for a government to maintain significant foreign exchange reserve balances, sufficient to allow it to intervene effectively. If the country runs out of foreign exchange reserves, it will be unable to buy back its domestic currency and will be forced to devalue.

Floating Exchange Rate Countries. Under a floating exchange rate system, the government of a country has no responsibility to peg its foreign exchange rate. The fact that the current and capital account balances do not sum to zero will automatically (in theory) alter the exchange rate in the direction necessary to obtain a BOP near zero. For example, a country running a sizable current account deficit, with a capital and financial accounts balance of zero will have a net BOP deficit. An excess supply of the domestic currency will appear on world markets. Like all goods in excess supply, the market will rid itself of the imbalance by lowering the price. Thus, the domestic currency will fall in value, and the BOP will move back toward zero. Exchange rate markets do not always follow this theory, particularly in the short to intermediate term. This delay is known as the *J-curve effect* (see the next section "Trade

Balances and Exchange Rates"). The deficit gets worse in the short run, but moves back toward equilibrium in the long run.

Managed Floats. Although still relying on market conditions for day-to-day exchange rate determination, countries operating with managed floats often find it necessary to take action to maintain their desired exchange rate values. Therefore, they seek to alter the market's valuation of a specific exchange rate by influencing the motivations of market activity, rather than through direct intervention in the foreign exchange markets.

The primary action taken by such governments is to change relative interest rates, thus influencing the economic fundamentals of exchange rate determination. In the context of the equation discussed, a change in domestic interest rates is an attempt to alter the term $(CI-CO)$, especially the short-term portfolio component of these capital flows, in order to restore an imbalance caused by the deficit in the current account. The power of interest rate changes on international capital and exchange rate movements can be substantial. A country with a managed float that wishes to defend its currency may choose to raise domestic interest rates to attract additional capital from abroad. This step will alter market forces and create additional market demand for the domestic currency. In this process, the government signals to exchange market participants that it intends to take measures to preserve the currency's value within certain ranges. The process also raises the cost of local borrowing for businesses, however, so the policy is seldom without domestic critics.

The BOP and Interest Rates

Apart from the use of interest rates to intervene in the foreign exchange market, the overall level of a country's interest rates compared to other countries has an impact on the financial account of the balance of payments. Relatively low real interest rates should normally stimulate an outflow of capital seeking higher interest rates in other country currencies. However, in the case of the United States, the opposite effect has occurred. Despite relatively low real interest rates and large BOP deficits on current account, the U.S. BOP financial account has experienced offsetting financial inflows due to relatively attractive U.S. growth rate prospects, high levels of productive innovation, and perceived political safety. Thus, the financial account inflows have helped the United States to maintain its lower interest rates and to finance its exceptionally large fiscal deficit. However, it is beginning to appear that the favorable inflow on the financial account is diminishing while the U.S. balance on current account is worsening.

The BOP and Inflation Rates

Imports have the potential to lower a country's inflation rate. In particular, imports of lower-priced goods and services place a limit on what domestic competitors charge for comparable goods and services. Thus, foreign competition substitutes for domestic competition to maintain a lower rate of inflation than might have been the case without imports.

On the other hand, to the extent that lower-priced imports substitute for domestic production and employment, gross domestic product will be lower and the balance on current account will be more negative.

Trade Balances and Exchange Rates

A country's import and export of goods and services is affected by changes in exchange rates. The transmission mechanism is in principle quite simple: changes in exchange rates change relative prices of imports and exports, and changing prices in turn result in changes in quantities demanded through the price elasticity of demand. Although the theoretical economics appear straightforward, the reality of global business is more complex.

Trade and Devaluation

Countries occasionally devalue their own currencies as a result of persistent and sizable trade deficits. Many countries in the not-too-distant past have intentionally devalued their currencies in an effort to make their exports more price-competitive on world markets. The devaluation of the New Taiwan dollar in 1997 during the Asian financial crisis is believed by many to have been one such competitive devaluation. These competitive devaluations are often considered self-destructive, however, as they also make imports relatively more expensive. So what is the logic and likely results of intentionally devaluing the domestic currency to improve the trade balance?

The J-Curve Adjustment Path

International economic analysis characterizes the trade balance adjustment process as occurring in three stages: 1) the *currency contract period*; 2) the *pass-through period*; and 3) the *quantity adjustment period*. These three stages, and the resulting time-adjustment path of the trade balance in whole, is illustrated in Exhibit 4.8. Assuming that the trade balance is already in deficit prior to the devaluation, a devaluation at time t_1 results initially in a further deterioration in the trade balance before an eventual improvement—the path of adjustment taking on the shape of a flattened "j."

In the first period, the *currency contract period*, a sudden unexpected devaluation of the domestic currency has a somewhat uncertain impact, simply because all of the contracts for exports and imports are already in effect. Firms operating under these agreements are required to fulfill their obligations, regardless of whether they profit or suffer losses. Assume that the United States experienced a sudden fall in the value of the U.S. dollar. Most exports

---

EXHIBIT 4.8   Trade Balance Adjustment to Exchange Rate Changes: The J-Curve

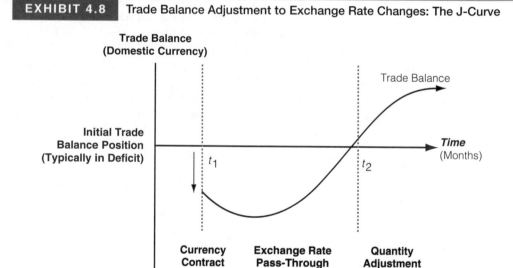

If export products are predominantly priced and invoiced in domestic currency, and imports are predominantly priced and invoiced in foreign currency, a sudden devaluation of the domestic currency can possibly result—initially—in a deterioration of the balance on trade. After exchange rate changes are passed-through to product prices, and markets have time to respond to price changes by altering market demands, the trade balance will improve. The currency contract period may last from three to six months, with pass-through and quality adjustment following for an additional three to six months.

were priced in U.S. dollars but most imports were contracts denominated in foreign currency. The result of a sudden depreciation would be an increase in the size of the trade deficit at time t_1, because the cost to U.S. importers of paying their import bills would rise as they spent more and more dollars to buy the foreign currency they needed, while the revenues earned by U.S. exporters would remain unchanged. Although this is the commonly cited scenario regarding trade balance adjustment, there is little reason to believe that most U.S. imports are denominated in foreign currency and most exports in U.S. dollars.

The second period of the trade balance adjustment process is termed the *pass-through period*. As exchange rates change, importers and exporters eventually must pass these exchange rate changes through to their own product prices. For example, a foreign producer selling to the U.S. market after a major fall in the value of the U.S. dollar will have to cover its own domestic costs of production. This need will require that the firm charge higher dollar prices in order to earn its own local currency in large enough quantities. The firm must raise its prices in the U.S. market. U.S. import prices rise substantially, eventually passing through the full exchange rate changes into prices. American consumers see higher import-product prices on the shelf. Similarly, the U.S. export prices are now cheaper compared to foreign competitors' because the dollar is cheaper. Unfortunately for U.S. exporters, many of the inputs for their final products may actually be imported, causing them also to suffer from rising prices after the fall of the dollar.

The third and final period, the *quantity adjustment period*, achieves the balance of trade adjustment that is expected from a domestic currency devaluation or depreciation. As the import and export prices change as a result of the pass-through period, consumers both in the United States and in the U.S. export markets adjust their demands to the new prices. Imports are relatively more expensive; therefore the quantity demanded decreases. Exports are relatively cheaper; therefore the quantity demanded increases. The balance of trade—the expenditures on exports less the expenditures on imports—improves.

Unfortunately, these three adjustment periods do not occur overnight. Countries like the United States, that have experienced major exchange rate changes, also have seen this adjustment take place over a prolonged period. Empirical studies have concluded that for industrial countries, the total time elapsing between time t_1 and t_2 can vary from 3 to 12 months—sometimes longer. To complicate the process, new exchange rate changes often occur before the adjustment is completed. Trade adjustment to exchange rate changes does not occur in a sterile laboratory environment, but in the messy and complex world of international business and economic events.

Trade Balance Adjustment Path: The Equations

A country's trade balance is essentially the net of import and export revenues, where each is a multiple of prices ($P_X^{\$}$ and P_M^{fc})—the prices of exports and imports, respectively. Export prices are assumed to be denominated in U.S. dollars, and import prices are denominated in foreign currency. The quantity of exports and the quantity of imports are denoted as Q_x and Q_M respectively. Import expenditures are then expressed in U.S. dollars by multiplying the foreign currency denominated expenditures by the spot exchange rate, $S^{\$/\text{fc}}$. The U.S. trade balance, expressed in U.S. dollars, is then expressed as follows:

$$\text{U.S. trade balance} = (P_X^{\$} Q_x) - (S^{\$/\text{fc}} P_M^{\text{fc}} Q_M)$$

The immediate impact of a devaluation of the domestic currency is to increase the value of the spot exchange rate S, resulting in an immediate deterioration in the trade balance (currency contract period). Only after a period in which the current contracts have matured, and new prices reflecting partial to full pass-through have been instituted, would improvement in the trade balance been evident (pass-through period). In the final stage, in which the price elasticity of demand has time to take effect (quantity adjustment period), is the actual trade balance—in theory—which is expected to rise above where it started in Exhibit 4.8.

Capital Mobility

The degree to which capital moves freely cross-border is critically important to a country's balance of payments. We have already seen how the U.S., while experiencing a deficit in its current account balance over the past 20 years, has simultaneously enjoyed a financial account surplus. This financial account surplus has probably been one of the major reasons for the ability of the U.S. dollar to maintain its value over this period. Many other countries however, for example Brazil in 1998–1999 and Argentina in 2001–2002, have experienced massive financial account outflows, contributing to their economic and financial crises.

Historical Patterns of Capital Mobility

Before leaving our discussion of the balance of payments, we need to gain additional insights into the history of capital mobility and the contribution of capital outflows—*capital flight*—to balance of payments crises. Has capital always been free to move in and out of a country? Definitely not. The ability of foreign investors to own property, buy businesses, or purchase stocks and bonds in other countries has been controversial.

Exhibit 4.9 divides the last 150 years of economic history into five distinct *exchange rate eras* and the associated implications of capital mobility (or lack thereof). These exchange rate eras obviously reflect the exchange rate regimes we discussed and detailed in Chapter 3, but also reflect the evolution of cross-border political economy beliefs and policies of both industrialized and emerging market nations over this period.

The Gold Standard (1860–1914). Although an era of growing capital openness in which trade and capital began to flow more freely, it was an era dominated by industrialized nation economies that were dependent on gold convertibility to maintain confidence in the system.

The Inter-War Years (1914–1945). An era of retrenchment, in which major economic powers returned to policies of isolationism and protectionism, restricting trade and nearly eliminating capital mobility. The devastating results included financial crisis, a global depression, and rising international political and economic disputes which drove nations into a second world war.

The Bretton Woods Era (1945–1971). The dollar-based fixed exchange rate system under Bretton Woods gave rise to a long period of economic recovery and growing openness of both international trade and capital flows in and out of more and more countries. Many researchers (for example Obstfeld and Taylor, 2001) believe it was the rapid growth in the speed and volume of capital flows that ultimately led to the failure of Bretton Woods—global capital could no longer be held in check.

The Floating Era (1971–1997). The *Floating Era*, saw the rise of a growing schism between the industrialized and the emerging market nations. The industrialized nations (primary currencies) moved to—or were driven to—floating exchange rates by capital mobility. The emerging markets (secondary currencies), in an attempt to both promote economic development but maintain control over their economies and currencies, opened trade but maintained restrictions on capital flows. Despite these restrictions, the era ended with the onslaught of the Asian Financial Crisis in 1997, when these same emerging market currencies found they still could not hold back capital mobility.

The Emerging Era (1997–Present). The emerging economies, led by China and India, attempt to gradually open their markets to global capital. But, as the Impossible Trinity taught the industrial nations in previous years, the increasing mobility of capital now requires that they give up either the ability to manage their currency values or conduct independent monetary

EXHIBIT 4.9	The Evolution of Capital Mobility

Exchange Rate Era	The Gold Standard	The Inter-War Years	The Bretton Woods Era	The Floating Era	The Emerging Era
Cross-Border Political Economy	Growing openness in trade, with growing, but limited, capital mobility	Protectionism & isolationism	Growing belief in the benefits of open economies	Industrialized (primary) nations open; emerging states (secondary) restrict capital flows to maintain economic control	More and more emerging nations open their markets to capital at the expense of reduced economic independence
Implication	Trade dominates capital in total influence on exchange rates	Rising barriers to the movement of both trade & capital	Trade increasingly dominated by capital; era ends as capital flows	Capital flows dominate trade; emerging nations suffer devaluations	Capital flows increasingly drive economic growth and health

1860   1914   1945   1971   1997   Present

The last 150 years has seen periods of increasing capital mobility, with periods of retrenchment, but a growing openness in trade and capital flows that is now spreading to the emerging economies. This growing mobility, however, has forced more and more countries—following the principles of the Impossible Trinity—to yield explicit control over the fixed value of their currencies.

policies. By 2010 and 2011 more and more emerging market currencies "suffer" appreciation as capital flows grow in magnitude and speed.

The 2008–2011 period reinforced what some call the double-edged sword of global capital movements. The credit crisis of 2008, beginning in the United States, quickly spread to the global economy, pulling and pushing down industrial and emerging market economies alike. But in the post credit crisis period, global capital now flowed toward the emerging markets. Although funding and fueling their rapid economic recoveries, it came—in the words of one journalist—with luggage. The increasing pressure on emerging market currencies to appreciate is partially undermining their export competitiveness. The flow of global capital does indeed appear relentless.

Capital Flight

A final issue is capital flight. Although no single accepted definition of capital flight exists, Ingo Walter's discussion is useful:

> *International flows of direct and portfolio investments under ordinary circumstances are rarely associated with the capital flight phenomenon. Rather, it is when capital transfers by residents conflict with political objectives that the term "flight" comes into general usage.*[1]

Although it is not limited to heavily indebted countries, the rapid and sometimes illegal transfer of convertible currencies out of a country poses significant economic and political problems. Many heavily indebted countries have suffered significant capital flight, which has compounded their problems of debt service.

[1]Ingo Walter, "The Mechanisms of Capital Flight," in *Capital Flight and Third World Debt*, edited by Donald R. Lessard and John Williamson, Institute for International Economics, Washington, D.C., 1987, p. 104.

Five primary mechanisms exist by which capital may be moved from one country to another:

1. **Transfers via the usual international payments mechanisms** (regular bank transfers) are obviously the easiest and lowest cost, and are legal. Most economically healthy countries allow free exchange of their currencies, but of course for such countries "capital flight" is not a problem.

2. **Transfer of physical currency by bearer** (the proverbial smuggling out of cash in the false bottom of a suitcase) is more costly and, for transfers out of many countries, illegal. Such transfers may be deemed illegal for balance of payments reasons or to make difficult the movement of money from the drug trade or other illegal activities.

3. Cash is transferred into collectibles or precious metals, which are then transferred across borders.

4. **Money laundering** is the cross-border purchase of assets that are then managed in a way that hides the movement of money and its ownership.

5. **False invoicing of international trade transactions** occurs when capital is moved through the underinvoicing of exports or the overinvoicing of imports, where the difference between the invoiced amount and the actual agreed upon payment is deposited in banking institutions in a country of choice.

Summary of Learning Objectives

Learn how nations measure their own levels of international economic activity, and how that creates the balance of payments

◆ The BOP is the summary statement of all international transactions between one country and all other countries.

◆ The BOP is a flow statement, summarizing all the international transactions that occur across the geographic boundaries of the nation over a period of time, typically a year.

◆ Although in theory the BOP must always balance, in practice there are substantial imbalances as a result of statistical errors and mis-reporting of current account and financial/capital account flows.

Examine the economic relationships underlying the two basic subcomponents of the balance of payments—the current account and financial account balances

◆ The two major subaccounts of the balance of payments, the current account and the financial/capital account, summarize the current trade and international capital flows of the country respectively.

◆ The current account and financial/capital account are typically inverse on balance, one in surplus and the other in deficit.

◆ Although most nations strive for current account surpluses, it is not clear that a balance on current or capi-tal account, or a surplus on current account, is either sustainable or desirable.

Consider the financial dimensions of international economic activity, and how they differ between merchandise and services trade

◆ Although merchandise trade is more easily observed (e.g., goods flowing through ports of entry), today, the growth of services trade is more significant to the balance of payments for many of the world's largest industrialized countries.

Identify balance of payment activities by nations in the pursuit of domestic and global economic and political policies

◆ Monitoring of the various subaccounts of a country's balance of payment activity is helpful to decision-makers and policymakers on all levels of government and industry in detecting the underlying trends and movements of fundamental economic forces driving a country's international economic activity.

Examine how exchange rate changes and volatility influence trade balances over time

◆ Changes in exchange rates change relative prices of imports and exports, and changing prices in turn result in changes in quantities demanded through the price elasticity of demand.

◆ A devaluation results initially in a further deterioration in the trade balance before an eventual improvement—the path of adjustment taking on the shape of a flattened "j."

Evaluate the history of capital mobility, and the conditions that lead in times of crisis to capital flight

◆ The ability of capital to move instantaneously and massively cross-border has been one of the major factors in the severity of recent currency crises. In cases such as Malaysia in 1997 and Argentina in 2001, the national governments concluded that they had no choice but to impose drastic restrictions on the ability of capital to flow.

◆ Although not limited to heavily indebted countries, the rapid and sometimes illegal transfer of convertible currencies out of a country poses significant economic and political problems. Many heavily indebted countries have suffered significant capital flight, which has compounded their problems of debt service.

MINI-CASE

Global Remittances

"Remittances are a vital source of financial support that directly increases the income of migrants' families," said Hans Timmer, director of development prospects at the World Bank. "Remittances lead to more investments in health, education, and small business. With better tracking of migration and remittance trends, policy makers can make informed decisions to protect and leverage this massive capital inflow which is triple the size of official aid flows," Timmer said.

— "Remittances to Developing Countries Resilient in the Recent Crisis," Press Release No. 2011/168DEC, The World Bank, November 8, 2010.

One area within the balance of payments that has received intense interest in the past decade is that of *remittances*. The term *remittance* is a bit tricky. According to the International Monetary Fund (IMF), *remittances* are international transfers of funds sent by migrant workers from the country where they are working to people, typically family members, in the country from which they originated.[1] According to the IMF, a *migrant* is a person who comes to a country and stays, or intends to stay, for a year or more. As shown in Exhibit 1, a brief overview of global remittances would include the following:

◆ The World Bank estimates that $414 billion was remitted in 2009, with $316 billion of that going to developing countries. These remittance transactions were made by more than 190 million people, roughly 3% of the world's population.

◆ The top remittance sending countries in 2009 were the United States, Saudi Arabia, Switzerland, Russia, and Germany. Worldwide, the top recipient countries in 2009 were India, China, Mexico, the Philippines, and France.

◆ Remittances make up a very small, often negligible cash outflow from sending countries like the United States. They do, however, represent a more significant volume, for example as a percent of GDP, for smaller receiving countries, developing countries, sometimes more than 25%. In many cases, this is greater than all development capital and aid flowing to these same countries.

The historical record on global remittances is short. As illustrated in Exhibit 2, it has shown dramatic growth in the post-2000 period, until suffering its first real decline since 1985 in the 2009 global economic slowdown.

Remittances largely reflect the income which is earned by migrant or guest workers in one country (source country) and then returned to families or related parties in their home countries (receiving countries). Therefore it is, not surprising that although there are more migrant worker flows between developing countries, the high-income developed economies remain the main source of remittances. The global economic recession of 2009 resulted in reduced economic activities like construction and manufacturing in the major source countries; as a result, remittance cash flows fell in 2009 but rebounded slightly in 2010.

Most remittances are frequent small payments made through wire transfers or a variety of informal channels (some even carried by hand). The United States Bureau of Economic Analysis (BEA), which is responsible for the compilation and reporting of U.S. balance of payments statistics, classifies migrant remittances as "current transfers" in the *current account*. Wider definitions of remittances may also include capital assets which migrants take with them to host countries, and similar assets which they bring back with them to their home countries. These values, when compiled, are generally reported under the *capital account* of the balance of payments exactly who a 'migrant' is is also an area of some debate. Transfers back to their home country made by individuals who may be working in a country (for example, an expat working for an MNE) but not considered

---

[1]"Remittances: International Payments by Migrants," Congressional Budget Office, May 2005.

EXHIBIT 1   Cross-Border Remittances, 2009

Amount of formal remittances inflow by migrants' origin country

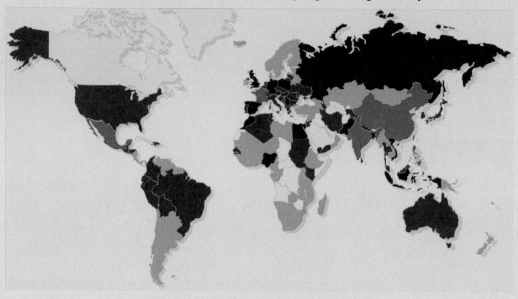

Amount of Formal Remittances (US$ billions)

☐ No data   ■ Less than $1   ■ $1 to $4.9   ■ $5 to $14.9   ■ $15 or more

Source: Development Prospects Group, World Bank. Map ©2010 by the Migration Policy Institute.

EXHIBIT 2   Global Remittances—World Inflows

Billions of U.S. dollars

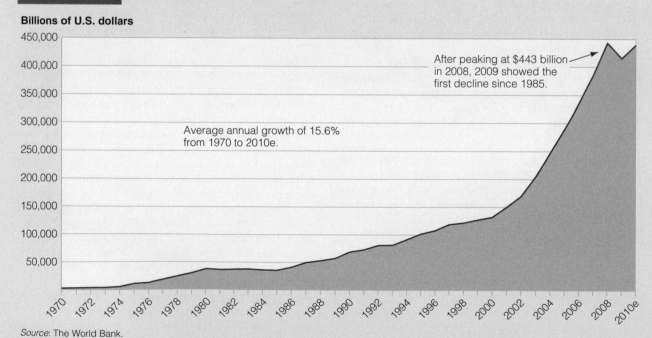

After peaking at $443 billion in 2008, 2009 showed the first decline since 1985.

Average annual growth of 15.6% from 1970 to 2010e.

Source: The World Bank.

'residents,' may also be considered global remittances under current transfers in the current account.

Remittance Prices

Given the development impact of remittance flows, we will facilitate a more efficient transfer and improved use of remittances and enhance cooperation between national and international organizations, in order to implement the recommendations of the 2007 Berlin G8 Conference and of the Global Remittances Working Group established in 2009 and coordinated by the World Bank. We will aim to make financial services more accessible to migrants and to those who receive remittances in the developing world. We will work to achieve in particular the objective of a reduction of the global average costs of transferring remittances from the present 10% to 5% in five years through enhanced information, transparency, competition and cooperation with partners, generating a significant net increase in income for migrants and their families in the developing world.

—The G8 Final Declaration on Responsible Leadership for a Sustainable Future, paragraph 134.

Some organizations have focused on the costs borne by migrants in transferring funds back to their home countries. The primary concern has been excessive remittance charges—the imposition of what many consider exploitive charges related to the transfer of these frequent small payments. The G8 countries, in an initiative entitled "5 × 5"—the reduction of transfer costs from an average of 10% to 5% in five years—seek to use a variety of market forces such as

transparency to improve the efficiency and reduce remittance prices globally.[2] *Remittance Prices Worldwide* (RPW), initiated by the World Bank in September 2008, is the primary body that is creating and sustaining a global database which monitors remittance price activity across geographic regions.

Little was known of global remittance costs until the World Bank began collecting data in the Remittance Prices Worldwide (RPW) database.[3] The database, updated twice yearly collects data on the average cost of transactions conducted along a variety of *country corridors* globally (country pairs). The most recent survey conducted in the second half of 2010 covered 200 individual corridors—remittances originating in 29 countries and received in 86 countries. The average cost of a migrant remittance transaction was 8.89% for all corridors surveyed for the third quarter of 2010 (most recent data available). The most recent survey found, assuming $200 per transfer, that the highest cost was that of the Tanzania-Kenya corridor (a remittance from Tanzania to Kenya) at $47.27 per $200 transaction, a 23.6% charge.

The cost of remittances is a combination of the fees charged at any stage of the transaction and the exchange rate used to convert the local currency into the currency of the destination country.[4] Fees charged may occur at the origin (for transactions, transaction size, currency conversion), while fees at the destination may include many of the same. One relatively simple example is that presented in Exhibit 3, a transaction described by a major RSP (remittance service provider) in Mexico. In this case, the transfer cost comprises two components, a transaction fee which differs by RSP, and a calculated foreign exchange charge based on the exchange rate used in the transaction

EXHIBIT 3   Remittances from the United States to Mexico: A Price Comparison

	Gross Remittance				Remittance Cost			
	(1)	(2)	(3)	(4)	(5)	(6)	(7)	(8)
Service Provider	Amount Remitted (US$)	RSP's FX Rate (Pesos/US$)	Amount Received (pesos)	Amount Received (US$ equivalent)	Transfer Fee (US$)	FX Cost (US$)	Full Cost (US$)	Full Cost (percent)
A	$300	10.53	3,159	$299.43	$5.00	$0.57	$5.57	1.9%
B	$300	10.55	3,165	$300.00	$8.00	$0.00	$8.00	2.7%
C	$300	10.50	3,150	$298.58	$8.00	$1.42	$9.42	3.1%
Reference Rate		10.55						

Source: Based on published reports from PROFECO, the Federal Consumer Protection Commission of Mexico, as presented in "General Principles for International Remittance Services," Bank for International Setlements and The World Bank, January 2007, p. 32. Note that the official reference exchange rate, Peso 1055/US$, is the same as the rate used by remittance service provider (RSP) "B."
Notes: (3) = (1) × (2); (4) = (3) / Reference FX Rate; (6) = (1) − (4); (7) = (5) + (6): (8) = (7)/(1).

[2]"Rome Roadmap for Remittances," G8 Summit, The World Bank, November 9, 2009.

[3]*Remittance Prices Worldwide*, The World Bank, Issue No. 1 2, November 2010, remittanceprices.worldbank.org.

[4]"Remittance Price Comparison Databases: Minimum Requirements and Overall Policy Strategy, Guidance and Special Purpose Note," Remittances Working Group, The World Bank Group, p. 2.

EXHIBIT 4   Highest Cost Corridors for Remittances

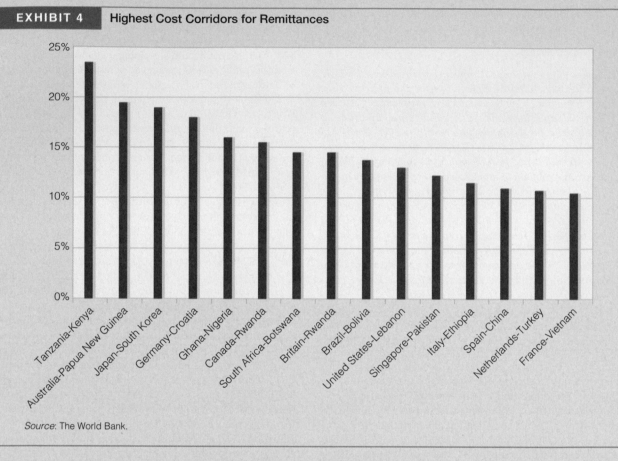

Source: The World Bank.

compared to an official reference rate for that date. In this case—as opposed to the rates quoted globally in the World Bank project—the full cost percentage of remittance is quite small and competitive.

As opposed to the remittance costs quoted by PROFECO in Exhibit 3, the World Bank's survey of global remittances across multiple corridors unveiled a number of individual transfer corridors where the costs were by all indications, exploitive. The most expensive are noted in Exhibit 4.

Growing Controversies

With the growth in global remittances has come a growing debate as to what role they do or should play in a country's balance of payments, and more importantly, economic development. In some cases, like India, there is growing resistance from the central bank and other banking institutions to allow online payment services like PayPal to process remittances. In other countries, like Honduras, Guatemala, and Mexico, there is growing debate on whether the remittances flow to families or are actually payments made to a variety of Central American smugglers—human trafficking smugglers.

In Mexico for example, remittances now make up the second largest source of foreign exchange earnings, second only to oil exports. The Mexican government has increas-ingly viewed remittances as an integral component of its balance of payments, and in some ways, a "plug" to replace declining export competition and dropping foreign direct investment. But there is also growing evidence that remittances flow to those who need it most, the lowest income component of the Mexican population, and therefore mitigate poverty and support consumer spending. (Former President Vicente Fox was quoted as saying that Mexico's workers in other countries remitting income home to Mexico are "heroes.") Mexico's own statistical agencies also disagree on both the size of the funds remittances received, as well as to whom the income is returning (family or nonfamily interests).

CASE QUESTIONS

1. Where are remittances across borders included within the balance of payments? Are they current or financial account components?

2. Under what conditions—for example, for which countries currently—are remittances significant contributors to the economy and overall balance of payments?

3. Why is the cost of remittances the subject of such intense international scrutiny?

Questions

1. **Balance of Payments Defined.** The measurement of all international economic transactions between the residents of a country and foreign residents is called the balance of payments (BOP). What institution provides the primary source of similar statistics for balance of payments and economic performance worldwide?

2. **Importance of BOP.** Business managers and investors need BOP data to anticipate changes in host-country economic policies that might be driven by BOP events. From the perspective of business managers and investors, list three specific signals that a country's BOP data can provide.

3. **Economic Activity.** What are the two main types of economic activity measured by a country's BOP?

4. **Balance.** Why does the BOP always "balance"?

5. **BOP Accounting.** If the BOP were viewed as an accounting statement, would it be a balance sheet of the country's wealth, an income statement of the country's earnings, or a funds flow statement of money into and out of the country?

6. **Current Account.** What are the main component accounts of the current account? Give one debit and one credit example for each component account for the United States.

7. **Real versus Financial Assets.** What is the difference between a "real" asset and a "financial" asset?

8. **Direct versus Portfolio Investments.** What is the difference between a direct foreign investment and a portfolio foreign investment? Give an example of each. Which type of investment is a multinational industrial company more likely to make?

9. **Capital and Financial Accounts.** What are the main components of the financial accounts? Give one debit and one credit example for each component account for the United States.

10. **Classifying Transactions.** Classify the following as a transaction reported in a subcomponent of the current account or the capital and financial accounts of the two countries involved:
    a. A U.S. food chain imports wine from Chile.
    b. A U.S. resident purchases a euro-denominated bond from a German company.
    c. Singaporean parents pay for their daughter to study at a U.S. university.
    d. A U.S. university gives a tuition grant to a foreign student from Singapore.
    e. A British Company imports Spanish oranges, paying with Eurodollars on deposit in London.
    f. The Spanish orchard deposits half the proceeds in a Eurodollar account in London.
    g. A London-based insurance company buys U.S. corporate bonds for its investment portfolio.
    h. An American multinational enterprise buys insurance from a London insurance broker.
    i. A London insurance firm pays for losses incurred in the United States because of an international terrorist attack.
    j. Cathay Pacific Airlines buys jet fuel at Los Angeles International Airport so it can fly the return segment of a flight back to Hong Kong.
    k. A California-based mutual fund buys shares of stock on the Tokyo and London stock exchanges.
    l. The U.S. army buys food for its troops in South Asia from local venders. A California-based mutual fund buys shares of stock on the Tokyo and London stock exchanges.
    m. A California-based mutual fund buys shares of stock on the Tokyo and London stock exchanges.
    n. A Yale graduate gets a job with the International Committee of the Red Cross in Bosnia and is paid in Swiss francs.
    o. The Russian government hires a Norwegian salvage firm to raise a sunken submarine.
    p. A Colombian drug cartel smuggles cocaine into the United States, receives a suitcase of cash, and flies back to Colombia with that cash.
    q. The U.S. government pays the salary of a foreign service officer working in the U.S. embassy in Beirut.
    r. A Norwegian shipping firm pays U.S. dollars to the Egyptian government for passage of a ship through the Suez Canal.
    s. A German automobile firm pays the salary of its executive working for a subsidiary in Detroit.
    t. An American tourist pays for a hotel in Paris with his American Express card.
    u. A French tourist from the provinces pays for a hotel in Paris with his American Express card.
    v. A U.S. professor goes abroad for a year on a Fullbright grant.

11. **The Balance.** What are the main summary statements of the balance of payments accounts and what do they measure?

12. **Drugs and Terrorists.** Where in the balance of payments accounts do the flows of "laundered" money by drug dealers and international terrorist organizations flow?

13. **Capital Mobility—United States.** The U.S. dollar has maintained or increased its value over the past 20 years despite running a gradually increasing current account deficit. Why has this phenomenon occurred?

14. **Capital Mobility—Brazil.** Brazil has experienced periodic depreciation of its currency over the past 20 years despite occasionally running a current account surplus. Why has this phenomenon occurred?

15. **BOP Transactions.** Identify the correct BOP account for each of the following transactions:
   a. A German-based pension fund buys U.S. government 30-year bonds for its investment portfolio.
   b. Scandinavian Airlines System (SAS) buys jet fuel at Newark Airport for its flight to Copenhagen.
   c. Hong Kong students pay tuition to the University of California, Berkeley.
   d. The U.S. Air Force buys food in South Korea to supply its air crews.
   e. A Japanese auto company pays the salaries of its executives working for its U.S. subsidiaries.
   f. A U.S. tourist pays for a restaurant meal in Bangkok.
   g. A Colombian citizen smuggles cocaine into the United States, receives cash, and smuggles the dollars back into Colombia.
   h. A U.K. corporation purchases a euro-denominated bond from an Italian MNE.

Problems

Brazil's Current Account

Use the following Brazilian balance of payments data from the IMF (all items are for the current account) to answer questions 1 through 5.

1. What is Brazil's balance on goods?
2. What is Brazil's balance on services?
3. What is Brazil's balance on goods and services?
4. What is Brazil's balance on goods, services, and income?
5. What is Brazil's current account balance?

Brazil's Current Account

(millions of US$)	2000	2001	2002	2003	2004	2005	2006	2007	2008	2009
Goods: exports	55,086	58,223	60,362	73,084	96,475	118,308	137,807	160,649	197,942	152,995
Goods: imports	−55,783	−55,572	−47,241	−48,290	−62,809	−73,606	−91,350	−120,617	−173,107	−127,705
Services: credit	9,498	9,322	9,551	10,447	12,584	16,048	19,462	23,954	30,451	27,728
Services: debit	−16,660	−17,081	−14,509	−15,378	−17,260	−24,356	−29,116	−37,173	−47,140	−46,974
Income: credit	3,621	3,280	3,295	3,339	3,199	3,194	6,438	11,493	12,511	8,826
Income: debit	−21,507	−23,023	−21,486	−21,891	−23,719	−29,162	−33,927	−40,784	−53,073	−42,510
Current transfers: credit	1,828	1,934	2,627	3,132	3,582	4,050	4,846	4,972	5,317	4,736
Current transfers: debit	−307	−296	−237	−265	−314	−493	−541	−943	−1,093	−1,398

Russia's Balance of Payments

Use the following Russian (Russian Federation) balance of payments data from the IMF to answer questions 6 through 9.

6. Is Russia experiencing a net capital inflow?
7. What is Russia's total for Groups A and B?
8. What is Russia's total for Groups A through C?
9. What is Russia's total for Groups A through D?

Russia's (Russian Federation's) Balance of Payments

(millions US$)	2000	2001	2002	2003	2004	2005	2006	2007	2008	2009
A. Current account balance	46,839	33,935	29,116	35,410	59,512	84,602	94,686	77,768	103,661	49,433
B. Capital account balance	10,676	−9,378	−12,396	−993	−1,624	−12,764	191	−10,224	496	−11,869
C. Financial account balance	−34,295	−3,732	921	3,024	−5,128	1,025	3,071	94,730	−131,807	−31,637
D. Net errors and omissions	−9,297	−9,558	−6,078	−9,179	−5,870	−7,895	9,518	−13,347	−11,268	−2,564
E. Reserves and related items	−13,923	−11,266	−11,563	−28,262	−46,890	−64,968	−107,466	−148,928	38,919	−3,363

India's Current Account

Use the following India balance of payments data from the IMF (all items are for the current account) to answer questions 10 through 14.

10. What is India's balance on goods?

11. What is India's balance on services?

12. What is India's balance on goods and services?

13. What is India's balance on goods, services, and income?

14. What is India's current account balance?

India's Current Account

(millions of US$)	1998	1999	2000	2001	2002	2003	2004	2005	2006	2007	2008	2009
Goods: exports	34,076	36,877	43,247	44,793	51,141	60,893	77,939	102,175	123,768	153,784	198,598	168,223
Goods: imports	−44,828	−45,556	−53,887	−51,212	−54,702	−68,081	−95,539	−134,692	−166,572	−208,611	−290,959	−247,040
Services: credit	11,691	14,509	16,684	17,337	19,478	23,902	38,281	52,527	69,730	86,929	104,215	90,598
Services: debit	−14,540	−17,271	−19,187	−20,099	−21,039	−24,878	−35,641	−47,287	−58,696	−70,805	−88,261	−80,996
Income: credit	1,806	1,919	2,521	3,524	3,188	3,491	4,690	5,646	8,199	12,650	15,593	13,734
Income: debit	−5,443	−5,629	−7,414	−7,666	−7,097	−8,386	−8,742	−12,296	−14,445	−19,166	−18,891	−20,248
Current transfers: credit	10,402	11,958	13,548	15,140	16,789	22,401	20,615	24,512	30,015	38,885	52,065	51,197
Current transfers: debit	−67	−35	−114	−407	−698	−570	−822	−869	−1,299	−1,742	−3,313	−2,095

China's (Mainland) Balance of Payments

Use the following Chinese (Mainland) balance of payments data from the IMF to answer questions 15 through 18.

15. Is China experiencing a net capital inflow or outflow?

16. What is China's total for Groups A and B?

17. What is China's total for Groups A through C?

18. What is China's total for Groups A through D?

China's (Mainland) Balance of Payments

(millions US$)	1998	1999	2000	2001	2002	2003	2004	2005	2006	2007	2008	2009
A. Current account balance	31,472	21,115	20,518	17,401	35,422	45,875	68,659	160,818	253,268	371,833	436,107	297,142
B. Capital account balance	−47	−26	−35	−54	−50	−48	−69	4,102	4,020	3,099	3,051	3,958
C. Financial account balance	−6,275	5,204	1,958	34.832	32,341	52,774	110,729	58,862	2,642	70,410	15,913	142,756
D. Net errors and omissions	−18,902	−17,641	−11,748	−4,732	7,504	17,985	10,531	27,192	24,721	15,309	24,481	−43,347
E. Reserves and related items	−6,248	−8,652	−10,693	−47,447	−75,217	−116,586	−189,849	−250,975	−284,651	−460,651	−479,553	−400,508

Euro Area Balance of Payments

Use the following Euro Area balance of payments data from the IMF to answer questions 19 through 22.

19. Is the Euro Area experiencing a net capital inflow?

20. What is the Euro Area's total for Groups A and B?

21. What is the Euro Area's total for Groups A through C?

22. What is the Euro Area's total for Groups A through D?

Euro Area Balance of Payments

(billions US$)	1998	1999	2000	2001	2002	2003	2004	2005	2006	2007	2008	2009
A. Current account balance	31.3	−25.5	−81.8	−19.7	44.5	24.9	81.2	19.2	−0.3	24.8	−187.8	−64.5
B. Capital account balance	13.9	13.5	8.4	5.6	10.3	14.3	20.5	14.2	11.7	5.4	14.2	8.4
C. Financial account balance	−86.1	2.6	50.9	−41.2	−15.3	−47.6	−122.9	−71.4	−27.2	−7.5	169.8	96.8
D. Net errors and omissions	31.2	−2.2	6.4	38.8	−36.5	−24.4	5.6	15.0	18.4	−17.1	8.6	19.1
E. Reserves and related items	9.6	11.6	16.2	16.4	−3.0	32.8	15.6	23.0	−2.5	−5.6	−4.8	−59.7

Australia's Current Account

Use the following data from the International Monetary Fund to answer questions 23 through 26.

23. What is Australia's balance on goods?

24. What is Australia's balance on services?

25. What is Australia's balance on goods and services?

26. What is Australia's current account balance?

Australia's Current Account

(millions US$)	1998	1999	2000	2001	2002	2003	2004	2005	2006	2007	2008
Goods: exports	55,884	56,096	64,052	63,676	65,099	70,577	87,207	107,011	124,913	142,421	189,057
Goods: imports	−61,215	−65,857	−68,865	−61,890	−70,530	−85,946	−105,238	−120,383	−134,509	−160,205	−193,972
Services: credit	16,181	17,399	18,677	16,689	17,906	21,205	26,362	31,047	33,088	40,496	45,240
Services: debit	−17,272	−18,330	−18,388	−16,948	−18,107	−21,638	−27,040	−30,505	−32,219	−39,908	−48,338
Income: credit	6,532	7,394	8,984	8,063	8,194	9,457	13,969	16,445	21,748	32,655	37,320
Income: debit	−17,842	−18,968	−19,516	−18,332	−19,884	−24,245	−35,057	−44,166	−54,131	−73,202	−76,719
Current transfers: credit	2,651	3,003	2,622	2,242	2,310	2,767	3,145	3,333	3,698	4,402	4,431
Current transfers: debit	−2,933	−3,032	−2,669	−2,221	−2,373	−2,851	−3,414	−3,813	−4,092	−4,690	−4,805

27. Trade Deficits and J-Curve Adjustment Paths. Assume the United States has the following import/export volumes and prices. It undertakes a major "devaluation" of the dollar, say 18% on average against all major trading partner currencies. What is the pre-devaluation and post-devaluation trade balance?

	Values
Initial spot exchange rate, $/fc	2.00
Price of exports, dollars ($)	20.0000
Price of imports, foreign currency (fc)	12.0000
Quantity of exports, units	100
Quantity of imports, units	120
Percentage devaluation of the dollar	18.00%
Price elasticity of demand, imports	(0.900)

Internet Exercises

1. **World Organizations and the Economic Outlook.** The IMF, World Bank, and United Nations are only a few of the major world organizations that track, report, and aid international economic and financial development. Using these Web sites and others which may be linked, briefly summarize the economic outlook for the developed and emerging nations of the world. For example, the full text of Chapter 1 of the *World Economic Outlook* published annually by the World Bank is available through the IMF's Web page.

International Monetary Fund	www.imf.org/
United Nations	www.unsystem.org/
The World Bank Group	www.worldbank.org/
Europa (EU) Homepage	europa.eu/
Bank for International Settlements	www.bis.org/

2. **St. Louis Federal Reserve.** The Federal Reserve Bank of St. Louis provides a large amount of recent open-economy macroeconomic data online. Use the following addresses to track down recent BOP and GDP data for the major industrial countries.

Recent international economic data	research.stlouisfed.org/publications/iet/
Balance of payments statistics	research.stlouisfed.org/fred2/categories/125

3. **U.S. Bureau of Economic Analysis.** Use the following Bureau of Economic Analysis (U.S. government) and the Ministry of Finance (Japanese government) Web sites to find the most recent balance of payments statistics for both countries.

Bureau of Economic Analysis	www.bea.doc.gov/bea/
Ministry of Finance	/www.mof.go.jp/

4. **World Trade Organization and Doha.** Visit the WTO's Web site and find the most recent evidence presented by the WTO on the progress of talks on issues including international trade in services and international recognition of intellectual property.

World Trade Organization	www.wto.org/

Current Multinational Financial Challenges: The Credit Crisis of 2007–2009

CHAPTER

5

Confidence in markets and institutions, it's a lot like oxygen.
When you have it, you don't even think about it. Indispensable.
You can go years without thinking about it. When it's gone
for five minutes, it's the only thing you think about. The
confidence has been sucked out of the credit markets
and institutions. —Warren Buffett, October 1, 2008.

LEARNING OBJECTIVES

◆ Learn how a variety of economic, regulatory, and social forces led to the real estate market growth and collapse.

◆ Examine the various dimensions of defining and classifying individual borrowers in terms of their credit quality.

◆ Consider the role that financial derivatives and securitization played in the formation of the international credit crisis.

◆ Identify the characteristics and components of a number of the instrumental financial derivatives contributing to the spread of the credit crisis including collateralized debt obligations (CDOs), structured investment vehicles (SIVs), and credit default swaps (CDSs).

◆ Examine how LIBOR, the most widely used cost of money, reacted to the growing tensions and risk perceptions between international financial institutions during the crisis.

◆ Evaluate the various remedies and prescriptions being pushed forward by a variety of governments and international organizations for the infected global financial organism.

Beginning in the summer of 2007, first the United States, followed by the European and Asian financial markets, incurred financial crises. This chapter provides an overview of the origins, dissemination, and repercussions of these credit crises on the conduct of global business. The impacts on the multinational enterprise have been significant and lasting. This chapter is a new addition to this text—representing, in our eyes, the significance of the subject. No student of multinational business should be without a clear understanding of the causes and consequences of this breakdown in global financial markets. The Mini-Case at the end of this chapter, *Letting Go of Lehman Brothers,* highlights an example of the crisis.

113

The Seeds of Crisis: Subprime Debt

The origins of the current crisis lie within the ashes of the equity bubble and subsequent collapse of the equity markets at the end of the 1990s. As the so-called *dot.com bubble* collapsed in 2000 and 2001, capital flowed increasingly toward the real estate sectors in the United States. Some economists have argued that much of the wealth accumulated from the equity markets during that period was now used to push housing prices and general real estate demands upward. Although corporate lending was still relatively slow, the U.S. banking sector found mortgage lending a highly profitable and rapidly expanding market. The following years saw investment and speculation in the real estate sector increase rapidly. This included both residential housing and commercial real estate. As prices rose and speculation increased, a growing number of the borrowers were of lower and lower credit quality. These borrowers and their associated mortgage agreements, the *subprime debt* which has been so widely discussed, now carried higher debt service obligations with lower and lower income and cash flow capabilities. In traditional financial management terms, *debt-service coverage* was increasingly inadequate.

Repeal of Glass-Steagall

The market was also more competitive than ever, as a number of deregulation efforts in the United States in 1999 and 2000 now opened up these markets to more and more financial organizations and institutions than ever before. One of the major openings was the U.S. Congress' passage of the Gramm-Leach-Bliley Financial Services Modernization Act of 1999, which repealed the last vestiges of the Glass-Steagall Act of 1933, eliminating the last barriers between commercial and investment banks. The Act now allowed commercial banks to enter into more areas of risk, including underwriting and proprietary dealing.[1] One key result was that the banks now competed aggressively for the loan business of customers of all kinds, offering borrowers more and more creative mortgage forms at lower and lower interest rates—at least initial interest rates.

Another negative result of banking deregulation was that extra pressure was placed on the existing regulators. The Federal Deposit Insurance Corporation (FDIC) was established to insure the deposits of customers in commercial banks. The FDIC's main tools were to require an adequate capital base for each bank and to conduct periodic inspections to assure the credit quality of the banks' loans. This worked very well for the period 1933–1999. There were very few bank failures and almost no major failures.

Investment banks and stock brokerage firms were regulated by the Securities and Exchange Commission (SEC). These banks and brokerage firms dealt in much riskier activities than the commercial banks. These activities included stock and bond underwriting, active participation in derivatives and insurance markets and investments in subprime debt and other mortgages, using their own equity and debt capital—not the deposits of consumers.

The Housing Sector and Mortgage Lending

One of the key outcomes of this new market openness and competitiveness was that many borrowers who in previous times could not have qualified for mortgages now could. Many of these loans were quite transparent in terms of both risks and returns. Borrowers often borrowed at floating rates, often priced at LIBOR, plus a small interest rate spread. The

---

[1]The Act now allowed corporate combinations like that between Citibank, a commercial bank, and the Travelers Group, an insurance company. The combined entity could now provide banking, insurance, and underwriting services under a variety of different brands. This combination would have been strictly forbidden under the Glass-Steagall and Bank Holding Company Acts.

loans would then reset at much higher fixed rates within two to five years. Other forms included loan agreements that were interest only in the early years, requiring a subsequent step up in payments with principal reduction or complete refinancing at later dates. In some cases, the interest-only loan payment structures were at initial interest rates that were far below market rates.

Credit Quality. Mortgage loans in the U.S. marketplace are normally categorized as *prime* (or A-paper), *Alt-A* (Alternative-A paper), and *subprime*, in increasing order of riskiness.[2] A prime mortgage would be categorized as *conforming* (also referred to as a *conventional loan*), meaning it would meet the guarantee requirements and resale to Government-Sponsored Enterprises (GSEs), Fannie Mae and Freddie Mac. Alt-A mortgages, however, would still be considered a relatively low risk loan and the borrower creditworthy, but for some reason were not initially conforming. (They could, however, still be sold to GSEs if certain minimums like 20% down payments were included.) As the housing and real estate markets boomed in 2003 and 2004, more and more mortgages were originated by lenders which were in the Alt-A category, as it was the preferred loan for many non–owner-occupied properties. Investors wishing to buy homes for resale purposes, *flipping*, would typically qualify for an Alt-A mortgage, but not a prime. By the end of 2008, there was more than $1.3 trillion in Alt-A debt outstanding.

The third category of mortgage loans, *subprime*, is difficult to define. In principle, it reflects borrowers who do not meet underwriting criteria. Subprime borrowers have a higher perceived risk of default, normally as a result of some credit history elements, which may include bankruptcy, loan delinquency, default, or simply limited experience or history of debt. They are nearly exclusively floating-rate structures, and carry significantly higher interest rate spreads over the floating bases like LIBOR.

Subprime borrowers typically pay a 2% premium over prime—the *subprime differential*. From a traditional lender's perspective, the key metric for any loan is the *termination profile*, the likelihood that the borrower will either prepay or default on the loan. Historically, the actual interest rate any specific borrower would pay is determined by a host of factors including the borrower's credit score, the specific mortgage loan-to-value (LTV) ratio, and the size of the down payment. Interestingly, the interest rate charged does not change significantly until the down payment drops below 10%.

Subprime lending was itself the result of deregulation. Until 1980, most states in the United States had stringent interest rate caps on lenders/borrowers. Even if a lender was willing to extend a mortgage to a subprime borrower—at a higher interest rate, and the borrower was willing to pay the higher rate, state law prohibited it. With the passage of the 1980 Depository Institutions Deregulation and Monetary Control Act (DIDMCA) federal law superceded state law. But it wasn't until the passage of the Tax Reform Act of 1986 that subprime debt became a viable market. The TRA of 1986 eliminated tax deductibility of consumer loans, but allowed tax deductibility on interest charges associated with both a primary residence and a second mortgage loan. The subprime loan was born.

The growing demand for loans or mortgages by these borrowers led more and more originators to provide the loans at above market rates beginning in the late 1990s. By the 2003–2005 period, these subprime loans were a growing segment of the market.[3] As illustrated

---

[2]*Prime* is the 30-year fixed interest rate reported by the Freddie Mac Primary Mortgage Market Survey. *Subprime* is the average 30-year fixed interest rate at origination as calculated by the Loan Performance data set. *Subprime premium* is the difference between the prime and subprime rates.

[3]Subprime mortgages may have never exceeded 7% to 8% of all outstanding mortgage obligations by 2007, but by the end of 2008, they were the source of more than 65% of bankruptcy filings by homeowners in the United States.

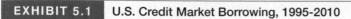

EXHIBIT 5.1   U.S. Credit Market Borrowing, 1995-2010

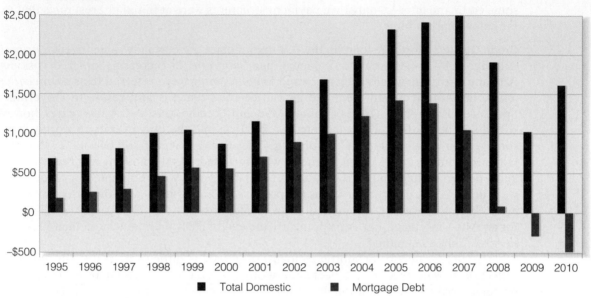

Billions of U.S. dollars

Total Domestic   Mortgage Debt

Source: Flow of Funds Accounts of the United States, Annual Flows and Outstandings, Board of Governors of the Federal Reserve System, Washington, DC, FFA 1995–2004 and FFA, 2005–2010, March 10, 2011, p. 2.

in Exhibit 5.1, the growth in both total domestic borrowing and mortgage-based borrowing in the United States in the post-2000 period was rapid. However, the collapse in mortgage borrowing as a result of the 2008 credit crisis was even more dramatic.

Asset Values. One of the key financial elements of this growing debt was the value of the assets collateralizing the mortgages—the houses and real estate itself. As the market demands pushed up prices, housing assets rose in market value. The increased values were then used as collateral in refinancing, and in some cases, additional debt in the form of second mortgages based on the rising equity value of the home.

Unfortunately, one particularly complex component of this process was that as existing homes rose in value, many homeowners were now enticed and motivated to refinance existing mortgages. As a result, many mortgage holders who were previously stable became more indebted and were participants in more aggressively constructed loan agreements. The mortgage brokers and loan originators themselves also provided fuel to the fire, as the continuing prospects for refinancing generated additional fee income, a staple of the industry's returns. The industry was itself providing the feedstock for its own growth. Students of financial history will recognize this as a common story behind some of the most famous financial bubbles in history.

Mortgage debt as a percentage of household disposable income continued to climb in the United States rapidly in the post-2000 business environment. But it was not a uniquely American issue, as debt obligations were rising in a variety of countries including Great Britain, France, Germany, and Australia. Exhibit 5.2 illustrates the rising household debt levels for three selected countries through mid-2008. In the end, Great Britain was significantly more indebted in mortgage debt than even the United States.

The U.S. Federal Reserve, at the same time, intentionally aided the debt growth mechanism by continuing to lower interest rates. The Fed's monetary policy actions were

EXHIBIT 5.2	Household Debt as a Percentage of Disposable Income, 1990–2008

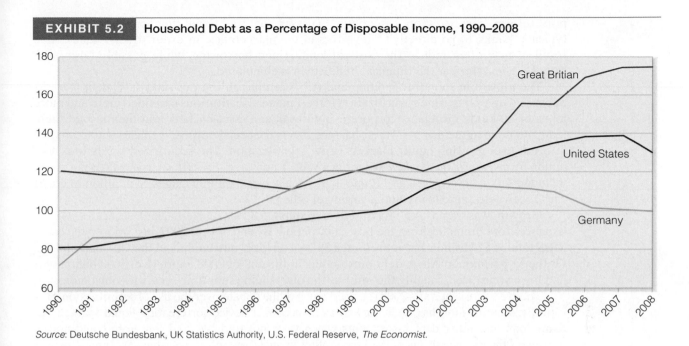

Source: Deutsche Bundesbank, UK Statistics Authority, U.S. Federal Reserve, *The Economist.*

predictably to lower interest rates to aid the U.S. economy in its recovery from the 2000–2001 recession. These lower rates provided additional incentive and aid for borrowers of all kinds to raise new and ever cheaper debt.

The Transmission Mechanism: Securitization and Derivatives of Securitized Debt

If subprime debt was the malaria, then securitization was the mosquito carrier, the airborne transmission mechanism of the protozoan parasite. The transport vehicle for the growing lower quality debt was a combination of securitization and repackaging provided by a series of new financial derivatives.

Securitization

Securitization has long been a force of change in global financial markets. *Securitization* is the process of turning an illiquid asset into a liquid salable asset. The key element is in the interpretation of the word *liquid*. *Liquid*, in the field of finance, is the ability to exchange an asset for cash, instantly, at fair market value.[4] Although a multitude of countries had used securitization as a method of creating liquid markets for debt and equity funding since World War II, the United States had been one of the last major industrial countries to use securitization in its savings and loan and commercial banking systems. The 1980s, however, saw the introduction of securitization in U.S. debt markets, and its growth had been unchecked since. In its

---

[4]Liquidity is not widely understood. A relevant example would be the ability of a homeowner to sell his home for cash today. Although he could do it, he would most likely receive a cash payment which is far below the asset's true value—the fair market value.

purest form, securitization essentially bypasses the traditional financial intermediaries, typically banks, to go directly to investors in the marketplace in order to raise funds. As a result, it may often reduce the costs of lending and borrowing, while possibly raising the returns to investors, as the financial middleman is eliminated.

The growth in subprime lending and Alt-A lending in the post-2000 U.S. debt markets depended upon this same securitization force. Financial institutions extended more and more loans of all kinds, mortgage, corporate, industrial, and asset-backed, and then moved these loan and bond agreements off their balance sheets to special purpose vehicles and ultimately into the ever-growing liquid markets using securitization. The securitized assets took two major forms, *mortgage-backed securities* (MBSs) and *asset-backed securities* (ABSs). ABSs included second mortgages and home-equity loans based on mortgages, in addition to credit card receivables, auto loans, and a variety of others.

Growth was rapid. As illustrated in Exhibit 5.3, mortgage-backed securities (MBS) issuances rose dramatically in the post-2000 period. By end of year 2007, just prior to the crisis, MBS totaled $27 trillion and represented 39% of all loans outstanding in the U.S. marketplace. Of the $1.3 trillion in Alt-A debt outstanding at the end of 2008, more than $600 billion of it had been securitized, roughly the same as the outstanding subprime securities outstanding.

The credit crisis of 2007–2008 renewed much of the debate over the use of securitization. Historically, securitization has been viewed as a successful device for creating liquid markets for many loan and other debt instruments which were not tradable, and therefore could not be moved off the balance sheets of banks and other financial organizations which are originating the debt. By securitizing the debt, portfolios of loans and other debt instruments could be packaged and resold into a more liquid market, freeing up the originating institutions to make more loans and increase access to debt financing for more mortgage seekers or commercial loan borrowers.

EXHIBIT 5.3   Annual Issuances of MBSs, 1995-2009

Billions of 2009 U.S. dollars

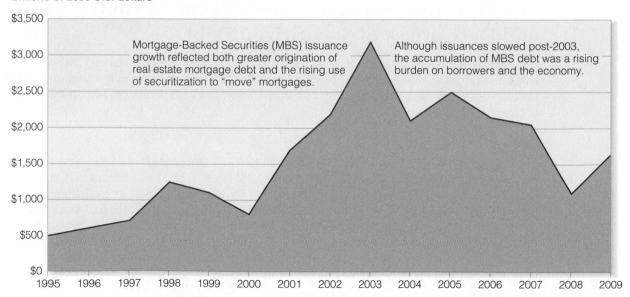

Source: *Fannie Mae, Freddie Mac, and the Federal Role in the Secondary Mortgage Market*, Congressional Budget Office, December 2010, p. 11.

The problem, however, is that securitization may degrade credit quality. As long as the lender, the originator, was "stuck" with the loan, the lender was keen to assure the quality of the loan and the capability of the borrower to repay in a timely manner. The lender had a vested interest in continuing to monitor borrower behavior over the life of the debt.

Securitization, however, severed that link. Now the originator could originate and sell, not being held accountable for the ultimate capability of the borrower to fulfill the loan obligation. Critics argue that securitization provides incentives for rapid and possibly sloppy credit quality assessment. Originators could now focus on generating more and more fees through more loans, origination, while not being concerned over the actual loan performance over time. The originate-to-distribute (OTD) model was now fragmenting traditional banking risks and returns. Under the OTD framework, once the loan was made and resold, the ability for any institution trading the portfolio of loans to track and monitor borrower behavior was negligible.

Proponents of securitization acknowledge that it did allow more subprime mortgages and loans to be written. But those same credits allowed more and more home buyers and commercial operators lower-cost financing, making home ownership and small business activities more affordable and more accessible. Moreover, although there was clearly abuse in the origination of subprime mortgages, many believe that the U.S. system was particularly vulnerable, not having sufficient requirements or principles in place over key credit quality criteria like credit histories. Proponents of securitization argue that if these errors are corrected, securitization would have the ability to truly reach its objectives of creating more liquid and efficient markets without degrading the quality of the instruments and obligations.

Of course, securitization alone did not assure a market for the obligations. Securitization simply changed their form, but there was still the need for a market for the nonconforming obligations.

Structured Investment Vehicles

The organization that filled that market niche, the buyer of much of the securitized nonconforming debt, was the *structured investment vehicle* (SIV). This was the ultimate financial intermediation device: it borrowed short and invested long. The SIV was an off-balance sheet entity first created by Citigroup in 1988. It was designed to allow a bank to create an investment entity that would invest in long-term and higher yielding assets such as speculative grade bonds, mortgage-backed securities (MBSs), and collateralized debt obligations (CDOs), while funding itself through commercial paper (CP) issuances. CP has long been one of the lowest-cost funding sources for any business. The problem, of course, is that the buyers of CP issuances must have full faith in the credit quality of the business unit. And that, in the end, was the demise of the SIV.

Exhibit 5.4 provides a brief overview of the SIV's basic structure. The funding of the typical SIV was fairly simple: using minimal equity, the SIV borrowed very short—commercial paper, interbank, or medium-term-notes. Sponsoring banks provided backup lines of credit to assure the highest credit ratings for CP issuances. The SIV then used the proceeds to purchase portfolios of higher yielding securities that held investment grade credit ratings. The SIV then generated an interest margin, roughly 0.25% on average, acting as a middleman in the shadow banking process.

It is the credit quality of many of the purchased assets—for example, collateralized debt obligations (CDOs), as described in the following section, which has been the subject of much *ex post* debate. A portfolio of subprime mortgages, which by definition are not of investment grade credit quality, was often awarded investment grade quality because of the belief in portfolio theory. The theory held that whereas a single large subprime borrower constituted significant risk, a portfolio of subprime borrowers which was securitized (chopped up

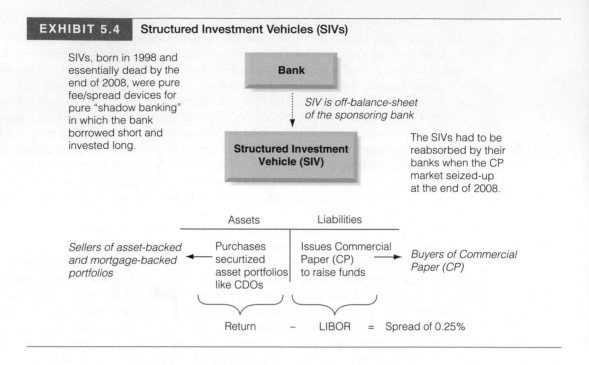

EXHIBIT 5.4   Structured Investment Vehicles (SIVs)

SIVs, born in 1998 and essentially dead by the end of 2008, were pure fee/spread devices for pure "shadow banking" in which the bank borrowed short and invested long.

Bank

SIV is off-balance-sheet of the sponsoring bank

Structured Investment Vehicle (SIV)

The SIVs had to be reabsorbed by their banks when the CP market seized-up at the end of 2008.

Assets   Liabilities

Sellers of asset-backed and mortgage-backed portfolios ← Purchases securtized asset portfolios like CDOs | Issues Commercial Paper (CP) to raise funds → *Buyers of Commercial Paper (CP)*

Return   –   LIBOR   =   Spread of 0.25%

pieces in a sense), represented significantly less risk of credit default and could therefore be awarded investment grade status.

The theory proved false, however. As the housing boom collapsed in 2007, the subprime mortgages underlying these CDOs failed, causing the value of the SIV's asset portfolios to be instantly written down in value (mark-to-market accounting required real-time revaluation of the assets). As the asset values fell, buyers of SIV-based CP disappeared. Because the sponsoring banks of many SIVs had to provide backup lines of credit for their SIVs to obtain A1/P1 credit quality to begin with, the banks were forced to step back in and fund their own SIVs. In the second half of 2007 and the first half of 2008, most SIVs were either closed down or re-consolidated with their sponsoring banks. By October 2008, SIVs were a thing of the past.

In the end, both the birth and death of the SIV were somewhat symbolic of the three major forces many believe were behind the credit crisis of 2007 and 2008: complex financial instruments, off-balance sheet accounting entities, and increased use of leverage.

> *SIVs are only one part of the story of credit problems in 2007 and 2008, but they are instructive because they include three features that contributed disturbance elsewhere. First, they involved the use of innovative securities, which were hard to value in the best of circumstances and which had little history to indicate how they might behave in a severe market downturn. Second, risks were underestimated: the SIVs were a form of highly leveraged speculation, which was dependent on the assumption that the markets would always supply liquidity. Finally, they were off balance sheet entities: few in the markets (or perhaps in the regulatory agencies) had an accurate idea of the scope or nature of their activities until the trouble came. The result of the interaction of these factors with a sharp housing market downturn is the most sustained period of instability in U.S. financial markets since the Great Depression.*

> —"Averting Financial Crisis," CRS Report for Congress, by Mark Jickling,
> Congressional Research Service, October 8, 2008.

As the credit crisis of 2008 deepened into the recession of 2009, many lawmakers and regulators in a variety of countries and continents debated the possible regulation of financial derivatives that may have contributed to the crisis. Both the European Union and the United States governments looked hard and close at two specific derivatives— *collateralized debt obligations* (CDOs) and *credit default swaps* (CDSs)—to determine what role they played in the crisis, and if and how they might be brought under greater control.

Collateralized Debt Obligations (CDOs)

One of the key instruments in this new growing securitization was the *collateralized debt obligation*, or CDO, pictured in Exhibit 5.5. Banks originating mortgage loans, and corporate loans and bonds, could now create a portfolio of these debt instruments and package them as an asset-backed security. Once packaged, the bank passed the security to a *special purpose vehicle* (SPV) (not to be confused with the previously described SIV), often located in an off-shore financial center like the Cayman Islands for legal and tax advantages.[5] SPVs offered a number of distinct advantages, such as the ability to remain off-balance sheet if financed and operated properly. From there the CDO was sold into a growing market through underwriters. This freed up the bank's financial resources to originate more and more loans, earning a variety of fees. A typical fee was 1.1% upfront to the CDO underwriter. The collateral in the CDO was the real estate or aircraft or heavy equipment or other property the loan was used to purchase.

EXHIBIT 5.5   The Collateralized Debt Obligation (CDO)

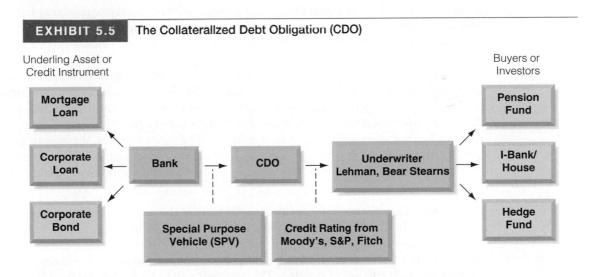

The Collateralized Debt Obligation, CDO, is a derivative instrument created from bank-originated mortgages and loans, combined with similar debt obligations into a portfolio, and then re-sold through investment banking underwriters to a variety of investors. The credit rating of the CDO, based on its constituent components, is critical to the salability to investors.

---

[5]Some readers may remember the ignominious past of the SPV from its widespread use by Enron in acquiring more and more debt—off-balance sheet—to feed its continuously failing business model in the late 1990s.

These CDOs were sold to the market in categories representing the credit quality of the borrowers in the mortgages—*senior tranches* (rated AAA), *mezzanine* or *middle tranches* (AA down to BB), and *equity tranches* (below BB, junk bond status, many of which were unrated). The actual marketing and sales of the CDOs was done by the major investment banking houses which now found the fee income easy and profitable. These houses, Lehman Brothers, Bear Stearns, AIG, and others, would later rue the day they committed their future to their new addiction to CDOs. Exhibit 5.5 traces this flow of CDOs to buyer.

Although at first glance this appeared relatively straightforward, in practice it turned out to be quite messy. A collection of corporate bonds or subprime mortgages would be combined into a portfolio—the CDO. The CDO would then be passed to a ratings firm, firms such as Moody's, S&P, and Fitch, for a rating for the security. The rating firms were paid for their rating, and were often under severe pressure to complete their analysis and rating of the CDO quickly. As a result, it was common practice to use the ratings information provided by the underwriter, rather than doing ground-up credit analysis on their own. A second, and somewhat confounding issue, was that it was also possible for a collection of bonds, say BB bonds, to be rated above BB when combined into a CDO. In the end, the ratings provided by the ratings firms were critical for the underwriter to be able to market the CDOs quickly and at a favorable price. Many investing institutions had strict investment policy statements in place which required investment grade status (BBB and above) for purchase.

The CDO now became the preferred asset *du jour*, as financial institutions of all kinds, from pension funds to hedge funds, purchased the assets and earned the relatively high rates of interest and returns as the economy, real estate, and mortgage lending markets boomed from 2001 to 2007. These markets, aided substantially by slowly performing equity markets and relatively low interest rates, benefited from investors moving rapidly toward real estate investment and speculation. By 2007, the CDO market had reached a record level of more than $600 billion.

Of course, the actual value of the CDO was no better or worse than its two primary value drivers. The first was the performance of the debt collateral it held, the ongoing payments being made by the original borrowers on their individual mortgages. If for any reason those borrowers were unable to make timely debt service payments, from changing interest rates or income levels, CDO values would fall. The second driver, the one to go unnoticed until crisis occurred, was the willingness of the many institutions and traders of CDOs to continue to make a market in the derivative. This liquidity component would later prove to be disastrous.

Ownership. One of the concerns about CDOs from the very beginning, voiced by a number of people including Warren Buffett, the famous American investor, was that the CDO originator had no continuing link or responsibility to the mortgage. Once the mortgage loan was made and the CDO structured and sold, the mortgage lender had no further responsibility toward the performance of the loan. This was commonly seen as a fatal flaw. It provided a significant incentive for mortgage originators to make more and more loans of questionable credit quality, earning their fees while passing the securities along to the marketplace. Of course, the buyers in the market were also responsible for their due diligence on the quality of the assets they were buying. They too found it somewhat easy to pass the CDOs along to more and more market participants, whether they are institutions like Freddie Mac in the United States, or commercial or investment banking organizations in London, Paris, Hong Kong, or Tokyo.

Mind the Gap. A second feature of potential failure was how the CDOs fit within the organizational structures of the financial institutions themselves. The original mortgage loans were a highly illiquid asset, and were typically carried on what might be called the "loan book" of a financial institution. Once the mortgages were combined into a securitized portfolio, the CDO, they were now traded in a market that was relatively invisible, with no real regulation or reporting of market activity. The CDOs were carried on the "market book" of the financial institutions. In a number of organizations, these different books meant different departments, people, and monitoring activities. Accountability often failed.

The CDO market reached what some investment bankers characterized as a "feeding frenzy" in the fall of 2006, as the appetite for new issues seemed insatiable. *Synthetic CDOs* were born. These were structures in which the CDO itself did not actually hold debt, but were constructed purely of derivative contracts combined to "mimic" the cash flows of many other CDOs. One issue, the *Mantoloking CDO* offered by Merrill Lynch in October 2006, was representative of another new extreme. *Mantoloking* was a "CDO-squared," a CDO that held other CDOs. As more and more CDOs were created, all of the subprime components that were not wanted or acceptable to potential investors were grouped; Mantoloking was effectively a dumping ground.[6] The CDO-squared instruments not only held lower and lower quality loans and bonds, but also they were typically highly subordinated CDOs to the original instruments that they supported.

Regardless of the CDO's weaknesses, it became a mainstay of investment banking activity globally by 2007. By the time the first real cracks in the market appeared in 2007, the CDO had spread far and wide within the global financial marketplace. Many would later argue that it would act as a cancer to the future of the system's health. The beginning of the end was the collapse of two Bear Stearns' hedge funds in July 2007. Both funds were made up nearly entirely of CDOs. Within a month the market for CDOs was completely illiquid. Anyone trying to liquidate a CDO was met with bids approaching $0.08 on the dollar. The market effectively collapsed, as illustrated in Exhibit 5.6.

EXHIBIT 5.6   Global CDO Issuance, 2004–2008 (billions of U.S. dollars)

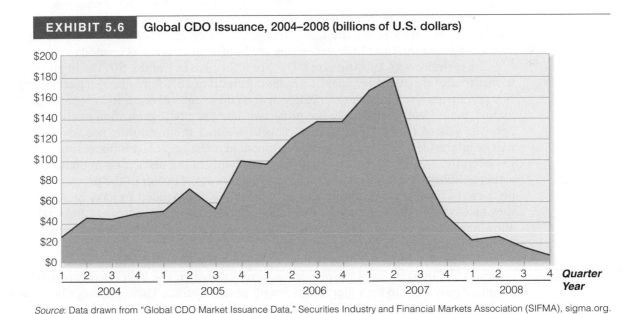

Source: Data drawn from "Global CDO Market Issuance Data," Securities Industry and Financial Markets Association (SIFMA), sigma.org.

---

[6]"Frenzy," Jill Drew, *The Washington Post*, Tuesday, December 16, 2008, p. A1.

Credit Default Swaps (CDSs)

> *Despite its forbidding name, the CDS is a simple idea: it allows an investor to buy insurance against a company defaulting on its debt payments. When it was invented, the CDS was a useful concept because more people felt comfortable owning corporate debt if they could eliminate the risk of the issuer failing. The extra appetite for debt helped lower the cost of capital.*

> —"Derivatives: Giving Credit Where It Is Due," *The Economist*, November 6, 2008.

The second derivative of increasing note—or concern—was the *credit default swap* (CDS). The credit default swap was a contract, a derivative, which derived its value from the credit quality and performance of any specified asset. The CDS was new, invented by a team at J.P. Morgan in 1997, and designed to shift the risk of default to a third party. In short, it was a way to bet whether a specific mortgage or security would either fail to pay on time or fail to pay at all. In some cases, for hedging, it provided insurance against the possibility that a borrower might not pay. In other instances, it was a way in which a speculator could bet against the increasingly risky securities (like the CDO), to hold their value. And uniquely, you could make the bet without ever holding or being directly exposed to the credit instrument itself.

The CDS was completely outside the regulatory boundaries, having obtained unique protection as a result of the Commodity Futures Modernization Act of 2000. The CDS was in fact a position or play which had been outlawed for more than a century—that is, until major financial market deregulatory steps were taken in 1999 and 2000. A *bucket shop* was a type of gambling house in which one could speculate on whether stocks were going to rise or fall in price without owning the stock. Note that this is not the same as a *short position*. A *short position* is when a speculator bets on a security to fall in price, and agrees to sell an actual share to a second party at a future date at a specified price. The speculator is hoping that the share price does fall, so that it can be purchased on the open market at a lower price. It could then use that share to fulfill the resale obligation. In order to write or sell the positions one needed only to find a counterparty willing to take the opposite position (as opposed to actually owning the shares). As a result, the CDS market, estimated at $62 trillion at its peak, grew to a size many times the size of the underlying credit instruments it was created to protect.

The cash flows and positions of CDSs are illustrated in Exhibit 5.7. The organization that wishes to acquire insurance against a potential credit quality fall (a hedger), or any organization possessing a view that a specific negative credit event will occur in the near-term (a speculator), is the *protection buyer*. The *protection seller* is any organization wishing to take the opposite side of the transaction, regardless of whether the institution has any specific holdings or interests in the asset or credit instrument in question. It is this dimension of CDSs that has been the subject of concern; that the participants in the market do not have to have any actual holdings or interests in the credit instruments at the center of the protection. They simply have to have a viewpoint. It turns out that they also needed to have more money than they had to fulfill their promise of protection. Another growing concern is that CDSs actually allow banks to sever their links to their borrowers, thereby reducing incentives to screen and monitor the ability of borrowers to repay.

The top of Exhibit 5.7 illustrates what is generally expected to happen over time to the positions and obligations of the protection buyer and seller. The buyer makes regular nominal premium payments to the seller for the length of the contract. There is no significant negative credit event during the term of the contract, and the protection seller earns its premiums over time, never having to payoff a significant claim. In essence, it's simple insurance.

The bottom half of Exhibit 5.7, however, tells a very different story. This is the case in which, say in period 4 of the swap agreement, the credit instrument at the core of the contract

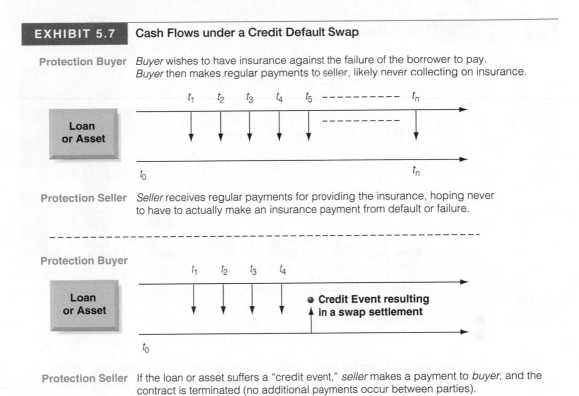

EXHIBIT 5.7   Cash Flows under a Credit Default Swap

Protection Buyer   *Buyer* wishes to have insurance against the failure of the borrower to pay.
Buyer then makes regular payments to seller, likely never collecting on insurance.

Protection Seller   *Seller* receives regular payments for providing the insurance, hoping never
to have to actually make an insurance payment from default or failure.

Protection Seller   If the loan or asset suffers a "credit event," *seller* makes a payment to *buyer*, and the
contract is terminated (no additional payments occur between parties).

suffers a credit event (e.g., bankruptcy). Then the protection seller has to fulfill its obligation to make a settlement payment to the protection buyer. All that is needed for a successful contract completion is for the protection seller to actually have sufficient capital or insurance of its own to cover its obligations. But to quote Shakespeare, "ay, that's the rub."[7] Questions continue over the adequacy of capital. According to *The Economist*, the sellers of CDSs in 2007 were widespread across a variety of financial institutions. Everyone then piled into the market: 44% banks, 32% hedge funds, 17% insurance companies, 4% pension funds, and 3% other.[8]

As a result of the CDS market growth in a completely deregulated segment, there was no real record or registry of issuances, no requirements on writers and sellers that they had adequate capital to assure contractual fulfilment, and no real market for assuring liquidity—depending on one-to-one counterparty settlement. As seen in Exhibit 5.8, the market boomed. New proposals for regulation of the market have centered on first requiring participants to have an actual exposure to a credit instrument or obligation. This eliminated the outside speculators simply wishing to take a position in the market. Also needed was the formation of some type of clearinghouse to provide systematic trading and valuation of all CDS positions at all times.

Critics of regulation argue that the market has weathered many challenges, such as the failures of Bear Stearns and Lehman Brothers (at one time estimated to have been a seller of 10% of global CDS obligations), the near failure of AIG, and the defaults of Freddie Mac and

[7]From Hamlet's famous "to be or not to be" speech by William Shakespeare, 1603.

[8]"Credit Derivatives: The Great Untangling," *The Economist*, November 6, 2008.

| EXHIBIT 5.8 | Credit Default Swap Market Growth |

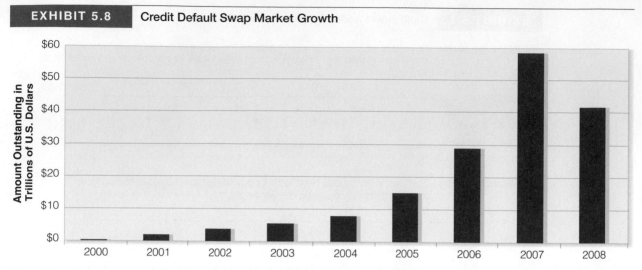

Source: Data drawn from Amounts Outstanding of Over-the-Counter-Derivatives, by Risk Category and Instrument, *BIS Quarterly Review*, June 2009, bis.org.

Fannie Mae. Despite these challenges, the CDS market continues to function and may have learned its lessons. Proponents argue that increased transparency of activity alone might provide sufficient information for growing market resiliency and liquidity.

> *All of which leaves a $55 trillion question. If companies fail en masse, what will happen to the derivatives that insure against default, known as credit default swaps (CDS)? The collapse of Lehman Brothers, an investment bank, and other financial disasters, raise fears that the sellers of these products, namely banks and insurance firms, will not honour their commitments. A cascade of defaults could be multiplied many times through derivatives, blowing yet another hole in the financial system. Once considered a marvelous tool of risk management, CDSs now look as though they will magnify, not mitigate, risk.*
>
> —"Dirty Words: Derivatives, Defaults, Disaster . . . ,"
> by Henry Tricks, *The World*, November 19, 2008.

Credit Enhancement

A final element quietly at work in credit markets beginning in the late 1990s was the process of *credit enhancement*. *Credit enhancement* is the method of making investments more attractive to prospective buyers by reducing their perceived risk. In the mid-1990s underwriters of a variety of asset-backed securities (ABSs) often used bond insurance agencies to make their products "safer" for both them and the prospective buyers. These bond insurance agencies were third parties, not a direct part of the underwriting and sale, but a guarantor in the case of default. The practice was widely used specifically in the underwriting of home equity loan ABSs.

Beginning in 1998, however, a more innovative approach to credit enhancement was introduced in the form of *subordination*. The process of *subordination*, illustrated in Exhibit 5.9, combined different asset pools (corporate bonds, MBSs, ABSs, etc.) of differing credit quality into different tranches by credit quality. Senior tranches contained high-quality loans, with mezzanine and junior tranches made up of relatively lower-quality loans such as Alt-A and jumbo loans. These were loans that were in many ways nonconforming—technically,

---

EXHIBIT 5.9   CDO Construction and Credit Enhancement

CDOs were constructed as portfolios of securitized instruments which mixed assets of differing risk in order to provide greater returns to investors. A typical CDO would combine tranches based on both debt rating (AAA, A, etc.) and equity.

By including lower credit quality tranche components, it was hoped that the overall return on the CDO would be enhanced while overall risk—as a result of the portfolio—was acceptable.

Subordination	Tranche and Rating	Possible Interest Return	Cash Waterfall
Senior Mezzanine Debt	AAA	LIBOR + 50 bp	
	A	LIBOR + 150 bp	
Junior Mezzanine Debt	BBB	LIBOR + 300 bp	
	BB	LIBOR + 800 bp	
Equity	Unrated	Residual	

In the event of portfolio asset default and failure, the *cash waterfall* would fill from the top-down, with lower mezzanine and equity/residual positions likely receiving little of cash flow on redemption.

---

but were still considered of relatively high quality and believed to be of low risk to the investor. The final tranches, the subordinated tranches, were composed of subprime loans which were clearly considered higher risk, and as a result were paying higher interest. It was the higher interest of the subprime components that made the entire combined package higher yield, possessing a higher weighted average interest return. These subordinated structures were particularly attractive to the senior tranche holders as they earned a higher return as a result of the junior and mezzanine components, but held first-call rights on being repaid in the event of default.

A third method of credit enhancement in the post high-tech bubble era (post 2000) was the use of the credit default swaps (CDSs) described in the previous section. A credit default swap could be used by the buyer of a CDO holding a variety of asset-backed or mortgage-backed securities to gain additional protection against the default of the CDOs at what proved to be relatively cheap rates.

The Fallout: The Crisis of 2007–2009

The housing market began to falter in late 2005, with increasing signs of collapse throughout 2006. The bubble finally burst in the spring of 2007. The United States was not alone, as housing markets in the United Kingdom and Australia followed similar paths. What followed was a literal domino effect of collapsing loans and securities, followed by the funds and institutions that were their holders. In July 2007, two hedge funds at Bear Stearns holding a variety of CDOs and other mortgage-based assets failed. Soon thereafter, Northern Rock, a major British banking organization, was rescued from the brink of collapse by the Bank of England. In early September 2007, global financial markets turned to near panic, as a multitude of financial institutions on several continents suffered bank runs. Interest rates rose, equity markets fell, and the first stages of crisis rolled through the global economy.

2008 proved even more volatile than 2007. Crude oil prices—as well as nearly every other commodity price—rose at astronomical rates in the first half of the year. The massive growth in the Chinese and Indian economies, and in fact in many emerging markets globally, continued unabated. And just as suddenly, it stopped. Crude oil peaked at $147/barrel in July, and then plummeted, as did nearly every other commodity price including copper, nickel, timber, concrete, and steel.

As mortgage markets faltered, the U.S. Federal Reserve stepped in. On August 10, 2008, the Fed purchased a record $38 billion in mortgage-backed securities in an attempt to inject liquidity into the credit markets. On September 7, 2008, the U.S. government announced that it was placing Fannie Mae (the Federal National Mortgage Association) and Freddie Mac (the Federal Home Loan Mortgage Corporation) into conservatorship. In essence, the government was taking over the institutions as result of their near insolvency. Over the following week, Lehman Brothers, one of the oldest investment banks on Wall Street, struggled to survive. Finally on September 14, Lehman filed for bankruptcy. As described in the Mini-Case at the end of this chapter, this was by the far the largest single bankruptcy in American history.

On Monday, September 15, the markets reacted. Equity markets plunged. In many ways much more important for the financial security of multinational enterprises, U.S. dollar LIBOR rates shot skywards, as illustrated in Exhibit 5.10, as a result of the growing international perception of financial collapse by U.S. banking institutions. The following day, American International Group (AIG), the U.S. insurance conglomerate, received an $85 billion injection from the U.S. Federal Reserve in exchange for an 80% equity interest. AIG had extensive credit default swap exposure. Although dollar markets seemingly calmed, the following weeks saw renewed periods of collapse and calm as more and more financial institutions failed, merged, or were bailed out by a bewildering array of bailout packages and capital injections.

EXHIBIT 5.10   USD and JPY LIBOR Rates (September–October 2008)

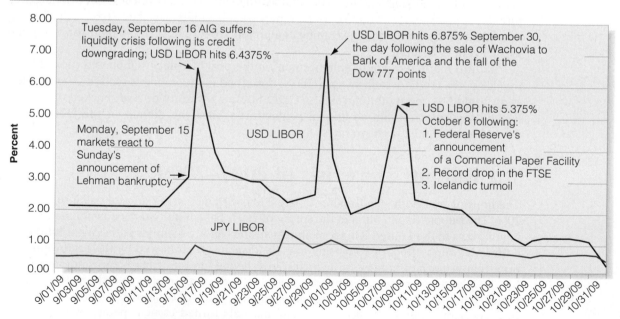

Source: British Bankers Association (BBA). Overnight lending rates.

The credit crisis now began in full force. Beginning in September 2008 and extending into the spring of 2009, the world's credit markets—lending of all kinds—nearly stopped. The corporate lending markets now demonstrated the following complex combination of crisis conditions:

◆ In the end, the risky investment banking activities undertaken post-deregulation, especially in the mortgage market, overwhelmed the banks' commercial banking activities.

◆ The indebtedness of the corporate sector was tiered, with the biggest firms actually being extremely well positioned to withstand the crisis. The middle and lower tier companies by size, however, were heavily dependent on debt, particularly short-term debt for working capital financing. Many were now having trouble in both servicing existing debt and gaining access to new debt to stave off declining business conditions.

◆ The Fortune 500 companies had two balance sheet characteristics that seemed to have predicted the crisis. First, the right-hand side of their balance sheets was extremely clean. They held record-low levels of debt, having reduced borrowing and paying down debt over the previous five-year period. Second, they were holding record-high levels of cash and marketable securities on the left-hand side of their balance sheets. This gave them ready cash even if their bank lines did dry up.

◆ Even within the top tier, the lowest indebted firms, the repercussions continued. Many corporate treasurers in the Fortune 500 now discovered that much of their marketable security portfolio, invested so safely and carefully with high-quality mutual funds and banks, had actually been invested in a variety of securities, derivatives, and funds that were now failing, despite all policy statements in place and supposedly adhered to.

◆ All corporate borrowers were suddenly confronted by banks reducing their access to credit. Companies that did not have preexisting lines of credit could not gain access to funds at any price. Companies with preexisting lines of credit were now receiving notification that their lines were being reduced. (This was particularly heavy in London, but also seen in New York.) As a result, many companies, although not needing the funds, chose to draw down their existing lines of credit before they could be reduced. This was clearly a panic response, and in fact worked to reduce credit availability for all.

◆ The commercial paper market nearly ceased to operate in September and October. Although the CP market had always been a short-term money market, more than 90% of all issuances in September 2008 were overnight. The markets no longer trusted the credit quality of any counterparty—whether they be hedge funds, money market funds, mutual funds, investment banks, commercial banks, or corporations. The U.S. Federal Reserve stepped in quickly, announcing that it would now buy billions in CP issuances in order to add liquidity into the system.

◆ Traditional commercial bank lending for working capital financing, automobile loans, student loans, and credit card debt were squeezed out by the huge losses from the investment banking activities. Thus began the credit squeeze worldwide, a decline of asset prices, increased unemployment, burgeoning real estate foreclosures, and a general global economic malaise.

Global Contagion

Although it is difficult to ascribe causality, the rapid collapse of the mortgage-backed securities markets in the United States definitely spread to the global marketplace. Capital invested in equity and debt instruments in all major financial markets fled not only for cash, but for cash in traditional safe-haven countries and markets. Equity markets fell worldwide, while capital fled many of the world's most promising emerging markets. Exhibit 5.11 illustrates clearly how markets fell in September and October 2008, and how they remained volatile ("jittery" in the Street's lexicon) in the months that followed.

EXHIBIT 5.11   Selected Stock Markets during the Crisis

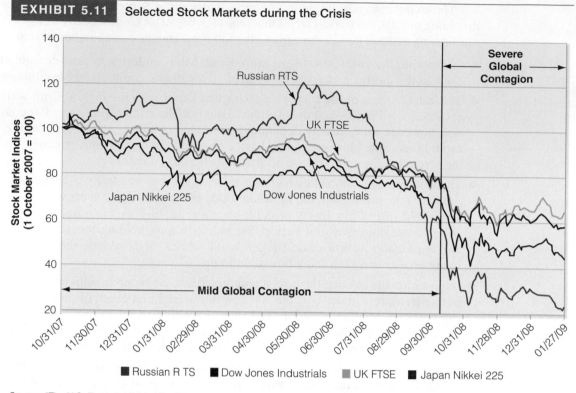

Source: "The U.S. Financial Crisis: The Global Dimension with Implications for U.S. Policy," Dick K. Nanto Congressional Research Service, Washington D.C., January 29, 2009, p.11.

The impact was felt immediately in the currencies of a multitude of the more financially open emerging markets. Many currencies now fell against the traditional three safe-haven currencies, the dollar, the euro, and the yen: the Icelandic krona, Hungarian forint, Pakistani rupee, Indian rupee, South Korean won, Mexican peso, Brazilian real, to name a few.

The spring of 2009, saw a mortgage marketplace that continued to deteriorate. Alt-A mortgages were now reaching record delinquency levels, higher than even subprime mortgages. It was now apparent that many of the mortgages that were pumped into the system near the end of the housing boom as Alt-A or "near-prime" mortgages were in fact subprime. Although possessing an historical average delinquency rate of less than 1%, the Alt-A mortgage debt originated in 2006 was now above 11%. Credit ratings of outstanding securities were at horrendous levels. Moody's, for example, downgraded more than $59 billion in Alt-A securities in a three-day period alone in January 2009, most of which fell instantly to speculative grade. Eventually it was expected that 25% of all Alt-A mortgage security debt would fail.

By January 2009, the credit crisis was having additionally complex impacts on global markets—and global firms. As financial institutions and markets faltered in many industrial countries, pressure of all kinds, business, market, and political, increased to focus on the needs of "their own." A new form of antiglobalization force arose, the differentiation of the domestic from the multinational. This new form of *financial mercantilism* focused on supporting the home-country financial and nonfinancial firms first, all others second. Multinational companies, even in emerging markets, now saw increasing indicators that they were being assessed higher credit risks and lower credit qualities, even though they theoretically had greater business diversity and the wherewithal to withstand the onslaught. The financial press categorized the credit dynamics as *homeward flow*. Credit conditions and a variety of new government bailout plans were underway in Australia, Belgium, Canada, France, Germany, Iceland, Ireland, Italy, Luxembourg, Spain, Sweden, the United Kingdom, and the United States.

The credit crisis, which had first started in the summer of 2007, now moved to a third stage. The first stage had been the failure of specific mortgage-backed securities. These had caused the fall of specific funds and instruments. The second stage had seen the crisis spread to the very foundations of the organizations at the core of the global financial system, the commercial and investment banks on all continents. This third new stage had been feared from the beginning—a credit-induced global recession of potential depression-like depths. Not only had lending stopped, but also in many cases, borrowing and investing had ceased. Although interest rates in U.S. dollar markets hovered little above zero, the price was not the issue. The prospects for investment returns of all types were now dim. The corporate sector did not see economic opportunities and returns to new investment. Budgets were slashed, layoffs continued, and the economies of the industrial world retrenched.

What's Wrong with LIBOR?

Today's failure of confidence is based on three related issues: the solvency of banks, their ability to fund themselves in illiquid markets and the health of the real economy.

—"The Credit Crunch: Saving the System," *The Economist*, October 9, 2008.

The global financial markets have always depended upon commercial banks for their core business activity. In turn, the banks have always depended on the interbank market for the liquid linkage to all of their nonbank activity, their loans and financing of multinational business. But throughout 2008 and early 2009, the interbank market was, in one analyst's words, "behaving badly." LIBOR was clearly the culprit.

The interbank market has historically operated, on its highest levels, as a "no-name" market. This meant that for the banks at the highest level of international credit quality, interbank transactions could be conducted without discriminating by name. Therefore, they traded among themselves at no differential credit risk premiums. A major money center bank trading on such a level was said to be *trading on the run*. Banks that were considered to be of slightly less credit quality, sometimes reflecting more country risk than credit risk, paid slightly higher to borrow in the interbank market. The market itself still preferred not to price on an individual basis, often categorizing many banks by tier.

But much of this changed in the summer of 2007 as many subprime mortgages began to fail. As they fell, the derivatives that had fed on those mortgages fell, the Collateralized Debt Obligations (CDOs), and with them a number of hedge funds. As individual financial institutions, commercial and investment banks alike, started suffering more and more losses related to bad loans and credits, the banks themselves became the object of much debate.

LIBOR's Role

In the spring of 2008, the British Bankers Association (BBA), the organization charged with the daily tabulation and publication of LIBOR Rates, became worried about the validity of its own published rate. The growing stress in the financial markets had actually created incentives for banks surveyed for LIBOR calculation to report lower rates than they were actually paying. A bank that had historically been considered to be *on the run*, but now suddenly reported having to pay higher rates in the interbank market, would be raising concerns that it no longer was of the same steadfast credit quality. The BBA collects quotes from 16 banks of seven different countries daily, including the United States, Switzerland, and Germany. Rate quotes are collected for 15 different maturities, ranging from one day to one year across 10 different currencies.[9] But the BBA has become concerned that even its survey wording—"at what rate

---

[9]After collecting the 16 quotes by maturity and currency, the BBA eliminates the four highest and four lowest rates reported, and averages the remaining ones to determine various published LIBOR rates.

could the bank borrow a reasonable amount?"—was leading to some reporting irregularities. There were increasing differences in the interpretation of "reasonable."

As the crisis deepened in September and October 2008, many corporate borrowers began to argue publicly that LIBOR rates published were in fact understating their problems. Many loan agreements with banks have *market disruption* clauses that allow banks to actually charge corporate borrowers their "real cost of funds," not just the published LIBOR. When markets are under stress and banks have to pay more and more to fund themselves, they need to pass the higher costs on to their corporate clients. Of course, this is only for corporate borrowers with pre-existing loan agreements with the banks. Corporate borrowers attempting to arrange new loan agreements were being quoted ever-higher prices at considerable spreads over LIBOR.

LIBOR, although only one of several key interest rates in the global marketplace, has been the focus of much attention and anxiety of late. In addition to its critical role in the interbank market, it has become widely used as the basis for all floating rate debt instruments of all kinds. This includes mortgages, corporate loans, industrial development loans, and the multitudes of financial derivatives sold throughout the global marketplace. The BBA recently estimated that LIBOR was used in the pricing of more than $360 trillion in assets globally. LIBOR's central role in the markets is illustrated in Exhibit 5.12. It was therefore a source of much concern when LIBOR rates literally skyrocketed in September 2008.

In principle, central banks around the world set the level of interest rates in their currencies and economies. But these rates are for lending between the central bank and the banks of the banking system. The result is that although the central bank sets the rate it lends at, it does not dictate the rate at which banks lend either between themselves or to non-bank borrowers. As illustrated in Exhibit 5.13, in July and August prior to the September crises, 3-month LIBOR was averaging just under 80 basis points higher than the 3-month interest rate swap index—the difference being termed the *TED Spread*. TED is an acronym for T-bill and ED (the ticker symbol for the Eurodollar futures contract). In September and October 2008,

---

EXHIBIT 5.12   LIBOR and the Crisis in Lending

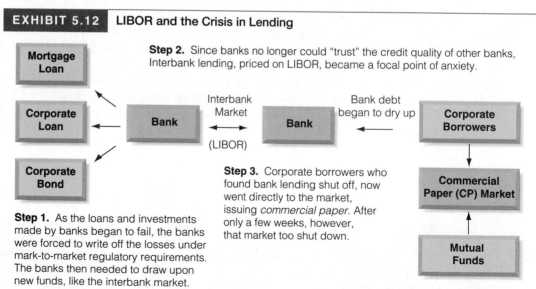

Step 2. Since banks no longer could "trust" the credit quality of other banks, Interbank lending, priced on LIBOR, became a focal point of anxiety.

Mortgage Loan

Corporate Loan

Corporate Bond

Bank — Interbank Market (LIBOR) — Bank

Bank debt began to dry up

Corporate Borrowers

Commercial Paper (CP) Market

Mutual Funds

Step 1. As the loans and investments made by banks began to fail, the banks were forced to write off the losses under mark-to-market regulatory requirements. The banks then needed to draw upon new funds, like the interbank market.

Step 3. Corporate borrowers who found bank lending shut off, now went directly to the market, issuing *commercial paper*. After only a few weeks, however, that market too shut down.

Step 4. Mutual funds and other nonbank investors were no longer willing to invest in CP as corporate borrowers began to suffer from falling business conditions and failure to pay.

however, the spread rose to more than 350 basis points, 3.5%, as the crisis caused many banks to question the credit quality of other banks. Even this spread proved misleading. The fact was that many banks were completely "locked-out" of the interbank market. Regardless of what they may or may not have been willing to pay for funds, they could not get them.

What is also apparent from Exhibit 5.13 is the impact of the various U.S. Treasury and Federal Reserve actions to "re-float" the market. As banks stopped lending in mid- to late-September, and many interbank markets became illiquid, the U.S. financial authorities worked feverishly to inject funds into the marketplace. The result was the rapid reduction in the 3-month Interest Rate Swap Index. The TED Spread remained relatively wide only a short period of time, with LIBOR actually falling to under 1.5% by the end of 2008. In January 2009, the TED Spread returned to a more common spread of under 80 basis points.[10]

Of course, the larger, more creditworthy companies do not have to borrow exclusively from banks, but may issue debt directly to the market in the form of *commercial paper*. In September 2008, when many commercial banks were no longer answering the phone, many corporate borrowers did just that. The commercial paper market, however, also quickly fell as many of the market's traditional buyers of commercial paper—other commercial banks, hedge funds, private equity funds, and even the SIVs discussed earlier—all now shied away from buying the paper. By mid-October, the commercial paper market saw issuances fall from an already low $1.75 billion weekly to just above $1.4 billion. Even CP sold by the traditionally secure General Electric jumped 40 basis points. Many of the buyers of CP now worried that the declining economy would result in an increasing default rate by CP issuers. As the CP market locked-up, the corporate sector saw another door to capital close.

EXHIBIT 5.13   The U.S. Dollar TED Spread (July 2008–January 2009)

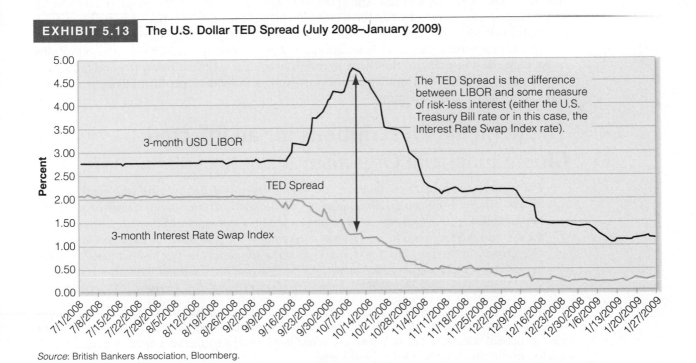

Source: British Bankers Association, Bloomberg.

---

[10]The TED Spread is often calculated using the maturity equivalent to LIBOR in U.S. Treasuries, in this case, the 3-month U.S. Treasury Bill yield. In fact, in late 2008 the U.S. 3-month Treasury Bill yield hovered around zero.

GLOBAL FINANCE IN PRACTICE   5.1

Financial Fraud and Financial Recovery

The purported fraudulent activity behind much of the global credit crisis involved the rather complex relationships between financial institutions and their customers and partners of all kinds. Simply put, much of it involved the abuse of trust.

In the spring of 2011, the American International Group (AIG), filed a series of lawsuits against other Wall Street investment banking and financial services firms. AIG had been the recipient of enormous quantities of bailout capital at the height of the September 2008 crisis. As a result, although still a possession of the U.S. government, any funds recouped from fraudulent investing or lending activities would go toward repaying taxpayers.

One example of this financial pursuit was in AIG's filing in the Supreme Court of the State of New York against ICP Asset management.* In its complaint, AIG asserted that "the

scheme perpetrated by the ICP Defendants involved numerous breaches of their contractual and fiduciary duties to AIG-FP." It also noted that most of the facts, circumstances, and allegations were the same as those filed by the Securities and Exchange Commission (SEC) in its complaint filed against ICP.

ICP was the underwriter of several large failed CDOs called Triaxx-1 and Triaxx-2. The proceeds earned from the sale of the CDOs were used to purchase residential mortgage-backed securities. AIG asserts that ICP then not only entered into a series of credit default swaps ensuring against the failure of the underlying notes, but also purchased hundreds of millions of dollars of the senior notes themselves, ultimately exposing AIG to significant loss.

*Technically, the listed defendants were ICP Asset Management, LLC, ICP Securities, LLC, Institutional Credit Partners, LLC, Triaxx Prime CDO 2007-1, Ltd., Triaxx Funding High Grade I, Ltd. Moore Capital Management, LP, and John Does 1-10.

The credit crisis was worsened by the destabilizing effects of speculators betting that particular CDOs would fail. The trick was to create and sell CDOs with enough risky mortgages that the CDO was likely to fail. The speculator bought credit default swaps (CDSs) which should repay what was lost when the CDO failed. The investors lost their money.[11]

Although legal suits like these will most likely wind their way through the American court system for many years, the basic question of *fiduciary responsibility*—the responsibility to act in the best interests of the client, to carry out their responsibilities with good faith, honesty, integrity, loyalty and undivided service—versus individual profit motives, is in many ways at the heart of the dilemma.

The Remedy: Prescriptions for an Infected Global Financial Organism

Put crudely, the bright new finance is the highly leveraged, lightly regulated, market-based system of allocating capital dominated by Wall Street. It is the spivvy successor to "traditional banking," in which regulated commercial banks lent money to trusted clients and held the debt on their books. The new system evolved over the past three decades and saw explosive growth in the past few years thanks to three simultaneous but distinct developments: deregulation, technological innovation and the growing international mobility of capital.
    —"The World Economy: Taming the Beast," *The Economist*, October 8, 2008.

So where now for the global financial markets? Dismissing the absolute extremes, on one end that capitalism has failed, and on the other end that extreme regulation is the only solution, what practical solutions fall in between? What if we return to the sequence of events which has led to the most recent global credit crisis?

[11]Two recommended books chronicling the risky practices of some Wall Street firms and their executives are *The End of Wall Street* by Roger Lowenstein (Penguin Press, New York, 2010) and *The Big Short* by Michael Lewis (W.W. Norton and Company, New York and London, 2010).

Debt

Was the mortgage boom itself the problem? The market largely boomed as a result of the combination of few competing investments (equity markets had fallen) with the low cost and great availability of capital. Of greater concern was the originate-to-distribute behavior combined with questionable credit assessments and classifications. New guidelines for credit quality and access to mortgages are already underway.

As illustrated by *Global Finance in Practice 5.2*, there were a number of additional surprises—unintended consequences—from the financial bailout.

Securitization

Was the financial technique of combining assets into packaged portfolios for trading the problem, or the lack of transparency and accountability for the individual elements within the portfolio? Although portfolio theory itself has been used for risk reduction since the 1960s, it was always used in the construction of assets with uncorrelated movements. In the case of mortgage-backed securities, however, the portfolio components were so similar that the only benefit was that the holder "hoped" that all the same securities would not fall into delinquency simultaneously. This was not the premise of portfolio theory.

Derivatives

This is not the first time that derivatives have been the source of substantial market failures, and it will most likely not be the last. They are the core of financial technological innovation. But derivatives are only devices and tools, and they are not better or worse than those using them. The creation of complex mortgage-backed assets and derivative structures which ultimately made the securities nearly impossible to value, particularly in thin markets, was in hindsight a very poor choice. Renewed regulatory requirements, increasing reporting, and greater degrees of transparency in pricing and valuation will aid in pulling derivatives back from the brink.

Deregulation

Regulation itself is complex enough in today's rapidly changing financial marketplace, and deregulation has the tendency to put very dangerous tools and toys in the hands of the uninitiated. Certain corrections have clearly been needed from the beginning. For example,

---

GLOBAL FINANCE IN PRACTICE   **5.2**

Refinancing Opportunities and the Credit Crisis

One of the more unusual outcomes of the credit crisis in the fall of 2008 was the opportunity for many companies to buy back their own debt at fractions of face value. The crisis had driven secondary market prices of debt, particularly speculative grade debt, extremely low. In some cases, outstanding debt was trading at 30% of face value. Now, if the issuing company had available cash, or access to new lower cost sources of debt, it could repurchase its outstanding debt at fire sale prices. The actual repurchase could be from the public market, or via a debt tender, where an offer would be extended directly to all current debt holders.

A multitude of companies including FreeScale, First Data, GenTek, and Weyerhauser have taken advantage of the opportunity to retire more costly debt at discount prices. Many companies currently held by private equity investors, who have access to additional financial resources, have moved aggressively to repurchase. Firms have focused particularly on debt issuances which are coming due in the short-term, particularly if they feared difficulty in refinancing.

There have been a number of unintended consequences, however. A number of the distressed financial institutions have used some of the government funds provided under bailout lending to repurchase their own debt. Morgan Stanley reported earnings of more than $2.1 billion in the fourth quarter of 2008 from just buying back $12 billion of its own debt. Although this does indeed shore up the balance sheets, the primary intent of the government-backed capital had been to renew lending and financing by the banks to the nonbank financial sector—commercial businesses—in hopes of restarting general business activity, not to generate bank profits from the refinancing of its own portfolio.

the lack of regulatory oversight and exchange trading of credit default swaps is already in the works. There are many today who argue that financial markets do indeed need to be regulated, but of course the degree and type is unclear. This will be a growing arena of debate in the coming years.

Capital Mobility

Capital is more mobile today than ever before. This increased capital mobility, when combined with the growth in capital markets in general and the new openness in many economies in particular, will likely produce more and more cases of financial-induced crisis. The dilemmas of Iceland and New Zealand in recent years are only the beginning of this phenomenon.

Illiquid Markets

This finally, will be the most troublesome. Most of the mathematics and rational behavior behind the design of today's sophisticated financial products, derivatives, and investment vehicles are based on principles of orderly and liquid markets. When the trading of highly commoditized securities or positions as clean as overnight bank loans between banks becomes the core source of instability in the system then all traditional knowledge and assumptions of finance have indeed gone out the window. *Global Finance in Practice 5.3* explains why history-based models can lead to flawed conclusions—at least in the eyes of one rather famous investor.

Troubled Asset Recovery Plan (TARP)

After a difficult debate and several failed attempts, the U.S. Congress passed the Troubled Asset Recovery Plan (TARP). It was signed by President G.W. Bush in October 2008. TARP authorized the U.S. government to use up to $700 billion to support—*bail-out*—the riskiest large banks. At that time, the U.S. stock market was at its lowest level in four years.

The bailout was especially useful in shoring up the largest banks and their insurers, such as AIG, that were deemed "too big to fail." (The "too big to fail" tag goes far back in financial history, and indicates that if these large institutions were allowed to collapse, they would take a multitude of smaller institutions with them, both financial and nonfinancial. A failure ripple-effect of this magnitude is simply considered unacceptable by most governments.) For example, AIG gained access to $85 billion of federal bailout funds because it was the largest issuer of CDSs. If these had been allowed to fail, they would have clearly caused

---

GLOBAL FINANCE IN PRACTICE   5.3

Warren Buffett on the Credit Crisis

The type of fallacy involved in projecting loss experience from a universe of noninsured bonds onto a deceptively similar universe in which many bonds are insured pops up in other areas of finance. "Back-tested" models of many kinds are susceptible to this sort of error. Nevertheless, they are frequently touted in financial markets as guides to future action. (If merely looking up past financial data would tell you what the future holds, the Forbes 400 would consist of librarians.)

Indeed, the stupefying losses in mortgage-related securities came in large part because of flawed, history-based models used by salesmen, rating agencies, and investors. These parties looked at loss experience over periods when home prices rose only moderately and speculation in houses was negligible. They then made this experience a yardstick for evaluating future losses. They blissfully ignored the fact that house prices had recently skyrocketed, loan practices had deteriorated and many buyers had opted for houses they couldn't afford. In short, universe "past" and universe "current" had very different characteristics. But lenders, government and media largely failed to recognize this all-important fact.

Investors should be skeptical of history-based models. Constructed by a nerdy sounding priesthood using esoteric terms such as beta, gamma, sigma, and the like, these models tend to look impressive. Too often, though, investors forget to examine the assumptions behind the symbols. Our advice: Beware of geeks bearing formulas.

Source: Berkshire Hathaway Annual Report, 2008, Letter to Shareholders, pp. 14–15.

the failure of a number of other major financial institutions. The U.S. government received an 80% equity interest in AIG in return for its capital injection.

Liquidity versus Capital

Starting as early as August 10, 2008, the U.S. Federal Reserve purchased billions of dollars of mortgage-backed securities, CDOs, in an attempt to inject liquidity into the credit market. Although liquidity was indeed a major portion of the problem, massive write-offs of failed mortgages by the largest banks were equally serious. The write-offs weakened the equity capital positions of these institutions. It would, therefore, be necessary for the private sector or the government to inject new equity capital into the riskiest banks and insurers—insolvency in addition to illiquidity.

The U.S. Federal Reserve and U.S. Treasury both encouraged the private sector banks to solve their own problems. This could be done by new equity issues, conversion of investment banks to commercial banks to get direct access to the Fed, and depositors funds and mergers. But the market for new equity issues for these weakened banks was unfavorable at this time; as a result, mergers were the strongest remaining alternative. The largest stock brokerage in the United States, Merrill Lynch, was merged into Bank of America. Morgan Stanley, a leading investment bank, sold a 20% equity interest to Mitsubishi Bank of Tokyo. Wachovia Bank was merged into Wells Fargo. Lehman Brothers was courted by Barclays Bank (U.K.) but failed to reach a timely agreement. It was then forced to declare bankruptcy, the largest bank failure in many years. Lehman's failure had many of the ripple effects feared, as its role in the commercial paper market could not be replaced. The Mini-Case at the end of this chapter chronicles the demise of Lehman Brothers.

The bailout included governmental institutions as well as private institutions. On September 7, 2008, the government announced it was placing Fannie Mae (the Federal National Mortgage Association) and Freddie Mac (the Federal Home Loan Mortgage Corporation) into conservatorship. In essence, the government was taking over the institutions as a result of their near insolvencies.

Golden Parachutes

A number of failing banks and other firms forced their top executives to resign or be fired. Many of these executives had previously negotiated contractual agreements that compensated them handsomely if they were separated from the firm, and this became an area of significant debate during the bailout.

Financial Reform 2010

The most recent response by the U.S. government to the excesses revealed by the credit crisis of 2007–2009 was the passage of the Financial Reform Law of 2010. Some key features follow:

◆ An Office of Financial Research was established. Financial firms must release confidential information that could help spot future potential market crises. The office can demand all the data necessary from financial firms, including banks, hedge funds, private equity funds, and brokerages.

◆ The Federal Deposit Insurance Corporation (FDIC) would permanently increase its protection of bank deposit accounts from the previous $100,000 to $250,000 per account.

◆ The SEC can sue lawyers, accountants, and other professionals, who know about a deceptive act, even if they weren't the wrongdoer.

◆ The Treasury will set up an office to monitor and modernize state regulation of insurance.

◆ Institutions must disclose the amount of short selling in each stock. Brokers must notify investors that they can stop their shares from being borrowed for a short sale.

EXHIBIT 5.14   The Global Financial Crash

Cross-Border Capital Inflows
(trillion US$, 2008 exchange rates)

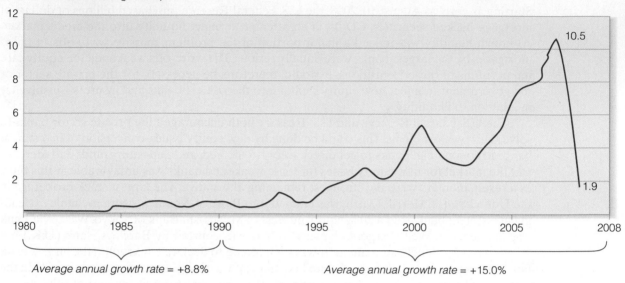

Average annual growth rate = +8.8%   Average annual growth rate = +15.0%

Source: "Global Capital Markets: Entering a New Era," McKinsey Global Institute, September 2009, p.14.

The Future

As long as the impacts of the global financial crisis are still under study, it is also clear that the sheer magnitude of the crisis may have been even larger than originally suspected. As illustrated by the analysis of global cross-border capital flows by McKinsey in Exhibit 5.14, international capital flows plummeted in 2008 to levels not seen since 2002. Although the global economy and capital markets have started the long road back to recovery, the lingering impacts of sparse capital flowing to companies and countries around the globe will have long-term impacts on the growth potential of much of the developing world.

Summary of Learning Objectives

Learn how a variety of economic, regulatory, and social forces led to the real estate market growth and collapse

◆ The seeds of the credit crisis were sown in the deregulation of the commercial and investment banking sectors in the 1990s.

◆ The flow of capital into the real estate sector in the post-2000 period reflected changes in social and economic forces in the U.S. economy.

Examine the various dimensions of defining and classifying individual borrowers in terms of their credit quality

◆ Mortgage loans in the U.S. marketplace are normally categorized as *prime* (A-paper), *Alt-A* (Alternative-A paper), and *subprime*, in increasing order of riskiness.

◆ Subprime borrowers, historically not considered creditworthy for mortgages, became an acceptable credit risk as a result of major deregulation initiatives.

Consider the role that financial derivatives and securitization played in the formation of the international credit crisis

◆ The transport vehicle for the growing distribution of lower-quality debt was a combination of securitization and re-packaging provided by a series of new financial derivatives.

◆ Securitization allowed the re-packaging of different combinations of credit-quality mortgages in order to make them more attractive for resale to other financial institutions; derivative construction increased the liquidity in the market for these securities.

Identify the characteristics and components of a number of the instrumental financial derivatives contributing to the spread of the credit crisis including collateralized debt obligations (CDOs), structured investment vehicles (SIVs), and credit default swaps (CDSs)

◆ The *structured investment vehicle* (SIV) was the ultimate financial intermediation device: It borrowed short and invested long.

◆ The SIV was an off-balance sheet entity designed to allow a bank to create an investment entity that would invest in long-term and higher yielding assets such as speculative grade bonds, mortgage-backed securities (MBSs) and collateralized debt obligations (CDOs), while funding itself through commercial paper (CP) issuances.

◆ The CDO, *collateralized debt obligation*, is a portfolio of debt instruments—mortgages—which are re-packaged as an asset-backed security. Once packaged, the bank passes the security to a *special purpose vehicle* (SPV).

◆ The *credit default swap* (CDS) is a contract, a derivative, which derived its value from the credit quality and performance of any specified asset. The CDS was designed to shift the risk of default to a third-party. In short, it was a way to bet whether a specific mortgage or security would either fail to pay on time or fail to pay at all.

Examine how LIBOR, the most widely used cost of money, reacted to the growing tensions and risk perceptions between international financial institutions during the crisis

◆ LIBOR, although only one of several key interest rates in the global marketplace, plays a critical role in the interbank market as the basis for all floating rate debt instruments of all kinds. This includes mortgages, corporate loans, industrial development loans, and the multitudes of financial derivatives sold throughout the global marketplace.

◆ With the onset of the credit crisis in September 2008, LIBOR rates skyrocketed between major international banks, indicating a growing fear of counterparty default in a market historically considered the highest quality and most liquid in the world.

Evaluate the various remedies and prescriptions being pushed forward by a variety of governments and international organizations for the infected global financial organism

◆ The U.S. Congress passed the Troubled Asset Recovery Plan (TARP), which authorized the U.S. government to use up to $700 billion to bail out the riskiest large banks.

◆ The U.S. Federal Reserve purchased billions in mortgage-backed securities, CDOs, in the months following the credit crisis in an attempt to inject liquidity into the credit markets.

◆ As a result of the massive write-offs of failed mortgages by the largest banks, the banks suffered weakened equity capital positions, making it necessary for the private sector and the government to inject new equity capital into the riskiest banks and insurers.

MINI-CASE

Letting Go of Lehman Brothers[1]

There are other things the Treasury might do when a major financial firm assumed to be "too big to fail" comes knocking, asking for free money. Here's one: Let it fail.

Not as chaotically as Lehman Brothers was allowed to fail. If a failing firm is deemed "too big" for that honor, then it should be explicitly nationalized, both to limit its effect on other firms and to protect the guts of the system. Its shareholders should be wiped out, and its

management replaced. Its valuable parts should be sold off as functioning businesses to the highest bidders— perhaps to some bank that was not swept up in the credit bubble. The rest should be liquidated, in calm markets. Do this and, for everyone except the firms that invented the mess, the pain will likely subside.

—"How to Repair a Broken Financial World," by Michael Lewis and David Einhorn, *The New York Times*, January 4, 2009.

Should Lehman Brothers have been allowed to fail? This is one of the lasting debates over the U.S. government's actions, or in this case inaction, in its attempts to fix the failing U.S. financial system in late 2008. Allowing Lehman to fail—it filed for bankruptcy on September 15, 2008—was in the eyes of many in the global financial markets the individual event that caused the global credit crisis which followed.

Lehman Brothers was founded in 1850 in Alabama by a pair of enterprising brothers. After moving the firm to New York following the American Civil War, the firm had long been considered one of the highest return, highest risk small investment banking firms on Wall Street. Although it had lived and nearly died by the sword many times over the years, by 2008 the firm was holding an enormous portfolio of failing mortgage-backed securities and the future was not bright.

Lehman's demise was not a shock, but a slow and painful downward spiral. After two major Bear Stearn's hedge funds collapsed in July 2007, Lehman was the constant focus of much speculation over its holdings of many of the distressed securities behind the credit crisis—the collateralized debt obligations and credit default swaps that had flooded the market as a result of the real estate and mortgage lending boom of the 2000 to 2007 period.

Too Big to Fail

The "too big to fail" doctrine has long been a mainstay of the U.S. financial system. The U.S. Federal Reserve has long held the responsibility as the *lender of last resort*, the institution that is charged with assuring the financial stability and viability of the U.S. financial system. Although it has exercised its powers only rarely in history, the Fed, in conjunction with the Comptroller of the Currency and the Federal Deposit Insurance Corporation (FDIC), has on a few occasions determined that an individual large bank's failure would threaten the health and functioning of the financial system. In those cases, for example Continental Illinois of Chicago in 1984, the three organizations had stepped in to effectively nationalize the institution and arrange for its continued operation to prevent what were believed to be disastrous results.

The doctrine, however, had largely been confined to commercial banks, not investment banks who made their money by intentionally taking on riskier classes of securities and positions on behalf of their investors—who expected greater returns. Lehman was clearly a risk taker. But the distinction between commercial and investment banking was largely gone, as more and more deregulation efforts had successfully reduced the barriers between taking deposits and making consumer and commercial loans, with traditional investment banking activities of underwriting riskier debt and equity issuances with a lessened fiduciary responsibility.

Many critics have argued that for some reason Lehman was singled out for failure. One week prior to Lehman's bankruptcy, the Federal Reserve and U.S. Treasury under Secretary of the Treasury Hank Paulson, Jr., had bailed out both Fannie Mae and Freddie Mac, putting them into U.S. government receivership. Two days following Lehman's bankruptcy filings, the Federal Reserve had extended AIG, an insurance conglomerate, an $85 billion loan package to prevent its failure. So why not Lehman?

Why Not Lehman?

Lehman had already survived one near miss. When Bear Stearns had failed in March 2008 and its sale arranged by the U.S. government, Lehman had been clearly in the cross-hairs of the financial speculators, particularly the short sellers. Its longtime CEO, Richard Fuld Jr., had been a vocal critic of the short sellers who continued to pound Lehman in the summer of 2008. But CEO Fuld had been encouraged by investors, regulators, and critics to find a way out of its mess following the close call in March. Secretary Paulson had gone on record following Lehman's June earnings reports (which showed massive losses) that if Lehman had not arranged a sale by the end of the third quarter there would likely be a crisis.

But repeated efforts by Fuld at finding buyers for different parts of the company failed, from Wall Street to the Middle East to Asia. Fuld has since argued that one of the reasons he wasn't able to arrange a sale was the U.S. government was not offering the same attractive guarantees it had put forward when arranging the sale of Bear Stearns.[2] The Fed has successfully arranged the sale of Bear Stearns to J.P. Morgan Chase only after the Fed agreed to cover $29 billion in losses. In fact, in August 2008, just weeks prior to its failure, Lehman believed it had found two suitors, Bank of America and Barclays, that would quickly step up if the Federal Reserve would guarantee $65 billion in potential bad loans on Lehman's books. The Fed declined.

Another proposal that had shown promise had been a self-insurance approach by Wall Street. Lehman would be split into a "good bank" and a "bad bank." The good bank would be composed of the higher quality assets and securities, and would be purchased by either Bank of America or Barclays. The bad bank would be a dumping ground of failing mortgage-backed securities which would be purchased by a consortium of 12 to 15 Wall Street financial institutions, not requiring any government funding or taxpayer dollars. The plan ultimately failed when the potential bad

---

[2]Fuld's own wealth and compensation had been the subject of much criticism. It has been estimated that Fuld's total compensation by Lehman over the previous five years was more than $500 million, and that his personal wealth was more than $1 billion early in 2008 (prior to the fall in Lehman's share price).

bank borrowers could not face their own losses and acquire Lehman's losses, while either Bank of America or Barclays walked away with high quality assets at the price of a song. In the end, only one day after Lehman's collapse, Barclays announced that it would buy Lehman's United States capital markets division for $1.75 billion, a "steal" according to one analyst.

Secretary Paulson has argued that in fact his hands were tied. The Federal Reserve is required by law only to lend to, and is limited by, the amount of asset collateral any specific institution has to offer against rescue loans. (This is in fact the defining principle behind the Fed's discount window operations.) But many critics have argued that it was not possible to determine the collateral value of the securities held by Lehman or AIG or Fannie Mae and Freddie Mac accurately at this time because of the credit crisis and the illiquidity of markets. Secretary Paulson had never been heard to make the argument before the time of the bankruptcy.

It also became readily apparent that following the AIG rescue the U.S. authorities moved quickly to try to create a systemic solution, rather than continuing to be bounced from one individual institutional crisis to another. Secretary Paulson has noted that it was increasingly clear that a larger solution was required, and that saving Lehman would not have stopped the larger crisis. Others have noted, however, that Lehman was one of the largest commercial paper issuers in the world. In the days following Lehman's collapse, the commercial paper market literally locked up. The seizing of the commercial paper market in turn eliminated the primary source of liquid funds between mutual banks, hedge funds, and banks of all kinds. The crisis was now in full bloom.

Executives on Wall Street and officials in European financial capitals have criticized Mr. Paulson and Mr. Bernanke for allowing Lehman to fail, an event that sent shock waves through the banking system, turning a financial tremor into a tsunami.

"For the equilibrium of the world financial system, this was a genuine error," Christine Lagarde, France's finance minister, said recently. Frederic Oudea, chief executive of Société Générale, one of France's biggest banks, called the failure of Lehman "a trigger" for events leading to the global crash. Willem Sels, a credit strategist with Dresdner Kleinwort, said that "it is clear that when Lehman defaulted, that is the date your money markets freaked out. It is difficult to not find a causal relationship."

—"The Reckoning: Struggling to Keep Up as the Crisis Raced On," by Joe Nocera and Edmund L. Andrews, *The New York Times*, October 22, 2008.

CASE QUESTIONS

1. Do you think that the U.S. government treated some financial institutions differently during the crisis? Was that appropriate?

2. Many experts argue that when the government bails out a private financial institution it creates a problem called "moral hazard," meaning that if the institution knows it will be saved, it actually has an incentive to take on more risk, not less. What do you think?

3. Do you think that the U.S. government should have allowed Lehman Brothers to fail?

Questions

1. **Three Forces.** What were the three major forces behind the credit crisis of 2007 and 2008?

2. **MBS.** What is a mortgage-backed security (MBS)?

3. **SIV.** What is a structured investment vehicle (SIV)?

4. **CDO.** What is a collateralized debt obligation (CDO)?

5. **CDS.** What is a credit default swap (CDS)?

6. **LIBOR's Role.** Why does LIBOR receive so much attention in the global financial markets?

7. **Interbank Market.** Why do you think it is important for many of the world's largest commercial and investment banks to be considered on-the-run in the interbank market?

8. **LIBOR Treasury Spread.** Why were LIBOR rates so much higher than Treasury yields in 2007 and 2008? What is needed to return LIBOR rates to the lower, more stable levels of the past?

Problems

1. **U.S. Treasury Bill Auction Rates—March 2009.** The interest yields on U.S. Treasury securities in early 2009 fell to very low levels as a result of the combined events surrounding the global financial crisis. Calculate the simple and annualized yields for the 3-month and 6-month Treasury bills auctioned on March 9, 2009, listed here.

	3-Month T-Bill	6-Month T-Bill
Treasury bill, face value	$10,000.00	$10,000.00
Price at sale	$9,993.93	$9,976.74
Discount	$6.07	$23.26

2. **The Living Yield Curve.** *SmartMoney* magazine has what they term a *Living Yield Curve* graphic on their Internet page. This yield curve graphic simulates the U.S. dollar Treasury yield curve from 1977 through the current day. Using this graphic at

www.smartmoney.com (then go to investing/bonds/living-yield-curve), answer the following questions:

a. After checking the box labeled "Average," what is the average 90-day Treasury bill rate for the 1977 to current day time interval?

b. In what year does the U.S. Treasury yield curve appear to have reached its highest levels for the 1977 to 2009 or 2010 period?

c. In what year does the U.S. Treasury yield curve appear to have reached its lowest levels for the 1977 to 2009 or 2010 period?

3. **Credit Crisis, 2008.** The global credit crisis became globally visible in September 2007. Interest rates, particularly extremely short-term interest rates, will often change quickly (typically up) as indications that markets are under severe stress. The interest rates shown in the table below are for selected dates in September and October 2008. Different publications define the *TED Spread* different ways, but one measure is the differential between the overnight LIBOR interest rate and the 3-month U.S. Treasury bill rate.

a. Calculate the spread between the two market rates shown here in September and October 2008.

b. On what date is the spread the narrowest? The widest?

c. When the spread widens dramatically, presumably demonstrating some form of financial anxiety or crisis, which of the rates moves the most and why?

4. **U.S. Treasury Bill Auction Rates—May 2009.** The interest yields on U.S. Treasury securities continued to fall in the spring of 2009. Calculate the discount, and then the simple and annualized yields for the 3-month and 6-month Treasury bills auctioned on May 4, 2009, listed here.

	3-Month T-Bill	6-Month T-Bill
Treasury bill, face value	$10,000.00	$10,000.00
Price at sale	$9,995.07	$9,983.32

5. **Underwater Mortgages.** Bernie Madeoff pays $240,000 for a new four-bedroom 2,400-square-foot home outside Tonopah, Nevada. He plans to make a 20% down payment, but is having trouble deciding whether he wants a 15-year fixed rate (6.400%) or a 30-year fixed rate (6.875%) mortgage.

a. What is the monthly payment for both the 15- and 30-year mortgages, assuming a fully amortizing loan of equal payments for the life of the mortgage? Use a spreadsheet calculator for the payments.

b. Assume that instead of making a 20% down payment, he makes a 10% down payment, and finances the remainder at 7.125% fixed interest for 15 years. What is his monthly payment?

c. Assume that the home's total value falls by 25%. If the homeowner is able to sell the house, but now at the new home value, what would be his gain or loss on the home and mortgage assuming all of the mortgage principal remains? Use the same assumptions as in part a.

6. **Ted Spread, 2009.** If we use the same definition of the TED Spread noted in problem 3, the differential between the overnight LIBOR rate and the 3-month

Date	Overnight USD LIBOR	3-Month U.S. Treasury	TED Spread
9/8/2008	2.15%	1.70%	_____
9/9/2008	2.14%	1.65%	_____
9/10/2008	2.13%	1.65%	_____
9/11/2008	2.14%	1.60%	_____
9/12/2008	2.15%	1.49%	_____
9/15/2008	3.11%	0.83%	_____
9/16/2008	6.44%	0.79%	_____
9/17/2008	5.03%	0.04%	_____
9/18/2008	3.84%	0.07%	_____
9/19/2008	3.25%	0.97%	_____
9/22/2008	2.97%	0.85%	_____
9/23/2008	2.95%	0.81%	_____
9/24/2008	2.69%	0.45%	_____
9/25/2008	2.56%	0.72%	_____
9/26/2008	2.31%	0.85%	_____

Date	Overnight USD LIBOR	3-Month U.S. Treasury	TED Spread
9/29/2008	2.57%	0.41%	_____
9/30/2008	6.88%	0.89%	_____
10/1/2008	3.79%	0.81%	_____
10/2/2008	2.68%	0.60%	_____
10/3/2008	2.00%	0.48%	_____
10/6/2008	2.37%	0.48%	_____
10/7/2008	3.94%	0.79%	_____
10/8/2008	5.38%	0.65%	_____
10/9/2008	5.09%	0.55%	_____
10/10/2008	2.47%	0.18%	_____
10/13/2008	2.47%	0.18%	_____
10/14/2008	2.18%	0.27%	_____
10/15/2008	2.14%	0.20%	_____
10/16/2008	1.94%	0.44%	_____
10/17/2008	1.67%	0.79%	_____

U.S. Treasury bill rate, we can see how the market may have calmed by the spring of 2009. Use the following data to answer the questions below:

a. Calculate the TED Spread for the dates shown.
b. On which dates is the spread the narrowest and the widest?
c. Looking at both the spread and the underlying data series, how would you compare these values with the rates and spreads in problem 3?

Date	Overnight USD LIBOR	3-Month U.S. Treasury	TED Spread
3/12/2009	0.33%	0.19%	_____
3/13/2009	0.33%	0.18%	_____
3/16/2009	0.33%	0.22%	_____
3/17/2009	0.31%	0.23%	_____
3/18/2009	0.31%	0.21%	_____
3/19/2009	0.30%	0.19%	_____
3/20/2009	0.28%	0.20%	_____
3/23/2009	0.29%	0.19%	_____
3/24/2009	0.29%	0.21%	_____
3/25/2009	0.29%	0.18%	_____
3/26/2009	0.29%	0.14%	_____
3/27/2009	0.28%	0.13%	_____
3/30/2009	0.29%	0.12%	_____
3/31/2009	0.51%	0.20%	_____
4/1/2009	0.30%	0.21%	_____
4/2/2009	0.29%	0.20%	_____
4/3/2009	0.27%	0.20%	_____
4/6/2009	0.28%	0.19%	_____
4/7/2009	0.28%	0.19%	_____
4/8/2009	0.26%	0.18%	_____
4/9/2009	0.26%	0.18%	_____
4/14/2009	0.27%	0.17%	_____

Internet Exercises

1. **The New York Times and Times Topics.** The online version of the *The New York Times* has a special section entitled "Times Topics"—issues of continuing interest and coverage by the publication. The current financial crisis is covered and updated regularly here.

The New York Times and *Times Topics*	topics.nytimes.com/topics/ reference/timestopics/ subjects/c/credit_crisis/

2. **British Bankers Association and LIBOR.** The British Bankers Association (BBA), the author of LIBOR, provides both current data for LIBOR of varying maturities as well as timely studies of interbank market behavior and practices.

British Bankers Association and LIBOR	www.bbalibor.com

3. **Bank for International Settlements.** The Bank for International Settlements (BIS) publishes regular assessments of international banking activity. Use the BIS Web site to find up-to-date analysis of the ongoing credit crisis.

Bank for International Settlements	www.bis.org/

4. **Federal Reserve Bank of New York.** The New York Fed maintains an interactive map of mortgage and credit card delinquencies for the United States. Use the following Web site to view the latest in default rates according to the Fed.

Federal Reserve Bank of New York	data.newyorkfed.org/ creditconditionsmap/

Foreign Exchange Theory and Markets

CHAPTER 6

The Foreign Exchange Market

CHAPTER 7

International Parity Conditions

CHAPTER 8

Foreign Currency Derivatives and Swaps

6

The Foreign Exchange Market

The best way to destroy the capitalist system is to debauch the currency. By a continuing process of inflation, governments can confiscate, secretly and unobserved, an important part of the wealth of their citizens. —John Maynard Keynes.

LEARNING OBJECTIVES

◆ Examine the what, when, where, and why of currency trading in the global marketplace.

◆ Understand the definitions and distinctions between spot, forward, swaps, and other types of foreign exchange financial instruments.

◆ Learn the forms of currency quotations used by currency dealers, financial institutions, and agents of all kinds when conducting foreign exchange transactions.

◆ Analyze the interaction between changing currency values, cross exchange rates, and the opportunities arising from intermarket arbitrage.

The foreign exchange market provides the physical and institutional structure through which the money of one country is exchanged for that of another country, the rate of exchange between currencies is determined, and foreign exchange transactions are physically completed. *Foreign exchange* means the money of a foreign country; that is, foreign currency bank balances, banknotes, checks, and drafts. A *foreign exchange transaction* is an agreement between a buyer and seller that a fixed amount of one currency will be delivered for some other currency at a specified rate. This chapter describes the following features of the foreign exchange market:

◆ Its geographical extent
◆ Its three main functions
◆ Its participants
◆ Its immense daily transaction volume
◆ Types of transactions, including spot, forward, and swap transactions
◆ Methods of stating exchange rates, quotations, and changes in exchange rates

The chapter concludes with the Mini-Case, ***The Saga of the Venezuelan Bolivar Fuerte***, which details the continuing devaluation of the Venezuelan currency in 2010 and 2011.

Geographical Extent of the Foreign Exchange Market

The foreign exchange market spans the globe, with prices moving and currencies trading somewhere every hour of every business day. Major world trading starts each morning in Sydney and Tokyo, moves west to Hong Kong and Singapore, passes on to Bahrain, shifts to the main European markets of Frankfurt, Zurich, and London, jumps the Atlantic to New York, goes west to Chicago, and ends in San Francisco and Los Angeles. Many large international banks operate foreign exchange trading rooms in each major geographic trading center in order to serve important commercial accounts on a 24-hour-a-day basis. Global currency trading is indeed a 24-hour-a-day process. As shown in Exhibit 6.1, the volume of currency transactions ebbs and flows across the globe as the major currency trading centers of London, New York, and Tokyo open and close throughout the day. Exhibit 6.2 provides a general mapping of which trading centers are open when, and which centers do and do not overlap with other city markets.

In some countries, a portion of foreign exchange trading is conducted on an official trading floor by open bidding. Closing prices are published as the official price, or "fixing," for the day, and certain commercial and investment transactions are based on this official price. Business firms in countries with exchange controls, for example, China (mainland), often must surrender foreign exchange earned from exports to the central bank at the daily fixing price.

Banks engaged in foreign exchange trading are connected by highly sophisticated telecommunications networks, with dealers and brokers exchanging currency quotes instantaneously. The foreign exchange departments of many nonbank business firms also use Internet-based networks, but often access trading through the major bank trading rooms. Reuters, Telerate, and Bloomberg are the leading suppliers of foreign exchange rate information and trading systems. A growing part of the industry is automated trading, in which corporate buyers and sellers trade currencies through Internet-based platforms provided or hosted by major money center banks. Although the largest currency transactions are still handled by humans via telephone, the use of computer trading has grown dramatically in recent years.

EXHIBIT 6.1   Measuring Foreign Exchange Market Activity: Average Electronic Conversions per Hour

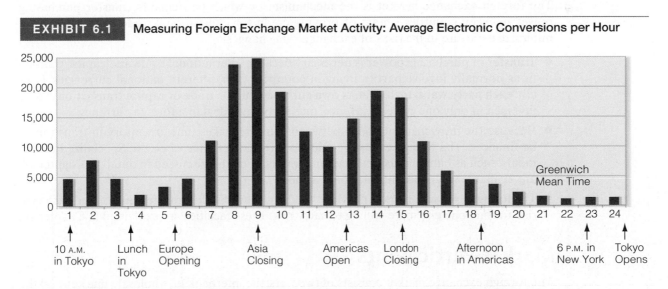

Source: Federal Reserve Bank of New York, "The Foreign Exchange Market in the United States," 2001, www.ny.frb.org.

EXHIBIT 6.2	Global Currency Trading: The Trading Day

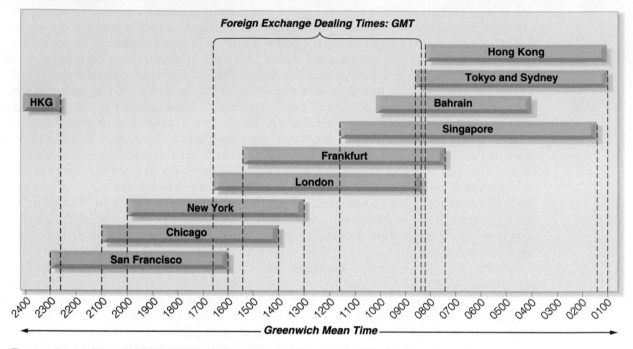

The currency trading day literally extends 24 hours per day. The busiest time of the day, however, is when New York and London overlap, the world's most liquid time of day.

Functions of the Foreign Exchange Market

The foreign exchange market is the mechanism by which participants transfer purchasing power between countries, obtain or provide credit for international trade transactions, and minimize exposure to the risks of exchange rate changes.

◆ Transfer of purchasing power is necessary because international trade and capital transactions normally involve parties living in countries with different national currencies. Usually each party, wants to deal in its own currency, but the trade or capital transaction can be invoiced in only one currency. Hence, one party must deal in a foreign currency.

◆ Because the movement of goods between countries takes time, inventory in transit must be financed. The foreign exchange market provides a source of credit. Specialized instruments, such as bankers' acceptances and letters of credit, discussed in detail in Chapter 19, are available to finance international trade.

◆ The foreign exchange market provides "hedging" facilities for transferring foreign exchange risk to someone else more willing to carry risk. These facilities are explained in Chapter 10.

Market Participants

The foreign exchange market consists of two tiers: the interbank or wholesale market, and the client or retail market. Individual transactions in the interbank market are usually for large sums that are multiples of a million U.S. dollars or the equivalent value in other currencies. By contrast, contracts between a bank and its clients are usually for specific amounts.

Five broad categories of participants operate within these two tiers: 1) bank and nonbank foreign exchange dealers; 2) individuals and firms conducting commercial or investment transactions; 3) speculators and arbitragers; 4) central banks and treasuries; and 5) foreign exchange brokers.

Bank and Nonbank Foreign Exchange Dealers

Banks, and a few nonbank foreign exchange dealers, operate in both the interbank and client markets. They profit from buying foreign exchange at a "bid" price and reselling it at a slightly higher "offer" (also called an "ask") price. Competition among dealers worldwide narrows the spread between bids and offers and so contributes to making the foreign exchange market "efficient" in the same sense as in securities markets.

Dealers in the foreign exchange departments of large international banks often function as "market makers." Such dealers stand willing at all times to buy and sell those currencies in which they specialize and thus maintain an "inventory" position in those currencies. They trade with other banks in their own monetary centers and with other centers around the world in order to maintain inventories within the trading limits set by bank policy. Trading limits are important because foreign exchange departments of many banks operate as profit centers, and individual dealers are compensated on a profit incentive basis.

Currency trading is quite profitable for commercial and investment banks. Many of the major currency-trading banks in the United States derive between 10% and 20% on average of their annual net income from currency trading. But currency trading is also very profitable for the bank's traders who typically earn a bonus based on the profitability to the bank of their individual trading activities.

Small- to medium-size banks are likely to participate but not be market makers in the interbank market. Instead of maintaining significant inventory positions, they buy from and sell to larger banks to offset retail transactions with their own customers. Of course, even market-making banks do not make markets in every currency. They trade for their own account in those currencies of most interest to their customers and become participants when filling customer needs in less important currencies. *Global Finance in Practice 6.1* describes a typical foreign exchange dealer's day on the job.

GLOBAL FINANCE IN PRACTICE   **6.1**

The Foreign Exchange Dealer's Day

How do foreign exchange dealers prepare for their working day? Foreign exchange dealing in Europe is officially opened at 8 A.M., but the dealer's work starts at least one hour earlier. Every morning, the chief dealers give their staff guidelines for their dealing activities. They will reassess their strategy on the basis of their estimation of the market over the next few months. They will also decide their tactics for the day, based on the following factors:

◆ **Trading Activities in the Past Few Hours in New York and the Far East.** Because of the time difference, banks in New York will have continued trading for several hours longer than the banks in Europe, while in the Far East the working day is already closing when the European day begins.

◆ **New Economic and Political Developments.** Following the theoretical forces that determine exchange rates, changes in interest rates, economic indicators, and monetary aggregates are the fundamental factors influencing exchange rates. Political events such as military conflicts, social unrest, the fall of a government, and so on, can also influence and sometimes even dominate the market scene.

◆ **The Bank's Own Foreign Exchange Position.** Early in the morning, market makers use electronic information systems to catch up on any events of the past night which might impact exchange rates. Charts (graphic presentations of rate movements) and screen-based rate boards allow dealers to study the latest developments in foreign exchange rates in New York and the Far East. As soon as this preparatory work is completed, the dealers will be ready for international trades (between 8 A.M. and 5 P.M.). The day starts with a series of telephone calls between the key market players, the aim being to sound out what intentions are. Until recently, brokers also acted as intermediaries in foreign exchange and money market operations.

Source: Foreign Exchange and Money Market Transactions, UBS Investment Bank, pp. 54–55.

Individuals and Firms Conducting Commercial and Investment Transactions

Importers and exporters, international portfolio investors, MNEs, tourists, and others use the foreign exchange market to facilitate execution of commercial or investment transactions. Their use of the foreign exchange market is necessary, but nevertheless incidental, to their underlying commercial or investment purpose. Some of these participants use the market to hedge foreign exchange risk as well.

Speculators and Arbitragers

Speculators and arbitragers seek to profit from trading in the market itself. They operate in their own interest, without a need or obligation to serve clients or to ensure a continuous market. Whereas dealers seek profit from the spread between bids and offers in addition to what they might gain from changes in exchange rates, speculators seek all of their profit from exchange rate changes. Arbitragers try to profit from simultaneous exchange rate differences in different markets.

A large proportion of speculation and arbitrage is conducted on behalf of major banks by traders employed by those banks. Thus, banks act both as exchange dealers and as speculators and arbitragers. (However, banks seldom admit to speculating; they characterize themselves as "taking an aggressive position"!) As described in *Global Finance in Practice 6.2*, however, trading is not for the weak of heart.

GLOBAL FINANCE IN PRACTICE   6.2

My First Day of Foreign Exchange Trading

For my internship I was working for the Treasury Front and Back Office of a major investment bank's New York branch on Wall Street. I was, for the first half of my internship, responsible for the timely input and verification of all foreign exchange, money market, securities, and derivative products. My job consisted of the input of all types of trades into the back office systems, the verification through confirmation or documentation of trade details, the verification and payment/receipt of funds regarding variation margins on future transactions, interest rate swaps, caps, floors, FRAs and options, and the maintenance of U.S. dollar positions for the end of day settlement. That was the boring part of my internship.

The second half was much more interesting. I received training in currency trading. I started on the spot desk, worked there for two weeks, and then moved to the swap desk for the remaining three weeks of my internship. From the first day of training in the front office I knew I would have to stay on my toes. The first two weeks of my training I was assigned to the spot desk where my supervisor was a senior trader, female, 23 years old, blonde, blue eyes, and extremely ambitious.

On the very first day, about 11 A.M., she bet on the rise of the Japanese yen after the elections of the new Japanese Prime Minister. She had a long position on the yen and was short on the dollar. Unfortunately she lost $700,000 in less than 10 minutes. It is still unclear for me why she made such a bet. The *Wall Street Journal* and the *Financial Times* (both papers were used heavily in the trading room) were very negative regarding the new Prime Minister's ability to reverse the financial crisis in Japan. It was clear that her position was based purely on emotions, instinct, savvy—anything but fundamentals.

To understand the impact of a $700,000 loss that my blonde *alien* made, you must understand that every trader on a spot desk has to make eight times his or her wage in commission. Let's say that my supervisor was making $80,000 a year. She would then need to make $640,000 in commission on spreads during that year to keep her job. A loss of $700,000 put her in a very bad position, and she knew it. But to her credit, she remained quite confident and did not appear shaken.

But after my first day I was pretty shaken. I understood after this that being a trader was not my cup of tea. It is not because of the stress of the job—and it is obviously very stressful. It was more that most of the skills of the job had nothing to do with what I had been learning in school for many years. And when I saw and experienced how hard these people partied up and down the streets of New York many nights—and then traded hundreds of millions of dollars in minutes the following day, well, I just did not see this as my career track.

Source: Reminiscences of an anonymous intern.

Central Banks and Treasuries

Central banks and treasuries use the market to acquire or spend their country's foreign exchange reserves as well as to influence the price at which their own currency is traded. They may act to support the value of their own currency because of policies adopted at the national level or because of commitments entered into through membership in joint float agreements, such as that of the European Monetary System (EMS) central banks that preceded introduction of the euro. Consequently, motive is not to earn a profit as such, but rather to influence the foreign exchange value of their currency in a manner that will benefit the interests of their citizens. In many instances they do their job best when they willingly take a loss on their foreign exchange transactions. As willing loss takers, central banks and treasuries differ in motive and behavior from all other market participants.

Foreign Exchange Brokers

Foreign exchange brokers are agents who facilitate trading between dealers without themselves becoming principals in the transaction. They charge a small commission for this service. They maintain instant access to hundreds of dealers worldwide via open telephone lines. At times a broker may maintain a dozen or more such lines to a single client bank, with separate lines for different currencies and for spot and forward markets.

It is a broker's business to know at any moment exactly which dealers want to buy or sell any currency. This knowledge enables the broker to find an opposite party for a client without revealing the identity of either party until after a transaction has been agreed upon. Dealers use brokers to expedite the transaction and to remain anonymous, since the identity of participants may influence short-term quotes.

Continuous Linked Settlement and Fraud

In 2002, the Continuous Linked Settlement (CLS) system was introduced. The CLS system eliminates losses if either party of a foreign exchange transaction is unable to settle with the other party. It links the Real-Time Gross Settlement (RTGS) systems in seven major currencies. It is expected eventually to result in a same-day settlement which will replace the traditional two-day transaction period.

The CLS system should help counteract fraud in the foreign exchange markets as well. In the United States, the Commodity Futures Modernization Act of 2000 gives the responsibility for regulating foreign exchange trading fraud to the U.S. Commodity Futures Trading Commission (CFTC).

Transactions in the Interbank Market

Transactions in the foreign exchange market can be executed on a *spot*, *forward*, or *swap* basis. A broader definition of the foreign exchange market includes foreign currency options, futures, and swaps, which are covered in Chapter 8. A *spot* transaction requires almost immediate delivery of foreign exchange. A *forward* transaction requires delivery of foreign exchange at some future date, either on an "outright" basis or through a "futures" contract. A *swap* transaction is the simultaneous exchange of one foreign currency for another.

Spot Transactions

A *spot* transaction in the interbank market is the purchase of foreign exchange, with delivery and payment between banks to take place, normally, on the second following business day. The Canadian dollar settles with the U.S. dollar on the first following business day. Exhibit 6.3 provides a structured map of when settlement occurs within the European market.

EXHIBIT 6.3   Foreign Exchange Settlement in Europe

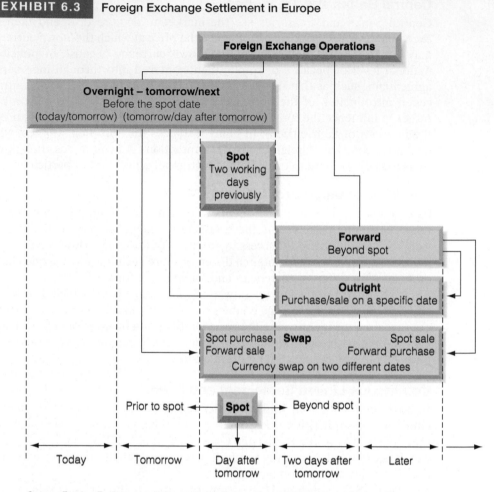

Source: Foreign Exchange and Money Market Transactions, UBS Investment Bank, p. 58.

The date of settlement is referred to as the "value date." On the value date, most dollar transactions in the world are settled through the computerized Clearing House Interbank Payments System (CHIPS) in New York, which provides for calculation of net balances owed by any one bank to another and for payment by 6:00 P.M. that same day in Federal Reserve Bank of New York funds. Other central banks and settlement services providers operate similarly in other currencies around the world.

A typical spot transaction in the interbank market might involve a U.S. bank contracting on a Monday for the transfer of £10,000,000 to the account of a London bank. If the spot exchange rate were $1.8420/£, the U.S. bank would transfer £10,000,000 to the London bank on Wednesday, and the London bank would transfer $18,420,000 to the U.S. bank at the same time. A spot transaction between a bank and its commercial customer would not necessarily involve a wait of two days for settlement.

Outright Forward Transactions

An *outright forward* transaction (usually called just "forward") requires delivery at a future value date of a specified amount of one currency for a specified amount of another currency. The exchange rate is established at the time of the agreement, but payment and delivery are not required until maturity. Forward exchange rates are normally quoted for value dates of one, two, three, six, and twelve months. Actual contracts can be arranged for other numbers of months or, on occasion, for periods of more than one year. Payment is on the second business day after the even-month anniversary of the trade. Thus, a 2-month forward transaction entered into on March 18 will be for a value date of May 20, or the next business day if May 20 falls on a weekend or holiday.

Note that as a matter of terminology we can speak of "buying forward" or "selling forward" to describe the same transaction. A contract to deliver dollars for euros in six months is both "buying euros forward for dollars" and "selling dollars forward for euros."

Swap Transactions

A *swap* transaction in the interbank market is the simultaneous purchase and sale of a given amount of foreign exchange for two different value dates. Both purchase and sale are conducted with the same counterparty. A common type of swap is a "spot against forward." The dealer buys a currency in the spot market and simultaneously sells the same amount back to the same bank in the forward market. Since this is executed as a single transaction with one counterparty, the dealer incurs no unexpected foreign exchange risk. Swap transactions and outright forwards combined made up 57% of all foreign exchange market activity in April 2010.

Forward-Forward Swaps. A more sophisticated swap transaction is called a "forward-forward" swap. A dealer sells £20,000,000 forward for dollars for delivery in, say, two months at $1.8420/£ and simultaneously buys £20,000,000 forward for delivery in three months at $1.8400/£. The difference between the buying price and the selling price is equivalent to the interest rate differential, that is the *interest rate parity* described in Chapter 7, between the two currencies. Thus, a swap can be viewed as a technique for borrowing another currency on a fully collateralized basis.

Nondeliverable Forwards (NDFs). Created in the early 1990s, the *nondeliverable forward* (NDF), is now a relatively common derivative offered by the largest providers of foreign exchange derivatives. NDFs possess the same characteristics and documentation requirements as traditional forward contracts, except that they are settled only in U.S. dollars; the foreign currency being sold forward or bought forward is not delivered. The dollar-settlement feature reflects the fact that NDFs are contracted offshore—for example, in New York for a Mexican investor—and so are beyond the reach and regulatory frameworks of the home country governments (Mexico in this case). NDFs are traded internationally using standards set by the International Swaps and Derivatives Association (ISDA). Although originally envisioned to be a method of currency hedging, it is now estimated that more than 70% of all NDF trading is for speculation purposes.

NDFs are used primarily for emerging market currencies, currencies that typically do not have open spot market currency trading, liquid money markets, or quoted Eurocurrency interest rates. Although most NDF trading focused on Latin America in the 1990s, many Asian currencies have been very widely traded in the post-1997 Asian crisis era. In general, NDF markets normally develop for country currencies having large cross-border capital movements, but still being subject to convertibility restrictions. Trading in recent years has been dominated by the Korean won, Chilean peso, Taiwanese dollar, Brazilian reais, and Chinese renminbi.

Pricing of NDFs reflects basic interest differentials, as with regular forward contracts, plus some additional premium charged by the bank for dollar settlement. If, however, there is no accessible or developed money market for interest rate setting, the pricing of the NDF takes on a much more speculative element. Without true interest rates, traders often price on the basis of what they believe spot rates may be at the time of settlement.

NDFs are traded and settled outside the country of the subject currency, and therefore are beyond the control of the country's government. In the past this has created a difficult situation, in which the NDF market then serves as something of a gray market in the trading of that currency. For example, in late 2001, Argentina was under increasing pressure to abandon its fixed exchange rate regime of one peso equaling one U.S. dollar. The NDF market began quoting rates of ARS1.05/USD and ARS1.10/USD, in effect a devalued peso, for NDFs settling within the next year. This led to increasing speculative pressure against the peso (and to the ire of the Argentine government).

NDFs, however, have proven to be something of an imperfect replacement for traditional forward contracts. The problems with NDFs typically involve its "fixing of spot rate on the fixing date," the spot rate at the end of the contract used to calculate the settlement. In times of financial crisis, for example, with the Venezuelan bolivar in 2003, the government of the subject currency may suspend foreign exchange trading in the spot market for an extended period of time. Without an official fixing rate, the NDF cannot be settled. In the case of Venezuela, the problem was compounded when a new official "devalued bolivar" was announced, but still not traded.

Size of the Foreign Exchange Market

The Bank for International Settlements (BIS), in conjunction with central banks around the world, conducts a survey of currency trading activity every three years. The most recent survey, conducted in April 2010, estimated *daily* global net turnover in the foreign exchange market to be $3.2 trillion. The BIS data for surveys between 1989 and 2010 is shown in Exhibit 6.4.

EXHIBIT 6.4   Global Foreign Exchange Market Turnover, 1989–2010 (average daily turnover in April, billions of U.S. dollars)

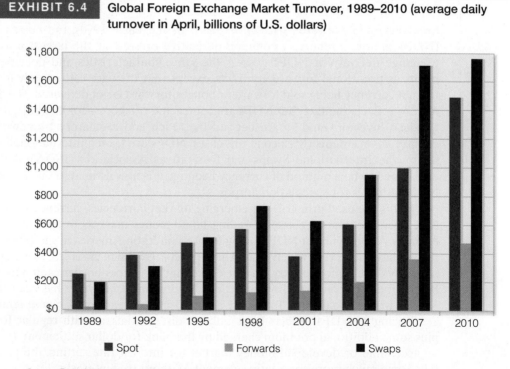

Source: Bank for International Settlements, "Triennial Central Bank Survey: Foreign Exchange and Derivatives Market Activity in April 2010: Preliminary Results," September 2010, www.bis.org.

Global foreign exchange turnover in Exhibit 6.4 is divided into three categories of currency instruments: spot transactions, forward transactions, and swap transactions. While spot market growth between 2007 and 2010 was dramatic, rising from $1.005 trillion to $1.495 trillion (48% growth in only three years), outright forwards rose from $0.362 trillion to $0.475 trillion (30% growth), with swaps growing only marginally, from $1.714 to $1.765 trillion. As we will discuss in Chapter 8, the low level of interest rates around the globe in recent years, combined with slowing economic growth and new debt issuances, has obviously had a dampening impact on the swap market.

Geographical Distribution

Exhibit 6.5 shows the proportionate share of foreign exchange trading for the most important national markets in the world between 1992 and 2010. (Note that although the data is collected and reported on a national basis, "United States" should largely be interpreted as "New York" because the great majority of foreign exchange trading takes place in the major city of each country. This is most true for "United Kingdom" and "London.")

EXHIBIT 6.5   Top 10 Geographic Trading Centers in the Foreign Exchange Market, 1992–2010 (average daily turnover in April)

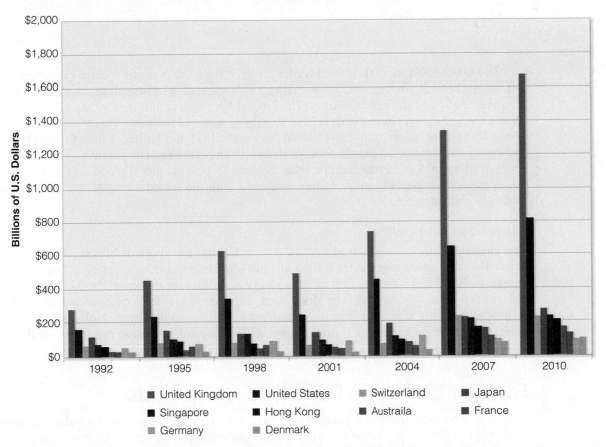

Source: Bank for International Settlements, "Triennial Central Bank Survey: Foreign Exchange and Derivatives Market Activity in April 2010: Preliminary Results," September 2010, www.bis.org.

EXHIBIT 6.6   Foreign Exchange Market Turnover by Currency Pair
(daily averages in April)

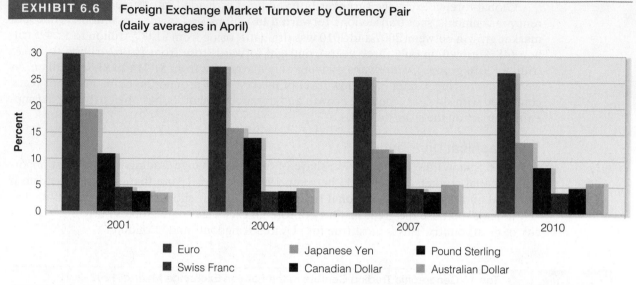

Source: Bank for International Settlements, "Triennial Central Bank Survey: Foreign Exchange and Derivatives Market Activity in April 2010: Preliminary Results," September 2010, www.bis.org.

The United Kingdom (London) continues to be the world's major foreign exchange market in traditional foreign exchange market activity with $1,854 billion in average daily turnover, 36.7% of the global market. The United Kingdom is followed by the United States with 17.9%, Japan (Tokyo) with 6.2%, Singapore with 5.3%, Switzerland with 5.2%, and Hong Kong now reaching 4.7% of global trading. Indeed, the United Kingdom and United States together make up nearly 55% of daily currency trading. The relative growth of currency trading in Asia versus Europe over the past 15 years is pronounced, as the growth of the Asian economies and markets has combined with the introduction of the euro to shift currency exchange activity.

Currency Composition

The currency composition of trading, as shown in Exhibit 6.6, also indicates significant global shifts. Because all currencies are traded against some other currency—pairs, all percentages shown in Exhibit 6.6 are for that currency versus another; in this case, the U.S. dollar. The dollar/euro cross along with the dollar/yen cross continue to dominate global trading. Although the "big three" (dollar, euro, and yen) continue to dominate global trades, it will probably not be long before a fourth, not yet on the map—the Chinese renminbi—will move into greater prominence.

Foreign Exchange Rates and Quotations

A *foreign exchange rate* is the price of one currency expressed in terms of another currency. A *foreign exchange quotation* (or *quote*) is a statement of willingness to buy or sell at an announced rate. As we delve into the terminology of currency trading, keep in mind basic pricing, say the price of an orange. If the price is $1.20/orange, the "price" is $1.20, the "unit" is the orange.

Currency Symbols

Quotations may be designated by traditional currency symbols or by ISO 4217 codes. The latter were developed in recent decades for use in electronic communications. Both traditional symbols and currency codes are given in full at the end of this book, but the major ones used throughout this chapter are the following:

Currency	Traditional Symbol	ISO 4217 Code
U.S. dollar	$	USD
European euro	€	EUR
Great Britain pound	£	GBP
Japanese yen	¥	JPY
Mexican peso	Ps	MXN

Today, all wholesale trading, that is, the trading of currencies between major banks in the global marketplace, uses the three-letter ISO codes. Although there are no hard and fast rules in the retail markets and in business periodicals, European and American periodicals have a tendency to use the traditional currency symbols, while many publications in Asia and the Middle East have embraced the use of ISO codes. The physical paper currency (banknotes) of most countries continue to use the country's traditional currency symbol.

Spot Market Quotes

Foreign exchange quotations follow a number of different systems and abbreviations (many are quite confusing, so stay focused). Exhibit 6.7 provides a brief overview of the most common quotation conventions, in this case, focusing on the European euro and U.S. dollar.

Dollar Rates. The *base currency* used to quote a currency's value is typically the U.S. dollar. Termed *European terms*, this means that whenever a currency's value is quoted, it is quoted in terms of number of units of currency to equal one U.S. dollar.

For example, if a trader in Zurich, whose home currency is the Swiss franc (CHF), were to request a quote from an Oslo-based trader on the Norwegian krone (NOK), the Norwegian trader will quote the value of the NOK against the USD, not the CHF. The result is that most currencies are quoted per dollar—Japanese yen per U.S. dollar, Norwegian krone per U.S. dollar, Mexican pesos per U.S. dollar, Brazilian real per U.S. dollar, Malaysian ringgit per U.S. dollar, Chinese renminbi per U.S. dollar, and so on.

EXHIBIT 6.7 Foreign Currency Quotations Convention

European terms
Foreign currency price of one dollar (USD)

EUR0.8214 = USD1.00

Called:
"Direct quote" on the USD in Europe
"Indirect quote" on the USD outside Europe

EUR is the *base*, or *price*, currency
USD is the *foreign*, or *unit*, currency

American terms
U.S. dollar price of one euro (EUR)

USD1.2174 = EUR1.00

Called:
"Direct quote" on the EUR in the United States
"Indirect quote" on the EUR In Europe

USD is the *base*, or *price*, currency
EUR is the *foreign*, or *unit*, currency

These quotes are reciprocals:

$$\frac{1}{EUR0.8214/USD} = USD1.2714/EUR$$

American terms are used in quoting rates for most foreign currency options and futures, as well as in retail markets that deal with tourists and personal remittances. Foreign exchange traders may also use nicknames for major currencies. "Cable" means the exchange rate between U.S. dollars and U.K. pound sterling, the name dating from the time when transactions in dollars and pounds were carried out over the Transatlantic telegraph cable. A Canadian dollar is a "loonie," named after the water fowl on Canada's one-dollar coin. "Kiwi" stands for the New Zealand dollar, "Aussie" for the Australian dollar, "Swissie" for Swiss francs, and "Sing dollar" for the Singapore dollar.

There are two major exceptions to this rule of using European terms: the euro and the U.K.'s pound sterling. The euro and the U.K. pound sterling are both normally quoted in *American terms*; the U.S. dollar price of one euro and the U.S. dollar price of one pound sterling. Additionally, Australian dollars and New Zealand dollars are normally quoted on American terms. Sterling is quoted as the foreign currency price of one pound for historical reasons. For centuries, the British pound sterling consisted of 20 shillings, each of which equaled 12 pence. Multiplication and division with the nondecimal currency were difficult. The custom evolved for foreign exchange prices in London, then the undisputed financial capital of the world, to be stated in foreign currency units per pound. This practice remained even after sterling changed to decimals in 1971.

The euro was first introduced as a substitute or replacement for domestic currencies like the Deutsche mark and French franc. To make the transition simple for the residents and users of these historical currencies, all quotes were made on a "domestic currency per euro" basis. This held true for its quotation against the U.S. dollar; hence, "U.S. dollars per euro" being the common quotation used today.

Direct and Indirect Quotations. A *direct quote* is the price of a foreign currency in domestic currency units. An *indirect quote* is the price of the domestic currency in foreign currency units.

In retail exchange in many countries (such as currency exchanged in hotels or airports) it is common practice to quote the *home currency* as the *price* and the *foreign currency* as the *unit*. A woman walking down the Avenue des Champs-Elysèes in Paris might see the following quote:

$$EUR0.8214 = USD1.00$$

In France, the home currency is the euro and the foreign currency is the dollar. This quotation in France is termed a *direct quote on the dollar* or a *price quote on the dollar*. Verbally, she might say to herself "0.8214 euros per dollar," or "it will cost me 0.8214 euros to get one dollar."

At the same time a man walking down Broadway in New York City may see the following quote in a bank window:

$$USD1.2174 = EUR1.00$$

The *home currency* is the dollar (the *price*), the *foreign currency* is the euro (the *unit*). In New York, this would be a *direct quote on the euro* (the home currency price of one unit of foreign currency) and an *indirect quote on the dollar* (the foreign currency price of one unit of home currency). Again, verbally, he would probably say "I will pay $1.2174 dollars per euro." These are *American terms*.

The two quotes are obviously equivalent (at least to four decimal places), one being the reciprocal of the other:

$$\frac{1}{EUR0.8214/USD} = USD1.2174/EUR$$

Bid and Ask Rates. Although a newspaper or magazine article will state an exchange rate as a single value, the market for buying and selling currencies, whether it be retail or wholesale, uses two different rates, one for buying and one for selling. Exhibit 6.8 provides a sample of how these quotations may be seen in the market for the dollar/euro.

A *bid* is the price (i.e., exchange rate) in one currency at which a dealer will buy another currency. An *ask* is the price (i.e., exchange rate) at which a dealer will sell the other currency. Dealers *bid* (buy) at one price and *ask* (sell) at a slightly higher price, making their profit from the spread between the buying and selling prices. The bid-ask spread may be quite large for currencies that are traded infrequently, in small volumes, or both.

Bid and ask quotations in the foreign exchange markets are superficially complicated by the fact that the bid for one currency is also the offer for the opposite currency. A trader seeking to buy dollars with euros is simultaneously offering to sell euros for dollars.

As illustrated in Exhibit 6.8, however, the full outright quotation (the full price to all of its decimal points) is typically shown only for the bid rate. Traders, however, tend to abbreviate when talking on the phone or putting quotations on a video screen. The first term, the *bid*, of a spot quotation may be given in full: that is, "1.2170." However, the second term, the *ask*, will probably be expressed only as the digits that differ from the bid. Hence, the bid and ask for spot euros would probably be shown "1.2170/78" on a video screen. In some cases between professional traders, they may only quote the last two digits of both the bid and ask, "70-78", because they know what the other figures are. Closing rates for 47 currencies (plus the SDR) as quoted by the *Wall Street Journal* are presented in Exhibit 6.9.

The *Wall Street Journal* gives American terms quotes under the heading "USD equivalent" and European terms quotes under the heading "Currency per USD." Quotes are given on an outright basis for spot, with forwards of one, three, and six months provided for a few select currencies. Quotes are for trading among banks in amounts of $1 million or more, as quoted at 4 P.M. EST by Reuters. The *Journal* does not state whether these are bid, ask, or mid-rate quotations.

EXHIBIT 6.8   Bid, Ask, and Mid-Point Quotations

In text documents of any kind, the exchange rate may be stated as *mid-point quote*, the average of *bid* and *ask*, of $1.2174/€.

For example, the *Wall Street Journal* would quote the following currencies as follows:

	Last Bid		Last Bid
Euro (EUR/USD)	1.2170	Brazilian Real (USD/BRL)	1.6827
Japanese Yen (USD/JPY)	83.16	Canadian Dollar (USD/CAD)	0.9930
U.K. Pound (GBP/USD)	1.5552	Mexican Peso (USD/MXN)	12.2365

EXHIBIT 6.9 Exchange Rates: New York Closing Snapshot

U.S.-dollar foreign-exchange rates in late New York trading, Tuesday, January 4, 2011

Country	Currency	Symbol	Code	USD Equivalent	Currency per USD
Americas					
Argentina*	peso	Ps	ARS	0.252	3.9683
Brazil	real	R$	BRL	0.602	1.6611
Canada	dollar	C$	CAD	1.0015	0.9985
1-month forward				1.0009	0.9991
3-months forward				0.9995	1.0005
6-months forward				0.9968	1.0032
Chile	peso	$	CLP	0.00205	487.8
Colombia	peso	Col$	COP	0.0005276	1895.38
Ecuador	U.S. dollar	$	USD	1	1
Mexico*	new peso	$	MXN	0.0818	12.2324
Peru	new sol	S/.	PEN	0.3568	2.8027
Uruguay†	peso	$U	UYU	0.0502	19.92
Venezuela	boliviar fuerte	Bs	VND	0.23285056	4.2946
Asia-Pacific					
Australia	dollar	A$	AUD	1.0055	0.9945
China	yuan	¥	CNY	0.1514	6.607
Hong Kong	dollar	HK$	HKG	0.1287	7.7695
India	rupee	Rs	INR	0.02226	44.9236
Indonesia	rupiah	Rp	IDR	0.0001113	8985
Japan	yen	¥	JPY	0.012189	82.04
1-month forward				0.012193	82.01
3-months forward				0.012201	81.96
6-months forward				0.012215	81.87
Malaysia §	ringgit	RM	MYR	0.3263	3.0647
New Zealand	dollar	NZ$	NZD	0.7666	1.3045
Pakistan	rupee	Rs.	PKR	0.01166	85.763
Philippines	peso	₱	PHP	0.023	43.554
Singapore	dollar	S$	SGD	0.7765	1.2878
South Korea	won	W	KRW	0.0008885	1125.49
Taiwan	dollar	T$	TWD	0.03428	29.172
Thailand	baht	B	THB	0.03324	30.084
Vietnam	dong	d	VND	0.00005	19499
Europe					
Czech Republic**	koruna	Kc	CZK	0.05343	18.716
Denmark	krone	Dkr	DKK	0.1784	5.6054
Euro area	euro	€	EUR	1.3297	0.752
Hungary	forint	Ft	HUF	0.00482	207.47
Norway	krone	NKr	NOK	0.1705	5.8651
Poland	zloty	—	PLN	0.342	2.924
Romania	leu	L	RON	0.3112	3.2131
Russia ‡	ruble	R	RUB	0.03268	30.6
Sweden	krona	SKr	SEK	0.1487	6.7249
Switzerland	franc	Fr.	CHF	1.0537	0.949
1-month forward				1.0541	0.9487
3-months forward				1.0548	0.948
6-months forward				1.056	0.947
Turkey**	lira	YTL	TRY	0.6483	1.5426
United Kingdom	pound	£	GBP	1.5585	0.6416
1-month forward				1.5581	0.6418
3-months forward				1.5573	0.6421
6-months forward				1.5557	0.6428
Middle East/Africa					
Bahrain	dinar	—	BHD	2.6524	0.377
Egypt*	pound	£	EGP	0.1727	5.7921
Israel	shekel	Shk	ILS	0.2841	3.5199
Jordan	dinar	—	JOD	1.4109	0.7088
Kenya	shilling	KSh	KES	0.01234	81.05
Kuwait	dinar	—	KWD	3.5564	0.2812
Lebanon	pound	—	LBP	0.000666	1501.5
Saudi Arabia	riyal	SR	SAR	0.2667	3.7495
South Africa	rand	R	ZAR	0.1498	6.6756
United Arab Emirates	dirham	—	AED	0.2723	3.6724
IMF ††	special drawing right	—	SDR	1.5464	0.6467

Notes: *Floating rate †Financial §Government rate and ‡Russian Central Bank rate **Commercial rate ††Special Drawing Rights (SDR); from the International Monetary Fund; based on exchange rates for U.S., British and Japanese currencies. Based on trading among banks of $1 million and more, as quoted at 4 p.m. ET by Reuters. Rates are drawn from the *Wall Street Journal* for January 5, 2011.

A final note. The order of currencies in quotations used by traders can be quite confusing (at least the authors of this book think so). As noted by one major international banking publication:

The notation EUR/USD is the system used by traders, although mathematically it would be more correct to express the exchange rate the other way around, as it shows how many USD have to be paid to obtain EUR 1.

This is why the currency quotes in Exhibit 6.8—EUR/USD, USD/JPY, or GBP/USD—are quoted and used in business and the rest of this text as $1.2170/€, ¥83.16/$, and $1.5552/£. International finance is not for the weak of heart!

Cross Rates

Many currency pairs are only inactively traded, so their exchange rate is determined through their relationship to a widely traded third currency. For example, a Mexican importer needs Japanese yen to pay for purchases in Tokyo. Both the Mexican peso (MXN) and the Japanese yen (JPY) are commonly quoted against the U.S. dollar (USD). Using the following quotes from Exhibit 6.9:

| Japanese yen | JPY82.04/USD |
| Mexican peso | MXN12.2324/USD |

the Mexican importer can buy one U.S. dollar for MXN12.2324, and with that dollar can buy JPY 82.04. The cross rate calculation would be as follows:

$$\frac{\text{Japanese yen/U.S. dollar}}{\text{Mexican pesos/U.S. dollar}} = \frac{\text{JPY82.04/USD}}{\text{MXN12.2324/USD}} = \text{JPY6.7068/MXN}$$

The cross rate could also be calculated as the reciprocal:

$$\frac{\text{Mexican peso/U.S. dollar}}{\text{Japanese yen/U.S. dollar}} = \frac{\text{MXN12.2324/USD}}{\text{JPY82.04/USD}} = \text{MXN0.1491/JPY}$$

Cross rates often appear in financial publications in the form of a matrix, as shown in Exhibit 6.10 from the *Wall Street Journal* (same day quotes as in Exhibit 6.9). This matrix shows the amount of each currency (rows) needed to buy a unit of the currency—*bid rates*—of

EXHIBIT 6.10   Key Currency Cross Rates, Tuesday, January 4, 2011

Snapshot of foreign exchange cross rates at 4 P.M. EST.

	Dollar	Euro	Pound	Sfranc	Peso	Yen	CdnDlr
Canada	0.9985	1.3277	1.5562	1.0521	0.0816	0.0122	....
Japan	82.041	109.09	127.86	86.447	6.7069	....	82.164
Mexico	12.232	16.265	19.064	12.889	....	0.1491	12.251
Switzerland	0.949	1.2619	1.4791	....	0.0776	0.0116	0.9505
U.K.	0.6416	0.8532	....	0.6761	0.0525	0.0078	0.6426
Euro	0.752	....	1.1721	0.7924	0.0615	0.0092	0.7532
U.S.	....	1.3297	1.5585	1.0537	0.0818	0.0122	1.0015

Source: Thomson Reuters.

the country on the column. For example, reading across the row labeled "Japan," it takes 82.041 Japanese yen to buy one U.S. dollar, 109.09 yen to buy one euro, and 6.7069 yen to buy one Mexican peso.

Intermarket Arbitrage

Cross rates can be used to check on opportunities for intermarket arbitrage. Suppose the following exchange rates are quoted:

Citibank quotes U.S. dollars per euro	USD1.3297/EUR
Barclays Bank quotes U.S. dollars per pound sterling	USD1.5585/GBP
Dresdner Bank quotes euros per pound sterling	EUR1.1722/GBP

The cross rate between Citibank and Barclays Bank is

$$\frac{USD1.5585/GBP}{USD1.3297/EUR} = EUR1.1721/GBP$$

This cross rate is not the same as Dresdner Bank's quotation of EUR1.1722/GBP, so an opportunity exists to profit from arbitrage between the three markets. Exhibit 6.11 shows the steps in what is called *triangular arbitrage*.

A market trader at Citibank New York, with USD1,000,000, can sell that sum spot to Barclays Bank for USD1,000,000 ÷ USD1.5585/GBP = GBP641,643. Simultaneously, these pounds can be sold to Dresdner Bank for GBP641,643 × EUR1.1722/GBP = EUR752,133, and the trader can then immediately sell these euros to Citibank for dollars: EUR752,133 × USD1.3297/EUR = USD1,000,112. The profit on one such "turn" is a risk-free USD112 (not much, but it's digital!). Such triangular arbitrage can continue until exchange rate equilibrium is reestablished; that is, until the calculated cross rate equals the actual quotation, less any tiny margin for transaction costs.

EXHIBIT 6.11   Triangular Arbitrage by a Market Trader

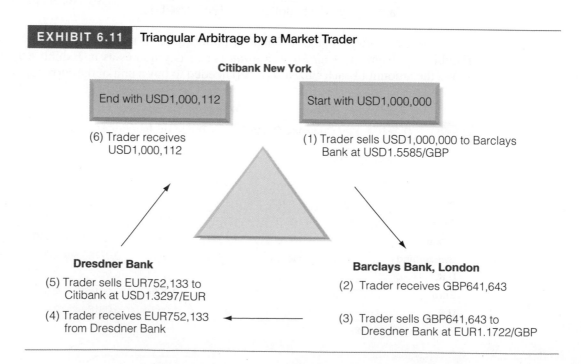

Citibank New York

End with USD1,000,112

Start with USD1,000,000

(6) Trader receives USD1,000,112

(1) Trader sells USD1,000,000 to Barclays Bank at USD1.5585/GBP

Dresdner Bank

(5) Trader sells EUR752,133 to Citibank at USD1.3297/EUR

(4) Trader receives EUR752,133 from Dresdner Bank

Barclays Bank, London

(2) Trader receives GBP641,643

(3) Trader sells GBP641,643 to Dresdner Bank at EUR1.1722/GBP

Percentage Change in Spot Rates

Assume that the Mexican peso has recently changed in value from MXP10.00/USD to MXP11.00/USD. Your home currency is the U.S. dollar. What is the percent change in the value of the Mexican peso? The calculation depends upon the designated home currency.

Foreign Currency Terms. When the foreign currency price (the price) of the home currency (the unit) is used, Mexican pesos per U.S. dollar in this case, the formula for the percent change in the foreign currency becomes

$$\%\Delta = \frac{\text{Beginning rate} - \text{Ending rate}}{\text{Ending rate}} \times 100 = \frac{\text{MXP10.00/USD} - \text{MXP11.00/USD}}{\text{MXP11.00/USD}} \times 100 = -9.09\%$$

The Mexican peso fell in value 9.09% against the dollar. Note that it takes more pesos per dollar, and the calculation resulted in a negative value, both characteristics of a fall in value.

Home Currency Terms. When the home currency price (the price) for a foreign currency (the unit) is used, therefore the reciprocals of the numbers used above, the formula for the percent change in the foreign currency is

$$\%\Delta = \frac{\text{Ending rate} - \text{Beginning rate}}{\text{Beginning rate}} \times 100 = \frac{\text{USD0.09091/MXP} - \text{USD0.1000/MXP}}{\text{USD0.1000/MXP}} \times 100 = -9.09\%$$

The calculation yields the identical percentage change, a fall in the value of the peso by 9.09%. Although many people find the second calculation, the home currency term calculation, as the more "intuitive" because it reminds them of many percentage change calculations, one must be careful to remember that these are exchanges of currency for currency, and which currency is designated as home currency matters.

Forward Quotations

Although spot rates are typically quoted on an outright basis, meaning all digits expressed, forward rates are typically quoted in terms of points or *pips*, the last digits of a currency quotation, depending on currency quotation convention. Forward rates of one year or less maturity are termed *cash rates*, longer than one-year *swap rates*. A forward quotation expressed in points is not a foreign exchange rate as such. Rather it is the *difference* between the forward rate and the spot rate. Consequently, the spot rate itself can never be given on a points basis.

Consider the spot and forward point quotes in Exhibit 6.12. The bid and ask spot quotes are outright quotes, but the forwards are stated as points from the spot rate. The 3-month points quotations for the Japanese yen in Exhibit 6.12 are "−143" *bid* and "−140" *ask*. The first number ("−143") refers to points away from the spot *bid*, and the second number ("−140") to points away from the spot *ask*. Given the outright quotes of 118.27 *bid* and 118.37 *ask*, the outright 3-month forward rates are calculated as follows:

	Bid	Ask
Outright spot	JPY118.27	JPY118.37
Plus points (3 months)	−1.43	−1.40
Outright forward	JPY116.84	JPY116.97

EXHIBIT 6.12   Spot and Forward Quotations for the Euro and Japanese yen

	Term	Euro: Spot and Forward ($/€)				Japanese yen: Spot and Forward (¥/$)			
		Bid		Ask		Bid		Ask	
		Points	Rate	Points	Rate	Points	Rate	Points	Rate
	Spot		1.0897		1.0901		118.27		118.37
Cash rates	1 week	3	1.0900	4	1.0905	−10	118.17	−9	118.28
	1 month	17	1.0914	19	1.0920	−51	117.76	−50	117.87
	2 months	35	1.0932	36	1.0937	−95	117.32	−93	117.44
	3 months	53	1.0950	54	1.0955	−143	116.84	−140	116.97
	4 months	72	1.0969	76	1.0977	−195	116.32	−190	116.47
	5 months	90	1.0987	95	1.0996	−240	115.87	−237	116.00
	6 months	112	1.1009	113	1.1014	−288	115.39	−287	115.50
	9 months	175	1.1072	177	1.1078	−435	113.92	−429	114.08
	1 year	242	1.1139	245	1.1146	−584	112.43	−581	112.56
Swap rates	2 years	481	1.1378	522	1.1423	−1150	106.77	−1129	107.08
	3 years	750	1.1647	810	1.1711	−1748	100.79	−1698	101.39
	4 years	960	1.1857	1039	1.1940	−2185	96.42	−2115	97.22
	5 years	1129	1.2026	1276	1.2177	−2592	92.35	−2490	93.47

The forward *bid* and *ask* quotations in Exhibit 6.12 longer than two years are called *swap rates*. As mentioned earlier, many forward exchange transactions in the interbank market involve a simultaneous purchase for one date and sale (reversing the transaction) for another date. This "swap" is a way to borrow one currency for a limited time while giving up the use of another currency for the same time. In other words, it is a short-term borrowing of one currency combined with a short-term loan of an equivalent amount of another currency. The two parties could, if they wanted, charge each other interest at the going rate for each of the currencies. However, it is easier for the party with the higher-interest currency to simply pay the net interest differential to the other. The swap rate expresses this net interest differential on a points basis rather than as an interest rate.

Forward Quotations in Percentage Terms

The percent per annum deviation of the forward from the spot rate is termed the *forward premium*. However, the *forward premium*—which may be either a positive (a premium) or negative value (a discount)—depends on which currency is the home, or base currency as with the calculation of percentage changes in spot rates. Assume the following spot rate for our discussion of *foreign currency terms* and *home currency terms*.

	Foreign currency (price)/ home currency (unit)	Home currency (price)/ foreign currency (unit)
Spot rate	¥118.27/$	USD0.0084552/JPY
3-month forward	¥116.84/$	USD0.0085587/JPY

Foreign Currency Terms. When the foreign currency is used as the price of the home currency (the unit), and substituting JPY/USD spot and forward rates, as well as the number of days forward (90), the forward premium on the yen (f^{JPY}) is calculated as follows:

$$f^{JPY} = \frac{Spot - Forward}{Forward} \times \frac{360}{90} \times 100 = \frac{118.27 - 116.84}{116.84} \times \frac{360}{90} \times 100 = +4.90\%$$

The sign is positive indicating that the Japanese yen is selling forward at a premium of 4.90% against the U.S. dollar.

Home Currency Terms. When the home currency (the dollar) is used as the price for the foreign currency (the yen), the reciprocals of the spot and forward rates used in the previous calculation, the calculation of the forward premium on the yen (f^{JPY}) is

$$f^{JPY} = \frac{Forward - Spot}{Spot} \times \frac{360}{90} \times 100 = \frac{0.0084552 - 0.0085587}{0.0085587} \times \frac{360}{90} \times 100 = +4.90\%$$

Again, result is identical to the previous premium calculation: a positive 4.90% premium of the yen against the dollar.

Summary of Learning Objectives

Examine the what, when, where, and why of currency trading in the global marketplace

♦ The three functions of the foreign exchange market are to transfer purchasing power, provide credit, and minimize foreign exchange risk.

♦ The foreign exchange market is composed of two tiers: the interbank market and the client market. Participants within these tiers include bank and nonbank foreign exchange dealers, individuals and firms conducting commercial and investment transactions, speculators and arbitragers, central banks and treasuries, and foreign exchange brokers.

♦ Geographically the foreign exchange market spans the globe, with prices moving and currencies traded somewhere every hour of every business day.

Understand the definitions and distinctions between spot, forward, swaps, and other types of foreign exchange financial instruments

♦ A foreign exchange *rate* is the price of one currency expressed in terms of another currency. A foreign exchange *quotation* is a statement of willingness to buy or sell currency at an announced price.

♦ Transactions within the foreign exchange market are executed either on a spot basis, requiring settlement two days after the transaction, or on a forward or swap basis, which requires settlement at some designated future date.

Learn the forms of currency quotations used by currency dealers, financial institutions, and agents of all kinds when conducting foreign exchange transactions

♦ *European terms* quotations are the foreign currency price of a U.S. dollar. *American terms* quotations are the dollar price of a foreign currency.

♦ Quotations can also be *direct* or *indirect*. A direct quote is the home currency price of a unit of foreign currency, while an indirect quote is the foreign currency price of a unit of home currency.

♦ Direct and indirect are *not* synonyms for American and European terms, because the home currency will change depending on who is doing the calculation, while European terms are always the foreign currency price of a dollar.

Analyze the interaction between changing currency values, cross exchange rates, and the possible opportunities arising from intermarket arbitrage

♦ A cross rate is an exchange rate between two currencies, calculated from their common relationships with a third currency. When cross rates differ from the direct rates between two currencies, intermarket arbitrage is possible.

MINI-CASE

The Saga of the Venezuelan Bolivar Fuerte

Una economía fuerte, un bolívar fuerte, un país fuerte.
Translation: A strong economy, a strong bolívar,
a strong country.

The Venezuelan bolivar dropped in the country's parallel currency market Monday after the government's official devaluation late last week. The value of the bolivar fell to VEF9.25 to the dollar, according to LechugaVerde.com, a website widely used by locals to track the rate of the Venezuelan currency in the black market.

—"Venezuela Bolivar Falls In Parallel Market After Devaluation," by Kejal Vyas, *Wall Street Journal*, January 3, 2011.

Unfortunately for the Venezuelan people, their currency, the Venezuelan *bolivar fuerte*, had proven anything but strong. On January 1, 2011, President Hugo Chávez devalued the bolivar fuerte—the "strong bolivar"—again, the fifth time in the past decade.

Current Regime

This last devaluation was more of an adjustment. The previous devaluation, January 1, 2008, had fixed the bolivar fuerte (BsF) at BsF4.30/$ for general economic and exchange purposes, but a preferred rate of BsF2.60/$ for food, medicine, and heavy machinery imports considered essential.[1] The 2011 devaluation eliminated the preferred rate, moving all import transactions to BsF4.30/$. This was not a minor elimination, as many analysts believed that in 2010 alone roughly 40% of all dollar-transactions were at the 2.6 rate. Even with this magnitude of change the bolivar fuerte is still considered overvalued; the black market rate of BsF8/$ was the current exchange as the devaluation occurred. The bolivar's history is detailed in Exhibit 1.

EXHIBIT 1   The Venezuelan Bolivar's Decline, 1996–2011

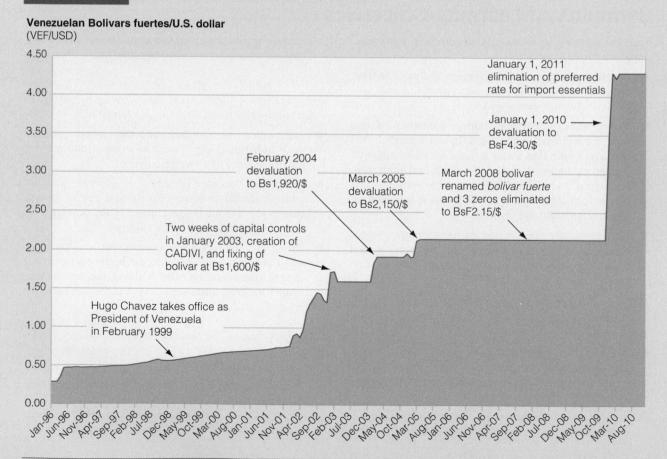

---

[1]"Venezuela to Devalue Currency," by Kejal Vyas and David Luhnow, *Wall Street Journal*, December 31, 2010.

Even this fixed exchange rate was subject to significant restrictions. CADIVI (Comisión de Administración de Divisas), the official government agency for the exchange of currency, limited Venezuelan residents to an annual total of $3,000 when traveling abroad, and $400 for Internet-based electronic purchases. Although the country had managed to go a number of years between devaluations, the 2008 and 2010 devaluations were clear losses for the purchasing power of the richest oil exporting country in South America.

The fight by the Venezuelan government and the Venezuelan Central Bank (BCV) to assert its independence from the manipulation of the outside world, specifically the United States, knew few bounds. When Hugo Chávez signed into law the currency reform measures in May 2010 to stop speculation of any kind, including foreign currency bonds in the form of equity securities on the Venezuelan stock exchange, it was made very clear what the objective was:[2]

> *Whoever, in one or multiple transactions, within one calendar year, without intervention of the BCV, buys, sells, or in any way offers, transfers, or receives foreign currency between an amount of 10,000 dollars to 20,000 dollars, of the United States of America or their equivalent . . . will be sanctioned with a fine valued at double the amount of the operation, in bolivars.*

Chávez had repeatedly devalued the bolivar during his reign in office. In 2003, after the imposition of currency controls, the bolivar was fixed at Bs1,600/$. In February 2004, the bolivar was devalued from Bs1,600/$ to Bs1,920/$. In 2005, it experienced another devaluation, to Bs2,150/$. In January 2008, the bolivar was replaced with the *bolivar fuerte* (BsF) and re-denominated, knocking off three zeros from the currency value, from Bs2,150/$ to BsF2.15/$. All bank accounts and business agreements and contracts were instantly re-denominated into bolivar fuertes by decree. January 1, 2010, a full five years later, saw the bolivar devalued massively, from BsF2.15/$ to BsF4.3/$.

Of course this did not eliminate a third exchange rate in effect, the Transaction System for Foreign Currency Denominated Securities (SITME), another government organization established to set the rate used by businesses to gain access to critical hard currency like the U.S. dollar in order to pay for inputs and other imported components. That rate, set at an even more costly BsF5.30/$, allowed commercial business to gain limited access to foreign currency—at a very high price.

Alternative Markets

The Venezuelan people had struggled so long with an artificially valued currency that they had become some of the most adept in the world at working through *black markets* and *alternative markets*. The "black" or parallel market was a semi-legal market that used brokered desk trading, yet was still not formally authorized much less regulated by the Venezuelan government.

The black market for bolivars, quoted in newspapers until recently, served a major purpose. Although the government set the official exchange rate, it still did not meet all of the demand for dollars even at that rate. As a result, the black market rate became the key indicator of value changes from supply and demand. Grocery stores, restaurants, merchants of all kinds used the black market rates to base their prices and price changes. When the black market rate started rising rapidly, business owners started increasing prices to make up for the loss in value of receiving what they considered discounted bolivars. Chávez and the Venezuelan government then, repeatedly, chastised business and threatened business owners raising prices with losing their companies. Despite all official efforts, black market trading was estimated at an astounding $100 million per day.[3]

One of the most innovative developments in this dysfunctional marketplace had been the selective use of alternative currencies throughout Venezuela. One such example was the *cimarón*, a round piece of stamped cardboard, introduced in a number of rural markets in exchange for goods. The principle was that someone coming to the country markets with goods for barter could exchange them for cimarón, then the cimarón for other goods. What the cimarón could not be exchanged for was bolivar fuertes. According to José Guerra, the former head of research at the country's Central Bank, the cimarón was a relic from Venezuela's past in which landowners paid their peasant workers, their serfs, in tokens which could only be used for goods on their own estates.[4] Although promoted by the government as another step in being "freed" from capitalist ways, the alternative currencies had seen only limited use.

The Chávez Objective

Venezuela's constant battle with inflation has been the underlying economic force driving official devaluation and black market depreciation. Averaging anywhere between 20% and 35% per year over the past decade, inflation has undermined all attempts by the government to reign in the value of its own currency. The devaluations alone contribute to inflation, as more and more domestic

[2] "Venezuela Temporarily Closes Parallel Currency Market," by Tamara Pearson, Venezuelanalysis.com, May 18, 2010.

[3] "Currency Woes Dog Venezuelans After Devaluation," by Darcy Crowe, *Wall Street Journal*, May 10, 2010.

[4] "Venezuela's Alternative Currencies," *The Economist*, December 18, 2008, print edition.

currency must then be used to buy the same—or fewer goods—following devaluation. The poor typically suffer the brunt of the devaluation, as they spend the greatest percentages of their incomes on food and other basic necessities, the majority of which are imported.

The Chávez regime, however, has repeatedly used the devaluation of the bolivar to increase the domestic monetary resources it earns from its oil exports. Oil, priced in dollars on the world market, generates U.S. dollar earnings. After each devaluation, each dollar of oil export revenue generates more bolivars or bolivar fuerte for government spending within Venezuela.

South America's largest oil-producing nation will devalue its currency by weakening the exchange rate used in the central bank-administered bond trading market, or Sitme, by 18.5 percent to 6.50 bolivars per U.S. dollar from 5.30 at present, according to the median

estimate of eight analysts surveyed by Bloomberg. Five of the analysts said the adjustment, which helps boost government revenue from oil exports, will occur by March 31.

—"Venezuela to Devalue Bolivar for Second Time This Quarter," By Charlie Devereux and Dominic Carey, *Bloomberg,* January 7, 2011.

CASE QUESTIONS

1. Why must a country's currency be devalued? What is failing in the economy?

2. What benefit did the Venezuelan regime in power gain from the repeated devaluation of the bolivar?

3. By the time you read this you will know whether the analysts predicting the future of the bolivar were correct. How did they do?

Questions

1. **Definitions.** Define the following terms:
   a. Foreign exchange market
   b. Foreign exchange transaction
   c. Foreign exchange

2. **Functions of the Foreign Exchange Market.** What are the three major functions of the foreign exchange market?

3. **Market Participants.** For each of the foreign exchange market participants, identify their motive for buying or selling foreign exchange.

4. **Transaction.** Define each of the following types of foreign exchange transactions:
   a. Spot
   b. Outright forward
   c. Forward-forward swaps

5. **Foreign Exchange Market Characteristics.** With reference to foreign exchange turnover in 2001 rank the following:
   a. The relative size of spot, forwards, and swaps as of 2001
   b. The five most important geographic locations for foreign exchange turnover
   c. The three most important currencies of denomination

6. **Foreign Exchange Rate Quotations.** Define and give an example of the following:
   a. Bid quote
   b. Ask quote

7. **Reciprocals.** Convert the following indirect quotes to direct quotes and direct quotes to indirect quotes:
   a. Euro: €1.22/$ (indirect quote)
   b. Russia: Rbl30/$ (indirect quote)
   c. Canada: $0.72/C$ (direct quote)
   d. Denmark: $0.1644/DKr (direct quote)

8. **Geographical Extent of the Foreign Exchange Market.**
   a. What is the geographical location of the foreign exchange market?
   b. What are the two main types of trading systems for foreign exchange?
   c. How are foreign exchange markets connected for trading activities?

9. **American and European Terms.** With reference to interbank quotations, what is the difference between American terms and European terms?

10. **Direct and Indirect Quotes.**
   a. Define and give an example of a direct quote between the U.S. dollar and the Mexican peso, where the United States is designated as the home country.
   b. Define and give an example of an indirect quote between the Japanese yen and the Chinese renminbi (yuan), where China is designated as the home country.

Problems

1. **Munich to Moscow.** On your post-graduation celebratory trip you decide to travel from Munich, Germany to Moscow, Russia. You leave Munich with

15,000 euros in your wallet. Wanting to exchange all of them for Russian rubles, you obtain the following quotes:

Spot rate on the dollar/euro cross rate	$1.3214/€
Spot rate on the ruble/dollar cross rate	Rbl 30.96/$

a. What is the Russian ruble/euro cross rate?
b. How many rubles will you obtain for your euros?

2. **Jumping to Japan.** After spending a week in Moscow you get an email from your friend in Japan. He can get you a very good deal on a plane ticket and wants you to meet him in Osaka next week to continue your post-graduation celebratory trip. You have 450,000 rubles left in your money pouch. In preparation for the trip you want to exchange your Russian rubles for Japanese yen so you get the following quotes:

Spot rate on the rubles/dollar cross rate	Rbl 30.96/$
Spot rate on the yen/dollar cross rate	¥ 84.02/$

a. What is the Russian ruble/euro cross rate?
b. How many rubles will you obtain for your euros?

3. **Visiting Guatemala.** Isaac Díez Peris lives in Rio de Janeiro. While attending school in Spain he meets Juan Carlos Cordero from Guatemala. Over the summer holiday Isaac decides to visit Juan Carlos in Guatemala City for a couple of weeks. Isaac's parents give him some spending money, R$4,500. Isaac wants to exchange it for Guatemalan quetzals (GTQ). He collects the following rates:

Spot rate on the GTQ/€ cross rate	GTQ 10.5799/€
Spot rate on the €/reais cross rate	€0.4462/R$

a. What is the Brazilian reais/Guatemalan quetzal cross rate?
b. How many quetzals will Isaac get for his reais?

4. **Trading in Zurich.** Andreas Broszio just started as an analyst for Credit Suisse in Zurich, Switzerland. He receives the following quotes for Swiss francs against the dollar for spot, 1-month forward, 3-months forward, and six months forward.

Spot exchange rate:

Bid rate	SF 1.2575/$
Ask rate	SF 1.2585/S
1-month forward	10 to 15
3-months forward	14 to 22
6-months forward	20 to 30

a. Calculate outright quotes for bid and ask, and the number of points spread between each.
b. What do you notice about the spread as quotes evolve from spot toward six months?
c. What is the 6-month Swiss bill rate?

5. **Crisis in the Pacific.** The Asian financial crisis which began in July 1997 wreaked havoc throughout the currency markets of East Asia.
   a. Which of the following currencies had the largest depreciations or devaluations during the July to November period?
   b. Which seemingly survived the first five months of the crisis with the least impact on their currencies?

Country	Currency	July 1997 (per US$)	November 1997 (per US$)
China	yuan	8.40	8.40
Hong Kong	dollar	7.75	7.73
Indonesia	rupiah	2,400	3,600
Korea	won	900	1,100
Malaysia	ringgit	2.50	3.50
Philippines	peso	27	34
Singapore	dollar	1.43	1.60
Taiwan	dollar	27.80	32.70
Thailand	baht	25.0	40.0

6. **Forward Premiums on the Japanese Yen.** Use the following spot and forward bid-ask rates for the Japanese yen/U.S. dollar (¥/$) exchange rate from September 16, 2010, to answer the following questions:
   a. What is the mid-rate for each maturity?
   b. What is the annual forward premium for all maturities?
   c. Which maturities have the smallest and largest forward premiums?

Period	¥/$ Bid Rate	¥/$ Ask Rate
spot	85.41	85.46
1 month	85.02	85.05
2 months	84.86	84.90
3 months	84.37	84.42
6 months	83.17	83.20
12 months	82.87	82.91
24 months	81.79	81.82

7. **Bloomberg Currency Cross Rates.** Use the following cross rate table from Bloomberg to answer the following questions.
   a. Japanese yen per U.S. dollar?
   b. U.S. dollars per Japanese yen?
   c. U.S. dollars per euro?
   d. Euros per U.S. dollar?
   e. Japanese yen per euro?
   f. Euros per Japanese yen?

Currency	USD	EUR	JPY	GBP	CHF	CAD	AUD	HKD
HKD	7.7736	10.2976	0.0928	12.2853	7.9165	7.6987	7.6584	
AUD	1.015	1.3446	0.0121	1.6042	1.0337	1.0053		0.1306
CAD	1.0097	1.3376	0.0121	1.5958	1.0283		0.9948	0.1299
CHF	0.9819	1.3008	0.0117	1.5519		0.9725	0.9674	0.1263
GBP	0.6328	0.8382	0.0076		0.6444	0.6267	0.6234	0.0814
JPY	83.735	110.9238		132.3348	85.2751	82.9281	82.4949	10.7718
EUR	0.7549		0.009	1.193	0.7688	0.7476	0.7437	0.0971
USD		1.3247	0.0119	1.5804	1.0184	0.9904	0.9852	0.1286

g. Canadian dollars per U.S. dollar?
h. U.S. dollars per Canadian dollar?
i. Australian dollars per U.S. dollar?
j. U.S. dollars per Australian dollar?
k. British pounds per U.S. dollar?
l. U.S. dollars per British pound?
m. U.S. dollars per Swiss franc?
n. Swiss francs per U.S. dollar?

8. **Forward Premiums on the Dollar/Euro ($/€).** Use the following spot and forward bid-ask rates for the U.S. dollar/euro (US$/€) exchange rate from December 10, 2010, to answer the following questions:
   a. What is the mid-rate for each maturity?
   b. What is the annual forward premium for all maturities?
   c. Which maturities have the smallest and largest forward premiums?

Period	US$/€ Bid Rate	US$/€ Ask Rate
spot	1.3231	1.3232
1 month	1.3230	1.3231
2 months	1.3228	1.3229
3 months	1.3224	1.3227
6 months	1.3215	1.3218
12 months	1.3194	1.3198
24 months	1.3147	1.3176

9. **Triangular Arbitrage Using the Swiss Franc.** The following exchange rates are available to you. (You can buy or sell at the stated rates.) Assume you have an initial SF12,000,000. Can you make a profit via triangular arbitrage? If so, show the steps and calculate the amount of profit in Swiss francs.

Mt. Fuji Bank	¥ 92.00/$
Mt. Rushmore Bank	SF1.02/$
Mt Blanc Bank	¥ 90.00/SF

10. **Forward Premiums on the Australian Dollar.** Use the following spot and forward bid-ask rates for the U.S. dollar/Australian dollar (US$/A$) exchange rate from December 10, 2010, to answer the following questions:
    a. What is the mid-rate for each maturity?
    b. What is the annual forward premium for all maturities?
    c. Which maturities have the smallest and largest forward premiums?

Period	US$/A$ Bid Rate	US$/A$ Ask Rate
spot	0.98510	0.98540
1 month	0.98131	0.98165
2 months	0.97745	0.97786
3 months	0.97397	0.97441
6 months	0.96241	0.96295
12 months	0.93960	0.94045
24 months	0.89770	0.89900

11. **Transatlantic Arbitrage.** A corporate treasury working out of Vienna with operations in New York simultaneously calls Citibank in New York City and Barclays in London. The banks give the following quotes on the euro simultaneously.

Citibank NYC	Barclays London
$0.7551-61/€	$0.7545-75/€

Using $1 million or its euro equivalent, show how the corporate treasury could make geographic arbitrage profit with the two different exchange rate quotes.

12. **Canuck Exports.** A Canadian exporter, Canuck Exports, will be receiving six payments of €12,000, ranging from now to 12 months in the future. Since the company keeps cash balances in both Canadian dollars and U.S. dollars, it can choose which currency

to change the euros to at the end of the various periods. Which currency appears to offer the better rates in the forward market?

Period	Days Forward	C$/euro	US$/euro
spot		1.3360	1.3221
1 month	30	1.3368	1.3230
2 months	60	1.3376	1.3228
3 months	90	1.3382	1.3224
6 months	180	1.3406	1.3215
12 months	360	1.3462	1.3194

13. Venezuelan Bolivar (A). The Venezuelan government officially floated the Venezuelan bolivar (Bs) in February 2002. Within weeks, its value had moved from the pre-float fix of Bs778/$ to Bs1025/$.
a. Is this a devaluation or depreciation?
b. By what percentage did its value change?

14. Venezuelan Bolivar (B). The Venezuelan political and economic crisis deepened in late 2002 and early 2003. On January 1, 2003, the bolivar was trading at Bs1400/$. By February 1, its value had fallen to Bs1950/$. Many currency analysts and forecasters were predicting that the bolivar would fall an additional 40% from its February 1 value by early summer 2003.
a. What was the percentage change in January?
b. Its forecast value for June 2003?

15. Indirect Quotation on the Dollar. Calculate the forward premium on the dollar (the dollar is the home currency) if the spot rate is €1.3300/$ and the 3-month forward rate is €1.3400/$.

16. Direct Quotation on the Dollar. Calculate the forward discount on the dollar (the dollar is the home currency) if the spot rate is $1.5800/£ and the 6-month forward rate is $1.5550/£.

17. Mexican Peso - European Euro Cross Rate. Calculate the cross rate between the Mexican peso (Ps) and the euro (€) from the following spot rates: Ps12.45/$ and €0.7550/$.

18. Pura Vida. Calculate the cross rate between the Costa Rican colón (₡) and the Canadian dollar (C$) from the following spot rates: C500.29/$ and C$1.02/$.

19. Around the Horn. Assuming the following quotes, calculate how a market trader at Citibank with $1,000,000 can make an intermarket arbitrage profit.

Citibank quotes U.S. dollar per pound	$1.5900/£
National Westminster quotes euros per pound	€1.2000/£
Deutschebank quotes U.S. dollar per euro	$0.7550/€

20. Great Pyramids. Inspired by his recent trip to the Great Pyramids, Citibank trader Ruminder Dhillon wonders if he can make an intermarket arbitrage profit using Libyan dinars and Saudi riyals. He has $1,000,000 to work with so he gathers the following quotes:

Citibank quotes U.S. dollar per Libyan dinar	$1.9324/LYD
National Bank of Kuwait quotes Saudi riyal per Libyan dinar	SAR1.9405/LYD
Barclay quotes U.S. dollar per Saudi riyal	$0.2667/SAR

Internet Exercises

1. Bank for International Settlements. The Bank for International Settlements (BIS) publishes a wealth of effective exchange rate indices. Use its database and analyses to determine the degree to which the dollar, the euro, and the yen (the "big three currencies") are currently overvalued or undervalued.

Bank for International Settlements — bis.org/statistics/eer/index.htm

2. Bank of Canada Exchange Rate Index (CERI). The Bank of Canada regularly publishes an index of the Canadian dollar's value, the CERI. The CERI is a multilateral trade-weighted index of the Canadian dollar's value against other major global currencies relevant to the Canadian economy and business landscape. Use the CERI from the Bank of Canada's Web site to evaluate the relative strength of the *loonie* in recent years.

Bank of Canada exchange rates — www.bankofcanada.ca/en/rates/ceri.html

3. Forward Quotes. OzForex Foreign Exchange Services provides representative forward rates on a multitude of currencies online. Use the following Web site to search out forward exchange rate quotations on a variety of currencies. (Note the London, New York, and Sydney times listed on the quotation screen.)

OzForex — ozforex.com.au/fxoptions/optiondynamics.htm

4. Federal Reserve Statistical Release. The United States Federal Reserve provides daily updates of the value of the major currencies traded against the U.S. dollar on its Web site. Use the Fed's Web site to determine the relative weights used by the Fed to determine the index of the dollar's value.

Federal Reserve — www.federalreserve.gov/releases/h10/update/

5. **Exotic Currencies.** Although major currencies like the U.S. dollar and the Japanese yen dominate the headlines, there are nearly as many currencies as countries in the world. Many of these currencies are traded in extremely thin and highly regulated markets, making their convertibility suspect. Finding quotations for these currencies is sometimes very difficult. Use the following Web pages to see how many African currency quotes you can find.

Forex-Markets.com	www.forex-markets.com/quotes_exotic.htm
Oanda.com	oanda.com

6. **Daily Market Commentary.** Many different online currency trading and consulting services provide daily assessments of global currency market activity.

Use the following GCI site to find the market's current assessment of how the euro is trading against both the U.S. dollar and the Canadian dollar.

GCI Financial Ltd	www.gcitrading.com/fxnews/

7. **Pacific Exchange Rate Service.** The Pacific Exchange Rate Service Web site, managed by Professor Werner Antweiler of the University of British Columbia, possesses a wealth of current information on currency exchange rates and related statistics. Use the service to plot the recent performance of currencies which have recently suffered significant devaluations or depreciations, such as the Argentine peso, the Venezuelan bolivar, the Turkish lira, and the Egyptian pound.

Pacific Exchange Rate Service	fx.sauder.ubc.ca/plot.html

International Parity Conditions

CHAPTER 7

. . . if capital freely flowed towards those countries where it could be most profitably employed, there could be no difference in the rate of profit, and no other difference in the real or labour price of commodities, than the additional quantity of labour required to convey them to the various markets where they were to be sold.

—David Ricardo, *On the Principles of Political Economy and Taxation,* 1817, Chapter 7.

LEARNING OBJECTIVES

◆ Examine how price levels and price level changes (inflation) in countries determine the exchange rate at which their currencies are traded.

◆ Show how interest rates reflect inflationary forces within each country and currency.

◆ Explain how forward markets for currencies reflect expectations held by market participants about the future spot exchange rate.

◆ Analyze how, in equilibrium, the spot and forward currency markets are aligned with interest differentials and differentials in expected inflation.

What are the determinants of exchange rates? Are changes in exchange rates predictable? These are fundamental questions that managers of MNEs, international portfolio investors, importers and exporters, and government officials must deal with every day. This chapter describes the core financial theories surrounding the determination of exchange rates. Chapter 9 will introduce two other major theoretical schools of thought regarding currency valuation, and combine the three different theories in a variety of real-world applications.

The economic theories that link exchange rates, price levels, and interest rates are called *international parity conditions*. In the eyes of many, these international parity conditions form the core of the financial theory that is considered unique to the field of international finance. These theories do not always work out to be "true" when compared to what students and practitioners observe in the real world, but they are central to any understanding of how multinational business is conducted and funded in the world today. And, as is often the case, the mistake is not always in the theory itself, but in the way it is interpreted or applied in practice. This chapter concludes with a Mini-Case, *Emerging Market Carry-Trades*, which demonstrates how both the theory and practice of international parity conditions sometimes combine to form unusual opportunities for profit.

Prices and Exchange Rates

If identical products or services can be sold in two different markets, and no restrictions exist on the sale or transportation costs of moving the product between markets, the product's price should be the same in both markets. This is called the *law of one price*.

A primary principle of competitive markets is that prices will equalize across markets if frictions or costs of moving the products or services between markets do not exist. If the two markets are in two different countries, the product's price may be stated in different currency terms, but the price of the product should still be the same. Comparing prices would require only a conversion from one currency to the other. For example,

$$P^\$ \times S = P^\yen$$

where the price of the product in U.S. dollars ($P^\$$), multiplied by the spot exchange rate (S, yen per U.S. dollar), equals the price of the product in Japanese yen ($P^\yen$). Conversely, if the prices of the two products were stated in local currencies, and markets were efficient at competing away a higher price in one market relative to the other, the exchange rate could be deduced from the relative local product prices:

$$S = \frac{P^\yen}{P^\$}$$

Purchasing Power Parity and the Law of One Price

If the law of one price were true for all goods and services, the *purchasing power parity* (PPP) exchange rate could be found from any individual set of prices. By comparing the prices of identical products denominated in different currencies, one could determine the "real" or PPP exchange rate that should exist if markets were efficient. This is the absolute version of the theory of purchasing power parity. Absolute PPP states that the spot exchange rate is determined by the relative prices of similar baskets of goods.

The "Big Mac Index," as it has been christened by *The Economist* (see Exhibit 7.1) and calculated regularly since 1986, is a prime example of the law of one price. Assuming that the Big Mac is indeed identical in all countries listed, it serves as one form of comparison of whether currencies are currently trading at market rates which are close to the exchange rate implied by Big Macs in local currencies.

For example, using Exhibit 7.1, in China a Big Mac costs yuan 13.2 (local currency), while in the United States the same Big Mac costs $3.73. The actual spot exchange rate was yuan 6.78/$ at this time. The price of a Big Mac in China in U.S. dollar terms was therefore

$$\frac{\text{Price of Big Mac in China in Yuan}}{\text{Yuan/\$ spot rate}} = \frac{\text{Yuan } 13.2}{\text{Yuan } 6.78/\$} = \$1.95$$

This is the value in column 2 of Exhibit 7.1 for China. *The Economist* then calculates the *implied purchasing power parity rate of exchange* using the actual price of the Big Mac in China (yuan 13.2) over the price of the Big Mac in the United States in U.S. dollars ($3.73):

$$\frac{\text{Price of Big Mac in China in Yuan}}{\text{Price of Big Mac in the U.S. in \$}} = \frac{\text{Yuan } 13.2}{\$3.73} = \text{Yuan } 3.54/\$$$

This is the value in column 4 of Exhibit 7.1 for China. In principle, this is what the Big Mac Index is saying the exchange rate between the yuan and the dollar should be according to the theory.

EXHIBIT 7.1	Selected Rates from the Big Mac Index

Country and Currency		(1) Big Mac Price in Local Currency	(2) Actual Dollar Exchange Rate on July 1	(3) Big Mac Price in Dollars	(4) Implied PPP of the Dollar	(5) Under/over Valuation against Dollar
United States	$	3.73	—	3.73	—	—
Britain	£	2.29	1.52	3.48*	1.63*	−7%
Canada	C$	4.17	1.04	4.01	1.12	7%
China	Yuan	13.2	6.78	1.95	3.54	−48%
Denmark	DK	28.50	5.81	4.91	7.64	32%
Euro area	€	3.38	1.28	4.33*	1.10*	16%
Japan	¥	320	87.2	3.67	85.8	−2%
Russia	Rouble	71.0	30.4	2.34	19.0	−37%
Switzerland	SFr	6.50	1.05	6.19	1.74	66%
Thailand	Baht	70.0	32.3	2.17	18.8	−42%

*These exchange rates are stated in US$ per unit of local currency, $/£ and $/€.

**Percentage under/over valuation against the dollar is calculated as (Implied−Actual)/(Actual), except for the Britain and Euro area calculations, which are (Actual−Implied)/(Implied)

Source: Data drawn from "The Big Mac Index," *The Economist,* July 22, 2010.

Now comparing this implied PPP rate of exchange, yuan 3.54/$, with the actual market rate of exchange at that time, yuan 6.78/$, the degree to which the yuan is either *undervalued* (−%) or *overvalued* (+%) versus the U.S. dollar is calculated as follows:

$$\frac{\text{Implied Rate} - \text{Actual Rate}}{\text{Actual Rate}} = \frac{\text{Yuan } 3.54/\$ - \text{Yuan } 6.78/\$}{\text{Yuan } 6.78/\$} = -48\%$$

In this case, the Big Mac Index indicates that the Chinese yuan is undervalued by 48% versus the U.S. dollar as indicated in the far right-hand column for China in Exhibit 7.1. *The Economist* is also quick to note that although this indicates a sizable undervaluation of the managed value of the Chinese yuan versus the dollar, the theory of purchasing power parity is supposed to indicate where the value of currencies should go over the long-term, and not necessarily its value today.

It is important to understand why the Big Mac may be a good candidate for the application of the law of one price and measurement of under or overvaluation. First, the product itself is nearly identical in each and every market. This is the result of product consistency, process excellence, and McDonald's brand image and pride. Second, and just as important, the product is a result of predominantly local materials and input costs. This means that its price in each country is representative of domestic costs and prices and not imported ones—which would be influenced by exchange rates themselves. But as *The Economist* points out, the Big Mac Index is not perfect.

The index was never intended to be a precise predictor of currency movements, simply a take-away guide to whether currencies are at their "correct" long-run level. Curiously, however, burgernomics has an impressive record in predicting exchange rates: currencies that show up as overvalued often tend to weaken in later years. But you must always remember

the Big Mac's limitations. Burgers cannot sensibly be traded across borders and prices are distorted by differences in taxes and the cost of non-tradable inputs, such as rents.
— "Happy 20th Anniversary," *The Economist*, May 25, 2006.

A less extreme form of this principle would be that in relatively efficient markets the price of a basket of goods would be the same in each market. Replacing the price of a single product with a price index allows the PPP exchange rate between two countries to be stated as

$$S = \frac{PI^{¥}}{PI^{\$}}$$

where $PI^{¥}$ and $PI^{\$}$ are price indices expressed in local currency for Japan and the United States, respectively. For example, if the identical basket of goods cost ¥1,000 in Japan and $10 in the United States, the PPP exchange rate would be

$$\frac{¥1000}{\$10} = ¥100/\$.$$

Just in case you are starting to believe that PPP is just about numbers, *Global Finance in Practice 7.1* reminds you of the human side of the equation.

Relative Purchasing Power Parity

If the assumptions of the absolute version of PPP theory are relaxed a bit, we observe what is termed *relative purchasing power parity*. Relative PPP holds that PPP is not particularly helpful in determining what the spot rate is today, but that the relative change in prices between

---

GLOBAL FINANCE IN PRACTICE   7.1

The Immiseration of the North Korean People—The "Revaluation" of the North Korean Won

The principles of purchasing power are not just a theoretical principle, they can also capture the problems, poverty, and misery of a people. The devaluation of the North Korean won (KPW) in November 2009 was one such case.

The North Korean government has been trying to stop the growth and activity in the street markets of its country for decades. For many years the street markets have been the lone opportunity for most of the Korean people to earn a living. Under the communist state's stewardship, the quality of life for its 24 million people has continued to deteriorate. Between 1990 and 2008, the country's infant mortality rate had increased 30%, and life expectancy had fallen by three years. The United Nations estimated that one in three children under the age of five suffered malnutrition. Although most of the working population worked officially for the government, many were underpaid (or in many cases not paid), that they often bribed their bosses to allow them to leave work early to try to scrape out a living in the street markets of the underground economy.

But it was this very basic market economy which President Kim Jong-il and the governing regime wished to stamp out. On November 30, 2009, the Korean government made a surprise announcement to its people: a new, more valuable Korean won would replace the old one. "You have until the end of the day to exchange your old won for new won." All old 1,000 won notes would be replaced with 10 won notes, knocking off two zeros from the officially recognized value of the currency. This meant that everyone holding old won, their cash and savings, would now officially be worth 1/100th of what it was previously. Exchange was limited to 100,000 old won. People who had worked and saved for decades to accumulate what was roughly $200 or $300 in savings outside of North Korea were wiped out; their total life savings were essentially worthless. By officially denouncing the old currency, the North Korean people would be forced to exchange their holdings for new won. The government would indeed undermine the underground economy.

The results were devastating. After days of street protests, the government raised the 100,000 ceiling to 150,000. By late January 2010, inflation was rising so rapidly that Kim Jong-il apologized to the people for the revaluation's impact on their lives. The government administrator who had led the revaluation was arrested, and in February 2010, executed "for his treason."

two countries over a period of time determines the change in the exchange rate over that period. More specifically, *if the spot exchange rate between two countries starts in equilibrium, any change in the differential rate of inflation between them tends to be offset over the long run by an equal but opposite change in the spot exchange rate.*

Exhibit 7.2 shows a general case of relative PPP. The vertical axis shows the percentage change in the spot exchange rate for foreign currency, and the horizontal axis shows the percentage difference in expected rates of inflation (foreign relative to home country). The diagonal parity line shows the equilibrium position between a change in the exchange rate and relative inflation rates. For instance, point P represents an equilibrium point where inflation in the foreign country, Japan, is 4% lower than in the home country, the United States. Therefore, relative PPP would predict that the yen would appreciate by 4% per annum with respect to the U.S. dollar.

The main justification for purchasing power parity is that if a country experiences inflation rates higher than those of its main trading partners, and its exchange rate does not change, its exports of goods and services become less competitive with comparable products produced elsewhere. Imports from abroad become more price-competitive with higher-priced domestic products. These price changes lead to a deficit on current account in the balance of payments unless offset by capital and financial flows.

Empirical Tests of Purchasing Power Parity

Extensive testing of both the absolute and relative versions of purchasing power parity and the law of one price has been done.[1] These tests have, for the most part, not proved PPP to be accurate in predicting future exchange rates. Goods and services do not in

EXHIBIT 7.2   Relative Purchasing Power Parity (PPP)

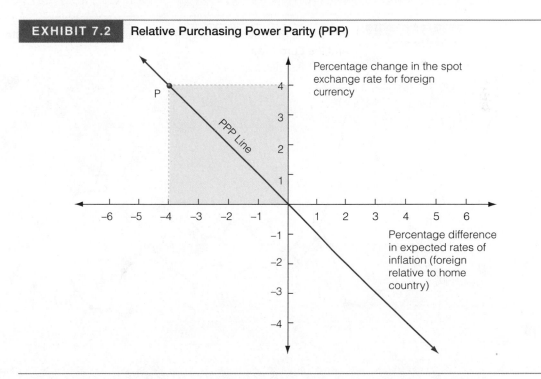

[1]See, for example, Kenneth Rogoff, "The Purchasing Power Parity Puzzle," *Journal of Economic Literature*, Volume 34, Number 2, June 1996, pp. 647–668; and Barry K. Goodwin, Thomas Greenes, and Michael K. Wohlgenant, "Testing the Law of One Price When Trade Takes Time," *Journal of International Money and Finance*, March 1990, pp. 21–40.

reality move at zero cost between countries, and in fact many services are not "tradable"—for example, haircuts. Many goods and services are not of the same quality across countries, reflecting differences in the tastes and resources of the countries of their manufacture and consumption.

Two general conclusions can be made from these tests: 1) PPP holds up well over the very long run but poorly for shorter time periods and 2) the theory holds better for countries with relatively high rates of inflation and underdeveloped capital markets.

Exchange Rate Indices: Real and Nominal

Because any single country trades with numerous partners, we need to track and evaluate its individual currency value against all other currency values in order to determine relative purchasing power. The objective is to discover whether its exchange rate is "overvalued" or "undervalued" in terms of PPP. One of the primary methods of dealing with this problem is the calculation of *exchange rate indices*. These indices are formed by trade-weighting the bilateral exchange rates between the home country and its trading partners.

The *nominal effective exchange rate index* uses actual exchange rates to create an index, on a weighted average basis, of the value of the subject currency over time. It does not really indicate anything about the "true value" of the currency, or anything related to PPP. The nominal index simply calculates how the currency value relates to some arbitrarily chosen base period, but it is used in the formation of the real effective exchange rate index. The *real effective exchange rate index* indicates how the weighted average purchasing power of the currency has changed relative to some arbitrarily selected base period. Exhibit 7.3 plots the real effective exchange rate indexes for the United States and Japan over the past 22 years.

EXHIBIT 7.3   IMF's Real Effective Exchange Rate Indexes for the United States, Japan, and the Euro Area

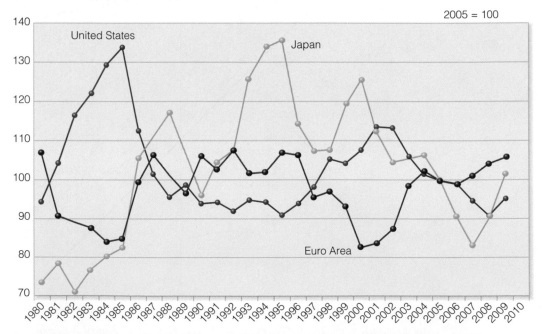

Source: *International Financial Statistics*, IMF, annual, CPI-weighted real effective exchange rates, series RECZF.

The real effective exchange rate index for the U.S. dollar, $E_R^\$$, is found by multiplying the nominal effective exchange rate index, $E_N^\$$ by the ratio of U.S. dollar costs, $C^\$$, over foreign currency costs, C^{FC}, both in index form:

$$E_R^\$ = E_N^\$ \times \frac{C^\$}{C^{FC}}$$

If changes in exchange rates just offset differential inflation rates—if purchasing power parity holds—all the real effective exchange rate indices would stay at 100. If an exchange rate strengthened more than was justified by differential inflation, its index would rise above 100. If the real effective exchange rate index is above 100, the currency would be considered "overvalued" from a competitive perspective. An index value below 100 would suggest an "undervalued" currency.

Exhibit 7.3 shows that the real effective exchange rate of the dollar, yen, and euro have changed over the past three decades. The dollar's index value was substantially above 100 in the 1980s (overvalued), but has remained below 100 (undervalued) since the late 1980s (it did rise slightly above 100 briefly in 1995–1996 and again in 2001–2002). The Japanese yen's real effective rate has remained above 100 for nearly the entire 1980 to 2006 period (overvalued). The euro, whose value has been back-calculated for the years prior to its introduction in 1999, has been largely below 100 and undervalued in its real lifetime.

Apart from measuring deviations from PPP, a country's real effective exchange rate is an important tool for management when predicting upward or downward pressure on a country's balance of payments and exchange rate, as well as an indicator of the desirability to produce for export from that country. *Global Finance in Practice 7.2* shows deviations from PPP in the twentieth century.

Exchange Rate Pass-Through

Incomplete *exchange rate pass-through* is one reason that a country's real effective exchange rate index can deviate for lengthy periods from its PPP-equilibrium level of 100. The degree to which the prices of imported and exported goods change as a result of exchange rate changes is termed *pass-through*. Although PPP implies that all exchange rate changes are passed-through by equivalent changes in prices to trading partners, empirical research in the 1980s questioned this long-held assumption. For example, sizable current account deficits of the United States in the 1980s and 1990s did not respond to changes in the value of the dollar.

To illustrate exchange rate pass-through, assume that BMW produces an automobile in Germany and pays all production expenses in euros. When the firm exports the auto to the United States, the price of the BMW in the U.S. market should simply be the euro value converted to dollars at the spot exchange rate:

$$P_{BMW}^\$ = P_{BMW}^{\text{€}} \times S$$

where $P_{BMW}^\$$ is the BMW price in dollars, $P_{BMW}^{\text{€}}$ is the BMW price in euros, and S is the number of dollars per euro. If the euro appreciated 10% versus the U.S. dollar, the new spot exchange rate should result in the price of the BMW in the United States rising a proportional 10%. If the price in dollars increases by the same percentage change as the exchange rate, the pass-through of exchange rate changes is complete (or 100%).

However, if the price in dollars rises by less than the percentage change in exchange rates (as is often the case in international trade), the pass-through is *partial*, as illustrated in

GLOBAL FINANCE IN PRACTICE   7.2

Deviations from Purchasing Power Parity in the Twentieth Century

The recent seminal work by Dimson, Marsh, and Staunton (2002) found that for the 1900–2000 period, relative purchasing power parity generally held. They noted also, however, that significant short-run deviations from PPP did occur. "When deviations from PPP appear to be present, it is likely that exchange rates are responding not only to relative inflation but also to other economic and political factors. Changes in productivity differentials, such as Japan's post-war productivity growth in the traded-goods sector, can bring similar wealth effects, with domestic inflation that does not endanger the country's exchange rate."

"While real exchange rates do not appear to exhibit a long-term upward or downward trend, they are clearly volatile, and on a year-to-year basis, PPP explains little of the fluctuations in foreign exchange rates. Some of the extreme changes (in the table) reflect exchange rates or inflation indexes that are not representative, typically (as in Germany) because of wartime controls, and this may amplify the volatility of real exchange rate changes. Given the potential measurement error in inflation indexes, and the fact that real exchange rates involve a ratio of two different price index series, it is all the more striking that, with the exception of South Africa, all real exchange rates appreciate or depreciate annually by no more than a fraction of one percentage point."

Source: Elroy Dimson, Paul Marsh, and Mike Staunton, *Triumph of the Optimists: 101 Years of Global Investment Returns,* Princeton University Press, 2002, pp. 97–98.

Real Exchange Rate Changes against the U.S. Dollar, Annually 1900–2000

Country	Geometric Mean (%)	Arithmetic Mean (%)	Standard Deviation (%)	Minimum Change (Year, %)	Maximum Change (Year, %)
Australia	−0.6	−0.1	10.7	1931: −39.0	1933: 54.2
Belgium	0.2	1.0	13.3	1919: −32.1	1933: 54.2
Canada	−0.5	−0.4	4.6	1931: −18.1	1933: 12.9
Denmark	0.1	1.0	12.7	1946: −50.3	1933: 37.2
France	−0.4	2.5	24.0	1946: −78.3	1943: 141.5
Germany	−0.1	15.1	134.8	1945: −75.0	1948: 1302.0
Ireland	−0.1	0.5	11.2	1946: −37.0	1933: 56.6
Italy	−0.2	4.0	39.5	1946: −64.9	1944: 335.2
Japan	0.2	3.2	29.5	1945: −78.3	1946: 253.0
The Netherlands	−0.1	0.8	12.6	1946: −61.6	1933: 55.7
South Africa	−1.3	−0.7	10.5	1946: −35.3	1986: 37.3
Spain	−0.4	1.1	18.8	1946: −56.4	1939: 128.7
Sweden	−0.4	0.2	10.7	1919: −38.0	1933: 43.5
Switzerland	0.2	0.8	11.2	1936: −29.0	1933: 53.3
United Kingdom	−0.3	0.3	11.7	1946: −36.7	1933: 55.2

Exhibit 7.4. The 71% pass-through (U.S. dollar prices rose only 14.29% when the euro appreciated 20%) implies that BMW is absorbing a portion of the adverse exchange rate change. This absorption could result from smaller profit margins, cost reductions, or both. For example, components and raw materials imported to Germany cost less in euros when the euro appreciates. It is also likely that some time may pass before all exchange rate changes are finally reflected in the prices of traded goods, including the period over which previously signed contracts are delivered upon. It is obviously in the interest of BMW to keep the appreciation of the euro from raising the price of its automobiles in major export markets.

The concept of *price elasticity of demand* is useful when determining the desired level of pass-through. Recall that the own-price elasticity of demand for any good is the percentage

---

EXHIBIT 7.4   Exchange Rate Pass-Through

Pass-through is the measure of response of imported and exported product prices to exchange rate changes. Assume that the price in dollars and euros of a BMW automobile produced in Germany and sold in the United States at the spot exchange rate is

$$P_{BMW}^{\$} = P_{BMW}^{€} \times (\$/€) = €35{,}000 \times \$1{,}000/€ = \$35{,}000$$

If the euro were to appreciate 20% versus the U.S. dollar, from \$1.0000/€ to \$1.2000/€, the price of the BMW in the U.S. market should theoretically be \$42,000. But if the price of the BMW in the U.S. does not rise by 20%—for example, it rises only to \$40,000—then the degree of pass-through is partial;

$$\frac{P_{BMW,2}^{\$}}{P_{BMW,1}^{\$}} - \frac{\$40{,}000}{\$35{,}000} = 1.1429, \text{ or a } 14.29\% \text{ increase.}$$

The degree of pass-through is measured by the proportion of the exchange rate change reflected in dollar prices. In this example, the dollar price of the BMW rose only 14.29%, while the euro appreciated 20% against the U.S. dollar. The degree of pass-through is partial: 14.29% ÷ 20.00%, or approximately 0.71. Only 71% of the exchange rate change was passed-through to the U.S. dollar price. The remaining 29% of the exchange rate change has been absorbed by BMW.

---

change in quantity of the good demanded as a result of the percentage change in the good's own price:

$$\text{Price elasticity of demand} = e_p = \frac{\%\Delta Q_d}{\%\Delta P}$$

where Q_d is quantity demanded and P is product price. If the absolute value of e_p is less than 1.0, then the good is relatively "inelastic." If it is greater than 1.0, it is a relatively "elastic" good.

A German product that is relatively price-inelastic, meaning that the quantity demanded is relatively unresponsive to price changes, may often demonstrate a high degree of pass-through. This is because a higher dollar price in the United States market would have little noticeable effect on the quantity of the product demanded by consumers. Dollar revenue would increase, but euro revenue would remain the same. However, products that are relatively price-elastic would respond in the opposite way. If the 20% euro appreciation resulted in 20% higher dollar prices, U.S. consumers would decrease the number of BMWs purchased. If the price elasticity of demand for BMWs in the United States were greater than one, total dollar sales revenue of BMWs would decline.

Interest Rates and Exchange Rates

We have already seen how prices of goods in different countries should be related through exchange rates. We now consider how interest rates are linked to exchange rates.

The Fisher Effect

The Fisher effect, named after economist Irving Fisher, states that nominal interest rates in each country are equal to the required real rate of return plus compensation for expected inflation. More formally, this is derived from $(1 + r)(1 + \pi) - 1$:

$$i = r + \pi + r\pi$$

where i is the nominal rate of interest, r is the real rate of interest, and π is the expected rate of inflation over the period of time for which funds are to be lent. The final compound term,

$r\pi$, is frequently dropped from consideration due to its relatively minor value. The Fisher effect then reduces to (approximate form):

$$i = r + \pi$$

The Fisher effect applied to the United States and Japan would be as follows:

$$i^\$ = r^\$ + \pi^\$; i^¥ = r^¥ + \pi^¥$$

where the superscripts \$ and ¥ pertain to the respective nominal (i), real r, and expected inflation (π) components of financial instruments denominated in dollars and yen, respectively. We need to forecast the future rate of inflation, not what inflation has been. Predicting the future can be difficult.

Empirical tests using *ex-post* national inflation rates have shown that the Fisher effect usually exists for short-maturity government securities such as Treasury bills and notes. Comparisons based on longer maturities suffer from the increased financial risk inherent in fluctuations of the market value of the bonds prior to maturity. Comparisons of private sector securities are influenced by unequal creditworthiness of the issuers. All the tests are inconclusive to the extent that recent past rates of inflation are not a correct measure of future expected inflation.

The International Fisher Effect

The relationship between the percentage change in the spot exchange rate over time and the differential between comparable interest rates in different national capital markets is known as the *international Fisher effect*. "Fisher-open," as it is often termed, states that the spot exchange rate should change in an equal amount but in the opposite direction to the difference in interest rates between two countries. More formally,

$$\frac{S_1 - S_2}{S_2} = i^\$ - i^¥$$

where $i^\$$ and $i^¥$ are the respective national interest rates, and S is the spot exchange rate using indirect quotes (an indirect quote on the dollar is, for example, ¥/\$) at the beginning of the period (S_1) and the end of the period (S_2). This is the approximation form commonly used in industry. The precise formulation is as follows:

$$\frac{S_1 - S_2}{S_2} = \frac{i^\$ - i^¥}{1 + i^¥}$$

Justification for the international Fisher effect is that investors must be rewarded or penalized to offset the expected change in exchange rates. For example, if a dollar-based investor buys a 10-year yen bond earning 4% interest, instead of a 10-year dollar bond earning 6% interest, the investor must be expecting the yen to appreciate vis-à-vis the dollar by at least 2% per year during the 10 years. If not, the dollar-based investor would be better off remaining in dollars. If the yen appreciates 3% during the 10-year period, the dollar-based investor would earn a bonus of 1% higher return. However, the international Fisher effect predicts that with unrestricted capital flows, an investor should be indifferent to whether his bond is in dollars or yen, because investors worldwide would see the same opportunity and compete it away.

Empirical tests lend some support to the relationship postulated by the international Fisher effect, although considerable short-run deviations occur. A more serious criticism has been posed, however, by recent studies that suggest the existence of a foreign exchange risk premium for most major currencies. Also, speculation in uncovered interest arbitrage (on pages 187–188) creates distortions in currency markets. Thus, the expected change in exchange rates might consistently be more than the difference in interest rates.

The Forward Rate

A *forward rate* is an exchange rate quoted today for settlement at some future date. A forward exchange agreement between currencies states the rate of exchange at which a foreign currency will be *bought forward* or *sold forward* at a specific date in the future (typically after 30, 60, 90, 180, 270, or 360 days).

The forward rate is calculated for any specific maturity by adjusting the current spot exchange rate by the ratio of euro currency interest rates of the same maturity for the two subject currencies. For example, the 90-day forward rate for the Swiss franc/U.S. dollar exchange rate ($F_{90}^{SF/\$}$) is found by multiplying the current spot rate ($S^{SF/\$}$) by the ratio of the 90-day euro-Swiss franc deposit rate (i^{SF}) over the 90-day Eurodollar deposit rate ($i^{\$}$):

$$F_{90}^{SF/\$} = S^{SF/\$} \times \frac{\left[1 + \left(i^{SF} \times \frac{90}{360}\right)\right]}{\left[1 + \left(i^{\$} \times \frac{90}{360}\right)\right]}$$

Assuming a spot rate of SF1.4800/\$, a 90-day euro Swiss franc deposit rate of 4.00% per annum, and a 90-day Eurodollar deposit rate of 8.00% per annum, the 90-day forward rate is SF1.4655/\$:

$$F_{90}^{SF/\$} = SF1.4800/\$ \times \frac{\left[1 + \left(0.0400 \times \frac{90}{360}\right)\right]}{\left[1 + \left(0.0800 \times \frac{90}{360}\right)\right]} = SF1.4800/\$ \times \frac{1.01}{1.02} = SF1.4655/\$$$

The *forward premium* or *discount* is the percentage difference between the spot and forward exchange rate, stated in annual percentage terms. When the foreign currency price of the home currency is used, as in this case of SF/\$, the formula for the percent-per-annum premium or discount becomes

$$f^{SF} = \frac{\text{Spot} - \text{Forward}}{\text{Forward}} \times \frac{360}{\text{days}} \times 100$$

Substituting the SF/\$ spot and forward rates, as well as the number of days forward (90),

$$f^{SF} = \frac{SF1.4800/\$ - SF1.4655/\$}{SF1.4655/\$} \times \frac{360}{90} \times 100 = +3.96\% \text{ per annum}$$

The sign is positive, indicating that the Swiss franc is *selling forward at a 3.96% per annum premium* over the dollar (it takes 3.96% more dollars to get a franc at the 90-day forward rate).

As illustrated in Exhibit 7.5, the forward premium on the Eurodollar forward exchange rate series arises from the differential between Eurodollar interest rates and Swiss franc interest rates. Because the forward rate for any particular maturity utilizes the specific interest rates for that term, the forward premium or discount on a currency is visually obvious — the currency with the higher interest rate (in this case the U.S. dollar) will sell forward at a discount, and the currency with the lower interest rate (in this case the Swiss franc) will sell forward at a premium.

The forward rate is calculated from three observable data items — the spot rate, the foreign currency deposit rate, and the home currency deposit rate — and is not a forecast of the future spot exchange. It is, however, frequently used by managers within MNEs as a forecast, with mixed results, as the following section describes.

EXHIBIT 7.5   Currency Yield Curves and the Forward Premium

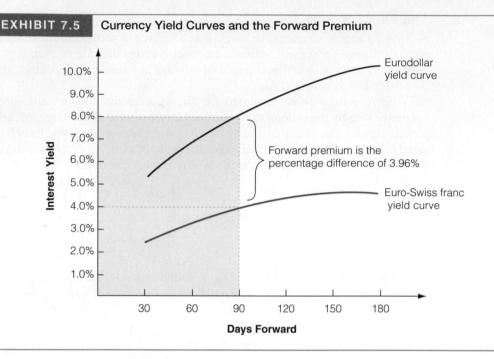

Interest Rate Parity (IRP)

The theory of *interest rate parity* (IRP) provides the link between the foreign exchange markets and the international money markets. The theory states: *The difference in the national interest rates for securities of similar risk and maturity should be equal to, but opposite in sign to, the forward rate discount or premium for the foreign currency, except for transaction costs.*

Exhibit 7.6 shows how the theory of interest rate parity works. Assume that an investor has $1,000,000 and several alternative but comparable Swiss franc (SF) monetary investments. If the investor chooses to invest in a dollar money market instrument, the investor would earn the dollar rate of interest. This results in $(1 + i^\$)$ at the end of the period, where $i^\$$ is the dollar rate of interest in decimal form. The investor may, however, choose to invest in a Swiss franc money market instrument of identical risk and maturity for the same period. This action would require that the investor exchange the dollars for francs at the spot rate of exchange, invest the francs in a money market instrument, sell the francs forward (in order to avoid any risk that the exchange rate would change), and at the end of the period convert the resulting proceeds back to dollars.

A dollar-based investor would evaluate the relative returns of starting in the top-left corner and investing in the dollar market (straight across the top of the box) compared to investing in the Swiss franc market (going down and then around the box to the top-right corner). The comparison of returns would be as follows:

$$(1 + i^\$) = S^{SF/\$} \times (1 + i^{SF}) \times \frac{1}{F^{SF/\$}}$$

where S = the spot rate of exchange and F = the forward rate of exchange. Substituting in the spot rate (SF1.4800/$) and forward rate (SF1.4655/$) and respective interest rates ($i^\$ = 0.02$, $i^{SF} = 0.01$) from Exhibit 7.6, the interest rate parity condition is as follows:

$$(1 + 0.02) = 1.4800 \times (1 + 0.01) \times \frac{1}{1.4655}$$

EXHIBIT 7.6   Interest Rate Parity (IRP)

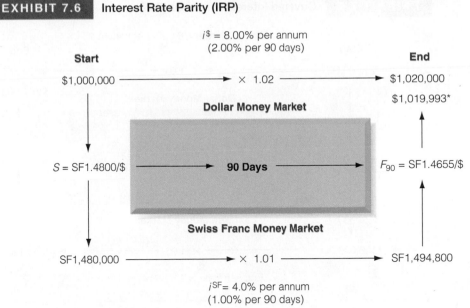

$i^\$ = 8.00\%$ per annum
(2.00% per 90 days)

Start

$1,000,000 ———————→ × 1.02 ———————→ $1,020,000

$1,019,993*

Dollar Money Market

$S = SF1.4800/\$$ ———————→ **90 Days** ———————→ $F_{90} = SF1.4655/\$$

Swiss Franc Money Market

SF1,480,000 ———————→ × 1.01 ———————→ SF1,494,800

$i^{SF} = 4.0\%$ per annum
(1.00% per 90 days)

*Note that the Swiss franc investment yields $1,019,993, $7 less on a $1 million investment.

The left-hand side of the equation is the gross return the investor would earn by investing in dollars. The right-hand side is the gross return the investor would earn by exchanging dollars for Swiss francs at the spot rate, investing the franc proceeds in the Swiss franc money market, and simultaneously selling the principal plus interest in Swiss francs forward for dollars at the current 90-day forward rate.

Ignoring transaction costs, if the returns in dollars are equal between the two alternative money market investments, the spot and forward rates are considered to be at IRP. The transaction is "covered," because the exchange rate back to dollars is guaranteed at the end of the 90-day period. Therefore, as shown in Exhibit 7.6, in order for the two alternatives to be equal, any differences in interest rates must be offset by the difference between the spot and forward exchange rates (in approximate form):

$$\frac{F}{S} = \frac{(1 + i^{SF})}{(1 + i^\$)} \text{ or } \frac{SF1.4655/\$}{SF1.4800/\$} = \frac{1.01}{1.02} = 0.9902 \approx 1\%$$

Covered Interest Arbitrage (CIA)

The spot and forward exchange markets are not constantly in the state of equilibrium described by interest rate parity. When the market is not in equilibrium, the potential for "riskless" or arbitrage profit exists. The arbitrager who recognizes such an imbalance will move to take advantage of the disequilibrium by investing in whichever currency offers the higher return on a covered basis. This is called *covered interest arbitrage* (CIA).

Exhibit 7.7 describes the steps that a currency trader, most likely working in the arbitrage division of a large international bank, would implement to perform a CIA transaction. The currency trader, Fye Hong, may utilize any of a number of major eurocurrencies that his bank holds to conduct arbitrage investments. The morning conditions indicate to Fye Hong that a CIA transaction that exchanges 1 million U.S. dollars for Japanese yen,

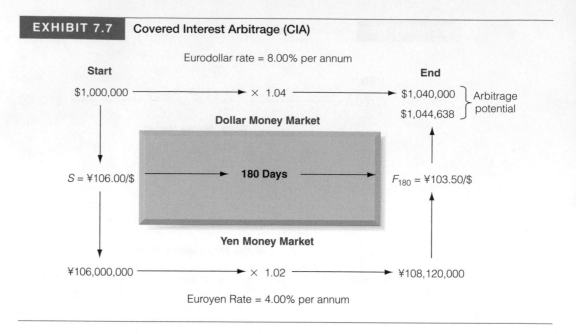

EXHIBIT 7.7 Covered Interest Arbitrage (CIA)

invested in a six month euroyen account and sold forward back to dollars, will yield a profit of $4,638 ($1,044,638 − $1,040,000) over and above that available from a eurodollar investment. Conditions in the exchange markets and euromarkets change rapidly however, so if Fye Hong waits even a few minutes, the profit opportunity may disappear. Fye Hong executes the following transaction:

Step 1: Convert $1,000,000 at the spot rate of ¥106.00/$ to ¥106,000,000 (see "Start" in Exhibit 7.7).

Step 2: Invest the proceeds, ¥106,000,000, in a euroyen account for six months, earning 4.00% per annum, or 2% for 180 days.

Step 3: Simultaneously sell the future yen proceeds (¥108,120,000) forward for dollars at the 180-day forward rate of ¥103.50/$. This action "locks in" gross dollar revenues of $1,044,638 (see "End" in Exhibit 7.7).

Step 4: Calculate the cost (opportunity cost) of funds used at the eurodollar rate of 8.00% per annum, or 4% for 180 days, with principal and interest then totaling $1,040,000. Profit on CIA ("End") is $4,638 ($1,044,638 − $1,040,000).

Note that all profits are stated in terms of the currency in which the transaction was initialized, but that a trader may conduct investments denominated in U.S. dollars, Japanese yen, or any other major currency.

Rule of Thumb. All that is required to make a covered interest arbitrage profit is for interest rate parity not to hold. Depending on the relative interest rates and forward premium, Fye Hong would have started in Japanese yen, invested in U.S. dollars, and sold the dollars forward for yen. The profit would then end up denominated in yen. But how would Fye Hong decide in which direction to go around the box in Exhibit 7.7?

The key to determining whether to start in dollars or yen is to compare the differences in interest rates to the forward premium on the yen (the *cost of cover*). For example, in

Exhibit 7.7, the difference in 180-day interest rates is 2.00% (dollar interest rates are higher by 2.00%). The premium on the yen for 180 days forward is as follows:

$$f^{\yen} = \frac{\text{Spot} - \text{Forward}}{\text{Forward}} \times \frac{360}{180} \times 100 = \frac{\yen106.00/\$ - \yen103.50/\$}{\yen103.50/\$} \times 200 = 4.8309\%$$

In other words, by investing in yen and selling the yen proceeds forward at the forward rate, Fye Hong earns 4.83% per annum, whereas he would earn only 4% per annum if he continues to invest in dollars.

> **Arbitrage Rule of Thumb:** *If the difference in interest rates is greater than the forward premium (or expected change in the spot rate), invest in the higher interest yielding currency. If the difference in interest rates is less than the forward premium (or expected change in the spot rate), invest in the lower interest yielding currency.*

Using this rule of thumb should enable Fye Hong to choose in which direction to go around the box in Exhibit 7.7. It also guarantees that he will always make a profit if he goes in the right direction. This rule assumes that the profit is greater than any transaction costs incurred.

This process of CIA drives the international currency and money markets toward the equilibrium described by interest rate parity. Slight deviations from equilibrium provide opportunities for arbitragers to make small riskless profits. Such deviations provide the supply and demand forces that will move the market back toward parity (equilibrium).

Covered interest arbitrage opportunities continue until interest rate parity is reestablished, because the arbitragers are able to earn risk-free profits by repeating the cycle as often as possible. Their actions, however, nudge the foreign exchange and money markets back toward equilibrium for the following reasons:

1. The purchase of yen in the spot market and the sale of yen in the forward market narrows the premium on the forward yen. This is because the spot yen strengthens from the extra demand and the forward yen weakens because of the extra sales. A narrower premium on the forward yen reduces the foreign exchange gain previously captured by investing in yen.

2. The demand for yen-denominated securities causes yen interest rates to fall, and the higher level of borrowing in the United States causes dollar interest rates to rise. The net result is a wider interest differential in favor of investing in the dollar.

Uncovered Interest Arbitrage (UIA)

A deviation from covered interest arbitrage is *uncovered interest arbitrage* (UIA), wherein investors borrow in countries and currencies exhibiting relatively low interest rates and convert the proceeds into currencies that offer much higher interest rates. The transaction is "uncovered," because the investor does not sell the higher yielding currency proceeds forward, choosing to remain uncovered and accept the currency risk of exchanging the higher yield currency into the lower yielding currency at the end of the period. Exhibit 7.8 demonstrates the steps an uncovered interest arbitrager takes when undertaking what is termed the "yen carry-trade."

The "yen carry-trade" is an age-old application of UIA. Investors, from both inside and outside Japan, take advantage of extremely low interest rates in Japanese yen (0.40% per annum) to raise capital. Investors exchange the capital they raise for other currencies like U.S. dollars or euros. Then they reinvest these dollar or euro proceeds in dollar or euro money markets where the funds earn substantially higher rates of return (5.00% per annum

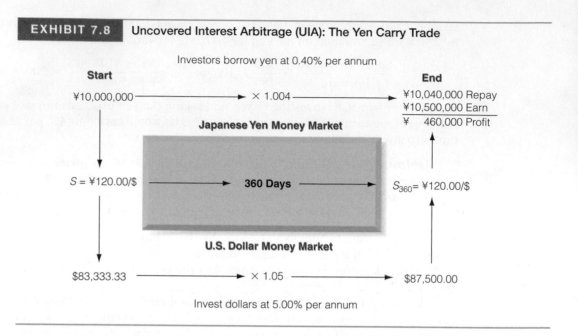

EXHIBIT 7.8   Uncovered Interest Arbitrage (UIA): The Yen Carry Trade

Investors borrow yen at 0.40% per annum

Start		End
¥10,000,000 —————→ × 1.004 —————→		¥10,040,000 Repay ¥10,500,000 Earn ¥ 460,000 Profit

Japanese Yen Money Market

S = ¥120.00/$ —————→ **360 Days** —————→ S_{360} = ¥120.00/$

U.S. Dollar Money Market

$83,333.33 —————→ × 1.05 —————→ $87,500.00

Invest dollars at 5.00% per annum

in Exhibit 7.8). At the end of the period—a year, in this case—they convert the dollar proceeds back into Japanese yen in the spot market. The result is a tidy profit over what it costs to repay the initial loan.

The trick, however, is that the spot exchange rate at the end of the year must not change significantly from what it was at the beginning of the year. If the yen were to appreciate significantly against the dollar, as it did in late 1999, moving from ¥120/$ to ¥105/$, these "uncovered" investors would suffer sizable losses when they convert their dollars into yen to repay the yen they borrowed. The higher return does indeed come at higher risk!

Equilibrium between Interest Rates and Exchange Rates

Exhibit 7.9 illustrates the conditions necessary for equilibrium between interest rates and exchange rates. The vertical axis shows the difference in interest rates in favor of the foreign currency, and the horizontal axis shows the forward premium or discount on that currency. The interest rate parity line shows the equilibrium state, but transaction costs cause the line to be a band rather than a thin line. Transaction costs arise from foreign exchange and investment brokerage costs on buying and selling securities. Typical transaction costs in recent years have been in the range of 0.18% to 0.25% on an annual basis. For individual transactions like Fye Hong's arbitrage activities in the previous example on covered interest arbitrage (CIA), there is no explicit transaction cost per trade; rather, the costs of the bank in supporting Fye Hong's activities are the transaction costs. Point X shows one possible equilibrium position, where a 4% lower rate of interest on yen securities would be offset by a 4% premium on the forward yen.

The disequilibrium situation, which encouraged the interest rate arbitrage in the previous CIA example, is illustrated by point U. It is located off the interest rate parity line because the lower interest on the yen is −4% (annual basis), whereas the premium on the forward yen is slightly over 4.8% (annual basis). Using the formula for forward premium presented earlier, we find the premium on the yen thus:

$$\frac{¥106.00/\$ - 103.50/\$}{¥103.50/\$} \times \frac{360 \text{ days}}{180 \text{ days}} \times 100 = 4.83\%$$

EXHIBIT 7.9	Interest Rate Parity (IRP) and Equilibrium

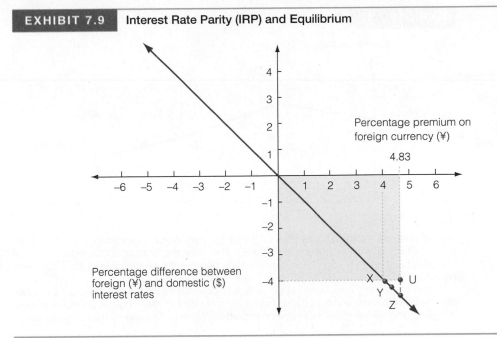

The situation depicted by point U is unstable, because all investors have an incentive to execute the same covered interest arbitrage. Except for a bank failure, the arbitrage gain is virtually risk-free.

Some observers have suggested that political risk does exist, because one of the governments might apply capital controls that would prevent execution of the forward contract. This risk is fairly remote for covered interest arbitrage between major financial centers of the world, especially because a large portion of funds used for covered interest arbitrage is in Eurodollars. The concern may be valid for pairings with countries not noted for political and fiscal stability.

The net result of the disequilibrium is that fund flows will narrow the gap in interest rates and/or decrease the premium on the forward yen. In other words, market pressures will cause point U in Exhibit 7.9 to move toward the interest rate parity band. Equilibrium might be reached at point Y, or at any other locus between X and Z, depending on whether forward market premiums are more or less easily shifted than interest rate differentials.

Forward Rate as an Unbiased Predictor of the Future Spot Rate

Some forecasters believe that foreign exchange markets for the major floating currencies are "efficient" and forward exchange rates are *unbiased predictors* of future spot exchange rates.

Exhibit 7.10 demonstrates the meaning of "unbiased prediction" in terms of how the forward rate performs in estimating future spot exchange rates. If the forward rate is an unbiased predictor of the future spot rate, the expected value of the future spot rate at time 2 equals the present forward rate for time 2 delivery, available now, $E_1(S_2) = F_{1,2}$.

Intuitively, this means that the distribution of possible actual spot rates in the future is centered on the forward rate. The fact that it is an unbiased predictor, however, does not mean that the future spot rate will actually be equal to what the forward rate predicts. Unbiased prediction simply means that the forward rate will, on average, overestimate and

EXHIBIT 7.10   Forward Rate as Unbiased Predictor for Future Spot Rate

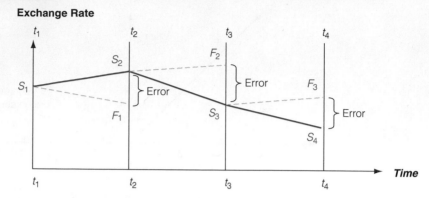

The forward rate available today (F_t, $t + 1$), time t, for delivery at future time $t + 1$, is used as a "predictor" of the spot rate that will exist at that day in the future. Therefore, the forecast spot rate for time S_{t2} is F_1; the actual spot rate turns out to be S_2. The vertical distance between the prediction and the actual spot rate is the forecast error.

When the forward rate is termed an "unbiased predictor of the future spot rate," it means that the forward rate overestimates or underestimates the future spot rate with relatively equal frequency and amount. It therefore "misses the mark" in a regular and orderly manner. The sum of the errors equals zero.

underestimate the actual future spot rate in equal frequency and degree. The forward rate may, in fact, never actually equal the future spot rate.

The rationale for this relationship is based on the hypothesis that the foreign exchange market is reasonably efficient. Market efficiency assumes that 1) all relevant information is quickly reflected in both the spot and forward exchange markets; 2) transaction costs are low; and 3) instruments denominated in different currencies are perfect substitutes for one another.

Empirical studies of the efficient foreign exchange market hypothesis have yielded conflicting results. Nevertheless, a consensus is developing that rejects the efficient market hypothesis. It appears that the forward rate is not an unbiased predictor of the future spot rate and that it does pay to use resources to attempt to forecast exchange rates.

If the efficient market hypothesis is correct, a financial executive cannot expect to profit in any consistent manner from forecasting future exchange rates, because current quotations in the forward market reflect all that is presently known about likely future rates. Although future exchange rates may well differ from the expectation implicit in the present forward market quotation, we cannot know today which way actual future quotations will differ from today's forward rate. The expected mean value of deviations is zero. The forward rate is therefore an "unbiased" estimator of the future spot rate.

Tests of foreign exchange market efficiency, using longer time periods of analysis, conclude that either exchange market efficiency is untestable or, if it is testable, that the market is not efficient. Furthermore, the existence and success of foreign exchange forecasting services suggest that managers are willing to pay a price for forecast information even though they can use the forward rate as a forecast at no cost. The "cost" of buying this information is, in many circumstances, an "insurance premium" for financial managers who might get fired for using their own forecast, including forward rates, when that forecast proves incorrect. If they "bought" professional advice that turned out wrong, the fault was not in their forecast!

If the exchange market is not efficient, it would be sensible for a firm to spend resources on forecasting exchange rates. This is the opposite conclusion to the one in which exchange markets are deemed efficient.

Prices, Interest Rates, and Exchange Rates in Equilibrium

Exhibit 7.11 illustrates all of the fundamental parity relations simultaneously, in equilibrium, using the U.S. dollar and the Japanese yen. The forecasted inflation rates for Japan and the United States are 1% and 5%, respectively; a 4% differential. The nominal interest rate in the U.S. dollar market (1-year government security) is 8%, a differential of 4% over the Japanese nominal interest rate of 4%. The spot rate, S_1, is ¥104/$, and the 1-year forward rate is ¥100/$.

◆ **Relation A: Purchasing Power Parity (PPP).** According to the relative version of purchasing power parity, the spot exchange rate one year from now, S_2, is expected to be ¥100/$:

$$S_2 = S_1 \times \frac{1 + \pi^{¥}}{1 + \pi^{\$}} = ¥104/\$ \times \frac{1.01}{1.05} = ¥100/\$$$

This is a 4% change and equal, but opposite in sign, to the difference in expected rates of inflation (1% − 5% or 4%).

◆ **Relation B: The Fisher Effect.** The real rate of return is the nominal rate of interest less the expected rate of inflation. Assuming efficient and open markets, the real rates of return should be equal across currencies. Here, the real rate is 3% in U.S. dollar markets ($r = i - \pi = 8\% - 5\%$), and in Japanese yen markets (4% − 1%). Note that the 3% real rate of return is not in Exhibit 7.11, but rather the Fisher effect's relationship—that nominal interest rate differentials equal the difference in expected rates of inflation, −4%.

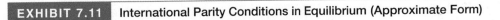

EXHIBIT 7.11 International Parity Conditions in Equilibrium (Approximate Form)

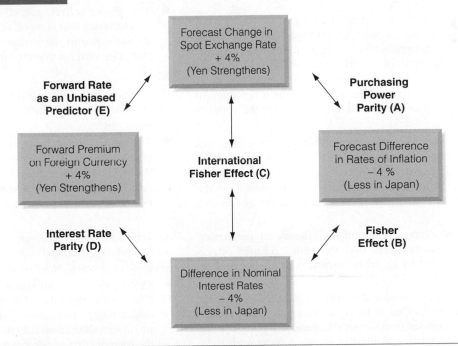

◆ **Relation C: International Fisher Effect.** The forecast change in the spot exchange rate, in this case 4%, is equal to, but opposite in sign to, the differential between nominal interest rates:

$$\frac{S_1 - S_2}{S_2} \times 100 = i^{¥} - i^{\$} = 4\% - 8\% = -4\%$$

◆ **Relation D: Interest Rate Parity (IRP).** According to the theory of interest rate parity, the difference in nominal interest rates is equal to, but opposite in sign to, the forward premium. For this numerical example, the nominal yen interest rate (4%) is 4% less than the nominal dollar interest rate (8%):

$$i^{¥} - i^{\$} = 4\% - 8\% = -4\%$$

and the forward premium is a positive 4%:

$$f^{¥} = \frac{S_1 - F}{F} \times 100 = \frac{¥104/\$ - ¥100/\$}{¥100/\$} \times 100 = 4\%$$

◆ **Relation E: Forward Rate as an Unbiased Predictor.** Finally, the 1-year forward rate on the Japanese yen, ¥100/$, if assumed to be an unbiased predictor of the future spot rate, also forecasts ¥100/$.

Summary of Learning Objectives

Examine how price levels and price level changes (inflation) in countries determine the exchange rate at which their currencies are traded.

◆ Parity conditions have traditionally been used by economists to help explain the long-run trend in an exchange rate.

◆ Under conditions of freely floating rates, the expected rate of change in the spot exchange rate, differential rates of national inflation and interest, and the forward discount or premium are all directly proportional to each other and mutually determined. A change in one of these variables has a tendency to change all of them with a feedback on the variable that changes first.

◆ If the identical product or service can be sold in two different markets, and there are no restrictions on its sale or transportation costs of moving the product between markets, the product's price should be the same in both markets. This is called the law of one price.

◆ The absolute version of the theory of purchasing power parity states that the spot exchange rate is determined by the relative prices of similar baskets of goods.

◆ The relative version of the theory of purchasing power parity states that if the spot exchange rate between two countries starts in equilibrium, any change in the differential rate of inflation between them tends to be offset over the long run by an equal but opposite change in the spot exchange rate.

Show how interest rates reflect inflationary forces within each country and currency.

◆ The Fisher effect, named after economist Irving Fisher, states that nominal interest rates in each country are equal to the required real rate of return plus compensation for expected inflation.

Explain how forward markets for currencies reflect expectations held by market participants about the future spot exchange rate.

◆ The international Fisher effect, "Fisher-open" as it is often termed, states that the spot exchange rate should change in an equal amount but in the opposite direction to the difference in interest rates between two countries.

Analyze how, in equilibrium, the spot and forward currency markets are aligned with interest differentials and differentials in expected inflation.

◆ The theory of interest rate parity (IRP) states that the difference in the national interest rates for securities of similar risk and maturity should be equal to, but opposite in sign to, the forward rate discount or premium for the foreign currency, except for transaction costs.

◆ When the spot and forward exchange markets are not in equilibrium as described by interest rate parity, the potential for "riskless" or arbitrage profit exists. This is called covered interest arbitrage (CIA).

◆ Some forecasters believe that for the major floating currencies, foreign exchange markets are "efficient" and forward exchange rates are unbiased predictors of future spot exchange rates.

MINI-CASE

Emerging Market Carry Trades

The weak economic outlook for the euro zone is the primary factor driving the change in that trade. Minor differences in interest rates between the euro and either the dollar or the Japanese yen are less important right now, strategists said. Rates in the U.S. and Japan are near 0%, while they are at 1% in Europe.

—"Euro Becomes Increasingly Popular Choice to Fund Carry Trades," The *Wall Street Journal*, December 21, 2010.

Incredibly low interest rates in both the United States and Europe, accompanied by dim economic performance and continuing concern over fiscal deficits, has led to a most unexpected outcome: a new form of carry trade which shorts the dollar and euro.

The *carry trade* has long been associated with Japan and the relatively low interest rates which its financial community has made available to multinational investors. A form of uncovered interest rate arbitrage (UIA), the Japanese carry trade was based on an investor raising funds in Japan at low interest rates and then exchanging the proceeds for a foreign currency in which the interest

rates promised higher relative returns. Then, at the end of the term, the investor could potentially exchange the foreign currency returns, plus interest, back to Japanese yen to settle the obligation and also, hopefully, a profit. The entire risk-return profile of the strategy, however, was based on the exchange rate at the end of the period being relatively unchanged from the initial spot rate.

The global financial crisis of 2007–2009 has left a marketplace in which the U.S. Federal Reserve and the European Central Bank have pursued easy money policies. Both central banks, in an effort to maintain high levels of liquidity and support fragile commercial banking systems, have kept interest rates at near-zero levels. Now global investors, those who see opportunities for profit in an anemic global economy, are using those same low-cost funds in the U.S. and Europe to fund uncovered interest arbitrage activities. But what is making this "emerging market carry trade" so unique is not the interest rates, but the fact that investors are shorting two of the world's core currencies: the dollar and the euro.

Consider the strategy outlined in Exhibit 1. An investor borrows EUR 20 million at an incredibly low rate, say 1.00% per annum or 0.50% for 180 days. The EUR 20 million are then exchanged for Indian rupees (INR), the current spot rate being INR 60.4672 = EUR 1.00. The resulting INR

EXHIBIT 1   The Euro/Emerging Market Carry Trade

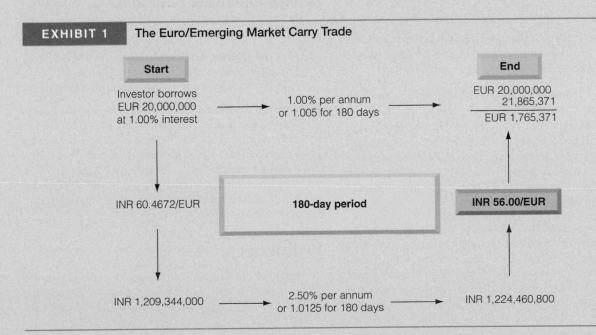

1,209,344,000 are put into an interest bearing deposit with any of a number of Indian banks attempting to attract capital. The rate of interest offered, 2.50%, is not particularly high, but is greater than that available in the dollar, euro, or even yen markets. But the critical component of the strategy is not to earn the higher rupee interest (although that does help), it is the expectations of the investor over the direction of the INR per EUR exchange rate.

The European economy yielded very weak economic growth in 2010, and all indications were that 2011 would not be much better. Low interest rates, although expected to persist, had not done much to support the euro's value. Like the dollar, many forecasts were for the euro to fall against many of the world's currencies—including the Indian rupee. The Indian economy, however, had been growing rapidly; in fact, nearly too fast. Inflationary pressures had kept inflation for 2010 at just under 10%, and it was expected to remain at 7% or higher throughout 2011. The State Bank of India, India's central bank, was expected to tighten monetary growth to fight inflationary pressures, sending rupee interest rates—and the rupee itself, higher on world markets. In the exhibit the investor is shown expecting a spot rate at the end of the 180-day arbitrage position at INR 56.00/EUR. The expected yield on position, a whopping 8.83% (EUR 1,765,371 profit on an initial investment of EUR 20 million). An extremely attractive rate of return in a global marketplace of sub-5% investment yields.

CASE QUESTIONS

1. Why are interest rates so low in the traditional core markets of USD and EUR?

2. What makes this "emerging market carry trade" so different from traditional forms of uncovered interest arbitrage?

3. Why are many investors shorting the dollar and the euro?

Questions

1. **Purchasing Power Parity.** Define the following terms:
   a. The law of one price
   b. Absolute purchasing power parity
   c. Relative purchasing power parity

2. **Nominal Effective Exchange Rate Index.** Explain how a nominal effective exchange rate index is constructed.

3. **Real Effective Exchange Rate Index.** What formula is used to convert a nominal effective exchange rate index into a real effective exchange rate index?

4. **Real Effective Exchange Rates: Japan and the United States.** Exhibit 7.3 compares the real effective exchange rates for the United States and Japan. If the comparative real effective exchange rate was the main determinant, does the United States or Japan have a competitive advantage in exporting? Which of the two has an advantage in importing? Explain why.

5. **Exchange Rate Pass-Through.** Incomplete *exchange rate pass-through* is one reason that a country's real effective exchange rate can deviate for lengthy periods from its purchasing power equilibrium level of 100. What is meant by the term *exchange rate pass-through*?

6. **The Fisher Effect.** Define the *Fisher effect*. To what extent do empirical tests confirm that the *Fisher effect* exists in practice?

7. **The International Fisher Effect.** Define the *international Fisher effect*. To what extent do empirical tests confirm that the *international Fisher effect* exists in practice?

8. **Interest Rate Parity.** Define *interest rate parity*. What is the relationship between *interest rate parity* and forward rates?

9. **Covered Interest Arbitrage.** Define the terms *covered interest arbitrage* and *uncovered interest arbitrage*. What is the difference between these two transactions?

10. **Forward Rate as an Unbiased Predictor of the Future Spot Rate.** Some forecasters believe that foreign exchange markets for the major floating currencies are "efficient" and forward exchange rates are *unbiased predictors* of future spot exchange rates. What is meant by "unbiased predictor" in terms of how the forward rate performs in estimating future spot exchange rates?

Problems

1. **Starbucks in Croatia.** Starbucks opened its first store in Zagreb, Croatia in October 2010. In Zagreb, the price of a tall vanilla latte is 25.70kn. In New York City,

the price of a tall vanilla latte is $2.65. The exchange rate between Croatian kunas (kn) and U.S. dollars is kn5.6288/$. According to purchasing power parity, is the Croatian kuna overvalued or undervalued?

2. **Crisis at the Heart of Carnaval.** The Argentine peso was fixed through a currency board at Ps1.00/$ throughout the 1990s. In January 2002, the Argentine peso was floated. On January 29, 2003, it was trading at Ps3.20/$. During that one year period, Argentina's inflation rate was 20% on an annualized basis. Inflation in the United States during that same period was 2.2% annualized.
   a. What should have been the exchange rate in January 2003 if PPP held?
   b. By what percentage was the Argentine peso undervalued on an annualized basis?
   c. What were the probable causes of undervaluation?

3. **Traveling Down Under.** Terry Lamoreaux owns homes in Sydney, Australia and Phoenix, Arizona. He travels between the two cities at least twice a year. Because of his frequent trips he wants to buy some new, high-quality luggage. He's done his research and has decided to purchase a Briggs and Riley three-piece luggage set. There are retail stores in Phoenix and Sydney. Terry was a finance major and wants to use purchasing power parity to determine if he is paying the same price regardless of where he makes his purchase.
   a. If the price of the three-piece luggage set in Phoenix is $850 and the price of the same three-piece set in Sydney is $930, using purchasing power parity, is the price of the luggage truly equal if the spot rate is A$1.0941/$?
   b. If the price of the luggage remains the same in Phoenix one year from now, determine the price of the luggage in Sydney in one year's time if PPP holds true. The U.S. Inflation rate is 1.15% and the Australian inflation rate is 3.13%.

4. **Takeshi Kamada—CIA Japan.** Takeshi Kamada, a foreign exchange trader at Credit Suisse (Tokyo), is exploring covered interest arbitrage possibilities. He wants to invest $5,000,000 or its yen equivalent, in a covered interest arbitrage between U.S. dollars and Japanese yen. He faced the following exchange rate and interest rate quotes.

Arbitrage funds available	$5,000,000
Spot rate (¥/$)	118.60
180-day forward rate (¥/$)	117.80
180-day U.S. dollar interest rate	4.800%
180-day Japanese yen interest rate	3.400%

5. **Takeshi Kamada—UIA Japan.** Takeshi Kamada, Credit Suisse (Tokyo), observes that the ¥/$ spot rate has been holding steady, and both dollar and yen interest rates have remained relatively fixed over the past week. Takeshi wonders if he should try an uncovered interest arbitrage (UIA) and thereby save the cost of forward cover. Many of Takeshi's research associates—and their computer models—are predicting the spot rate to remain close to ¥118.00/$ for the coming 180 days. Using the same data as in problem 4, analyze the UIA potential.

6. **Japanese/United States Parity Conditions.** Derek Tosh is attempting to determine whether U.S./Japanese financial conditions are at parity. The current spot rate is a flat ¥89.00/$, while the 360-day forward rate is ¥84.90/$. Forecast inflation is 1.100% for Japan, and 5.900% for the United States. The 360-day euro yen deposit rate is 4.700%, and the 360-day euro dollar deposit rate is 9.500%.
   a. Diagram and calculate whether international parity conditions hold between Japan and the United States.
   b. Find the forecasted change in the Japanese yen/U.S. dollar (¥/$) exchange rate one year from now.

7. **Corolla Exports and Pass-Through.** Assume that the export price of a Toyota Corolla from Osaka, Japan is ¥2,150,000. The exchange rate is ¥87.60/$. The forecast rate of inflation in the United States is 2.2% per year and in Japan is 0.0% per year. Use this data to answer the following questions on exchange rate pass-through.
   a. What was the export price for the Corolla at the beginning of the year expressed in U.S. dollars?
   b. Assuming purchasing power parity holds, what should be the exchange rate at the end of the year?
   c. Assuming 100% pass-through of exchange rate, what will be the dollar price of a Corolla at the end of the year?
   d. Assuming 75% pass-through, what will be the dollar price of a Corolla at the end of the year?

8. **Copenhagen Covered (A).** Heidi Høi Jensen, a foreign exchange trader at J.P.Morgan Chase, can invest $5 million, or the foreign currency equivalent of the bank's short-term funds, in a covered interest arbitrage with Denmark. Using the following quotes, can Heidi make a covered interest arbitrage (CIA) profit?

Arbitrage funds available	$5,000,000
Spot exchange rate (kr/$)	6.1720
3-month forward rate (kr/$)	6.1980
U.S. dollar 3-month interest rate	3.000%
Danish kroner 3-month interest rate	5.000%

9. Copenhagen Covered (B)—Part a. Heidi Høi Jensen is now evaluating the arbitrage profit potential in the same market after interest rates change. (Note that any time the difference in interest rates does not exactly equal the forward premium, it must be possible to make a CIA profit one way or another.)

Arbitrage funds available	$5,000,000
Spot exchange rate (kr/$)	6.1720
3-month forward rate (kr/$)	6.1980
U.S. dollar 3-month interest rate	4.000%
Danish kroner 3-month interest rate	5.000%

10. Copenhagen Covered (B)—Part b. Heidi Høi Jensen is now evaluating the arbitrage profit potential in the same market after interest rates change. (Note that any time the difference in interest rates does not exactly equal the forward premium, it must be possible to make a CIA profit one way or another.)

Arbitrage funds available	$5,000,000
Spot exchange rate (kr/$)	6.1720
3-month forward rate (kr/$)	6.1980
U.S. dollar 3-month interest rate	3.000%
Danish kroner 3-month interest rate	6.000%

11. Casper Landsten—CIA. Casper Landsten is a foreign exchange trader for a bank in New York. He has $1 million (or its Swiss franc equivalent) for a short term money market investment and wonders if he should invest in U.S. dollars for three months, or make a CIA investment in the Swiss franc. He faces the following quotes:

Arbitrage funds available	$1,000,000
Spot exchange rate (SFr/$)	1.2810
3-month forward rate (SFr/$)	1.2740
U.S. dollar 3-month interest rate	4.800%
Swiss franc 3-month interest rate	3.200%

12. Casper Landsten—UIA. Casper Landsten, using the same values and assumptions as in problem 11, decides to seek the full 4.800% return available in U.S. dollars by not covering his forward dollar receipts—an uncovered interest arbitrage (UIA) transaction. Assess this decision.

13. Casper Landsten—Thirty Days Later. One month after the events described in problems 10 and 11, Casper Landsten once again has $1 million (or its Swiss franc equivalent) to invest for three months. He now faces the following rates. Should he again enter into a covered interest arbitrage (CIA) investment?

Arbitrage funds available	$1,000,000
Spot exchange rate (SFr/$)	1.3392
3-month forward rate (SFr/$)	1.3286
U.S. dollar 3-month interest rate	4.750%
Swiss franc 3-month interest rate	3.625%

14. Pulau Penang Island Resort. Theresa Nunn is planning a 30-day vacation on Pulau Penang, Malaysia, one year from now. The present charge for a luxury suite plus meals in Malaysian ringgit (RM) is RM1,045/day. The Malaysian ringgit presently trades at RM3.1350/$. She determines that the dollar cost today for a 30-day stay would be $10,000. The hotel informs her that any increase in its room charges will be limited to any increase in the Malaysian cost of living. Malaysian inflation is expected to be 2.75% per annum, while U.S. inflation is expected to be 1.25%.

a. How many dollars might Theresa expect to need one year hence to pay for her 30-day vacation?

b. By what percent will the dollar cost have gone up? Why?

15. Statoil of Norway's Arbitrage. Statoil, the national oil company of Norway, is a large, sophisticated, and active participant in both the currency and petrochemical markets. Although it is a Norwegian company, because it operates within the global oil market, it considers the U.S. dollar as its functional currency, not the Norwegian krone. Ari Karlsen is a currency trader for Statoil, and has immediate use of either $3 million (or the Norwegian krone equivalent). He is faced with the following market rates, and wonders whether he can make some arbitrage profits in the coming 90 days.

Arbitrage funds available	$3,000,000
Spot exchange rate (Nok/$)	6.0312
3-month forward rate (Nok/$)	6.0186
U.S. dollar 3-month interest rate	5.000%
Norwegian krone 3-month interest rate	4.450%

16. **Separated by the Atlantic.** Separated by more than 3,000 nautical miles and five time zones, money and foreign exchange markets in both London and New York are very efficient. The following information has been collected from the respective areas:

Assumptions	London	New York
Spot exchange rate ($/€)	1.3264	1.3264
1-year Treasury bill rate	3.900%	4.500%
Expected inflation rate	Unknown	1.250%

    a. What do the financial markets suggest for inflation in Europe next year?

    b. Estimate today's 1-year forward exchange rate between the dollar and the euro?

17. **Chamonix Chateau Rentals.** You are planning a ski vacation to Mt. Blanc in Chamonix, France, one year from now. You are negotiating the rental of a chateau. The chateau's owner wishes to preserve his real income against both inflation and exchange rate changes, and so the present weekly rent of €9,800 (Christmas season) will be adjusted upward or downward for any change in the French cost of living between now and then. You are basing your budgeting on purchasing power parity (PPP). French inflation is expected to average 3.5% for the coming year, while U.S. dollar inflation is expected to be 2.5%. The current spot rate is $1.3620/€. What should you budget as the U.S. dollar cost of the 1-week rental?

Spot exchange rate ($/€)	$1.3620
Expected US inflation for coming year	2.500%
Expected French inflation for coming year	3.500%
Current chateau nominal weekly rent (€)	€ 9,800.00

18. **East Asiatic Company—Thailand.** The East Asiatic Company (EAC), a Danish company with subsidiaries throughout Asia, has been funding its Bangkok subsidiary primarily with U.S. dollar debt because of the cost and availability of dollar capital as opposed to Thai baht-denominated (B) debt. The treasurer of EAC-Thailand is considering a 1-year bank loan for $250,000. The current spot rate is B32.06/$, and the dollar-based interest is 6.75% for the 1-year period. 1-year loans are 12.00% in baht.

    a. Assuming expected inflation rates of 4.3% and 1.25% in Thailand and the United States, repectively, for the coming year, according to purchase power parity, what would be the effective cost of funds in Thai baht terms?

    b. If EAC's foreign exchange advisers believe strongly that the Thai government wants to push the value of the baht down against the dollar by 5% over the coming year (to promote its export competitiveness in dollar markets), what might be the effective cost of funds in baht terms?

    c. If EAC could borrow Thai baht at 13% per annum, would this be cheaper than either part (a) or part (b)?

19. **Maltese Falcon.** The infamous solid gold falcon, initially intended as a tribute by the Knights of Rhodes to the King of Spain in appreciation for his gift of the island of Malta to the order in 1530, has recently been recovered. The falcon is 14 inches high and solid gold, weighing approximately 48 pounds. Assume that gold prices have risen to $440/ounce, primarily as a result of increasing political tensions. The falcon is currently held by a private investor in Istanbul, who is actively negotiating with the Maltese government on its purchase and prospective return to its island home. The sale and payment are to take place in March 2004, and the parties are negotiating over the price and currency of payment. The investor has decided, in a show of goodwill, to base the sales price only on the falcon's specie value—its gold value.

    The current spot exchange rate is 0.39 Maltese lira (ML) per U.S. dollar. Maltese inflation is expected to be about 8.5% for the coming year, while U.S. inflation, on the heels of a double-dip recession, is expected to come in at only 1.5%. If the investor bases value in the U.S. dollar, would he be better off receiving Maltese lira in one year—assuming purchasing power parity, or receiving a guaranteed dollar payment assuming a gold price of $420 per ounce.

20. **Malaysian Risk.** Clayton Moore is the manager of an international money market fund managed out of London. Unlike many money funds that guarantee their investors a near risk-free investment with variable interest earnings, Clayton Moore's fund is a very aggressive fund that searches out relatively high interest earnings around the globe, but at some risk. The fund is pound-denominated. Clayton is currently evaluating a rather interesting opportunity in Malaysia. Since the Asian Crisis of 1997, the Malaysian government enforced a number of currency and capital restrictions to protect and preserve the value of the Malaysian ringgit. The ringgit was fixed to the U.S. dollar at RM3.80/$ for seven years. In 2005, the Malaysian government allowed the currency to float against several major currencies. The current spot rate today is RM3.13485/$. Local currency time deposits of

180-day maturities are earning 8.900% per annum. The London eurocurrency market for pounds is yielding 4.200% per annum on similar 180-day maturities. The current spot rate on the British pound is $1.5820/£, and the 180-day forward rate is $1.5561/£.

21. **The Beer Standard.** In 1999, *The Economist* reported the creation of an index, or standard, for the evaluation of African currency values using the local prices of beer. Beer, instead of Big Macs, was chosen as the product for comparison because McDonald's had not penetrated the African continent beyond South Africa, and beer met most of the same product and market characteristics required for the construction of a proper currency index. Investec, a South African investment banking firm, has replicated the process of creating a measure of purchasing power parity (PPP) like

that of the Big Mac Index of *The Economist*, for Africa.

The index compares the cost of a 375 milliliter bottle of clear lager beer across Sub-Sahara Africa. As a measure of PPP, the beer needs to be relatively homogeneous in quality across countries, and must possess substantial elements of local manufacturing, inputs, distribution, and service, in order to actually provide a measure of relative purchasing power. The beer is first priced in local currency (purchased in the taverns of the locals, and not in the high-priced tourist centers), then converted to South African rand. The price of the beer in rand is then compared to form one measure of whether the local currency is under-valued (−%) or overvalued (+%) versus the South African rand. Use the data in the table and complete the calculation of whether the individual currencies are undervalued or overvalued.

Country	Beer	Beer Prices Local Currency	Local Currency	In rand	Implied PPP Rate	Spot Rate (3/15/99)
South Africa	Castle	Rand	2.30	—	—	—
Botswana	Castle	Pula	2.20	2.94	0.96	0.75
Ghana	Star	Cedi	1,200.00	3.17	521.74	379.10
Kenya	Tusker	Shilling	41.25	4.02	17.93	10.27
Malawi	Carlsberg	Kwacha	18.50	2.66	8.04	6.96
Mauritius	Phoenix	Rupee	15.00	3.72	6.52	4.03
Namibia	Windhoek	N$	2.50	2.50	1.09	1.00
Zambia	Castle	Kwacha	1,200.00	3.52	521.74	340.68
Zimbabwe	Castle	Z$	9.00	1.46	3.91	6.15

Internet Exercises

1. **Big Mac Index Updated.** Use *The Economist*'s Web site to find the latest edition of the Big Mac Index of currency overvaluation and undervaluation. (You will need to do a search for "Big Mac Currencies.") Create a worksheet to compare how the British pound, the euro, the Swiss franc, and the Canadian dollar have changed from the version presented in this chapter.

The Economist   www.economist.com/markets/ Bigmac/Index.cfm

2. **Purchasing Power Parity Statistics.** The Organization for Economic Cooperation and Development (OECD) publishes detailed measures of prices and purchasing power for its member countries. Go to the OECD's Web site and download the spreadsheet file

with the historical data for purchasing power for the member countries.

OECD Purchasing Power   www.oecd.org/department/ 0,3355,en_2649_34357_1_1_1_ 1_1,00.html

3. **International Interest Rates.** A number of Web sites publish current interest rates by currency and maturity. Use the *Financial Times* Web site listed here to isolate the interest rate differentials between the U.S. dollar, the British pound, and the euro for all maturities up to and including one year.

Financial Times Market Data www.ft.com/markets

Data Listed by the *Financial Times*:

International money rates (bank call rates for major currency deposits)

Money rates (LIBOR and CD rates, etc.)

10-year spreads (individual country spreads versus the euro and U.S. 10-year treasuries) *Note*: Which countries actually have lower 10-year government bond rates than the United States and the euro? Probably Switzerland and Japan. Check.

Benchmark government bonds (sampling of representative government issuances by major countries and recent price movements) Note which countries are showing longer maturity benchmark rates.

Emerging market bonds (government issuances, Brady bonds, etc.)

Eurozone rates (miscellaneous bond rates for assorted European-based companies; includes debt ratings by Moodys and S&P)

4. **World Bank's International Comparison Program.** The World Bank has an ongoing research program that focuses on the relative purchasing power of 107 different economies globally, specifically in terms of household consumption. Download the latest data tables and highlight which economies seem to be showing the greatest growth in recent years in relative purchasing power.

World Bank International Comparison Program web.worldbank.org/WBSITE/EXTERNAL/ DATASTATISTICS/ICPEXT/0,,pagePK:62002243~ theSitePK:270065,00.html

APPENDIX

An Algebraic Primer
to International Parity Conditions

The following is a purely algebraic presentation of the parity conditions explained in this chapter. It is offered to provide those who wish additional theoretical detail and definition ready access to the step-by-step derivation of the various conditions.

The Law of One Price

The *law of one price* refers to the state in which, in the presence of free trade, perfect substitutability of goods, and costless transactions, the equilibrium exchange rate between two currencies is determined by the ratio of the price of any commodity i denominated in two different currencies. For example,

$$S_t = \frac{P_{i,t}^{\$}}{P_{i,t}^{SF}}$$

where $P_i^{\$}$ and P_i^{SF} refer to the prices of the same commodity i, at time t, denominated in U.S. dollars and Swiss francs, respectively. The spot exchange rate, S_t, is simply the ratio of the two currency prices.

Purchasing Power Parity

The more general form in which the exchange rate is determined by the ratio of two price indexes is termed the absolute version of purchasing power parity (PPP). Each price index reflects the currency cost of the identical "basket" of goods across countries. The exchange rate that equates purchasing power for the identical collection of goods is then stated as follows:

$$S_t = \frac{P_t^{\$}}{P_t^{SF}}$$

where $P_t^{\$}$ and P_t^{SF} are the price index values in U.S. dollars and Swiss francs at time t, respectively. If π represents the rate of inflation in each country, the spot exchange rate at time $t + 1$ would be

$$S_{t+1} = \frac{P_t^{\$}(1 + \pi^{\$})}{P_t^{SF}(1 + \pi^{SF})} = S_t \left[\frac{(1 + \pi^{\$})}{(1 + \pi^{SF})} \right]$$

The change from period t to $t + 1$ is then

$$\frac{S_{t+1}}{S_t} = \frac{\dfrac{P_t^{\$}(1 + \pi^{\$})}{P_t^{SF}(1 + \pi^{SF})}}{\dfrac{P_t^{\$}}{P_t^{SF}}} = \frac{S_t \left[\dfrac{(1 + \pi^{\$})}{(1 + \pi^{SF})} \right]}{S_t} = \frac{(1 + \pi^{\$})}{(1 + \pi^{SF})}$$

Isolating the percentage change in the spot exchange rate between periods t and $t + 1$ is then

$$\frac{S_{t+1} - S_t}{S_t} = \frac{S_t\left[\frac{(1 + \pi^\$)}{(1 + \pi^{SF})}\right] - S_t}{S_t} = \frac{(1 + \pi^\$) - (1 + \pi^{SF})}{(1 + \pi^{SF})}$$

This equation is often approximated by dropping the denominator of the right-hand side if it is considered to be relatively small. It is then stated as

$$\frac{S_{t+1} - S_t}{S_t} = (1 + \pi^\$) - (1 + \pi^{SF}) = \pi^\$ - \pi^{SF}$$

Forward Rates

The forward exchange rate is that contractual rate which is available to private agents through banking institutions and other financial intermediaries who deal in foreign currencies and debt instruments. The annualized percentage difference between the forward rate and the spot rate is termed the forward premium,

$$f^{SF} = \left[\frac{F_{t,\,t+1} - S_t}{S_t}\right] \times \left[\frac{360}{n_{t,\,t+1}}\right]$$

where f^{SF} is the forward premium on the Swiss franc, $F_{t,\,t+1}$ is the forward rate contracted at time t for delivery at time $t + 1$, S_t is the current spot rate, and $n_{t,\,t+1}$ is the number of days between the contract date (t) and the delivery date ($t + 1$).

Covered Interest Arbitrage (CIA) and Interest Rate Parity (IRP)

The process of covered interest arbitrage is when an investor exchanges domestic currency for foreign currency in the spot market, invests that currency in an interest-bearing instrument, and signs a forward contract to "lock in" a future exchange rate at which to convert the foreign currency proceeds (gross) back to domestic currency. The net return on CIA is

$$\text{Net return} = \left[\frac{(1 + i^{SF})\,F_{t,\,t+1}}{S_t}\right] - (1 + i^\$)$$

where S_t and $F_{t,t+1}$ are the spot and forward rates (\$/SF), i^{SF} is the nominal interest rate (or yield) on a Swiss franc-denominated monetary instrument, and $i^\$$ is the nominal return on a similar dollar-denominated instrument.

If they possess exactly equal rates of return—that is, if CIA results in zero riskless profit—interest rate parity (IRP) holds, and appears as

$$(1 + i^\$) = \left[\frac{(1 + i^{SF})\,F_{t,\,t+1}}{S_t}\right]$$

or alternatively as

$$\frac{(1 + i^\$)}{(1 + i^{SF})} = \frac{F_{t,\,t+1}}{S_t}$$

If the percent difference of both sides of this equation is found (the percentage difference between the spot and forward rate is the forward premium), then the relationship between the forward premium and relative interest rate differentials is

$$\frac{F_{t,t+1} - S_t}{S_t} = f^{SF} = \frac{i^{\$} - i^{SF}}{i^{\$} + i^{SF}}$$

If these values are not equal (thus, the markets are not in equilibrium), there exists a potential for riskless profit. The market will then be driven back to equilibrium through CIA by agents attempting to exploit such arbitrage potential, until CIA yields no positive return.

Fisher Effect

The Fisher effect states that all nominal interest rates can be decomposed into an implied real rate of interest (return) and an expected rate of inflation:

$$i^{\$} = [(1 + r^{\$})(1 + \pi^{\$})] - 1$$

where $r^{\$}$ is the real rate of return, and $\pi^{\$}$ is the expected rate of inflation, for dollar-denominated assets. The subcomponents are then identifiable:

$$i^{\$} = r^{\$} + \pi^{\$} + r^{\$}\pi^{\$}$$

As with PPP, there is an approximation of this function that has gained wide acceptance. The cross-product term of $r^{\$}\pi^{\$}$ is often very small and therefore dropped altogether:

$$i^{\$} = r^{\$} + \pi^{\$}$$

International Fisher Effect

The international Fisher effect is the extension of this domestic interest rate relationship to the international currency markets. If capital, by way of covered interest arbitrage (CIA), attempts to find higher rates of return internationally resulting from current interest rate differentials, the real rates of return between currencies are equalized (e.g., $r^{\$} = r^{SF}$):

$$\frac{S_{t+1} - S_t}{S_t} = \frac{(1 + i^{\$}) - (1 + i^{SF})}{(1 + i^{SF})} = \frac{i^{\$} - i^{SF}}{(1 + i^{SF})}$$

If the nominal interest rates are then decomposed into their respective real and expected inflation components, the percentage change in the spot exchange rate is

$$\frac{S_{t+1} - S_t}{S_t} = \frac{(r^{\$} + \pi^{\$} + r^{\$}\pi^{\$}) - (r^{SF} + \pi^{SF} + r^{SF}\pi^{SF})}{1 + r^{SF} + \pi^{SF} + r^{SF}\pi^{SF}}$$

The international Fisher effect has a number of additional implications, if the following requirements are met: (1) capital markets can be freely entered and exited; (2) capital markets possess investment opportunities that are acceptable substitutes; and (3) market agents have complete and equal information regarding these possibilities.

Given these conditions, international arbitragers are capable of exploiting all potential riskless profit opportunities, until real rates of return between markets are equalized

$(r^{\$} = r^{SF})$. Thus, the expected rate of change in the spot exchange rate reduces to the differential in the expected rates of inflation:

$$\frac{S_{t+1} - S_t}{S_t} = \frac{\pi^{\$} + r^{\$}\pi^{\$} - \pi^{SF} - r^{SF}\pi^{SF}}{1 + r^{SF} + \pi^{SF} + r^{SF}\pi^{SF}}$$

If the approximation forms are combined (through the elimination of the denominator and the elimination of the interactive terms of r and π), the change in the spot rate is simply

$$\frac{S_{t+1} - S_t}{S_t} = \pi^{\$} - \pi^{SF}$$

Note the similarity (identical in equation form) of the approximate form of the international Fisher effect to purchasing power parity, discussed previously (the only potential difference is that between *ex post* and *ex ante*, or expected, inflation).

8

Foreign Currency Derivatives and Swaps

Unless derivatives contracts are collateralized or guaranteed, their ultimate value also depends on the creditworthiness of the counterparties to them. In the meantime, though, before a contract is settled, the counterparties record profits and losses—often huge in amount—in their current earnings statements without so much as a penny changing hands. The range of derivatives contracts is limited only by the imagination of man (or sometimes, so it seems, madmen). — Warren Buffett, Berkshire Hathaway Annual Report, 2002.

LEARNING OBJECTIVES

◆ Explain how foreign currency futures are quoted, valued, and used for speculation purposes.

◆ Illustrate how foreign currency futures differ from forward contracts.

◆ Analyze how foreign currency options are quoted, valued, and used for speculation purposes.

◆ Explain how foreign currency options are valued.

◆ Define interest rate risk, and examine how can it be managed.

◆ Explain interest rate swaps and how they can be used to manage interest rate risk.

◆ Analyze how interest rate swaps and cross currency swaps can be used to manage both foreign exchange risk and interest rate risk simultaneously.

Financial management of the multinational enterprise in the twenty-first century will certainly include the use of *financial derivatives*. These *derivatives*, so named because their values are derived from an underlying asset like a stock or a currency, are powerful tools used in business today for two very distinct management objectives, *speculation* and *hedging*. The financial manager of an MNE may purchase these financial derivatives in order to take positions in the expectation of profit, speculation, or may use these instruments to reduce the risks associated with the everyday management of corporate cash flow, hedging. Before these financial instruments can be used effectively, however, the financial manager must understand certain basics about their structure and pricing.

In this chapter, we cover the primary foreign currency financial derivatives used today in multinational financial management: *foreign currency futures, foreign currency options, interest rate swaps, and cross currency interest rate swaps*. We focus on the fundamentals of their valuation and their use for speculative purposes. Chapter 10 will describe how these foreign currency derivatives can be used to hedge commercial transactions, hedging. The Mini-Case at the end of this chapter, **McDonald's Corporation British Pound Exposure** illustrates how one major multinational company, McDonald's, has used currency derivatives quite success- fully over time.

A word of caution—of reservation—before proceeding further. Financial derivatives are powerful tools in the hands of careful and competent financial managers. They can also be destructive devices when used recklessly and carelessly. The history of finance is littered with cases in which financial managers—either intentionally or unintentionally—took huge posi- tions resulting in significant losses for their companies, and occasionally, their outright col- lapse. In the right hands and with the proper controls, however, financial derivatives may provide management with opportunities to enhance and protect their corporate financial performance. User beware.

Foreign Currency Futures

A *foreign currency futures contract* is an alternative to a forward contract that calls for future delivery of a standard amount of foreign exchange at a fixed time, place, and price. It is simi- lar to futures contracts that exist for commodities (hogs, cattle, lumber, etc.), interest-bearing deposits, and gold.

Most world money centers have established foreign currency futures markets. In the United States, the most important market for foreign currency futures is the International Monetary Market (IMM) of Chicago, a division of the Chicago Mercantile Exchange.

Contract Specifications

Contract specifications are established by the exchange on which futures are traded. Using the Chicago IMM as an example, the major features of standardized futures trading are illus- trated by the Mexican peso futures traded on the Chicago Mercantile Exchange (CME), as shown in Exhibit 8.1. These are taken from the *Wall Street Journal*.

Each futures contract is for 500,000 Mexican pesos, this is the *notional principal*. Trading in each currency must be done in an even multiple of currency units. The method of stating exchange rates is in American terms, the U.S. dollar cost (price) of a foreign currency (unit), $/MXN, where the CME is mixing the old dollar symbol with the ISO 4217 code for the peso, MXN. In Exhibit 8.1 this is U.S. dollars per Mexican peso. Contracts mature on the third Wednesday of January, March, April, June, July, September, October, or December.

EXHIBIT 8.1   Mexican Peso (CME)—MXN 500,000; $ per 10MXN

| | | | | | | Lifetime | | |
Maturity	Open	High	Low	Settle	Change	High	Low	Open Interest
Mar	.10953	.10988	.10930	.10958	...	.11000	.09770	34,481
June	.10790	.10795	.10778	.10773	...	.10800	.09730	3,405
Sept	.10615	.10615	.10610	.10573	...	.10615	.09930	1,481

All contracts are for 500,000 Mexican pesos. "Open" means the opening price on the day. "High" means the high price on the day. "Low" indicates the low- est price on the day. "Settle" is the closing price on the day. "Change" indicates the change in the settle price from the previous day's close. "High" and "Low" to the right of Change indicate the highest and lowest prices this specific contract (as defined by its maturity) has experienced over its trading history. "Open Interest" indicates the number of contracts outstanding.

Contracts may be traded through the second business day prior to the Wednesday on which they mature. Unless holidays interfere, the last trading day is the Monday preceding the maturity date.

One of the defining characteristics of futures is the requirement that the purchaser deposits a sum as an initial *margin* or *collateral*. This requirement is similar to requiring a performance bond, and it can be met by a letter of credit from a bank, Treasury bills, or cash. In addition, a *maintenance margin* is required. The value of the contract is marked to market daily, and all changes in value are paid in cash daily. *Marked to market* means that the value of the contract is revalued using the closing price for the day. The amount to be paid is called the *variation margin*.

Only about 5% of all futures contracts are settled by the physical delivery of foreign exchange between buyer and seller. Most often, buyers and sellers offset their original position prior to delivery date by taking an opposite position. That is, an investor will normally close out a futures position by selling a futures contract for the same delivery date. The complete buy/sell or sell/buy is called a "round turn."

Customers pay a commission to their broker to execute a round turn and a single price is quoted. This practice differs from that of the interbank market, where dealers quote a bid and an offer and do not charge a commission. All contracts are agreements between the client and the exchange clearinghouse, rather than between the two clients involved. Consequently, clients need not worry that a specific counterparty in the market will fail to honor an agreement (counterparty risk). The clearinghouse is owned and guaranteed by all members of the exchange.

Using Foreign Currency Futures

Any investor wishing to speculate on the movement of the Mexican peso versus the U.S. dollar could pursue one of the following strategies. Keep in mind that the principle of a futures contract is that if a speculator buys a futures contract, they are locking in the price at which they must buy that currency on the specified future date, and if they sell a futures contract, they are locking in the price at which they must sell that currency on that future date.

Short Positions. If Amber McClain, a speculator working for International Currency Traders, believes that the Mexican peso will fall in value versus the U.S. dollar by March, she could sell a March futures contract, taking a short position. By selling a March contract, Amber locks in the right to sell 500,000 Mexican pesos at a set price. If the price of the peso falls by the maturity date as she expects, Amber has a contract to sell pesos at a price above their current price on the spot market. Hence, she makes a profit.

Using the quotes on Mexican peso (MXN) futures in Exhibit 8.1, Amber sells one March futures contract for 500,000 pesos at the closing price, termed the settle price, of $.10958/MXN. The value of her position at maturity—at the expiration of the futures contract in March—is then

$$\text{Value at maturity (Short position)} = -\text{Notional principal} \times (\text{Spot} - \text{Futures})$$

Note that the short position is entered into the valuation as a negative notional principal. If the spot exchange rate at maturity is $.09500/MXN, the value of her position on settlement is

$$\text{Value} = -\text{MXN } 500{,}000 \times (\$.09500/\text{MXN} - \$.10958/\text{MXN}) = \$7{,}290$$

Amber's expectation proved correct; the Mexican peso fell in value versus the U.S. dollar. We could say that "Amber ends up buying at $.09500 and sells at $.10958 per peso."

All that was really required of Amber to speculate on the Mexican peso's value was that she formed an opinion on the Mexican peso's future exchange value versus the U.S. dollar. In this case, she opined that it would fall in value by the March maturity date of the futures contract.

Long Positions. If Amber McClain expected the peso to rise in value versus the dollar in the near term, she could take a long position, by buying a March future on the Mexican peso. Buying a March future means that Amber is locking in the price at which she must buy Mexican pesos at the future's maturity date. Amber's futures contract at maturity would have the following value:

$$\text{Value at maturity (Long position)} = \text{Notional principal} \times (\text{Spot} - \text{Futures})$$

Again using the March settle price on Mexican peso futures in Exhibit 8.1, $.10958/MXN, if the spot exchange rate at maturity is $.1100/MXN, Amber has indeed guessed right. The value of her position on settlement is then

$$\text{Value} = \text{MXN500,000} \times (\$.11000/\text{MXN} - \$.10958/\text{MXN}) = \$210$$

In this case, Amber makes a profit in a matter of months of $210 on the single futures contract. We could say that "Amber buys at $.10958 and sells at $.11000 per peso."

But what happens if Amber's expectation about the future value of the Mexican peso proves wrong? For example, if the Mexican government announces that the rate of inflation in Mexico has suddenly risen dramatically, and the peso falls to $.08000/MXN by the March maturity date, the value of Amber's futures contract on settlement is

$$\text{Value} = \text{MXN500,000} \times (\$.08000/\text{MXN} - \$.10958/\text{MXN}) = (\$14,790)$$

In this case, Amber McClain suffers a speculative loss.

Futures contracts could obviously be used in combinations to form a variety of more complex positions. When we are combining contracts, however, valuation is fairly straightforward and additive in character.

Foreign Currency Futures versus Forward Contracts

Foreign currency futures contracts differ from forward contracts in a number of important ways. Individuals find futures contracts useful for speculation because they usually do not have access to forward contracts. For businesses, futures contracts are often considered inefficient and burdensome because the futures position is marked to market on a daily basis over the life of the contract. Although this does not require the business to pay or receive cash daily, it does result in more frequent margin calls from its financial service providers than the business typically wants.

Currency Options

A *foreign currency option* is a contract that gives the option purchaser (the buyer) the right, but not the obligation, to buy or sell a given amount of foreign exchange at a fixed price per unit for a specified time period (until the maturity date). The most important phrase in this definition is "but not the obligation"; this means that the owner of an option possesses a valuable choice.

In many ways buying an option is like buying a ticket to a benefit concert. The buyer has the right to attend the concert, but does not have to. The buyer of the concert ticket risks nothing more than what she pays for the ticket. Similarly, the buyer of an option cannot lose more than what he pays for the option. If the buyer of the ticket decides later not to attend the concert—prior to the day of the concert, the ticket can be sold to someone else who wishes to go.

◆ There are two basic types of options, *calls* and *puts*. A call is an option to buy foreign currency, and a *put* is an option to sell foreign currency.

◆ The buyer of an option is termed the *holder*, while the seller of an option is referred to as the *writer* or *grantor*.

Every option has three different price elements: 1) the *exercise* or *strike price*, the exchange rate at which the foreign currency can be purchased (call) or sold (put); 2) the *premium*, the cost, price, or value of the option itself; and 3) the underlying or actual spot exchange rate in the market.

An *American option* gives the buyer the right to exercise the option at any time between the date of writing and the expiration or maturity date. A *European option* can be exercised only on its expiration date, not before. Nevertheless, American and European options are priced almost the same because the option holder would normally sell the option itself before maturity. The option would then still have some "time value" above its "intrinsic value" if exercised (explained later in this chapter).

◆ The *premium* or option price is the cost of the option, usually paid in advance by the buyer to the seller. In the *over-the-counter market* (options offered by banks), premiums are quoted as a percentage of the transaction amount. Premiums on exchange-traded options are quoted as a domestic currency amount per unit of foreign currency.

◆ An option whose exercise price is the same as the spot price of the underlying currency is said to be *at-the-money* (ATM). An option that would be profitable, excluding the cost of the premium, if exercised immediately is said to be *in-the-money* (ITM). An option that would not be profitable, again excluding the cost of the premium, if exercised immediately is referred to as *out-of-the-money* (OTM).

Foreign Currency Options Markets

In the past three decades the use of foreign currency options as a hedging tool and for speculative purposes has blossomed into a major foreign exchange activity. A number of banks in the United States and other capital markets offer flexible foreign currency options on transactions of $1 million or more. The bank market, or over-the-counter market as it is called, offers custom-tailored options on all major trading currencies for any period up to one year, and in some cases, two to three years.

In December 1982, the Philadelphia Stock Exchange introduced trading in standardized foreign currency option contracts in the United States. The Chicago Mercantile Exchange and other exchanges in the United States and abroad have followed suit. Exchange-traded contracts are particularly appealing to speculators and individuals who do not normally have access to the over-the-counter market. Banks also trade on the exchanges because it is one of several ways they can offset the risk of options they have transacted with clients or other banks.

Increased use of foreign currency options is a reflection of the explosive growth in the use of other kinds of options and the resultant improvements in option pricing models. The original option pricing model developed by Black and Scholes in 1973 has been commercialized since then by numerous firms offering software programs and even built-in routines for handheld calculators. Several commercial programs are available for option writers and traders to utilize.

Options on the Over-the-Counter Market. Over-the-counter (OTC) options are most frequently written by banks for U.S. dollars against British pounds sterling, Swiss francs, Japanese yen, Canadian dollars, and most recently, the euro.

The main advantage of over-the-counter options is that they are tailored to the specific needs of the firm. Financial institutions are willing to write or buy options that vary by amount (notional principal), strike price, and maturity. Although the over-the-counter markets were relatively illiquid in the early years, the market has grown to such proportions that liquidity is now quite good. On the other hand, the buyer must assess the writing bank's ability to fulfill the option contract. Termed counterparty risk, the financial risk associated with the counterparty is an increasing issue in international markets as a result of the increasing use of financial contracts like options and swaps by MNE management. Exchange-traded options are more the territory of individuals and financial institutions themselves than of business firms.

If an investor wishes to purchase an option in the over-the-counter market, the investor will normally place a call to the currency option desk of a major money center bank, specify the currencies, maturity, strike rate(s), and ask for an *indication*—a bid-offer quote. The bank will normally take a few minutes to a few hours to price the option and return the call.

Options on Organized Exchanges. Options on the physical (underlying) currency are traded on a number of organized exchanges worldwide, including the Philadelphia Stock Exchange (PHLX) and the Chicago Mercantile Exchange.

Exchange-traded options are settled through a clearinghouse, so that buyers do not deal directly with sellers. The clearinghouse is the counterparty to every option contract and it guarantees fulfillment. Clearinghouse obligations are in turn the obligation of all members of the exchange, including a large number of banks. In the case of the Philadelphia Stock Exchange, clearinghouse services are provided by the Options Clearing Corporation (OCC).

Currency Option Quotations and Prices

Typical quotes in the *Wall Street Journal* for options on Swiss francs are shown in Exhibit 8.2. The *Journal*'s quotes refer to transactions completed on the Philadelphia Stock Exchange on the previous day. Quotations usually are available for more combinations of strike prices and expiration dates than were actually traded and thus reported in the newspaper. Currency option strike prices and premiums on the U.S. dollar are typically quoted as direct quotations on the U.S. dollar and indirect quotations on the foreign currency ($/SF, $/¥, etc.).

Exhibit 8.2 illustrates the three different prices that characterize any foreign currency option. The three prices that characterize an "August 58.5 call option" (highlighted in Exhibit 8.2) are the following:

1. **Spot Rate.** In Exhibit 8.2, "Option and Underlying" means that 58.51 cents, or $0.5851, was the spot dollar price of one Swiss franc at the close of trading on the preceding day.

EXHIBIT 8.2   Swiss Franc Option Quotations (U.S. cents/SF)

Option and Underlying	Strike Price	Calls—Last			Puts—Last		
		Aug	Sep	Dec	Aug	Sep	Dec
58.51	56.0	–	–	2.76	0.04	0.22	1.16
58.51	56.5	–	–	–	0.06	0.30	–
58.51	57.0	1.13	–	1.74	0.10	0.38	1.27
58.51	57.5	0.75	–	–	0.17	0.55	–
58.51	58.0	0.71	1.05	1.28	0.27	0.89	1.81
58.51	58.5	0.50	–	–	0.50	0.99	–
58.51	59.0	0.30	0.66	1.21	0.90	1.36	–
58.51	59.5	0.15	0.40	–	2.32	–	–
58.51	60.0	–	0.31	–	2.32	2.62	3.30

Each option = 62,500 Swiss francs. The August, September, and December listings are the option maturities or expiration dates.

---

2. **Exercise Price.** The exercise price, or "Strike price" listed in Exhibit 8.2, means the price per franc that must be paid if the option is exercised. The August call option on francs of 58.5 means $0.5850/SF. Exhibit 8.2 lists nine different strike prices, ranging from $0.5600/SF to $0.6000/SF, although more were available on that date than are listed here.

3. **Premium.** The premium is the cost or price of the option. The price of the August 58.5 call option on Swiss francs was 0.50 U.S. cents per franc, or $0.0050/SF. There was no trading of the September and December 58.5 call on that day. The premium is the market value of the option, and therefore the terms premium, cost, price, and value are all interchangeable when referring to an option.

The August 58.5 call option premium is 0.50 cents per franc, and in this case, the August 58.5 put's premium is also 0.50 cents per franc. Since one option contract on the Philadelphia Stock Exchange consists of 62,500 francs, the total cost of one option contract for the call (or put in this case) is SF62,500 × $0.0050/SF = $312.50.

Buyer of a Call

Options differ from all other types of financial instruments in the patterns of risk they produce. The option owner, the holder, has the choice of exercising the option or allowing it to expire unused. The owner will exercise it only when exercising is profitable, which means only when the option is in the money. In the case of a call option, as the spot price of the underlying currency moves up, the holder has the possibility of unlimited profit. On the down side, however, the holder can abandon the option and walk away with a loss never greater than the premium paid.

Hans Schmidt is a currency speculator in Zurich, Switzerland. The position of Hans as a buyer of a call is illustrated in Exhibit 8.3. Assume he purchases the August call option on

| EXHIBIT 8.3 | Profit and Loss for the Buyer of a Call Option |

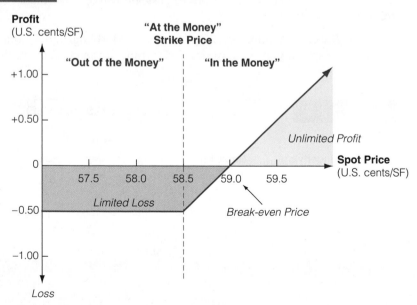

The buyer of a call option on SF, with a strike price of 58.5 cents/SF, has a limited loss of 0.50 cents/SF at spot rates less than 58.5 ("out of the money"), and an unlimited profit potential at spot rates above 58.5 cents/SF ("in the money").

Swiss francs described previously, the one with a strike price of 58.5 ($0.5850/SF), and a premium of $0.005/SF. The vertical axis measures profit or loss for the option buyer at each of several different spot prices for the franc up to the time of maturity.

At all spot rates below the strike price of 58.5, Hans would choose not to exercise his option. This is obvious because at a spot rate of 58.0 for example, he would prefer to buy a Swiss franc for $.580 on the spot market rather than exercising his option to buy a franc at $0.585. If the spot rate remains below 58.0 until August when the option expired, Hans would not exercise the option. His total loss would be limited to only what he paid for the option, the $0.005/SF purchase price. At any lower price for the franc, his loss would similarly be limited to the original $0.005/SF cost.

Alternatively, at all spot rates above the strike price of 58.5, Hans would exercise the option, paying only the strike price for each Swiss franc. For example, if the spot rate were 59.5 cents per franc at maturity, he would exercise his call option, buying Swiss francs for $0.585 each instead of purchasing them on the spot market at $0.595 each. He could sell the Swiss francs immediately in the spot market for $0.595 each, pocketing a gross profit of $0.010/SF, or a net profit of $0.005/SF after deducting the original cost of the option of $0.005/SF. Hans' profit, if the spot rate is greater than the strike price, with strike price $0.585, a premium of $0.005, and a spot rate of $0.595, is

$$\begin{aligned} \text{Profit} &= \text{Spot Rate} - (\text{Strike Price} + \text{Premium}) \\ &= \$0.595/\text{SF} - (\$0.585/\text{SF} + \$0.005/\text{SF}) \\ &= \$0.005/\text{SF} \end{aligned}$$

More likely, Hans would realize the profit through executing an offsetting contract on the options exchange rather than taking delivery of the currency. Because the dollar price of a franc could rise to an infinite level (off the upper right-hand side of Exhibit 8.3), maximum profit is unlimited. The buyer of a call option thus possesses an attractive combination of outcomes: limited loss and unlimited profit potential.

Note that *break-even price* of $0.590/SF is the price at which Hans neither gains nor loses on exercising the option. The premium cost of $0.005, combined with the cost of exercising the option of $0.585, is exactly equal to the proceeds from selling the francs in the spot market at $0.590. Note that he will still exercise the call option at the break-even price. This is because by exercising it he at least recoups the premium paid for the option. At any spot price above the exercise price but below the break-even price, the gross profit earned on exercising the option and selling the underlying currency covers part (but not all) of the premium cost.

Writer of a Call

The position of the writer (seller) of the same call option is illustrated in Exhibit 8.4. If the option expires when the spot price of the underlying currency is below the exercise price of 58.5, the option holder does not exercise. What the holder loses, the writer gains. The writer keeps as profit the entire premium paid of $0.005/SF. Above the exercise price of 58.5, the writer of the call must deliver the underlying currency for $0.585/SF at a time when the value of the franc is above $0.585. If the writer wrote the option "naked," that is, without owning the currency, that writer will now have to buy the currency at spot and take the loss. The amount of such a loss is unlimited and increases as the price of the underlying currency rises. Once again, what the holder gains, the writer loses, and vice versa. Even if the writer already owns the currency, the writer will experience an opportunity loss, surrendering against the option the same currency that could have been sold for more in the open market.

EXHIBIT 8.4 | Profit and Loss for the Writer of a Call Option

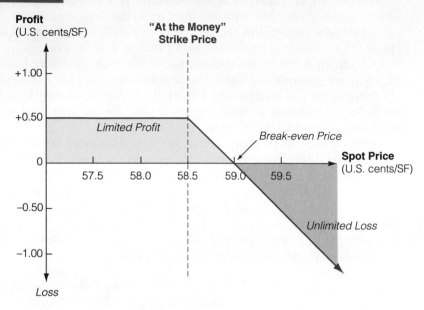

The writer of a call option on SF, with a strike price of 58.5 cents/SF, has a limited profit of 0.50 cents/SF at spot rates less than 58.5, and an unlimited loss potential at spot rates above (to the right of) 59.0 cents/SF.

For example, the profit to the writer of a call option of strike price \$0.585, premium \$0.005, a spot rate of \$0.595/SF is

$$
\begin{aligned}
\text{Profit} &= \text{Premium} - (\text{Spot Rate} - \text{Strike Price}) \\
&= \$0.005/\text{SF} - (\$0.595/\text{SF} - \$0.585/\text{SF}) \\
&= -\$0.005/\text{SF}
\end{aligned}
$$

but only if the spot rate is greater than or equal to the strike rate. At spot rates less than the strike price, the option will expire worthless and the writer of the call option will keep the premium earned. The maximum profit that the writer of the call option can make is limited to the premium. The writer of a call option would have a rather unattractive combination of potential outcomes: limited profit potential and unlimited loss potential, but there are ways to limit such losses through other offsetting techniques.

Buyer of a Put

Hans' position as buyer of a put is illustrated in Exhibit 8.5. The basic terms of this put are similar to those we just used to illustrate a call. The buyer of a put option, however, wants to be able to sell the underlying currency at the exercise price when the market price of that currency drops (not rises as in the case of a call option). If the spot price of a franc drops to, say, \$0.575/SF, Hans will deliver francs to the writer and receive \$0.585/SF. The francs can now be purchased on the spot market for \$0.575 each and the cost of the option was \$0.005/SF, so he will have a net gain of \$0.005/SF.

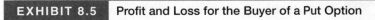

EXHIBIT 8.5   Profit and Loss for the Buyer of a Put Option

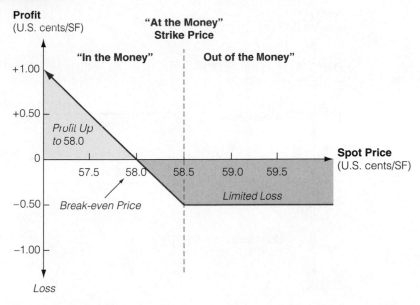

The buyer of a put option on SF, with a strike price of 58.5 cents/SF, has a limited loss of 0.50 cents/SF at spot rates greater than 58.5 ("out of the money"), and an unlimited profit potential at spot rates less than 58.5 cents/SF ("in the money") up to 58.0 cents.

Explicitly, the profit to the holder of a put option if the spot rate is less than the strike price, with a strike price $0.585/SF, premium of $0.005/SF, and a spot rate of $0.575/SF, is

$$
\begin{aligned}
\text{Profit} &= \text{Strike Price} - (\text{Spot Rate} + \text{Premium}) \\
&= \$0.585/\text{SF} - (\$0.575/\text{SF} + \$0.005/\text{SF}) \\
&= \$0.005/\text{SF}
\end{aligned}
$$

The break-even price for the put option is the strike price less the premium, or $0.580/SF in this case. As the spot rate falls further and further below the strike price, the profit potential would continually increase, and Hans' profit could be unlimited (up to a maximum of $0.580/SF, when the price of a franc would be zero). At any exchange rate above the strike price of 58.5, Hans would not exercise the option, and so would lose only the $0.005/SF premium paid for the put option. The buyer of a put option has an almost unlimited profit potential with a limited loss potential. Like the buyer of a call, the buyer of a put can never lose more than the premium paid up front.

Writer of a Put

The position of the writer who sold the put to Hans is shown in Exhibit 8.6. Note the symmetry of profit/loss, strike price, and break-even prices between the buyer and the writer of the put. If the spot price of francs drops below 58.5 cents per franc, Hans will exercise the option. Below a price of 58.5 cents per franc, the writer will lose more than the premium received from writing the option ($0.005/SF), falling below break-even. Between $0.580/SF and $0.585/SF the writer will lose part, but not all, of the premium received. If the spot price is above $0.585/SF, Hans will not exercise the option, and the option writer will pocket the entire premium of $0.005/SF.

EXHIBIT 8.6   Profit and Loss for the Writer of a Put Option

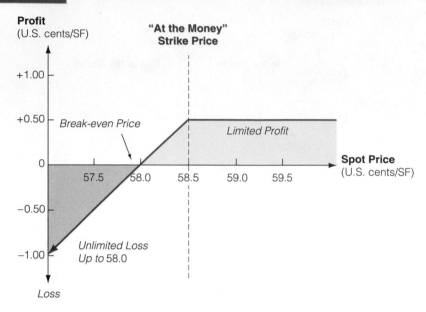

The writer of a put option on SF, with a strike price of 58.5 cents/SF, has a limited profit of 0.50 cents/SF at spot rates greater than 58.5, and an unlimited loss potential at spot rates less than 58.5 cents/SF up to 58.0 cents.

The profit (loss) earned by the writer of a $0.585 strike price put, premium $0.005, at a spot rate of $0.575, is

$$\text{Profit (loss)} = \text{Premium} - (\text{Strike Price} - \text{Spot Rate})$$
$$= \$0.005/\text{SF} - (\$0.585/\text{SF} - \$0.575/\text{SF})$$
$$= -\$0.005/\text{SF}$$

but only for spot rates that are less than or equal to the strike price. At spot rates greater than the strike price, the option expires out-of-the-money and the writer keeps the premium. The writer of the put option has the same basic combination of outcomes available to the writer of a call: limited profit potential and unlimited loss potential. *Global Finance in Practice 8.1* describes one of the largest, and most successful, currency option speculations ever made—that by Andrew Krieger against the New Zealand kiwi.

GLOBAL FINANCE IN PRACTICE   **8.1**

The New Zealand Kiwi, Key, and Krieger

What has long been considered one of the most dramatic currency plays in history has moved back into the limelight. New Zealand elected Mr. John Key as its new Prime Minister in November 2008. Key's career has been a long and storied one, a large part of it involving speculation on foreign currencies. Strangely enough, Key had at one time worked with

another currency speculator, Andrew Krieger, who is believed to have single-handedly caused the fall of the New Zealand dollar, the kiwi, in 1987.

Then, Andrew Krieger was a 31-year-old currency trader for Bankers Trust of New York (BT). Following the U.S. stock market crash in October 1987, the world's currency markets moved rapidly to exit the dollar. Many of the world's other currencies—including small ones which were in stable, open, industrialized markets like that of New Zealand—became the subject of interest. As the world's currency traders dumped dollars and bought kiwis, the value of the kiwi rose rapidly.

Krieger believed that the markets were overreacting, and would overvalue the kiwi. So he took a short position on the kiwi, betting on its eventual fall. And he did so in a big way, not limiting his positions to simple spot or forward market positions, but through currency options as well. (Krieger supposedly had approval for positions rising to nearly $700 million in size, while all other BT traders were restricted to $50 million.) Krieger, on behalf of BT, is purported to have shorted 200 million kiwi—more than the entire New Zealand money supply at the time. His view proved correct. The kiwi fell, and Krieger was able to earn millions in currency gains for BT. Ironically, only months later, Krieger resigned from BT when annual bonuses were announced and he reportedly earned only $3 million on the more than $300 million he had made for the bank.

Eventually, the New Zealand central bank lodged complaints with BT, in which the CEO at the time, Charles S. Sanford Jr., seemingly added insult to injury when he reportedly remarked "We didn't take too big a position for Bankers Trust, but we may have taken too big a position for that market."

Option Pricing and Valuation

Exhibit 8.7 illustrates the profit/loss profile of a European-style call option on British pounds. The call option allows the holder to buy British pounds at a strike price of $1.70/£. It has a 90-day maturity.

The value of this call option is actually the sum of two components:

$$\text{Total Value (premium)} = \text{Intrinsic Value} + \text{Time Value}$$

The pricing of any currency option combines six elements. For example, this European-style call option on British pounds has a premium of $0.033/£ (3.3 cents per pound) at a spot rate of $1.70/£. This premium is calculated using the following assumptions: a spot rate of $1.70/£, a 90-day maturity, a $1.70/£ forward rate, both U.S. dollar and British pound interest rates of 8.00% per annum, and an option volatility for the 90-day period of 10.00% per annum.

EXHIBIT 8.7   Option Intrinsic Value, Time Value, and Total Value

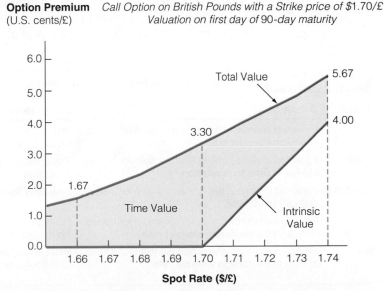

Option Premium   *Call Option on British Pounds with a Strike price of $1.70/£*
(U.S. cents/£)   *Valuation on first day of 90-day maturity*

Spot Rate ($/£)

216 PART 2 Foreign Exchange Theory and Markets

Intrinsic value is the financial gain if the option is exercised immediately. It is shown by the solid line in Exhibit 8.7, which is zero until it reaches the strike price, then rises linearly (1 cent for each 1-cent increase in the spot rate). Intrinsic value will be zero when the option is *out-of-the-money*—that is, when the strike price is above the market price—as no gain can be derived from exercising the option. When the spot rate rises above the strike price, the intrinsic value becomes positive because the option is always worth at least this value if exercised. On the date of maturity an option will have a value equal to its intrinsic value (zero time remaining means zero time value).

◆ When the spot rate is $1.74/£, the option is *in-the-money* and has an *intrinsic value* of $1.74–$1.70/£, or 4 cents per pound.

◆ When the spot rate is $1.70/£, the option is *at-the-money* and has an *intrinsic value* of $1.70–$1.70/£, or zero cents per pound.

◆ When the spot rate is $1.66/£, the option is *out-of-the-money* and has no intrinsic value. This is shown by the intrinsic value lying on the horizontal axis. Only a fool would exercise this call option at this spot rate instead of buying pounds more cheaply on the spot market.

The *time value* of an option exists because the price of the underlying currency, the spot rate, can potentially move further and further into the money before the option's expiration. Time value is shown in Exhibit 8.7 as the area between the *total value* of the option and its intrinsic value. An investor will pay something today for an out-of-the-money option (i.e., zero intrinsic value) on the chance that the spot rate will move far enough before maturity to move the option in-the-money. Consequently, the price of an option is always somewhat greater than its intrinsic value, since there is always some chance that the intrinsic value will rise between the present and the expiration date.

If currency options are to be used effectively, either for the purposes of speculation or risk management (covered in Chapters 10 and 11), the individual trader needs to know how option values—premiums—react to their various components. Exhibit 8.8 summarizes six basic sensitivities.

Although rarely noted, standard foreign currency options are priced around the forward rate because the current spot rate and both the domestic and foreign interest rates (home currency and foreign currency rates) are included in the option premium calculation. Regardless of the specific strike rate chosen and priced, the forward rate is central to valuation. The option-pricing formula calculates a subjective probability distribution centered on

EXHIBIT 8.8 Summary of Option Premium Components

Greek	Definition	Interpretation
Delta	Expected change in the option premium for a small change in the **spot rate**	The higher the delta, the more likely the option will move in-the-money
Theta	Expected change in the option premium for a small change in **time to expiration**	Premiums are relatively insensitive until the final 30 or so days
Lambda	Expected change in the option premium for a small change in **volatility**	Premiums rise with increases in volatility
Rho	Expected change in the option premium for a small change in the **domestic interest rate**	Increases in domestic interest rates cause increasing call option premiums
Phi	Expected change in the option premium for a small change in the **foreign interest rate**	Increases in foreign interest rates cause decreasing call option premiums

the forward rate. This approach does not mean that the market expects the forward rate to be equal to the future spot rate, it is simply a result of the arbitrage-pricing structure of options.

The forward rate focus also provides helpful information for the trader managing a position. When the market prices a foreign currency option, it does so without any bullish or bearish sentiment on the direction of the foreign currency's value relative to the domestic currency. If the trader has specific expectations about the future spot rate's direction, those expectations can be put to work. A trader will not be inherently betting against the market.

Interest Rate Risk

All firms—domestic or multinational, small or large, leveraged or unleveraged—are sensitive to interest rate movements in one way or another. Although a variety of interest rate risks exist in theory and industry, this book focuses on the financial management of the nonfinancial firm. Hence, our discussion is limited to the interest rate risks associated with the multinational firm. The interest rate risks of financial firms, such as banks, are not covered here.

The single largest interest rate risk of the nonfinancial firm is debt service. The debt structure of the MNE will possess differing maturities of debt, different interest rate structures (such as fixed versus floating-rate), and different currencies of denomination. Interest rates are currency-specific. Each currency has its own interest rate yield curve and credit spreads for borrowers. Therefore, the multicurrency dimension of interest rate risk for the MNE is a serious concern. As illustrated in Exhibit 8.9, even the interest rate calculations vary on occasion across currencies and countries. *Global Finance in Practice 8.2* provides additional evidence on the use of fixed versus floating-rate instruments in today's marketplace.

The second most prevalent source of interest rate risk for the MNE lies in its holdings of interest-sensitive securities. Unlike debt, which is recorded on the right-hand side of the firm's balance sheet, the marketable securities portfolio of the firm appears on the left-hand side. Marketable securities represent potential earnings or interest inflows to the firm. Ever-increasing competitive pressures have pushed financial managers to tighten their management of both the left and right sides of the firm's balance sheet.

EXHIBIT 8.9   International Interest Rate Calculations

International interest rate calculations differ by the number of days used in the period's calculation and their definition of how many days there are in a year (for financial purposes). The following example highlights how the different methods result in different 1-month payments of interest on a $10 million loan, 5.500% per annum interest, for an exact period of 28 days.

Practice	Day Count in Period	Days/Year	$10 million @ 5.500% per annum	
			Days Used	Interest Payment
International	Exact number of days	360	28	$42,777.78
British	Exact number of days	365	28	$42,191.78
Swiss (Eurobond)	Assumed 30 days/month	360	30	$45,833.33

GLOBAL FINANCE IN PRACTICE   **8.2**

A Fixed-Rate or Floating-Rate World?

The *BIS Quarterly Review* of March 2009 provides a detailed statistical breakdown of the types of international notes and bonds newly issued and outstanding, by issuer, by type of instrument, and by currency of denomination. The data provides some interesting insights into the international securities market.

◆ At of end of year 2008 there were $22.7 trillion outstanding in international notes and bonds issued by all types of institutions.

◆ The market continues to be dominated by issuances of financial institutions. The issuers by dollar value were as follows: financial institutions, $17.9 trillion or 79%; governments, $1.8 trillion or 8%; international organizations, $0.6 trillion or 3%; and corporate issuers, $2.4 trillion or 10% of the total outstanding.

◆ The instruments are still largely fixed-rate issuances, with 64% of all outstanding issuances being fixed-rate, 34% floating-rate, and roughly 2% equity-related.

◆ The euro continues to dominate international note and bond issuances, making up more than 48% of the total. The euro is followed by the dollar, 36%, the pound sterling, 8%, the Japanese yen, 3%, and the Swiss franc, just under 2%.

The data continues to support two long-standing fundamental properties of the international debt markets.

◆ First, that the euro's domination reflects the long-term use of the international security markets by the institutions in the countries constituting the euro—Western Europe.

◆ Second, that fixed-rate issuances are still the foundation of the market. Although floating-rate issuances did rise marginally in the 2003–2006 period, the international credit crisis of 2007–2008 and the response by central banks to push interest rates downwards created new opportunities for the issuance of longer-term fixed-rate issuances by issuers of all kinds.

Source: Data drawn from Table 13B, *BIS Quarterly Review*, March 2009, p. 91, www.bis.org/statistics/secstats.htm.

Credit Risk and Repricing Risk

Prior to describing the management of the most common interest rate pricing risks, it is important to distinguish between credit risk and repricing risk. Credit risk, sometimes termed roll-over risk, is the possibility that a borrower's creditworth, at the time of renewing a credit, is reclassified by the lender. This can result in changing fees, changing interest rates, altered credit line commitments, or even denial. Repricing risk is the risk of changes in interest rates charged (earned) at the time a financial contract's rate is reset.

Consider the following debt strategies being considered by a corporate borrower. Each is intended to provide $1 million in financing for a 3-year period.

Strategy 1: Borrow $1 million for three years at a fixed rate of interest.

Strategy 2: Borrow $1 million for three years at a floating rate, LIBOR + 2%, to be reset annually.

Strategy 3: Borrow $1 million for one year at a fixed rate, then renew the credit annually.

Although the lowest cost of funds is always a major selection criteria, it is not the only one. If the firm chooses strategy 1, it assures itself of the funding for the full three years at a known interest rate. It has maximized the predictability of cash flows for the debt obligation. What it has sacrificed, to some degree, is the ability to enjoy a lower interest rate in the event that interest rates fall over the period. Of course, it has also eliminated the risk that interest rates could rise over the period, increasing debt servicing costs.

Strategy 2 offers what strategy 1 did not, flexibility (repricing risk). It too assures the firm of full funding for the 3-year period. This eliminates credit risk. Repricing risk is, however, alive and well in strategy 2. If LIBOR changes dramatically by the second or third year, the LIBOR rate change is passed through fully to the borrower. The spread, however, remains fixed (reflecting the credit standing that has been locked in for the full three years). Flexibility comes at a cost in this case, the risk that interest rates could go up as well as down.

Strategy 3 offers more flexibility and more risk. First, the firm is borrowing at the shorter end of the yield curve. If the yield curve is positively sloped, as is commonly the case in major industrial markets, the base interest rate should be lower. But the short end of the yield curve is also the more volatile. It responds to short-term events in a much more pronounced fashion than longer-term rates. The strategy also exposes the firm to the possibility that its credit rating may change dramatically by the time for credit renewal, for better or worse. Noting that credit ratings in general are established on the premise that a firm can meet its debt-service obligations under worsening economic conditions, firms that are highly creditworthy (investment-rated grades) may view strategy 3 as a more relevant alternative than do firms of lower quality (speculative grades). This is not a strategy for firms that are financially weak.

Although the previous example gives only a partial picture of the complexity of funding decisions within the firm, it demonstrates the many ways credit risks and repricing risks are inextricably intertwined. The expression *interest rate exposure* is a complex concept, and the proper measurement of the exposure prior to its management is critical. We now proceed to describe the interest rate risk of the most common form of corporate debt, floating-rate loans.

Interest Rate Derivatives

Like foreign currency, interest rates have derivatives in the form of futures, forwards, and options. In addition, and likely of more importance, is the interest rate swap.

Interest Rate Futures

Unlike foreign currency futures, *interest rate futures* are relatively widely used by financial managers and treasurers of nonfinancial companies. Their popularity stems from the relatively high liquidity of the interest rate futures markets, their simplicity in use, and the rather standardized interest rate exposures most firms possess. The two most widely used futures contracts are the Eurodollar futures traded on the Chicago Mercantile Exchange (CME) and the U.S. Treasury Bond Futures of the Chicago Board of Trade (CBOT). Interestingly, the third-largest volume of a traded futures contract in the latter 1990s was the U.S. dollar/Brazilian *real* currency futures contract traded on the Bolsa de Mercadorias y Futuros in Brazil.

To illustrate the use of futures for managing interest rate risks we will focus on the 3-month Eurodollar futures contracts. Exhibit 8.10 presents Eurodollar futures for two years (they actually trade 10 years into the future).

EXHIBIT 8.10	Eurodollar Futures Prices					
Maturity	**Open**	**High**	**Low**	**Settle**	**Yield**	**Open Interest**
June 10	94.99	95.01	94.98	95.01	4.99	455,763
Sept	94.87	94.97	94.87	94.96	5.04	535,932
Dec	94.60	94.70	94.60	94.68	5.32	367,036
Mar 11	94.67	94.77	94.66	94.76	5.24	299,993
June	94.55	94.68	94.54	94.63	5.37	208,949
Sept	94.43	94.54	94.43	94.53	5.47	168,961
Dec	94.27	94.38	94.27	94.36	5.64	130,824

Typical presentation by the *Wall Street Journal*. Only regular quarterly maturities shown. All contracts are for $1 million; points of 100%. Open interest is number of contracts outstanding.

The yield of a futures contract is calculated from the *settlement price*, which is the closing price for that trading day. For example, a financial manager examining the Eurodollar quotes in Exhibit 8.10 for a March 2011 contract would see that the *settlement price* on the previous day was 94.76, an annual yield of 5.24%:

$$\text{Yield} = (100.00 - 94.76) = 5.24\%$$

Since each contract is for a 3-month period (quarter) and a notional principal of $1 million, each basis point is actually worth $2,500 (.01 × $1,000,000 × 90/360).

If a financial manager were interested in hedging a floating-rate interest payment due in March 2011, she would need to *sell a future*, to take a short position. This strategy is referred to as a short position because the manager is selling something she does not own (as in shorting common stock). If interest rates rise by March—as the manager fears—the futures price will fall and she will be able to close the position at a profit. This profit will roughly offset the losses associated with rising interest payments on her debt. If the manager is wrong, however, and interest rates actually fall by the maturity date, causing the futures price to rise, she will suffer a loss that will wipe out the "savings" derived by making a lower floating-rate interest payment than she expected. So by selling the March 2011 futures contract, the manager will be locking in an interest rate of 5.24%.

Obviously interest rate futures positions could be—and are on a regular basis—purchased purely for speculative purposes. Although that is not the focus of the managerial context here, the example shows how any speculator with a directional view on interest rates could take positions in expectations of profit.

As mentioned previously, the most common interest rate exposure of the nonfinancial firm is interest payable on debt. Such exposure is not, however, the only interest rate risk. As more and more firms aggressively manage their entire balance sheet, the interest earnings from the left-hand side are under increasing scrutiny. If financial managers are expected to earn higher interest on interest-bearing securities, they may well find a second use of the interest rate futures market: to lock in future interest earnings. Exhibit 8.11 provides an overview of these two basic interest rate exposures and the strategies needed to manage interest rate futures.

Forward Rate Agreements

A *forward rate agreement* (FRA) is an interbank-traded contract to buy or sell interest rate payments on a notional principal. These contracts are settled in cash. The buyer of an FRA obtains the right to lock in an interest rate for a desired term that begins at a future date. The contract specifies that the seller of the FRA will pay the buyer the increased interest expense

---

EXHIBIT 8.11   Interest Rate Futures Strategies for Common Exposures

Exposure or Position	Futures Action	Interest Rates	Position Outcome
Paying interest on future date	Sell a Futures (short position)	If rates go up	Futures price falls; short earns a profit
		If rates go down	Futures price rises; short earns a loss
Earning interest on future date	Buy a Futures (long position)	If rates go up	Futures price falls; long earns a loss
		If rates go down	Futures price rises; long earns a profit

on a nominal sum (the notional principal) of money if interest rates rise above the agreed rate, but the buyer will pay the seller the differential interest expense if interest rates fall below the agreed rate. Maturities available are typically 1, 3, 6, 9, and 12 months, much like traditional forward contracts for currencies.

Like foreign currency forward contracts, FRAs are useful on individual exposures. They are contractual commitments of the firm that allow little flexibility to enjoy favorable movements, such as when LIBOR is falling as described above. Firms also use FRAs if they plan to invest in securities at future dates but fear that interest rates might fall prior to the investment date. Because of the limited maturities and currencies available, however, FRAs are not widely used outside the largest industrial economies and currencies.

Interest Rate Swaps

Swaps are contractual agreements to exchange or swap a series of cash flows. These cash flows are most commonly the interest payments associated with debt service, such as the floating-rate loan described above.

◆ If the agreement is for one party to swap its fixed interest rate payment for the floating interest rate payments of another, it is termed an *interest rate swap*.

◆ If the agreement is to swap currencies of debt service obligation—for example, Swiss franc interest payments in exchange for U.S. dollar interest payments—it is termed a *currency swap*.

◆ A single swap may combine elements of both interest rate and currency swaps.

In any case, however, the swap serves to alter the firm's cash flow obligations, as in changing floating-rate payments into fixed-rate payments associated with an existing debt obligation. The swap itself is not a source of capital, but rather an alteration of the cash flows associated with payment. What is often termed the *plain vanilla swap* is an agreement between two parties to exchange fixed-rate for floating-rate financial obligations. This type of swap forms the largest single financial derivative market in the world.

The two parties may have various motivations for entering into the agreement. For example, a very common position is as follows. A corporate borrower of good credit standing has existing floating-rate debt service payments. The borrower, after reviewing current market conditions and forming expectations about the future, may conclude that interest rates are about to rise. In order to protect the firm against rising debt-service payments, the company's treasury may enter into a swap agreement to pay *fixed/receive floating*. This means the firm will now make fixed interest rate payments and receive from the swap counterparty floating interest rate payments. The floating-rate payments that the firm receives are used to service the debt obligation of the firm, so the firm, on a net basis, is now making fixed interest rate payments. Using derivatives it has synthetically changed floating-rate debt into fixed-rate debt. It has done so without going through the costs and intricacies of refinancing existing debt obligations.

Similarly, a firm with fixed-rate debt that expects interest rates to fall can change fixed-rate debt to floating-rate debt. In this case, the firm would enter into a *pay floating/receive fixed* interest rate swap. Exhibit 8.12 presents a summary table of the recommended interest rate swap strategies for firms holding either fixed-rate debt or floating-rate debt.

The cash flows of an interest rate swap are interest rates applied to a set amount of capital (*notional principal*). For this reason they are also referred to as *coupon swaps*. Firms entering into interest rate swaps set the notional principal so that the cash flows resulting from the interest rate swap cover their interest rate management needs.

Interest rate swaps are contractual commitments between a firm and a swap dealer and are completely independent of the interest rate exposure of the firm. That is, the firm may

EXHIBIT 8.12	Interest Rate Swap Strategies	
Position	**Expectation**	**Interest Rate Swap Strategy**
Fixed-Rate Debt	Rates to go up	Do nothing
	Rates to go down	Pay floating/Receive fixed
Floating-Rate Debt	Rates to go up	Pay fixed/Receive floating
	Rates to go down	Do nothing

enter into a swap for any reason it sees fit and then swap a notional principal that is less than, equal to, or even greater than the total position being managed. For example, a firm with a variety of floating-rate loans on its books may enter into interest rate swaps for only 70% of the existing principal, if it wishes. The reason for entering into a swap, and the swap position the firm enters into, is purely at management's discretion. It should also be noted that the interest rate swap market is filling a gap in market efficiency. If all firms had free and equal access to capital markets, regardless of interest rate structure or currency of denomination, the swap market would most likely not exist. The fact that the swap market not only exists but flourishes and provides benefits to all parties is in some ways the proverbial "free lunch."

Currency Swaps

Since all swap rates are derived from the yield curve in each major currency, the fixed-to floating-rate interest rate swap existing in each currency allows firms to swap across currencies. Exhibit 8.13 lists typical swap rates for the euro, the U.S. dollar, the Japanese yen, and the

EXHIBIT 8.13		Interest Rate and Currency Swap Quotes						
	Euro-E		**Swiss franc**		**U.S. dollar**		**Japanese yen**	
Years	**Bid**	**Ask**	**Bid**	**Ask**	**Bid**	**Ask**	**Bid**	**Ask**
1	2.99	3.02	1.43	1.47	5.24	5.26	0.23	0.26
2	3.08	3.12	1.68	1.76	5.43	5.46	0.36	0.39
3	3.24	3.28	1.93	2.01	5.56	5.59	0.56	0.59
4	3.44	3.48	2.15	2.23	5.65	5.68	0.82	0.85
5	3.63	3.67	2.35	2.43	5.73	5.76	1.09	1.12
6	3.83	3.87	2.54	2.62	5.80	5.83	1.33	1.36
7	4.01	4.05	2.73	2.81	5.86	5.89	1.55	1.58
8	4.18	4.22	2.91	2.99	5.92	5.95	1.75	1.78
9	4.32	4.36	3.08	3.16	5.96	5.99	1.90	1.93
10	4.42	4.46	3.22	3.30	6.01	6.04	2.04	2.07
12	4.58	4.62	3.45	3.55	6.10	6.13	2.28	2.32
15	4.78	4.82	3.71	3.81	6.20	6.23	2.51	2.56
20	5.00	5.04	3.96	4.06	6.29	6.32	2.71	2.76
25	5.13	5.17	4.07	4.17	6.29	6.32	2.77	2.82
30	5.19	5.23	4.16	4.26	6.28	6.31	2.82	2.88
LIBOR	3.0313	3.0938	1.3125	1.4375	4.9375	5.0625	0.1250	0.2188

Typical presentation by the *Financial Times*. Bid and ask spreads as of close of London business. US$ is quoted against 3-month LIBOR; Japanese yen against 6-month LIBOR; Euro and Swiss franc against 6-month LIBOR.

Swiss franc. These swap rates are based on the government security yields in each of the individual currency markets, plus a credit spread applicable to investment grade borrowers in the respective markets.

Note that the swap rates in Exhibit 8.13 are not rated or categorized by credit ratings. This is because the swap market itself does not carry the credit risk associated with individual borrowers. Individual borrowers with obligations priced at LIBOR plus a spread will keep the spread. The fixed spread, a credit risk premium, is still borne by the firm itself. For example, lower-rated firms may pay spreads of 3% or 4% over LIBOR, while some of the world's largest and most financially sound MNEs may actually raise capital at rates of LIBOR −0.40%. The swap market does not differentiate the rate by the participant; all swap at fixed rates versus LIBOR in the respective currency.

The usual motivation for a currency swap is to replace cash flows scheduled in an undesired currency with flows in a desired currency. The desired currency is probably the currency in which the firm's future operating revenues (inflows) will be generated. Firms often raise capital in currencies in which they do not possess significant revenues or other natural cash flows. The reason they do so is cost; specific firms may find capital costs in specific currencies attractively priced to them under special conditions. Having raised the capital, however, the firm may wish to swap its repayment into a currency in which it has future operating revenues.

The utility of the currency swap market to an MNE is significant. An MNE wishing to swap a 10-year fixed 6.04% U.S. dollar cash flow stream could swap to 4.46% fixed in euro, 3.30% fixed in Swiss francs, or 2.07% fixed in Japanese yen. It could swap from fixed dollars not only to fixed rates, but also to floating LIBOR rates in the various currencies as well. All are possible at the rates quoted in Exhibit 8.13.

Prudence in Practice

In the following chapters we will illustrate how derivatives can be used to reduce the risks associated with the conduct of multinational financial management. It is critical, however, that the user of any financial tool or technique—including financial derivatives—follow sound principles and practices. Many a firm has been ruined as a result of the misuse of derivatives. A word to the wise: Do not fall victim to what many refer to as the *gambler's dilemma*—confusing luck with talent.

Major corporate financial disasters related to financial derivatives continue to be a problem in global business. As is the case with so many issues in modern society, technology is not at fault, rather human error in its use. We conclude our discussion of financial derivatives with a note of caution and humility from an essay in the *Harvard Business Review* by Peter Bernstein:

> *More than any other development, the quantification of risk defines the boundary between modern times and the rest of history. The speed, power, movement, and instant communication that characterize our age would have been inconceivable before science replaced superstition as a bulwark against risks of all kinds.*
>
> *It is hubris that we believe that we can put reliable and stable numbers on the impact of a politician's power, on the probability of a takeover boom like the one that occurred in the 1980s, on the return on the stock market over the next 2, 20, or 50 years, or on subjective factors like utility and risk aversion. It is equally silly to limit our deliberations only to those variables that do lend themselves to quantification, excluding all serious consideration of the unquantifiable. It is irrational to confuse probability with timing and to assume that an event with low probability is therefore not imminent. Such confusion, however, is by*

no means unusual. And it surely is naive to define discontinuity as anomaly instead of as normality; only the shape and the timing of the disturbances are hidden from us, not their inevitability.

Finally, the science of risk management is capable of creating new risks even as it brings old risk under control. Our faith in risk management encourages us to take risk we otherwise would not take. On most counts, that is beneficial. But we should be wary of increasing the total amount of risk in the system. Research shows that the security of seat belts encourages drivers to behave more aggressively, with the result that the number of accidents rises even as the seriousness of injury in any one accident may diminish.[1]

Summary of Learning Objectives

Explain how foreign currency futures are quoted, valued, and used for speculation purposes.

◆ A foreign currency futures contract is an exchange-traded agreement calling for future delivery of a standard amount of foreign exchange at a fixed time, place, and price.

◆ Foreign currency futures contracts are in reality standardized forward contracts. Unlike forward contracts, however, trading occurs on the floor of an organized exchange rather than between banks and customers. Futures also require collateral and are normally settled through the purchase of an offsetting position.

Illustrate how foreign currency futures differ from forward contracts.

◆ Futures differ from forward contracts by size of contract, maturity, location of trading, pricing, collateral/margin requirements, method of settlement, commissions, trading hours, counterparties, and liquidity.

◆ Financial managers typically prefer foreign currency forwards over futures out of simplicity of use and position maintenance. Financial speculators typically prefer foreign currency futures over forwards because of the liquidity of the futures markets.

Analyze how foreign currency options are quoted, valued, and used for speculation purposes.

◆ Foreign currency options are financial contracts that give the holder the right, but not the obligation, to buy (in the case of calls) or sell (in the case of puts) a specified amount of foreign exchange at a predetermined price on or before a specified maturity date.

◆ The use of a currency option as a speculative device for the buyer of an option arises from the fact that an option gains in value as the underlying currency rises (for calls) or falls (for puts). The amount of loss when the underlying currency moves opposite to the desired direction is limited to the premium of the option.

◆ The use of a currency option as a speculative device for the writer (seller) of an option arises from the option premium. If the option—either a put or call—expires out-of-the-money (valueless), the writer of the option has earned, and retains, the entire premium.

◆ Speculation is an attempt to profit by trading on expectations about prices in the future. In the foreign exchange market, one speculates by taking a position in a foreign currency and then closing that position after the exchange rate has moved; a profit results only if the rate moves in the direction that the speculator expected.

Explain how foreign currency options are valued.

◆ Currency option valuation, the determination of the option's premium, is a complex combination of the current spot rate, the specific strike rate, the forward rate (which itself is dependent on the current spot rate and interest differentials), currency volatility, and time to maturity.

◆ The total value of an option is the sum of its intrinsic value and time value. Intrinsic value depends on the relationship between the option's strike price and the current spot rate at any single point in time, whereas time value estimates how this current intrinsic value may change—for the better—prior to the option's maturity or expiration.

---

[1]Reprinted by permission of *Harvard Business Review*. Excerpt from "The New Religion of Risk Management" by Peter L. Bernstein, March–April 1996. Copyright 1996 by the Harvard Business School Publishing Corporation; all rights reserved.

Define interest rate risk, and examine how can it be managed.

◆ The single largest interest rate risk of the nonfinancial firm is debt-service. The debt structure of the MNE will possess differing maturities of debt, different interest rate structures (such as fixed versus floating-rate), and different currencies of denomination.

◆ The increasing volatility of world interest rates, combined with the increasing use of short-term and variable-rate debt by firms worldwide, has led many firms to actively manage their *interest rate risks*.

◆ The primary sources of interest rate risk to a multinational nonfinancial firm are short-term borrowing and investing, as well as long-term sources of debt.

◆ The techniques and instruments used in interest rate risk management in many ways resemble those used in currency risk management: the old tried and true methods of lending and borrowing.

◆ The primary instruments and techniques used for interest rate risk management include forward rate agreements (FRAs), forward swaps, interest rate futures, and interest rate swaps.

Explain interest rate swaps and how they can be used to manage interest rate risk.

◆ The interest rate and currency swap markets allow firms that have limited access to specific currencies and interest rate structures to gain access at relatively low costs. This in turn allows these firms to manage their currency and interest rate risks more effectively.

Analyze how interest rate swaps and cross currency swaps can be used to manage both foreign exchange risk and interest rate risk simultaneously.

◆ A cross currency interest rate swap allows a firm to alter both the currency of denomination of cash flows in debt service, but also to alter the fixed-to-floating or floating-to-fixed interest rate structure.

MINI-CASE

McDonald's Corporation's British Pound Exposure

McDonald's Corporation has investments in more than 100 countries. It considers its equity investment in foreign affiliates capital which is at risk, subject to hedging depending on the individual country, currency, and market.

British Subsidiary as an Exposure

McDonald's parent company has three different pound-denominated exposures arising from its ownership and operation of its British subsidiary.

1. The British subsidiary has equity capital which is a pound-denominated asset of the parent company.

2. In addition to the equity capital invested in the British affiliate, the parent company provides intra-company debt in the form of a 4-year £125 million loan. The loan is denominated in British pounds and carries a fixed 5.30% per annum interest payment.

3. The British subsidiary pays a fixed percentage of gross sales in royalties to the parent company. This too is pound-denominated. The three different exposures sum to a significant exposure problem for McDonald's.

An additional technical detail further complicates the situation. When the parent company makes an intra-company loan as that to the British subsidiary, it must designate—according to U.S. accounting and tax law practices—whether the loan is considered to be *permanently invested* in that country. (Although on the surface it seems illogical to consider four years "permanent," the loan itself could simply be continually rolled-over by the parent company and never actually be repaid.) If not considered permanent, the foreign exchange gains and losses related to the loan flow directly to the parent company's profit and loss statement (P&L), according to FAS #52. If, however, the loan is designated as permanent, the foreign exchange gains and losses related to the intracompany loan would flow only to the CTA (cumulative translation adjustment) on the consolidated balance sheet. To date, McDonald's has chosen to designate the loan as *permanent*. The functional currency of the British affiliate for consolidation purposes is the local currency, the British pound.

Anka Gopi is both the Manager for Financial Markets/Treasury and a McDonald's shareholder. She is currently reviewing the existing hedging strategy employed by McDonald's against the pound exposure. The company has been hedging the pound exposure by entering into a cross-currency U.S. dollar/British pound sterling swap. The current swap is a 7-year swap to receive dollars and pay pounds. Like all cross-currency swaps, the agreement requires McDonald's-U.S. to make regular pound-denominated interest payments and a bullet principal repayment (notional principal) at the end of the swap agreement. McDonald's considers the large notional principal payment a hedge against the equity investment in its British affiliate.

According to accounting practice, a company may elect to take the interest associated with a foreign currency-denominated loan and carry that directly to the parent company's P&L This has been done in the past, and McDonald's has benefited from the inclusion of this interest payment.

FAS #133, *Accounting for Derivative Instruments and Hedging Activities*, issued in June 1998, was originally intended to be effective for all fiscal quarters within fiscal years beginning after June 15, 1999 (for most firms this meant January 1, 2000). The new standard, however, was so complex and potentially of such material influence to U.S.-based MNEs, that the Financial Accounting Standards Board has been approached by dozens of major firms and asked to postpone mandatory implementation. The standard's complexity, combined with the workloads associated with Y2K (year 2000) risk controls, persuaded the Financial Accounting Standards Board to delay FAS #133's mandatory implementation date indefinitely.

Issues for Discussion. Anka Gopi, however, still wishes to consider the impact of FAS #133 on the hedging strategy currently employed. Under FAS #133, the firm will have to mark-to-market the entire cross-currency swap position, including principal, and carry this to *other comprehensive income* (OCI). OCI, however, is actually a form of income required under U.S. GAAP and reported in the footnotes to the financial statements, but not the income measure used in reported earnings per share. Although McDonald's has been carrying the interest payments on the swap to income, it has not previously had to carry the present value of the swap principal to OCI. In Anka Gopi's eyes, this poses a substantial material risk to OCI.

Anka Gopi also wished to reconsider the current strategy. She began by listing the pros and cons of the current strategy, comparing these to alternative strategies, and then deciding what if anything should be done about it at this time.

CASE QUESTIONS

1. How does the cross-currency swap effectively hedge the three primary exposures McDonald's has relative to its British subsidiary?

2. How does the cross-currency swap hedge the long-term equity position in the foreign subsidiary?

3. Should Anka—and McDonald's—worry about OCI?

Questions

1. **Options versus Futures.** Explain the difference between foreign currency *options* and *futures* and when either might be most appropriately used.

2. **Trading Location for Futures.** Check the *Wall Street Journal* to find where in the United States foreign exchange future contracts are traded.

3. **Futures Terminology.** Explain the meaning and probable significance for international business of the following contract specifications:
   a. Specific-sized contract
   b. Standard method of stating exchange rates
   c. Standard maturity date
   d. Collateral and maintenance margins
   e. Counterparty

4. **A Futures Trade.** A newspaper shows the prices below for the previous day's trading in U.S. dollar-euro currency futures. What do the terms shown indicate?

Month:	December
Open:	0.9124
Settlement:	0.9136
Change:	+0.0027
High:	0.9147
Low:	0.9098
Estimated volume	29,763
Open interest:	111,360
Contract size:	€125,000

5. **Puts and Calls.** What is the basic difference between a *put* on British pounds sterling and a *call* on sterling?

6. **Call Contract Elements.** You read that exchange-traded American call options on pounds sterling having a strike price of 1.460 and a maturity of next March are now quoted at 3.67. What does this mean if you are a potential buyer?

7. **The Option Cost.** What happens to the premium you paid for the above option in the event you decide to let the option expire unexercised? What happens to this amount in the event you do decide to exercise the option?

8. **Buying a European Option.** You have the same information as in question 4, except that the pricing is for a European option. What is different?

9. **Writing Options.** Why would anyone write an option, knowing that the gain from receiving the option premium is fixed but the loss if the underlying price goes in the wrong direction can be extremely large?

10. **Option Valuation.** The value of an option is stated to be the sum of its *intrinsic value* and its *time value*. Explain what is meant by these terms.

11. **Reference Rates.** What is an interest "reference rate" and how is it used to set rates for individual borrowers?

12. Risk and Return. Some corporate treasury departments are organized as a service center (cost center), while others are set up as profit centers. What is the difference and what are the implications for the firm?

13. Forecast Types. What is the difference between a specific forecast and a directional forecast?

14. Policy Statements. Explain the difference between a goal statement and a policy statement?

15. Credit and Repricing Risk. From the point of view of a borrowing corporation, what are credit and repricing risks. Explain steps a company might take to minimize both.

16. Forward Rate Agreement. How can a business firm that has borrowed on a floating rate basis use a forward rate agreement to reduce interest rate risk?

17. Eurodollar Futures. A newspaper reports that a given June Eurodollar futures settled at 93.55. What was the annual yield? How many dollars does this represent?

18. Defaulting on an Interest Rate Swap. Smith Company and Jones Company enter into an interest rate swap, with Smith paying fixed interest to Jones, and Jones paying floating interest to Smith. Smith now goes bankrupt and so defaults on its remaining interest payments. What is the financial damage to Jones Company?

19. Currency Swaps. Why would one company, with interest payments due in pounds sterling, want to swap those payments for interest payments due in U.S. dollars?

20. Counterparty Risk. How does exchange trading in swaps remove any risk that the counterparty in a swap agreement will not complete the agreement?

Problems

1. Peleh's Puts. Peleh writes a put option on Japanese yen with a strike price of $0.008000/¥ (¥125.00/$) at a premium of 0.0080¢ per yen and with an expiration date six months from now. The option is for ¥12,500,000. What is Peleh's profit or loss at maturity

if the ending spot rates are ¥110/$, ¥115/$, ¥120/$, ¥125/$, ¥130/$, ¥135/$, and ¥140/$?

2. Sallie Schnudel. Sallie Schnudel trades currencies for Keystone Funds in Jakarta. She focuses nearly all of her time and attention on the U.S. dollar/Singapore dollar ($/S$) cross-rate. The current spot rate is $0.6000/S$. After considerable study, she has concluded that the Singapore dollar will appreciate versus the U.S. dollar in the coming 90 days, probably to about $0.7000/S$. She has the following options on the Singapore dollar to choose from:

Option	Strike Price	Premium
Put on Sing $	$0.6500/S$	$0.00003/S$
Call on Sing $	$0.6500/S$	$0.00046/S$

a. Should Sallie buy a put on Singapore dollars or a call on Singapore dollars?
b. What is Sallie's break-even price on the option purchased in part (a)?
c. Using your answer from part (a), what is Sallie's gross profit and net profit (including premium) if the spot rate at the end of 90 days is indeed $0.7000/S$?
d. Using your answer from part (a), what is Sallie's gross profit and net profit (including premium) if the spot rate at the end of 90 days is $0.8000/S$?

3. Ventosa Investments. Jamie Rodriguez, a currency trader for Chicago-based Ventosa Investments, uses the futures quotes on the British pound (£) shown at the bottom of the page to speculate on the value of the pound.
a. If Jamie buys 5 June pound futures, and the spot rate at maturity is $1.3980/£, what is the value of her position?
b. If Jamie sells 12 March pound futures, and the spot rate at maturity is $1.4560/£, what is the value of her position?
c. If Jamie buys 3 March pound futures, and the spot rate at maturity is $1.4560/£, what is the value of her position?
d. If Jamie sells 12 June pound futures, and the spot rate at maturity is $1.3980/£, what is the value of her position?

British Pound Futures, US$/pound (CME)   **Contract = 62,500 pounds**

Maturity	Open	High	Low	Settle	Change	High	Open Interest
March	1.4246	1.4268	1.4214	1.4228	0.0032	1.4700	25,605
June	1.4164	1.4188	1.4146	1.4162	0.0030	1.4550	809

4. **Amber McClain.** Amber McClain, the currency speculator we met in the chapter, sells eight June futures contracts for 500,000 pesos at the closing price quoted in Exhibit 8.1.
   a. What is the value of her position at maturity if the ending spot rate is $0.12000/Ps?
   b. What is the value of her position at maturity if the ending spot rate is $0.09800/Ps?
   c. What is the value of her position at maturity if the ending spot rate is $0.11000/Ps?

5. **Blade Capital (A).** Christoph Hoffeman trades currency for Blade Capital of Geneva. Christoph has $10 million to begin with, and he must state all profits at the end of any speculation in U.S. dollars. The spot rate on the euro is $1.3358/€, while the 30-day forward rate is $1.3350/€.
   a. If Christoph believes the euro will continue to rise in value against the U.S. dollar, so that he expects the spot rate to be $1.3600/€ at the end of 30 days, what should he do?
   b. If Christoph believes the euro will depreciate in value against the U.S. dollar, so that he expects the spot rate to be $1.2800/€ at the end of 30 days, what should he do?

6. **Blade Capital (B).** Christoph Hoffeman of Blade Capital now believes the Swiss franc will appreciate versus the U.S. dollar in the coming 3-month period. He has $100,000 to invest. The current spot rate is $0.5820/SF, the 3-month forward rate is $0.5640/SF, and he expects the spot rates to reach $0.6250/SF in three months.
   a. Calculate Christoph's expected profit assuming a pure spot market speculation strategy.
   b. Calculate Christoph's expected profit assuming he buys or sells SF three months forward.

7. **Vatic Capital.** Cachita Haynes works as a currency speculator for Vatic Capital of Los Angeles. Her latest speculative position is to profit from her expectation that the U.S. dollar will rise significantly against the Japanese yen. The current spot rate is ¥120.00/$. She must choose between the following 90-day options on the Japanese yen:

Option	Strike Price	Premium
Put on yen	¥125/$	$0.00003/S$
Call on yen	¥125/$	$0.00046/S$

   a. Should Cachita buy a put on yen or a call on yen?
   b. What is Cachita's break-even price on the option purchased in part (a)?
   c. Using your answer from part (a), what is Cachita's gross profit and net profit (including premium) if the spot rate at the end of 90 days is ¥140/$?

8. **Calling All Profits.** Assume a call option on euros is written with a strike price of $1.2500/€ at a premium of 3.80¢ per euro ($0.0380/€) and with an expiration date three months from now. The option is for €100,000. Calculate your profit or loss should you exercise before maturity at a time when the euro is traded spot at the following:
   a. $1.10/€
   b. $1.15/€
   c. $1.20/€
   d. $1.25/€
   e. $1.30/€
   f. $1.35/€
   g. $1.40/€

9. **Mystery at Baker Street.** Arthur Doyle is a currency trader for Baker Street, a private investment house in London. Baker Street's clients are a collection of wealthy private investors who, with a minimum stake of £250,000 each, wish to speculate on the movement of currencies. The investors expect annual returns in excess of 25%. Although officed in London, all accounts and expectations are based in U.S. dollars.

   Arthur is convinced that the British pound will slide significantly—possibly to $1.3200/£—in the coming 30 to 60 days. The current spot rate is $1.4260/£. Arthur wishes to buy a put on pounds which will yield the 25% return expected by his investors. Which of the following put options would you recommend he purchase? Prove your choice is the preferable combination of strike price, maturity, and up-front premium expense.

Strike Price	Maturity	Premium
$1.36/£	30 days	$0.00081/£
$1.34/£	30 days	$0.00021/£
$1.32/£	30 days	$0.00004/£
$1.36/£	60 days	$0.00333/£
$1.34/£	60 days	$0.00150/£
$1.32/£	60 days	$0.00060/£

10. **Contrarious Calandra.** Calandra Panagakos works for CIBC Currency Funds in Toronto. Calandra is something of a contrarian—as opposed to most of the forecasts, she believes the Canadian dollar (C$) will appreciate versus the U.S. dollar over the coming 90 days. The current spot rate is $0.6750/C$. Calandra may choose between the following options on the Canadian dollar.

Option	Strike Price	Premium
Put on C$	$0.7000	$0.00003/S$
Call on C$	$0.7000	$0.00049/S$

a. Should Calandra buy a put on Canadian dollars or a call on Canadian dollars?

b. What is Calandra's break-even price on the option purchased in part (a)?

c. Using your answer from part (a), what is Calandra's gross profit and net profit (including premium) if the spot rate at the end of 90 days is indeed $0.7600?

d. Using your answer from part (a), what is Calandra's gross profit and net profit (including premium) if the spot rate at the end of 90 days is $0.8250?

11. **Chavez S.A.** Chavez S.A., a Venezuelan company, wishes to borrow $8,000,000 for eight weeks. A rate of 6.250% per annum is quoted by potential lenders in New York, Great Britain, and Switzerland using, respectively, international, British, and the Swiss-Eurobond definitions of interest (day count conventions). From which source should Chavez borrow?

12. **Botany Bay Corporation.** Botany Bay Corporation of Australia seeks to borrow US$30,000,000 in the Eurodollar market. Funding is needed for two years. Investigation leads to three possibilities. Compare the alternatives and make a recommendation.

1. Botany Bay could borrow the US$30,000,000 for two years at a fixed 5% rate of interest.

2. Botany Bay could borrow the US$30,000,000 at LIBOR + 1.5%. LIBOR is currently 3.5%, and the rate would be reset every six months.

3. Botany Bay could borrow the US$30,000,000 for one year only at 4.5%. At the end of the first year Botany Bay Corporation would have to negotiate for a new 1-year loan.

13. **Raid Gauloises.** Raid Gauloises is a rapidly growing French sporting goods and adventure racing outfitter. The company has decided to borrow €20,000,000 via a euro-euro floating rate loan for four years. Raid must decide between two competing loan offers from two of its banks.

Banque de Paris has offered the 4-year debt at euro-LIBOR + 2.00% with an up-front initiation fee of 1.8%. Banque de Sorbonne, however, has offered euro-LIBOR + 2.5%, a higher spread, but with no loan initiation fees up front, for the same term and principal. Both banks reset the interest rate at the end of each year.

Euro-LIBOR is currently 4.00%. Raid's economist forecasts that LIBOR will rise by 0.5 percentage points each year. Banque de Sorbonne,

however, officially forecasts euro-LIBOR to begin trending upward at the rate of 0.25 percentage points per year. Raid Gauloises's cost of capital is 11%. Which loan proposal do you recommend for Raid Gauloises?

14. **Schifano Motors.** Schifano Motors of Italy recently took out a 4-year €5 million loan on a floating rate basis. It is now worried, however, about rising interest costs. Although it had initially believed interest rates in the Euro-zone would be trending downward when taking out the loan, recent economic indicators show growing inflationary pressures. Analysts are predicting that the European Central Bank will slow monetary growth driving interest rates up.

Schifano is now considering whether to seek some protection against a rise in euro-LIBOR, and is considering a forward rate agreement (FRA) with an insurance company. According to the agreement, Schifano would pay to the insurance company at the end of each year the difference between its initial interest cost at LIBOR + 2.50% (6.50%) and any fall in interest cost due to a fall in LIBOR. Conversely, the insurance company would pay to Schifano 70% of the difference between Schifano's initial interest cost and any increase in interest costs caused by a rise in LIBOR.

Purchase of the floating rate agreement will cost €100,000, paid at the time of the initial loan. What are Schifano's annual financing costs now if LIBOR rises and if LIBOR falls? Schifano uses 12% as its weighted average cost of capital. Do you recommend that Schifano purchase the FRA?

15. **Chrysler LLC.** Chrysler LLC, the now privately held company sold off by DaimlerChrysler, must pay floating rate interest three months from now. It wants to lock in these interest payments by buying an interest rate futures contract. Interest rate futures for three months from now settled at 93.07, for a yield of 6.93% per annum.

a. If the floating interest rate three months from now is 6.00%, what did Chrysler gain or lose?

b. If the floating interest rate three months from now is 8.00%, what did Chrysler gain or lose?

16. **CB Solutions.** Heather O'Reilly, the treasurer of CB Solutions, believes interest rates are going to rise, so she wants to swap her future floating rate interest payments for fixed rates. Presently, she is paying LIBOR + 2% per annum on $5,000,000 of

Assumptions	Values	Swap Rates	3-year Bid	3-year Ask
Notional principal	$ 10,000,000	U.S. dollar	5.56%	5.59%
Spot exchange rate, SFr/$	1.5000	Swiss franc—SFr	1.93%	2.01%
Spot exchange rate, $/euro	1.1200			

debt for the next two years, with payments due semiannually. LIBOR is currently 4.00% per annum. Heather has just made an interest payment today, so the next payment is due six months from today.

Heather finds that she can swap her current floating rate payments for fixed payments of 7.00% per annum. (CB Solution's weighted average cost of capital is 12%, which Heather calculates to be 6% per 6-month period, compounded semiannually).

a. If LIBOR rises at the rate of 50 basis points per 6-month period, starting tomorrow, how much does Heather save or cost her company by making this swap?

b. If LIBOR falls at the rate of 25 basis points per 6-month period, starting tomorrow, how much does Heather save or cost her company by making this swap?

17. **Lluvia and Paraguas.** Lluvia Manufacturing and Paraguas Products both seek funding at the lowest possible cost. Lluvia would prefer the flexibility of floating rate borrowing, while Paraguas wants the security of fixed rate borrowing. Lluvia is the more creditworthy company. They face the following rate structure. Lluvia, with the better credit rating, has lower borrowing costs in both types of borrowing.

Lluvia wants floating rate debt, so it could borrow at LIBOR + 1%. However it could borrow fixed at 8% and swap for floating rate debt. Paraguas wants fixed rate debt, so it could borrow fixed at 12%. However, it could borrow floating at LIBOR +2% and swap for fixed rate debt. What should they do?

18. **Trident's Cross Currency Swap: SFr for US$.** Trident Corporation entered into a 3-year cross currency interest rate swap to receive U.S. dollars and pay Swiss francs. Trident, however, decided to unwind the swap after one year—thereby having two years left on the settlement costs of unwinding

the swap after one year. Repeat the calculations for unwinding, but assume that the rates shown above now apply.

19. **Trident's Cross Currency Swap: Yen for Euros.** Use the table of swap rates in the chapter (Exhibit 8.13), and assume Trident enters into a swap agreement to receive euros and pay Japanese yen, on a notional principal of €5,000,000. The spot exchange rate at the time of the swap is ¥104/€.

a. Calculate all principal and interest payments, in both euros and Swiss francs, for the life of the swap agreement.

b. Assume that one year into the swap agreement Trident decides it wants to unwind the swap agreement and settle it in euros. Assuming that a 2-year fixed rate of interest on the Japanese yen is now 0.80%, and a 2-year fixed rate of interest on the euro is now 3.60%, and the spot rate of exchange is now ¥114/€, what is the net present value of the swap agreement? Who pays whom what?

20. **Falcor.** Falcor is the U.S.-based automotive parts supplier that was spun-off from General Motors in 2000. With annual sales of over $26 billion, the company has expanded its markets far beyond traditional automobile manufacturers in the pursuit of a more diversified sales base. As part of the general diversification effort, the company wishes to diversify the currency of denomination of its debt portfolio as well. Assume Falcor enters into a $50 million 7-year cross currency interest rate swap to do just that—pay euros and receive dollars. Using the data in Exhibit 8.13,

a. Calculate all principal and interest payments in both currencies for the life of the swap.

b. Assume that three years later Falcor decides to unwind the swap agreement. If 4-year fixed rates of interest in euros have now risen to 5.35%, 4-year fixed rate dollars have fallen to 4.40%, and the current spot exchange rate is $1.02/€, what is the net present value of the swap agreement? Who pays whom what?

Pricing Your Own Options

An Excel workbook entitled FX Option Pricing *is downloadable from the book's Web site. The workbook has five spreadsheets constructed for pricing currency options for the following five currency pairs: U.S. dollar/euro, U.S. dollar/* *Japanese yen, euro/Japanese yen, U.S. dollar/British pound, and euro/British pound. The dollar/euro pair is shown in the table at the top of the next page. Use the appropriate spreadsheet from the workbook to answer questions 21–25.*

Pricing Currency Options on the Euro

	A U.S.-based firm wishing to buy or sell euros (the foreign currency)		A European firm wishing to buy or sell dollars (the foreign currency)	
	Variable	Value	Variable	Value
Spot rate (domestic/foreign)	S_0	$1.2480	S_0	€0.8013
Strike rate (domestic/foreign)	X	$1.2500	X	€0.8000
Domestic interest rate (%p.a.)	r_d	1.453%	r_d	2.187%
Foreign interest rate (%p.a.)	r_f	2.187%	r_f	1.453%
Time (years, 365 days)	T	1.000	T	1.000
Days equivalent		365.00		365.00
Volatility (%p.a.)	s	10.500%	s	10.500%
Call option premium (per unt fc)	c	$0.0461	c	€0.0366
Put option premium (per unit fc)	p	$0.0570	p	€0.0295
(European pricing)				
Call option premium (%)	c	3.69%	c	4.56%
Put option premium (%)	p	4.57%	p	3.68%

21. **U.S. Dollar/Euro.** The table above indicates that a 1-year call option on euros at a strike rate of $1.25/€ will cost the buyer $0.0632/€, or 4.99%. But that assumed a volatility of 12.000% when the spot rate was $1.2674/€. What would that same call option cost if the volatility was reduced to 10.500% when the spot rate fell to $1.2480/€?

22. **U.S. Dollar/Japanese Yen.** What would be the premium expense, in home currency, for a Japanese firm to purchase an option to sell 750,000 U.S. dollars, assuming the initial values listed in the FX Option Pricing workbook?

23. **Euro/Japanese Yen.** A French firm is expecting to receive JPY 10.4 million in 90 days as a result of an export sale to a Japanese semiconductor firm. What will it cost, in total, to purchase an option to sell the yen at €0.0072/JPY?

24. **U.S. Dollar/British Pound.** Assuming the same initial values for the dollar/pound cross rate in the FX Option Pricing workbook, how much more would a call option on pounds be if the maturity was doubled

from 90 to 180 days? What percentage increase is this for twice the length of maturity?

25. **Euro/British Pound.** How would the call option premium change on the right to buy pounds with euros if the euro interest rate changed to 4.000% from the initial values listed in the FX Option Pricing workbook?

Internet Exercises

1. **Financial Derivatives and the ISDA.** The International Swaps and Derivatives Association (ISDA) publishes a wealth of information about financial derivatives, their valuation and their use, in addition to providing master documents for their contractual use between parties. Use the following ISDA Internet site to find the definitions to 31 basic financial derivative questions and terms:

   ISDA   www.isda.org/educat/faqs.html

2. **Risk Management of Financial Derivatives.** If you think this book is long, take a look at the freely

downloadable U.S. Comptroller of the Currency's handbook on risk management related to the care and use of financial derivatives!

Comptroller of the Currency   www.occ.treas.gov/handbook/deriv.pdf

3. **Option Pricing.** OzForex Foreign Exchange Services is a private firm with an enormously powerful foreign currency derivative-enabled Web site. Use the following site to evaluate the various "Greeks" related to currency option pricing.

OzForex   www.ozforex.com.au/reference/fxoptions/

4. **Garman-Kohlhagen Option Formulation.** For those brave of heart and quantitatively adept, check out the following Internet site's detailed presentation of the Garman-Kohlhagen option formulation used widely in business and finance today.

Riskglossary.com   www.riskglossary.com/link/garman_kohlhagen_1983.htm

5. **Chicago Mercantile Exchange.** The Chicago Mercantile Exchange trades futures and options on a variety of currencies, including the Brazilian real. Use the following site to evaluate the uses of these currency derivatives:

Chicago Mercantile Exchange   www.cme.com/trading/dta/del/product_list.html?ProductType=cur

6. **Implied Currency Volatilities.** The single unobservable variable in currency option pricing is the volatility, since volatility inputs are the expected standard deviation of the daily spot rate for the coming period of the option's maturity. Use the New York Federal Reserve's Web site to obtain current implied currency volatilities for major trading cross-rate pairs.

Federal Reserve Bank of New York   www.ny.frb.org/markets/impliedvolatility.html

7. **Montreal Exchange.** The Montreal Exchange is a Canadian exchange devoted to the support of financial derivatives in Canada. Use its Web site to view the latest on MV volatility—the volatility of the Montreal Exchange Index itself—in recent trading hours and days.

Montreal Exchange   www.m-x.ca/marc_options_en.php

PART

3

Foreign Exchange Exposure

CHAPTER 9

Foreign Exchange Rate Determination and Forecasting

CHAPTER 10

Transaction and Translation Exposure

CHAPTER 11

Operating Exposure

Foreign Exchange Rate Determination and Forecasting

The herd instinct among forecasters makes sheep look like independent thinkers. —Edgar R. Fiedler.

LEARNING OBJECTIVES

◆ Examine how the supply and demand for any currency can be viewed as an asset choice issue within the portfolio of investors.

◆ Explore how the three major approaches to exchange rate determination—parity conditions, the balance of payments, and the asset approach—combine to explain the numerous emerging market currency crises experienced in recent years.

◆ Observe how forecasters combine technical analysis with the three major theoretical approaches to forecasting exchange rates.

What determines the exchange rate between currencies? This has proven to be a very difficult question to answer. Companies and agents need foreign currency for buying imports, or may earn foreign currency by exporting. Investors, investing in interest-bearing instruments in foreign countries and currencies, fixed-income securities like bonds, shares in publicly traded companies, or other new types of hybrid instruments in foreign markets, all need foreign currency. Tourists, migrant workers, speculators on currency movements—all of these economic agents buy and sell and supply and demand currencies every day. This chapter offers some basic theoretical frameworks to try to organize these elements, forces, and principles.

Chapter 7 described the international parity conditions that integrate exchange rates with inflation and interest rates and provided a theoretical framework for both the global financial markets and the management of international financial business. Chapter 4 provided a detailed analysis of how an individual country's international economic activity, its balance of payments, can impact exchange rates. This chapter extends those discussions of exchange rate determination to the third school, the asset market approach.

Exhibit 9.1 provides an overview of the many determinants of exchange rates. This road map is first organized by the three major schools of thought (parity conditions, balance of payments approach, asset market approach), and second by the individual drivers within those approaches. At first glance the idea that there are three sets of theories may appear daunting, but it is important to remember that these are not *competing theories*, but rather *complementary theories*. Without the depth and breadth of the various approaches combined, our ability to capture the complexity of the global market for currencies is lost. The chapter concludes with the Mini-Case, ***The Japanese Yen Intervention of 2010***, detailing Japan's return to its guidance of market value.

EXHIBIT 9.1   The Determinants of Foreign Exchange Rates

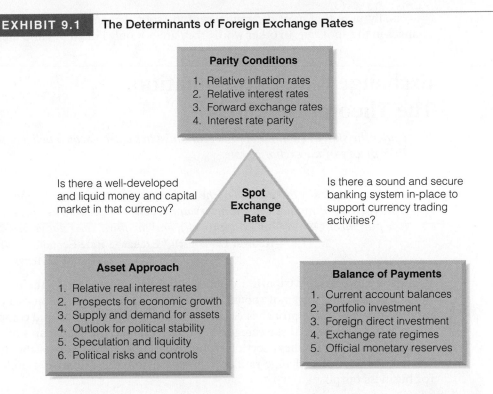

Parity Conditions

1. Relative inflation rates
2. Relative interest rates
3. Forward exchange rates
4. Interest rate parity

Is there a well-developed and liquid money and capital market in that currency?

Spot Exchange Rate

Is there a sound and secure banking system in-place to support currency trading activities?

Asset Approach

1. Relative real interest rates
2. Prospects for economic growth
3. Supply and demand for assets
4. Outlook for political stability
5. Speculation and liquidity
6. Political risks and controls

Balance of Payments

1. Current account balances
2. Portfolio investment
3. Foreign direct investment
4. Exchange rate regimes
5. Official monetary reserves

In addition to gaining an understanding of the basic theories, it is equally important to gain a working knowledge of how the complexities of international political economy, societal and economic infrastructures, and random political, economic, or social events affect the exchange rate markets. Here are a few examples:

◆ *Infrastructure weaknesses* were among the major causes of the exchange rate collapses in emerging markets in the late 1990s. On the other hand, infrastructure strengths help explain why the U.S. dollar continued to be strong, at least until the September 11, 2001 terrorist attack on the United States, despite record balance of payments deficits on current account.

◆ *Speculation* contributed greatly to the emerging market crises. Some characteristics of speculation are hot money flowing into and out of currencies, securities, real estate, and commodities. Uncovered interest arbitrage caused by exceptionally low borrowing interest rates in Japan coupled with high real interest rates in the United States was a problem in much of the 1990s. Borrowing yen to invest in safe U.S. government securities, hoping that the exchange rate did not change, was popular.

◆ *Cross-border foreign direct investment and international portfolio investment* into the emerging markets dried up during the recent crises. This has proven to be a very serious issue both for MNEs from the industrialized countries operating in emerging markets, and even more serious for the multinationals that call these emerging market countries home.

◆ *Foreign political risks* were much reduced in recent years as capital markets became less segmented from each other and more liquid. More countries adopted democratic forms of government. However, recent occurrences of terrorism within the U.S. may be changing perceptions of political risk.

Finally, note that most *determinants* of the spot exchange rate are also in turn *affected by* changes in the spot rate. In other words, they are not only linked but also mutually determined.

Exchange Rate Determination: The Theoretical Thread

Under the skin of an international economist lies a deep-seated belief in some variant of the PPP theory of the exchange rate.

—Paul Krugman, 1976.

There are basically three views of the exchange rate. The first takes the exchange rate as the relative price of monies (the monetary approach); the second, as the relative price of goods (the purchasing-power-parity approach); and the third, the relative price of bonds.

—Rudiger Dornbusch, "Exchange Rate Economics: Where Do We Stand?,
Brookings Papers on Economic Activity 1, 1980, pp. 143–194.

Professor Dornbusch's tripartite categorization of exchange rate theory is a good starting point, but in some ways not robust enough—in our humble opinion—to capture the multitude of theories and approaches. So, in the spirit of both tradition and completeness, we have amended Dornbusch's three categories with several additional streams of thought in the following discussion. The next section will provide a brief overview of the many different, but related, theories of exchange rate determination, and their relative usefulness in forecasting for business purposes.

Purchasing Power Parity Approaches

The most widely accepted for all exchange rate determination theories, the theory of *purchasing power parity* (PPP) states that the long-run equilibrium exchange rate is determined by the ratio of domestic prices relative to foreign prices, as explained in Chapter 7. PPP is both the oldest and most widely followed of the exchange rate theories, as most theories of exchange rate determination have PPP elements embedded within their frameworks.

There are a number of different versions of PPP, the *Law of One Price, Absolute Purchasing Power Parity*, and *Relative Purchasing Power Parity* (discussed in detail in Chapter 7). The latter of the three theories, *Relative Purchasing Power Parity*, is thought to be the most relevant to possibly explaining what drives exchange rate values. In essence, it states that changes in relative prices between countries drive the change in exchange rates over time.

If, for example, the current spot exchange rate between the Japanese yen and U.S. dollar was ¥90.00 = $1.00, and Japanese and U.S. prices were to change at 2% and 1% over the coming period, respectively, the spot exchange rate next period would be ¥90.89/$.

$$S_{t+1} = S_t \times \frac{1 + \Delta \text{ in Japanese prices}}{1 + \Delta \text{ in U.S. prices}} = ¥90.00/\$ \times \frac{1.02}{1.01} = ¥90.89/\$.$$

Although PPP seems to possess a core element of common sense, it has proven to be quite poor at forecasting exchange rates. The problems are both theoretical and empirical. The theoretical problems lie primarily with its basic assumption that the *only thing* that matters is relative price changes. Yet many currency supply and demand forces are driven by other forces including investment incentives and economic growth. The empirical issues are primarily in deciding which measures or indexes of prices to use across countries, in addition to the ability to provide a "predicted change in prices" with the chosen indexes.

Balance of Payments (Flows) Approaches

After purchasing power parity, the most frequently used theoretical approach to exchange rate determination is probably that involving the supply and demand for currencies in the foreign exchange market. These exchange rate *flows* reflect current account and financial account transactions recorded in a nation's balance of payments, as described in Chapter 4. The basic *balance of payments approach* argues that the equilibrium exchange rate is found when the net inflow (outflow) of foreign exchange arising from current account activities matches the net outflow (inflow) of foreign exchange arising from financial account activities.

The balance of payments approach continues to enjoy a wide degree of appeal as the balance of payments transactions are one of the most frequently captured and reported of international economic activity. Trade surpluses and deficits, current account growth in service activity, and recently the growth and significance of international capital flows continue to fuel this theoretical fire.

Criticisms of the balance of payments approach arise from the theory's emphasis on *flows* of currency and capital rather than *stocks* of money or financial assets. Relative stocks of money or financial assets play no role in exchange rate determination in this theory, a weakness explored in the following monetary and asset market approaches.

Curiously, the balance of payments approach is largely dismissed by the academic community today, while the practitioner public—market participants including currency traders themselves—still rely on different variations of the theory for much of their decision making.

Monetary Approaches

The *monetary approach* in its simplest form states that the exchange rate is determined by the supply and demand for national monetary stocks, as well as the expected future levels and rates of growth of monetary stocks. Other financial assets, such as bonds, are not considered relevant for exchange rate determination as both domestic and foreign bonds are viewed as perfect substitutes. It is all about money stocks.

The monetary approach focuses on changes in the supply and demand for money as the primary determinant of inflation. Changes in relative inflation rates in turn are expected to alter exchange rates through a purchasing power parity affect. The monetary approach then assumes that prices are flexible in the short run as well as the long run, so that the transmission mechanism of inflationary pressure is immediate in impact.

In monetary models of exchange rate determination, real economic activity is relegated to a role in which it only influences exchange rates through any alterations to the demand for money. The theory is also criticized on its omission of a number of factors which generally are agreed by area experts as important to exchange rate determination, including 1) the failure of PPP to hold in the short to medium term; 2) money demand appears to be relatively unstable over time; and 3) the level of economic activity and the money supply appear to be interdependent, not independent. Therefore, we will not pursue the monetary approach further.

Asset Market Approach (Relative Price of Bonds)

The *asset market approach*, sometimes called the *relative price of bonds* or *portfolio balance approach*, argues that exchange rates are determined by the supply and demand for financial assets of a wide variety. Shifts in the supply and demand for financial assets alter exchange rates. Changes in monetary and fiscal policy alter expected returns and perceived relative risks of financial assets, which in turn alter rates.

Many of the macroeconomic theoretical developments in the 1980s and 1990s focused on how monetary and fiscal policy changes altered the relative perceptions of return and risk to the stocks of financial assets driving exchange rate changes. The frequently cited works of Mundell-Fleming are in this genre. Theories of *currency substitution*, the ability of individual and commercial investors to alter the composition of their monetary holdings in their portfolios, follow the same basic premises of the portfolio balance and re-balance framework.

Unfortunately, for all of the good work and research over the past 50 years, the ability to forecast exchange rate values in the short term to long term is—in the words of the authors below—*sorry*. Although academics and practitioners alike agree that in the long-run fundamental principles such as purchasing power and external balances drive currency values, none of the fundamental theories has proven that useful in the short to medium term.

> *. . . the case for macroeconomic determinants of exchange rates is in a sorry state . . . [The] results indicate that no model based on such standard fundamentals like money supplies, real income, interest rates, inflation rates and current account balances will ever succeed in explaining or predicting a high percentage of the variation in the exchange rate, at least at short- or medium-term frequencies.*
>
> —Jeffrey A. Frankel and Andrew K. Rose, "A Survey of Empirical Research on Nominal Exchange Rates," *NBER Working Paper* no. 4865, 1994.

Technical Analysis

The forecasting inadequacies of fundamental theories has led to the growth and popularity of *technical analysis*, the belief that the study of past price behavior provides insights into future price movements. The primary feature of technical analysis is the assumption that exchange rates, or for that matter any market-driven price, follows trends. And those trends may be analyzed and projected to provide insights into short-term and medium-term price movements in the future.

Most theories of technical analysis differentiate fair value from market value. Fair value is the true long-term value which the price will eventually retain. The market value is subject to a multitude of changes and behaviors arising from widespread market participant perceptions and beliefs.

The Asset Market Approach to Forecasting

The *asset market approach* assumes that whether foreigners are willing to hold claims in monetary form depends on an extensive set of investment considerations or drivers. These drivers, as previously depicted in Exhibit 9.1, include the following elements:

◆ Relative real interest rates are a major consideration for investors in foreign bonds and short-term money market instruments.

◆ Prospects for economic growth and profitability are an important determinant of cross-border equity investment in both securities and foreign direct investment.

◆ Capital market liquidity is particularly important to foreign institutional investors. Cross-border investors are not only interested in the ease of buying assets, but also in the ease of selling those assets quickly for fair market value if desired.

◆ A country's economic and social infrastructure is an important indicator of its ability to survive unexpected external shocks and to prosper in a rapidly changing world economic environment.

◆ Political safety is exceptionally important to both foreign portfolio and direct investors. The outlook for political safety is usually reflected in political risk premiums for a country's securities and for purposes of evaluating foreign direct investment in that country.

◆ The credibility of corporate governance practices is important to cross-border portfolio investors. A firm's poor corporate governance practices can reduce foreign investors' influence and cause subsequent loss of the firm's focus on shareholder wealth objectives.

◆ *Contagion* is defined as the spread of a crisis in one country to its neighboring countries and other countries with similar characteristics—at least in the eyes of cross-border investors. Contagion can cause an "innocent" country to experience capital flight with a resulting depreciation of its currency.

◆ Speculation can both cause a foreign exchange crisis or make an existing crisis worse. We will observe this effect through the three illustrative cases that follow shortly.

Foreign investors are willing to hold securities and undertake foreign direct investment in highly developed countries based primarily on relative real interest rates and the outlook for economic growth and profitability. All the other drivers described in Exhibit 9.1 are assumed to be satisfied.

For example, during the 1981–1985 period, the U.S. dollar strengthened despite growing current account deficits. This strength was due partly to relatively high real interest rates in the United States. Another factor, however, was the heavy inflow of foreign capital into the U.S. stock market and real estate, motivated by good long-run prospects for growth and profitability in the United States.

The same cycle was repeated in the United States in the period between 1990 and 2000. Despite continued worsening balances on current account, the U.S. dollar strengthened in both nominal and real terms due to foreign capital inflow motivated by rising stock and real estate prices, a low rate of inflation, high real interest returns, and a seemingly endless "irrational exuberance" about future economic prospects. This time the "bubble" burst following the September 11, 2001 terrorist attacks on the United States. The attack and its aftermath caused a negative reassessment of long-term growth and profitability prospects in the United States (as well as a newly formed level of political risk for the United States itself). This negative outlook was reinforced by a very sharp drop in the U.S. stock markets based on lower expected earnings. Further damage to the economy was caused by a series of revelations about failures in corporate governance of several large corporations (including overstatement of earnings, insider trading, and self-serving executives).

Loss of confidence in the U.S. economy led to a large withdrawal of foreign capital from U.S. security markets. As would be predicted by both the balance of payments and asset market approaches, the U.S. dollar depreciated. Indeed, its nominal rate depreciated by 18% between mid-January and mid-July 2002 relative to the euro alone.

The experience of the United States, as well as other highly developed countries, illustrates why some forecasters believe that exchange rates are more heavily influenced by economic prospects than by the current account. One scholar summarizes this belief using an interesting anecdote.

> *Many economists reject the view that the short-term behavior of exchange rates is determined in flow markets. Exchange rates are asset prices traded in an efficient financial market. Indeed, an exchange rate is the relative price of two currencies and therefore is determined by the willingness to hold each currency. Like other asset prices, the exchange rate is determined by expectations about the future, not current trade flows.*
>
> *A parallel with other asset prices may illustrate the approach. Let's consider the stock price of a winery traded on the Bordeaux stock exchange. A frost in late spring results in a poor harvest, in terms of both quantity and quality. After the harvest the wine is finally sold, and the income is much less than the previous year. On the day of the final sale there is no reason for the stock price to be influenced by this flow. First, the poor income has already been discounted for several months in the winery stock price. Second, the stock price is affected by future, in addition to current, prospects. The stock price is based on expectations of future earnings, and the major cause for a change in stock price is a revision of these expectations.*
>
> *A similar reasoning applies to exchange rates: Contemporaneous international flows should have little effect on exchange rates to the extent they have already been expected.*

Only news about future economic prospects will affect exchange rates. Since economic expectations are potentially volatile and influenced by many variables, especially variables of a political nature, the short-run behavior of exchange rates is volatile.
— Bruno Solnik, *International Investments*, 3rd Edition, Reading,
MA: Addison Wesley, 1996, p. 58. Reprinted with permission of Pearson Education, Inc.

The asset market approach to forecasting is also applicable to emerging markets. In this case, however, a number of additional variables contribute to exchange rate determination. These variables, as described previously, are illiquid capital markets, weak economic and social infrastructure, political instability, corporate governance, contagion effects, and speculation. These variables will be illustrated in the sections on crises that follow.

Currency Market Intervention

A fundamental problem with exchange rates is that no commonly accepted method exists to estimate the effectiveness of official intervention into foreign exchange markets. Many interrelated factors affect the exchange rate at any given time, and no quantitative model exists that is able to provide the magnitude of any causal relationship between intervention and an exchange rate when so many interdependent variables are acting simultaneously.
— "Japan's Currency Intervention: Policy Issues," Dick K. Nanto,
CRS Report to Congress, July 13, 2007, CRS-7.

The value of a country's currency is of significant interest to an individual government's economic and political policies and objectives. Those interests sometimes extend beyond the individual country, but may actually reflect some form of collective country interest. Although many countries have moved from fixed exchange rate values long ago, the governments and central bank authorities of the multitude of floating rate currencies still privately and publicly profess what value their currency "should hold" in their eyes, regardless of whether the market for that currency agrees at that time. *Foreign currency intervention*, the active management, manipulation, or intervention in the market's valuation of a country's currency, is a component of currency valuation and forecast that cannot be overlooked.

Motivations for Intervention

There is a long-standing saying that "what worries bankers is inflation, but what worries elected officials is unemployment." The principle is actually quite useful in understanding the various motives for currency market intervention. Depending upon whether a country's central bank is an independent institution (e.g., the U.S. Federal Reserve), or a subsidiary of its elected government (as the Bank of England was for many years), the bank's policies may either fight inflation or fight slow economic growth.

Historically, a primary motive for a government to pursue currency value change was to keep the country's currency cheap so that foreign buyers would find its exports cheap. This policy, long referred to as "beggar-thy-neighbor," gave rise to several competitive devaluations over the years. It has not, however, fallen out of fashion. The Asian financial crisis of 1997 (discussed in detail in the following section), resulted in a number of countries devaluing their currency when they did not have to; they devalued their currencies intentionally to remain competitive with neighboring countries with competing export products. The slow economic growth and continuing employment problems in many countries in 2010 and 2011 led to some countries, the United States and the European Union being prime examples, working to hold their currency values down.

Alternatively, the fall in the value of the domestic currency will sharply reduce the purchasing power of its people. If the economy is forced, for a variety of reasons, to continue to purchase imported products (e.g., petroleum imports because of no domestic substitute), a currency devaluation or depreciation may prove highly inflationary—and in the extreme, impoverish the country's people. This was a partial outcome of the Argentine crisis of 1999 discussed in the following section, and a result of the multitude of devaluations which President Hugo Chavez of Venezuela has directed over the past decade.

It is frequently noted that most countries would like to see stable exchange rates, to not get into the entanglements associated with manipulating currency values. Unfortunately, that would also imply that not only are they happy with the current level, but also that the level or rate of exchange is existing within a global economy which itself is not changing. One must look no further than the continuing highly public debate between the United States and China over the value of the yuan. The U.S. believes it is undervalued, making Chinese exports to the United States overly cheap, which in turn, results in a growing current account deficit of the United States and current account surplus of China.

The International Monetary Fund, as one of its basic principles (Article IV), encourages members to avoid pursuing "currency manipulation" to gain competitive advantages over other members. The IMF defines manipulation as "protracted large-scale intervention in one direction in the exchange market."

Intervention Methods

There are a multitude of ways in which an individual or collective set of governments and central banks can alter the value of their currencies. It should be noted, however, that the methods of market intervention used are very much determined by the size of the country's economy, the magnitude of global trading in its currency, and the depth and breadth of development in its domestic financial markets. A short list of the intervention methods would include the following:

Direct Intervention. This is the active buying and selling of the domestic currency against foreign currencies. This traditionally required a central bank to act like any other trader in the currency market—albeit a big one. If the goal was to increase the value of the domestic currency, the central bank would purchase its own currency using its foreign exchange reserves, at least to the acceptable limits of depleting its reserves that it could endure.

If the goal was to decrease the value of its currency—to fight an appreciation of its currency's value on the foreign exchange market—it would sell its own currency in exchange for foreign currency, typically major hard currencies like the dollar and euro. Although there are no physical limits to its ability to sell its own currency (it could theoretically continue to "print money" endlessly), central banks are cautious to the degree to which they may potentially change their monetary supplies through intervention.

Direct intervention was the primary method used for many years, but beginning in the 1970s, the world's currency markets grew enough that any individual player, even a central bank, may find itself insufficient in resources to move the market. As one trader stated a number of years ago, "We at the bank found ourselves little more than a grain of sand on the beach of the market." *Global Finance in Practice 9.1* provides one suggested strategy for this lack of market-weight.

One solution to the market size challenge has been the occasional use of *coordinated intervention*, in which several major countries, or a collective such as the G8 of industrialized countries, agree that a specific currency's value is out of alignment with their collective interests. In that situation, they may work collectively, to intervene and push a currency's value in a desired direction. The September 1985 Plaza Agreement, an agreement signed at the Plaza Hotel in New York City by the members of the Group of Ten, was one such coordinated intervention agreement. The members, collectively, had concluded that currency values had

GLOBAL FINANCE IN PRACTICE   9.1

Rules of Thumb for Effective Intervention

There are a number of factors, features, and tactics, according to many currency traders that determine the effectiveness of an intervention effort.

◆ **Don't Lean Into the Wind.** Markets that are moving significantly in one direction, like the strengthening of the Japanese yen in the fall of 2010, are very tough to turn. Termed "leaning into the wind," intervention during a strong market movement will most likely result in a very expensive failure. Currency traders argue that central banks should time their intervention very carefully, choosing moments when trading volumes are light and direction nearly flat. Don't lean into the wind, read it.

◆ **Coordinate Timing and Activity.** Use traders or associates in a variety of geographic markets and trading centers, possibly other central banks, if at all possible. The markets are much more likely to be influenced if they believe the intervention activity is reflecting a grass-roots movement, and not the singular activity of a single trading entity or bank.

◆ **Use Good News.** Particularly when trying to quell a currency fall, time the intervention to coincide with positive economic, financial, or business news closely associated with a country's currency market. Traders often argue that 'markets wish to celebrate good news,' and currencies may be no different.

◆ **Don't Be Cheap.** Overwhelm them. Traders fear missing the moment, and a large, coordinated, well-timed intervention can make them fear they are leaning in the wrong direction. A successful intervention is in many ways a battle of psychology; play on their insecurities. If it appears the intervention is gradually having the desired impact, throw ever-increasing assets into the battle. Don't get cheap.

become too volatile or too extreme in movement for sound economic policy management. The problem with coordinated intervention is, of course, reaching agreement between nations. This has proven to be a major sticking point in the principle's use.

Indirect Intervention. This is the alteration of economic or financial fundamentals which are thought to be drivers of capital to flow in and out of specific currencies. This was a logical development for market manipulation given the growth in size of the global currency markets relative to the financial resources of central banks.

The most obvious and widely used factor here is interest rates. Following the financial principles outlined previously in parity conditions, higher real rates of interest attract capital. If a central bank wishes to "defend its currency" for example, it might follow a restrictive monetary policy which would drive real rates of interest up. The method is therefore no longer limited to the quantity of foreign exchange reserves held by the country, but only by its willingness to suffer the domestic impacts of higher real interest rates in order to attract capital inflows and therefore drive up the demand for its currency.

Alternatively, a country wishing for its currency to fall in value, particularly when confronted with a continual appreciation of its value against major trading partner currencies, the central bank may work to lower real interest rates, reducing the returns to capital.

Because indirect intervention uses tools of monetary policy, a fundamental dimension of economic policy, the magnitude and extent of impacts may reach far beyond currency value. Overly stimulating economic activity, or increasing money supply growth beyond real economic activity, may prove inflationary. The use of such broad-based tools like interest rates to manipulate currency values requires a determination of importance, in many cases the choice to pursue international economic goals at the expense of domestic economic policy goals.

It is also important to remember that intervention may fail. One very real example of intervention failure occurred in 1992 when the United Kingdom attempted to defend the value of the British pound against a rapidly rising Deutsche Mark. As a member of the European Exchange Rate Mechanism (ERM) of the EMS of the time, the pound's value against the Deutsche Mark had to be maintained within a narrow band. The Bank of England, after increasing key interest rates three times in six hours on one day, pulled the currency from the ERM. (A global currency speculator of significance at the time, George Soros, is reported to have made millions of dollars betting against the pound.) The United Kingdom was said to have suffered a "humiliating defeat," although it was a currency war, not a military one.

Capital Controls. This is the restriction of access to foreign currency by government. This involves limiting the ability to exchange domestic currency for foreign currency. When access and exchange is permitted, trading often takes place only with official designees of the government or central bank, and only at dictated exchange rates.

Often, governments will limit access to foreign currencies to commercial trade: for example, allowing access to hard currency for the purchase of imports "of import" only. Access for investment purposes, particularly short-term portfolio purposes in which investors are investing in and out of interest-bearing accounts, purchasing or selling fixed income or equity securities or other funds, is often prohibited or limited.

The Chinese regulation of access and trading of the Chinese yuan is a prime example over the use of capital controls over currency value. In addition to the government's setting of the daily rate of exchange, access to the exchange is limited by a difficult and timely bureaucratic process for approval, and is limited to commercial trade transactions alone.

Understanding the motivations and methods for currency market intervention are critical to any analysis of the determination of future exchange rates. And although it is often impossible to determine, in the end, whether subtle intervention was successful, it appears to be an area of growing market activity, particularly for countries trying to "emerge" to higher levels of economic income and wealth.

Disequilibrium: Exchange Rates in Emerging Markets

Although the three different schools of thought on exchange rate determination (*parity conditions*, *balance of payments approach*, and *asset approach*) described earlier make understanding exchange rates appear to be straightforward, that is rarely the case. The large and liquid capital and currency markets follow many of the principles outlined so far relatively well in the medium to long term. The smaller and less liquid markets, however, frequently demonstrate behaviors that seemingly contradict theory. The problem lies not in the theory, but in the relevance of the assumptions underlying the theory. An analysis of the emerging market crises illustrates a number of these seeming contradictions.

After a number of years of relative global economic tranquility, the second half of the 1990s was racked by a series of currency crises that shook all emerging markets. The devaluation of the Mexican peso in December 1994 was a harbinger. The Asian crisis of July 1997, the Russian ruble's collapse in August 1998, and the fall of the Argentine peso in 2002 provide a spectrum of emerging market economic failures, each with its own complex causes and unknown outlooks. These crises also illustrated the growing problem of capital flight and short-run international speculation in currency and securities markets. We will use each of the individual crises to focus on a specific dimension of the causes and consequences.

The Asian Crisis of 1997

The roots of the Asian currency crisis extended from a fundamental change in the economics of the region, the transition of many Asian nations from being net exporters to net importers. Starting as early as 1990 in Thailand, the rapidly expanding economies of the Far East began importing more than they exported, requiring major net capital inflows to support their currencies. As long as the capital continued to flow in—capital for manufacturing plants, dam projects, infrastructure development, and even real estate speculation—the pegged exchange rates of the region could be maintained. When the investment capital inflows stopped, however, crisis was inevitable.

The most visible roots of the crisis were in the excesses of capital inflows into Thailand in 1996 and early 1997. With rapid economic growth and rising profits forming the backdrop,

Thai firms, banks, and finance companies had ready access to capital on the international markets, finding U.S. dollar debt cheap offshore. Thai banks continued to raise capital internationally, extending credit to a variety of domestic investments and enterprises beyond what the Thai economy could support. As capital flows into the Thai market hit record rates, financial flows poured into investments of all kinds, including manufacturing, real estate, and even equity market margin-lending. As the investment "bubble" expanded, some participants raised questions about the economy's ability to repay the rising debt. The baht came under attack.

Currency Collapse. In May and June 1997, more and more rumors circulated throughout the globe's currency traders that the Thai baht was weak, and that a number of major investors were now speculating on its fall. The Thai government and central bank quickly intervened in the foreign exchange markets directly (using up precious hard currency reserves) and indirectly (by raising interest rates to attempt to stop the continual outflow). Thai investment ground quickly to a halt. Foreign capital, which had flowed into Thailand freely in the months and years previous, stopped.

A second round of speculative attacks in late June and early July proved too much for the Thai authorities. On July 2, 1997, the Thai central bank finally allowed the baht to float (or sink in this case). The baht fell 17% against the U.S. dollar and more than 12% against the Japanese yen in a matter of hours. By November, the baht had fallen from THB25/USD to nearly THB40/USD, a fall of about 38%, as illustrated in Exhibit 9.2.

Within days, in Asia's own version of what is called the *tequila effect*, a number of neighboring Asian nations, some with and some without similar characteristics to Thailand, came under speculative attack by currency traders and capital markets. ("Tequila effect" is the term used to describe how the Mexican peso crisis of December 1994 quickly spread to other Latin American currency and equity markets, a form of financial panic termed *contagion*.)

EXHIBIT 9.2   The Thai Baht and the Asian Crisis

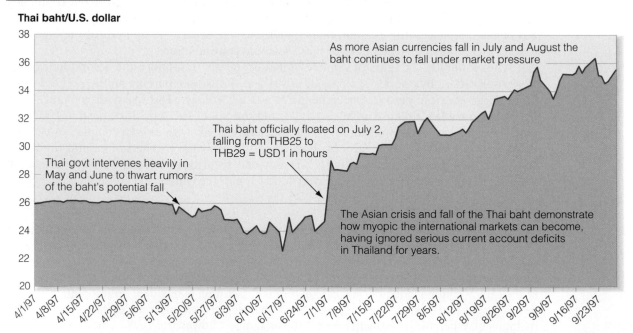

Thai baht/U.S. dollar

Thai govt intervenes heavily in May and June to thwart rumors of the baht's potential fall

Thai baht officially floated on July 2, falling from THB25 to THB29 = USD1 in hours

As more Asian currencies fall in July and August the baht continues to fall under market pressure

The Asian crisis and fall of the Thai baht demonstrate how myopic the international markets can become, having ignored serious current account deficits in Thailand for years.

The Philippine peso, the Malaysian ringgit, and the Indonesian rupiah all fell in the months following the July baht devaluation.

In late October 1997, Taiwan caught the markets off balance with a surprise competitive devaluation of 15%. The Taiwanese devaluation seemed only to renew the momentum of the crisis. Although the Hong Kong dollar survived (at great expense to the central bank's foreign exchange reserves), the Korean won (KRW) was not so lucky. In November 1997, the historically stable won also fell victim, falling from KRW900/USD to more than KRW1100. The only currency that had not fallen besides the Hong Kong dollar was the Chinese renminbi, which was not freely convertible. Although the renminbi was not devalued, there was rising speculation that the Chinese government would soon devalue it for competitive reasons. It did not.

Causal Complexities. The Asian economic crisis—for it was more than just a currency collapse—had many roots besides traditional balance of payments difficulties. The causes were different in each country, yet, there are specific underlying similarities which allow comparison: corporate socialism, corporate governance, banking stability, and management.

Although Western markets have long known the volatility of the free market, the countries of the post-World War II Asia have largely known only stability. Because of the influence of government and politics in the business arena, even in the event of failure, it was believed that government would not allow firms to fail, workers to lose their jobs, or banks to close. Practices that had persisted for decades without challenge, such as lifetime employment, were now no longer sustainable.

Little doubt exists that many local firms operating within the Far Eastern business environments were often largely controlled either by families or by groups related to the governing party or body of the country. This tendency has been labeled *cronyism*. Cronyism means that the interests of minority stockholders and creditors are often secondary at best to the primary motivations of corporate management. When management did not focus on "the bottom line," the bottom line deteriorated.

The banking sector has fallen behind. Bank regulatory structures and markets have been deregulated nearly without exception across the globe. The central role played by banks in the conduct of business, however, had largely been ignored and underestimated. As firms across Asia collapsed, government coffers were emptied and speculative investments made by the banks themselves failed. Without banks, the "plumbing" of business conduct was shut down.

The Asian economic crisis had global impacts. What started as a currency crisis quickly became a regionwide recession. (The magnitude of economic devastation in Asia is still largely unappreciated by Westerners. At a 1998 conference sponsored by the Milken Institute, a speaker noted that the world's preoccupation with the economic problems of Indonesia was incomprehensible because "the total gross domestic product of Indonesia is roughly the size of North Carolina." The following speaker observed, however, that the last time he had checked, "North Carolina did not have a population of 220 million people.") The slowed economies of the region quickly caused major reductions in world demands for many products, especially commodities. World oil, metal, and agricultural products markets all saw severe price falls as demand fell. These price drops were immediately noticeable in declining earnings and growth prospects for other emerging economies. The problems of Russia in 1998 were reflections of those declines.

In the aftermath, the international speculator and philanthropist George Soros was the object of much criticism, primarily by the Prime Minister of Malaysia, Dr. Mahathir Mohamad, for being the cause of the crisis because of massive speculation by his and other hedge funds. Soros, however, was likely only the messenger. *Global Finance in Practice 9.2* details the Soros debate.

GLOBAL FINANCE IN PRACTICE   9.2

Was George Soros to Blame for the Asian Crisis?

We have worked 30 to 40 years to develop our countries to this level, but along comes a man with a few billion dollars, and who in a period of just two weeks, has undone most of the work we have done. As a result, the people of our countries suffer. You talk about human rights and protecting people. But they must be protected from people like Soros who has so much money and so much power and totally thoughtless because he is not only hurting the people of Myanmar, but the poor people in Indonesia, Malaysia, the Philippines and Thailand.

—Prime Minister Datuk Seri Dr. Mahathir Mohamad of Malaysia *New Straits Times*, Kuala Lumpur, July 27, 1997.

For Thailand to blame Mr Soros for its plight is rather like condemning an undertaker for burying a suicide.

—*The Economist*, August 2, 1997, p. 57.

George Soros is probably the most famous currency speculator—and possibly the most successful—in global history. Admittedly responsible for much of the European financial crisis of 1992 and the fall of the French franc in 1993, he once again was the recipient of critical attention in 1997 following the fall of the Thai baht and Malaysian ringgit. Prime

Minister Mahathir of Malaysia blamed Soros for the collapse of the ringgit, as the quote indicates.

Nine years later, in 2006, Mahathir and Soros met for the first time. Mahathir apologized and withdrew his previous accusations. In Soros's book published in 1998, *The Crisis of Global Capitalism: Open Society Endangered*, Soros explained his role in the crisis as follows:

The financial crisis that originated in Thailand in 1997 was particularly unnerving because of its scope and severity. . . . By the beginning of 1997, it was clear to Soros Fund Management that the discrepancy between the trade account and the capital account was becoming untenable. We sold short the Thai baht and the Malaysian ringgit early in 1997 with maturities ranging from six months to a year. (That is, we entered into contracts to deliver at future dates Thai Baht and Malaysian ringgit that we did not currently hold.) Subsequently Prime Minister Mahathir of Malaysia accused me of causing the crisis, a wholly unfounded accusation. We were not sellers of the currency during or several months before the crisis; on the contrary, we were buyers when the currencies began to decline—we were purchasing ringgit to realize the profits on our earlier speculation. (Much too soon, as it turned out. We left most of the potential gain on the table because we were afraid that Mahathir would impose capital controls. He did so, but much later.)

The Russian Crisis of 1998

"A stable ruble is the anchor of an inflation-free economy," according to Alexander Livshits, deputy head of President Boris Yeltsin's administration. He added that the loss of a stable ruble "will start rocking our ship again. The result is well known—nausea."

The crisis of August 1998 was the culmination of a continuing deterioration in general economic conditions in Russia. During the period from 1995 to 1998, Russian borrowers—both governmental and nongovernmental—had borrowed heavily on the international capital markets. Servicing this debt soon became a growing problem, as servicing dollar debt requires earning dollars. The Russian current account, a surprisingly healthy surplus, was not finding its way into internal investment and external debt service. Capital flight accelerated, as hard-currency earnings flowed out as fast as they found their way in. Finally, in the spring of 1998, even Russian export earnings began to decline. Russian exports were predominantly commodity-based, and global commodity prices had been falling since the start of the Asian crisis in 1997.

The Russian currency, the ruble (RUB), operated under a managed float. This meant that the Central Bank of Russia allowed the ruble to trade within a band. The exchange rate band had been adjusted continually throughout 1996, 1997, and the first half of 1998. Theoretically, the Central Bank allowed the exchange rate and associated band to slide daily at a 1.5% per month rate. Automatically, the Central Bank announced an official exchange rate each day at which it was willing to buy and sell rubles, always within the official band. In the event that the ruble's rate came under pressure at the limits of the band, the Central Bank intervened in the market by buying and selling rubles, usually buying, using the country's foreign exchange reserves.

The August Collapse. On August 7, 1998, the Russian Central Bank announced that its currency reserves had fallen by $800 million in the last week of July. Prime Minister Kiriyenko said that Russia would issue an additional $3 billion in foreign bonds to help pay its rising debt, a full $1 billion more than had been previously scheduled. The ruble, however, continued to trade within a very narrow range.

On August 10, Russian stocks fell more than 5% as investors feared a Chinese currency (renminbi) devaluation. The Chinese currency was the only Asian currency of size not devalued in 1997 and 1998. Devaluation would aid Chinese exports in cutting into Russian export sales. Analysts worldwide speculated that international markets were waiting to see if the Russian government would increase its tax revenues as it had promised the IMF throughout the year. Russian oil companies were publicly warned by the Russian government to pay past due taxes. (Russian tax collections averaged $1 billion per month in 1998, less than those of New York City.) By Wednesday of that week, Russian financing choices narrowed further as the government canceled the government debt auction for the third week in a row.

The following days saw a continuing series of press releases assuring the markets and general population that the government had everything under control. The government stated that the "panic" was psychological, not fiscal, and repeated, as it had in recent days, that it had money to meet its obligations through the fall of the year. The Russian Central Bank continued to trade rubles throughout Friday at RUB6.30/USD, but at many unofficial exchanges throughout Moscow the rate was RUB7.00/USD or more. President Boris Yeltsin, in a speech in the ancient city of Novgorode, stated

"There will be no devaluation—that's firm and definite."

He went on to add,

"That would signify that there was a disaster and that everything was collapsing. On the contrary, everything is going as it should."

"As it should" turned out to mean devaluation. On Monday, August 17, the floodgates were released. The Russian Central Bank announced that the ruble would be allowed to fall by 34% this year, from RUB6.30/USD to about RUB9.50. The government then announced a 90-day moratorium on all repayment of foreign debt, debt owed by Russian banks and all private borrowers, in order to avert a banking collapse.

The currency's fall continued into the following week, as illustrated in Exhibit 9.3. On Thursday, August 27, Acting Prime Minister Viktor Chernomyrdin traveled to the Ukraine to meet with the visiting head of the IMF, Michael Camdessus. A sense of urgency was felt after the ruble fell from RUB10.0/USD to RUB13.0 the previous day alone. In related matters, the Central Bank of Russia, in an attempt to defray criticism of its management of the ruble's devaluation, disclosed that it had expended $8.8 billion in the preceding eight weeks defending the ruble's value. On August 28, the Moscow currency exchange closed after 10 minutes of trading as the ruble continued to fall.

The Aftermath. It is hard to say when a crisis begins or ends, but for the Russian people and the Russian economy, the deterioration of the economic conditions continued. What is likely of more substantial concern is the toll the crisis has taken on Russian society. For many, the collapse of the ruble and the loss of Russia's access to the international capital markets brought into question the benefits of a free-market economy, long championed by the advocates of Western-style democracy.

EXHIBIT 9.3   The Fall of the Russian Ruble

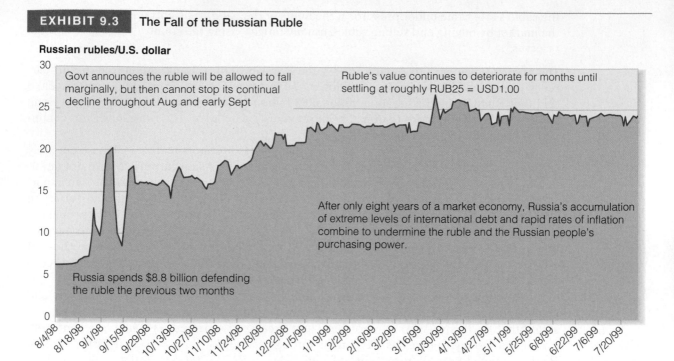

Russian rubles/U.S. dollar

Govt announces the ruble will be allowed to fall marginally, but then cannot stop its continual decline throughout Aug and early Sept

Ruble's value continues to deteriorate for months until settling at roughly RUB25 = USD1.00

After only eight years of a market economy, Russia's accumulation of extreme levels of international debt and rapid rates of inflation combine to undermine the ruble and the Russian people's purchasing power.

Russia spends $8.8 billion defending the ruble the previous two months

The Argentine Crisis of 2002

Now, most Argentines are blaming corrupt politicians and foreign devils for their ills. But few are looking inward, at mainstream societal concepts such as viveza criolla, an Argentine cultural quirk that applauds anyone sly enough to get away with a fast one. It is one reason behind massive tax evasion here: One of every three Argentines does so—and many like to brag about it.

—"Once-Haughty Nation's Swagger Loses Its Currency,"
Anthony Faiola, *The Washington Post*, March 13, 2002.

Argentina's economic ups and downs have historically been tied to the health of the Argentine peso. South America's southernmost resident—which oftentimes considered itself more European than Latin American—had been wracked by hyperinflation, international indebtedness, and economic collapse in the 1980s. By early 1991 the people of Argentina had had enough. Economic reform in the early 1990s was a common goal of the Argentine people. They were not interested in quick fixes, but lasting change and a stable future. They nearly got it.

The Currency Board. In 1991, the Argentine peso had been fixed to the U.S. dollar at a one-to-one rate of exchange. The policy was a radical departure from traditional methods of fixing the rate of a currency's value. Argentina adopted a *currency board*, a structure—rather than merely a commitment—to limiting the growth of money in the economy. Under a currency board, the central bank may increase the money supply in the banking system only with increases in its holdings of hard currency reserves. The reserves were in this case U.S. dollars. By removing the ability of government to expand the rate of growth of the money supply, Argentina believed it was eliminating the source of inflation which had devastated its standard of living.

The idea was simple: limit the rate of growth in the country's money supply to the rate at which the country receives net inflows of U.S. dollars as a result of trade growth and general surplus. It was both a recipe for conservative and prudent financial management, and a decision to eliminate the power of politicians, elected and unelected, to exercise judgment both good and bad. It was an automatic and unbendable rule. And from the beginning, it had shown the costs and benefits of its rigor.

Although hyperinflation had indeed been the problem, the "cure" was a restrictive monetary policy which slowed economic growth. The first and foremost cost of the slower economic growth had been in unemployment. Beginning with a decade low unemployment rate in 1991, unemployment rose to double-digit levels in 1994 and stayed there. The real GDP growth rate, which opened the decade with booming levels over 10%, settled into recession in late 1998. GDP growth "shrank" in 1999 (−3.5%) and 2000 (−0.4%).

As part of the continuing governmental commitment to the currency board's fixed exchange rate for the peso, Argentine banks allowed depositors to hold their money in either form—pesos or dollars. This was intended to provide a market-based discipline to the banking and political systems, and to demonstrate the government's unwavering commitment to maintaining the peso's value parity with the dollar. Although intended to build confidence in the system, in the end it proved disastrous to the Argentine banking system.

Economic Crisis of 2001. The 1998 recession proved to be unending. Three and a half years later, Argentina was still in recession. By 2001, crisis conditions had revealed three very important underlying problems with Argentina's economy: 1) the Argentine peso was overvalued; 2) the currency board regime had eliminated monetary policy alternatives for macroeconomic policy; and 3) the Argentine government budget deficit—and deficit spending—was out of control. The peso had indeed been stabilized. But inflation had not been eliminated, and the other factors which are important in the global market's evaluation of a currency's value— economic growth, corporate profitability, etc.—had not necessarily always been positive. The inability of the peso's value to change with market forces led many to believe increasingly that it was overvalued, and that the overvaluation gap was rising as time passed.

Argentina's large neighbor to the north, Brazil, had also suffered many of the economic ills of hyperinflation and international indebtedness. Brazil's response, the *Real Plan*, was introduced in July 1994. The real plan worked, for a while, but eventually collapsed in January 1999 as a result of the rising gap between the real's official value and the market's assessment of its true value. With the fall of the Brazilian real, however, Brazilian consumers could no longer afford Argentine exports. Argentine exports became some of the most expensive in all of South America as other countries saw their currencies slide marginally against the dollar over the decade. But not the Argentine peso.

The Currency Board and Monetary Policy. The increasingly sluggish economic growth in Argentina warranted expansionary economic policies argued many policymakers in and out of the country. But the currency board's basic premise was that the money supply to the financial system could not be expanded any further or faster than the ability of the economy to capture dollar reserves. This eliminated monetary policy as an avenue for macroeconomic policy formulation, leaving only fiscal policy for economic stimulation.

Government spending was not slowing, however. As the unemployment rate grew higher, as poverty and social unrest grew, government—both in the civil center of Argentina, Buenos Aires, and in the outer provinces—was faced with growing expansionary spending needs to close the economic and social gaps. Government spending continued to increase, but tax receipts did not. Lower income led to lower taxes on income. Argentina turned to the international markets to aid in the financing of its government's deficit spending. The total foreign debt of the country began rising dramatically. Only a number of IMF capital injections prevented the total foreign debt of the country from skyrocketing. When the decade was over, however, total foreign debt had effectively doubled, and the economy's earning power had not.

Social Repercussions. As economic conditions continued to deteriorate, banks suffered increasing runs. Depositors, fearing that the peso would be devalued, lined up to withdraw their money, both Argentine peso cash balances and U.S. dollar cash balances. Pesos were converted to dollars, once again adding fuel to the growing fire of currency collapse. The government, fearing that the increasing financial drain on banks would cause their collapse, closed the banks. Consumers, unable to withdrawal more than $250 per week, were instructed to use debit cards and credit cards to make purchases and conduct the everyday transactions required by society.

Riots in the streets of Buenos Aires in December 2001 intensified the need for rapid change. As the new year of 2002 arrived, the second president in two weeks, Fernando de la Rua, was driven from office. He was succeeded by a Peronist, President Adolfo Rodriguez Saa, who lasted all of one week as president before he too was driven from office. President Saa did, however, leave his legacy. In his one week as President of Argentina, President Adolfo Rodriguez Saa declared the largest sovereign debt default in history. Argentina announced it would not be able to make interest payments due on $155 billion in government debt.

Devaluation. On Sunday, January 6, 2002, in the first act of his presidency, President Eduardo Duhalde devalued the peso from ARS1.00/USD to ARS1.40. But the economic pain continued. Two weeks after the devaluation, the banks were still closed. Most of the state governments outside of Buenos Aires, basically broke and without access to financing resources, began printing their own money—*script*—promissary notes of the provincial governments. The provincial governments were left with little choice as the economy of Argentina was nearing complete collapse as people and businesses could not obtain money to conduct the day-to-day commercial transactions of life.

On February 3, 2002, the Argentine government announced that the peso would be floated, as seen in Exhibit 9.4. The government would no longer attempt to fix or manage its value to any specific level, allowing the market to find or set the exchange rate. The value of the peso now began a slow but gradual depreciation.[1] As the year wore on the country was confronted with issue after issue of social, political, and economic collapse.

A former Harvard professor and member of the U.S. President's Council of Economic Advisors summed up the hard lessons of the Argentine story.

> *In reality, the Argentines understood the risk that they were taking at least as well as the IMF staff did. Theirs was a calculated risk that might have produced good results. It is true, however, that the IMF staff did encourage Argentina to continue with the fixed exchange rate and currency board. Although the IMF and virtually all outside economists believe that a floating exchange rate is preferable to a "fixed but adjustable" system, in which the government recognizes that it will have to devalue occasionally, the IMF (as well as some outside economists) came to believe that the currency board system of a firmly fixed exchange rate (a "hard peg" in the jargon of international finance) is a viable long-term policy for an economy. Argentina's experience has proved that wrong.[2]*

[1]When a currency that is under a fixed exchange rate regime is officially altered in its value—downward—it is termed a *devaluation*. When a currency which is freely floated on exchange markets moves downward in value it is termed *depreciation*.

[2]"Argentina's Fall," Martin Feldstein, *Foreign Affairs*, March/April 2002.

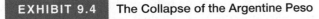

EXHIBIT 9.4   The Collapse of the Argentine Peso

Argentine pesos/U.S. dollar

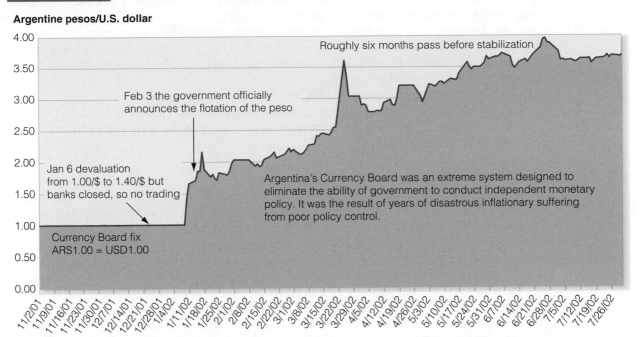

Forecasting in Practice

Numerous foreign exchange forecasting services exist, many of which are provided by banks and independent consultants. In addition, some multinational firms have their own in-house forecasting capabilities. Predictions can be based on elaborate econometric models, technical analysis of charts and trends, intuition, and a certain measure of gall.

Whether any of the forecasting services are worth their cost depends partly on our motive for forecasting as well as the required accuracy of the forecast. For example, long-run forecasts may be motivated by a multinational firm's desire to initiate a foreign investment in Japan, or perhaps to raise long-term funds denominated in Japanese yen. Or a portfolio manager may be considering diversifying for the long term in Japanese securities. The longer the time horizon of the forecast, the more inaccurate but also the less critical the forecast is likely to be. The forecaster will typically use annual data to display long-run trends in such economic fundamentals as Japanese inflation, growth, and BOP.

Short-term forecasts are typically motivated by a desire to hedge a receivable, payable, or dividend for perhaps a period of three months. In this case, the long-run economic fundamentals may not be as important as technical factors in the marketplace, government intervention, news, and passing whims of traders and investors. Accuracy of the forecast is critical, since most of the exchange rate changes are relatively small even though the day-to-day volatility may be high.

Forecasting services normally undertake fundamental economic analysis for long-term forecasts, and some base their short-term forecasts on the same basic model. Others base their short-term forecasts on technical analysis similar to that conducted in security analysis. They attempt to correlate exchange rate changes with various other variables, regardless of whether there is any economic rationale for the correlation. The chances of these forecasts being consistently useful or profitable depend on whether one believes the foreign exchange market is efficient. The more efficient the market is, the more likely it is that exchange rates are "random walks," with past price behavior providing no clues to the future. The less efficient the foreign exchange market is, the better the chance that forecasters may get lucky and find a key relationship that holds, at least for the short run. If the relationship is really consistent, however, others will soon discover it and the market will become efficient again with respect to that piece of information.

Exhibit 9.5 summarizes the various forecasting periods, regimes, and the authors' suggested methodologies. Opinions, however, are subject to change without notice! (And remember, if authors could predict the movement of exchange rates with regularity, we surely wouldn't write books.)

Technical Analysis

Technical analysts, traditionally referred to as *chartists*, focus on price and volume data to determine past trends that are expected to continue into the future. The single most important element of technical analysis is that future exchange rates are based on the current exchange rate. Exchange rate movements, similar to equity price movements, can be subdivided into three periods: 1) day-to-day movement, which is seemingly random; 2) short-term movements extending from several days to trends lasting several months; 3) long-term movements, which are characterized by up and down long-term trends. Long-term technical analysis has gained new popularity as a result of recent research into the possibility that long-term "waves" in currency movements exist under floating exchange rates.

The longer the time horizon of the forecast, the more inaccurate the forecast is likely to be. Whereas forecasting for the long run must depend on economic fundamentals of exchange rate determination, many of the forecast needs of the firm are short- to medium-term in their

EXHIBIT 9.5	Exchange Rate Forecasting in Practice	
Forecast Period	**Regime**	**Recommended Forecast Methods**
SHORT-RUN	*Fixed-Rate*	1. Assume the fixed rate is maintained 2. Indications of stress on fixed rate? 3. Capital controls; black market rates 4. Indicators of government's capability to maintain fixed-rate? 5. Changes in official foreign currency reserves

	Floating-Rate	1. Technical methods which capture trend
		2. Forward rates as forecasts
		   (a) <30 days, assume a random walk
		   (b) 30–90 days, forward rates
		3. 90–360 days, combine trend with fundamental analysis
		4. Fundamental analysis of inflationary concerns
		5. Government declarations and agreements regarding exchange rate goals
		6. Cooperative agreements with other countries

LONG-RUN	*Fixed-Rate*	1. Fundamental analysis 2. BOP management 3. Ability to control domestic inflation 4. Ability to generate hard currency reserves to use for intervention 5. Ability to run trade surpluses
	Floating-Rate	1. Focus on inflationary fundamentals and PPP 2. Indicators of general economic health such as economic growth and stability 3. Technical analysis of long-term trends; new research indicates possibility of long-term technical "waves"

time horizon and can be addressed with less theoretical approaches. Time series techniques infer no theory or causality but simply predict future values from the recent past. Forecasters freely mix fundamental and technical analysis, presumably because forecasting is like playing horseshoes—getting close is all that counts. *Global Finance in Practice 9.3* provides a short analysis of how accurate one very prestigious currency forecaster was over a 3-year period.

Cross-Rate Consistency in Forecasting

International financial managers must often forecast their home currency exchange rates for the set of countries in which the firm operates, not only to decide whether to hedge or to make an investment, but also as part of preparing multicountry operating budgets in the home country's currency. These are the operating budgets against which the performance of foreign subsidiary managers will be judged. Checking the reasonableness of the cross rates implicit in individual forecasts acts as a reality check to the original forecasts.

GLOBAL FINANCE IN PRACTICE   9.3

JPMorgan Chase Forecast of the Dollar/Euro

There are many different foreign exchange forecasting services and service providers. JPMorgan Chase (JPMC) is one of the most prestigious and widely used.[1] A review of JPMC's forecasting accuracy for the U.S. dollar/euro spot exchange rate ($/€) for the 2002 to 2005 period, in 90-day increments, is presented in the exhibit. The graph shows the actual spot exchange rate for the period and JPMC's forecast for the spot exchange rate for the same period.

There is good news and there is bad news. The good news is that JPMC hit the actual spot rate dead on in both May and November 2002. The bad news is that after that, they missed. Somewhat worrisome is when the forecast got the direction wrong. For example, in February 2004, JPMC had forecast the spot rate to move from the current rate of $1.27/€ to $1.32/€, but in fact, the dollar had appreciated dramatically in the following 3-month period to close at $1.19/€. This was in fact a massive difference. Again, in November 2004, JPMC had forecast the spot rate to move from the current spot rate of $1.30/€ to $1.23/€, but in fact, the actual spot rate proved to be $1.32/€.

The lesson learned is probably that regardless of how professional and prestigious a forecaster may be, and how accurate they may have been in the past, forecasting the future—by anyone for anything—is challenging to say the least.

[1]This analysis uses exchange rate data as published in the print edition of *The Economist*, appearing quarterly. The source of the exchange rate forecasts, as noted in *The Economist*, is JPMorgan Chase.

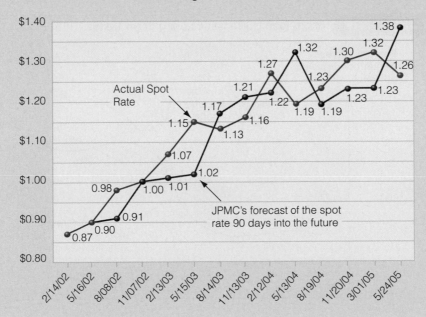

To illustrate, assume the U.S. parent home office forecasts the yen-to-dollar exchange rate a year hence to be ¥120/$ and the U.K. pound sterling rate to be $1.50/£. This creates an implied spot rate one year hence of ¥180/£. However, both the Japanese and the British financial managers, with good reason, have forecast a spot rate one year hence of ¥150/£.

Obviously the two foreign subsidiary managers (forecasting ¥150/£) and the home office (with an implicit forecast of ¥180/£) cannot both be correct. The time to reconcile these conflicting forecasts is the present, not one year hence when managers in Japan or the United Kingdom claim that their performance against budget is better than measured by the U.S. parent. Additionally, checking the reasonableness of implied cross rates is an exercise in improving the accuracy of the forecasting process.

Forecasting: What to Think?

Obviously, with the variety of theories and practices, forecasting exchange rates into the future is a daunting task. Here is a synthesis of our thoughts and experience:

◆ It appears from decades of theoretical and empirical studies that exchange rates do adhere to the fundamental principles and theories outlined in the previous sections. Fundamentals do apply in the long term. There is, therefore, something of a *fundamental equilibrium path* for a currency's value.

◆ It also seems that in the short term, a variety of random events, institutional frictions, and technical factors may cause currency values to deviate significantly from their long-term fundamental path. This is sometimes referred to as *noise*. Clearly, therefore, we might expect deviations from the long-term path not only to occur, but also to occur with some regularity and relative longevity.

Exhibit 9.6 illustrates this synthesis of forecasting thought. The long-term equilibrium path of the currency—although relatively well defined in retrospect—is not always apparent in the short term. The exchange rate itself may deviate in something of a cycle or wave about the long-term path.

EXHIBIT 9.6   Short-Term Noise versus Long-Term Trends

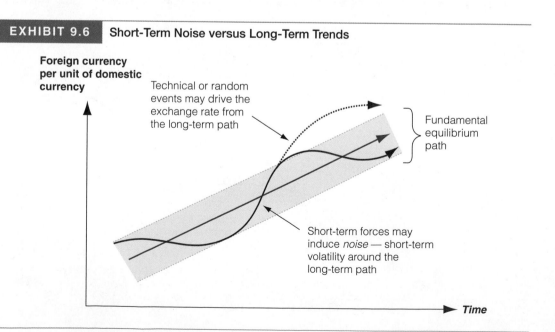

If market participants both agree on the general long-term path and possess *stabilizing expectations*, the currency's value will periodically return to the long-term path. It is critical, however, that when the currency's value rises above the long-term path, most market participants see it as being overvalued and respond by selling the currency—causing its price to fall. Similarly, when the currency's value falls below the long-term path, market participants respond by buying the currency driving its value up. This is what is meant by *stabilizing expectations*: Market participants continually respond to deviations from the long-term path by buying or selling to drive the currency back to the long-term path.

If, for some reason, the market becomes unstable, as illustrated by the dotted deviation path in Exhibit 9.6, the exchange rate may move significantly away from the long-term path for longer periods of time. Causes of these destabilizing markets, weak infrastructure (such as the banking system), and political or social events that dictate economic behaviors, are often the actions of speculators and inefficient markets.

Exchange Rate Dynamics: Making Sense of Market Movements

Although the various theories surrounding exchange rate determination are clear and sound, it may appear on a day-to-day basis that the currency markets do not pay much attention to the theories, they don't read the books! The difficulty is understanding which fundamentals are driving markets at which points in time.

One example of this relative confusion over exchange rate dynamics is the phenomenon known as *overshooting*. Assume that the current spot rate between the dollar and the euro, as illustrated in Exhibit 9.7, is S_0. The U.S. Federal Reserve announces an expansionary monetary policy which cuts U.S. dollar interest rates. If euro-denominated interest rates remain unchanged, the new spot rate expected by the exchange markets on the basis of interest differentials is S_1. This immediate change in the exchange rate is typical

---

EXHIBIT 9.7   Exchange Rate Dynamics: Overshooting

If the U.S. Federal Reserve were to announce a change in monetary policy, an expansion in money supply growth, it could potentially result in an "overshooting" exchange rate change.

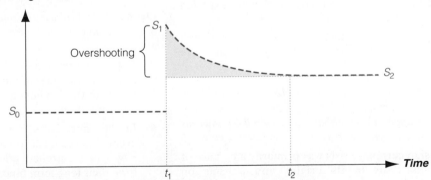

The Fed announces a monetary expansion at a time t_1. This results immediately in lower dollar interest rates. The foreign exchange markets immediately respond to the lower dollar interest rates by driving the value of the dollar down from S_0 to S_1. This new rate is based on *interest differentials*. However, in the coming days and weeks, as the fundamental price effects of the monetary policy actions work their way through the economy, *purchasing power parity* takes hold and the market moves toward a longer term valuation of the dollar—by time t_2—of S_2, a weaker dollar than S_0, but not as weak as initially set at S_1.

of how the markets react to *news*, distinct economic and political events which are observable. The immediate change in the value of the dollar/euro is therefore based on interest differentials.

As time passes, however, the price impacts of the monetary policy change start working their way through the economy. As price changes occur over the medium to long term, purchasing power parity forces drive the market dynamics, and the spot rate moves from S_1 toward S_2. Although both S_1 and S_2 were rates determined by the market, they reflected the dominance of different theoretical principles. As a result, the initial lower value of the dollar of S_1 is often explained as an *overshooting* of the longer-term equilibrium value of S_2.

This is of course only one possible series of events and market reactions. Currency markets are subject to new *news* every hour of every day, making it very difficult to forecast exchange rate movements in short periods of time. In the longer term, as shown here, the markets do customarily return to fundamentals of exchange rate determination.

Summary of Learning Objectives

Examine how the supply and demand for any currency can be viewed as an asset choice issue within the portfolio of investors.

◆ The asset approach to forecasting suggests that whether foreigners are willing to hold claims in monetary form depends partly on relative real interest rates and partly on a country's outlook for economic growth and profitability.

◆ Longer-term forecasting, over one year, requires a return to the basic analysis of exchange rate fundamentals such as BOP, relative inflation rates, relative interest rates, and the long-run properties of purchasing power parity.

◆ Technical analysts (chartists) focus on price and volume data to determine past trends that are expected to continue into the future.

◆ Exchange rate forecasting in practice is a mix of both fundamental and technical forms of exchange rate analysis.

Explore how the three major approaches to exchange rate determination—parity conditions, the balance of payments, and the asset approach—combine to explain the numerous emerging market currency crises experienced in recent years.

◆ The Asian currency crisis was primarily a balance of payments crisis in its origins and impacts on exchange rate determination. A weak economic and financial infrastructure, corporate governance problems and speculation were also contributing factors.

◆ The Russian ruble crisis of 1998 was a complex combination of speculative pressures best explained by the asset approach to exchange rate determination.

◆ The Argentine crisis of 2002 was probably a combination of a disequilibrium in international parity conditions (differential rates of inflation) and balance of payments disequilibrium (current account deficits combined with financial account outflows).

Observe how forecasters combine technical analysis with the three major theoretical approaches to forecasting exchange rates.

◆ In the long term, it does appear that exchange rates follow a fundamental equilibrium path, one consistent with the fundamental theories of exchange rate determination.

◆ In the short term, however, a variety of random events, institutional frictions, and technical factors may cause currency values to deviate significantly from their long-term fundamental path.

MINI-CASE

The Japanese Yen Intervention of 2010[1]

We will take decisive steps if necessary, including intervention, while continuing to closely watch currency market moves from now on.

— Yoshihiko Noda, Finance Minister of Japan,
September 13, 2010.

Japan has been the subject of continued criticism for nearly two decades over its frequent intervention in the foreign exchange markets. Trading partners have accused it of market manipulation, while Japan has argued that it is a country and economy which is inherently global in its economic structure, relying on its international competitiveness for its livelihood, and currency stability is its only desire.

The debate was renewed in September 2010 when Japan intervened in the foreign exchange markets for the first time in nearly six years. Japan reportedly bought nearly 20 billion U.S. dollars in exchange for Japanese yen in an attempt to stop the continuing appreciation of the yen. Finance Ministry officials had stated publicly that 82 yen per dollar was probably the limit of their tolerance for yen appreciation.

As illustrated in Exhibit 1, the Bank of Japan intervened on September 13 as the yen approached 82 yen per dollar. (The Bank of Japan is independent in its ability to conduct Japanese monetary policy, but as the organizational subsidiary of the Japanese Ministry of Finance, it must conduct foreign exchange operations on behalf of the Japanese government.) Japanese officials reportedly notified authorities in both the United States and the European Union of their activity, but noted that they had not asked for permission or support.

The intervention resulted in public outcry from Beijing to Washington to London over the "new era of currency intervention." Although market intervention is always looked down upon by free market proponents, the move by Japan was seen as particularly frustrating as it came at a time when the United States was continuing to pressure China to revalue its currency, the renminbi. As noted by economist Nouriel Roubini, "We are in a world where everyone wants

| **EXHIBIT 1** | Intervention and the Japanese Yen, 2010 |

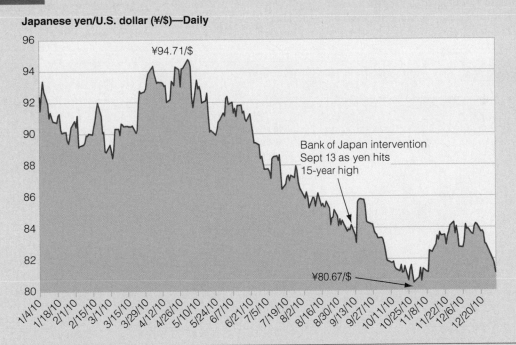

Japanese yen/U.S. dollar (¥/$)—Daily

¥94.71/$

Bank of Japan intervention Sept 13 as yen hits 15-year high

¥80.67/$

[1]This Mini-Case draws from a number of sources including "Japan's Currency Intervention: Policy Issues," Dick K. Nanto, CRS Report for Congress, July 13, 2007; IMF Country Report No. 05/273, Japan: 2005 Article IV Consultation Staff Report, August 2005; "Interventions and the Japanese Economic Recovery," Takatoshi Ito, paper presented at the University of Michigan Conference on Policy Options for Japan and the United States, October 2004; "Towards a New Era of Currency Intervention," Mansoor Mohi-Uddin, *Financial Times*, September 22, 2010; "Currency Intervention's Mixed Record of Success," Russell Hotten, *BBC News*, September 16, 2010.

a weak currency," a marketplace in which all countries are looking to stimulate their domestic economies through exceptionally low interest rates and corresponding weak currency values—"a global race to the bottom."

Ironically, as illustrated in Exhibit 1, it appears that the intervention was largely unsuccessful. When the Bank of Japan started buying dollars in an appreciating yen market—the so-called "leaning into the wind" strategy—it was hoping to either stop the appreciation, change the direction of the spot rate movement, or both. In either pursuit, it appears to have failed. As one analyst commented, it turned out to be a "short-term fix to a long-term problem." Although the yen spiked downward (more yen per dollar) for a few days, it returned once again to an appreciating path within a week.

Japan's frequent interventions, described in Exhibit 2, have been the subject of much study. In an August 2005 study by the IMF, it was noted that between 1991 and 2005, the Bank of Japan had intervened on 340 days, the European Central Bank on 4 days (since its inception in 1998), and the U.S. Federal Reserve on 22 days. Although the IMF has never found Japanese intervention to be officially "currency manipulation," an analysis by Takatoshi Ito in 2004 concluded that there was on average a one-yen per dollar change in market rates, roughly 1%, as a result of Japanese intervention over time.

It is not clear at this time whether or not Japan will "sterilize" the intervention, meaning neutralize the additional yen impact on the money supply by buying bonds domestically. Although this has been the tendency historically, given the current deflation forces in Japan, it may not be necessary.

Japan's interventions are not, however, a lone example of attempted market manipulation. The Swiss National Bank repeatedly intervened in 2009 to stop the appreciation of the Swiss franc against both the dollar and the euro, and recently, in January 2011, Chile had aggressively sold Chilean pesos against the U.S. dollar to stop its continued appreciation.

There is no historical case in which [yen] selling intervention succeeded in immediately stopping the pre-existing long term uptrend in the Japanese yen.
—Tohru Sasaki, Currency Strategist, JPMorgan.

CASE QUESTIONS

1. Could the Bank of Japan continually intervene to try to stop the appreciation of the yen? Is there any limit to its ability to intervene?

2. Why is a stronger yen such a bad thing for Japan? Isn't a stronger currency value an indication of confidence by the global markets in the economy and policies of a country?

3. If currency intervention has such a poor record, why do you think countries like Japan or Switzerland or Chile continue to do it?

EXHIBIT 2   The History of Japanese Intervention

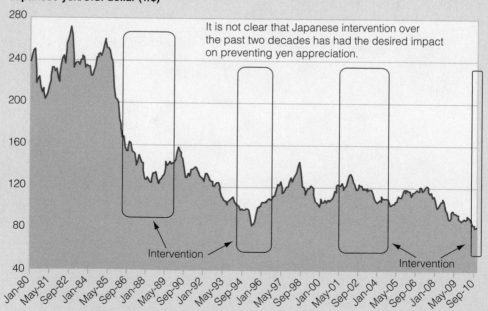

Japanese yen/U.S. dollar (¥/$)

It is not clear that Japanese intervention over the past two decades has had the desired impact on preventing yen appreciation.

Questions

1. **Term Forecasting.** What are the major differences between short-term and long-term forecasts for the following:
   a. A fixed exchange rate
   b. A floating exchange rate

2. **Exchange Rate Dynamics.** What is meant by the term "overshooting"? What causes it and how is it corrected?

3. **Fundamental Equilibrium.** What is meant by the term "fundamental equilibrium path" for a currency value? What is "noise"?

4. **Asset Market Approach to Forecasting.** Explain how the asset market approach can be used to forecast future spot exchange rates. How does the asset market approach differ from the BOP approach to forecasting?

5. **Technical Analysis.** Explain how technical analysis can be used to forecast future spot exchange rates. How does technical analysis differ from the BOP and asset market approaches to forecasting?

6. **Forecasting Services.** Numerous exchange rate forecasting services exist. Trident's CFO Maria Gonzalez is considering whether to subscribe to one of these services at a cost of $20,000 per year. The price includes online access to the forecasting services' computerized econometric exchange rate prediction model. What factors should Maria consider when deciding whether or not to subscribe?

7. **Cross-Rate Consistency in Forecasting.** Explain the meaning of *"cross-rate consistency"* as used by MNEs. How do MNEs use a check of cross-rate consistency in practice?

8. **Infrastructure Weakness.** *Infrastructure weakness* was one of the causes of the emerging market crisis in Thailand in 1997. Define infrastructure weakness and explain how it could affect a country's exchange rate.

9. **Infrastructure Strength.** Explain why infrastructure strengths have helped to offset the large BOP deficits on current account in the United States.

10. **Speculation.** The emerging market crises of 1997–2002 were worsened because of rampant speculation. Do speculators cause such crisis or do they simply respond to market signals of weakness? How can a government manage foreign exchange speculation?

11. **Foreign Direct Investment.** Swings in foreign direct investment flows into and out of emerging markets contribute to exchange rate volatility. Describe one concrete historical example of this phenomenon during the last 10 years.

12. **Thailand's Crisis of 1997.** What were the main causes of Thailand's crisis of 1997? What lessons were learned and what steps were eventually taken to normalize Thailand's economy?

13. **Russia's Crisis of 1998.** What were the main causes of Russia's crisis of 1998? What lessons were learned and what steps were taken to normalize Russia's economy?

14. **Argentina's Crisis of 2001–2002.** What were the main causes of Argentina's crisis of 2001–2002? What lessons were learned and what steps were taken to normalize Argentina's economy?

Problems

1. **Trepak (The Russian Dance).** The Russian ruble (RUB) traded at RUB 29.00/USD on January 2, 2009. On December 11, 2010, its value had fallen to RUB 31.45/USD. What was the percentage change in its value?

2. **Center of the World.** The Ecuadorian sucre (S) suffered from hyper-inflationary forces throughout 1999. Its value moved from S5,000/$ to S25,000/$. What was the percentage change in its value?

3. **Reais Reality.** The Brazilian reais' (R$) value was R$1.80/$ on Thursday, January 24, 2008. Its value fell to R$2.39/$ on Monday, January 26, 2009. What was the percentage change in its value?

4. **That's Loonie.** The Canadian dollar's value against the U.S. dollar has seen some significant changes over recent history. Use the following graph of the C$/US$ exchange rate for the 30-year period between 1980 and end-of-year 2010 to estimate the percentage change in the Canadian dollar's value (it's affectionately known as the "loonie") versus the dollar for the following periods.
   a. January 1980–December 1985
   b. January 1986–December 1991
   c. January 1992–December 2001
   d. January 2002–December 2006
   e. January 2007–December 2008
   f. January 2009–December 2010

**Monthly Average Exchange Rates:
Canadian Dollars/U.S. Dollar**

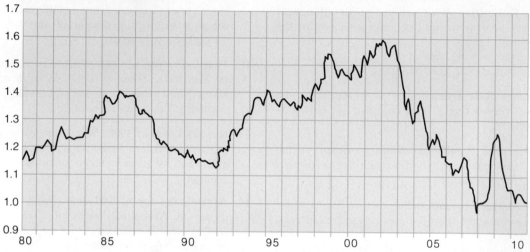

Source: PACIFIC Exchange Rates © 2010 by Prof. Werner Antweiler,
University of British Columbia, Vancouver BC, Canada.

5. **Paris to Tokyo.** The Japanese yen-euro cross rate is one of the more significant currency values for global trade and commerce. The graph below shows this cross rate from when the euro was launched in January 1999 through the end-of-year 2010. Estimate the change in the value of the yen over the following three periods of change.
   a. Jan 1999–Aug 2001
   b. Sep 2001–June 2008
   c. July 2008–Dec 2010

6. **Lowering the Lira.** The Turkish lira (TL) was officially devalued by the Turkish government in February 2001 during a severe political and economic crisis. The Turkish government announced on February 21 that the lira would be devalued by 20%. The spot exchange rate on February 20 was TL68,000/$.
   a. What was the exchange rate after devaluation?
   b. What was percentage change after falling to TL100,000/$?

**Monthly Average Exchange Rates:
Japanese Yen/European Euro**

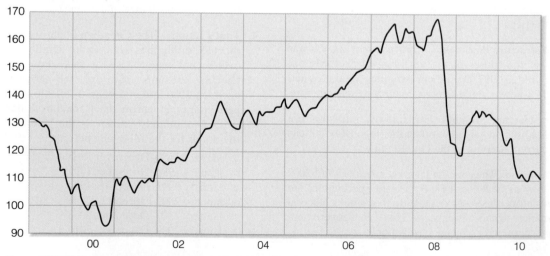

Source: PACIFIC Exchange Rates © 2010 by Prof. Werner Antweiler,
University of British Columbia, Vancouver BC, Canada.

7. **Cada Seis Años.** Mexico was famous—or infamous—for many years in having two things every six years (*cada seis años* in Spanish): a presidential election and a currency devaluation. This was the case in 1976, 1982, 1988, and 1994. In its last devaluation on December 20, 1994, the value of the Mexican peso (Ps) was officially changed from Ps3.30/$ to Ps5.50/$. What was the percentage devaluation?

8. **Brokedown Palace.** The Thai baht (THB) was devalued by the Thai government from THB25/$ to THB29/$ on July 2, 1997. What was the percentage devaluation of the baht?

9. **Forecasting the Argentine Peso.** As illustrated in the graph on the next page, the Argentine peso moved from its fixed exchange rate of Ps1.00/$ to over Ps2.00/$ in a matter of days in early January 2002. After a brief period of high volatility, the peso's value appeared to settled down into a range varying between 2.0 and 2.5 pesos per dollar. If you were forecasting the Argentine peso further into the future, how would you use the information in the graphic—the value of the peso freely floating in the weeks following devaluation—to forecast its future value?

Daily Exchange Rates:
Argentine Pesos/U.S. Dollar

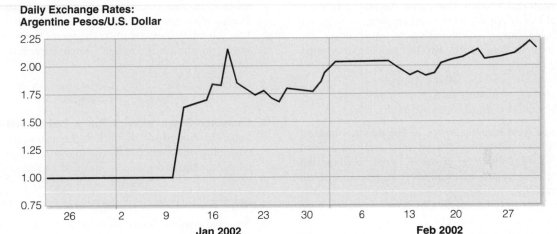

Forecasting the Pan-Pacific Pyramid

Using the table below containing economic, financial, and business indicators from October 20, 2007, issue of *The Economist* (print edition) to answer problems 10 through 15.

	Gross Domestic Product				Industrial Production	Unemployment Rate
Country	Latest Qtr	Qtr*	Forecast 2007e	Forecast 2008e	Recent Qtr	Latest
Australia	4.3%	3.8%	4.1%	3.5%	4.6%	4.2%
Japan	1.6%	−1.2%	2.0%	1.9%	4.3%	3.8%
United States	1.9%	3.8%	2.0%	2.2%	1.9%	4.7%

	Consumer Prices			Interest Rates	
Country	Year Ago	Latest	Forecast 2007e	3-month Latest	1-yr Govt Latest
Australia	4.0%	2.1%	2.4%	6.90%	6.23%
Japan	0.9%	−0.2%	0.0%	0.73%	1.65%
United States	2.1%	2.8%	2.8%	4.72%	4.54%

	Trade Balance	Current Account		Current Units (per US$)	
Country	Last 12 mos (billion $)	Last 12 mos (billion $)	Forecast 07 (% of GDP)	Oct 17th	Year Ago
Australia	−13.0	−$47.0	−5.7%	1.12	1.33
Japan	98.1	$197.5	4.6%	117	119
United States	−810.7	−$793.2	−5.6%	1.00	1.00

Source: Data abstracted from *The Economist*, October 20, 2007, print edition. Unless otherwise noted, percentages are percentage changes over one year. Rec Qtr = recent quarter. Values for 2007e are estimates or forecasts.

10. **Current Spot Rates.** What are the current spot exchange rates for the following cross rates?
    a. Japanese yen/U.S. dollar exchange rate
    b. Japanese yen/Australian dollar exchange rate
    c. Australian dollar/U.S. dollar exchange rate

11. **Purchasing Power Parity Forecasts.** Assuming purchasing power parity, and assuming that the forecasted change in consumer prices is a good proxy of predicted inflation, forecast the following cross rates:
    a. Japanese yen/U.S. dollar in one year
    b. Japanese yen/Australian dollar in one year
    c. Australian dollar/U.S. dollar in one year

12. **International Fischer Forecasts.** Assuming International Fisher applies to the coming year, forecast the following future spot exchange rates using the government bond rates for the respective country currencies:
    a. Japanese yen/U.S. dollar in one year
    b. Japanese yen/Australian dollar in one year
    c. Australian dollar/U.S. dollar in one year

13. **Implied Real Interest Rates.** If the nominal interest rate is the government bond rate, and the current change in consumer prices is used as expected inflation, calculate the implied "real" rates of interest by currency.
    a. Australian dollar "real" rate
    b. Japanese yen "real" rate
    c. U.S. dollar "real" rate

14. **Forward Rates.** Using the spot rates and 3-month interest rates above, calculate the 90-day forward rates for:
    a. Japanese yen/U.S. dollar exchange rate
    b. Japanese yen/Australian dollar exchange rate
    c. Australian dollar/U.S. dollar exchange rate

15. **Real Economic Activity and Misery.** Calculate the country's Misery Index (unemployment + inflation) and then use it like interest differentials to forecast the future spot exchange rate, one year into the future.
    a. Japanese yen/U.S. dollar exchange rate in one year
    b. Japanese yen/Australian dollar exchange rate in one year
    c. Australian dollar/U.S. dollar exchange rate in one year

Internet Exercises

1. **Recent Economic and Financial Data.** Use the following Web sites to obtain recent economic and financial data used for all approaches to forecasting presented in this chapter.

Economist.com	www.economist.com
FT.com	www.ft.com
EconEdLink	www.econedlink.org/datalinks/index.cfm

2. **OzForex Weekly Comment.** The OzForex Foreign Exchange Services Web site provides a weekly commentary on major political and economic factors and events which move current markets. Using their Web site, see what they expect to happen in the coming week on the three major global currencies—the dollar, yen, and euro.

OzForex	www.ozforex.com.au/marketwatch.htm

3. **Exchange Rates, Interest Rates, and Global Markets.** The magnitude of market data can seem overwhelming on occasion. Use the following Bloomberg markets page to organize your mind and your global data.

Bloomberg Financial News	www.bloomberg.com/markets

4. **National Bank of Slovakia and the Slovakia Koruna.** The National Bank of Slovakia has been publishing spot and forward rates of selected currencies versus the Slovakia koruna for several years. Using the following Web site, compile spot rates, 3-month forward rates, and 6-month forward rates for a recent 2-year period. After graphing the data, does it appear that the forward rate has predicted the future direction of the spot rate?

National Bank of Slovakia	www.nbs.sk/KL/INDEXA.HTM

5. **Banque Canada and the Canadian Dollar Forward Market.** Using the following Web site to find the latest spot and forward quotes of the Canadian dollar against the Bahamian dollar and the Brazilian real.

Banque Canada	www.bank-banque-canada.ca/fmd/exchange.htm

Transaction and Translation Exposure

There are two times in a man's life when he should not speculate: when he can't afford it and when he can.

— "Following the Equator," *Pudd'nhead Wilson's New Calendar*, Mark Twain.

LEARNING OBJECTIVES

◆ Distinguish between the three major foreign exchange exposures experienced by firms.

◆ Analyze the pros and cons of hedging foreign exchange transaction exposure.

◆ Examine the alternatives available to a firm to manage a large and significant transaction exposure.

◆ Evaluate the institutional practices and concerns of conducting foreign exchange risk management.

◆ Demonstrate how translation practices result in a foreign exchange exposure for the multinational enterprise.

◆ Explain the meaning behind the designation of a foreign subsidiary's "functional currency."

◆ Illustrate both the theoretical and practical differences between the two primary methods of translating foreign currency denominated financial statements into the currency reporting of the parent company.

◆ Compare translation exposure with operating expense.

◆ Analyze the costs and benefits of managing translation exposure.

Foreign exchange exposure is a measure of the potential for a firm's profitability, net cash flow, and market value to change because of a change in exchange rates. An important task of the financial manager is to measure foreign exchange exposure and to manage it so as to maximize the profitability, net cash flow, and market value of the firm. This chapter describes and details both types of accounting exposure: transaction exposure and translation exposure. The chapter concludes with a Mini-Case, ***Banbury Impex (India)***, which involves a recent exposure management problem in India.

Types of Foreign Exchange Exposure

What happens to a firm when foreign exchange rates change? There are two distinct categories of foreign exchange exposure for the firm, those that are based in accounting and those that arise from economic competitiveness. The accounting exposures, specifically described as *transaction exposure* and *translation exposure*, arise from contracts and accounts being denominated in foreign currency. The economic exposure, which we will describe as *operating exposure*, is the potential change in the value of the firm from its changing global competitiveness as determined by exchange rates. Exhibit 10.1 shows schematically the three main types of foreign exchange exposure: *transaction*, *translation*, and *operating*.

Transaction Exposure

Transaction exposure measures changes in the value of outstanding financial obligations incurred prior to a change in exchange rates but not due to be settled until after the exchange rates change. Thus, it deals with changes in cash flows that result from existing contractual obligations.

Translation Exposure

Translation exposure is the potential for accounting-derived changes in owner's equity to occur because of the need to "translate" foreign currency financial statements of foreign subsidiaries into a single reporting currency to prepare worldwide consolidated financial statements.

Operating Exposure

Operating exposure, also called *economic exposure*, *competitive exposure*, or *strategic exposure*, measures the change in the present value of the firm resulting from any change in future operating cash flows of the firm caused by an *unexpected* change in exchange rates. The change in value depends on the effect of the exchange rate change on future sales volume, prices, and costs.

Transaction exposure and operating exposure exist because of unexpected changes in future cash flows. The difference between the two is that transaction exposure is concerned with future cash flows already contracted for, while operating exposure focuses on expected (not yet contracted for) future cash flows that might change because a change in exchange rates has altered international competitiveness.

EXHIBIT 10.1   Corporate Foreign Exchange Exposure

Resulting from Accounting	Resulting from Economics
Transaction Exposure	**Operating Exposure**
Impact of settling outstanding obligations entered into before change in exchange rates but to be settled after change in exchange rates	Change in expected future cash flows arising from an unexpected change in exchange rates
Translation Exposure	Changes in future cash flows arising from firm and competitor firm responses
Changes in income and owners' equity in consolidated financial statements caused by a change in exchange rates	

Time and Exchange Rate Changes →

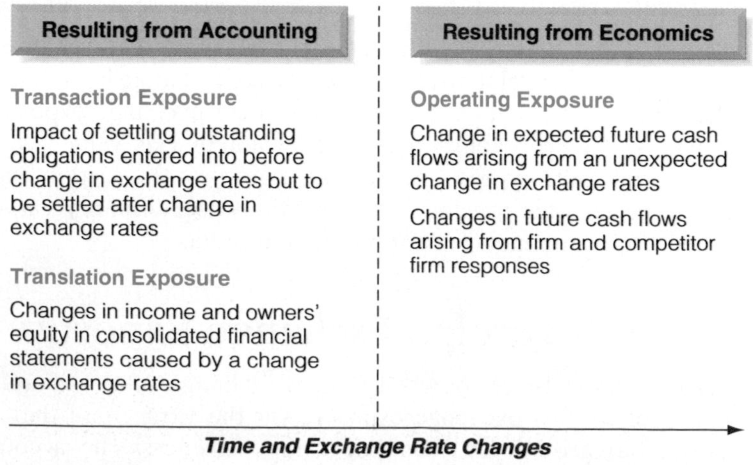

Why Hedge?

MNEs possess a multitude of cash flows that are sensitive to changes in exchange rates, interest rates, and commodity prices. Chapters 10 and 11 focus exclusively on the sensitivity of the individual firm's value and future cash flows to exchange rates. We begin by exploring the question of whether exchange rate risk should or should not be managed.

Hedging Defined

Many firms attempt to manage their currency exposures through *hedging*, which is the taking of a position, either acquiring a cash flow, an asset, or a contract that will rise (fall) in value and offset a fall (rise) in the value of an existing position. Hedging protects the owner of the existing asset from loss. However, it also eliminates any gain from an increase in the value of the asset hedged against. The question remains: What is to be gained by the firm from hedging?

According to financial theory, the value of a firm is the net present value of all expected future cash flows. The fact that these cash flows are *expected* emphasizes that nothing about the future is certain. If the reporting currency value of many of these cash flows is altered by exchange rates changes, a firm that hedges its currency exposures reduces some of the variance in the value of its future expected cash flows. *Currency risk* can then be defined as the variance in expected cash flows arising from unexpected exchange rate changes.

Exhibit 10.2 illustrates the distribution of expected net cash flows of the individual firm. Hedging these cash flows narrows the distribution of the cash flows about the mean of the distribution. Currency hedging reduces risk. Reduction of risk is not, however, the same as adding value or return. The value of the firm depicted in Exhibit 10.2 would be increased only if hedging actually shifted the mean of the distribution to the right. In fact, if hedging is not

---

EXHIBIT 10.2   Hedging's Impact on the Expected Cash Flows of the Firm

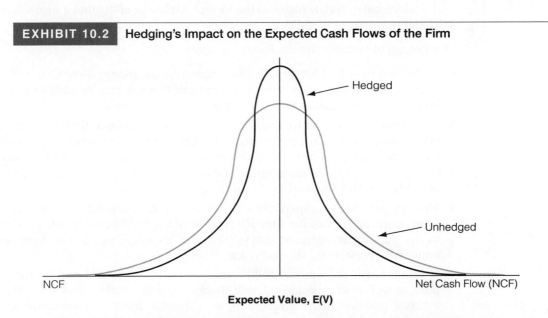

Hedging reduces the variability of expected cash flows about the mean of the distribution. This reduction of distribution variance is a reduction of risk.

"free," meaning that the firm must expend resources to hedge, then hedging will add value only if the rightward shift is sufficiently large to compensate for the cost of hedging.

The Pros and Cons of Hedging

Is a reduction in the variability of cash flows sufficient reason for currency risk management? Opponents of currency hedging commonly make the following arguments:

◆ Shareholders are more capable of diversifying currency risk than is the management of the firm. If stockholders do not wish to accept the currency risk of any specific firm, they can diversify their portfolios to manage the risk in a way that satisfies their individual preferences and risk tolerance.

◆ Currency risk management does not increase the expected cash flows of the firm. Currency risk management does, however, consume firm resources and so reduces cash flow. The impact on value is a combination of the reduction of cash flow (which lowers value) and the reduction in variance (which increases value).

◆ Management often conducts hedging activities that benefit management at the expense of the shareholders. The field of finance called *agency theory* frequently argues that management is generally more risk-averse than are shareholders.

◆ Managers cannot outguess the market. If and when markets are in equilibrium with respect to parity conditions, the expected net present value of hedging should be zero.

◆ Management's motivation to reduce variability is sometimes driven by accounting reasons. Management may believe that it will be criticized more severely for incurring foreign exchange losses than for incurring similar or even higher cash costs in avoiding the foreign exchange loss. Foreign exchange losses appear in the income statement as a highly visible separate line item or as a footnote, but the higher costs of protection are buried in operating or interest expenses.

◆ Efficient market theorists believe that investors can see through the "accounting veil" and therefore have already factored the foreign exchange effect into a firm's market valuation. Hedging would only add cost.

Proponents of hedging cite the following arguments:

◆ Reduction in risk of future cash flows improves the planning capability of the firm. If the firm can more accurately predict future cash flows, it may be able to undertake specific investments or activities that it might otherwise not consider.

◆ Reduction of risk in future cash flows reduces the likelihood that the firm's cash flows will fall below a level sufficient to make debt-service payments in order for its continued operation. This minimum cash flow point, often referred to as the point of *financial distress*, lies left of the center of the distribution of expected cash flows. Hedging reduces the likelihood of the firm's cash flows falling to this level.

◆ Management has a comparative advantage over the individual shareholder in knowing the actual currency risk of the firm. Regardless of the level of disclosure provided by the firm to the public, management always possesses an advantage in the depth and breadth of knowledge concerning the real risks.

◆ Markets are usually in disequilibrium because of structural and institutional imperfections, as well as unexpected external shocks (such as an oil crisis or war). Management is in a better position than shareholders to recognize disequilibrium conditions and to take advantage of single opportunities to enhance firm value through *selective hedging* (the hedging of exceptional exposures or the occasional use of hedging when management has a definite expectation of the direction of exchange rates).

Measurement of Transaction Exposure

Transaction exposure measures gains or losses that arise from the settlement of existing financial obligations whose terms are stated in a foreign currency. Transaction exposure arises from any of the following:

◆ Purchasing or selling on credit goods or services when prices are stated in foreign currencies

◆ Borrowing or lending funds when repayment is to be made in a foreign currency

◆ Being a party to an unperformed foreign exchange forward contract

◆ Otherwise acquiring assets or incurring liabilities denominated in foreign currencies

The most common example of transaction exposure arises when a firm has a receivable or payable denominated in a foreign currency. Exhibit 10.3 demonstrates how this exposure is born. The total transaction exposure consists of *quotation, backlog*, and *billing exposures*.

A transaction exposure is created at the first moment the seller quotes a price in foreign currency terms to a potential buyer (t_1). The quote can be either verbal, as in a telephone quote, or, as in written bid or a printed price list. With the placing of an order (t_2), the potential exposure created at the time of the quotation (t_1) is converted into actual exposure, called *backlog exposure* because the product has not yet been shipped or billed. Backlog exposure lasts until the goods are shipped and billed (t_3), at which time it becomes *billing exposure*. Billing exposure remains until payment is received by the seller (t_4).

Purchasing or Selling on Open Account. Suppose that Trident Corporation, a U.S. firm, sells merchandise on open account to a Belgian buyer for €1,800,000, with payment to be made in 60 days. The spot exchange rate on the date of the sale is \$1.1200/€, and the seller expects to exchange the euros received for €1,800,000 × \$1.1200/€ = \$2,016,000 when payment is received. The \$2,016,000 is the value of the sale which is posted to the firm's books. Accounting practices stipulate that the foreign currency transaction be listed at the spot exchange rate in effect on the date of the transaction.

Transaction exposure arises because of the risk that Trident will receive something other than the \$2,016,000 expected and booked. For example, if the euro weakens to \$1.1000/€ when

---

EXHIBIT 10.3   The Life Span of Transaction Exposure

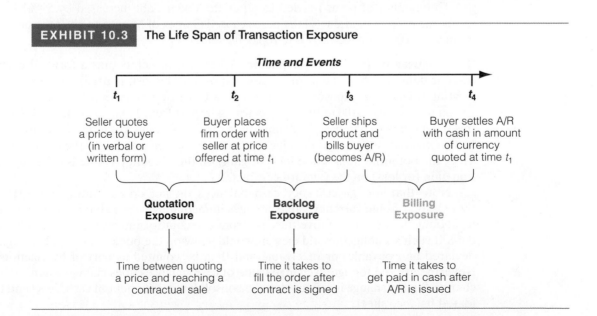

payment is received, the U.S. seller will receive only €1,800,000 × $1.1000/€ = $1,980,000, or some $180,000 less.

Transaction settlement: €1,800,000 × $1.1000/€	=	$1,980,000
Transaction booked: €1,800,000 × $1.1200/€	=	$2,016,000
Foreign exchange gain (loss) on sale	=	($180,000)

If the euro should strengthen to $1.3000/€, however, Trident receives €1,800,000 × $1.3000/€ = $2,340,000, an increase of $180,000 over the amount expected. Thus, exposure is the chance of either a loss or a gain on the resulting dollar settlement versus what the sale was booked at.

The U.S. seller might have avoided transaction exposure by invoicing the Belgian buyer in dollars. Of course, if the U.S. company attempted to sell only in dollars it might not have obtained the sale in the first place. Even if the Belgian buyer agrees to pay in dollars, transaction exposure is not eliminated. Instead, it is transferred to the Belgian buyer, whose dollar account payable has an unknown cost—to it—60 days hence.

Borrowing and Lending. A second example of transaction exposure arises when funds are borrowed or loaned, and the amount involved is denominated in a foreign currency. For example, in 1994, PepsiCo's largest bottler outside of the United States was Grupo Embotellador de Mexico (Gemex). In mid-December 1994, Gemex, a Mexican company, had U.S. dollar debt of $264 million. At that time, Mexico's *new peso* ("Ps") was traded at Ps3.45/US$, a pegged rate that had been maintained with minor variations since January 1, 1993, when the new currency unit had been created. On December 22, 1994, the peso was allowed to float because of economic and political events within Mexico, and in one day it sank to Ps4.65/US$. For most of the following January it traded in a range near Ps5.50/US$.

Dollar debt in mid-December 1994: US$264,000,000 × Ps3.45/US$ =	Ps910,800,000
Dollar debt in mid-January 1995: US$264,000,000 × Ps5.50/US$ =	Ps1,452,000,000
Dollar debt increase measure in Mexican pesos	Ps541,200,000

The number of pesos needed to repay the dollar debt increased by 59%! In U.S. dollar terms, the drop in the value of the pesos caused Gemex of Mexico to need the peso-equivalent of an additional US$98,400,000 to repay its debt.

Other Causes of Transaction Exposure. When a firm enters into a forward exchange contract, it deliberately creates transaction exposure. This risk is usually incurred to hedge an existing transaction exposure. For example, a U.S. firm might want to offset an existing obligation to purchase ¥100 million to pay for an import from Japan in 90 days. One way to offset this payment is to purchase ¥100 million in the forward market today for delivery in 90 days. In this manner any change in value of the Japanese yen relative to the dollar is neutralized. Thus, the potential transaction loss (or gain) on the account payable is offset by the transaction gain (or loss) on the forward contract.

Note that foreign currency cash balances do not create transaction exposure, even though their home currency value changes immediately with a change in exchange rates. No legal obligation exists to move the cash from one country and currency to another at a future date. If such an obligation did exist, it would show on the books as a payable (e.g., dividends declared and payable) or receivable and then be counted as part of transaction exposure. Nevertheless, the foreign exchange value of cash balances does change when exchange rates change. Such a change is reflected in the consolidated statement of cash flows and the consolidated balance sheet.

Contractual Hedges. Foreign exchange transaction exposure can be managed by *contractual*, *operating*, and *financial hedges*. The main contractual hedges employ the forward, money, futures, and options markets. Operating and financial hedges employ the use of risk-sharing agreements, leads and lags in payment terms, swaps, and other strategies to be discussed in later chapters.

The term *natural hedge* refers to an offsetting operating cash flow, a payable arising from the conduct of business. A *financial hedge* refers to either an offsetting debt obligation (such as a loan) or some type of financial derivative such as an interest rate swap. Care should be taken to distinguish hedges in the same way finance distinguishes cash flows—*operating* from *financing*. The following case illustrates how contractual hedging techniques may be used to protect against transaction exposure.

Trident's Transaction Exposure

Maria Gonzalez is the chief financial officer of Trident. She has just concluded negotiations for the sale of a turbine generator to Regency, a British firm, for £1,000,000. This single sale is quite large in relation to Trident's present business. Trident has no other current foreign customers, so the currency risk of this sale is of particular concern. The sale is made in March with payment due three months later in June. Exhibit 10.4 summarizes the financial and market information Maria has collected for the analysis of her currency exposure problem. The unknown—the *transaction exposure*—is the actual realized value of the receivable in U.S. dollars at the end of 90 days.

Trident operates on relatively narrow margins. Although Maria and Trident would be very happy if the pound appreciated versus the dollar, concerns center on the possibility that

---

EXHIBIT 10.4   Trident's Transaction Exposure

U.S. Dollar Market

Trident's weighted average cost of capital = 12.00% (3.00% for 90 days)
US$ 3-month borrowing rate = 8.00% per annum (2.00% for 90 days)
US$ 3-month investment rate = 6.00% per annum (1.50% for 90 days)

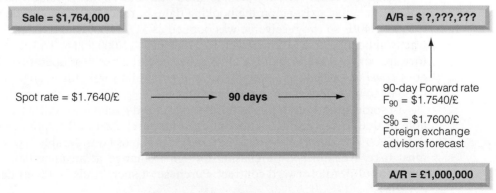

Spot rate = $1.7640/£

Sale = $1,764,000

A/R = $?,???,???

90 days

90-day Forward rate
F_{90} = $1.7540/£

S_{90}^e = $1.7600/£
Foreign exchange
advisors forecast

A/R = £1,000,000

UK£ 3-month investment rate = 8.00% per annum (2.00% for 90 days)
UK£ 3-month borrowing rate = 10.00% per annum (2.50% for 90 days)

British Pound Market

June (3-month) put option for £1,000,000 with a strike rate of $1.75/£; premium of 1.5%

the pound will fall. When Trident had priced and budgeted this contract, it had set a very slim minimum acceptable margin at a sales price of $1,700,000; Trident wanted the deal for both financial and strategic purposes. The *budget rate*, the lowest acceptable dollar per pound exchange rate, was therefore established at $1.70/£. Any exchange rate below this budget rate would result in Trident realizing no profit on the deal.

Four alternatives are available to Trident to manage the exposure: 1) remain unhedged; 2) hedge in the forward market; 3) hedge in the money market; or 4) hedge in the options market.

Unhedged Position

Maria may decide to accept the transaction risk. If she believes the foreign exchange advisor, she expects to receive £1,000,000 × $1.76 = $1,760,000 in three months. However, that amount is at risk. If the pound should fall to, say, $1.65/£, she will receive only $1,650,000. Exchange risk is not one-sided, however; if the transaction is left uncovered and the pound strengthened even more than forecast by the advisor, Trident will receive considerably more than $1,760,000. The essence of an unhedged approach is as follows.

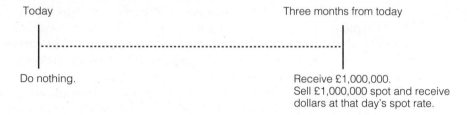

Forward Market Hedge

A *forward hedge* involves a forward (or futures) contract and a source of funds to fulfill that contract. The forward contract is entered into at the time the transaction exposure is created. In Trident's case, that would be in March, when the sale to Regency was booked as an account receivable.

When a foreign currency denominated sale such as this is made, it is booked at the spot rate of exchange existing on the booking date. In this case, the spot rate on the date of sale was $1.7640/£, so the receivable was booked as $1,764,000. Funds to fulfill the forward contract will be available in June, when Regency pays £1,000,000 to Trident. If funds to fulfill the forward contract are on hand or are due because of a business operation, the hedge is considered *covered*, *perfect*, or *square* because no residual foreign exchange risk exists. Funds on hand or to be received are matched by funds to be paid.

In some situations, funds to fulfill the forward exchange contract are not already available or due to be received later, but must be purchased in the spot market at some future date. Such a hedge is *open* or *uncovered*. It involves considerable risk because the hedger must take a chance on purchasing foreign exchange at an uncertain future spot rate in order to fulfill the forward contract. Purchase of such funds at a later date is referred to as *covering*.

Should Trident wish to hedge its transaction exposure with a forward, it will sell £1,000,000 forward today at the 3-month forward rate of $1.7540/£. This is a *covered transaction* in which the firm no longer has any foreign exchange risk. In three months the firm will receive £1,000,000 from the British buyer, deliver that sum to the bank against its forward sale, and receive $1,754,000. This would be recorded on Trident's income statement as a foreign exchange loss of $10,000 ($1,764,000 as booked, $1,754,000 as settled).

The essence of a forward hedge is as follows:

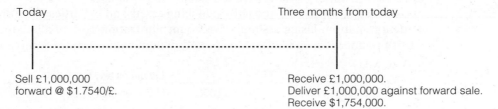

Today

Sell £1,000,000
forward @ $1.7540/£.

Three months from today

Receive £1,000,000.
Deliver £1,000,000 against forward sale.
Receive $1,754,000.

If Maria's forecast of future rates was identical to that implicit in the forward quotation, that is, $1.7540/£, expected receipts would be the same whether or not the firm hedges. However, realized receipts under the unhedged alternative could vary considerably from the certain receipts when the transaction is hedged. Never underestimate the value of predictability of outcomes (and 90 nights of solid sleep).

Money Market Hedge

Like a forward market hedge, a *money market hedge* also involves a contract and a source of funds to fulfill that contract. In this instance, the contract is a loan agreement. The firm seeking the money market hedge borrows in one currency and exchanges the proceeds for another currency. Funds to fulfill the contract—that is, to repay the loan—are generated from business operations, in this case, the account receivable.

A money market hedge can cover a single transaction, such as Trident's £1,000,000 receivable, or repeated transactions. Hedging repeated transactions is called *matching*. It requires the firm to match the expected foreign currency cash inflows and outflows by currency and maturity. For example, if Trident had numerous sales denominated in pounds to British customers over a long period of time, it would have somewhat predictable U.K. pound cash inflows. The appropriate money market hedge technique here would be to borrow U.K. pounds in an amount matching the typical size and maturity of expected pound inflows. Then, if the pound depreciated or appreciated, the foreign exchange effect on cash inflows in pounds would be offset by the effect on cash outflows in pounds from repaying the pound loan plus interest.

The structure of a money market hedge resembles that of a forward hedge. The difference is that the cost of the money market hedge is determined by different interest rates than the interest rates used in the formation of the forward rate. The difference in interest rates facing a private firm borrowing in two separate country markets may be different from the difference in risk-free government bill rates or Eurocurrency interest rates in these same markets. In efficient markets interest rate parity should ensure that these costs are nearly the same, but not all markets are efficient at all times.

To hedge in the money market, Maria will borrow pounds in London at once, immediately convert the borrowed pounds into dollars, and repay the pound loan in three months with the proceeds from the sale of the generator. She will need to borrow just enough to repay both the principal and interest with the sale proceeds. The borrowing interest rate will be 10% per annum, or 2.5% for three months. Therefore, the amount to borrow now for repayment in three months is

$$\frac{£1,000,000}{1 + 0.025} = £975,610$$

Maria would borrow £975,610 now, and in three months repay that amount plus £24,390 of interest with the account receivable. Trident would exchange the £975,610 loan proceeds for dollars at the current spot exchange rate of $1.7640/£, receiving $1,720,976 at once.

The money market hedge, if selected by Trident, creates a pound-denominated liability, the pound loan, to offset the pound-denominated asset, the account receivable. The money market hedge works as a hedge by matching assets and liabilities according to their currency of denomination. Using a simple T-account illustrating Trident's balance sheet, the loan in British pounds is seen to offset the pound-denominated account receivable:

Assets		Liabilities and Net Worth	
Account receivable	£1,000,000	Bank loan (principal)	£975,610
		Interest payable	24,390
	£1,000,000		£1,000,000

The loan acts as a *balance sheet hedge* against the pound-denominated account receivable.

To compare the forward hedge with the money market hedge one must analyze how Trident's loan proceeds will be utilized for the next three months. Remember that the loan proceeds are received today but the forward contract proceeds are received in three months. For comparison purposes, one must either calculate the future value of the loan proceeds or the present value of the forward contract proceeds. Since the primary uncertainty here is the dollar value in three months, we will use future value here.

As both the forward contract proceeds and the loan proceeds are relatively certain, it is possible to make a clear choice between the two alternatives based on the one that yields the higher dollar receipts. This result, in turn, depends on the assumed rate of investment or use of the loan proceeds.

At least three logical choices exist for an assumed investment rate for the loan proceeds for the next three months. First, if Trident is cash rich, the loan proceeds might be invested in U.S. dollar money market instruments that yield 6% per annum. Second, Maria might simply use the pound loan proceeds to pay down dollar loans that currently cost Trident 8% per annum. Third, Maria might invest the loan proceeds in the general operations of the firm, in which case the cost of capital of 12% per annum would be the appropriate rate. The field of finance generally uses the company's cost of capital to move capital forward and backward in time, and we will therefore use the WACC of 12% (3% for the 90-day period here) to calculate the future value of proceeds under the money market hedge:

$$\$1,720,976 \times 1.03 = \$1,772,605$$

A break-even rate can now be calculated between the forward hedge and the money market hedge. Assume that r is the unknown 3-month investment rate, expressed as a decimal, that would equalize the proceeds from the forward and money market hedges. We have

$$\text{(Loan proceeds)} \times (1 + \text{rate}) = \text{(forward proceeds)}$$
$$\$1,720,976 \times (1 + r) = \$1,754,000$$
$$r = 0.0192$$

One can convert this 3-month (90 days) investment rate to an annual whole percentage equivalent, assuming a 360-day financial year, as follows:

$$0.0192 \times \frac{360}{90} \times 100 = 7.68\%$$

In other words, if Maria Gonzalez can invest the loan proceeds at a rate higher than 7.68% per annum, she would prefer the money market hedge. If she can only invest at a rate lower than 7.68%, she would prefer the forward hedge.

The essence of a money market hedge is as follows:

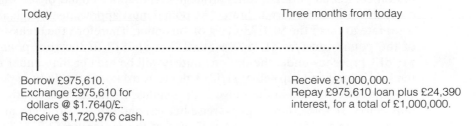

Today

Borrow £975,610.
Exchange £975,610 for
  dollars @ $1.7640/£.
Receive $1,720,976 cash.

Three months from today

Receive £1,000,000.
Repay £975,610 loan plus £24,390
interest, for a total of £1,000,000.

The money market hedge therefore results in cash received up-front (at the start of the period), which can then be carried forward in time for comparison with the other hedging alternatives.

Options Market Hedge

Maria Gonzalez could also cover her £1,000,000 exposure by purchasing a put option. This technique allows her to speculate on the upside potential for appreciation of the pound while limiting downside risk to a known amount. Maria could purchase from her bank a 3-month put option on £1,000,000 at an at-the-money (ATM) strike price of $1.75/£ with a premium cost of 1.50%. The cost of the option—the premium—is

$$(\text{Size of option}) \times (\text{premium}) \times (\text{spot rate}) = \text{cost of option}$$
$$£1,000,000 \times 0.015 \times \$1.7640 = \$26,460$$

Because we are using future value to compare the various hedging alternatives, it is necessary to project the premium cost of the option forward three months. We will use the cost of capital of 12% per annum or 3% per quarter. Therefore, the premium cost of the put option as of June would be $26,460(1.03) = $27,254. This is equal to $0.0273 per pound ($27,254 ÷ £1,000,000).

When the £1,000,000 is received in June, the value in dollars depends on the spot rate at that time. The upside potential is unlimited, the same as in the unhedged alternative. At any exchange rate above $1.75/£, Trident would allow its option to expire unexercised and would exchange the pounds for dollars at the spot rate. If the expected rate of $1.76/£ materializes, Trident would exchange the £1,000,000 in the spot market for $1,760,000. Net proceeds would be $1,760,000 minus the $27,254 cost of the option, or $1,732,746.

In contrast to the unhedged alternative, downside risk is limited with an option. If the pound depreciates below $1.75/£, Maria would exercise her option to sell (put) £1,000,000 at $1.75/£, receiving $1,750,000 gross, but $1,722,746 net of the $27,254 cost of the option. Although this downside result is worse than the downside of the forward or money market hedges, the upside potential is unlimited.

The essence of the at-the-money (ATM) put option market hedge is as follows:

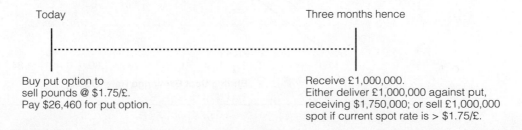

Today

Buy put option to
sell pounds @ $1.75/£.
Pay $26,460 for put option.

Three months hence

Receive £1,000,000.
Either deliver £1,000,000 against put,
receiving $1,750,000; or sell £1,000,000
spot if current spot rate is > $1.75/£.

We can calculate a trading range for the pound that defines the break-even points for the option compared with the other strategies. The upper bound of the range is determined by comparison with the forward rate. The pound must appreciate enough above the $1.7540 forward rate to cover the $0.0273/£ cost of the option. Therefore, the break-even upside spot price of the pound must be $1.7540 + $0.0273 = $1.7813. If the spot pound appreciates above $1.7813, proceeds under the option strategy will be greater than under the forward hedge. If the spot pound ends up below $1.7813, the forward hedge would be superior in retrospect.

The lower bound of the range is determined by the unhedged strategy. If the spot price falls below $1.75/£, Maria will exercise her put and sell the proceeds at $1.75/£. The net proceeds will be $1.75/£ less the $0.0273 cost of the option, or $1.7221/£. If the spot rate falls below $1.7221/£, the net proceeds from exercising the option will be greater than the net proceeds from selling the unhedged pounds in the spot market. At any spot rate above $1.7221/£, the spot proceeds from remaining unhedged will be greater.

Foreign currency options have a variety of hedging uses. A put option is useful to construction firms or other exporters when they must submit a fixed price bid in a foreign currency without knowing until some later date whether their bid is successful. Similarly, a call option is useful to hedge a bid for a foreign business or firm if a potential future foreign currency payment may be required. In either case, if the bid is rejected, the loss is limited to the cost of the option.

Comparison of Alternatives

Exhibit 10.5 shows the value of Trident's £1,000,000 account receivable over a range of possible ending spot exchange rates and hedging alternatives. This exhibit makes it clear that the firm's *view* of likely exchange rate changes aids in the hedging choice.

◆ If the exchange rate is expected to move against Trident—to the left of $1.76/£, the money market hedge is the clearly preferred alternative—a guaranteed value of $1,772,605.

EXHIBIT 10.5   Valuation of Cash Flows under Hedging Alternatives for Trident with Option

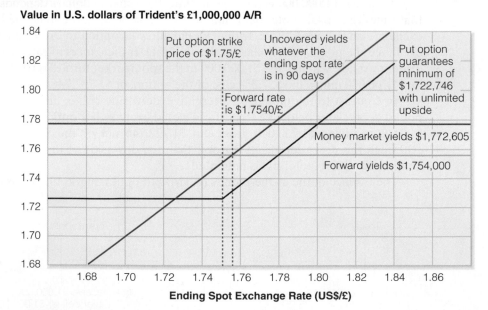

Value in U.S. dollars of Trident's £1,000,000 A/R

◆ If the exchange rate is expected to move in Trident's favor, to the right of $1.76/£, the choice of the hedge is more complex, and lies between remaining unhedged, the money market hedge, or the put option.

Remaining unhedged is most likely an unacceptable choice. If Maria's expectations regarding the future spot rate proved wrong, and the spot rate fell below $1.70/£, she would not reach her budget rate. The put option offers a unique alternative. If the exchange rate moves in Trident's favor, the put option offers nearly the same upside potential as the unhedged alternative except for the up-front costs. If, however, the exchange rate moves against Trident, the put option limits the downside risk to $1,722,746.

Strategy Choice and Outcome

Trident, like all firms attempting to hedge transaction exposure, must decide on a strategy before the exchange rate changes occur. How will Maria Gonzalez choose among the alternative hedging strategies? She must select on the basis of two decision criteria: 1) the *risk tolerance* of Trident, as expressed in its stated policies; and 2) her own *view*, or expectation of the direction (and distance) the exchange rate will move over the coming 90-day period.

Trident's *risk tolerance* is a combination of management's philosophy toward transaction exposure and the specific goals of treasury activities. Many firms believe that currency risk is simply a part of doing business internationally, and therefore, start their analysis from an unhedged baseline. Other firms, however, view currency risk as unacceptable, and either start their analysis from a full forward contract cover baseline, or simply mandate that all transaction exposures be fully covered by forward contracts regardless of the value of other hedging alternatives. The treasury in most firms operates as a cost or *service center* for the firm. On the other hand, if the treasury operates as a *profit center*, it might tolerate taking more risk.

The final choice among hedges—if Maria Gonzalez does expect the pound to appreciate—combines both the firm's risk tolerance, its view, and its confidence in its view. Transaction exposure management with contractual hedges requires managerial judgment.

Management of an Account Payable

The management of an account payable, where the firm would be required to make a foreign currency payment at a future date, is similar but not identical in form. If Trident had a £1,000,000 account payable in 90 days, the hedging choices would appear as follows:

Remain Unhedged. Trident could wait 90 days, exchange dollars for pounds at that time, and make its payment. If Trident expects the spot rate in 90 days to be $1.7600/£, the payment would be expected to cost $1,760,000. This amount is, however, uncertain; the spot exchange rate in 90 days could be very different from that expected.

Forward Market Hedge. Trident could buy £1,000,000 forward, locking in a rate of $1.7540/£, and a total dollar cost of $1,754,000. This is $6,000 less than the expected cost of remaining unhedged, and therefore clearly preferable to the first alternative.

Money Market Hedge. The money market hedge is distinctly different for a payable as opposed to a receivable. To implement a money market hedge in this case, Trident would exchange U.S. dollars spot and invest them for 90 days in a pound-denominated interest-bearing account. The principal and interest in British pounds at the end of the 90-day period would be used to pay the £1,000,000 account payable.

In order to assure that the principal and interest exactly equal the £1,000,000 due in 90 days, Trident would discount the £1,000,000 by the pound investment interest rate of 8% for 90 days in order to determine the pounds needed today:

$$\frac{£1,000,000}{\left[1 + \left(.08 \times \dfrac{90}{360}\right)\right]} = £980,392.16$$

This £980,392.16 needed today would require $1,729,411.77 at the current spot rate of $1.7640/£:

$$£980,392.16 \times \$1.7640/£ = \$1,729,411.77$$

Finally, in order to compare the money market hedge outcome with the other hedging alternatives, the $1,729,411.77 cost today must be carried forward 90 days to the same future date as the other hedge choices. If the current dollar cost is carried forward at Trident's WACC of 12%, the total cost of the money market hedge is $1,781,294.12. This is higher than the forward hedge and therefore unattractive.

$$\$1,729,411.77 \times \left[1 + \left(.12 \times \dfrac{90}{360}\right)\right] = \$1,781,294.12$$

Option Hedge. Trident could cover its £1,000,000 account payable by purchasing a *call option* on £1,000,000. A June call option on British pounds with a near at-the-money strike price of $1.75/£ would cost 1.5% (premium) or

$$£1,000,000 \times 0.015 \times \$1.7640/£ = \$26,460$$

This premium, regardless of whether the call option is exercised or not, will be paid up-front. Its value carried forward 90 days at the WACC of 12%, would raise its end of period cost to $27,254.

If the spot rate in 90 days is less than $1.75/£, the option would be allowed to expire and the £1,000,000 for the payable purchased on the spot market. The total cost of the call option hedge if the option is not exercised is theoretically smaller than any other alternative (with the exception of remaining unhedged, because the option premium is still paid and lost). If the spot rate in 90 days exceeds $1.75/£, the call option would be exercised. The total cost of the call option hedge if exercised is as follows:

Exercise call option (£1,000,000 × $1.75/£)	$1,750,000
Call option premium (carried forward 90 days)	27,254
Total maximum expense of call option hedge	$1,777,254

The four hedging methods of managing a £1,000,000 account payable for Trident are summarized in Exhibit 10.6. The costs of the forward hedge and money market hedge are certain. The cost using the call option hedge is calculated as a maximum, and the cost of remaining unhedged is highly uncertain.

As with Trident's account receivable, the final hedging choice depends on the confidence of Maria's exchange rate expectations, and her willingness to bear risk. The forward hedge provides the lowest cost of making the account payable payment that is certain. If the dollar strengthens against the pound, ending up at a spot rate less than $1.75/£, the call option could potentially be the lowest cost hedge. Given an expected spot rate of $1.76/£, however, the forward hedge appears the preferred alternative.

EXHIBIT 10.6   Valuation of Hedging Alternatives for an Account Payable

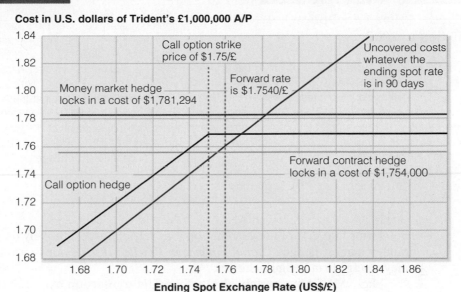

Cost in U.S. dollars of Trident's £1,000,000 A/P

Call option strike price of $1.75/£

Money market hedge locks in a cost of $1,781,294

Forward rate is $1.7540/£

Uncovered costs whatever the ending spot rate is in 90 days

Call option hedge

Forward contract hedge locks in a cost of $1,754,000

Ending Spot Exchange Rate (US$/£)

Risk Management in Practice

As many different approaches to exposure management exist as there are firms. A variety of surveys of corporate risk management practices in recent years in the United States, the United Kingdom, Finland, Australia, and Germany, indicate no real consensus exists regarding the best approach. The following is our attempt to assimilate the basic results of these surveys and combine them with our own personal experiences.

Which Goals?   The treasury function of most private firms, the group typically responsible for transaction exposure management, is usually considered a cost center. It is not expected to add profit to the firm's bottom-line (which is not the same thing as saying it is not expected to add value to the firm). Currency risk managers are expected to err on the conservative side when managing the firm's money.

Which Exposures?   Transaction exposures exist before they are actually booked as foreign currency-denominated receivables and payables. However, many firms do not allow the hedging of quotation exposure or backlog exposure as a matter of policy. The reasoning is straightforward: until the transaction exists on the accounting books of the firm, the probability of the exposure actually occurring is considered to be less than 100%. Conservative hedging policies dictate that contractual hedges be placed only on existing exposures.

An increasing number of firms, however, are actively hedging not only backlog exposures, but also selectively hedging quotation and *anticipated exposures*. *Anticipated exposures* are transactions for which there are—at present—no contracts or agreements between parties, but are anticipated on the basis of historical trends and continuing business relationships. Although this may appear to be overly speculative on the part of these firms, it may be that hedging expected foreign-currency payables and receivables for future periods is the most conservative approach to protect the firm's future operating revenues.

Which Contractual Hedges?   As might be expected, transaction exposure management programs are generally divided along an "option-line," those that use options and those that do

GLOBAL FINANCE IN PRACTICE   10.1

The Credit Crisis and Option Volatilities in 2009

The global credit crisis had a number of lasting impacts on corporate foreign exchange hedging practices in late 2008 and early 2009. Currency volatilities rose to some of the highest levels seen in years, and stayed there. This caused option premiums to rise so dramatically that many companies were much more selective in their use of currency options in their risk management programs.

The dollar-euro volatility was a prime example. As recently as July 2007, the implied volatility for the most widely traded currency cross was below 7% for maturities from one week to three years. By October 31, 2008, the 1-month implied volatility had reached 29%. Although this was seemingly the peak, 1-month implied volatilities were still over 20% on January 30, 2009.

This makes options very expensive. For example, the premium on a 1-month call option on the euro with a strike rate forward-at-the-money at the end of January 2009 rose from $0.0096/€ to $0.0286/€ when volatility is 20%, not 7%. For a notional principal of €1 million, that is an increase in price from $9,580 to $28,640. That will put a hole in any treasury department's budget.

not. Firms that do not use currency options rely almost exclusively on forward contracts and money market hedges. *Global Finance in Practice 10.1* demonstrates how market condition may change firm hedging choices.

Many MNEs have established rather rigid transaction exposure risk management policies which mandate *proportional hedging*. These policies generally require the use of forward contract hedges on a percentage (e.g., 50, 60, or 70%) of existing transaction exposures. As the maturity of the exposures lengthens, the percentage forward-cover required decreases. The remaining portion of the exposure is then selectively hedged on the basis of the firm's risk tolerance, view of exchange rate movements, and confidence level. Although rarely acknowledged by the firms themselves, selective hedging is essentially speculation. Significant question remains as to whether a firm or a financial manager can consistently predict the future direction of exchange rates.

Translation Exposure

Translation exposure, the second category of accounting exposures, arises because financial statements of foreign subsidiaries—which are stated in foreign currency—must be restated in the parent's reporting currency for the firm to prepare consolidated financial statements. Foreign subsidiaries of U.S. companies, for example, must restate local euro, pound, yen, etc., statements into U.S. dollars so the foreign values can be added to the parent's U.S. dollar-denominated balance sheet and income statement. This accounting process is called "translation." *Translation exposure* is the potential for an increase or decrease in the parent's net worth and reported net income caused by a change in exchange rates since the last translation.

Although the main purpose of translation is to prepare consolidated statements, translated statements are also used by management to assess the performance of foreign subsidiaries. Although such assessment might be performed from the local currency statements, restatement of all subsidiary statements into the single "common denominator" of one currency facilitates management comparison.

Overview of Translation

There are two financial statements for each subsidiary which must be translated for consolidation: the *income statement* and the *balance sheet*. (Statements of cash flow are not translated from the foreign subsidiaries.) The consolidated statement of cash flow is constructed from the consolidated statement of income and consolidated balance sheet. Because the consolidated results for any multinational firm are constructed from all of its subsidiary operations, including foreign subsidiaries, the possibility of a change in consolidated net income or consolidated net worth from period to period, as a result of a change in exchange rates, is high.

For any individual financial statement, internally, if the same exchange rate were used to remeasure each and every line item on the individual statement, the income statement and balance sheet, there would be no imbalances resulting from the remeasurement. But if a different exchange rate were used for different line items on an individual statement, an imbalance would result. Different exchange rates are used in remeasuring different line items because translation principles are a complex compromise between historical and current values. The question, then, is what is to be done with the imbalance?

Subsidiary Characterization. Most countries specify the translation method to be used by a foreign subsidiary based on its business operations. For example, a foreign subsidiary's business can be categorized as either an *integrated foreign entity* or a *self-sustaining foreign entity*. An *integrated foreign entity* is one which operates as an extension of the parent company, with cash flows and general business lines that are highly interrelated with those of the parent. A *self-sustaining foreign entity* is one which operates in the local economic environment independent of the parent company. The differentiation is important to the logic of translation. A foreign subsidiary should be valued principally in terms of the currency that is the basis of its economic viability.

It is not unusual for a single company to have both types of foreign subsidiaries, *integrated* and *self-sustaining*. For example, a U.S.-based manufacturer that produces subassemblies in the United States which are then shipped to a Spanish subsidiary for finishing and resale in the European Union would likely characterize the Spanish subsidiary as an *integrated foreign entity*. The dominant currency of economic operation is likely the U.S. dollar. That same U.S. parent may also own an agricultural marketing business in Venezuela that has few cash flows or operations related to the U.S. parent company or U.S. dollar. The Venezuelan subsidiary may source all inputs and sell all products in Venezuelan bolivar. Because the Venezuelan subsidiary's operations are independent of its parent, and its functional currency is the Venezuelan bolivar, it would be classified as a *self-sustaining foreign entity*.

Functional Currency. A foreign subsidiary's *functional currency* is the currency of the primary economic environment in which the subsidiary operates and in which it generates cash flows. In other words, it is the dominant currency used by that foreign subsidiary in its day-to-day operations. It is important to note that the geographic location of a foreign subsidiary and its functional currency may be different. The Singapore subsidiary of a U.S. firm may find that its functional currency is the U.S. dollar (*integrated* subsidiary), the Singapore dollar (*self-sustaining* subsidiary), or a third currency such as the British pound (also a *self-sustaining* subsidiary). The United States, rather than distinguishing a foreign subsidiary as either integrated or self-sustaining, requires that the functional currency of the subsidiary be determined.

Management must evaluate the nature and purpose of each of its individual foreign subsidiaries to determine the appropriate functional currency for each. If a foreign subsidiary of a U.S.-based company is determined to have the U.S. dollar as its functional currency, it is essentially an extension of the parent company (equivalent to the integrated foreign entity designation used by most countries). If, however, the functional currency of the foreign subsidiary is determined to be different from the U.S. dollar, the subsidiary is considered a separate entity from the parent (equivalent to the self-sustaining entity designation).

Translation Methods

Two basic methods for translation are employed worldwide, the *current rate method* and the *temporal method*. Regardless of which method is employed, a translation method must not only designate at what exchange rate individual balance sheet and income statement items are remeasured, but also designate where any imbalance is to be recorded, either in current income or in an equity reserve account in the balance sheet.

Current Rate Method. The current rate method is the most prevalent in the world today. Under this method, all financial statement line items are translated at the "current" exchange rate with few exceptions.

◆ *Assets and Liabilities.* All assets and liabilities are translated at the current rate of exchange; that is, at the rate of exchange in effect on the balance sheet date.

◆ *Income Statement Items.* All items, including depreciation and cost of goods sold, are translated at either the actual exchange rate on the dates the various revenues, expenses, gains, and losses were incurred or at an appropriately weighted average exchange rate for the period.

◆ *Distributions.* Dividends paid are translated at the exchange rate in effect on the date of payment.

◆ *Equity Items.* Common stock and paid-in capital accounts are translated at historical rates. Year-end retained earnings consist of the original year-beginning retained earnings plus or minus any income or loss for the year.

Gains or losses caused by translation adjustments are *not* included in the calculation of consolidated net income. Rather, translation gains or losses are reported separately and accumulated in a separate equity reserve account (on the consolidated balance sheet) with a title such as "cumulative translation adjustment" (CTA), but it depends on the country. If a foreign subsidiary is later sold or liquidated, translation gains or losses of past years accumulated in the CTA account are reported as one component of the total gain or loss on sale or liquidation. The total gain or loss is reported as part of the net income or loss for the time period in which the sale or liquidation occurs.

Temporal Method. Under the temporal method, specific assets and liabilities are translated at exchange rates consistent with the timing of the item's creation. The *temporal method* assumes that a number of individual line item assets such as inventory and net plant and equipment are restated regularly to reflect market value. If these items were not restated but were instead carried at historical cost, the temporal method becomes the *monetary/nonmonetary method* of translation, a form of translation that is still used by a number of countries today. Line items include the following:

◆ *Monetary assets* (primarily cash, marketable securities, accounts receivable, and long-term receivables) and *monetary liabilities* (primarily current liabilities and long-term debt). These are translated at current exchange rates. *Nonmonetary assets and liabilities* (primarily inventory and fixed assets) are translated at historical rates.

◆ *Income Statement Items.* These are translated at the average exchange rate for the period, except for items such as depreciation and cost of goods sold that are directly associated with nonmonetary assets or liabilities. These accounts are translated at their historical rate.

◆ *Distributions.* Dividends paid are translated at the exchange rate in effect on the date of payment.

◆ *Equity Items.* Common stock and paid-in capital accounts are translated at historical rates. Year-end retained earnings consist of the original year-beginning retained earnings plus or minus any income or loss for the year, plus or minus any imbalance from translation.

Under the temporal method, gains or losses resulting from remeasurement are carried directly to current consolidated income, and not to equity reserves. Hence, foreign exchange gains and losses arising from the translation process do introduce volatility to consolidated earnings.

U.S. Translation Procedures. The United States differentiates foreign subsidiaries on the basis of functional currency, not subsidiary characterization. A note on terminology: Under U.S. accounting and translation practices, use of the current rate method is termed "translation" while use of the temporal method is termed "remeasurement." The primary principles of U.S. translation are summarized as follows:

◆ If the financial statements of the foreign subsidiary of a U.S. company are maintained in U.S. dollars, translation is not required.

◆ If the financial statements of the foreign subsidiary are maintained in the local currency and the local currency is the *functional currency*, they are translated by the *current rate method*.

◆ If the financial statements of the foreign subsidiary are maintained in the local currency and the U.S. dollar is the *functional currency*, they are remeasured by the *temporal method*.

◆ If the financial statements of foreign subsidiaries are in the local currency and neither the local currency nor the dollar is the functional currency, then the statements must first be remeasured into the functional currency by the temporal method, and then translated into dollars by the current rate method.

◆ U.S. translation practices have a special provision for translating statements of foreign subsidiaries operating in *hyperinflation countries*. These are countries where cumulative inflation has been 100% or more over a 3-year period. In this case, the subsidiary must use the temporal method.

A final note: The selection of the functional currency is determined by the economic realities of the subsidiary's operations, and is not a discretionary management decision on preferred procedures or elective outcomes. Since many U.S.-based multinationals have numerous foreign subsidiaries, some dollar-functional and some foreign currency-functional, currency gains and losses may be passing through both current consolidated income and/or accruing in equity reserves.

International Translation Practices. Many of the world's largest industrial countries use International Accounting Standards Committee (IASC), and therefore the same basic translation procedure. A foreign subsidiary is an *integrated foreign entity* or a *self-sustaining foreign entity*; *integrated foreign entities* are typically remeasured using the *temporal method* (or some slight variation thereof); and *self-sustaining foreign entities* are translated at the *current rate method*, also termed the *closing-rate method*.

Trident Corporation's Translation Exposure

Trident Corporation, first introduced in Chapter 1 and shown in Exhibit 10.7, is a U.S.-based corporation, with a U.S. business unit, as well as foreign subsidiaries in both Europe and China. The company is publicly traded and its shares are traded on the New York Stock Exchange (NYSE).

Each subsidiary of Trident—the United States, Europe, and China—will have its own financial statement. Each set of financials will be constructed in the local currency (yuan, dollar, euro), but the subsidiary income statements and balance sheets will also be translated into U.S. dollars, the reporting currency of the company, for consolidation and reporting. As a

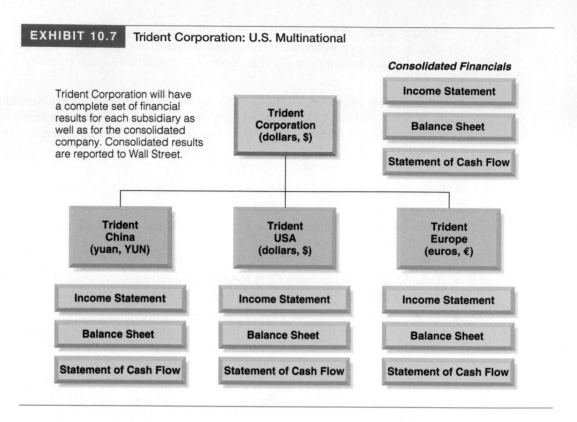

EXHIBIT 10.7 Trident Corporation: U.S. Multinational

Trident Corporation will have a complete set of financial results for each subsidiary as well as for the consolidated company. Consolidated results are reported to Wall Street.

U.S.-based corporation whose shares are traded on the NYSE, it will report all of its final results in U.S. dollars.

Trident Corporation's Translation Exposure: Income

Trident Corporation's sales and earnings by operating unit for 2009 and 2010 are described in Exhibit 10.8.

EXHIBIT 10.8 Trident Corporation, Selected Financial Results, 2009–2010

	Sales (millions, local currency)			Average Exchange Rate ($/€ and YUN/$)			Sales (millions of US$)		
	2009	2010	% Change	2009	2010	% Change	2009	2010	% Change
United States	$280	$300	7.1%	—	—		$280.0	$300.0	7.1%
Europe	€118	€120	1.7%	1.4000	1.3200	−5.71%	$165.2	$158.4	−4.1%
China	YUN600	YUN600	0.0%	6.8300	6.7000	1.94%	$87.8	$89.6	1.9%
Total							$533.0	$548.0	2.8%

	Earnings (millions, local currency)			Average Exchange Rate ($/€ and YUN/$)			Earnings (millions of US$)		
	2009	2010	% Change	2009	2010	% Change	2009	2010	% Change
United States	$28.2	$28.6	1.4%	—	—		$28.2	$28.6	1.4%
Europe	€10.4	€10.5	1.0%	1.4000	1.3200	−5.71%	$14.6	$13.9	−4.8%
China	YUN71.4	YUN71.4	0.0%	6.8300	6.7000	1.94%	$10.5	$10.7	1.9%
Total							$53.2	$53.1	−0.2%

- ◆ **Consolidated Sales.** For 2010, the company generated $300 million in sales in its U.S. unit, $158.4 million in its European subsidiary (€120 million at $1.32/€), and $89.6 million in its Chinese subsidiary (YUN600 million at YUN6.70/$). Total global sales for 2010 were $548.0 million. This constituted sales growth of 2.8% over 2009.

- ◆ **Consolidated Earnings.** The company's earnings (profits) fell in 2010, dropping to $53.1 million from $53.2 million in 2009. Although not a large fall, Wall Street would not react favorably to a fall in consolidated earnings.

A closer look at the sales and earnings by country, however, yields some interesting insights. Sales and earnings in the U.S. unit rose, sales growing 7.1% and earnings growing 1.4%. Since the U.S. unit makes up more than half of the total company's sales and profits, this is very important. The Chinese subsidiary's sales and earnings were identical in 2009 and 2010 when measured in local currency, Chinese yuan. The Chinese yuan, however, was revalued against the U.S. dollar by the Chinese government, from YUN6.83/$ to YUN6.70/$. The result was the dollar value of both Chinese sales and profits rose.

The European subsidiary's financial results are even more striking. Sales and earnings in Europe in euros grew from 2009 to 2010. Sales grew 1.7% while earnings increased 1.0%. But the euro depreciated against the dollar, falling from $1.40/€ to $1.32/€. This depreciation of 5.7% resulted in the financial results of European operations falling in dollar terms. As a result, Trident's consolidated earnings, as reported dollars, fell in 2010. One can imagine the discussion and debate within Trident, and with the analysts who follow the firm, of the fall in earnings reported to Wall Street.

Translation Exposure: Balance Sheet

Let us continue the example of Trident focusing here on the balance sheet of its European subsidiary. We will illustrate translation by both methods, the temporal method and current rate method, in order to show the very arbitrary nature of a translation gain or loss. The functional currency of Trident Europe is the euro, and the reporting currency of its parent, Trident Corporation, is the U.S. dollar.

Our analysis assumes that plant and equipment and long-term debt were acquired, and common stock issued, by Trident Europe some time in the past when the exchange rate was $1.2760/€. Inventory currently on hand was purchased or manufactured during the immediately prior quarter when the average exchange rate was $1.2180/€. At the close of business on Monday, December 31, 2010, the current spot exchange rate was $1.2000/€. When business reopened on January 3, 2011, after the New Year holiday, the euro had dropped in value versus the dollar to $1.0000/€.

Current Rate Method. Exhibit 10.9 illustrates translation loss using the current rate method. Assets and liabilities on the predepreciation balance sheet are translated at the current exchange rate of $1.2000/€. Capital stock is translated at the historical rate of $1.2760/€, and retained earnings are translated at a composite rate that is equivalent to having each past year's addition to retained earnings translated at the exchange rate in effect in that year.

The sum of retained earnings and the CTA account must "balance" the liabilities and net worth section of the balance sheet with the asset side. For this hypothetical example, we have assumed the two amounts used for the December 31 balance sheet. As shown in Exhibit 10.9, the "just before depreciation" dollar translation reports an accumulated translation loss from prior periods of $136,800. This balance is the cumulative gain or loss from translating euro statements into dollars in prior years.

After the depreciation, Trident Corporation translates assets and liabilities at the new exchange rate of $1.0000/€. Equity accounts, including retained earnings, are translated just as they were before depreciation, and as a result the cumulative translation loss

EXHIBIT 10.9   Trident Europe's Translation Loss after Depreciation of the Euro: Current Rate Method

Assets	In Euros (€)	December 31, 2010 Exchange Rate (US$/euro)	December 31, 2010 Translated Accounts (US$)	January 2, 2011 Exchange Rate (US$/euro)	January 2, 2011 Translated Accounts (US$)
Cash	1,600,000	1.2000	$ 1,920,000	1.0000	$ 1,600,000
Accounts receivable	3,200,000	1.2000	3,840,000	1.0000	3,200,000
Inventory	2,400,000	1.2000	2,880,000	1.0000	2,400,000
Net plant and equipment	4,800,000	1.2000	5,760,000	1.0000	4,800,000
Total	12,000,000		$14,400,000		$12,000,000
Liabilities and Net Worth					
Accounts payable	800,000	1.2000	$ 960,000	1.0000	$800,000
Short-term bank debt	1,600,000	1.2000	1,920,000	1.0000	1,600,000
Long-term debt	1,600,000	1.2000	1,920,000	1.0000	1,600,000
Common stock	1,800,000	1.2760	2,296,800	1.2760	2,296,800
Retained earnings	6,200,000	1.2000 (a)	7,440,000	1.2000 (b)	7,440,000
Translation adjustment (CTA)	—		$ (136,800)		$(1,736,800)
Total	12,000,000		$14,400,000		$12,000,000

(a) Dollar retained earnings before depreciation are the cumulative sum of additions to retained earnings of all prior years, translated at exchange rates in each year.

(b) Translated into dollars at the same rate as before depreciation of the euro.

increases to $1,736,800. The increase of $1,600,000 in this account (from a cumulative loss of $136,800 to a new cumulative loss of $1,736,800) is the translation loss measured by the current rate method.

This translation loss is a decrease in equity, measured in the parent's reporting currency, of "net exposed assets." An "exposed asset" is an asset whose value drops with the depreciation of the functional currency and rises with an appreciation of that currency. "Net" exposed assets in this context means exposed assets minus exposed liabilities. Net exposed assets are positive (that is, "long") if exposed assets exceed exposed liabilities. They are negative ("short") if exposed assets are smaller than exposed liabilities.

Temporal Method. Translation of the same accounts under the temporal method shows the arbitrary nature of any gain or loss from translation. This is illustrated in Exhibit 10.10. Monetary assets and monetary liabilities in the predepreciation euro balance sheet are translated at the current rate of exchange, but other assets and the equity accounts are translated at their historic rates. For Trident Europe, the historical rate for inventory differs from that for net plant and equipment because inventory was acquired more recently.

Under the temporal method, translation losses are not accumulated in a separate equity account but passed directly through each quarter's income statement. Thus, in the dollar balance sheet translated before depreciation, retained earnings were the cumulative result of earnings from all prior years translated at historical rates in effect each year, plus translation gains or losses from all prior years. In Exhibit 10.10, no translation loss appears in the predepreciation dollar balance sheet because any losses would have been closed to retained earnings.

The effect of the depreciation is to create an immediate translation loss of $160,000. This amount is shown as a separate line item in Exhibit 10.10 in order to focus attention on it for this example. Under the temporal method, this translation loss of $160,000 would pass

EXHIBIT 10.10	Trident Europe's Translation Loss after Depreciation of the Euro: Temporal Method

		December 31, 2010		January 2, 2011	
Assets	In Euros (€)	Exchange Rate (US$/euro)	Translated Accounts (US$)	Exchange Rate (US$/euro)	Translated Accounts (US$)
Cash	1,600,000	1.2000	$ 1,920,000	1.0000	$ 1,600,000
Accounts receivable	3,200,000	1.2000	3,840,000	1.0000	3,200,000
Inventory	2,400,000	1.2180	2,923,200	1.2180	2,923,200
Net plant and equipment	4,800,000	1.2760	6,124,800	1.2760	6,124,800
Total	12,000,000		$14,808,000		$13,848,000
Liabilities and Net Worth					
Accounts payable	800,000	1.2000	$ 960,000	1.0000	$ 800,000
Short-term bank debt	1,600,000	1.2000	1,920,000	1.0000	1,600,000
Long-term debt	1,600,000	1.2000	1,920,000	1.0000	1,600,000
Common stock	1,800,000	1.2760	2,296,800	1.2760	2,296,800
Retained earnings	6,200,000	1.2437 (a)	7,711,200	1.2437 (b)	7,711,200
Translation gain (loss)	—			(c)	$ (160,000)
Total	12,000,000		$14,808,000		$13,848,000

(a) Dollar retained earnings before depreciation are the cumulative sum of additions to retained earnings of all prior years, translated at exchange rates in each year.

(b) Translated into dollars at the same rate as before depreciation of the euro.

(c) Under the temporal method, the translation loss of $160,000 would be closed into retained earnings through the income statement rather than left as a separate line item as shown here. Ending retained earnings would actually be $7,711,200 − $160,000 = $7,551,200.

through the income statement, reducing reported net income and reducing retained earnings. Ending retained earnings would in fact be $7,711,200 minus $160,000, or $7,551,200. Whether gains and losses pass through the income statement under the temporal method depends upon the country.

Managerial Implications

In the case of Trident, the translation loss or gain was larger under the current rate method because inventory and net plant and equipment, as well as all monetary assets, are deemed exposed. When net exposed assets are larger, gains or losses from translation are also larger. If management expects a foreign currency to depreciate, it could minimize translation exposure by reducing net exposed assets. If management anticipates an appreciation of the foreign currency, it should increase net exposed assets to benefit from a gain.

Depending on the accounting method, management might select different assets and liabilities for reduction or increase. Thus, "real" decisions about investing and financing might be dictated by which accounting technique is required, when in fact, the method of reporting should be neutral in its influence on operating and financing decisions.

Managing Translation Exposure

The main technique to minimize translation exposure is called a *balance sheet hedge*. At times, some firms have attempted to hedge translation exposure in the forward market. Such action amounts to speculating in the forward market in the hope that a cash profit will be realized to offset the noncash loss from translation. Success depends on a precise prediction of future exchange rates, for such a hedge will not work over a range of possible future spot rates. In addition, the profit from the forward "hedge" (i.e., speculation) is taxable, but the translation loss does not reduce taxable income.

Balance Sheet Hedge Defined. A balance sheet hedge requires an equal amount of *exposed* foreign currency assets and liabilities on a firm's consolidated balance sheet. If this can be achieved for each foreign currency, net translation exposure will be zero. A change in exchange rates will change the value of exposed liabilities in an equal amount but in a direction opposite to the change in value of exposed assets. If a firm translates by the temporal method, a zero net exposed position is called *monetary balance*. Complete monetary balance cannot be achieved under the current rate method because total assets would have to be matched by an equal amount of debt, but the equity section of the balance sheet must still be translated at historic exchange rates.

The cost of a balance sheet hedge depends on relative borrowing costs. If foreign currency borrowing costs, after adjusting for foreign exchange risk, are higher than parent currency borrowing costs, the balance sheet hedge is costly, and vice versa. Normal operations, however, already require decisions about the magnitude and currency denomination of specific balance sheet accounts. Thus, balance sheet hedges are a compromise in which the denomination of balance sheet accounts is altered, perhaps at a cost in terms of interest expense or operating efficiency, to achieve some degree of foreign exchange protection.

To achieve a balance sheet hedge, Trident Corporation must either 1) reduce exposed euro assets without simultaneously reducing euro liabilities, or 2) increase euro liabilities without simultaneously increasing euro assets. One way to do this is to exchange existing euro cash for dollars. If Trident Europe does not have large euro cash balances, it can borrow euros and exchange the borrowed euros for dollars. Another subsidiary could borrow euros and exchange them for dollars. That is, the essence of the hedge is for the parent or any of its subsidiaries to create euro debt and exchange the proceeds for dollars.

Current Rate Method. Under the current rate method, Trident should borrow as much as €8,000,000. The initial effect of this first step is to increase both an exposed asset (cash) and an exposed liability (notes payable) on the balance sheet of Trident Europe, with no immediate effect on *net* exposed assets. The required follow-up step can take two forms: 1) Trident Europe could exchange the acquired euros for U.S. dollars and hold those dollars itself, or 2) it could transfer the borrowed euros to Trident Corporation, perhaps as a euro dividend or as repayment of intracompany debt. Trident Corporation could then exchange the euros for dollars. In some countries, local monetary authorities will not allow their currency to be so freely exchanged.

Another possibility would be for Trident Corporation or a sister subsidiary to borrow the euros, thus keeping the euro debt entirely off Trident's books. However, the second step is still essential to eliminate euro exposure; the borrowing entity must exchange the euros for dollars or other unexposed assets. Any such borrowing should be coordinated with all other euro borrowings to avoid the possibility that one subsidiary is borrowing euros to reduce translation exposure at the same time as another subsidiary is repaying euro debt. (Note that euros can be "borrowed," by simply delaying repayment of existing euro debt; the goal is to increase euro debt, not borrow in a literal sense.)

Temporal Method. If translation is by the temporal method, the much smaller amount of only €800,000 need be borrowed. As before, Trident Europe could use the proceeds of the loan to acquire U.S. dollars. However, Trident Europe could also use the proceeds to acquire inventory or fixed assets in Europe. Under the temporal method, these assets are not regarded as exposed and do not drop in dollar value when the euro depreciates.

When Is a Balance Sheet Hedge Justified?

If a firm's subsidiary is using the local currency as the functional currency, the following circumstances could justify when to use a balance sheet hedge:

◆ The foreign subsidiary is about to be liquidated, so that value of its CTA would be realized.

◆ The firm has debt covenants or bank agreements that state the firm's debt/equity ratios will be maintained within specific limits.

◆ Management is evaluated on the basis of certain income statement and balance sheet measures that are affected by translation losses or gains.

◆ The foreign subsidiary is operating in a hyperinflationary environment.

If a firm is using the parent's home currency as the functional currency of the foreign subsidiary, all transaction gains/losses are passed through to the income statement. Hedging this consolidated income to reduce its variability may be important to investors and bond rating agencies.

In the end, accounting exposure is a topic of great concern and complex choices for all multinationals. As demonstrated by *Global Finance in Practice 10.2*, despite the best of intentions and structures, business itself may dictate hedging outcomes.

GLOBAL FINANCE IN PRACTICE   10.2

When Business Dictates Hedging Results

GM Asia, a regional subsidiary of GM Corporation, U.S., held major corporate interests in a variety of countries and companies, including Daewoo Auto. GM had acquired control of Daewoo of South Korea's automobile operations in 2001. The following years had been very good for the Daewoo unit, and by 2009, GM Daewoo was selling automobile components and vehicles to more than 100 countries.

Daewoo's success meant that it had expected sales (receivables) from buyers all over the world. What was even more remarkable was that the global automobile industry now used the U.S. dollar more than ever as its currency of contract for cross-border transactions. This meant that Daewoo did not really have dozens of foreign currencies to manage, just one, the U.S. dollar. So Daewoo of Korea had, in late 2007 and early 2008, entered into a series of *forward exchange contracts*. These currency contracts locked in the Korean won value of the many dollar-denominated receivables the company *expected* to receive from international automobile sales in the coming year. In the eyes of many, this was a conservative and responsible currency hedging policy; that is, until the global financial crisis and the following collapse of global automobile sales.

The problem for Daewoo was not that the Korean won per U.S. dollar exchange rate had moved dramatically; it had not. The problem was that Daewoo's sales, like all other automobile industry participants, had collapsed. The sales had not taken place, and therefore the underlying exposures, the expected receivables in dollars by Daewoo, had not happened. But GM still had to contractually deliver on the forward contracts. It would cost GM Daewoo Won2,300 billion. GM's Daewoo unit was now broke, its equity wiped out by currency hedging gone bad. GM Asia needed money, quickly, and selling interests in its highly successful Chinese and Indian businesses was the only solution.

Summary of Learning Objectives

Distinguish between the three major foreign exchange exposures experienced by firms.

◆ MNEs encounter three types of currency exposure: transaction exposure; translation exposure, and operating exposure.

◆ *Transaction exposure* measures gains or losses that arise from the settlement of financial obligations whose terms are stated in a foreign currency.

◆ *Operating exposure*, also called *economic exposure*, measures the change in the present value of the firm resulting from any change in future operating cash flows of the firm caused by an *unexpected* change in exchange rates.

◆ *Translation exposure* is the potential for accounting-derived changes in owner's equity to occur because of the need to "translate" foreign currency financial statements of foreign affiliates into a single reporting currency to prepare worldwide consolidated financial statements.

Analyze the pros and cons of hedging foreign exchange transaction exposure.

◆ Considerable theoretical debate exists as to whether firms should hedge currency risk. Theoretically, hedging reduces the variability of the cash flows to the firm. It does not increase the cash flows to the firm. In fact, the costs of hedging may potentially lower them.

Examine the alternatives available to a firm to manage a large and significant transaction exposure.

◆ Transaction exposure can be managed by contractual techniques and certain operating strategies. Contractual hedging techniques include forward, futures, money market, and option hedges.

◆ The choice of which contractual hedge to use depends on the individual firm's currency risk tolerance and its expectation of the probable movement of exchange rates over the transaction exposure period.

◆ In general, if an exchange rate is expected to move in a firm's favor, the preferred contractual hedges are probably those which allow it to participate in some up-side potential, but protect it against significant adverse exchange rate movements.

◆ In general, if the exchange rate is expected to move against the firm, the preferred contractual hedge is one which locks in an exchange rate, such as the forward contract hedge or money market hedge.

Evaluate the institutional practices and concerns of conducting foreign exchange risk management in practice.

◆ Risk management in practice requires a firm's treasury department to identify its goals. Is treasury a cost center or profit center?

◆ Treasury must also choose which contractual hedges it wishes to use and what proportion of the currency risk should be hedged. Additionally, treasury must determine whether the firm should buy and/or sell currency options, a strategy that has historically been risky for some firms and banks.

Demonstrate how translation practices result in a foreign exchange exposure for the multinational enterprise.

◆ Translation exposure results from translating foreign–currency-denominated statements of foreign subsidiaries into the parent's reporting currency so the

parent can prepare consolidated financial statements. Translation exposure is the potential for loss or gain from this translation process.

Explain the meaning behind the designation of a foreign subsidiary's "functional currency."

◆ A foreign subsidiary's functional currency is the currency of the primary economic environment in which the subsidiary operates and in which it generates cash flows. In other words, it is the dominant currency used by that foreign subsidiary in its day-to-day operations.

Illustrate both the theoretical and practical differences between the two primary methods of converting foreign currency denominated financial statements into the reporting currency of the parent company.

◆ The two basic procedures for translation used in most countries today are the current rate method and the temporal method.

◆ Technical aspects of translation include questions about when to recognize gains or losses in the income statement, the distinction between functional and reporting currency, and the treatment of subsidiaries in hyperinflation countries.

Compare translation exposure with operating exposure.

◆ Translation gains and losses can be quite different from operating gains and losses, not only in magnitude but also in sign. Management may need to determine which is of greater significance prior to deciding which exposure is to be managed first.

Analyze the costs and benefits of managing translation exposure.

◆ The main technique for managing translation exposure is a balance sheet hedge. This calls for having an equal amount of exposed foreign currency assets and liabilities.

◆ Even if management chooses to follow an active policy of hedging translation exposure, it is nearly impossible to offset both transaction and translation exposure simultaneously. If forced to choose, most managers will protect against transaction losses because these are realized cash losses, rather than protect against translation losses.

MINI-CASE

Banbury Impex (India)[1]

As November 2010 came to a close, CEO Aadesh Lapura of Banbury Impex Private Limited, a textile company in India, sat in his office in solitude looking over his company's financial statements. It looked like 2010 would close with a small growth in sales and a small drop in profits. Although Banbury's profits were positive, the prospects of about 1.5% return on sales were simply not good enough moving forward. He now had two problems: negotiating a short-term prospective sale to a Turkish company, and increasing his overall profitability, which was a larger, long-term problem.

Lapura concluded that overall profitability—or lack thereof—was a result of two price forces. The first was the rapid rise in the price of cotton. A major cost driver in the textiles industry, cotton prices had risen dramatically in 2010. The second issue was clearly the rising value of the Indian rupee (INR) against the U.S. dollar (USD). Banbury's sales were all invoiced in U.S. dollars, and the dollar was falling. Profit margins were down, and he needed to move quickly.

Banbury Fabrics

Founded in 1997, Banbury Impex Private Ltd. was a family-owned enterprise that manufactured and exported apparel fabrics. The company expected sales close to INR 25.6 crores or USD 5.4 million (a *crore*, cr, is a unit in the Indian numbering system equal to 10 million) in 2010 as illustrated in Exhibit 1. Sales were flat, operating income was declining, and—to be honest—prospects bleak.

Banbury's sales were nearly all exported, mainly to the Middle East (50%), South America (30%), and Europe (10%). Banbury's products included a range of blended woven fabrics made from viscose, cotton, and wool. The company operated two weaving units based in India.

The company's sales growth had been slow over the past five years, averaging about 2.5% per year. However, management had been satisfied with 5% margins in 2006 and 2007 in a highly competitive business environment. Cash flows had remained relatively predictable as Lapura had managed foreign exchange risks by using forward contracts. Choosing to invoice all international sales in USD helped provide further stability in mitigating raw material costs as international cotton prices were priced in USD. All things considered, Banbury's profit projections for 2011 looked disastrously low.

The Indian Textile Industry

The Indian textile industry has been a major contributor to Indian GDP over the past several years. After dismantling the quota regime in 2005, the government had hoped

---

EXHIBIT 1	Banbury Impex Private Ltd—Sales and Income

	2006	2007	2008	2009	Expected 2010	Forecast 2011
Sales (USD)	5,000,000	5,100,000	5,202,000	5,306,040	5,412,161	5,520,404
Average rate (INR/USD)	44.6443	41.7548	43.6976	46.8997	44.8624	45.2500
Sales (INR)	223,221,500	212,949,480	227,314,915	248,851,684	242,802,523	249,798,282
Cost of goods sold (INR)	151,790,620	144,805,646	159,120,441	216,500,965	235,518,447	242,304,333
Cotton Costs	57,680,436	55,026,146	60,465,767	84,435,376	124,824,777	128,421,297
Direct Labor	19,732,781	28,961,129	38,188,906	47,630,212	49,458,874	48,460,867
Weaving Charges	44,019,280	40,545,581	31,824,088	47,630,212	32,972,583	33,922,607
Variable Overhead	30,358,124	20,272,790	28,641,679	36,805,164	28,262,214	31,499,563
Operating Income	71,430,880	68,143,834	68,194,475	32,350,719	7,284,076	7,493,948
Net Income	11,161,075	10,647,474	11,365,746	7,465,551	3,642,038	3,746,974
Return on Sales (% of sales)	5.0%	5.0%	5.0%	3.0%	1.5%	1.5%
COGS (% of Sales)	68%	68%	70%	87%	97%	97%
Cotton Costs (% of COGS)	38%	38%	38%	39%	53%	53%
Direct Labor (% of COGS)	13%	20%	24%	22%	21%	20%

---

[1]Copyright © 2010 Thunderbird, School of Global Management. All rights reserved. This case was prepared by Kyle Mineo, MBA '10, Saurabh Goyal, MBA '10, and Tim Erion, MBA '10, under the direction of Professor Michael Moffett for the purpose of classroom discussion only, and not to indicate either effective or ineffective management.

for textile exports to hit USD 50 billion by 2012, but as of 2010, they were only USD 22 billion.

The industry was both capital and labor intensive, as well as highly regulated. Companies operated on small margins in a highly competitive marketplace, and the global recession of 2008–2009 had battered the Indian industry even further. Challenges faced by the Indian textile industry included the following:

Rising Raw Material and Labor Costs. The chief raw materials used in textiles were cotton and other natural and poly-based yarn. Erratic monsoons, coupled with increased exports of cotton in the recent years, had caused the price of cotton to rise dramatically. During the past 12 months, cotton prices had increased more than 75%. A variety of government programs and restrictions had also contributed to a growing scarcity of skilled labor in the textile industry.

Competition from China and other Asian Countries. India and China account for the majority of global textile production. Due to low labor costs and strong government support and infrastructure, China had been able to stay ahead in competing with the BRIC (Brazil, Russia, India, and China) countries. As a consequence, Chinese textile products were priced more competitively in the global market, and prevented Indian companies from pushing through any price increases. Indian companies were now suffering falling margins and losing orders to other countries. Much of the Indian low-value market had already shifted to Bangladesh, as costs there were 50% cheaper than in India.

Appreciation of the Rupee. The rupee had grown increasingly volatile in recent years against the dollar, and over the past two years, appreciated by nearly 20%. This appreciation had made countries like Bangladesh and Vietnam more competitive on the global front. In early November, the rupee had risen to INR44/USD, the strongest in more than three years. It now hovered at 45. Further strengthening of the rupee against the dollar would most likely put many Indian textile companies out of business.

The Curious Case of High Cotton Prices
The cotton market had been nothing other than "crazy" recently. The monsoons in India had prompted many farmers to plant more cotton to meet the heightened demand. But, despite growing production, cotton prices had skyrocketed in the past year, reaching $1.50/lb, as illustrated in Exhibit 2. The increased demand from China

EXHIBIT 2   Curious Case of Rising Cotton Prices

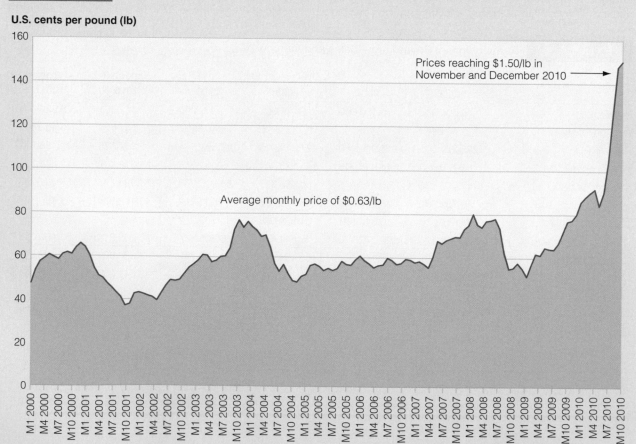

and the reduced inventories in the United States had driven the price up.

Although most market analysts continued to argue that cotton prices were abnormally high—and must fall sooner rather than later—they remained high and only seemed to go higher as the soothsayers predicted their fall. What frightened Lapura even more, were the market analysts who were now arguing that cotton prices had moved to a higher level, permanently.

Lapura was considering the use of cotton futures, a practice some of his competitors were already using. A recent check of futures prices had provided him some data on what prices he may be able to lock in now for cotton in the coming year, in U.S. cents per pound: March 2011: 113.09; July 2011: 102.06/; October 2011: 95.03. Although futures would eliminate the risk of further increases in cotton prices, he was still afraid he would be locking in the price at the top.

Currency of Invoice

As an Indian textile exporter, Lapura had never had choice about the currency of invoice—it would be the U.S. dollar. But maybe times had changed? The dollar had been falling against the rupee for some time now (as seen

in Exhibit 3), and as a result, the rupees generated from export sales were less and less. The problem was that as an exporter from what the world called an "emerging market," his hard currency choices were the U.S. dollar, the European euro, and the Japanese yen. And the rupee had been strengthening against all of them!

But what might the future bring? All three hard currencies were at record low rates of return—nominal interest rate yields—and not expected to change much in the immediate future. They were under careful watch by their central banks, with all three central banks pumping liquidity into the respective monetary systems following the credit crisis of 2008–2009. The most immediate likelihood was the rise of inflation in all three markets. Unfortunately, that would not help, as a rise in inflation would probably only drive their values down further against the rupee.

The Turkish Sale

Lapura's immediate problem was a $250,000 textile sale he had made to a Turkish customer. The contract allowed him to change the currency of invoice from the Turkish lira to the dollar or euro if he wished, but he had to decide by close of business day.

EXHIBIT 3   Indian Rupee/U.S. Dollar Spot Rate

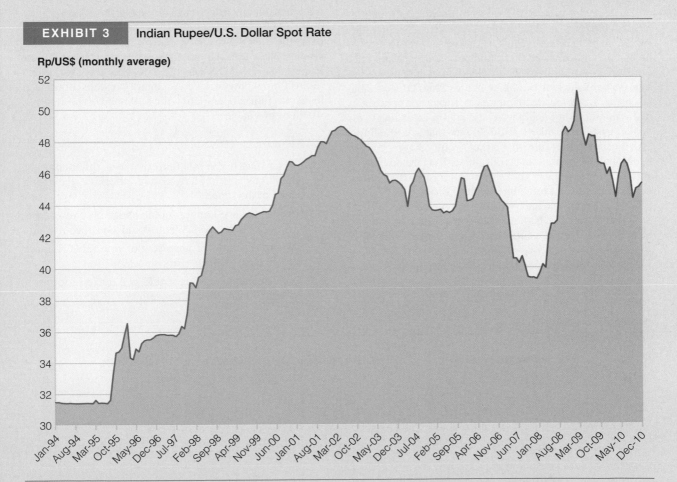

EXHIBIT 4   Forward Rate Quotes

Currency Cross	Symbols	Spot	Bank Quotes on Forward Rates		
			30 days	60 days	90 days
Indian rupees per U.S. dollar	USD/INR	45.8300	46.12	46.70	46.11
Indian rupees per euro	EURO/INR	60.9611	61.70	61.90	62.20
Japanese yen per rupee	INR/JPY	1.8250	1.81	1.81	1.80
Indian rupees per Turkish lira	TRY/INR	30.7192	30.96	30.95	30.87
Turkish lira per U.S. dollar	USD/LIRA	1.4793	1.49	1.48	1.48

Expected settlement on the invoice was January 30, 2011. But regardless of which currency he chose (the rupee not being one of the choices), he still had to decide how to hedge it.

Lapura had collected a variety of forward rates from his local bank for the dollar, euro, and Turkish lira, as listed in Exhibit 4. He eyed the dollar quotes the closest. The forwards would lock him into a rupee rate, which was slightly better than the current spot rate. Of course if the forwards were considered indicators of likely rate movement, they did indicate what he had long hoped for—a rise in the dollar.

He had also considered some form of money market hedge—borrowing Turkish lira against the receivable. Although he had been selling in Turkey for over five years, he had never borrowed there, and only had one bank relationship in Ankara. If he provided sales history to the Turkish bank, he may be able to use his $250,000 receivable as collateral. Domestic loan rates in Turkey for companies with similar credit quality were about 14% according to his bankers. But his bankers also told him that as a small foreign business, the Turkish market would charge him an additional 300 basis point credit spread. But if he did indeed get the money sooner rather than later, domestic Indian deposit rates were averaging a healthy 10.4%.

Currency options had recently become a hedging alternative in India. The National Stock Exchange of India in Mumbai had opened a currency options market in October 2010. With no experience with options, Lapura wondered if an option would provide better protection than a forward contract. The options market, at least for now, was limited to INR/USD options. Although Mr. Lapura could see the upside potential that an options contract might provide, he wondered how much the contract would hurt his slim margins if he had to exercise his contract. Put and call option quotes on the dollar, considered by Mr. Lapura, are listed in Exhibit 5.

Out of Time

Aadesh Lapura picked up his notes and knew it was time to call a family meeting. Times were tough and the family's livelihood was being threatened. Two things needed to be sorted out and quickly. With the last major sale of 2010 on the books—the Turkish sale, he knew he needed to protect the value of this sale from currency losses. Secondly, he needed to find a sustainable path to protecting the business over the long term. With India's continued economic growth, many analysts are forecasting a stronger Indian Rupee versus USD exchange rate into the foreseeable future. Competition was fierce. Lapura wondered how much longer his Indian operations—the livelihood of the family—would be profitable.

CASE QUESTIONS

1. Which factor do you think is more threatening to Banbury's profitability, cotton prices or the rising value of the rupee?

2. Do you believe Lapura should hedge his cotton costs with cotton futures? What would you recommend?

3. Which currency of invoice do you think Lapura should choose for the Turkish sale?

4. What recommendation would you make in terms of hedging the Turkish sale receipts?

EXHIBIT 5   Currency Option Quotes on the USD

Strike Rate (Rupee/USD)	Put Premium (Rupee/USD)	Call Premium (Rupee/USD)
44.00	0.005	1.890
45.25	0.035	0.440

Quotes for 60-day maturity, USD 1000 per contract.

Source: National Stock Exchange of India, nseindia.com.

Questions

1. **Foreign Exchange. Define the following terms:**
   a. *Foreign exchange exposure*
   b. The four types of foreign exchange exposure

2. **Hedging and Currency Risk. Define the following terms:**
   a. *hedging*
   b. *currency risk*

3. **Arguments against Currency Risk Management.** Describe six arguments against a firm pursuing an active currency risk management program?

4. **Arguments for Currency Risk Management.** Describe four arguments in favor of a firm pursuing an active currency risk management program?

5. **Transaction Exposure.** What are the four main types of transactions from which transaction exposure arises?

6. **Life Span of a Transaction Exposure.** Diagram the life span of an exposure arising from selling a product on open account. On the diagram define and show *quotation*, *backlog*, and *billing* exposures.

7. **Borrowing Exposure.** Give an example of a transaction exposure that arises from borrowing in a foreign currency.

8. **Cash Balances.** Explain why foreign currency cash balances do not cause transaction exposure.

9. **Contractual Hedges.** What are the four main contractual instruments used to hedge transaction exposure?

10. **Decision Criteria.** Ultimately, a treasurer must chose among alternative strategies to manage transaction exposure. Explain the two main decision criteria that must be used.

11. **Proportional Hedge.** Many MNEs have established transaction exposure risk management policies that mandate proportional hedging. Explain and give an example of how proportional hedging can be implemented.

12. **By Any Other Name.** What does the word *translation* mean? Why is translation exposure sometimes called *accounting exposure*?

13. **Converting Financial Assets.** In the context of preparing consolidated financial statements, are the words *translate* and *convert* synonyms?

14. **The Central Problem.** What is the central problem involved in consolidating the financial statements of a foreign subsidiary?

15. **Self-Sustaining Subsidiaries.** What is the difference between a *self-sustaining foreign subsidiary* and an *integrated foreign subsidiary*?

16. **Functional Currency.** What is a *functional currency*? What is a nonfunctional currency?

17. **Translating Assets.** What are the major differences in translating assets between the current rate method and the temporal method?

18. **Translating Liabilities.** What are the major differences in translating liabilities between the current rate method and the temporal method?

19. **Hyperinflation.** What is *hyperinflation* and what are the consequences for translating foreign financial statements?

20. **Foreign Exchange Losses by Any Other Name.** What is the primary difference between losses from transaction exposure, operating exposure, and translation exposure?

Problems

1. **P & G India.** Proctor and Gamble's affiliate in India, P & G India, procures much of its toiletries product line from a Japanese company. Because of the shortage of working capital in India, payment terms by Indian importers are typically 180 days or longer. P & G India wishes to hedge an 8.5 million Japanese yen payable. Although options are not available on the Indian rupee (Rs), forward rates are available against the yen. Additionally, a common practice in India is for companies like P & G India to work with a currency agent who will, in this case, lock in the current spot exchange rate in exchange for a 4.85% fee. Using the following exchange rate and interest rate data, recommend a hedging strategy.

2. **Siam Cement.** Siam Cement, the Bangkok-based cement manufacturer, suffered enormous losses with the coming of the Asian crisis in 1997. The company had been pursuing a very aggressive growth strategy in the mid-1990s, taking on massive quantities of foreign–currency-denominated debt (primarily U.S. dollars). When the Thai baht (B) was devalued from its pegged rate of B25.0/$ in July 1997, Siam's interest payments alone were over $900 million on its outstanding dollar debt (with an average interest rate of 8.40% on its U.S. dollar debt at that time). Assuming Siam Cement took out $50 million in debt in June 1997 at 8.40% interest, and had to repay it in one year when the spot exchange rate had stabilized at B42.0/$, what was the foreign exchange loss incurred on the transaction?

3. **BioTron Medical, Inc.** Brent Bush, CFO of a medical device distributor, BioTron Medical, Inc., was approached by a Japanese customer, Numata, with a proposal to pay cash (in yen) for its typical orders of ¥12,500,000 every other month if it were given a 4.5% discount. Numata's current terms are 30 days with no discounts. Using the following quotes and estimated cost of capital for Numata, Bush will compare the proposal with covering yen payments with forward contracts.

Spot rate:	¥111.40/$
30-day forward rate:	¥111.00/$
90-day forward rate:	¥110.40/$
180-day forward rate:	¥109.20/$
Numata's WACC	8.850%
BioTron's WACC	9.200%

4. **Embraer of Brazil.** Embraer of Brazil is one of the two leading global manufacturers of regional jets (Bombardier of Canada is the other). Regional jets are smaller than the traditional civilian airliners produced by Airbus and Boeing, seating between 50 and 100 people on average. Embraer has concluded an agreement with a regional U.S. airline to produce and deliver four aircraft one year from now for $80 million. Although Embraer will be paid in U.S. dollars, it also possesses a currency exposure of inputs—it must pay foreign suppliers 20 million for inputs one year from now (but they will be delivering the subcomponents throughout the year). The current spot rate on the Brazilian real (R$) is R$1.8240/$, but it has been steadily appreciating against the U.S. dollar over the past three years. Forward contracts are difficult to acquire and considered expensive. Citibank Brasil has not explicitly provided Embraer a forward rate quote, but has stated that it will probably be pricing a forward off the current 4.00% U.S. dollar Eurocurrency rate and the 10.50% Brazilian government deposit note.

5. **Vizor Pharmaceuticals.** Vizor Pharmaceuticals, a U.S.-based multinational pharmaceutical company, is evaluating an export sale of its cholesterol-reduction drug with a prospective Indonesian distributor. The purchase would be for 1,650 million Indonesian rupiah (Rp), which at the current spot exchange rate of Rp9,450/$, translates into nearly $175,000. Although not a big sale by company standards, company policy dictates that sales must be settled for at least a minimum gross margin, in this case, a cash settlement of $168,000. The current 90-day forward rate is Rp9,950/$. Although this rate appeared unattractive, Vizor had to contact several major banks before even finding a forward quote on the rupiah. The consensus of currency forecasters at the moment, however, is that the rupiah will hold relatively steady, possibly falling to Rp9,400/$ over the coming 90 to 120 days. Analyze the prospective sale and make a hedging recommendation.

6. **Mattel Toys.** Mattel is a U.S.-based company whose sales are roughly two-thirds in dollars (Asia and the Americas) and one-third in euros (Europe). In September, Mattel delivers a large shipment of toys (primarily Barbies and Hot Wheels) to a major distributor in Antwerp. The receivable, €30 million, is due in 90 days, standard terms for the toy industry in Europe. Mattel's treasury team has collected the following currency and market quotes. The company's foreign exchange advisors believe the euro will be at about $1.4200/€ in 90 days. Mattel's management does not use currency options in currency risk management activities. Advise Mattel on which hedging alternative is probably preferable.

Current spot rate ($/€)	$1.4158
Credit Suisse 90-day forward rate ($/€)	$1.4172
Barclays 90-day forward rate ($/€)	$1.4195
Mattel Toys WACC ($)	9.600%
90-day eurodollar interest rate	4.000%
90-day euro interest rate	3.885%
90-day eurodollar borrowing rate	5.000%
90-day euro borrowing rate	5.000%

7. **Bobcat Company.** Bobcat Company, U.S.-based manufacturer of industrial equipment, just purchased a Korean company that produces plastic nuts and bolts for heavy equipment. The purchase price was Won7,500 million. Won1,000 million has already been paid, and the remaining Won6,500 million is due in six months. The current spot rate is Won1,110/$, and the 6-month forward rate is Won1,175/$. The 6-month Korean won interest rate is 16% per annum, the 6-month U.S. dollar rate is 4% per annum. Bobcat can invest at these interest rates, or borrow at 2% per annum above those rates. A 6-month call option on won with a 1200/$ strike rate has a 3.0% premium, while the 6-month put option at the same strike rate has a 2.4% premium.

Bobcat can invest at the rates given above, or borrow at 2% per annum above those rates. Bobcat's weighted average cost of capital is 10%. Compare alternate ways that Bobcat might deal with its foreign exchange exposure. What do you recommend and why?

8. Aquatech. Aquatech is a U.S.-based company that manufactures, sells, and installs water purification equipment. On April 11, the company sold a system to the City of Nagasaki, Japan, for installation in Nagasaki's famous Glover Gardens (where Puccini's *Madame Butterfly* waited for the return of Lt. Pinkerton). The sale was priced in yen at ¥20,000,000, with payment due in three months.

Spot exchange rate:	¥118.255/$ (closing mid-rates)
1-month forward rate:	¥117.760/$, a 5.04% p.a. premium
3-month forward:	¥116.830/$, a 4.88% p.a. premium
1-year forward:	¥112.450/$, a 5.16% p.a. premium

Money Rates	United States	Japan	Differential
One month	4.8750%	0.09375%	4.78125%
Three months	4.9375%	0.09375%	4.84375%
Twelve months	5.1875%	0.31250%	4.87500%

Note: The interest rate differentials vary slightly from the forward discounts on the yen because of time differences for the quotes. The spot ¥118.255/$, for example, is a mid-point range. On April 11, the spot yen traded in London from ¥118.30/$ to ¥117.550/$.

Additional information: Aquatech's Japanese competitors are currently borrowing yen from Japanese banks at a spread of two percentage points above the Japanese money rate. Aquatech's weighted average cost of capital is 16%, and the company wishes to protect the dollar value of this receivable.

3-month options from Kyushu Bank:
- Call option on ¥20,000,000 at exercise price of ¥118.00/$: a 1% premium.
- Put option on ¥20,000,000, at exercise price of ¥118.00/$: a 3% premium.
- a. What are the costs and benefits of alternative hedges? Which would you recommend, and why?
- b. What is the break-even reinvestment rate when comparing forward and money market alternatives?

9. Compass Rose. Compass Rose, Ltd., a Canadian manufacturer of raincoats, does not selectively hedge its transaction exposure. Instead, if the date of the transaction is known with certainty, all foreign currency-denominated cash flows must utilize the following mandatory forward cover formula:

Compass Rose's Manadatory Forward Cover	0–90 days	91–180 days	>180 days
Paying the points forward	75%	60%	50%
Receiving the points forward	100%	90%	50%

Compass Rose expects to receive multiple payments in Danish kroner over the next year. DKr 3,000,000 is due in 90 days; DKr 2,000,000 is due in 180 days; and DKr 1,000,000 is due in one year. Using the following spot and forward exchange rates, what would be the amount of forward cover required by company policy by period?

10. Pupule Travel. Pupule Travel, a Honolulu, Hawaii–based 100% privately owned travel company, has signed an agreement to acquire a 50% ownership share of Taichung Travel, a Taiwan–based privately owned travel agency specializing in servicing inbound customers from the United States and Canada. The acquisition price is 7 million Taiwan dollars (T$7,000,000) payable in cash in three months.

Thomas Carson, Pupule Travel's owner, believes the Taiwan dollar will either remain stable or decline a little over the next three months. At the present spot rate of T$35/$, the amount of cash required is only $200,000, but even this relatively modest amount will need to be borrowed personally by Thomas Carson. Taiwanese interest-bearing deposits by nonresidents are regulated by the government, and are currently set at 1.5% per year. He has a credit line with Bank of Hawaii for $200,000 with a current borrowing interest rate of 8% per year. He does not believe that he can calculate a credible weighted average cost of capital since he has no stock outstanding and his competitors are all also privately owned without disclosure of their financial results. Since the acquisition would use up all his available credit, he wonders if he should hedge this transaction exposure. He has quotes from Bank of Hawaii shown in the following table:

Spot rate (T$/$)	33.40
3-month forward rate (T$/$)	32.40
3-month Taiwan dollar deposit rate	1.500%
3-month dollar borrowing rate	6.500%
3-month call option on T$	not available

Analyze the costs and risks of each alternative, and then make a recommendation as to which alternative Thomas Carson should choose.

11. Chronos Time Pieces. Chronos Time Pieces of Boston exports watches to many countries, selling in local currencies to stores and distributors. Chronos prides itself on being financially conservative. At least 70% of each individual transaction exposure is hedged, mostly in the forward market, but occasionally with options. Chronos's foreign exchange policy is such that the 70%

hedge may be increased up to a 120% hedge if devaluation or depreciation appears imminent. Chronos has just shipped to its major North American distributor. It has issued a 90-day invoice to its buyer for €1,560,000. The current spot rate is $1.2224/€, the 90-day forward rate is $1.2270/€. Chronos's treasurer, Manny Hernandez, has a very good track record in predicting exchange rate movements. He currently believes the euro will weaken against the dollar in the coming 90 to 120 days, possibly to around $1.16/€.

12. **Lucky 13.** Lucky 13 Jeans of San Antonio, Texas, is completing a new assembly plant near Guatemala City. A final construction payment of Q8,400,000 is due in six months. ("Q" is the symbol for Guatemalan quetzals.) Lucky 13 uses 20% per annum as its weighted average cost of capital. Today's foreign exchange and interest rate quotations are as follows:

Construction payment due in 6-months (A/P, quetzals)	8,400,000
Present spot rate (quetzals/$)	7.0000
6-month forward rate (quetzals/$)	7.1000
Guatemalan 6-month interest rate (per annum)	14.000%
U.S. dollar 6-month interest rate (per annum)	6.000%
Lucky 13's weighted average cost of capital (WACC)	20.000%

Lucky 13's treasury manager, concerned about the Guatemalan economy, wonders if Lucky 13 should be hedging its foreign exchange risk. The manager's own forecast is as follows:

Expected spot rate in 6-months (quetzals/$):

Highest expected rate (reflecting a significant devaluation)	8.0000
Expected rate	7.3000
Lowest expected rate (reflecting a strengthening of the quetzal)	6.4000

What realistic alternatives are available to Lucky 13 for making payments? Which method would you select and why?

13. **Burton Manufacturing.** Jason Stedman is the director of finance for Burton Manufacturing, a U.S.-based

manufacturer of handheld computer systems inventory management. Burton's system combines a low-cost active bar code used on inventory (the bar code tags emit an extremely low-grade radio frequency) with custom designed hardware and software which tracks the low-grade emissions for inventory control. Burton has completed the sale of a bar code system to a British firm, Pegg Metropolitan (UK), for a total payment of £1,000,000. The exchange rates shown at the bottom of this page were available to Burton on the following dates corresponding to the events of this specific export sale. Assume each month is 30 days.

14. **Micca Metals, Inc.** Micca Metals, Inc. is a specialty materials and metals company located in Detroit, Michigan. The company specializes in specific precious metals and materials which are used in a variety of pigment applications in many other industries including cosmetics, appliances, and a variety of high tinsel metal fabricating equipment. Micca just purchased a shipment of phosphates from Morocco for 6,000,000, dirhams, payable in six months. Micca's cost of capital is 8.600%.

Six-month call options on 6,000,000 dirhams at an exercise price of 10.00 dirhams per dollar are available from Bank Al-Maghrub at a premium of 2%. Six-month put options on 6,000,000 dirhams at an exercise price of 10.00 dirhams per dollar are available at a premium of 3%. Compare and contrast alternative ways that Micca might hedge its foreign exchange transaction exposure. What is your recommendation?

Assumptions	Values
Shipment of phosphates from Morocco, Moroccan dirhams	6,000,000
Micca's cost of capital (WACC)	14.000%
Spot exchange rate, dirhams/$	10.00
6-month forward rate, dirhams/$	10.40

15. **Maria Gonzalez and Trident.** Trident—the U.S.-based company discussed in this chapter, has concluded a second larger sale of telecommunications equipment

Date	Event	Spot Rate ($/£)	Forward Rate ($/£)	Days Forward of Forward Rate
February 1	Price quotation for Pegg	1.7850	1.7771	210
March 1	Contract signed for sale	1.7465	1.7381	180
	Contract amount, pounds	£1,000,000		
June 1	Product shipped to Pegg	1.7689	1.7602	90
August 1	Product received by Pegg	1.7840	1.7811	30
September 1	Grand Met makes payment	1.7290	—	—

to Regency (U.K.). Total payment of £3,000,000 is due in 90 days. Maria Gonzalez has also learned that Trident will only be able to borrow in the United Kingdom at 14% per annum (due to credit concerns of the British banks). Given the following exchange rates and interest rates, what transaction exposure hedge is now in Trident's best interest?

Assumptions	Value
90-day A/R in pounds	£3,000,000.00
Spot rate, US$ per pound ($/£)	$1.7620
90-day forward rate, US$ per pound ($/£)	$1.7550
3-month U.S. dollar investment rate	6.000%
3-month U.S. dollar borrowing rate	8.000%
3-month U.K. investment interest rate	8.000%
3-month U.K. borrowing interest rate	14.000%
Put options on the British pound: Strike rates, US$/pound ($/£)	
Strike rate ($/£)	$1.75
Put option premium	1.500%
Strike rate ($/£)	$1.71
Put option premium	1.000%
Trident's WACC	12.000%
Maria Gonzalez's expected spot rate in 90-day, US$ per pound ($/£)	$1.7850

16. **Larkin Hydraulics.** On May 1, Larkin Hydraulics, a wholly owned subsidiary of Caterpillar (U.S.), sold a 12-megawatt compression turbine to Rebecke-Terwilleger Company of the Netherlands for €4,000,000, payable €2,000,000 on August 1 and €2,000,000 on November 1. Larkin derived its price quote of €4,000,000 on April 1 by dividing its normal U.S. dollar sales price of $4.320,000 by the then current spot rate of $1.0800/€.

By the time the order was received and booked on May 1, the euro had strengthened to $1.1000/€, so the sale was in fact worth €4,000,000 × $1.1000/€ = $4,400,000. Larkin had already gained an extra $80,000 from favorable exchange rate movements. Nevertheless, Larkin's director of finance now wondered if the firm should hedge against a reversal of the recent trend of the euro. Four approaches were possible:

1. Hedge in the forward market: The 3-month forward exchange quote was $1.1060/€ and the 6-month forward quote was $1.1130/€.
2. Hedge in the money market: Larkin could borrow euros from the Frankfurt branch of its U.S. bank at 8.00% per annum.
3. Hedge with foreign currency options: August put options were available at strike price of $1.1000/€

for a premium of 2.0% per contract, and November put options were available at $1.1000/€ for a premium of 1.2%. August call options at $1.1000/€ could be purchased for a premium of 3.0%, and November call options at $1.1000/€ were available at a 2.6% premium.
4. Do nothing: Larkin could wait until the sales proceeds were received in August and November, hope the recent strengthening of the euro would continue, and sell the euros received for dollars in the spot market.

Larkin estimates the cost of equity capital to be 12% per annum. As a small firm, Larkin Hydraulics is unable to raise funds with long-term debt. U.S. T-bills yield 3.6% per annum. What should Larkin do?

17. **Tristan Narvaja, S.A. (A).** Tristan Narvaja, S.A., is the Uruguayan subsidiary of a U.S. manufacturing company. Its balance sheet for January 1 follows. The January 1 exchange rate between the U.S. dollar and the peso Uruguayo ($U) is $U20/$. Determine Tristan Narvaja's contribution to the translation exposure of its parent on January 1, using the current rate method.

Balance Sheet (thousands of pesos Uruguayo, $U)

Assets	January 1	Exchange Rate (U/US)
Cash	60,000	20.00
Accounts receivable	120,000	20.00
Inventory	120,000	20.00
Net plant and equipment	240,000	20.00
	540,000	
Liabilities and Net Worth		
Current liabilities	30,000	20.00
Long-term debt	90,000	20.00
Capital stock	300,000	15.00
Retained earnings	120,000	15.00
	540,000	

18. **Tristan Narvaja, S.A. (B).** Using the same balance sheet as in problem 17, calculate Tristan Narvaja's contribution to its parent's translation loss if the exchange rate on December 31 is $U22/$. Assume all peso accounts remain as they were at the beginning of the year.

19. **Tristan Narvaja, S.A. (C).** Calculate Tristan Narvaja's contribution to its parent's translation gain or loss using the current rate method if the exchange rate on December 31 is $U12/$. Assume all peso accounts remain as they were at the beginning of the year.

Balance Sheet of Cairo Ingot, Ltd.

Assets	Egyptian Pounds Statement	Before Exchange Rate Change	
		Exchange Rate (Egyptian £/UK£)	Translated Accounts British Pounds
Cash	16,500,000	5.50	£ 3,000,000.00
Accounts receivable	33,000,000	5.50	6,000,000
Inventory	49,500,000	5.50	9,000,000
Net plant and equipment	66,000,000	5.50	12,000,000
Total	165,000,000		£30,000,000.00
Liabilities and Net Worth			
Accounts payable	24,750,000	5.50	£ 4,500,000.00
Long-term debt	49,500,000	5.50	9,000,000
Invested capital	90,750,000	5.50	16,500,000
CTA account (loss)	–		–
Total	165,000,000		£30,000,000.00

20. **Cairo Ingot, Ltd.** Cairo Ingot, Ltd., is the Egyptian subsidiary of Trans-Mediterranean Aluminum, a British multinational that fashions automobile engine blocks from aluminum. Trans-Mediterranean's home reporting currency is the British pound. Cairo Ingot's December 31 balance sheet is shown at the top of this page. At the date of this balance sheet, the exchange rate between Egyptian pounds and British pounds sterling was £E5.50/UK£.
   a. What is Cairo Ingot's contribution to the translation exposure of Trans-Mediterranean on December 31, using the current rate method?
   b. Calculate the translation exposure loss to Trans-Mediterranean if the exchange rate at the end of the following quarter is £E6.00/£. Assume all balance sheet accounts are the same at the end of the quarter as they were at the beginning.

Internet Exercises

1. **Current Volatilities.** You wish to price your own options, but you need current volatilities on the euro, British pound, and Japanese yen. Using the following Web sites, collect spot rates and volatilities in order to price forward at-the-money put options for your option pricing analysis.

Federal Reserve Bank of New York	www.ny.frb.org/statistics
RatesFX.com	www.ratesfx.com/

2. **Hedging Objectives.** All multinational companies will state the goals and objectives of their currency risk management activities in their annual reports. Beginning with the following firms, collect samples of corporate "why hedge?" discussions for a contrast and comparison discussion.

Nestlé	www.nestle.com
Disney	www.disney.com
Nokia	www.nokia.com
BP	www.bp.com

3. **Changing Translation Practices: FASB.** The Financial Accounting Standards Board promulgates standard practices for the reporting of financial results by companies in the United States. It also, however, often leads the way in the development of new practices and emerging issues around the world. One major issue today is the valuation and reporting of financial derivatives and derivative agreements by firms. Use the FASB's home page and the Web pages of several of the major accounting firms and other interest groups around the world to see current proposed accounting standards and the current state of reaction to the proposed standards.

FASB home page	raw.rutgers.edu/raw/fasb/
Treasury Management Association	www.tma.org/

Operating Exposure

The essence of risk management lies in maximizing the areas where we have some control over the outcome while minimizing the areas where we have absolutely no control over the outcome and the linkage between effect and cause is hidden from us. —Peter Bernstein, *Against the Gods*, 1996.

LEARNING OBJECTIVES

◆ Examine how operating exposure arises through unexpected changes in both operating and financing cash flows.

◆ Analyze the sequence of how unexpected exchange rate changes alter the economic performance of a business unit through the sequence of volume, price, cost, and other key variable changes.

◆ Evaluate the strategic alternatives to managing operating exposure.

◆ Detail the proactive policies available to firms for managing operating exposure.

This chapter examines the economic exposure of a firm over time, what we term *operating exposure*. Operating exposure, also referred to as *economic exposure, competitive exposure,* or *strategic exposure*, measures any change in the present value of a firm resulting from changes in future operating cash flows caused by any unexpected change in exchange rates. Operating exposure analysis assesses the impact of changing exchange rates on a firm's own operations over coming months and years and on its competitive position vis-à-vis other firms. The goal is to identify strategic moves or operating techniques the firm might wish to adopt to enhance its value in the face of unexpected exchange rate changes.

Operating exposure and transaction exposure are related in that they both deal with future cash flows. They differ in terms of which cash flows management considers and why those cash flows change when exchange rates change. We begin by revisiting the structure of our firm, Trident Corporation, and how its structure dictates its likely operating exposure. The chapter continues with a series of strategies and structures used in the management of operating exposure, and concludes with a Mini-Case, ***Toyota's European Operating Exposure***.

Trident Corporation: A Multinational's Operating Exposure

The structure and operations of a multinational company determine the nature of its operating exposure. Trident Corporation's basic structure and currencies of operation are described in Exhibit 11.1. As a U.S.-based publicly traded company, ultimately all financial metrics and values have to be consolidated and expressed in U.S. dollars. That accounting exposure of the firm was described in Chapter 10. Operationally, however, the functional

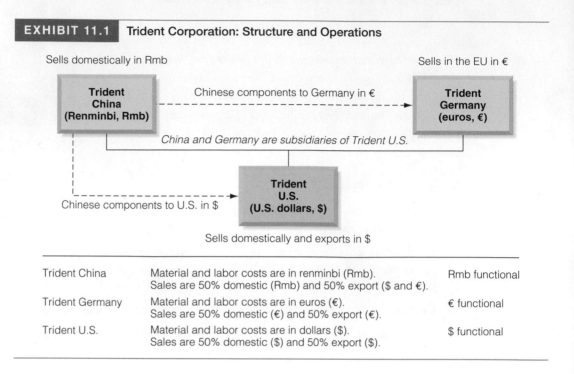

EXHIBIT 11.1   Trident Corporation: Structure and Operations

Trident China	Material and labor costs are in renminbi (Rmb). Sales are 50% domestic (Rmb) and 50% export ($ and €).	Rmb functional
Trident Germany	Material and labor costs are in euros (€). Sales are 50% domestic (€) and 50% export (€).	€ functional
Trident U.S.	Material and labor costs are in dollars ($). Sales are 50% domestic ($) and 50% export ($).	$ functional

currencies of the individual subsidiaries in combination determine the overall operating exposure of the firm in total.

The net operating cash flows of any individual business unit reflects where and to whom it sells against from whom and from where it buys:

$$\begin{matrix} \text{Net operating} \\ \text{cash flow} \end{matrix} = \begin{matrix} \text{Receivables over time} \\ \text{from sales} \end{matrix} - \begin{matrix} \text{Payables over time} \\ \text{for inputs and labor} \end{matrix}$$

For example, Trident Germany sells locally and exports, but all sales are invoiced in euros. All operating cash inflows are therefore in its home currency, the euro. On the cost side, labor costs are local and in euros, as well as many of its material input purchases being local and in euros. It also purchases components from Trident China, but those too are invoiced in euros. Trident Germany is clearly euro-functional, with all cash inflows and outflows in euros.

Trident Corporation U.S. is similar in structure to Trident Germany. All cash inflows from sales, domestic and international, are in U.S. dollars. All costs, labor and materials, sourced domestically and internationally, are invoiced in U.S. dollars. This includes purchases from Trident China. Trident U.S. is therefore obviously dollar functional.

Trident China is more complex. Cash outflows, labor and materials, are all domestic and paid in Chinese renminbi. Cash inflows, however, are generated across three different currencies as the company sells locally in renminbi, as well as exporting to both Germany in euros and the United States in dollars. On net, although having some cash inflows in both dollars and euros, the dominant currency cash flow is the renminbi.

Static versus Dynamic Operating Exposure

Measuring the operating exposure of a firm like Trident requires forecasting and analyzing all the firm's future individual transaction exposures together with the future exposures of all the firm's competitors and potential competitors worldwide. Exchange rate changes in the short term affect current and immediate contracts, generally termed *transactions*. But over the longer term, as prices change and competitors react, the more fundamental economic and competitive drivers of the business may alter all cash flows of all units. A simple example will clarify the point.

Assume Trident's three business units are roughly equal in size. In 2012, the dollar starts depreciating in the market against the euro at the same time the Chinese government continues the gradual revaluation of the renminbi. The operating exposure of each individual business unit then needs to be examined statically (transaction exposures) and dynamically (future business transactions not yet contracted for).

◆ **Trident China.** Sales in U.S. dollars will result in fewer renminbi proceeds in the immediate period. Sales in euros may stay roughly the same in renminbi proceeds depending on the relative movement of the Rmb against the euro. General profitability will fall in the short run. In the longer term, depending on the markets for its products and the nature of competition, it may need to raise the price it sells its export products for, even to its U.S. parent company.

◆ **Trident Germany.** Since this business unit's cash inflows and outflows are all in euros, there is no immediate transaction exposure or change. It may suffer some rising input costs in the future if Trident China does indeed eventually push through price increases of component sales. Profitability is unaffected in the short term.

◆ **Trident U.S.** Like Trident Germany, Trident U.S. has all local currency cash inflows and outflows. A fall in the value of the dollar will have no immediate (transaction exposure) impact, but may change over the medium to long term as input costs from China may rise over time as the Chinese subsidiary tries to regain prior profit margins. But, like Germany, short-term profitability is unaffected.

The net result for Trident is possibly a fall in the total profitability of the firm in the short term, primarily from the fall in profits of the Chinese subsidiary; that is, the short-term transaction/operating exposure impact. The fall in the dollar in the short term, however, is likely to have a positive impact on translation exposure, as profits and earnings in renminbi and euros translate into more and more dollars. Wall Street would likely like the results in the immediate quarter or two.

Operating and Financing Cash Flows

The cash flows of the MNE can be divided into *operating cash flows* and *financing cash flows*. Operating cash flows arise from intercompany (between unrelated companies) and intracompany (between units of the same company) receivables and payables, rent and lease payments for the use of facilities and equipment, royalty and license fees for the use of technology and intellectual property, and assorted management fees for services provided.

Financing cash flows are payments for the use of intercompany and intracompany loans (principal and interest) and stockholder equity (new equity investments and dividends). Each of these cash flows can occur at different time intervals, in different amounts, and in different currencies of denomination, and each has a different predictability of occurrence. We summarize cash flow possibilities in Exhibit 11.2 for Trident China and Trident U.S.

Expected versus Unexpected Changes in Cash Flow

Operating exposure is far more important for the long-run health of a business than changes caused by transaction or translation exposure. However, operating exposure is inevitably subjective because it depends on estimates of future cash flow changes over an

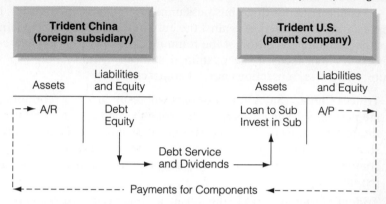

EXHIBIT 11.2   Financial and Operating Cash Flows between Parent and Subsidiary

Cash flows related to the financing of the subsidiary are *Financial Cash Flows*
Cash flows related to the business activities of the subsidiary are *Operating Cash Flows*

arbitrary time horizon. Thus, it does not spring from the accounting process but rather from the operating analysis. Planning for operating exposure is a total management responsibility depending upon the interaction of strategies in finance, marketing, purchasing, and production.

An *expected* change in foreign exchange rates is not included in the definition of operating exposure, because both management and investors should have factored this information into their evaluation of anticipated operating results and market value.

◆ From a management perspective, budgeted financial statements already reflect information about the effect of an expected change in exchange rates.

◆ From a debt service perspective, expected cash flow to amortize debt should already reflect the international Fisher effect. The level of expected interest and principal repayment should be a function of expected exchange rates rather than existing spot rates.

◆ From an investor's perspective, if the foreign exchange market is efficient, information about expected changes in exchange rates should be widely known and thus reflected in a firm's market value. Only unexpected changes in exchange rates, or an inefficient foreign exchange market, should cause market value to change.

◆ From a broader macroeconomic perspective, operating exposure is not just the sensitivity of a firm's future cash flows to unexpected changes in foreign exchange rates, but also its sensitivity to other key macroeconomic variables. This factor has been labeled as *macroeconomic uncertainty*.

Chapter 7 described the parity relationships among exchange rates, interest rates, and inflation rates. However, these variables are often in disequilibrium with one another. Therefore, unexpected changes in interest rates and inflation rates could also have a simultaneous but differential impact on future cash flows. As discussed in *Global Finance in Practice 11.1*, fixed exchange rates obviously add an additional complexity to managing future cash flows and general corporate currency risk.

GLOBAL FINANCE IN PRACTICE   **11.1**

Do Fixed Exchange Rates Increase Corporate Currency Risk in Emerging Markets?

It has long been argued that when firms know the exchange rate cannot or will not change, they will conduct their business as if currency exposure—at least against the major currency(s) which their home currency is fixed—will not occur. As one study of currency risk in India noted: "These results support the hypothesis that pegged exchange rates induce moral hazard and increase financial fragility."[1]

Moral hazard is the concept that a party, an agent, an individual, or a firm will take on more risk when it either knows or believes that a second party will handle, accommodate, or insure the negative repercussions of the firm's risk-taking decisions. In other words, a firm may take more risk when it knows that someone else will pick up the tab. In a fixed or managed exchange rate regime, that party is represented by the central bank which tells all those undertaking cross-currency contractual obligations and exposures that the exchange rate will not change.

Although there is still scant research on this specific practice for most of the emerging markets, it could prove to be a significant issue in the years to come as many emerging markets become the object of major new international capital flows—the so-called globalization of finance. If commercial firms in those markets are not aware of the risk which the country itself may be taking in opening the door to international capital flows, both in and out of the country, and the impact they may have on the country's exchange rate, they may be in for a wild ride in the immediate years to come.

[1]"Does the currency regime shape unhedged currency exposure?," by Ila Patnaik and Ajay Shah, *Journal of International Money and Finance*, 29, 2010, pp. 760–769. See also "Moral Hazard, Financial Crises, and the Choice of Exchange Rate Regimes," Apanard Angkinand and Thomas Willett, June 2006; and "Exchange-Rate Regimes for Emerging Markets: Moral Hazard and International Borrowing," by Ronald I. McKinnon and Huw Pill, Oxford Review of Economic Policy, Vol. 15, No. 3, 1999.

Measuring Operating Exposure

An unexpected change in exchange rates impacts a firm's expected cash flows at four levels, depending on the time horizon used, as summarized in Exhibit 11.3.

1. **Short Run.** The first-level impact is on expected cash flows in the 1-year operating budget. The gain or loss depends on the currency of denomination of expected cash flows. These are both existing transaction exposures and anticipated exposures. The currency of denomination cannot be changed for existing obligations, or even for implied obligations such as purchase or sales commitments. Apart from real or implied obligations, in the short run it is difficult to change sales prices or renegotiate factor costs. Therefore, realized cash flows will differ from those expected in the budget. However, as time passes, prices and costs can be changed to reflect the new competitive realities caused by a change in exchange rates.

EXHIBIT 11.3   Operating Exposure's Phases of Adjustment and Response

Phase	Time	Price Changes	Volume Changes	Structural Changes
Short Run	Less than one year	Prices are fixed/contracted	Volumes are contracted	No competitive market changes
Medium Run: Equilibrium	Two to five years	Complete pass-through of exchange rate changes	Volumes begin a partial response to prices	Existing competitors begin partial responses
Medium Run: Disequilibrium	Two to five years	Partial pass-through of exchange rate changes	Volumes begin a partial response to prices	Existing competitors begin partial responses
Long Run	More than five years	Completely flexible	Completely flexible	Threat of new entrants and changing competitor responses

2. **Medium Run: Equilibrium.** The second-level impact is on expected medium-run cash flows, such as those expressed in 2- to 5-year budgets, assuming parity conditions hold among foreign exchange rates, national inflation rates, and national interest rates. Under equilibrium conditions, the firm should be able to adjust prices and factor costs over time to maintain the expected level of cash flows. In this case, the currency of denomination of expected cash flows is not as important as the countries in which cash flows originate. National monetary, fiscal, and balance of payments policies determine whether equilibrium conditions will exist and whether firms will be allowed to adjust prices and costs.

    If equilibrium exists continuously, and a firm is free to adjust its prices and costs to maintain its expected competitive position, its operating exposure may be zero. Its expected cash flows would be realized and therefore its market value unchanged since the exchange rate change was anticipated. However, it is also possible that equilibrium conditions exist but the firm is unwilling or unable to adjust operations to the new competitive environment. In such a case, the firm would experience operating exposure because its realized cash flows would differ from expected cash flows. As a result, its market value might also be altered.

3. **Medium Run: Disequilibrium.** The third-level impact is on expected medium-run cash flows assuming disequilibrium conditions. In this case, the firm may not be able to adjust prices and costs to reflect the new competitive realities caused by a change in exchange rates. The primary problem may be the reactions of existing competitors. The firm's realized cash flows will differ from its expected cash flows. The firm's market value may change because of the unanticipated results.

4. **Long Run.** The fourth-level impact is on expected long-run cash flows, meaning those beyond five years. At this strategic level, a firm's cash flows will be influenced by the reactions of both existing and potential competitors, possible new entrants, to exchange rate changes under disequilibrium conditions. In fact, all firms that are subject to international competition, whether they are purely domestic or multinational, are exposed to foreign exchange operating exposure in the long run whenever foreign exchange markets are not continuously in equilibrium.

Measuring Operating Exposure: Trident Germany

Exhibit 11.4 presents the dilemma facing Trident as a result of an unexpected change in the value of the euro, the currency of economic consequence for the German subsidiary. Trident derives much of its reported profits (earnings and earnings per share—EPS—as reported to Wall Street) from its European subsidiary. If the euro unexpectedly falls in value, how will Trident Germany's revenues change (prices, in euro terms, and volumes)? How will its costs change (primarily input costs, in euro terms)? How will competitors respond? We explain the sequence of likely events over the short and medium run in the following section.

Base Case. Trident Germany manufactures in Germany, sells domestically and exports, and all sales are invoiced in euros. Accounts receivable are equal to one-fourth of annual sales, the average collection period being 90 days. Inventory is equal to 25% of annual direct costs. Trident Germany can expand or contract production volume without any significant change in per-unit direct costs or in general and administrative expenses. Depreciation on plant and equipment is €600,000 per year, and the corporate tax rate is 34%.

EXHIBIT 11.4   Trident and Trident Germany

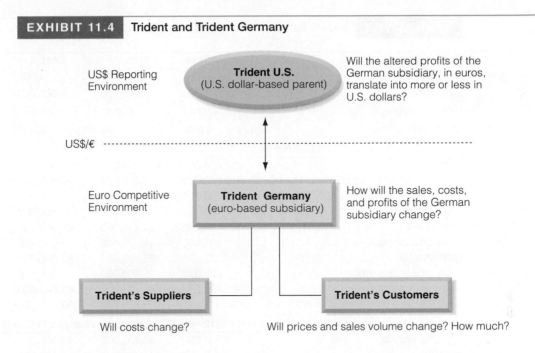

An unexpected depreciation in the value of the euro alters both the competitiveness of the subsidiary and the financial results which are consolidated with the parent company.

The December 31, 2011, balance sheet and alternative scenarios are shown in Exhibit 11.5. We assume that on January 1, 2012, before any commercial activity begins, the euro unexpectedly drops from $1.2000/€ to $1.0000/€. If no depreciation had occurred, Trident Germany was expected to perform in 2012 as shown in the base case of Exhibit 11.5, generating a dollar cash flow from operations for Trident of $2,074,320.

Operating exposure depends on whether an unexpected change in exchange rates causes unanticipated changes in sales volume, sales prices, or operating costs. Following a euro depreciation, Trident Germany might choose to maintain its domestic sales prices constant in euro terms, or it might try to raise domestic prices because competing imports are now priced higher in Europe. The firm might choose to keep export prices constant in terms of foreign currencies, in terms of euros, or somewhere in between (partial pass-through). The strategy undertaken depends to a large measure on management's opinion about the price elasticity of demand. On the cost side, Trident Germany might raise prices because of more expensive imported raw material or components, or perhaps because all domestic prices in Germany have risen and labor is now demanding higher wages to compensate for domestic inflation.

Trident Germany's domestic sales and costs might also be partly determined by the effect of the euro depreciation on demand. To the extent that the depreciation, by making prices of German goods initially more competitive, stimulates purchases of European goods in import-competing sectors of the economy as well as exports of German goods, German national income should increase. This assumes that the favorable effect of a euro depreciation on comparative prices is not immediately offset by higher domestic inflation. Thus, Trident Germany might be able to sell more goods domestically because of price and income effects and internationally because of price effects.

EXHIBIT 11.5	Trident Europe's Changing Cash Flows under Euro Depreciation			
Assumptions	**Base Case**	**Case 1**	**Case 2**	**Case 3**
Exchange rate, $/€	1.2000	1.0000	1.0000	1.0000
Sales volume (units)	1,000,000	1,000,000	2,000,000	1,000,000
Sales price per unit	€12.80	€12.80	€12.80	€15.36
Direct cost per unit	€9.60	€9.60	€9.60	€9.60
Annual Cash Flows before Adjustments				
Sales revenue	€12,800,000	€12,800,000	€25,600,000	€15,360,000
Direct cost of goods sold	9,600,000	9,600,000	19,200,000	9,600,000
Cash operating expenses (fixed)	890,000	890,000	890,000	890,000
Depreciation	600,000	600,000	600,000	600,000
Pretax profit	€1,710,000	€1,710,000	€4,910,000	€4,270,000
Income tax expense	581,400	581,400	1,669,400	1,451,800
Profit after tax	€1,128,600	€1,128,600	€3,240,600	€2,818,200
Add back depreciation	600,000	600,000	600,000	600,000
Cash flow from operations, in euros	€1,728,600	€1,728,600	€3,840,600	€3,418,200
Cash flow from operations, in dollars	$2,074,320	$1,728,600	$3,840,600	$3,418,200
Adjustments to Working Capital for 2012 and 2016 Caused by Changes in Conditions				
Accounts receivable	€3,200,000	€3,200,000	€6,400,000	€3,840,000
Inventory	2,400,000	2,400,000	4,800,000	2,400,000
Sum	€5,600,000	€5,600,000	€11,200,000	€6,240,000
Change from base conditions in 2012	€0	€0	€5,600,000	€640,000

Year	**Year-End Cash Flows**			
1 (2012)	$2,074,320	$1,728,600	($1,759,400)	$2,778,200
2 (2013)	$2,074,320	$1,728,600	$3,840,600	$3,418,200
3 (2014)	$2,074,320	$1,728,600	$3,840,600	$3,418,200
4 (2015)	$2,074,320	$1,728,600	$3,840,600	$3,418,200
5 (2016)	$2,074,320	$1,728,600	$9,440,600	$4,058,200

Year	**Change in Year-End Cash Flows from Base Conditions**			
1 (2012)	na	($345,720)	($3,833,720)	$703,880
2 (2013)	na	($345,720)	$1,766,280	$1,343,880
3 (2014)	na	($345,720)	$1,766,280	$1,343,880
4 (2015)	na	($345,720)	$1,766,280	$1,343,880
5 (2016)	na	($345,720)	$7,366,280	$1,983,880

	Present Value of Incremental Year-End Cash Flows			
	na	($1,033,914)	$2,866,106	$3,742,892

Note: Initial balance sheet for Trident Germany is the same as that presented in Exhibit 10.9. Analysis assumes accounts receivable at 25% of sales, inventory of 25% of direct cost, German tax rate of 34%, and Trident Germany's cost of capital at 20%.

To illustrate the effect of various postdepreciation scenarios on Trident Germany's operating exposure, consider three simple cases:

Case 1: Depreciation, no change in any variable

Case 2: Increase in sales volume, other variables remain constant

Case 3: Increase in sales price, other variables remain constant

To calculate the net change in present value under each of the scenarios, we will use a 5-year horizon for any change in cash flow induced by the change in the dollar/euro exchange rate.

Case 1: Depreciation; No Change in Any Variable. Assume that in the five years ahead no changes occur in sales volume, sales price, or operating costs. Profits for the coming year in euros will be as expected, and cash flow from operations will be €1,728,600, as shown in Exhibit 11.5. With a new exchange rate of $1.0000/€, this cash flow measured in dollars during 2012 will be €1,728,600 × $1.0000/€ = $1,728,600. Exhibit 11.5 shows that the change in year-end cash flows from the base case is a negative $345,720 for each of the next five years (2012–2016). Exhibit 11.5 shows that the discounted present value of this series of diminished dollar value cash flows is $1,033,914.

Case 2: Volume Increases; Other Variables Remain Constant. Assume that sales within Europe double following the depreciation because German-made telecom components are now more competitive with imports. Additionally, export volume doubles because German-made components are now cheaper in countries whose currencies have not weakened. The sales price is kept constant in euro terms because management of Trident Germany has not observed any change in local German operating costs and because it sees an opportunity to increase market share.

Exhibit 11.5 shows expected cash flow for the first year (2012) would be $3,840,600. This amount, however, is not available because a doubling of sales volume will require additional investment in accounts receivable and in inventory. Although a portion of this additional investment might be financed by increasing accounts payable, we assume additional working capital is financed by cash flow from operations.

At the end of 2012, accounts receivable will be equal to one-fourth of annual sales, or €6,400,000. This amount is twice receivables of €3,200,000 at the end of 2011, and the incremental increase of €3,200,000 must be financed from available cash. Year-end inventory would be equal to one-fourth of annual direct costs, or €4,800,000, an increase of €2,400,000 over the year-beginning level. Receivables and inventory together increase by €5,600,000. At the end of five years (2016), these incremental cash outflows will be recaptured because any investment in current assets eventually rolls back into cash.

Assuming no further change in volume, price, or costs, cash inflows for the five years would be as described in Exhibit 11.5. In this instance, the depreciation causes a major drop in first-year cash flow from the $2,074,320 anticipated in 2012 without depreciation to a negative cash flow of $1,759,400. However, the remaining four years' cash flow is substantially enhanced by the operating effects of the depreciation. Over time, Trident Germany generates significantly more cash for its owners. The depreciation produces an operating gain over time, rather than an operating *loss*.

The reason that Trident Corporation is better off in Case 2 following the depreciation is that sales volume doubled while the per-unit dollar-equivalent sales price fell only 16.67% — the percent amount of the currency depreciation. In other words, the product faced a price elasticity of demand greater than one.

Case 3: Sales Price Increases, Other Variables Remain Constant. Assume the euro sales price is raised from €12.80 to €15.36 per unit to maintain the same U.S. dollar-equivalent price (the change offsets the depreciation of the euro). Assume further that volume remains constant in spite of this price increase; that is, customers expect to pay the same dollar-equivalent price, and local costs do not change.

Trident Germany is now better off following the depreciation than it was before because the sales price, which is pegged to the international price level, increased. However, volume did not drop. The new level of accounts receivable would be one-fourth of the new sales level of €15,360,000, or €3,840,000, an increase of €640,000 over the base case. The investment in inventory is $2,400,000, which is the same as the base case because annual direct costs did not change.

Expected dollar cash flow in every year exceeds the cash flow of $2,074,320 that had been originally expected. The increase in working capital causes net cash flow to be only $2,778,200 in 2012, but thereafter, the cash flow is $3,418,200 per year, with an additional $640,000 working capital recovered in the fifth year. The key to this improvement is operating leverage. If costs are incurred in euros and do not increase after a depreciation, an increase in the sales price by the amount of depreciation will lead to sharply higher profits.

Other Possibilities. If any portion of sales revenues were incurred in other currencies, the situation would be different. Trident Germany might leave the foreign sales price unchanged, in effect raising the euro-equivalent price. Alternatively, it might leave the euro-equivalent price unchanged, thus lowering the foreign sales price in an attempt to gain volume. Of course, it could also position itself between these two extremes. Depending on elasticities and the proportion of foreign to domestic sales, total sales revenue might rise or fall.

If some or all raw material or components were imported and paid for in hard currencies, euro operating costs would increase after the depreciation of the euro. Another possibility is that local (not imported) euro costs would rise after a depreciation.

Measurement of Loss. Exhibit 11.5 summarizes the change in expected year-end cash flows for the three cases and compares them with the cash flow expected should no depreciation occur (base case). These changes are then discounted by Trident's assumed weighted average cost of capital of 20% to obtain the present value of the gain (loss) on operating exposure.

In Case 1, in which nothing changes after the euro is devalued, Trident incurs an operating loss with a present value of ($1,033,914). In Case 2, in which volume doubled with no price change after depreciation, Trident experienced an operating gain with a present value of $2,866,106. In Case 3, in which the euro sales price was increased and volume did not change, the present value of the operating gain from depreciation was $3,742,892. An almost infinite number of combinations of volume, price, and cost could follow any depreciation, and any or all of them might take effect over time.

Strategic Management of Operating Exposure

The objective of both operating and transaction exposure management is to anticipate and influence the effect of unexpected changes in exchange rates on a firm's future cash flows, rather than merely hoping for the best. To meet this objective, management can *diversify the firm's operating and financing base. Management can also change the firm's operating and financing policies.*

The key to managing operating exposure at the strategic level is for management to recognize a disequilibrium in parity conditions when it occurs and to be pre-positioned to react most appropriately. This task can best be accomplished if a firm diversifies internationally both its operating and its financing bases. Diversifying operations means diversifying sales, location of production facilities, and raw material sources. Diversifying the financing base means raising funds in more than one capital market and in more than one currency.

A diversification strategy permits the firm to react either actively or passively, depending on management's risk preference, to opportunities presented by disequilibrium conditions in the foreign exchange, capital, and product markets. Such a strategy does not require management to predict disequilibrium but only to recognize it when it occurs. It does require management to consider how competitors are pre-positioned with respect to their own operating exposures. This knowledge should reveal which firms would be helped or hurt competitively by alternative disequilibrium scenarios.

Diversifying Operations

If a firm's operations are diversified internationally, management is pre-positioned both to recognize disequilibrium when it occurs and to react competitively. Consider the case where purchasing power parity is temporarily in disequilibrium. Although the disequilibrium may have been unpredictable, management can often recognize its symptoms as soon as they occur. For example, management might notice a change in comparative costs in the firm's own plants located in different countries. It might also observe changed profit margins or sales volume in one area compared to another, depending on price and income elasticities of demand and competitors' reactions.

Recognizing a temporary change in worldwide competitive conditions permits management to make changes in operating strategies. Management might make marginal shifts in sourcing raw materials, components, or finished products. If spare capacity exists, production runs can be lengthened in one country and reduced in another. The marketing effort can be strengthened in export markets where the firm's products have become more price competitive because of the disequilibrium condition.

Even if management does not actively distort normal operations when exchange rates change, the firm should experience some beneficial portfolio effects. The variability of its cash flows is probably reduced by international diversification of its production, sourcing, and sales because exchange rate changes under disequilibrium conditions are likely to increase the firm's competitiveness in some markets while reducing it in others. In that case, operating exposure would be neutralized.

In contrast to the internationally diversified MNE, a purely domestic firm might be subject to the full impact of foreign exchange operating exposure even though it does not have foreign currency cash flows. For example, it could experience intense import competition in its domestic market from competing firms producing in countries with undervalued currencies.

A purely domestic firm does not have the option to react to an international disequilibrium condition in the same manner as an MNE. In fact, a purely domestic firm will not be positioned to recognize that a disequilibrium exists because it lacks comparative data from its own internal sources. By the time external data are available, it is often too late to react. Even if a domestic firm recognizes the disequilibrium, it cannot quickly shift production and sales into foreign markets in which it has had no previous presence.

Constraints exist that may limit the feasibility of diversifying production locations. The technology of a particular industry may require large economies of scale. High tech firms, such as Intel, prefer to locate in places where they have easy access to other high tech suppliers, a highly educated workforce, and one or more leading universities. Their R&D efforts are closely tied to initial production and sales activities.

Diversifying Financing

If a firm diversifies its financing sources, it will be pre-positioned to take advantage of temporary deviations from the international Fisher effect. If interest rate differentials do not equal expected changes in exchange rates, opportunities to lower a firm's cost of capital will exist. However, to be able to switch financing sources, a firm must already be well known in the international investment community, with banking contacts firmly established. Again, this is not typically an option for a domestic firm.

As we will demonstrate in Chapter 12, diversifying sources of financing, regardless of the currency of denomination, can lower a firm's cost of capital and increase its availability of capital. It could also diversify such risks as restrictive capital market policies, and other constraints if the firm is located in a segmented capital market. This is especially important for firms resident in emerging markets.

Proactive Management of Operating Exposure

Operating and transaction exposures can be partially managed by adopting operating or financing policies that offset anticipated foreign exchange exposures. Four of the most commonly employed proactive policies are 1) matching currency cash flows; 2) risk-sharing agreements; 3) back-to-back or parallel loans; and 4) cross-currency swaps.

Matching Currency Cash Flows

One way to offset an anticipated continuous long exposure to a particular currency is to acquire debt denominated in that currency. Exhibit 11.6 depicts the exposure of a U.S. firm with continuing export sales to Canada. In order to compete effectively in Canadian markets, the firm invoices all export sales in Canadian dollars. This policy results in a continuing receipt of Canadian dollars month after month. If the export sales are part of a continuing supplier relationship, the long Canadian dollar position is relatively predictable and constant. This endless series of transaction exposures could of course be continually hedged with forward contracts or other contractual hedges, as discussed in Chapter 10.

But what if the firm sought out a continual use, an outflow, for its continual inflow of Canadian dollars? If the U.S. firm were to acquire part of its debt-capital in the Canadian dollar markets, it could use the relatively predictable Canadian dollar cash inflows from export sales to service the principal and interest payments on Canadian dollar debt and be cash *flow matched*. The U.S.-based firm has hedged an operational cash inflow by creating a financial cash outflow, and so it does not have to actively manage the exposure with contractual financial instruments such as forward contracts. This form of hedging, sometimes referred to as matching, is effective in eliminating currency exposure when the exposure cash flow is relatively constant and predictable over time.

EXHIBIT 11.6   Debt Financing as a Financial Hedge

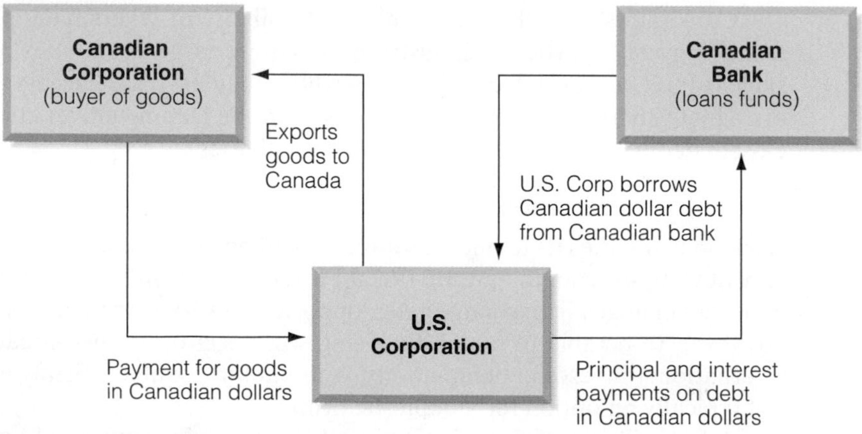

Exposure: The sale of goods to Canada creates a foreign currency exposure from the inflow of Canadian dollars.

Hedge: The Canadian dollar debt payments act as a financial hedge by requiring debt service, an outflow of Canadian dollars.

The list of potential matching strategies is nearly endless. A second alternative would be for the U.S. firm to seek out potential suppliers of raw materials or components in Canada as a substitute for U.S. or other foreign firms. The firm would then possess not only an operational Canadian dollar cash inflow, the receivable, but also a Canadian dollar operational cash outflow, a payable. If the cash flows were roughly the same in magnitude and timing, the strategy would be a natural hedge. The term "natural" refers to operating-based activities of the firm.

A third alternative, often referred to as currency switching, would be to pay foreign suppliers with Canadian dollars. For example, if the U.S. firm imported components from Mexico, the Mexican firms themselves might welcome payment in Canadian dollars because they are short Canadian dollars in their multinational cash flow network.

Currency Clauses: Risk-Sharing

An alternative arrangement for managing a long-term cash flow exposure between firms with a continuing buyer-supplier relationship is *risk-sharing*. Risk-sharing is a contractual arrangement in which the buyer and seller agree to "share" or split currency movement impacts on payments between them. If the two firms are interested in a long-term relationship based on product quality and supplier reliability and not on the whims of the currency markets, a cooperative agreement to share the burden of currency risk management may be in order.

If Ford's North American operations import automotive parts from Mazda (Japan) every month, year after year, major swings in exchange rates can benefit one party at the expense of the other. (Ford is a major stockholder of Mazda, but it does not exert control over its operations. Therefore, the risk-sharing agreement is particularly appropriate; transactions between the two are both intercompany and intracompany. A risk-sharing agreement solidifies the partnership.) One potential solution would be for Ford and Mazda to agree that all purchases by Ford will be made in Japanese yen at the current exchange rate, as long as the spot rate on the date of invoice is between, say, ¥115/$ and ¥125/$. If the exchange rate is between these values on the payment dates, Ford agrees to accept whatever transaction exposure exists (because it is paying in a foreign currency). If, however, the exchange rate falls outside this range on the payment date, Ford and Mazda will share the difference equally.

For example, Ford has an account payable of ¥25,000,000 for the month of March. If the spot rate on the date of invoice is ¥110/$, the Japanese yen would have appreciated versus the dollar, causing Ford's costs of purchasing automotive parts to rise. Since this rate falls outside the contractual range, Mazda would agree to accept a total payment in Japanese yen which would result from a difference of ¥5/$ (i.e., ¥115 – ¥110). Ford's payment would be

$$\left[\frac{¥25,000,000}{¥115.00/\$ - \left(\dfrac{¥5.00/\$}{2}\right)} \right] = \frac{¥25,000,000}{¥112.50/\$} = \$222,222.22$$

Ford's total payment in Japanese yen would be calculated using an exchange rate of ¥112.50/$, and saves Ford $5,050.51. At a spot rate of ¥110/$, Ford's costs for March would be $227,272.73. The risk-sharing agreement between Ford and Mazda allows Ford to pay $222,222.22, a savings of $5,050.51 over the cost without risk sharing (this "savings" is a reduction in an increased cost, not a true cost reduction). Both parties therefore incur costs and benefits from exchange rate movements outside the specified band. Note that the movement could just as easily have been in Mazda's favor if the spot rate had moved to ¥130/$.

The risk-sharing arrangement is intended to smooth the impact on both parties of volatile and unpredictable exchange rate movements. Of course, a sustained appreciation of one currency versus the other would require the negotiation of a new sharing agreement, but the ultimate goal of the agreement is to alleviate currency pressures on the continuing business relationship. Risk-sharing agreements like these have been in use for nearly 50 years on world markets. They became something of a rarity during the 1960s when exchange rates were relatively stable under the Bretton Woods Agreement. But with the return to floating exchange rates in the 1970s, firms with long-term customer-supplier relationships across borders have returned to some old ways of maintaining mutually beneficial long-term trade.

Back-to-Back Loans

A *back-to-back loan*, also referred to as a *parallel loan* or *credit swap*, occurs when two business firms in separate countries arrange to borrow each other's currency for a specific period of time. At an agreed terminal date they return the borrowed currencies. The operation is conducted outside the foreign exchange markets, although spot quotations may be used as the reference point for determining the amount of funds to be swapped. Such a swap creates a covered hedge against exchange loss, since each company, on its own books, borrows the same currency it repays. Back-to-back loans are also used at a time of actual or anticipated legal limitations on the transfer of investment funds to or from either country.

The structure of a typical back-to-back loan is illustrated in Exhibit 11.7. A British parent firm wanting to invest funds in its Dutch subsidiary locates a Dutch parent firm that wants to invest funds in the United Kingdom. Avoiding the exchange markets entirely, the British parent lends pounds to the Dutch subsidiary in the United Kingdom, while the Dutch parent lends euros to the British subsidiary in the Netherlands. The two loans would be for equal values at the current spot rate and for a specified maturity. At maturity, the two separate loans would each be repaid to the original lender, again without any need to use the foreign exchange markets. Neither loan carries any foreign exchange risk, and neither loan normally needs the approval of any governmental body regulating the availability of foreign exchange for investment purposes.

Parent company guarantees are not needed on the back-to-back loans because each loan carries the right of offset in the event of default of the other loan. A further agreement can

---

EXHIBIT 11.7   Back-to-Back Loans for Currency Hedging

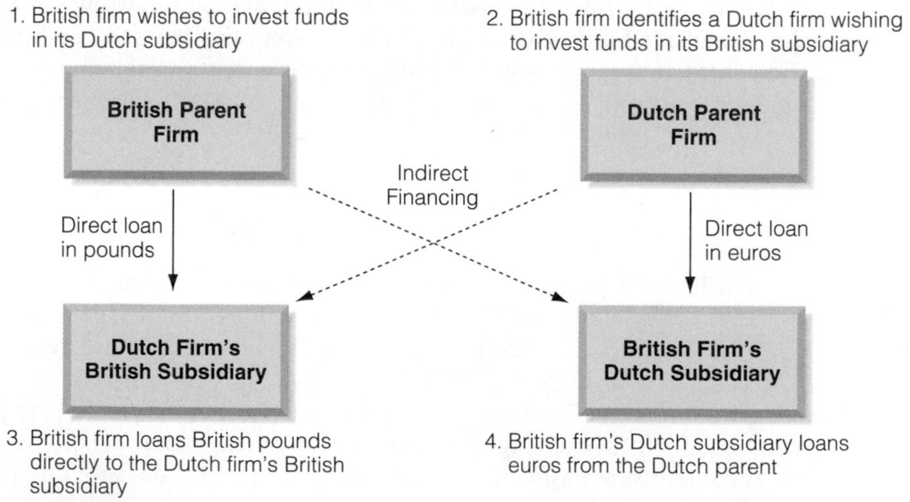

1. British firm wishes to invest funds in its Dutch subsidiary

2. British firm identifies a Dutch firm wishing to invest funds in its British subsidiary

British Parent Firm

Dutch Parent Firm

Indirect Financing

Direct loan in pounds

Direct loan in euros

Dutch Firm's British Subsidiary

British Firm's Dutch Subsidiary

3. British firm loans British pounds directly to the Dutch firm's British subsidiary

4. British firm's Dutch subsidiary loans euros from the Dutch parent

The back-to-back loan provides a method for parent-subsidiary cross-border financing without incurring direct currency exposure.

provide for maintenance of principal parity in case of changes in the spot rate between the two countries. For example, if the pound dropped by more than, say, 6% for as long as 30 days, the British parent might have to advance additional pounds to the Dutch subsidiary to bring the principal value of the two loans back to parity. A similar provision would protect the British if the euro should weaken. Although this parity provision might lead to changes in the amount of home currency each party must lend during the period of the agreement, it does not increase foreign exchange risk, because at maturity all loans are repaid in the same currency loaned.

There are two fundamental impediments to widespread use of the back-to-back loan. First, it is difficult for a firm to find a partner, termed a *counterparty*, for the currency, amount, and timing desired. Secondly, a risk exists that one of the parties will fail to return the borrowed funds at the designated maturity—although this risk is minimized because each party to the loan has, in effect, 100% collateral, albeit in a different currency. These disadvantages have led to the rapid development and wide use of the currency swap.

Cross Currency Swaps

A *cross currency swap* resembles a back-to-back loan except that it does not appear on a firm's balance sheet. As we noted briefly in Chapter 6, the term swap is widely used to describe a foreign exchange agreement between two parties to exchange a given amount of one currency for another and, after a period of time, to give back the original amounts swapped. Care should be taken to clarify which of the many different swaps is being referred to in a specific case.

In a currency swap, a firm and a swap dealer or swap bank agree to exchange an equivalent amount of two different currencies for a specified period of time. Currency swaps can be negotiated for a wide range of maturities up to at least 10 years. If funds are more expensive in one country than another, a fee may be required to compensate for the interest differential. The swap dealer or swap bank acts as a middleman in setting up the swap agreement.

A typical currency swap first requires two firms to borrow funds in the markets and currencies in which they are best known. For example, a Japanese firm would typically borrow yen on a regular basis in its home market. If, however, the Japanese firm were exporting to the United States and earning U.S. dollars, it might wish to construct a *matching cash flow hedge* which would allow it to use the U.S. dollars earned to make regular debt-service payments on U.S. dollar debt. If, however, the Japanese firm is not well known in the U.S. financial markets, it may have no ready access to U.S. dollar debt.

One way in which it could, in effect, borrow dollars, is to participate in a *cross-currency swap* (see Exhibit 11.8). The Japanese firm could swap its yen-denominated debt service payments with another firm that has U.S. dollar-debt service payments. This swap would have the Japanese firm "paying dollars" and "receiving yen." The Japanese firm would then have dollar-debt service without actually borrowing U.S. dollars. Simultaneously, a U.S. corporation could actually be entering into a cross-currency swap in the opposite direction—"paying yen" and "receiving dollars." The swap dealer is taking the role of a middleman.

Swap dealers arrange most swaps on a "blind basis," meaning that the initiating firm does not know who is on the other side of the swap arrangement—the counterparty. The firm views the dealer or bank as its counterparty. Because the swap markets are dominated by the major money center banks worldwide, the counterparty risk is acceptable. Because the swap dealer's business is arranging swaps, the dealer can generally arrange for the currency, amount, and timing of the desired swap.

Accountants in the United States treat the currency swap as a foreign exchange transaction rather than as debt and treat the obligation to reverse the swap at some later date as a forward exchange contract. Forward exchange contracts can be matched against assets, but they are entered in a firm's footnotes rather than as balance sheet items. The result is that

EXHIBIT 11.8   Using Cross-Currency Swaps

Both the Japanese corporation and the U.S. corporation would like to enter into a cross-currency swap which would allow them to use foreign currency cash inflows to service debt.

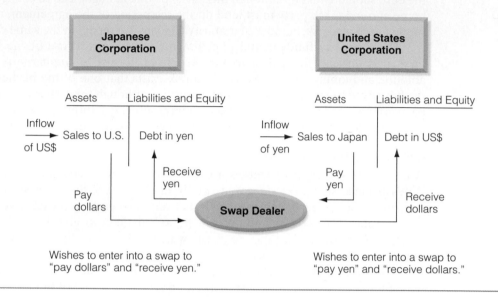

Wishes to enter into a swap to "pay dollars" and "receive yen."

Wishes to enter into a swap to "pay yen" and "receive dollars."

both translation and operating exposures are avoided, and neither a long-term receivable nor a long-term debt is created on the balance sheet.

Contractual Approaches: Hedging the Unhedgeable

Some MNEs now attempt to hedge their operating exposure with contractual strategies. A number of firms like Merck (U.S.) have undertaken long-term currency option positions, hedges designed to offset lost earnings from adverse exchange rate changes. This hedging of what many of these firms refer to as *strategic exposure or competitive exposure* seems to fly in the face of traditional theory.

The ability of firms to hedge the "unhedgeable" is dependent upon *predictability*: 1) the predictability of the firm's future cash flows, and 2) the predictability of the firm's competitor's responses to exchange rate changes. Although the management of many firms may believe they are capable of predicting their own cash flows, few in practice feel capable of accurately predicting competitor response. As illustrated by *Global Finance in Practice 11.2*, many firms still find even timely measurement of exposure a challenge.

Merck is an example of a firm whose management feels capable of both. The company possesses relatively predictable long-run revenue streams due to the product-niche nature of the pharmaceuticals industry. As a U.S.-based exporter to foreign markets, markets in which sales levels by product are relatively predictable and prices are often regulated by government, Merck can accurately predict net long-term cash flows in foreign currencies five and ten years into the future. Merck has a relatively undiversified operating structure. It is highly centralized in terms of where research, development, and production costs are located. Merck's managers feel Merck has no real alternatives but contractual hedging if it is to weather long-term unexpected exchange rate changes. Merck has purchased over-the-counter (OTC) long-term put options on foreign currencies versus the U.S. dollar as insurance against potential lost earnings from exchange rate changes. In Merck's case, the predictability of competitor response to exchange rate changes is less pertinent given the niche-market nature of pharmaceutical products.

A significant question remains as to the true effectiveness of hedging operating exposure with contractual hedges. The fact remains that even after feared exchange rate movements and put option position payoffs have occurred, the firm is competitively disadvantaged. The capital outlay required for the purchase of such sizable put option positions is capital not used for the potential diversification of operations, which in the long run might have more effectively maintained the firm's global market share and international competitiveness.

Summary of Learning Objectives

Examine how operating exposure arises through unexpected changes in operating and financing cash flows.

◆ *Foreign exchange exposure* is a measure of the potential for a firm's profitability, net cash flow, and market value to change because of a change in exchange rates. The three main types of foreign exchange risk are *operating*, *transaction*, and *translation* exposures.

◆ *Operating exposure* measures the change in value of the firm that results from changes in future operating cash flows caused by an unexpected change in exchange rates.

Analyze the sequence of how unexpected exchange rate changes alter the economic performance of a business unit through volume, price, cost and other key variable changes.

◆ An unexpected change in exchange rates impacts a firm's expected cash flow at four levels: 1) short run; 2) medium run, equilibrium case; 3) medium run, disequilibrium case; and 4) long run.

Evaluate the strategic alternatives to managing operating exposure.

◆ Operating strategies for the management of operating exposure emphasize the structuring of firm operations

in order to create matching streams of cash flows by currency. This is termed natural hedging.

◆ The objective of operating exposure management is to anticipate and influence the effect of unexpected changes in exchange rates on a firm's future cash flow, rather than being forced into passive reaction to such changes as was described in the Trident Europe case. This task can best be accomplished if a firm diversifies internationally both its operations and its financing base.

Detail the proactive policies available to firms for managing operating exposure.

◆ Proactive policies include matching currency of cash flow, currency risk sharing clauses, back-to-back loan structures, and cross-currency swap agreements.

◆ Strategies to change financing policies include matching currency cash flows, back-to-back loans and currency swaps.

◆ Contractual approaches (i.e., options and forwards) have occasionally been used to hedge operating exposure but are costly and possibly ineffectual.

Toyota's European Operating Exposure

It was January 2002, and Toyota Motor Europe Manufacturing (TMEM) had a problem. More specifically, Mr. Toyoda Shuhei, the new President of TMEM, had a problem. He was on his way to Toyota Motor Company's (Japan) corporate offices outside Tokyo to explain the continuing losses of the European manufacturing and sales operations. The CEO of Toyota Motor Company, Mr. Hiroshi Okuda, was expecting a proposal from Mr. Shuhei to reduce and eventually eliminate the European losses. The situation was intense given that TMEM was the only major Toyota subsidiary suffering losses.

Toyota and Auto Manufacturing

Toyota Motor Company was the number one automobile manufacturer in Japan, the third largest manufacturer in the world by unit sales (5.5 million units or one auto every six seconds), but number eight in sales in Continental Europe. The global automobile manufacturing industry had been experiencing, like many industries, continued consolidation in recent years as margins were squeezed, economies of scale and scope pursued, and global sales slowed.

Toyota was no different. It had continued to rationalize its manufacturing along regional lines. Toyota had continued to increase the amount of local manufacturing in North America. In 2001, over 60% of Toyota's North American sales were locally manufactured. But Toyota's European sales were nowhere close to this yet. Most of Toyota's automobile and truck manufacturing for Europe was still done in Japan. In 2001, only 24% of the autos sold in Europe were manufactured in Europe (including the United Kingdom), the remainder were imported from Japan (see Exhibit 1).

Toyota Motor Europe sold 634,000 automobiles in 2000. This was the second largest foreign market for Toyota, second only to North America. TMEM expected significant growth in European sales, and was planning to expand European manufacturing and sales to 800,000 units by 2005. But for fiscal 2001, the unit reported operating losses of ¥9.897 billion ($82.5 million at ¥120/$). TMEM had three assembly plants in the United Kingdom, one plant in Turkey, and one plant in Portugal. In November 2000, Toyota Motor Europe announced publicly that it would not generate positive profits for the next two years due to the weakness of the euro.

Toyota had recently introduced a new model to the European market, the Yaris, which was proving very successful. The Yaris, a super-small vehicle with a 1,000cc engine, had sold more than 180,000 units in 2000.

EXHIBIT 1   Toyota Motor's European Currency Operating Structure

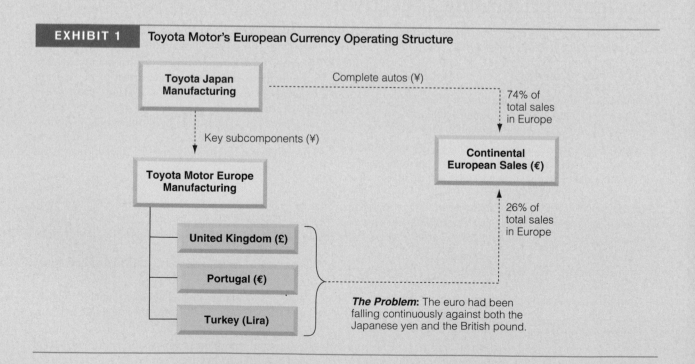

Although the Yaris had been specifically designed for the European market, the decision had been made early on to manufacture it in Japan.

Currency Exposure

The primary source of the continuing operating losses suffered by TMEM was the falling value of the euro. Over the recent two year period, the euro had fallen in value against both the Japanese yen and the British pound. As demonstrated in Exhibit 1, the cost base for most of the autos sold within the Continental European market was the Japanese yen. Exhibit 2 illustrates the slide of the euro against the Japanese yen.

As the yen rose against the euro, costs increased significantly when measured in euro terms. If Toyota wished to preserve its price competitiveness in the European market, it had to absorb most of the exchange rate changes and suffer reduced or negative margins on both completed cars and key subcomponents shipped to its European manufacturing centers. Deciding to manufacture the Yaris in Japan had only exacerbated the situation.

Management Response

Toyota management was not sitting passively by. In 2001, they had initiated some assembly operations in Valenciennes, France. Although a relatively small percentage of total European sales as of January 2002, Toyota planned to continue to expand its capacity and capabilities to source about 25% of European sales by 2004. Assembly of the Yaris was scheduled to be moved to Valenciennes in 2002. The continuing problem, however, was that it was an assembly facility, meaning that much of the expensive value-added content of the autos being assembled was still based in either Japan or the United Kingdom.

Mr. Shuhei, with the approval of Mr. Okuda, had also initiated a local sourcing and procurement program for the United Kingdom manufacturing operations. TMEM wished to decrease the number of key components imported from Toyota Japan to reduce the currency exposure of the U.K. unit. But again, the continuing problem of the British pound's value against the euro, as shown in Exhibit 3, reduced even the effectiveness of this solution.

CASE QUESTIONS

1. Why do you think Toyota waited so long to move much of its manufacturing for European sales to Europe?

2. If the British pound were to join the European Monetary Union would the problem be resolved? How likely do you think this is?

3. If you were Mr. Shuhei, how would you categorize your problems and solutions? What was a short-term problem? What was a long-term problem?

4. What measures would you recommend that Toyota Europe take to resolve the continuing operating losses?

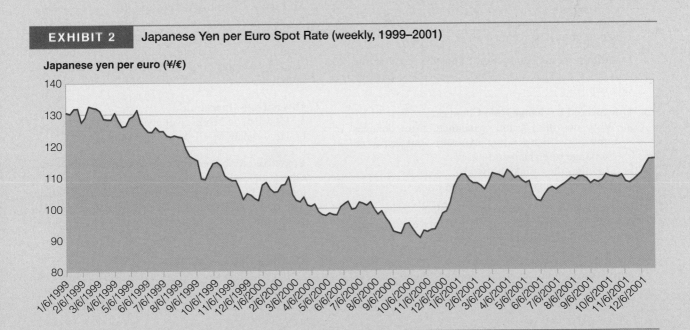

EXHIBIT 2   Japanese Yen per Euro Spot Rate (weekly, 1999–2001)

EXHIBIT 3   British pounds per Euro Spot Rate (weekly, 1999–2001)

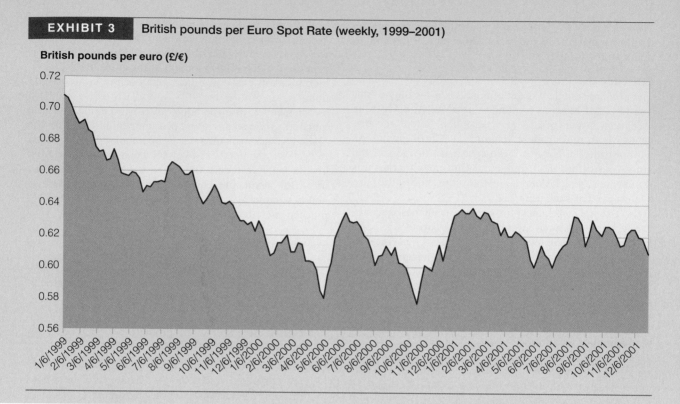

British pounds per euro (£/€)

Questions

1. **Definitions.** Define the following terms:
   a. Operating exposure
   b. Economic exposure
   c. Competitive exposure

2. **Operating versus Transaction Exposure.** Explain the difference between operating exposure and transaction exposure.

3. **Unexpected Exchange Rate Changes.**
   a. Why do unexpected exchange rate changes contribute to operating exposure, but expected exchange rate changes do not?
   b. Explain the time horizons used to analyze unexpected changes in exchange rates.

4. **Macroeconomic Uncertainty.** Explain how the concept of macroeconomic uncertainty expands the scope of analyzing operating exposure.

5. **Strategic Response.** The objective of both operating and transaction exposure management is to anticipate and influence the effect of unexpected changes in exchange rates on a firm's future cash flows. What strategic alternative policies exist to enable management to manage these exposures?

6. **Managing Operating Exposure.** The key to managing operating exposure at the strategic level is for management to recognize a disequilibrium in parity conditions when it occurs and to be prepositioned to react most appropriately. How can this task best be accomplished?

7. **Diversifying Operations.**
   a. How can an MNE diversify operations?
   b. How can an MNE diversify financing?

8. **Proactive Management of Operating Exposure.** Operating and transaction exposures can be partially managed by adopting operating or financing policies that offset anticipated foreign exchange exposures. What are four of the most commonly employed proactive policies?

9. **Matching Currency Exposure.**
   a. Explain how matching currency cash flows can offset operating exposure.
   b. Give an example of matching currency cash flows.

10. Risk Sharing. An alternative arrangement for managing operating exposure between firms with a continuing buyer-supplier relationship is risk sharing. Explain how risk sharing works.

11. Back-to-Back Loans. Explain how back-to-back loans can hedge foreign exchange operating exposure.

12. Currency Swaps. Explain how currency swaps can hedge foreign exchange operating exposure. What are the accounting advantages of currency swaps?

13. Contractual Hedging. Eastman Kodak is an MNE that has undertaken contractual hedging of its operating exposure.
   a. How do they accomplish this task?
   b. What assumptions do they make in order to justify contractual hedging of their operating exposure?
   c. How effective is such contractual hedging in your opinion? Explain your reasoning.

Problems

1. DeMagistris Fashion Company. DeMagistris Fashion Company, based in New York City, imports leather coats from Acuña Leather Goods, a reliable and longtime supplier, based in Buenos Aires, Argentina. Payment is in Argentine pesos. When the peso lost its parity with the U.S. dollar in January 2002, it collapsed in value to Ps4.0/$ by October 2002. The outlook was for a further decline in the peso's value. Since both DeMagistris and Acuña wanted to continue their longtime relationship, they agreed on a risk-sharing arrangement. As long as the spot rate on the date of an invoice is between Ps3.5/$ and Ps4.5/$ DeMagistris will pay based on the spot rate. If the exchange rate falls outside this range, they will share the difference equally with Acuña Leather Goods. The risk-sharing agreement will last for six months, at which time the exchange rate limits will be reevaluated. DeMagistris contracts to import leather coats from Acuña for Ps8,000,000 or $2,000,000 at the current spot rate of Ps4.0/$ during the next six months.
   a. If the exchange rate changes immediately to Ps6.00/$, what will be the dollar cost of six months of imports to DeMagistris?
   b. At Ps6.00/$, what will be the peso export sales in Acuña Leather Goods to DeMagistris Fashion Company?

2. Mauna Loa. Mauna Loa, a macadamia nut subsidiary of Hershey's with planations on the slopes of its namesake volcano in Hilo, Hawaii, exports macadamia nuts worldwide. The Japanese market is its biggest export market, with average annual sales invoiced in yen to Japanese customers of ¥1,200,000,000. At the present exchange rate of ¥125/$, this is equivalent to $9,600,000. Sales are relatively equally distributed during the year. They show up as a ¥250,00,000 account receivable on Mauna Loa's balance sheet. Credit terms to each customer allow for 60 days before payment is due. Monthly cash collections are typically ¥100,000,000.

Mauna Loa would like to hedge its yen receipts, but it has too many customers and transactions to make it practical to sell each receivable forward. It does not want to use options because they are considered to be too expensive for this particular purpose. Therefore, they have decided to use a "matching" hedge by borrowing yen.
   a. How much should Mauna Loa borrow in yen?
   b. What should be the terms of payment on the yen loan?

3. Murray Exports (A). Murray Exports (U.S.) exports heavy crane equipment to several Chinese dock facilities. Sales are currently 10,000 units per year at the yuan equivalent of $24,000 each. The Chinese yuan (renminbi) has been trading at Yuan8.20/$, but a Hong Kong advisory service predicts the renminbi will drop in value next week to Yuan9.00/$, after which it will remain unchanged for at least a decade. Accepting this forecast as given, Murray Exports faces a pricing decision in the face of the impending devaluation. It may either 1) maintain the same yuan price and in effect sell for fewer dollars, in which case Chinese volume will not change; or 2) maintain the same dollar price, raise the yuan price in China to offset the devaluation, and experience a 10% drop in unit volume. Direct costs are 75% of the U.S. sales price.
   a. What would be the short-run (one year) impact of each pricing strategy?
   b. Which do you recommend?

4. Murray Exports (B). Assume the same facts as in Murray Exports (A). Additionally, financial management believes that if it maintains the same yuan sales price, volume will increase at 12% per annum for eight years. Dollar costs will not change. At the end of 10 years, Murray Exports' patent expires and it will no longer export to China. After the yuan is devalued to Yuan9.20/$, no further devaluations are expected. If Murray Exports raises the yuan price so as to maintain its dollar price, volume will increase at only 1% per annum for eight years, starting from the lower initial base of 9,000 units. Again, dollar costs will not change, and at the end of eight years Murray Exports will stop exporting to China. Murray Exports' weighted average cost of capital is 10%. Given these considerations, what should be Murray Exports' pricing policy?

5. **MacLoren Automotive.** MacLoren Automtive manufactures British sports cars, a number of which are exported to New Zealand for payment in pounds sterling. The distributor sells the sports cars in New Zealand for New Zealand dollars. The New Zealand distributor is unable to carry all of the foreign exchange risk, and would not sell MacLoren models unless MacLoren could share some of the foreign exchange risk. MacLoren has agreed that sales for a given model year will initially be priced at a "base" spot rate between the New Zealand dollar and pound sterling set to be the spot mid-rate at the beginning of that model year. As long as the actual exchange rate is within ±5% of that base rate, payment will be made in pounds sterling. That is, the New Zealand distributor assumes all foreign exchange risk. However, if the spot rate at time of shipment falls outside of this ±5% range, MacLoren will share equally (i.e., 50/50) the difference between the actual spot rate and the base rate. For the current model year the base rate is NZ$1.6400/£.

   a. What are the outside ranges within which the New Zealand importer must pay at the then current spot rate?

   b. If MacLoren ships 10 sports cars to the New Zealand distributor at a time when the spot exchange rate is NZ$1.7000/£, and each car has an invoice cost £32,000, what will be the cost to the distributor in New Zealand dollars? How many pounds will MacLoren receive, and how does this compare with McLaren's expected sales receipt of £32,000 per car?

   c. If MacLoren Automotive ships the same 10 cars to New Zealand at a time when the spot exchange rate is NZ$1.6500/£, how many New Zealand dollars will the distributor pay? How many pounds will MacLoren Automotive receive?

   d. Does a risk-sharing agreement such as this one shift the currency exposure from one party of the transaction to the other?

   e. Why is such a risk-sharing agreement of benefit to MacLoren? To the New Zealand distributor?

6. **Trident Germany: Case 4.** Trident Germany decides not to change its domestic price of €12.80 per unit within Europe, but to raise its export price (in euros) from £12.80 per unit to €15.36 per unit, thus preserving its original dollar equivalent price of $15.36 per unit. Volume in both markets remains the same because no buyer perceives that the price has changed.

7. **Trident Germany: Case 5.** Trident Germany finds that domestic costs increase in proportion to the drop in value of the euro because of local inflation and a rise in the cost of imported raw materials and components. This rise in costs (+20%) applies to all cash costs, including direct costs and fixed cash operating costs. However, it does not apply to depreciation. Because of the increase in its costs, Trident Europe increases its sales price in euros from €12.80 per unit to €15.36 per unit.

8. **Risk-Sharing at Harley Davidson.** Harley-Davidson (U.S.) reportedly uses risk-sharing agreements with its own foreign subsidiaries and with independent foreign distributors. Because these foreign units typically sell to their local markets and earn local currency, Harley would like to ease their individual currency exposure problems by allowing them to pay for merchandise from Harley (U.S.) in their local functional currency. The spot rate between the U.S. dollar and the Australian dollar on January 1 is A$1.3052/US$. Assume that Harley uses this rate as the basis for setting its central rate or base exchange rate for the year at A$1.3000/US$. Harley agrees to price all contracts to Australian distributors at this exact exchange rate as long as the current spot rate on the order date is within ±2.5% of this rate. If the spot rate falls outside of this range, but is still within ±5% of the central rate, Harley will "share" equally (i.e., "50/50") the difference between the new spot rate and the neutral boundary with the distributor.

9. **Hurte-Paroxysm Products, Inc. (A).** Hurte-Paroxysm Products, Inc. (HP) of the United States, exports computer printers to Brazil, whose currency, the reais (symbol R$) has been trading at R$3.40/US$. Exports to Brazil are currently 50,000 printers per year at the reais equivalent of $200 each. A strong rumor exists that the reais will be devalued to R$4.00/$ within two weeks by the Brazilian government. Should the devaluation take place, the reais is expected to remain unchanged for another decade. Accepting this forecast as given, HP faces a pricing decision which must be made before any actual devaluation: HP may either 1) maintain the same reais price and in effect sell for fewer dollars, in which case Brazilian volume will not change, or 2) maintain the same dollar price, raise

the reais price in Brazil to compensate for the devaluation, and experience a 20% drop in volume. Direct costs in the United States are 60% of the U.S. sales price. What would be the short-run (1-year) implication of each pricing strategy? Which do you recommend?

10. **Hurte-Paroxysm Products, Inc. (B).** Assume the same facts as in Hurte-Paroxysm Products, Inc. (A). HP also believes that if it maintains the same price in Brazilian reais as a permanent policy, volume will increase at 10% per annum for six years, costs will not change. At the end of six years, HP's patent expires and it will no longer export to Brazil. After the reais is devalued to R$4.00/US$, no further devaluation is expected. If HP raises the price in reais so as to maintain its dollar price, volume will increase at only 4% per annum for six years, starting from the lower initial base of 40,000 units. Again, dollar costs will not change, and at the end of six years, HP will stop exporting to Brazil. HP's weighted average cost of capital is 12%. Given these considerations, what do you recommend for HP's pricing policy? Justify your recommendation.

Internet Exercises

1. **Operating Exposure: Recent Examples.** Using the following major periodicals as starting points, find a current example of a firm with a substantial operating exposure problem. To aid in your search, you might focus on businesses having major operations in countries with recent currency crises, either through depreciation or major home currency appreciation.

Financial Times	www.ft.com/
The Economist	www.economist.com/
The *Wall Street Journal*	www.wsj.com/

2. **SEC Edgar Files.** To analyze an individual firm's operating exposure more carefully, it is necessary to have more detailed information available than in the normal annual report. Choose a specific firm with substantial international operations, for example, Coca-Cola or PepsiCo, and search the Security and Exchange Commission's Edgar Files for more detailed financial reports of their international operations.

Search SEC EDGAR Archives	www.sec.gov/cgi-bin/ srch-edgar

Financing the Global Firm

CHAPTER 12
The Global Cost and Availability of Capital

CHAPTER 13
Sourcing Equity and Debt Globally

CHAPTER 14
Multinational Tax Management

12

The Global Cost and Availability of Capital

Ideas and leadership, however, are not enough. They need to be nurtured with money. Companies that cannot depend on steady access to the capital markets will not prosper . . . . What do investors want? First, of course, investors want performance: strong predictable earnings and sustainable growth. Second, they want transparency, accountability, open communications and effective corporate governance. Companies that fail to move toward international standards in each of these areas will fail to attract and retain international capital. —"The Brave New World of Corporate Governance," *Latinfinance*, May 2001.

LEARNING OBJECTIVES

◆ Examine how a firm headquartered in a country with an illiquid and segmented capital market achieves a lower global cost and greater availability of capital.

◆ Analyze the linkage between cost and availability of capital.

◆ Evaluate the effect of market liquidity and segmentation on the cost of capital.

◆ Explain how the weighted average cost of capital for an MNE compares with its domestic counterpart.

How can firms tap global capital markets for the purpose of minimizing their cost of capital and maximizing capital's availability? Why should they do so? This chapter explores these questions, concluding with a Mini-Case that details one of the most influential corporate financial strategies ever executed, ***Novo Industri A/S (Novo)***.

Financial Globalization and Strategy

Global integration of capital markets has given many firms access to new and cheaper sources of funds beyond those available in their home markets. These firms can then accept more long-term projects and invest more in capital improvements and expansion. If a firm is located in a country with illiquid and/or segmented capital markets, it can achieve this lower global cost and greater availability of capital by a properly designed and implemented strategy. The dimensions of the cost and availability of capital are presented in Exhibit 12.1. The impact of firm-specific characteristics, market liquidity for the firm's securities, and the definition and effect of market segmentation on the prices of a firm's capital are the focus of most of this chapter.

EXHIBIT 12.1   Dimensions of the Cost and Availability of Capital Strategy

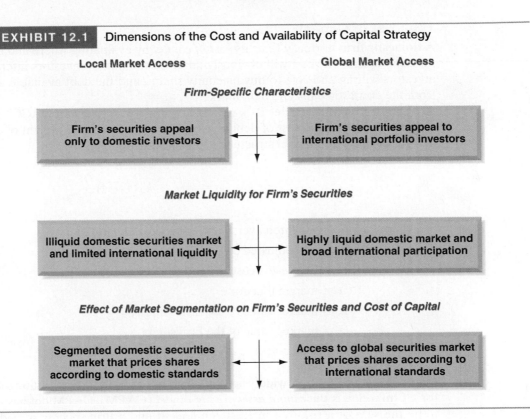

Local Market Access   Global Market Access

Firm-Specific Characteristics

Firm's securities appeal only to domestic investors ↔ Firm's securities appeal to international portfolio investors

Market Liquidity for Firm's Securities

Illiquid domestic securities market and limited international liquidity ↔ Highly liquid domestic market and broad international participation

Effect of Market Segmentation on Firm's Securities and Cost of Capital

Segmented domestic securities market that prices shares according to domestic standards ↔ Access to global securities market that prices shares according to international standards

A firm that must source its long-term debt and equity in a highly illiquid domestic securities market will probably have a relatively high cost of capital and will face limited availability of such capital, which in turn will lower its competitiveness both internationally and vis-à-vis foreign firms entering its home market. This category of firms includes both firms resident in emerging countries, where the capital market remains undeveloped, and firms too small to gain access to their own national securities markets. Many family-owned firms find themselves in this category because they choose not to utilize securities markets to source their long-term capital needs.

Firms resident in industrial countries with small capital markets often source their long-term debt and equity at home in these partially liquid domestic securities markets. The firms' cost and availability of capital is better than that of firms in countries with illiquid capital markets. However, if these firms can tap the highly liquid global markets, they can also strengthen their competitive advantage in sourcing capital.

Firms resident in countries with segmented capital markets must devise a strategy to escape dependence on that market for their long-term debt and equity needs. A national capital market is segmented if the required rate of return on securities in that market differs from the required rate of return on securities of comparable expected return and risk traded on other securities markets. Capital markets become segmented because of such factors as excessive regulatory control, perceived political risk, anticipated foreign exchange risk, lack of transparency, asymmetric availability of information, cronyism, insider trading, and many other market imperfections. Firms constrained by any of these conditions must develop a strategy to escape their own limited capital markets and source some of their long-term capital abroad.

The Cost of Capital

A domestic firm normally finds its *cost of capital* by evaluating where and from whom it will raise its capital. The cost will obviously differ on the mix of investors interested in the firm, investors willing and able to buy its equity shares, and the debt available to the firm, raised from the domestic bank and debt market.

The firm then calculates its *weighted average cost of capital* (WACC) by combining the cost of equity with the cost of debt in proportion to the relative weight of each in the firm's optimal long-term financial structure. More specifically,

$$k_{WACC} = k_e \frac{E}{V} + k_d(1-t)\frac{D}{V}$$

where k_{WACC} = weighted average after-tax cost of capital
k_e = risk-adjusted cost of equity
k_d = before-tax cost of debt
t = marginal tax rate
E = market value of the firm's equity
D = market value of the firm's debt
V = total market value of the firm's securities $(D + E)$

Cost of Equity. The most widely accepted and used method of calculating the cost of equity for a firm today is the *capital asset pricing model* (CAPM). CAPM defines the cost of equity to be the sum of a risk-free interest component and a firm-specific spread over and above that risk-free component, as seen in the following formula:

$$k_e = k_{rf} + \beta_j(k_m - k_{rf})$$

where k_e = expected (required) rate of return on equity
k_{rf} = rate of interest on risk-free bonds (Treasury bonds, for example)
β_j = coefficient of *systematic risk* for the firm
k_m = expected (required) rate of return on the market portfolio of stocks

The key component of CAPM is *beta*, the measure of *systematic risk*. *Systematic risk* is a measure of how the firm's returns vary with those of the market in which it trades. Beta is calculated as a function of the total variability of expected returns of the firm's stock relative to the market index (k_m) and the degree to which the variability of expected returns of the firm is correlated to the expected returns on the market index. More formally,

$$\beta_j = \frac{\rho_{jm}\sigma_j}{\sigma_m}$$

where β_j (beta) = measure of systematic risk for security j
ρ (rho) = correlation between security j and the market
σ_j (sigma) = standard deviation of the return on firm j
σ_m (sigma) = standard deviation of the market return

Beta will have a value of less than 1.0 if the firm's returns are less volatile than the market, 1.0 if the same as the market, or greater than 1.0 if more volatile—or risky—than the market. CAPM analysis assumes that the required return estimated is an indication of what more is necessary to keep an investor's capital invested in the equity considered. If the equity's return does not reach the expected return, CAPM assumes that individual investors will liquidate their holdings.

CAPM's biggest challenge is that the *beta* used needs to be for the future and not the past. A prospective investor is interested in how the individual firm's returns will vary in the coming periods. Unfortunately, since the future is not known, the *beta* used in any firm's estimate of equity cost is typically based on evidence from the recent past.

Cost of Debt. Firms acquire debt in either the form of loans from commercial banks—the most common form of debt, or as securities sold to the debt markets, instruments like notes and bonds. The normal procedure for measuring the cost of debt requires a forecast of interest rates for the next few years, the proportions of various classes of debt the firm expects to use, and the corporate income tax rate. The interest costs of the different debt components are then averaged according to their proportion in the debt structure. This before-tax average, k_d, is then adjusted for corporate income taxes by multiplying it by the expression $(1 - \text{tax rate})$, to obtain $k_d(1 - t)$, the weighted average after-tax cost of debt.

The weighted average cost of capital is normally used as the risk-adjusted discount rate whenever a firm's new projects are in the same general risk class as its existing projects. On the other hand, a project-specific required rate of return should be used as the discount rate if a new project differs from existing projects in business or financial risk.

International CAPM (ICAPM)

The traditional form of CAPM, the domestic CAPM used in the previous section, assumes the firm's equity trades in a purely domestic market. The *beta* and market risk premium $(k_m - k_{rf})$ therefore used in the cost of equity calculation were based on a purely domestic market of securities and choices. But what if globalization has opened up the global markets, integrating them, allowing investors to choose among stocks of a global portfolio?

International CAPM (ICAPM) assumes that there is a global market in which the firm's equity trades, and estimates of the firm's *beta*, β_j^g, and the market risk premium, $(k_m^g - k_{rf}^g)$, must then reflect this global portfolio.

$$k_e^{\text{global}} = k_{rf}^g + \beta_j^g (k_m^g - k_{rf}^g)$$

The value of the risk-free rate, k_{rf}^g, may not change (so that $k_{rf}^g = k_{rf}$), as a U.S. Treasury note may be the risk-free rate for a U.S.-based investor regardless of the domestic or international portfolio. The market return, k_m^g, will change, reflecting average expected global market returns for the coming periods. The firm's *beta*, β_j^g, will most assuredly change as it now will reflect the expected variations against a greater global portfolio. How that *beta* will change, however, depends.

Sample Calculation: Trident's Cost of Capital

Maria Gonzalez, Trident's Chief Financial Officer, wants to calculate the company's weighted average cost of capital in both forms, the traditional CAPM and then ICAPM.

Maria assumes the risk-free rate of interest (k_{rf}) as 4%, using the U.S. government 10-year Treasury bond rate. The expected rate of return of the market portfolio (k_m) is assumed to be 9%, the expected rate of return on the market portfolio held by a well-diversified domestic investor. Trident's estimate of its own systematic risk, its *beta*, against the domestic portfolio is 1.2. Trident's cost of equity is then

$$k_e = k_{rf} + \beta (k_m - k_{rf}) = 4.00\% + 1.2 (9.00\% - 5.00\%) = 10.00\%$$

Trident's cost of debt (k_d), the before tax cost of debt estimated by observing the current yield on Trident's outstanding bonds combined with bank debt, is 8%. Using 35% as the corporate income tax rate for the United States, Trident's after-tax cost of debt is then

$$k_d (1 - t) = 8.00 (1 - 0.35) = 8.00 (0.65) = 5.20\%$$

Trident's long-term capital structure is 60% equity (E/V) and 40% debt (D/V), where V is Trident's total market value. Trident's weighted average cost of capital (k_{WACC}) is then

$$k_{WACC} = k_e \frac{E}{V} + k_d (1 - t)\frac{D}{V} = 10.00\% (.60) + 5.20\% (.40) = 8.08\%$$

This is Trident's cost of capital using the traditional domestic CAPM estimate of the cost of equity.

But Maria Gonzalez wonders if this is the proper approach for Trident. As Trident has globalized its own business activities, the investor base that owns Trident's shares has also globally diversified. Trident's shares are now listed in London and Tokyo, in addition to their home listing on the New York Stock Exchange. Over 40% of Trident's stock is now held by foreign portfolio investors, as part of their globally diversified portfolios, while Trident's U.S. investors also typically hold globally diversified portfolios.

A second calculation of Trident's cost of equity, this time using the ICAPM, yields different results. Trident's beta, when calculated against a larger global equity market index which includes these foreign markets and their investors, is lower, 0.90. The expected market return for a larger globally integrated equity market is a lower value as well, 8.00%. The ICAPM cost of equity is a much lower value of 7.60%.

$$k_e^{global} = k_{rf}^g + \beta_j^g (k_m^g - k_{rf}^g) = 4.00\% + 0.90 (8.00\% - 4.00\%) = 7.60\%$$

Maria now recalculates Trident's WACC using the ICAPM estimate of equity costs, assuming the same debt and equity proportions and the same cost of current debt. Trident's WACC is now estimated at a lower cost of 6.64%.

$$k_{WACC}^{ICAPM} = k_e^{global}\frac{E}{V} + k_d (1 - t)\frac{D}{V} = 7.60\% (.60) + 5.20\% (.40) = 6.64\%$$

Maria believes that this is a more appropriate estimate of Trident's cost of capital. It is fully competitive with Trident's main rivals in the telecommunications hardware industry segment worldwide, which are mainly headquartered in the United States, the United Kingdom, Canada, Finland, Sweden, Germany, Japan, and the Netherlands. The key to Trident's favorable global cost and availability of capital going forward is its ability to attract and hold the international portfolio investors that own its stock.

ICAPM Considerations

In theory, the primary distinction in the estimation of the cost of equity for an individual firm using an internationalized version of the CAPM is the definition of the "market" and a recalculation of the firm's beta for that market. The three basic components of the CAPM model must then be reconsidered.

Nestlé, the Swiss-based multinational firm that produces and distributes a variety of confectionery products, serves as an excellent example of how the international investor may view the global cost of capital differently from a domestic investor, and what that means for Nestlé's estimate of its own cost of equity.[1] The numerical example for Nestlé is summarized in Exhibit 12.2.

In the case of Nestlé, a prospective Swiss investor might assume a risk-free return of 3.3%, an index of Swiss government bond issues, in Swiss francs. That same Swiss investor may also consider the expected market return might be an average return on a portfolio of Swiss equities, the *Financial Times* Swiss index, in Swiss francs, estimated at 10.2%. Assuming a risk-free rate of 3.30%, an expected market return of 10.2%, and a $\beta_{Nestlé}$ of 0.885, a Swiss investor would expect Nestlé to yield 9.4065% for the coming year.

$$k_e^{Nestlé} = k_{RF} + (k_M - k_{RF})\,\beta_{Nestlé} = 3.3 + (10.2 - 3.3)\,0.885 = 9.4065\%$$

But what if Swiss investors held internationally diversified portfolios instead? Both the expected market return k_M, and the beta estimate for Nestlé itself would be defined and determined differently. For the same time period as before, a global portfolio index such as the *Financial Times* index in Swiss francs (*FTA-Swiss*) would show a market return of 13.7% (as opposed to the domestic Swiss index return of 10.2%). In addition, a beta for Nestlé estimated on Nestlé's returns versus the global portfolio index would be much smaller, 0.585 (as opposed to the 0.885 found previously). An internationally diversified Swiss investor would expect a return on Nestlé of:

$$k_e^{Nestlé} = k_{RF} + (k_M - k_{RF})\,\beta_{Nestlé} = 3.3 + (13.7 - 3.3)\,0.585 = 9.3840\%$$

Admittedly, this is not a lot of difference in the end. However, given the magnitude of change in both the values of the market return average and the beta for the firm, it is obvious that the final result could easily have varied by several hundred basis points. The proper construction of the investor's portfolio and the proper portrayal of the investor's perceptions of

---

EXHIBIT 12.2   **The Cost of Equity for Nestlé of Switzerland**

Nestlé's estimate of its cost of equity will depend upon whether a Swiss investor is thought to hold a domestic portfolio of equity securities or a global portfolio.

Domestic Portfolio for Swiss Investor	Global Portfolio for Swiss Investor
k_{RF} = 3.3% (Swiss bond index yield)	k_{RF} = 3.3% (Swiss bond index yield)
k_M = 10.2% (Swiss market portfolio in SF)	k_M = 13.7% (*Financial Times* Global index in SF)
$\beta_{Nestlé}$ = 0.885 (Nestlé versus Swiss market portfolio)	$\beta_{Nestlé}$ = 0.585 (Nestlé versus FTA-Swiss index)

$$k_{Nestlé} = k_{RF} + \beta_{Nestlé}(k_M - k_{RF})$$

Required return on Nestlé:	Required return on Nestlé:
$k_e^{Nestlé}$ = 9.4065%	$k_e^{Nestlé}$ = 9.3840%

Source: All values are taken from Rene Stulz, "The Cost of Capital in Internationally Integrated Markets: The Case of Nestlé," *European Financial Management*, Volume 1, Number 1, March 1995, 11–22.

---

[1]René Stulz, "The Cost of Capital in Internationally Integrated Markets: The Case of Nestlé," *European Financial Management*, Volume 1, Number 1, March 1995, 11–22.

risk and opportunity cost are clearly important to identifying the global cost of a company's equity capital. In the end, it all depends on the specific case—which firm, which country market, which global portfolio.

We follow the practice here of describing the internationally diversified portfolio as the *global portfolio* rather than the *world portfolio*. The distinction is important. The *world portfolio* is an index of all securities in the world. However, even with the increasing trend of deregulation and financial integration, a number of securities markets still remain segmented or restricted in their access. Those securities actually available to an investor are the *global portfolio*.

There are, in fact, a multitude of different proposed formulations for calculating the international cost of capital. The problems with both formulation and data expand dramatically as the analysis is extended to rapidly developing or emerging markets. Harvey (2005) serves as a first place to start if you wish to expand your reading and research.[2]

Global Betas

International portfolio theory, covered in detail in Chapter 14, typically concludes that adding international securities to a domestic portfolio will reduce the portfolio's risks. Although this is fundamental to much of international financial theory, it still depends on individual firms in individual markets. Nestlé's beta went down when calculated using a global portfolio of equities, but that may not always be the case. Depending on the firm and its business line, the country in which it calls home, and the industry domestically and globally in which it competes, the global beta may go up or down.

One company often noted by researchers is Petrobrás, the national oil company of Brazil. Although government controlled, the company is publicly traded. Its shares are listed in São Paulo and New York. It operates in a global oil market in which prices and values are set in U.S. dollars. As a result, its domestic or home beta has been estimated at 1.3, but its global beta higher, at 1.7.[3] This is only one example of many.

Although it seems obvious to some that the returns to the individual firm should become less correlated to those of the market as the market is redefined ever-larger, it turns out to be more of a case of empirical analysis, not preconceived notions of correlation and covariance.

Equity Risk Premiums

In practice, calculating a firm's equity risk premium is much more controversial. Although the capital asset pricing model (CAPM) has now become very widely accepted in global business as the preferred method of calculating the cost of equity for a firm, there is rising debate over what numerical values should be used in its application, especially the *equity risk premium*. The *equity risk premium* is the average annual return of the market expected by investors over and above riskless debt, the term $(k_m - k_{rf})$.

Equity Risk Premium History. The field of finance does agree that a cost of equity calculation should be forward-looking, meaning that the inputs to the equation should represent what is expected to happen over the relevant future time horizon. As is typically the case, however, practitioners use historical evidence as the basis for their forward-looking projections. The current debate begins with a debate over what has happened in the past.

[2] "12 Ways to Calculate the International Cost of Capital," Campbell R. Harvey, Duke University, unpublished, October 14, 2005.

[3] *The Real Cost of Capital*, Tim Ogier, John Rugman and Lucinda Spicer, Financial Times Prentice Hall, Pearson Publishing, 2005, p. 139.

In a large study completed in 2001 by Dimson, Marsh, and Stanton (updated in 2003), the authors estimated the equity risk premium in 16 different developed countries for the 1900–2002 period. The study found significant differences in equity returns over bill and bond returns (proxies for the risk-free rate) over time by country.

◆ Comparing arithmetic returns over bills, Italy clearly had the highest equity risk premium (10.3%) with Germany (9.4%) and Japan (9.3%) following. Denmark, with an average arithmetic return of only 3.8%, had the lowest. The United States had an average arithmetic equity premium of 7.2%, while the United Kingdom had 5.9%. The average equity premium for the 16 listed countries was 6.9%. The world, as defined by the authors of the study, had an arithmetic premium of 5.7%.

◆ Comparing geometric returns, the authors found the highest equity risk premium relative to bills in Australia (6.8%) and France (6.4%), with Belgium and Denmark the lowest (2.2%). The average equity premium for the same 16 countries was 4.5%, the world, 4.4%.

There is little debate regarding the use of arithmetic returns over geometric returns. The mean arithmetic return is simply the average of the annual percentage changes in capital appreciation plus dividend distributions. This is a rate of return calculation with which every business student is familiar. The mean geometric return, however, is a more specialized calculation which takes into account only the beginning and ending values over an extended period of history. It then calculates the annual average rate of compounded growth to get from the beginning to the end, without paying attention to the specific path taken in between. Exhibit 12.3 provides a simple example of how the two methods would differ for a very short historical series of stock prices.

Arithmetic returns capture the year-to-year volatility in markets, which geometric returns do not. For this reason, most practitioners prefer the arithmetic, as it embodies more of the volatility so often characteristic of equity markets globally. Note that the geometric change will in all but a few extreme circumstances yield a smaller mean return.

The debate over which equity risk premium to use in practice was highlighted in this same study by looking at what equity risk premiums are being recommended for the United States by a variety of different sources. As illustrated in Exhibit 12.4, a hypothetical firm with a beta of 1.0 (estimated market risk equal to that of the market) might have a cost of equity as low as 9.000% and as high as 12.800% using this set of alternative values. Note that here the authors used geometric returns, not arithmetic returns. Fernandez and del Campo (2010), in their annual survey of market risk premiums used by analysts and academics, most recently

---

EXHIBIT 12.3   Arithmetic versus Geometric Returns: A Sample Calculation

Year	1	2	3	4	5	Mean
Share price	10	12	10	12	14	
Arithmetic change		+20.00%	−16.67%	+20.00%	+16.67%	+10.00%
Geometric change		+8.78%	+8.78%	+8.78%	+8.78%	+8.78%

Arithmetic change is calculated year-by-year as $(P_2/P_1 - 1)$. The simple average of the series is the mean. The geometric change is calculated using only the beginning and ending values, 10 and 14, and the geometric root of $[(14/10)^{1/4} - 1]$ is found (the $^{1/4}$ is in reference to four periods of change). The geometric change assumes reinvested compounding, whereas the arithmetic mean only assumes point to point investment.

EXHIBIT 12.4   Alternative Estimates of Cost of Equity for a Hypothetical U.S. Firm
Assuming $\beta = 1$ and $k_{rf} = 4\%$

Source	Equity Risk Premium $(k_m - k_{rf})$	Cost of Equity $k_{rf} + \beta\,(k_m - k_{rf})$	Differential
Ibbotson	8.800%	12.800%	3.800%
Finance textbooks	8.500%	12.500%	3.500%
Investor surveys	7.100%	11.100%	2.100%
Dimson, et al.	5.000%	9.000%	Baseline

Source: Equity risk premium quotes from "Stockmarket Valuations: Great Expectations," *The Economist*, January 31, 2002.

---

found the average risk premium used by U.S. and Canadian analysts is 5.1%, European analysts 5.0%, and British analysts 5.6%.[4]

How important is it for a company to accurately predict its cost of equity? The corporation must annually determine which potential investments it will accept and reject due to its limited capital resources. If the company is not accurately estimating its cost of equity—and therefore its general cost of capital—it will not be accurately estimating the net present value of potential investments if it uses its own cost of capital as the basis for discounting expected cash flows.

A final note on the cost of equity and the selection of betas. For many years there has been a significant gulf between academia and industry on the importance of cost of equity and capital estimations (see Exhibit 12.5). We won't take a stand ourselves here—taking the easy way out—but the reader should be well aware of the debate.

EXHIBIT 12.5   Corporate Cost of Equity and Capital Estimation

What gets measured, gets managed.
    —Anonymous

Financial academics love the details and debates associated with the calculation of a company's cost of equity and ultimately the cost of capital. Instability of betas, whether or not domestic or international cost of capital estimations are appropriate or executed correctly, the source and size of the equity risk premium used, the measure of the risk-free rate, the time period for estimation and forecast—the issues go on and on. Even where the estimates come from is under debate. One famous academic recently went on in-length in his blog that the cost of equity and the equity risk premium is too important to the future of the firm to leave to external service providers like Ibbotson, Duff, and Phelps, or an investment banking firm like CreditSuisse.

But in industry, one is very likely to encounter a near-indifference to the topic. In most companies today, either domestic or multinational, the cost of equity and its calculation is only revisited annually. Then, often executed with key inputs gathered from consultants or other third-party data providers, the company calculates the cost of equity and capital and carves it into stone for the year. In many cases, it then only provides a foundation for the establishment of a *hurdle rate*, the required return the company will post as the minimum necessary for investment consideration. As one former student relayed to us, when he asked how the cost of equity was calculated and had there been an update recently, he was told "It's 12%. End of discussion." Reader beware!

---

[4]"Market Risk Premium used in 2010 by Analysts and Companies: a survey with 2,400 answers," Pablo Fernandez and Javier del Campo, IESE Business School, May 17, 2010.

The Demand for Foreign Securities: The Role of International Portfolio Investors

Gradual deregulation of equity markets during the past three decades not only elicited increased competition from domestic players but also opened up markets to foreign competitors. International portfolio investment and cross-listing of equity shares on foreign markets have become commonplace.

What motivates portfolio investors to purchase and hold foreign securities in their portfolio? The answer lies in an understanding of "domestic" portfolio theory and how it has been extended to handle the possibility of global portfolios. More specifically, it requires an understanding of the principles of portfolio risk reduction, portfolio rate of return, and foreign currency risk.

Both domestic and international portfolio managers are asset allocators. Their objective is to maximize a portfolio's rate of return for a given level of risk, or to minimize risk for a given rate of return. International portfolio managers can choose from a larger bundle of assets than portfolio managers limited to domestic-only asset allocations. As a result, internationally diversified portfolios often have a higher expected rate of return, and they nearly always have a lower level of portfolio risk, since national securities markets are imperfectly correlated with one another.

Portfolio asset allocation can be accomplished along many dimensions depending on the investment objective of the portfolio manager. For example, portfolios can be diversified according to the type of securities. They can be composed of stocks only or bonds only or a combination of both. They also can be diversified by industry or by size of capitalization (small-cap, mid-cap, and large-cap stock portfolios).

For our purposes, the most relevant dimensions are diversification by country, geographic region, stage of development, or a combination of these (global). An example of diversification by country is the Korea Fund. It was at one time the only vehicle for foreign investors to hold South Korean securities, but foreign ownership restrictions have more recently been liberalized. A typical regional diversification would be one of the many Asian funds. These performed exceptionally well until the "bubble" burst in Japan and Southeast Asia during the second half of the 1990s. Portfolios composed of emerging market securities are examples of diversification by stage of development. They are composed of securities from different countries, geographic regions, and stage of development.

The Link between Cost and Availability of Capital

Trident's weighted average cost of capital (WACC) was calculated assuming that equity and debt capital would always be available at the same required rate of return even if Trident's capital budget expands. This is a reasonable assumption considering Trident's excellent access through the NYSE to international portfolio investors in global capital markets. It is a bad assumption, however, for firms resident in illiquid or segmented capital markets, small domestic firms, and family-owned firms resident in any capital market. We will now examine how market liquidity and market segmentation can affect a firm's cost of capital.

Improving Market Liquidity

Although no consensus exists about the definition of *market liquidity*, we can observe market liquidity by noting the degree to which a firm can issue a new security without depressing the existing market price, as well as the degree to which a change in price of its securities elicits a substantial order flow.

In the domestic case, an underlying assumption is that total availability of capital to a firm at any time is determined by supply and demand in the domestic capital markets. A firm should always expand its capital budget by raising funds in the same proportion as its optimal financial structure. As its budget expands in absolute terms, however, its marginal cost of capital will eventually increase. In other words, a firm can only tap the capital market for some limited amount in the short run before suppliers of capital balk at providing further funds, even if the same optimal financial structure is preserved. In the long run, this may not be a limitation, depending on market liquidity.

In the multinational case, a firm is able to improve market liquidity by raising funds in the euromarkets (money, bond, and equity), by selling security issues abroad, and by tapping local capital markets through foreign subsidiaries. Such activity should logically expand the capacity of an MNE to raise funds in the short run over what might have been raised if the firm were limited to its home capital market. This situation assumes that the firm preserves its optimal financial structure.

Market Segmentation

If all capital markets are fully integrated, securities of comparable expected return and risk should have the same required rate of return in each national market after adjusting for foreign exchange risk and political risk. This definition applies to both equity and debt, although it often happens that one or the other may be more integrated than its counterpart.

Capital market segmentation is a financial market imperfection caused mainly by government constraints, institutional practices, and investor perceptions. The following are the most important imperfections:

◆ Asymmetric information between domestic and foreign-based investors
◆ Lack of transparency
◆ High securities transaction costs
◆ Foreign exchange risks
◆ Political risks
◆ Corporate governance differences
◆ Regulatory barriers

Market imperfections do not necessarily imply that national securities markets are inefficient. A national securities market can be efficient in a domestic context and yet segmented in an international context. According to finance theory, a market is *efficient* if security prices in that market reflect all available relevant information and adjust quickly to any new relevant information. Therefore, the price of an individual security reflects its "intrinsic value" and any price fluctuations will be "random walks" around this value. Market efficiency assumes that transaction costs are low, that many participants are in the market, and that these participants have sufficient financial strength to move security prices. Empirical tests of market efficiency show that most major national markets are reasonably efficient.

An efficient national securities market might very well correctly price all securities traded in that market on the basis of information available to the investors who participate in that market. However, if that market is segmented, foreign investors would not be participants. Thus, securities in the segmented market would be priced on the basis of domestic rather than international standards.

In the rest of this chapter and in Chapter 13, we will use the term MNE to describe all firms that have access to a global cost and availability of capital. This includes qualifying MNEs, whether they are located in highly developed or emerging markets. It also includes large firms that are not multinational but have access to global capital markets. They too could be located in highly developed or emerging capital markets. We will use the term *domestic firm* (DF) for all firms that do not have access to a global cost and availability of capital, no matter where they are located.

Availability of capital depends on whether a firm can gain liquidity for its debt and equity securities and a price for those securities based on international rather than national standards. In practice, this means that the firm must define a strategy to attract international portfolio investors and thereby escape the constraints of its own illiquid or segmented national market.

The Effect of Market Liquidity and Segmentation

The degree to which capital markets are illiquid or segmented has an important influence on a firm's marginal cost of capital and thus on its weighted average cost of capital. The marginal cost of capital is the weighted average cost of the next currency unit raised. This is illustrated in Exhibit 12.6, which shows the transition from a domestic to a global marginal cost of capital.

Exhibit 12.6 shows that the MNE has a given marginal return on capital at different budget levels, represented in the line MRR. This demand is determined by ranking potential projects according to net present value or internal rate of return. Percentage rate of return to both users and suppliers of capital is shown on the vertical scale. If the firm is limited to raising funds in its domestic market, the line MCC_D shows the marginal domestic cost of capital (vertical axis) at various budget levels (horizontal axis). Remember that the firm continues to maintain the same debt ratio as it expands its budget, so that financial risk does not change. The optimal budget in the domestic case is $40 million, where the marginal return on capital

---

EXHIBIT 12.6   Market Liquidity, Segmentation, and the Marginal Cost of Capital

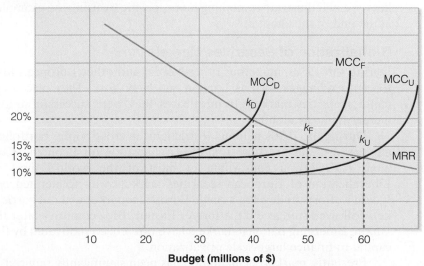

(MRR) just equals the marginal cost of capital (MCC_D). At this budget, the marginal domestic cost of capital, k_D, would be equal to 20%.

If the MNE has access to additional sources of capital outside an illiquid domestic capital market, the marginal cost of capital should shift to the right (the line MCC_F). In other words, foreign markets can be tapped for long-term funds at times when the domestic market is saturated because of heavy use by other borrowers or equity issuers, or when it is unable to absorb another issue of the MNE in the short run. Exhibit 12.6 shows that by a tap of foreign capital markets the firm has reduced its marginal international cost of capital, k_F to 15%, even while it raises an additional $10 million. This statement assumes that about $20 million is raised abroad, since only about $30 million could be raised domestically at a 15% marginal cost of capital.

If the MNE is located in a capital market that is both illiquid and segmented, the line MCC_U represents the decreased marginal cost of capital if it gains access to other equity markets. As a result of the combined effects of greater availability of capital and international pricing of the firm's securities, the marginal cost of capital, k_U, declines to 13% and the optimal capital budget climbs to $60 million.

Most of the tests of market segmentation suffer from the usual problem for models—namely, the need to abstract from reality in order to have a testable model. In our opinion a realistic test would be to observe what happens to a single security's price when it has been traded only in a domestic market, is "discovered" by foreign investors, and then is traded in a foreign market. Arbitrage should keep the market price equal in both markets. However, if during the transition we observe a significant change in the security's price uncorrelated with price movements in either of the underlying securities markets, we can infer that the domestic market was segmented.

In academic circles, tests based on case studies are often considered to be "casual empiricism," since no theory or model exists to explain what is being observed. Nevertheless, something may be learned from such cases, just as scientists learn from observing nature in an uncontrolled environment. Furthermore, case studies that preserve real-world complications may illustrate specific kinds of barriers to market integration and ways in which they might be overcome.

Unfortunately, few case studies have been documented in which a firm has "escaped" from a segmented capital market. In practice, escape usually means being listed on a foreign stock market such as New York or London, and/or selling securities in foreign capital markets. We will illustrate something more specific by using the example of Novo, the Mini-Case at the end of the chapter.

Globalization of Securities Markets

During the 1980s, numerous other Nordic and other European firms cross-listed on major foreign exchanges such as London and New York. They placed equity and debt issues in major securities markets. In most cases, they were successful in lowering their WACC and increasing its availability.

During the 1990s, national restrictions on cross-border portfolio investment were gradually eased under pressure from the Organization for Economic Cooperation and Development (OECD), a consortium of most of the world's most industrialized countries. Liberalization of European securities markets was accelerated because of the European Union's efforts to develop a single European market without barriers. Emerging nation markets followed suit, as did the former Eastern Bloc countries after the breakup of the Soviet Union. Emerging national markets have often been motivated by the need to source foreign capital to finance large-scale privatization.

Presently, market segmentation has been significantly reduced, although the liquidity of individual national markets remains limited. Most observers believe that for better or for worse we have achieved a global market for securities. The good news is that many firms have been assisted to become MNEs because they now have access to a global cost and availability of capital. The bad news is that the correlation among securities markets has increased, thereby reducing, but not eliminating, the benefits of international portfolio diversification. Globalization of securities markets has also led to more volatility and speculative behavior as shown by the emerging market crises of the 1995–2001 period, and the 2008–2009 global credit crisis.

Corporate Governance and the Cost of Capital. Would global investors be willing to pay a premium for a share in a good corporate governance company? A recent study of Norwegian and Swedish firms measured the impact of foreign board membership (Anglo-American) on firm value. They summarized their findings as follows:

> *Using a sample of firms with headquarters in Norway or Sweden the study indicates a significantly higher value for firms that have outsider Anglo-American board member(s), after a variety of firm-specific and corporate governance related factors have been controlled for. We argue that this superior performance reflects the fact that these companies have successfully broken away from a partly segmented domestic capital market by "importing" an Anglo-American corporate governance system. Such an "import" signals a willingness on the part of the firm to expose itself to improved corporate governance and enhances its reputation in the financial market.[5]*

Strategic Alliances

Strategic alliances are normally formed by firms that expect to gain synergies from one or more of the following joint efforts. They might share the cost of developing technology, or pursue complementary marketing activities. They might gain economies of scale or scope or a variety of other commercial advantages. However, one synergy that may sometimes by overlooked is the possibility for a financially strong firm to help a financially weak firm to lower its cost of capital by providing attractively priced equity or debt financing. This is illustrated in the *Global Finance in Practice 12.1* on the strategic alliance between Bang and Olufsen and Philips.

GLOBAL FINANCE IN PRACTICE 12.1

Bang & Olufsen and Philips N.V.

One excellent example of financial synergy that lowered a firm's cost of capital was provided by the cross-border strategic alliance of Philips N.V. of the Netherlands and Bang & Olufsen (B & O) of Denmark in 1990. Philips N.V. is one of the largest multinational firms in the world and the leading consumer electronics firm in Europe. B & O is a small European competitor but with a nice market niche at the high end of the audiovisual market.

Philips was a major supplier of components to B & O, a situation it wished to continue. It also wished to join

forces with B & O in the upscale consumer electronics market where Philips did not have the quality image enjoyed by B & O. Philips was concerned that financial pressure might force B & O to choose a Japanese competitor for a partner. That would be very unfortunate. B & O had always supported Philips' political efforts to gain EU support to make the few remaining European-owned consumer electronics firms more competitive than their strong Japanese competitors.

B & O's Motivation

B & O was interested in an alliance with Philips to gain more rapid access to its new technology and assistance in

[5]Lars Oxelheim and Trond Randøy, "The impact of foreign board membership on firm value," *Journal of Banking and Finance*, Vol. 27, No. 12, 2003, p. 2369.

converting that technology into B & O product applications. B & O wanted assurance of timely delivery of components at large volume discounts from Philips itself, as well as access to Philip's large network of suppliers under terms enjoyed by Philips. Equally important, B & O wanted to get an equity infusion from Philips to strengthen its own shaky financial position. Despite its commercial artistry, in recent years B & O had been only marginally profitable, and its publicly traded shares were considered too risky to justify a new public equity issue either in Denmark or abroad. It had no excess borrowing capacity.

The Strategic Alliance

A strategic alliance was agreed upon that would give each partner what it desired commercially. Philips agreed to invest DKK342 million (about $50 million) to increase the equity of B & O's main operating subsidiary. In return it received a 25% ownership of the expanded company.

When B & O's strategic alliance was announced to the public on May 3, 1990, the share price of B & O Holding, the listed company on the Copenhagen Stock Exchange, jumped by 35% during the next two days. It remained at that level until the Gulf War crisis temporarily depressed B & O's share price. The share price has since recovered and the expected synergies eventually materialized. B & O eventually bought back its shares from Philips at a price that had been predetermined at the start.

In evaluating what happened, we recognize that an industrial purchaser might be willing to pay a higher price for a firm that will provide it some synergies than would a portfolio investor who does not receive these synergies. Portfolio investors are only pricing firm's shares based on the normal risk versus return tradeoff. They cannot normally anticipate the value of synergies that might accrue to the firm from an unexpected strategic alliance partner. The same conclusion should hold for a purely domestic strategic alliance but this example happens to be a cross-border alliance.

The Cost of Capital for MNEs Compared to Domestic Firms

Is the weighted average cost of capital for MNEs higher or lower than for their domestic counterparts? The answer is a function of the marginal cost of capital, the relative after-tax cost of debt, the optimal debt ratio, and the relative cost of equity.

Availability of Capital

We saw earlier in this chapter that international availability of capital to MNEs, or to other large firms that can attract international portfolio investors, may allow them to lower their cost of equity and debt compared with most domestic firms. In addition, international availability permits an MNE to maintain its desired debt ratio, even when significant amounts of new funds must be raised. In other words, an MNE's marginal cost of capital is constant for considerable ranges of its capital budget. This statement is not true for most domestic firms. They must either rely on internally generated funds or borrow in the short and medium term from commercial banks.

Financial Structure, Systematic Risk, and the Cost of Capital for MNEs

Theoretically, MNEs should be in a better position than their domestic counterparts to support higher debt ratios because their cash flows are diversified internationally. The probability of a firm's covering fixed charges under varying conditions in product, financial, and foreign exchange markets should improve if the variability of its cash flows is minimized.

By diversifying cash flows internationally, the MNE might be able to achieve the same kind of reduction in cash flow variability as portfolio investors receive from diversifying their security holdings internationally. The same argument applies—namely, that returns are not perfectly correlated between countries. For example, in 2000 Japan was in recession but the United States was experiencing rapid growth. Therefore, we might have expected returns, on either a cash flow or an earnings basis, to be depressed in Japan and favorable in the United States. An MNE with operations located in both these countries could rely on its strong U.S. cash inflow to cover debt obligations, even if its Japanese subsidiary produced weak net cash inflows.

Despite the theoretical elegance of this hypothesis, empirical studies have come to the opposite conclusion.[6] Despite the favorable effect of international diversification of cash flows, bankruptcy risk was only about the same for MNEs as for domestic firms. However, MNEs faced higher agency costs, political risk, foreign exchange risk, and asymmetric information. These have been identified as the factors leading to lower debt ratios and even a higher cost of long-term debt for MNEs. Domestic firms rely much more heavily on short and intermediate debt, which lie at the low cost end of the yield curve.

Even more surprising, one study found that MNEs have a higher level of systematic risk than their domestic counterparts.[7] The same factors caused this phenomenon as caused the lower debt ratios for MNEs. The study concluded that the increased standard deviation of cash flows from internationalization more than offset the lower correlation from diversification.

As we stated earlier in this chapter, the systematic risk term, β_j, is defined as

$$\beta_j = \frac{\rho_{jm}\sigma_j}{\sigma_m}$$

where ρ_{jm} is the correlation coefficient between security j and the market; σ_j is the standard deviation of the return on firm j; and σ_m is the standard deviation of the market return. The MNE's systematic risk could increase if the decrease in the correlation coefficient, ρ_{jm}, due to international diversification, is more than offset by an increase in s_j, the standard deviation due to the aforementioned risk factors. This conclusion is consistent with the observation that many MNEs use a higher hurdle rate to discount expected foreign project cash flows. In essence, they are accepting projects they consider to be riskier than domestic projects, thus potentially skewing upward their perceived systematic risk. At the least, MNEs need to earn a higher rate of return than their domestic equivalents in order to maintain their market value.

A more recent study found that internationalization actually allowed emerging market MNEs to carry a higher level of debt and lowered their systematic risk.[8] This occurred because the emerging market MNEs are investing in more stable economies abroad, a strategy that lowers their operating, financial, foreign exchange, and political risks. The reduction in risk more than offsets their increased agency costs and allows the emerging market MNEs to enjoy higher leverage and lower systematic risk than their U.S.-based MNE counterparts.

[6]Lee, Kwang Chul and Chuck C.Y. Kwok, "Multinational Corporations vs. Domestic Corporations: International Environmental Factors and Determinants of Capital Structure," *Journal of International Business Studies*, Summer 1988, pp. 195–217.

[7]Reeb, David M., Chuck C.Y. Kwok, and H. Young Baek, "Systematic Risk of the Multinational Corporation, *Journal of International Business Studies*, Second Quarter 1998, pp. 263–279.

[8]Kwok, Chuck C.Y., and David M. Reeb, "Internationalization and Firm Risk: An Upstream-Downstream Hypothesis," *Journal of International Business Studies*, Vol. 31, Issue 4, 2000, pp. 611–630.

Solving a Riddle: Is the Weighted Average Cost of Capital for MNEs Really Higher than for Their Domestic Counterparts?

The riddle is that the MNE is supposed to have a lower marginal cost of capital (MCC) than a domestic firm because of the MNE's access to a global cost and availability of capital. On the other hand, the empirical studies we mentioned show that the MNE's weighted average cost of capital (WACC) is actually higher than for a comparable domestic firm because of agency costs, foreign exchange risk, political risk, asymmetric information, and other complexities of foreign operations.

The answer to this riddle lies in the link between the cost of capital, its availability, and the opportunity set of projects. As the opportunity set of projects increases, eventually the firm needs to increase its capital budget to the point where its marginal cost of capital is increasing. The optimal capital budget would still be at the point where the rising marginal cost of capital equals the declining rate of return on the opportunity set of projects. However, this would be at a higher weighted average cost of capital than would have occurred for a lower level of the optimal capital budget.

To illustrate this linkage, Exhibit 12.7 shows the marginal cost of capital given different optimal capital budgets. Assume that there are two different demand schedules based on the opportunity set of projects for both the multinational enterprise (MNE) and domestic counterpart (DC).

The line MRR_{DC} depicts a modest set of potential projects. It intersects the line MCC_{MNE} at 15% and a $100 million budget level. It intersects the MCC_{DC} at 10% and a $140 million budget level. At these low budget levels the MCC_{MNE} has a higher MCC and

---

EXHIBIT 12.7   The Cost of Capital for MNE and Domestic Counterpart Compared

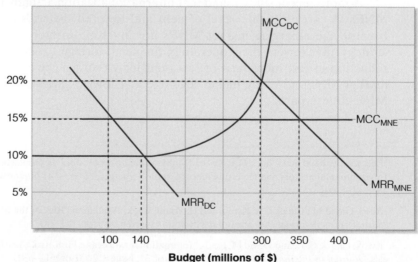

probably weighted average cost of capital than its domestic counterpart (DC), as discovered in the recent empirical studies.

The line MRR$_{MNE}$ depicts a more ambitious set of projects for both the MNE and its domestic counterpart. It intersects the line MCC$_{MNE}$ still at 15% and a $350 million budget. However, it intersects the MCC$_{DC}$ at 20% and a budget level of $300 million. At these higher budget levels, the MCC$_{MNE}$ has a lower MCC and probably weighted average cost of capital than its domestic counterpart, as predicted earlier in this chapter. In order to generalize this conclusion, we would need to know under what conditions a domestic firm would be willing to undertake the optimal capital budget despite its increasing the firm's marginal cost of capital. At some point the MNE might also have an optimal capital budget at the point where its MCC is rising.

Empirical studies show that neither mature domestic firms nor MNEs are typically willing to assume the higher agency costs or bankruptcy risk associated with higher MCCs and capital budgets. In fact, most mature firms demonstrate some degree of corporate wealth maximizing behavior. They are somewhat risk averse and tend to avoid returning to the market to raise fresh equity. They prefer to limit their capital budgets to what can be financed with free cash flows. Indeed, they have a so-called pecking order that determines the priority of which sources of funds they tap and in what order. This behavior motivates shareholders to monitor management more closely. They tie management's compensation to stock performance (options). They may also require other types of contractual arrangements that are collectively part of agency costs.

In conclusion, if both MNEs and domestic firms do actually limit their capital budgets to what can be financed without increasing their MCC, then the empirical findings that MNEs have higher WACC stands. If the domestic firm has such good growth opportunities that it chooses to undertake growth despite an increasing marginal cost of capital, then the MNE would have a lower WACC. Exhibit 12.8 summarizes these conclusions.

EXHIBIT 12.8   **Do MNEs Have a Higher or Lower Cost of Capital Than Their Domestic Counterparts?**

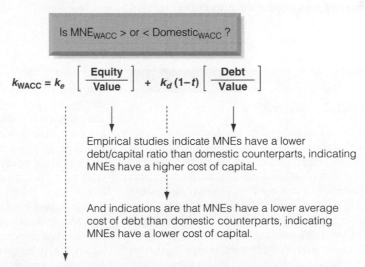

Is MNE$_{WACC}$ > or < Domestic$_{WACC}$?

$$k_{WACC} = k_e \left[\frac{\text{Equity}}{\text{Value}} \right] + k_d (1-t) \left[\frac{\text{Debt}}{\text{Value}} \right]$$

Empirical studies indicate MNEs have a lower debt/capital ratio than domestic counterparts, indicating MNEs have a higher cost of capital.

And indications are that MNEs have a lower average cost of debt than domestic counterparts, indicating MNEs have a lower cost of capital.

The cost of equity required by investors is higher for multinational firms than for domestic firms. Possible explanations are higher levels of *political risk, foreign exchange risk,* and higher *agency costs* of doing business in a multinational managerial environment. However, at relatively high levels of the optimal capital budget, the MNE would have a lower cost of capital.

Summary of Learning Objectives

Examine how a firm headquartered in a country with an illiquid and segmented capital market achieves a lower global cost of capital and greater availability of capital.

◆ Gaining access to global capital markets should allow a firm to lower its cost of capital. This can be achieved by increasing the market liquidity of its shares and by escaping from segmentation of its home capital market.

Analyze the linkage between cost and availability of capital.

◆ The cost and availability of capital is directly linked to the degree of market liquidity and segmentation. Firms having access to markets with high liquidity and a low level of segmentation should have a lower cost of capital and greater ability to raise new capital.

◆ A firm is able to increase its market liquidity by raising debt in the Euromarket, by selling security issues in individual national capital markets and as Euro-equities, and tapping local capital markets through foreign subsidiaries. Increased market liquidity causes the marginal cost of capital line to "flatten out to the right." This results in the firm being able to raise more capital at the same low marginal cost of capital, and thereby justify investing in more capital projects. The key is to attract international portfolio investors.

Evaluate the effect of market liquidity and segmentation on the cost of capital.

◆ A national capital market is segmented if the required rate of return on securities in that market

differs from the required rate of return on securities of comparable expected return and risk that are traded on other national securities markets. Capital market segmentation is a financial market imperfection caused by government constraints and investor perceptions. The most important imperfections are 1) asymmetric information; 2) transaction costs; 3) foreign exchange risk; 4) corporate governance differences; 5) political risk; and 6) regulatory barriers.

◆ Segmentation results in a higher cost of capital and less availability of capital.

◆ If a firm is resident in a segmented capital market, it can still escape from this market by sourcing its debt and equity abroad. The result should be a lower marginal cost of capital, improved liquidity for its shares, and a larger capital budget. The experience of Novo was suggested as a possible model for firms resident in small or emerging markets that are partially segmented and illiquid.

Explain how the weighted average cost of capital for an MNE compares with its domestic counterpart.

◆ Whether or not MNEs have a lower cost of capital than their domestic counterparts depends on their optimal financial structures, systematic risk, availability of capital, and the level of the optimal capital budget.

MINI-CASE

Novo Industri A/S (Novo)

Novo is a Danish multinational firm which produces industrial enzymes and pharmaceuticals (mostly insulin). In 1977, Novo's management decided to "internationalize" its capital structure and sources of funds. This decision was based on the observation that the Danish securities market was both illiquid and segmented from other capital markets. In particular, the lack of availability and high cost of equity capital in Denmark resulted in Novo having a higher cost of capital than its main multinational competitors, such as Eli Lilly (U.S.), Miles Laboratories (U.S.—a subsidiary of Bayer, Germany), and Gist Brocades (The Netherlands).

Apart from the cost of capital, Novo's projected growth opportunities signaled the eventual need to raise new long-term capital beyond what could be raised in the illiquid

Danish market. Since Novo is a technology leader in its specialties, planned capital investments in plant, equipment, and research could not be postponed until internal financing from cash flow became available. Novo's competitors would preempt any markets not served by Novo.

Even if an equity issue of the size required could have been raised in Denmark, the required rate of return would have been unacceptably high. For example, Novo's price/earnings ratio was typically around 5; that of its foreign competitors was well over 10. Yet Novo's business and financial risk appeared to be about equal to that of its competitors. A price/earnings ratio of 5 appeared appropriate for Novo only within a domestic Danish context when Novo was compared with other domestic firms of comparable business and financial risk.

If Denmark's securities markets were integrated with world markets, one would expect foreign investors to rush in and buy "undervalued" Danish securities. In that case, firms like Novo would enjoy an international cost of capital comparable to that of their foreign competitors. Strangely enough, no Danish governmental restrictions existed that would have prevented foreign investors from holding Danish securities. Therefore, one must look for investor perception as the main cause of market segmentation in Denmark at that time.

At least six characteristics of the Danish equity market were responsible for market segmentation: 1) asymmetric information base of Danish and foreign investors; 2) taxation; 3) alternative sets of feasible portfolios; 4) financial risk; 5) foreign exchange risk; and 6) political risk.

Asymmetric Information

Certain institutional characteristics of Denmark caused Danish and foreign investors to be uninformed about each other's equity securities. The most important information barrier was a Danish regulation that prohibited Danish investors from holding foreign private sector securities. Therefore, Danish investors had no incentive to follow developments in foreign securities markets or to factor such information into their evaluation of Danish securities. As a result, Danish securities might have been priced correctly in the efficient market sense relative to one another, considering the Danish information base, but priced incorrectly considering the combined foreign and Danish information base. Another detrimental effect of this regulation was that foreign securities firms did not locate offices or personnel in Denmark, since they had no product to sell. Lack of a physical presence in Denmark reduced the ability of foreign security analysts to follow Danish securities.

A second information barrier was lack of enough Danish security analysts following Danish securities. Only one professional Danish securities analysis service was published (Børsinformation), and that was in the Danish language. A few Danish institutional investors employed in-house analysts, but their findings were not available to the public. Almost no foreign security analysts followed Danish securities because they had no product to sell and the Danish market was too small (small-country bias).

Other information barriers included language and accounting principles. Naturally, financial information was normally published in Danish, using Danish accounting principles. A few firms, such as Novo, published English versions, but almost none used U.S. or British accounting principles or attempted to show any reconciliation with such principles.

Taxation

Danish taxation policy had all but eliminated investment in common stock by individuals. Until a tax law change in July 1981, capital gains on shares held for over two years were taxed at a 50% rate. Shares held for less than two years, or for "speculative" purposes, were taxed at personal income tax rates, with the top marginal rate being 75%. In contrast, capital gains on bonds were tax free. This situation resulted in bonds being issued at deep discounts because the redemption at par at maturity was considered a capital gain. Thus, most individual investors held bonds rather than stocks. This factor reduced the liquidity of the stock market and increased the required rate of return on stocks if they were to compete with bonds.

Feasible Set of Portfolios

Because of the prohibition on foreign security ownership, Danish investors had a very limited set of securities from which to choose a portfolio. In practice, Danish institutional portfolios were composed of Danish stocks, government bonds, and mortgage bonds. Since Danish stock price movements are closely correlated with each other, Danish portfolios possessed a rather high level of systematic risk. In addition, government policy had been to provide a relatively high real rate of return on government bonds after adjusting for inflation. The net result of taxation policies on individuals, and attractive real yields on government bonds was that required rates of return on stocks were relatively high by international standards.

From a portfolio perspective, Danish stocks provided an opportunity for foreign investors to diversify internationally. If Danish stock price movements were not closely correlated with world stock price movements, inclusion of Danish stocks in foreign portfolios should reduce these portfolio's systematic risk. Furthermore, foreign investors were not subject to the high Danish income tax rates because they are normally protected by tax treaties that typically limit their tax to 15% on dividends and capital gains. As a result of the international diversification potential, foreign investors might have required a lower rate of return on Danish stocks than Danish investors, other things being equal. However, other things were not equal because foreign investors perceived Danish stocks to carry more financial, foreign exchange, and political risk than their own domestic securities.

Financial, Foreign Exchange, and Political Risks

Financial leverage utilized by Danish firms was relatively high by U.S. and U.K. standards but not abnormal for Scandinavia, Germany, Italy, or Japan. In addition, most of the debt was short term with variable interest rates. Just how foreign investors viewed financial risk in Danish firms depended on what norms they follow in their home countries. We know from Novo's experience in tapping the Eurobond market in 1978, that Morgan Grenfell, its British investment banker, advised Novo to maintain a debt ratio (debt/total capitalization) closer to 50% rather than the traditional Danish 65% to 70%.

Foreign investors in Danish securities are subject to foreign exchange risk. Whether this is a plus or minus factor depends on the investor's home currency, perception about the future strength of the Danish krone, and its impact on a firm's operating exposure. Through personal contacts with foreign investors and bankers, Novo's management did not believe foreign exchange risk was a factor in Novo's stock price because its operations were perceived as being well diversified internationally. Over 90% of its sales were to customers located outside of Denmark.

With respect to political risk, Denmark was perceived as a stable Western democracy but with the potential to cause periodic problems for foreign investors. In particular, Denmark's national debt was regarded as too high for comfort, although this judgment had not yet shown up in the form of risk premiums on Denmark's Eurocurrency syndicated loans.

The Road to Globalization

Although Novo's management in 1977 wished to escape from the shackles of Denmark's segmented and illiquid capital market, many barriers had to be overcome. It is worthwhile to describe some of these obstacles, because they typify the barriers faced by other firms from segmented markets that wish to internationalize their capital sources.

Closing the Information Gap. Novo had been a family-owned firm from its founding in the 1920s by the two Pedersen brothers until 1974, when it went public and listed its "B" shares on the Copenhagen Stock Exchange. The "A" shares were held by the Novo Foundation; the "A" shares were sufficient to maintain voting control. However, Novo was essentially unknown in investment circles outside of Denmark. To overcome this disparity in the information base, Novo increased the level of its financial and technical disclosure in both Danish and English versions.

The information gap was further closed when Morgan Grenfell successfully organized a syndicate to underwrite and sell a $20 million convertible Eurobond issue for Novo in 1978. In connection with this offering, Novo listed its shares on the London Stock Exchange to facilitate conversion and to gain visibility. These twin actions were the key to dissolving the information barrier and, of course, they also raised a large amount of long-term capital on favorable terms, which would have been unavailable in Denmark.

Despite the favorable impact of the Eurobond issue on availability of capital, Novo's cost of capital actually increased when Danish investors reacted negatively to the potential dilution effect of the conversion right. During 1979, Novo's share price declined from around Dkr300 per share to around Dkr220 per share.

The Biotechnology Boom. During 1979, a fortuitous event occurred. Biotechnology began to attract the interest of the U.S. investment community, with several sensationally oversubscribed stock issues by such start-up firms as Genentech and Cetus. Thanks to the aforementioned domestic information gap, Danish investors were unaware of these events and continued to value Novo at a low price/earnings ratio of 5, compared with over 10 for its established competitors and 30 or more for these new potential competitors.

In order to profile itself as a biotechnology firm with a proven track record, Novo organized a seminar in New York City on April 30, 1980. Soon after the seminar a few sophisticated individual U.S. investors began buying Novo's shares and convertibles through the London Stock Exchange. Danish investors were only too happy to supply this foreign demand. Therefore, despite relatively strong demand from U.S. and British investors, Novo's share price increased only gradually, climbing back to the Dkr300 level by midsummer. However, during the following months, foreign interest began to snowball, and by the end of 1980 Novo's stock price had reached the Dkr600 level. Moreover, foreign investors had increased their proportion of share ownership from virtually nothing to around 30%. Novo's price/earnings ratio had risen to around 16, which was now in line with that of its international competitors but not with the Danish market. At this point one must conclude that Novo had succeeded in internationalizing its cost of capital. Other Danish securities remained locked in a segmented capital market. Exhibit 1 shows that the movement in the Danish stock market in general did not parallel the rise in Novo's share price, nor could it be explained by movement in the U.S. or U.K. stock markets as a whole.

Directed Share Issue in the United States. During the first half of 1981, under the guidance of Goldman Sachs and with the assistance of Morgan Grenfell and Copenhagen Handelsbank, Novo prepared a prospectus for SEC registration of a U.S. share offering and eventual listing on the New York Stock Exchange. The main barriers encountered in this effort, which would have general applicability, were connected with preparing financial statements that could be reconciled with U.S. accounting principles and the higher level of disclosure required by the SEC. In particular, industry segment reporting was a problem both from a disclosure perspective and an accounting perspective because the accounting data were not available internally in that format. As it turned out, the investment barriers in the U.S. were relatively tractable, although expensive and time consuming to overcome.

The more serious barriers were caused by a variety of institutional and governmental regulations in Denmark. The latter were never designed so that firms could issue shares at market value, since Danish firms typically issued stock at par value with preemptive rights. By this time, however, Novo's share price, driven by continued foreign buying, was so high

EXHIBIT 1   Novo's B-Share Price Performance

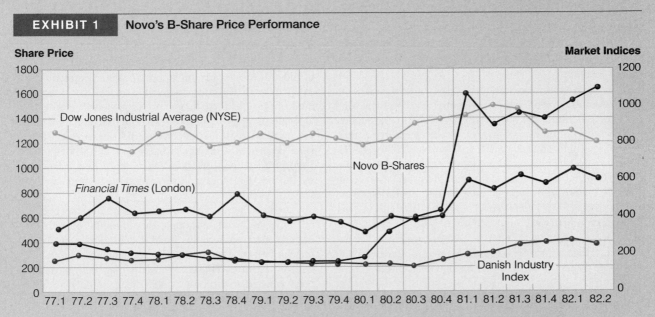

Source: Arthur I. Stonehill and Kåre B. Dullum, *Internationalizing the Cost of Capital: The Novo Experience and National Policy Implications*, London: John Wiley, 1982, p. 73. Reprinted with permission.

that virtually nobody in Denmark thought it was worth the price which foreigners were willing to pay. In fact, prior to the time of the share issue in July 1981 Novo's share price had risen to over Dkr1500, before settling down to a level around Dkr1400. Foreign ownership had increased to over 50% of Novo's shares outstanding!

Stock Market Reactions. One final piece of evidence on market segmentation can be gleaned from the way Danish and foreign investors reacted to the announcement of the proposed $61 million U.S. share issue on May 29, 1981. Novo's share price dropped 156 points the next trading day in Copenhagen, equal to about 10% of its market value. As soon as trading started in New York, the stock price immediately recovered all of its loss. The Copenhagen reaction was typical for an illiquid market. Investors worried about the dilution effect of the new share issue, because it would increase the number of shares outstanding by about 8%. They did not believe that Novo could invest the new funds at a rate of return which would not dilute future earnings per share. They also feared that the U.S. shares would eventually flow back to Copenhagen if biotechnology lost its glitter.

The U.S. reaction to the announcement of the new share issue was consistent with what one would expect in a liquid and integrated market. U.S. investors viewed the new issue as creating additional demand for the shares as Novo became more visible due to the selling efforts of a large aggressive syndicate. Furthermore, the marketing effort was directed at institutional investors who were previously

underrepresented among Novo's U.S. investors. They had been underrepresented because U.S. institutional investors want to be assured of a liquid market in a stock in order to be able to get out, if desired, without depressing the share price. The wide distribution effected by the new issue, plus SEC registration and a New York Stock Exchange listing, all added up to more liquidity and a global cost of capital.

Effect on Novo's Weighted Average Cost of Capital. During most of 1981 and the years thereafter Novo's share price was driven by international portfolio investors transacting on the New York, London, and Copenhagen stock exchanges. This reduced Novo's weighted average cost of capital and lowered its marginal cost of capital. Novo's systematic risk was reduced from its previous level, which was determined by nondiversified (internationally) Danish institutional investors and the Novo Foundation. However, its appropriate debt ratio level was also reduced to match the standards expected by international portfolio investors trading in the United States, United Kingdom, and other important markets. In essence, the U.S. dollar became Novo's functional currency when being evaluated by international investors. Theoretically, its revised weighted average cost of capital should have become a new reference hurdle rate when evaluating new capital investments in Denmark or abroad.

Other firms that follow Novo's strategy are also likely to have their weighted average cost of capital become a function of the requirements of international portfolio investors.

Firms resident in some of the emerging market countries have already experienced "dollarization" of trade and financing for working capital. This phenomenon might be extended to long-term financing and the weighted average cost of capital.

The Novo experience has been described in hopes that it can be a model for other firms wishing to escape from segmented and illiquid home equity markets. In particular, MNEs based in emerging markets often face barriers and lack of visibility similar to what Novo faced. They could benefit by following Novo's proactive strategy employed to attract international portfolio investors. However, a word of caution is advised. Novo had an excellent operating track record and a very strong worldwide market niche in two important industry sectors, insulin and industrial enzymes. This record continues to attract investors in Denmark and abroad. Other companies would also need to have such a favorable track record to attract foreign investors.

Globalization of Securities Markets

During the 1980s, numerous other Nordic and other European firms followed Novo's example. They cross-listed on major foreign exchanges such as London and New York. They placed equity and debt issues in major securities markets. In most cases, they were successful in lowering their WACC and increasing its availability.

During the 1980s and 1990s, national restrictions on cross-border portfolio investment were gradually eased under pressure from the Organization for Economic Cooperation and Development (OECD), a consortium of most of the world's most industrialized countries. Liberalization of European securities markets was accelerated because of the European Union's efforts to develop a single European market without barriers. Emerging nation markets followed suit, as did the former Eastern Bloc countries after the breakup of the Soviet Union. Emerging national markets have often been motivated by the need to source foreign capital to finance large-scale privatization.

At the present time, market segmentation has been significantly reduced, although the liquidity of individual national markets remains limited. Most observers believe that for better or for worse we have achieved a global market for securities. The good news is that many firms have been assisted to become MNEs because they now have access to a global cost and availability of capital. The bad news is that the correlation among securities markets has increased, thereby reducing, but not eliminating, the benefits of international portfolio diversification. Globalization of securities markets has also led to more volatility and speculative behavior as shown by the emerging market crises of the 1995–2001 period.

Questions

1. **Dimensions of the Cost and Availability of Capital.** Global integration has given many firms access to new and cheaper sources of funds beyond those available in their home markets. What are the dimensions of a strategy to capture this lower cost and greater availability of capital?

2. **Benefits.** What are the benefits of achieving a lower cost and greater availability of capital?

3. **Definitions.** Define the following terms:
   a. Systematic risk
   b. Unsystematic risk
   c. Beta (in the Capital Asset Pricing Model)

4. **Equity Risk Premiums**
   a. What is an equity risk premium?
   b. What is the difference between calculating an equity risk premium using arithmetic returns compared to geometric returns?
   c. In Exhibit 12.3, why are arithmetic mean risk premiums always higher than geometric mean risk premiums?

5. **Portfolio Investors.** Both domestic and international portfolio managers are *asset allocators*.
   a. What is their portfolio management objective?
   b. What is the main advantage that international portfolio managers have compared to portfolio managers limited to domestic-only asset allocation?

6. **Dimensions of Asset Allocation.** Portfolio asset allocation can be accomplished along many dimensions depending on the investment objective of the portfolio manager. Identify the various dimensions.

7. **Market Liquidity**
   a. Define what is meant by the term *market liquidity*.
   b. What are the main disadvantages for a firm to be located in an illiquid market?
   c. If a firm is limited to raising funds in its domestic capital market, what happens to its marginal cost of capital as it expands?
   d. If a firm can raise funds abroad what happens to its marginal cost of capital as it expands?

8. **Market Segmentation**
   a. Define market segmentation.
   b. What are the six main causes of market segmentation?

c. What are the main disadvantages for a firm to be located in a segmented market?

9. **Market Liquidity and Segmentation Effects.** What is the effect of market liquidity and segmentation on a firm's cost of capital?

10. **Novo Industri (A).** Why did Novo believe its cost of capital was too high compared to its competitors? Why did Novo's relatively high cost of capital create a competitive disadvantage?

11. **Novo Industri (B).** Novo believed that the Danish capital market was segmented from world capital markets. Explain the six characteristics of the Danish equity market that were responsible for its segmentation.

12. **Novo Industri A/S**
    a. What was Novo's strategy to internationalize its cost of capital?
    b. What is the evidence that Novo's strategy succeeded?

13. **Emerging Markets.** It has been suggested that firms located in illiquid and segmented emerging markets could follow Novo's proactive strategy to internationalize their own cost of capital. What are the preconditions that would be necessary to succeed in such a proactive strategy?

14. **Cost of Capital for MNEs Compared to Domestic Firms.** Theoretically, MNEs should be in a better position than their domestic counterparts to support higher debt ratios because their cash flows are diversified internationally. However, recent empirical studies have come to the opposite conclusion. These studies also concluded that MNEs have higher betas than their domestic counterparts.
    a. According to these empirical studies, why do MNEs have lower debt ratios than their domestic counterparts?
    b. According to these empirical studies, why do MNEs have higher betas than their domestic counterparts?

15. **The "Riddle."** The riddle is an attempt to explain under what conditions an MNE would have a higher or lower debt ratio and beta than its domestic counterpart. Explain and diagram what are these conditions.

16. **Emerging Market MNEs.** Apart from improving liquidity and escaping from a segmented home market, why might emerging market MNEs further lower their cost of capital by listing and selling equity abroad?

Problems

1. **Corcovado Pharmaceuticals.** Corcovado Pharmaceutical's cost of debt is 7%. The risk-free rate of interest is 3%. The expected return on the market portfolio is 8%. After effective taxes, Corcovado's effective tax rate is 25%. Its optimal capital structure is 60% debt and 40% equity.
    a. If Corcovado's beta is estimated at 1.1, what is its weighted average cost of capital?
    b. If Corcovado's beta is estimated at 0.8, significantly lower because of the continuing profit prospects in the global energy sector, what is its weighted average cost of capital?

2. **Colton Conveyance, Inc.** Colton Conveyance, Inc., is a large U.S. natural gas pipeline company that wants to raise $120 million to finance expansion. Deming wants a capital structure that is 50% debt and 50% equity. Its corporate combined federal and state income tax rate is 40%. Deming finds that it can finance in the domestic U.S. capital market at the rates listed below. Both debt and equity would have to be sold in multiples of $20 million, and these cost figures show the component costs, each, of debt and equity if raised half by equity and half by debt.

   A London bank advises Deming that U.S. dollars could be raised in Europe at the following costs, also in multiples of $20 million, while maintaining the 50/50 capital structure.

   Each increment of cost would be influenced by the total amount of capital raised. That is, if Deming first borrowed $20 million in the European market at 6% and matched this with an additional $20 million of equity, additional debt beyond this amount would cost 12% in the United States and 10% in Europe. The same relationship holds for equity financing.
    a. Calculate the lowest average cost of capital for each increment of $40 million of new capital, where Deming raises $20 million in the equity market and an additional $20 in the debt market at the same time.
    b. If Deming plans an expansion of only $60 million, how should that expansion be financed? What will be the weighted average cost of capital for the expansion?

3. **Trident's Cost of Capital.** Market conditions have changed. Maria Gonzalez now estimates the risk-free rate to be 3.60%, the company's credit risk premium is 4.40%, the domestic beta is estimated at 1.05, the international beta at .85, and the company's capital structure is now 30% debt. All other values remain

the same. For both the domestic CAPM and ICAPM, calculate the following:

a. Trident's cost of equity
b. Trident's cost of debt
c. Trident's weighted average cost of capital

4. Country Equity Risk Premiums. Using the century of equity market data presented in Exhibit 12.3, answer the following questions:

a. Which country had the largest differential between the arithmetic mean and geometric mean?
b. If a Swiss firm were attempting to calculate its cost of equity using this data, assuming a risk-free rate of 2.0% and a security beta of 1.4, what would be its estimated cost of equity using both the arithmetic mean and geometric means for the equity risk premium?

5. Kashmiri's Cost of Capital. Kashmiri is the largest and most successful specialty goods company based in Bangalore, India. It has not entered the North American marketplace yet, but is considering establishing both manufacturing and distribution facilities in the United States through a wholly owned subsidiary. It has approached two different investment banking advisors, Goldman Sachs and Bank of New York, for estimates of what its costs of capital would be several years into the future when it planned to list its American subsidiary on a U.S. stock exchange. Using the following assumptions by the two different advisors, calculate the prospective costs of debt, equity, and the WACC for Kashmiri (U.S.):

Assumptions	Symbol	Goldman Sachs	Bank of New York
Components of beta:	β		
Estimate of correlation between security and market	ρ_{jm}	0.90	0.85
Estimate of standard deviation of Tata's returns	σ_j	24.0%	30.0%
Estimate of standard deviation of market's return	σ_m	18.0%	22.0%
Risk-free rate of interest	k_{rf}	3.0%	3.0%
Estimate of Tata's cost of debt in U.S. market	k_d	7.5%	7.8%
Estimate of market return, forward-looking	k_m	9.0%	12.0%
Corporate tax rate	t	35.0%	35.0%
Proportion of debt	D/V	35%	40%
Proportion of equity	E/V	65%	60%

6. Cargill's Cost of Capital. Cargill is generally considered to be the largest privately held company in the world. Headquartered in Minneapolis, Minnesota, the company has been averaging sales of over $113 billion per year over the past five-year period. Although the company does not have publicly traded shares, it is still extremely important for it to calculate its weighted average cost of capital properly in order to make rational decisions on new investment proposals. Assuming a risk-free rate of 4.50%, an effective tax rate of 48%, and a market risk premium of 5.50%, estimate the weighted average cost of capital first for companies A and B, and then make a "guesstimate" of what you believe a comparable WACC would be for Cargill.

	Company A	Company B	Cargill
Company Sales	$10.5 billion	$45 billion	$113 billion
Company's beta	0.83	0.68	??
Credit Rating	AA	A	AA
Weighted average cost of debt	6.885%	7.125%	6.820%
Debt to total capital	34%	41%	28%
International sales/Sales	11%	34%	54%

7. The Tombs. You have joined your friends at the local watering hole, The Tombs, for your weekly debate on international finance. The topic this week is whether the cost of equity can ever be cheaper than the cost of debt. The group has chosen Brazil in the mid-1990s as the subject of the debate. One of the group members has torn a table of data out of a book (shown on the next page), which is then the subject of the analysis.

Larry argues that "it's all about expected versus delivered. You can talk about what equity investors expect, but they often find that what is delivered for years at a time is so small—even sometimes negative—that in effect, the cost of equity is cheaper than the cost of debt."

Moe interrupts: "But you're missing the point. The cost of capital is what the investor requires in compensation for the risk taken going into the investment. If he doesn't end up getting it, and that was happening here, then he pulls his capital out and walks."

Curly is the theoretician. "Ladies, this is not about empirical results; it is about the fundamental concept of risk-adjusted returns. An investor in equities knows he will reap returns only after all compensation has been made to debt providers. He is therefore always subject to a higher level of risk to his return than debt instruments, and as the capital asset pricing model states, equity investors set their expected returns as a risk-adjusted factor over and above the returns to risk-free instruments."

At this point, Larry and Moe simply stare at Curly, pause, and order more beer. Using the Brazilian data presented, comment on this week's debate at the Tombs.

Brazilian Economic Performance	1995	1996	1997	1998	1999
Inflation rate (IPC)	23.20%	10.00%	4.80%	−1.00%	10.50%
Bank lending rate	53.10%	27.10%	24.70%	29.20%	30.70%
Exchange rate (reais/$)	0.972	1.039	1.117	1.207	1.700
Equity returns (São Paulo Bovespa)	16.0%	28.0%	30.2%	−33.5%	151.9%

Genedak-Hogan

Use the following information to answer problems 8 through 10. Genedak-Hogan is an American conglomerate which is actively debating the impacts of international diversification of its operations on its capital structure and cost of capital. The firm is planning on reducing consolidated debt after diversification.

Assumptions	Symbol	Before Diversification	After Diversification
Correlation between G-H and the market	ρ_{jm}	0.88	0.76
Standard deviation of G-H's returns	σ_j	28.0%	26.0%
Standard deviation of market's returns	σ_m	18.0%	18.0%
Risk-free rate of interest	k_{rf}	3.0%	3.0%
Additional equity risk premium for internationalization	RPM	0.0%	3.0%
Estimate of G-H's cost of debt in U.S. market	k_d	7.2%	7.0%
Market risk premium	$k_m - k_{rf}$	5.5%	5.5%
Corporate tax rate	t	35.0%	35.0%
Proportion of debt	D/V	38%	32%
Proportion of equity	E/V	62%	68%

8. **Genedak-Hogan Cost of Equity.** Senior management at Genedak-Hogan is actively debating the implications of diversification on its cost of equity. Although both parties agree that the company's returns will be less correlated with the reference market return in the future, the financial advisors believe that the market will assess an additional 3.0% risk premium for "going international" to the basic CAPM cost of equity. Calculate Genedak-Hogan's cost of equity before and after international diversification of its operations, with and without the hypothetical additional risk premium, and comment on the discussion.

9. **Genedak-Hogan's WACC.** Calculate the weighted average cost of capital for Genedak-Hogan for before and after international diversification.
   a. Did the reduction in debt costs reduce the firm's weighted average cost of capital? How would you describe the impact of international diversification on its costs of capital?

   b. Adding the hypothetical risk premium to the cost of equity introduced in problem 8 (an added 3.0% to the cost of equity because of international diversification), what is the firm's WACC?

10. **Genedak-Hogan's WACC and Effective Tax Rate.** Many MNEs have greater ability to control and reduce their effective tax rates when expanding international operations. If Genedak-Hogan was able to reduce its consolidated effective tax rate from 35% to 32%, what would be the impact on its WACC?

Internet Exercises

1. **International Diversification via Mutual Funds.** All major mutual fund companies now offer a variety of internationally diversified mutual funds. The degree of international composition across funds, however, differs significantly. Use the Web sites listed, and others of interest, to
   a. Distinguish between international funds, global funds, worldwide funds, and overseas funds

b. Determine how international funds have been performing, in U.S. dollar terms, relative to mutual funds offering purely domestic portfolios

Fidelity	www.fidelity.com/funds/
T. Rowe Price	www.troweprice.com/
Merrill Lynch	www.ml.com/
Scudder	www.scudder.com/
Kemper	www.kemper.com/

2. **Center for Latin American Capital Markets Research.** Although most of the Latin American markets have suffered significant falls in trading following the Mexican peso crisis of December 1994 and the Brazilian real in January 1999, many of these markets may still be some of the most "undervalued" markets in the world. If you were given the task of investing US$1 million in a single equity market in Latin America or South America, which one would you invest in? Use the Internet to find recent market performance statistics to support your choice.

| Center for Latin American | www.netrus.net/users/ |
| Capital Markets Research | gmorles/ |

3. **Novo Industri.** Novo Industri A/S merged with Nordisk Gentofte in 1989. Nordisk Gentofte was Novo's main European competitor. The combined company, now called Novo Nordisk, has become the leading producer of insulin worldwide. Its main competitor is Eli Lilly of the United States. Using standard investor information, and the Web sites for Novo Nordisk and Eli Lilly, determine whether during the most recent five years, Novo Nordisk has maintained a cost of capital competitive with Eli Lilly. In particular, examine the P/E ratios, share prices, debt ratios, and betas. Try to calculate each firm's actual cost of capital.

Novo Nordisk	www.novonordisk.com
Eli Lilly and Company	www.lilly.com
BigCharts.com	www.bigcharts.com

4. **Cost of Capital Calculator.** Ibbotson and Associates of Chicago is one of the leading providers of quantitative estimates of the cost of capital across markets. Use the following Web site—specifically the *Cost of Capital Center*—to prepare an overview of the major theoretical approaches and the numerical estimates they yield for cross-border costs of capital.

| Ibbotson and Associates | www.ibbotson.com |

Sourcing Equity and Debt Globally

Do what you will, the capital is at hazard ... All that can be required of a trustee to invest, is, that he shall conduct himself faithfully and exercise a sound discretion. He is to observe how men of prudence, discretion, and intelligence manage their own affairs, not in regard to speculation, but in regard to the permanent disposition of their funds, considering the probable income, as well as the probable safety of the capital to be invested. —Prudent Man Rule, Justice Samuel Putnam, 1830.

LEARNING OBJECTIVES

◆ Design a strategy to source equity and debt globally.

◆ Analyze the motivations and goals of a firm cross-listing its shares on foreign equity markets.

◆ Analyze the motivations and goals of a firm issuing new equity shares on foreign equity markets.

◆ Understand the many barriers to penetrate effectively foreign equity markets through cross-listing and selling equity abroad.

◆ Examine the various financial instruments that can be used to source equity in the global equity markets.

◆ Extend the theory of optimal financial structure to the multinational enterprise (MNE).

◆ Analyze the factors that, in practice, determine the financial structure of foreign subsidiaries within the context of the MNE.

◆ Evaluate the various internal and external sources of funds available for the financing of foreign subsidiaries.

◆ Identify the relevant characteristics of different international debt instruments in financing both the MNE itself, and its various foreign affiliate components.

Chapter 12 analyzed why gaining access to global capital markets should lower a firm's marginal cost of capital and increase its availability by improving the market liquidity of its shares and by overcoming market segmentation. In order to implement such a lofty goal it is necessary to start by designing a strategy that will ultimately attract international investors. This involves identifying and choosing among alternative paths to access global markets. It also usually requires some restructuring of the firm, improving the quality and level of its disclosure, and making its accounting and reporting standards more transparent to potential foreign investors.

This chapter focuses on firms resident in less liquid, segmented, or emerging markets. They are the ones that need to tap liquid and unsegmented markets in order to attain the global cost and availability of capital. These firms are typically resident in emerging market countries and many of the smaller industrial country markets. Firms resident in the United States and United Kingdom already have full access to their own domestic liquid and unsegmented markets. Although they too source equity and debt abroad, it is unlikely to have as favorable an impact on their cost and availability of capital. In fact, sourcing funds abroad is often motivated only by the need to fund large foreign acquisitions rather than existing domestic or foreign operations.

The chapter starts with the design of a strategy to source both equity and debt capital globally. It then analyzes the optimal financial structure for an MNE and its subsidiaries, one that minimizes its cost of capital. This is followed by a discussion of the issues involved in raising equity capital. We then present a detailed analysis of international debt markets, including bank loans, syndicated credits, the Euronote market, and international bond market. The chapter ends with the Mini-Case, *Petrobrás of Brazil and the Cost of Capital*.

Designing a Strategy to Source Equity Globally

Designing a capital sourcing strategy requires management to agree upon a long-run financial objective and then choose among the various alternative paths to get there. Exhibit 13.1 is a visual presentation of alternative paths to the ultimate objective of attaining a global cost and availability of capital.

Normally, the choice of paths and implementation is aided by an early appointment of an investment bank as official advisor to the firm. Investment bankers are in touch with the potential foreign investors and their current requirements. They can also help navigate the various institutional requirements and barriers that must be satisfied. Their services include advising if, when, and where a cross-listing should be initiated. They usually prepare the required prospectus if an equity or debt issue is desired, help to price the issue, and maintain an aftermarket to prevent the share price from falling below its initial price.

Alternative Paths

Most firms raise their initial capital in their own domestic market (see Exhibit 13.1). Next, they are tempted to skip all the intermediate steps and drop to the bottom line, a Euroequity issue in global markets. This is the time when a good investment bank advisor will offer a "reality check." Most firms that have only raised capital in their domestic market are not well enough known to attract foreign investors. Remember from Chapter 12 that Novo was advised by its investment bankers to start with a convertible Eurobond issue and simultaneously cross-list their shares (and the bonds) in London. This was despite the fact that Novo had an outstanding track record with respect to growth, profitability, and dominance of two worldwide market niches.

Exhibit 13.1 shows that most firms should start sourcing abroad with an international bond issue. It could be placed on a less prestigious foreign market. This could be followed by an international bond issue in a target market or in the Eurobond market. The next step might be to cross-list and issue equity in one of the less prestigious markets so as to attract international investor attention. The next step could be to cross-list shares on a highly liquid

EXHIBIT 13.1   Alternative Paths to Globalize the Cost and Availability of Capital

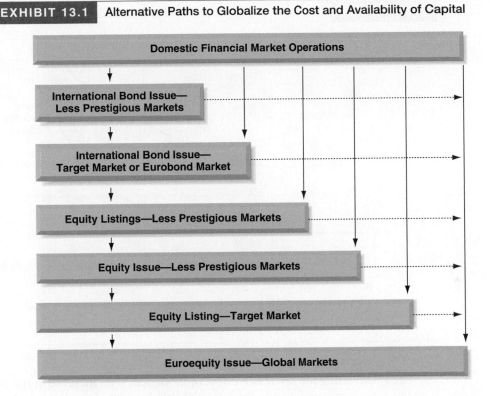

Source: Oxelhiem, Stonehill, Randøy, Vikkula, Dullum, and Modén, *Corporate Strategies in Internationalizing the Cost of Capital*, Copenhagen: Copenhagen Business School Press, 1998, p. 119.

prestigious foreign stock exchange such as London (LSE), NYSE-Euronext, or NASDAQ. The ultimate step would be to place a directed equity issue in a prestigious target market or a Euroequity issue in global equity markets.

Optimal Financial Structure

After many years of debate, most finance theorists now agree about whether an optimal financial structure exists for a firm, and if so, how it can be determined. The great debate between the so-called traditionalists and the Modigliani and Miller school of thought has apparently ended in a compromise. When taxes and bankruptcy costs are considered, a firm has an optimal financial structure determined by that particular mix of debt and equity that minimizes the firm's cost of capital for a given level of business risk. If the business risk of new projects differs from the risk of existing projects, the optimal mix of debt and equity would change to recognize trade-offs between business and financial risks.

Exhibit 13.2 illustrates how the cost of capital varies with the amount of debt employed. As the debt ratio, defined as total debt divided by total assets at market values, increases, the overall cost of capital (k_{WACC}) decreases because of the heavier weight of low-cost debt $[k_d(1 - t)]$ compared to high-cost equity (k_e). The low cost of debt is, of course, due to the tax deductibility of interest shown by the term $(1 - t)$.

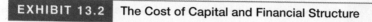

EXHIBIT 13.2   The Cost of Capital and Financial Structure

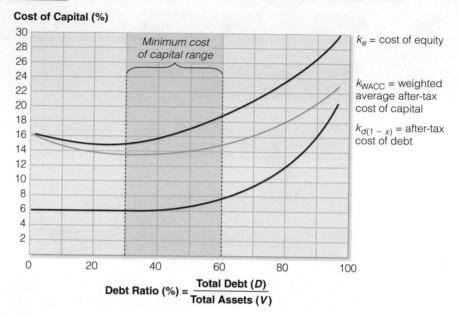

Partly offsetting the favorable effect of more debt is an increase in the cost of equity (k_e), because investors perceive greater financial risk. Nevertheless, the overall weighted average after-tax cost of capital (k_{WACC}) continues to decline as the debt ratio increases, until financial risk becomes so serious that investors and management alike perceive a real danger of insolvency. This result causes a sharp increase in the cost of new debt and equity, thus increasing the weighted average cost of capital. The low point on the resulting U-shaped cost of capital curve, which is at 14% in Exhibit 13.2, defines the debt ratio range in which the cost of capital is minimized.

Most theorists believe that the low point is actually a rather broad flat area encompassing a wide range of debt ratios, 30% to 60% in Exhibit 13.2, where little difference exists in the cost of capital. They also believe that, at least in the United States, the range of the flat area and the location of a particular firm's debt ratio within that range are determined by such variables as 1) the industry in which it competes; 2) volatility of its sales and operating income; and 3) the collateral value of its assets.

Optimal Financial Structure and the MNE

The domestic theory of optimal financial structures needs to be modified by four more variables in order to accommodate the case of the MNE. These variables, in order of appearance, are 1) availability of capital; 2) diversification of cash flows; 3) foreign exchange risk; and 4) expectations of international portfolio investors.

Availability of Capital. Chapter 12 demonstrated that access to capital in global markets allows an MNE to lower its cost of equity and debt compared with most domestic firms. It also permits an MNE to maintain its desired debt ratio, even when significant amounts of new funds must be raised. In other words, a multinational firm's marginal cost of capital is constant for considerable ranges of its capital budget. This statement is not true for most small domestic firms because they do not have access to the national equity or debt markets. They must either rely on internally generated funds or borrow for the short and medium terms from commercial banks.

Multinational firms domiciled in countries that have illiquid capital markets are in almost the same situation as small domestic firms unless they have gained a global cost and availability of capital. They must rely on internally generated funds and bank borrowing. If they need to raise significant amounts of new funds to finance growth opportunities, they may need to borrow more than would be optimal from the viewpoint of minimizing their cost of capital. This is equivalent to saying that their marginal cost of capital is increasing at higher budget levels.

Diversification of Cash Flows. As explained in Chapter 12, the theoretical possibility exists that multinational firms are in a better position than domestic firms to support higher debt ratios because their cash flows are diversified internationally. The probability of a firm's covering fixed charges under varying conditions in product, financial, and foreign exchange markets should increase if the variability of its cash flows is minimized.

By diversifying cash flows internationally, the MNE might be able to achieve the same kind of reduction in cash flow variability as portfolio investors receive from diversifying their security holdings internationally. Returns are not perfectly correlated between countries.

In contrast, a domestic German firm would not enjoy the benefit of cash flow international diversification but would have to rely entirely on its own net cash inflow from domestic operations. Perceived financial risk for the German firm would be greater than for a multinational firm because the variability of its German domestic cash flows could not be offset by positive cash flows elsewhere in the world.

As introduced in Chapter 12, the diversification argument has been challenged by empirical research findings that MNEs in the United States actually have lower debt ratios than their domestic counterparts. The agency costs of debt were higher for the MNEs, as were political risks, foreign exchange risks, and asymmetric information.

Foreign Exchange Risk and the Cost of Debt

When a firm issues foreign currency denominated debt, its effective cost equals the after-tax cost of repaying the principal and interest in terms of the firm's own currency. This amount includes the nominal cost of principal and interest in foreign currency terms, adjusted for any foreign exchange gains or losses.

For example, if a U.S.-based firm borrows Sfr1,500,000 for one year at 5.00% interest, and during the year the Swiss franc appreciates from an initial rate of Sfr1.5000/$ to Sfr1.4400/$, what is the dollar cost of this debt $(k_d^\$)$? The dollar proceeds of the initial borrowing are calculated at the current spot rate of Sfr1.5000/$:

$$\frac{\text{Sfr}1,500,000}{\text{Sfr}1.5000/\$} = \$1,000,000$$

At the end of one year the U.S.-based firm is responsible for repaying the Sfr1,500,000 principal plus 5.00% interest, or a total of Sfr1,575,000. This repayment, however, must be made at an ending spot rate of Sfr1.4400/$:

$$\frac{\text{Sfr}1,500,000 \times 1.05}{\text{Sfr}1.4400/\$} = \$1,093,750$$

The actual dollar cost of the loan's repayment is not the nominal 5.00% paid in Swiss franc interest, but 9.375%:

$$\left[\frac{\$1,093,750}{\$1,000,000} \right] - 1 = 0.09375 \approx 9.375\%$$

The dollar cost is higher than expected due to appreciation of the Swiss franc against the U.S. dollar.

This total home-currency cost is actually the result of the combined percentage cost of debt and percentage change in the foreign currency's value. We can find the total cost of borrowing Swiss francs by a U.S.-dollar based firm, $k_d^\$$, by multiplying one plus the Swiss franc interest expense, k_d^{Sfr}, by one plus the percentage change in the Sfr/$ exchange rate, s:

$$k_d^\$ = [(1 + k_d^{Sfr}) \times (1 + s)] - 1$$

where $k_d^{Sfr} = 5.00\%$ and $s = 4.1667\%$. The percentage change in the value of the Swiss franc versus the U.S. dollar, when the home currency is the U.S. dollar, is

$$\frac{S_1 - S_2}{S_2} \times 100 = \frac{Sfr1.5000/\$ - Sfr1.4400/\$}{Sfr1.4400/\$} \times 100 = +4.1667\%$$

The total expense, combining the nominal interest rate and the percentage change in the exchange rate, is

$$k_d^\$ = [(1 + .0500) \times (1 + .041667)] - 1 = .09375 \approx 9.375\%$$

The total percentage cost of capital is 9.375%, not simply the foreign currency interest payment of 5%. The after-tax cost of this Swiss franc denominated debt, when the U.S. income tax rate is 34%, is

$$k_d^\$(1 - t) = 9.375\% \times 0.66 = 6.1875\%$$

The firm would report the added 4.1667% cost of this debt in terms of U.S. dollars as a foreign exchange transaction loss, and it would be deductible for tax purposes.

Expectations of International Portfolio Investors

Chapter 12 highlighted the fact that the key to gaining a global cost and availability of capital is attracting and retaining international portfolio investors. Their expectations for a firm's debt ratio and overall financial structures are based on global norms that have developed over the past 30 years. Because a large proportion of international portfolio investors are based in the most liquid and unsegmented capital markets, such as the United States and the United Kingdom, their expectations tend to predominate and override individual national norms. Therefore, regardless of other factors, if a firm wants to raise capital in global markets, it must adopt global norms that are close to the U.S. and U.K. norms. Debt ratios up to 60% appear to be acceptable. Any higher debt ratio is more difficult to sell to international portfolio investors.

Financial Structure of Foreign Subsidiaries

If we accept the theory that minimizing the cost of capital for a given level of business risk and capital budget is an objective that should be implemented from the perspective of the consolidated MNE, then the financial structure of each subsidiary is relevant only to the extent that it affects this overall goal. In other words, an individual subsidiary does not really have an independent cost of capital. Therefore, its financial structure should not be based on an objective of minimizing it.

Financial structure norms for firms vary widely from one country to another but cluster for firms domiciled in the same country. This statement is the conclusion of a long line of empirical studies that have investigated the question, from 1969 to the present. Most of these international studies concluded that country-specific environmental variables are key determinants of debt ratios. Among these variables are historical development, taxation, corporate governance, bank influence, existence of a viable corporate bond market, attitude toward risk, government regulation, availability of capital, and agency costs.

Many other institutional differences also influence debt ratios in national capital markets, but firms trying to attract international portfolio investors must pay attention to debt ratio norms those investors expect. Since many international portfolio investors are influenced by the debt ratios that exist in the Anglo-American markets, there is a trend toward more global conformity. MNEs and other large firms dependent on attracting international portfolio investors are beginning to adopt similar debt ratio standards, even if domestic firms continue to use national standards.

Local Norms and the Financial Structure of Local Subsidiaries

Within the constraint of minimizing its consolidated worldwide cost of capital, should an MNE take differing country debt ratio norms into consideration when determining its desired debt ratio for foreign subsidiaries? For definition purposes the debt considered here should be only that borrowed from sources outside the MNE. This debt would include local and foreign currency loans as well as Eurocurrency loans. The reason for this definition is that parent loans to foreign subsidiaries are often regarded as equivalent to equity investment both by host countries and by investing firms. A parent loan is usually subordinated to other debt and does not create the same threat of insolvency as an external loan. Furthermore, the choice of debt or equity investment is often arbitrary and subject to negotiation between host country and parent firm.

Main Advantages of Localization. The main advantages of a finance structure for foreign subsidiaries that conforms to local debt norms are as follows:

◆ A localized financial structure reduces criticism of foreign subsidiaries that have been operating with too high a proportion of debt (judged by local standards), often resulting in the accusation that they are not contributing a fair share of risk capital to the host country. At the other end of the spectrum, a localized financial structure would improve the image of foreign subsidiaries that have been operating with too little debt and thus appear to be insensitive to local monetary policy.

◆ A localized financial structure helps management evaluate return on equity investment relative to local competitors in the same industry. In economies where interest rates are relatively high as an offset to inflation, the penalty paid reminds management of the need to consider price level changes when evaluating investment performance.

◆ In economies where interest rates are relatively high because of a scarcity of capital, and real resources are fully utilized (full employment), the penalty paid for borrowing local funds reminds management that unless return on assets is greater than the local price of capital—that is, negative leverage—they are probably misallocating scarce domestic real resources such as land and labor. This factor may not appear relevant to management decisions, but it will certainly be considered by the host country in making decisions with respect to the firm.

Main Disadvantages of Localization. The main disadvantages of localized financial structures are as follows:

◆ An MNE is expected to have a comparative advantage over local firms in overcoming imperfections in national capital markets through better availability of capital and the ability to diversify risk. Why should it throw away these important competitive advantages to conform to local norms established in response to imperfect local capital markets, historical precedent, and institutional constraints that do not apply to the MNE?

◆ If each foreign subsidiary of an MNE localizes its financial structure, the resulting consolidated balance sheet might show a financial structure that does not conform to any particular country's norm. The debt ratio would be a simple weighted average of the corresponding ratio of each country in which the firm operates. This feature could increase perceived financial risk and thus the cost of capital for the parent, but only if two additional conditions are present:

  1. The consolidated debt ratio is pushed completely out of the discretionary range of acceptable debt ratios in the flat area of the cost of capital curve, shown previously in Exhibit 13.2.

  2. The MNE is unable to offset high debt in one foreign subsidiary with low debt in other foreign or domestic subsidiaries at the same cost. If the International Fisher effect is working, replacement of debt should be possible at an equal after-tax cost after adjusting for foreign exchange risk. On the other hand, if market imperfections preclude this type of replacement, the possibility exists that the overall cost of debt, and thus the cost of capital, could increase if the MNE attempts to conform to local norms.

◆ The debt ratio of a foreign subsidiary is only cosmetic, because lenders ultimately look to the parent and its consolidated worldwide cash flow as the source of repayment. In many cases, debt of subsidiaries must be guaranteed by the parent firm. Even if no formal guarantee exists, an implied guarantee usually exists because almost no parent firm would dare to allow an affiliate to default on a loan. If it did, repercussions would surely be felt with respect to the parent's own financial standing, with a resulting increase in its cost of capital.

Compromise Solution. In our opinion, a compromise position is possible. Both multinational and domestic firms should try to minimize their overall weighted average cost of capital for a given level of business risk and capital budget, as finance theory suggests. However, if debt is available to a foreign subsidiary at equal cost to that which could be raised elsewhere, after adjusting for foreign exchange risk, then localizing the foreign subsidiary's financial structure should incur no cost penalty and yet would also enjoy the advantages listed above.

Financing the Foreign Subsidiary

In addition to choosing an appropriate financial structure for foreign subsidiaries, financial managers of multinational firms need to choose among alternative sources of funds to finance foreign subsidiaries. Sources of funds available to foreign subsidiaries can be classified as *internal to the MNE and external to the MNE.*

Ideally, the choice among the sources of funds should minimize the cost of external funds after adjusting for foreign exchange risk. The firm should choose internal sources in order to minimize worldwide taxes and political risk. Simultaneously, the firm should ensure that managerial motivation in the foreign subsidiaries is geared toward minimizing the firm's consolidated worldwide cost of capital, rather than the foreign subsidiary's cost of capital. Needless to say, this task is difficult if not impossible, and the tendency is to place more emphasis on one variable at the expense of others.

Internal Sources of Funding. Exhibit 13.3 provides an overview of the internal sources of financing for foreign subsidiaries. In general, although the equity provided by the parent is required, it is frequently kept to legal and operational minimums to reduce risk of invested capital. Equity investment can take the form of either cash or real goods (machinery, equipment, inventory, etc.).

Debt is the preferable form of subsidiary financing, but access to local host country debt is limited in the early stages of a foreign subsidiary's life. Without a history of proven operational capability and debt service capability, the foreign subsidiary must acquire its debt from the parent company or sister subsidiaries (initially) and from unrelated parties with a parental guarantee (after operations have been initiated).

Once the operational and financial capabilities of the foreign subsidiary have been established, its ability to generate funds internally may become critical for the subsidiary's growth. In special cases in which the subsidiary may be operating in a highly segmented market, such as an emerging market nation considered to be risky by the international investment and banking communities, the subsidiary's ability to generate its own funds (retained earnings, depreciation, etc.) from internal sources is important.

External Sources of Funding. Exhibit 13.4 provides an overview of the sources of foreign subsidiary financing external to the MNE. The sources are first decomposed into three categories: 1) debt from the parent's country; 2) debt from countries outside the parent's country; and 3) local equity.

EXHIBIT 13.3   Internal Financing of the Foreign Subsidiary

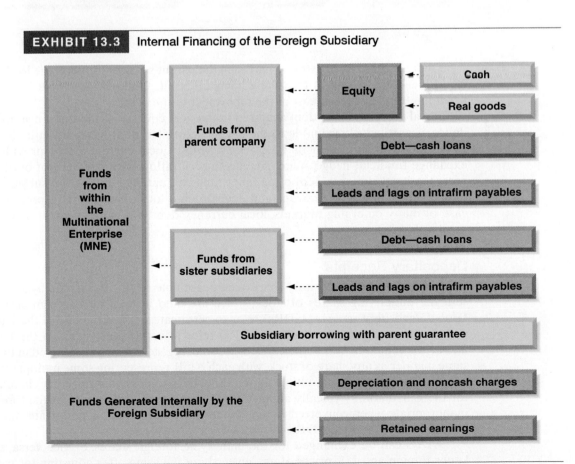

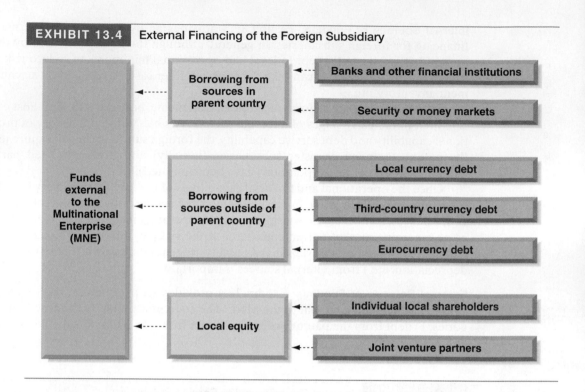

EXHIBIT 13.4   External Financing of the Foreign Subsidiary

Debt acquired from external parties in the parent's country reflects the lenders' familiarity with and confidence in the parent company itself, although the parent is in this case not providing explicit guarantees for the repayment of the debt.

Local currency debt, debt acquired in the host country of the foreign subsidiary's residence, is particularly valuable to the foreign subsidiary that has substantial local currency cash inflows arising from its business activities. Local currency debt provides a foreign exchange financial hedge, matching currency of inflow with currency of outflow. Gaining access to local currency debt often takes time and patience by foreign subsidiary management in establishing operations and developing a local market credit profile. And in the case of many emerging markets, local currency debt is in short supply for all borrowers, local or foreign.

Depositary Receipts

Depositary receipts (depositary shares) are negotiable certificates issued by a bank to represent the underlying shares of stock, which are held in trust at a foreign custodian bank. *Global depositary receipts* (GDRs) refer to certificates traded outside of the United States, and *American depositary receipts* (ADRs) refer to certificates traded in the United States and denominated in U.S. dollars. ADRs are sold, registered, and transferred in the U.S. in the same manner as any share of stock, with each ADR representing some multiple of the underlying foreign share. This multiple allows the ADRs to possess a price per share appropriate for the U.S. market (typically about $20 per share) even if the price of the foreign share is inappropriate when converted to U.S. dollars directly. Exhibit 13.5 illustrates the underlying issuance structure of an ADR.

ADRs can be exchanged for the underlying foreign shares, or vice versa, so arbitrage keeps foreign and U.S. prices of any given share the same after adjusting for transfer costs.

EXHIBIT 13.5   American Depositary Receipts (ADRs)

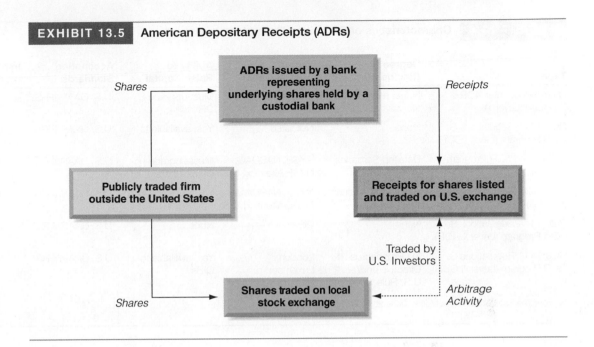

For example, investor demand in one market will cause a price rise there, which will cause an arbitrage rise in the other market even when investors there are not as bullish on the stock.

ADRs convey certain technical advantages to U.S. shareholders. Dividends paid by a foreign firm are passed to its custodial bank and then to the bank that issued the ADR. The issuing bank exchanges the foreign currency dividends for U.S. dollars and sends the dollar dividend to the ADR holders. ADRs are in registered form, rather than in bearer form. Transfer of ownership is facilitated because it is done in the United States in accordance with U.S. laws and procedures. In the event of death of a shareholder, the estate need not to go through probate in a foreign court system. Normally, trading costs are lower than when buying or selling the underlying shares in their home market. Settlement is usually faster in the United States. Withholding taxes are simpler because they're handled by the depositary bank.

ADRs are either *sponsored* or *unsponsored*. Sponsored ADRs are created at the request of a foreign firm wanting its shares traded in the United States. The firm applies to the Security and Exchange Commission (SEC) and a U.S. bank for registration and issuance of ADRs. The foreign firm pays all costs of creating such sponsored ADRs. If a foreign firm does not seek to have its shares traded in the United States but U.S. investors are interested, a U.S. securities firm may initiate creation of the ADRs. Such an ADR would be unsponsored, but the SEC still requires that all new ADR programs must have approval by the firm itself even if it is not a sponsored ADR.

Exhibit 13.6 summarizes the characteristics of ADRs in the United States. It shows three levels of commitment, distinguished by the necessary accounting standards, SEC registration requirement, time to completion, and costs. Level I ("over the counter" or pink sheets) is the easiest to satisfy. It facilitates trading in foreign securities that have been acquired by U.S. investors but the securities are not registered with the SEC. It is the least costly approach but might have a minimal impact on liquidity.

Level II applies to firms that want to list existing shares on the NYSE-EURONEXT, ASE, or NASDAQ markets. They must meet the full registration requirements of the SEC. This means reconciling their financial accounts with those used under U.S. GAAP, raising the

EXHIBIT 13.6   Characteristics of Depositary Receipt Programs

Type	Degree of Disclosure	Listing Alternatives	Ability to Raise Capital	Accounting Standards	Implementation Timetable
Over-the-Counter ADR Program (Level 1)	None: home country standards apply	Over-the-counter (OTC/OTCQX	Must upgrade DR facility	U.S. GAAP/IFRS	6 weeks
Rule 144A/Regulations S GDR Program (Level I GDR)	None	Not listed	Yes, available to QIBs	U.S. GAAP/IFRS	3 weeks
U.S.-Listed ADR Program (Level II)	Detailed Sarbanes Oxley	NYSE, NASDAQ, NYSE Alternext U.S.	Must upgrade DR facility	U.S. GAAP/IFRS	13 weeks
U.S.-Listed ADR Program (Level III)	Rigorous Sarbanes Oxley	NYSE, NASDAQ, NYSE Alternext U.S.	Yes, public offering	U.S. GAAP/IFRS	14 weeks
Rule 144A/Regulations S GDR Program (Level II GDR)	None	DIFX	None	U.S. GAAP/IFRS	2 weeks
Rule 144A/Regulations S GDR Program (Level III GDR)	EU Prospectus Directive and/or U.S. Rule 144A	London, Luxembourg, DIFX, U.S. Portal	Yes, available to QIBs	U.S. GAAP/IFRS	2 weeks

Source: The Bank of New York Mellon, June 2, 2009.

cost considerably. Level III applies to the sale of a new equity issued in the United States. It too requires full registration with the SEC and an elaborate stock prospectus. This is the most expensive alternative, but is the most likely to improve the stock's liquidity and escape from home market segmentation. Rule 144a programs will be described later in this chapter.

Global Registered Shares (GRSs)

Similar to ordinary shares, GRSs have the added benefit of being able to be traded on equity exchanges around the globe in a variety of currencies. ADRs, however, are quoted only in U.S. dollars and are traded only in the United States. GRSs can, theoretically, be traded with the sun, following markets as they open and close around the globe around the clock. The shares are traded electronically, therefore eliminating the specialized forms and depositaries required by share forms like ADRs.

GRSs are not really a recent innovation. In fact, they are nearly identical to the structure used for cross-border trading of Canadian company securities in the United States for decades. More than 70 Canadian firms are listed on the NYSE-Euronext, a two-way electronic linkage between the Depositary Trust Company in the United States and the Deutsche Börse Clearing Company in Germany, which facilitates the efficient quoting, trading, and settlement of shares in the respective currencies.

Foreign Equity Listing and Issuance

According to the alternative paths depicted earlier in Exhibit 13.1, a firm needs to choose one or more stock markets on which to cross-list its shares and sell new equity. Just where to go depends mainly on the firm's specific motives and the willingness of the host stock market to accept the firm. By cross-listing and selling its shares on a foreign stock exchange a firm typically tries to accomplish one or more of the following objectives:

◆ Improve the liquidity of its existing shares and support a liquid secondary market for new equity issues in foreign markets

◆ Increase its share price by overcoming mispricing in a segmented and illiquid home capital market

◆ Increase the firm's visibility and political acceptance to its customers, suppliers, creditors, and host governments

◆ Establish a secondary market for shares used to acquire other firms in the host market

◆ Create a secondary market for shares that can be used to compensate local management and employees in foreign subsidiaries

Improving Liquidity

Quite often foreign investors have acquired a firm's shares through normal brokerage channels, even though the shares are not listed in the investor's home market or not traded in the investor's preferred currency. Cross-listing is a way to encourage such investors to continue to hold and trade these shares, thus marginally improving secondary market liquidity. It is usually done through ADRs.

Firms domiciled in countries with small illiquid capital markets often outgrow those markets and are forced to raise new equity abroad. Listing on a stock exchange in the market in which these funds are to be raised is typically required by the underwriters to ensure post-issue liquidity in the shares.

The first section of this chapter suggested that firms start by cross-listing in a less liquid market, followed by having an equity issue in that market (see Exhibit 13.1). In order to maximize liquidity, however, the firm ideally should cross-list and issue equity in a more liquid market and eventually offer a global equity issue.

Size and Liquidity of the Market

In order to maximize liquidity, it is desirable to cross-list and/or sell equity in the most liquid markets. Stock markets have, however, been subject to two major forces in recent years, which are changing their very behavior and liquidity—*demutualization* and *diversification*.

Demutualization is the ongoing process by which the small controlling seat owners on a number of exchanges have been giving up their exclusive powers. As a result, the actual ownership of the exchanges has become increasingly public. *Diversification* represents the growing diversity of both products (derivatives, currencies, etc.) and foreign companies/shares being listed. This has increased the activities and profitability of many exchanges while simultaneously offering a more global mix for reduced cost and increased service.

Stock Exchanges

With respect to stock exchanges, New York and London are clearly the most liquid. The recent merger of the New York Stock Exchange (NYSE) and Euronext, which itself was a merger of stock exchanges in Amsterdam, Brussels, and Paris, has extended the NYSE lead over NASDAQ (New York) and the London Stock Exchange (LSE). Tokyo has fallen on hard times in recent years in terms of trading value, as many foreign firms have chosen to de-list from the Tokyo exchange in recent years. Few foreign firms remain cross-listed now in Tokyo. Deutsche Börse (Germany) has a fairly liquid market for domestic shares but a much lower level of liquidity for trading foreign shares. On the other hand, it is an appropriate target market for firms resident in the European Union, especially those that have adopted the euro. It is also used as a supplementary cross-listing location for firms that are already cross-listed on the LSE, NYSE, or NASDAQ.

Why are New York and London so dominant? They offer what global financial firms are looking for: plenty of skilled people, ready access to capital, good infrastructure, attractive regulatory and tax environments, and low levels of corruption. Location and the use of English, increasingly acknowledged as the language of global finance, are also important factors.

Global Derivatives

With respect to the global derivatives, Chicago continues to be the dominant location for derivative creation and trading. This lead was reinforced recently with the merger of the Chicago Mercantile Exchange (CME) with the Chicago Board of Trade (CBOT). Eurex (Frankfurt) and Euronext LIFFE (London) are also important liquid derivative markets. Other derivative exchanges are actively considering mergers to gain competitiveness and liquidity.

Electronic Trading

Most exchanges have moved heavily into electronic trading in recent years. For example, the role of the specialist on the floor of the NYSE has been greatly reduced with a corresponding reduction in employment by specialist firms. They are no longer responsible for ensuring an orderly movement for their stocks, but are still important in making more liquid markets for the less-traded shares. The same fate has reduced the importance of market makers on the London Stock Exchange. Now the U.S. stock market is actually a network of 50 different venues connected by an electronic system of published quotes and sales prices.

Hedge funds and other high frequency traders dominate the market. High frequency traders now account for 60% of daily volumes. Equity volume controlled by the NYSE fell from 80% in 2005 to 25% in 2010. Trades are executed immediately by computer. Spreads between buy and sell orders are in decimal points as low as a penny a share instead of an eighth of a point. Liquidity has greatly increased but so has the risk of unexpected swings in prices. For example, on May 6, 2010, the Dow Jones Average fell 9.2% at one point but eventually recovered by the end of the day. Nineteen billion shares were bought and sold.

Effect of Cross-Listing and Equity Issuance on Share Price

Although cross-listing and equity issuance can occur together, their impacts are separable and significant in and of themselves.

Cross-Listing

Does merely cross-listing on a foreign stock exchange have a favorable impact on share prices? It depends on the degree to which markets are segmented.

If a firm's home capital market is segmented, the firm could theoretically benefit by cross-listing in a foreign market if that market values the firm or its industry more than does the home market. This was certainly the situation experienced by Novo when it listed on the NYSE in 1981 (see Chapter 12). However, most capital markets are becoming more integrated with global markets. Even emerging markets are less segmented than they were just a few years ago.

A more comprehensive study consisted of 181 firms from 35 countries that instituted their first ADR program in the United States over the period from 1985 to 1995.[1] The author measured the stock price impact of the announcement of a cross-listing in the United States

[1]Darius P. Miller, "The Market Reaction to International Cross-Listings: Evidence from Depositary Receipts," *Journal of Financial Economics*, Vol. 51, 1999, pp. 102–123.

and found significant positive abnormal returns around the announcement date. These were retained in the immediate following period. As expected, the study showed that the abnormal returns were greater for firms resident in emerging markets with a low level of legal barriers to capital flows, than for firms resident in developed markets. Firms resident in emerging markets with heavy restrictions on capital flows received some abnormal returns, but not as high as firms resident in the other markets. This was due to the perceived limited liquidity of firms resident in markets with too many restrictions on capital flows.

Equity Issuance

It is well known that the combined impact of a new equity issue undertaken simultaneously with a cross-listing has a more favorable impact on stock price than cross-listing alone. This occurs because the new issue creates an instantly enlarged shareholder base. Marketing efforts by the underwriters prior to the issue engender higher levels of visibility. Post-issue efforts by the underwriters to support at least the initial offering price also reduce investor risk.

The study of 181 firms cross-listing in the United States contained 30 firms that initiated new equity issues (Level III ADRs). The author found a statistically significant abnormal return for these firms, even higher than for the firms that just cross-listed (Levels I and II). Furthermore, the highest abnormal return was for Chilean firms (8.23%). The Chilean market has one of the highest levels of restrictions affecting foreign investors. Since it is well known that stock prices react negatively to new domestic issues in the United States, something truly significant must be happening when foreign ADRs are sold in the United States.

Even U.S. firms can benefit by issuing equity abroad. A study of U.S. firms that issued equity abroad concluded that increased name recognition and accessibility from global equity issues leads to increased investor recognition and participation in both the primary and secondary markets.[2] Moreover, the ability to issue global shares can validate firm quality by reducing the information asymmetry between insiders and investors. Another conclusion was that U.S. firms may seize a window of opportunity to switch to global offerings when domestic demand for their shares is weak. Finally, the study found that U.S. firms announcing global equity offerings have significantly fewer negative market reactions by about one percentage point than what would have been expected had they limited their issues to the domestic market.

Increasing Visibility and Political Acceptance. MNEs list in markets where they have substantial physical operations. Commercial objectives are to enhance corporate image, advertise trademarks and products, get better local press coverage, and become more familiar with the local financial community in order to raise working capital locally.

Political objectives might include the need to meet local ownership requirements for a multinational firm's foreign joint venture. Local ownership of the parent firm's shares might provide a forum for publicizing the firm's activities and how they support the host country. This objective is the most important one for Japanese firms. The Japanese domestic market has both low-cost capital and high availability. Therefore, Japanese firms are not trying to increase the stock price, the liquidity of their shares, or the availability of capital.

Increasing Potential for Share Swaps with Acquisitions. Firms that follow a strategy of growth by acquisition are always looking for creative ways to fund these acquisitions rather than paying cash. Offering their shares as partial payment is considerably more attractive if

---

[2]Congsheng Wu and Chuck C.Y. Kwok, "Why Do U.S. Firms Choose Global Equity Offerings?," *Financial Management*, Summer 2002, pp. 47–65.

those shares have a liquid secondary market. In that case, the target's shareholders have an easy way to convert their acquired shares to cash if they do not prefer a share swap. However, a share swap is often attractive as a tax-free exchange.

Compensating Management and Employees. If an MNE wishes to use stock options and share purchase compensation plans for local management and employees, local listing would enhance the perceived value of such plans. It should reduce transaction and foreign exchange costs for the local beneficiaries.

Barriers to Cross-Listing and Selling Equity Abroad

Although a firm may decide to cross-list and/or sell equity abroad, certain barriers exist. The most serious barriers are the future commitment to providing full and transparent disclosure of operating results and balance sheets as well as a continuous program of investor relations.

The Commitment to Disclosure and Investor Relations

A decision to cross-list must be balanced against the implied increased commitment to full disclosure and a continuing investor relations program. For firms resident in the Anglo-American markets, listing abroad might not appear to be much of a barrier. For example, the SEC's disclosure rules for listing in the United States are so stringent and costly that any other market's rules are mere child's play. Reversing the logic, however, non-U.S. firms must really think twice before cross-listing in the United States. Not only are the disclosure requirements breathtaking, but also continuous timely quarterly information is required by U.S. regulators and investors. As a result, the foreign firm must provide a costly continuous investor relations program for its U.S. shareholders, including frequent "road shows" and the time-consuming personal involvement of top management.

Disclosure Is a Double-Edged Sword

The U.S. school of thought is that the worldwide trend toward requiring fuller, more transparent, and more standardized financial disclosure of operating results and financial positions may have the desirable effect of lowering the cost of equity capital. As we observed in 2002 and 2008, lack of full and accurate disclosure, and poor transparency worsened the U.S. stock market decline as investors fled to safer securities such as U.S. government bonds. This action increased the equity cost of capital for all firms. The other school of thought is that the U.S. level of required disclosure is an onerous, costly burden. It chases away many potential listers, thereby narrowing the choice of securities available to U.S. investors at reasonable transaction costs.

A study of 203 internationally traded shares concluded that there is a statistically significant relationship between the level of financial disclosure required and the markets on which the firms chose to list.[3] The higher the level of disclosure required, the less likely a firm would be to list in that market. However, for those firms that do list despite the disclosure and cost barriers, the payoff could be needed access to additional equity funding of a large factory or an acquisition in the United States. Daimler Benz took the painful step of cross-listing on the NYSE prior to raising equity in the United States to fund a new auto plant and, as it turned out later, to merge with Chrysler Corporation.

---

[3]Saudagaran, Shahrokh M. and Gary Biddle, "Foreign Listing Location: A Study of MNEs and Stock Exchanges in Eight Countries," *Journal of International Business Studies*, Volume 26, No. 2, Second Quarter 1995, pp. 319–341.

Alternative Instruments to Source Equity in Global Markets

Alternative instruments to source equity in global markets include the following:

◆ Sale of a *directed public share* issue to investors in a target market

◆ Sale of a *Euroequity public issue* to investors in more than one market, including both foreign and domestic markets

◆ Private placements under SEC Rule 144A

◆ Sale of shares to *private equity* funds

◆ Sale of shares to a foreign firm as part of a *strategic alliance*

Directed Public Share Issues

A *directed public share issue* is defined as one that is targeted at investors in a single country and underwritten in whole or in part by investment institutions from that country. The issue might or might not be denominated in the currency of the target market. The shares might or might not be cross-listed on a stock exchange in the target market.

The $61 million U.S. share issue by Novo in 1981 (Chapter 12) was a good example of a successful directed share issue that both improved the liquidity of Novo's shares and lowered its cost of capital. Novo repeated this success in 1983 with a $100 million share issue at $53 per share (ADR), compared to $36 per share two years earlier.

A directed share issue might be motivated by a need to fund acquisitions or major capital investments in a target foreign market. This is an especially important source of equity for firms that reside in smaller capital markets and that have outgrown that market. A foreign share issue, plus cross-listing, can provide it with improved liquidity for its shares and the means to use those shares to pay for acquisitions.

Nycomed, a small but well-respected Norwegian pharmaceutical firm, was an example of this type of motivation for a directed share issue combined with cross-listing. Its commercial strategy for growth was to leverage its sophisticated knowledge of certain market niches and technologies within the pharmaceutical field by acquiring other promising firms that possess relevant technologies, personnel, or market niches. Europe and the United States have provided fertile hunting grounds. The acquisitions were paid for partly with cash and partly with shares. Norway is too small a home capital market to fund these acquisitions for cash or to provide a liquid enough market to minimize Nycomed's marginal cost of capital.

Nycomed responded to the challenge by selling two successful directed share issues abroad. In June 1989 it cross-listed on the LSE (quoted on SEAQ International) and raised the equivalent of about $100 million in equity from foreign investors there. Then, in June 1992, it cross-listed on the NYSE and raised about $75 million with a share issue directed at U.S. investors. Nycomed eventually merged with Amersham, a British firm, and moved its headquarters to the United Kingdom.

Euroequity Public Issue

The gradual integration of the world's capital markets and increased international portfolio investment has spawned the emergence of a very viable Euroequity market. A firm can now issue equity underwritten and distributed in multiple foreign equity markets, sometimes simultaneously with distribution in the domestic market. The term "Euro" does not imply that the issuers or investors are located in Europe, nor does it mean the shares are sold in the currency "euro." It is a generic term for international securities issues originating and being sold anywhere in the world.

The largest and most spectacular issues have been made in conjunction with a wave of privatizations of government-owned enterprises. The Thatcher government in the United Kingdom created the model when it privatized British Telecom in December 1984. That issue was so large that it was necessary and desirable to sell *tranches* to foreign investors in addition to the sale to domestic investors. A tranche means an allocation of shares, typically to underwriters that are expected to sell to investors in their designated geographic markets. The objective is both to raise the funds and to ensure post-issue worldwide liquidity. Unfortunately, in the case of British Telecom, the issue was, in retrospect, underpriced. Most of the foreign shares, especially those placed in the United States, flowed back to London, leaving a nice profit behind for the U.S. underwriters and investors. Nevertheless, other large British privatization issues followed British Telecom, most notably British Steel in 1988.

Euroequity privatization issues have been particularly popular with international portfolio investors because most of the firms are very large, with excellent credit ratings and profitable quasi-government monopolies at the time of privatization. The British privatization model has been so successful that numerous others have followed. One of the largest Euroequity issues was made by Deutsche Telecom A.G. It was privatized by an initial public offering of $13.3 billion in November 1996.

Even government-owned firms in emerging capital markets have implemented privatization with the help of foreign tranches.

◆ Telefonos de Mexico, the giant Mexican telephone company, completed a $2 billion Euroequity issue in 1991. U.S.-based Southwestern Bell became a 10% shareholder, as did numerous other foreign institutional and individual investors. Telefonos de Mexico has a very liquid listing on the NYSE.

◆ One of the largest Euroequity offerings by a firm resident in a an illiquid market was the 1993 sale of shares for $3.04 billion by YPF Sociedad Anónima, Argentina's state-owned oil company. About 75% of its shares were placed in tranches outside of Argentina, with 46% in the United States alone. Its underwriting syndicate represented a virtual "who's who" of the world's leading investment banks.

It appears that many of the privatized firms have performed well after being privatized. A study of privatization concluded that privatized firms showed strong performance improvements without reducing employment security. The firms in the study had been fully or partially privatized via public equity issues during the period from 1961 to 1990. After privatization, the firms increased real sales, raised capital investment levels, improved efficiency, and expanded their employment. With respect to financial performance, their profitability improved, debt levels decreased, and dividend payments increased.[4]

Private Placement Under SEC Rule 144A

One type of directed issue with a long history as a source of both equity and debt is the private placement market. A *private placement* is the sale of a security to a small set of qualified institutional buyers. The investors are traditionally insurance companies and investment companies. Since the securities are not registered for sale to the public, investors have typically followed a "buy and hold" policy. In the case of debt, terms are often custom designed on a negotiated basis. Private placement markets now exist in most countries.

[4]William L. Megginson, Robert C. Nash, and Mathias Ian Randenborgh, "The Financial and Operating Performance of Newly Privatized Firms: An International Empirical Analysis," *Journal of Finance*, June 1994, pp. 403–452.

In 1990, the SEC approved Rule 144A. It permits qualified institutional buyers (QIBs) to trade privately placed securities without the previous holding period restrictions and without requiring SEC registration.

A *qualified institutional buyer* (QIB) is an entity (except a bank or a savings and loan) that owns and invests on a discretionary basis $100 million in securities of nonaffiliates. Banks and savings and loans must meet this test but also must have a minimum net worth of $25 million. The SEC has estimated that about 4,000 QIBs exist, mainly investment advisors, investment companies, insurance companies, pension funds, and charitable institutions. Simultaneously, the SEC modified its Regulation S to permit foreign issuers to tap the U.S. private placement market through an SEC Rule 144A issue, also without SEC registration. A trading system called PORTAL was established by the National Association of Securities Dealers (NASD) to support the distribution of primary issues and to create a liquid secondary market for these unregistered private placements.

Since SEC registration has been identified as the main barrier to foreign firms wishing to raise funds in the United States, SEC Rule 144A placements are proving attractive to foreign issuers of both equity and debt securities. Atlas Copco, the Swedish multinational engineering firm, was the first foreign firm to take advantage of SEC Rule 144A. It raised $49 million in the United States through an ADR equity placement as part of its larger $214 million Euroequity issue in 1990. Since then, several billion dollars a year have been raised by foreign issuers with private equity placements in the United States. However, it does not appear that such placements have a favorable effect on either liquidity or stock price.[5]

Private Equity Funds

Private equity funds are usually limited partnerships of institutional and wealthy investors, such as college endowment funds, that raise capital in the most liquid capital markets. They are best known for buying control of publicly owned firms, taking them private, improving management, and then reselling them after one to three years. They are resold in a variety of ways including selling the firms to other firms, other private equity funds, or taking them back public. The private equity funds themselves are frequently very large, but may also utilize a large amount of debt to fund their takeovers. These "alternatives" as they are called, demand fees of 2% of assets plus 20% of profits. In addition, in the United States their gains are taxed at the capital gains rate of 15% on "carried interest" instead of the usual 35% rate on ordinary income. Equity funds have had some highly visible successes.

Many mature family-owned firms resident in emerging markets are unlikely to qualify for a global cost and availability of capital even if they follow the strategy suggested in this chapter. Although they might be consistently profitable and growing, they are still too small, too invisible to foreign investors, lacking in managerial depth, and unable to fund the up-front costs of a globalization strategy. For these firms, *private equity funds* may be a solution.

Private equity funds differ from traditional venture capital funds. The latter usually operate mainly in highly developed countries. They typically invest in start-up firms with the goal of exiting the investment with an initial public offering (IPO) placed in those same highly liquid markets. Very little venture capital is available in emerging markets, partly because it would be difficult to exit with an IPO in an illiquid market. The same exiting problem faces the private equity funds, but they appear to have a longer time horizon. They invest in already mature and profitable companies. They are content with growing companies through better management and mergers with other firms.

[5]Boubakri, Narjess and Jean Claude Cosset, "The Financial and Operating Performance of Newly Privatized Firms: Evidence from Developing Countries," *The Journal of Finance*, Volume 53, No. 3, June 1998, pp. 1081–1110. This same conclusion was reached in the slightly more recent study by Miller 1999, op. cit.

International Debt Markets

The international debt markets offer the borrower a variety of different maturities, repayment structures, and currencies of denomination. The markets and their many different instruments vary by source of funding, pricing structure, maturity, and subordination or linkage to other debt and equity instruments. Exhibit 13.7 provides an overview of the three basic categories described in the following sections, along with their primary components as issued or traded in the international debt markets today. The three major sources of debt funding on the international markets are *international bank loans* and *syndicated credits*, the *Euronote market*, and the *international bond market*.

Bank Loans and Syndicated Credits

International Bank Loans. International bank loans have traditionally been sourced in the Eurocurrency markets. Eurodollar bank loans are also called "Eurodollar credits" or simply "Eurocredits." The latter title is broader because it encompasses nondollar loans in the Eurocurrency market. The key factor attracting both depositors and borrowers to the Eurocurrency loan market is the narrow interest rate spread within that market. The difference between deposit and loan rates is often less than 1%.

Eurocredits. Eurocredits are bank loans to MNEs, sovereign governments, international institutions, and banks denominated in Eurocurrencies and extended by banks in countries other than the country in whose currency the loan is denominated. The basic borrowing interest rate for Eurodollar loans has long been tied to the London Interbank Offered Rate (LIBOR), which is the deposit rate applicable to interbank loans within London. Eurodollars are lent for both short- and medium-term maturities, with transactions for six months or less regarded as routine. Most Eurodollar loans are for a fixed term with no provision for early repayment.

EXHIBIT 13.7   International Debt Markets and Instruments

Syndicated Credits. The syndication of loans has enabled banks to spread the risk of very large loans among a number of banks. Syndication is particularly important because many large MNEs need credit in excess of a single bank's loan limit. A syndicated bank credit is arranged by a lead bank on behalf of its client. Before finalizing the loan agreement, the lead bank seeks the participation of a group of banks, with each participant providing a portion of the total funds needed. The lead manager bank will work with the borrower to determine the amount of the total credit, the floating-rate base and spread over the base rate, maturity, and fee structure for managing the participating banks. The periodic expenses of the syndicated credit are composed of two elements:

1. The actual interest expense of the loan, normally stated as a spread in basis points over a variable-rate base such as LIBOR.

2. The commitment fees paid on any unused portions of the credit. The spread paid over LIBOR by the borrower is considered the risk premium, reflecting the general business and financial risk applicable to the borrower's repayment capability.

Global Finance in Practice 13.1 illustrates the pricing common to the syndicated loan markets, including interest expenses and the commitment and investment banking fees.

Euronote Market

The Euronote market is the collective term used to describe short- to medium-term debt instruments sourced in the Eurocurrency markets. Although a multitude of differentiated financial products exists, they can be divided into two major groups—*underwritten facilities* and *nonunderwritten facilities*. Underwritten facilities are used for the sale of Euronotes in a

---

GLOBAL FINANCE IN PRACTICE   13.1

Pricing and Structure of a Syndicated Eurocredit

Borrower:	Irish Aerospace, GPA Airbus, GPA Fokker, GPA Jetprop, GPA Rolls
Amount:	US$1.25 billion; Revolving loans/guarantees /letters of credit
Terms:	Eight years at 93.75 basis points over LIBOR, with a margin of 7/8% for GPA Airbus drawings
Arranger:	Citicorp Investment Bank
Lead Managers and Underwriters:	Citibank, Chase Investment Bank, Toronto-Dominion Bank, Citibank (Channel Islands) for a syndicate of Japanese leasing companies, Credit Suisse, Société Générale (London), Amsterdam-Rotterdam Bank, Bank of Nova Scotia, Bank of Tokyo International, Daiwa Bank, IBJ, Irish Intercontinental

A typical syndicated loan of this type would have up-front fees totaling 1.5% of the principal. The fees would be divided between three groups: 1) the lead arranger bank(s), which organizes the loan and participants; 2) the lead managing and underwriting banks, which aid in the syndication of the loan; and 3) the participating banks, which actually provide the capital.

If the 1.5% total fee was subdivided equally among the three groups, the proceeds of the loan after expenses of issuance and arrangement

$$\$1,250,000,000 - [(0.005 + 0.005 + 0.005) \times \$1,250,000,000] = \$1,231,250,000$$

The debt service payments over the 8-year period prior to principal repayment are LIBOR + 93.75 basis points; assuming an initial LIBOR rate of 9.00% (reset every six months for semiannual debt service payments):

$$\left[\frac{0.0900 + 0.009375}{2}\right] \times \$1,250,000,000 = \$62,109,375$$

The effective annual cost is thus

$$\left[\frac{\$62,109,375}{\$1,231,250,000}\right] \times 2 \times 100 = 10.09\%$$

The syndicated credit will cost Irish Aerospace 10.09% at the current LIBOR rate of 9.000%.

number of different forms. Nonunderwritten facilities are used for the sale and distribution of *Euro-commercial paper* (ECP) and *Euro medium-term notes* (EMTNs).

Euronote Facilities. A major development in international money markets was the establishment of facilities for sales of short-term, negotiable, promissory notes—*euronotes*. Among the facilities for their issuance were revolving underwriting facilities (rufs), note issuance facilities (nifs), and standby note issuance facilities (snifs). These facilities were provided by international investment and commercial banks. The euronote was a substantially cheaper source of short-term funds than were syndicated loans because the notes were placed directly with the investor public, and the securitized and underwritten form allowed the ready establishment of liquid secondary markets. The banks received substantial fees initially for their underwriting and placement services.

Euro-Commercial Paper (ECP). Euro-commercial paper (ECP), like commercial paper issued in domestic markets around the world, is a short-term debt obligation of a corporation or bank. Maturities are typically one, three, and six months. The paper is sold normally at a discount or occasionally with a stated coupon. Although the market is capable of supporting issues in any major currency, over 90% of issues outstanding are denominated in U.S. dollars.

Euro Medium-Term Notes (EMTNs). The Euro medium-term note (EMTN) market effectively bridges the maturity gap between ECP and the longer-term and less flexible international bond. Although many of the notes were initially underwritten, most EMTNs are now nonunderwritten.

The rapid initial growth of the EMTN market followed directly on the heels of the same basic instrument that began in the U.S. domestic market when the U.S. Securities and Exchange Commission (SEC) instituted Rule #415, allowing companies to obtain *shelf registrations* for debt issues. What this meant was that once the registration was obtained, the corporation could issue notes on a continuous basis without having to obtain new registrations for each additional issue. This, in turn, allowed a firm to sell short- and medium-term notes through a much cheaper and more flexible issuance facility than ordinary bonds.

The EMTN's basic characteristics are similar to those of a bond, with principal, maturity, and coupon structures and rates being comparable. The EMTN's typical maturities range from as little as nine months to a maximum of 10 years. Coupons are typically paid semiannually, and coupon rates are comparable to similar bond issues. The EMTN does, however, have three unique characteristics. 1) the EMTN is a facility, allowing continuous issuance over a period of time, unlike a bond issue which is essentially sold all at once; 2) because EMTNs are sold continuously, in order to make debt service (coupon redemption) manageable, coupons are paid on set calendar dates regardless of the date of issuance; 3) EMTNs are issued in relatively small denominations, from $2 million to $5 million, making medium-term debt acquisition much more flexible than the large minimums customarily needed in the international bond markets.

International Bond Market

The international bond market sports a rich array of innovative instruments created by imaginative investment bankers, who are unfettered by the usual controls and regulations governing domestic capital markets. Indeed, the international bond market rivals the international banking market in terms of the quantity and cost of funds provided to international borrowers. All international bonds fall within two generic classifications, *Eurobonds* and *foreign bonds*. The distinction between categories is based on whether the borrower is a domestic or a foreign resident, and whether the issue is denominated in the local currency or a foreign currency.

Eurobonds. A *Eurobond* is underwritten by an international syndicate of banks and other securities firms, and is sold exclusively in countries other than the country in whose currency the issue is denominated. For example, a bond issued by a firm resident in the United States, denominated in U.S. dollars, but sold to investors in Europe and Japan (not to investors in the United States), is a Eurobond.

Eurobonds are issued by MNEs, large domestic corporations, sovereign governments, governmental enterprises, and international institutions. They are offered simultaneously in a number of different national capital markets, but not in the capital market or to residents of the country in whose currency the bond is denominated. Almost all Eurobonds are in bearer form with call provisions and sinking funds.

The syndicate that offers a new issue of Eurobonds might be composed of underwriters from a number of countries, including European banks, foreign branches of U.S. banks, banks from offshore financial centers, investment and merchant banks, and nonbank securities firms.

◆ **The Straight Fixed-Rate Issue.**   The *straight fixed-rate issue* is structured like most domestic bonds, with a fixed coupon, set maturity date, and full principal repayment upon final maturity. Coupons are normally paid annually, rather than semiannually, primarily because the bonds are bearer bonds and annual coupon redemption is more convenient for the holders.

◆ **The Floating-Rate Note (FRN).**   The *FRN* normally pays a semiannual coupon which is determined using a variable-rate base. A typical coupon would be set at some fixed spread over LIBOR. This structure, like most variable-rate interest-bearing instruments, was designed to allow investors to shift more of the interest-rate risk of a financial investment to the borrower. Although many FRNs have fixed maturities, a number of major issues since 1985 are perpetuities. The principal will never be repaid. Thus, they provide many of the same financial functions as equity.

◆ **The Equity-Related Issue.**   The *equity-related international bond* resembles the straight fixed-rate issue in practically all price and payment characteristics, with the added feature that it is convertible to stock prior to maturity at a specified price per share (or alternatively, number of shares per bond). The borrower is able to issue debt with lower coupon payments due to the added value of the equity conversion feature.

Foreign Bonds. A *foreign bond* is underwritten by a syndicate composed of members from a single country, sold principally within that country, and denominated in the currency of that country. The issuer, however, is from another country. A bond issued by a firm resident in Sweden, denominated in dollars, and sold in the United States to U.S. investors by U.S. investment bankers, is a foreign bond. Foreign bonds have nicknames: foreign bonds sold in the United States are "Yankee bonds"; foreign bonds sold in Japan are "Samurai bonds"; and foreign bonds sold in the United Kingdom are "Bulldogs."

Unique Characteristics of Eurobond Markets

Although the Eurobond market evolved at about the same time as the Eurodollar market, the two markets exist for different reasons, and each could exist independently of the other. The Eurobond market owes its existence to several unique factors. They are the absence of regulatory interference, less stringent disclosure practices, and favorable tax treatment.

Absence of Regulatory Interference. National governments often impose tight controls on foreign issuers of securities denominated in the local currency and sold within their national boundaries. However, governments in general have less stringent limitations for securities denominated in foreign currencies and sold within their markets to holders of those foreign currencies. In effect, Eurobond sales fall outside the regulatory domain of any single nation.

Less Stringent Disclosure. Disclosure requirements in the Eurobond market are much less stringent than those of the Securities and Exchange Commission (SEC) for sales within the United States. U.S. firms often find that the registration costs of a Eurobond offering are less than those of a domestic issue and that less time is needed to bring a new issue to market. Non-U.S. firms often prefer Eurodollar bonds over bonds sold within the United States because they do not wish to undergo the costs, and disclosure, needed to register with the SEC. However, the SEC has relaxed disclosure requirements for certain private placements (Rule #144A), which has improved the attractiveness of the U.S. domestic bond and equity markets.

Favorable Tax Status. Eurobonds offer tax anonymity and flexibility. Interest paid on Eurobonds is generally not subject to an income withholding tax. As one might expect, Eurobond interest is not always reported to tax authorities. Eurobonds are usually issued in bearer form, meaning that the name and country of residence of the owner is not on the certificate. To receive interest, the bearer cuts an interest coupon from the bond and turns it in at a banking institution listed on the issue as a paying agent. European investors are accustomed to the privacy provided by bearer bonds and are very reluctant to purchase registered bonds, which require holders to reveal their names before they receive interest. Bearer bond status, of course, is also tied to tax avoidance.

Rating of Eurobonds and Other International Issues

Purchasers of Eurobonds do not rely only on bond-rating services or on detailed analyses of financial statements. The general reputation of the issuing corporation and its underwriters has been a major factor in obtaining favorable terms. For this reason, larger and better-known MNEs, state enterprises, and sovereign governments are able to obtain the lowest interest rates. Firms whose names are better known to the general public, possibly because they manufacture consumer goods, are often believed to have an advantage over equally qualified firms whose products are less widely known.

Rating agencies, such as Moody's and Standard and Poor's (S&Ps), provide ratings for selected international bonds for a fee. Moody's ratings for international bonds imply the same creditworthiness as for domestic bonds of U.S. issuers. Moody's limits its evaluation to the issuer's ability to obtain the necessary currency to repay the issue according to the original terms of the bond. The agency excludes any assessment of risk to the investor caused by changing exchange rates.

Moody's rates international bonds upon request of the issuer. Based on supporting financial statements and other material obtained from the issuer, it makes a preliminary rating and then informs the issuer who has an opportunity to comment. After Moody's determines its final rating, the issuer may decide not to have the rating published. Consequently, a disproportionately large number of published international ratings fall into the highest categories, since issuers about to receive a lower rating do not allow publication.

Moody's review of political risk includes study of the government system, the social environment, and the nation's external relations. Its review of economic risk looks at debt burden, international liquidity, balance of payments flexibility, economic structure, growth performance, economic management, and economic outlook. Moody's also evaluates the bonds of sovereign-supported entities by looking first at their creditworthiness on a stand-alone basis and then at the extent to which sovereign support either enhances or diminishes the borrower's financial strength. Credit ratings are critical to borrowers and investors alike. An MNE's credit rating determines its cost of funds.

Access to debt capital is, however, in the end, still a function of basic societal norms. Religion itself, may play a part in the use and availability of debt capital. *Global Finance in Practice 13.2* illustrates one area rarely seen by Westerners, Islamic Finance.

GLOBAL FINANCE IN PRACTICE 13.2

Islamic Finance

Muslims, the followers of Islam, now make up roughly one-fourth of the world's population. The countries of the world which are predominantly Muslim create roughly 10% of global GDP, and comprise a large share of the emerging market-place. Islamic law reaches into many dimensions of the individual and organizational behaviors for its practitioners—including business. Islamic finance, the specific area of our interest, imposes a number of restrictions on Muslims, which dramatically alter the funding and structure of Muslim businesses.

Under Islam, the *shari'ah* lays down a series of fundamental beliefs—restrictions in practice—regarding business and finance.

◆ Making money from money is not permissible

◆ Earning interest is prohibited

◆ Profit and loss should be shared

◆ Speculation, gambling, is prohibited

◆ Investments should support only *halal* activities

For the conduct of business, the key to understanding the prohibition on earning interest is to understand that profitability from investment should arise from the returns associated with carrying risk. For example, a traditional Western bank may extend a loan to a business. The bank is to receive its principal and interest in repayment and return regardless of the ultimate profitability of the business. In fact, the debt is paid off first. Similarly, an individual who deposits their money in a Western bank will receive an interest earning on their deposit regardless of the profitability of the bank and the bank's associated investments.

An Islamic bank, however, cannot pay interest to depositors—who are Muslims—under Islamic law. There-fore, the depositors in an Islamic bank are actually share-holders (much like credit unions in the West), and the returns they receive are a function of the profitability of the bank's investments. Their returns cannot be fixed or guaranteed, because that would break the principle of profit and loss being shared.

Recently, however, a number of Islamic banking institutions have opened in Europe and North America. A Muslim now can enter into a sequence of purchases which allows them to purchase a home without departing from Islamic principles. The buyer selects the property, which is then purchased by the Islamic bank. The bank in turn resells the house to the prospective buyer at a higher price. The buyer is allowed to pay off the purchase over a series of years. Although the difference in purchase prices is, by Western thinking, implicit interest, this structure does conform to the *shari'ah*. Unfortunately, in both the United States and the United Kingdom, the difference is not a tax deductible expense for the homeowner as interest would be.

Summary of Learning Objectives

Design a strategy to source equity and debt globally.

◆ Designing a capital sourcing strategy requires management to agree upon a long-run financial objective.

◆ The firm must then choose among the various alternative paths to get there, including where to cross-list its shares, and where to issue new equity, and in what form.

Analyze the motivations and goals of a firm cross-listing its shares on foreign equity markets.

A firm cross-lists its shares on foreign stock exchanges for some of the following reasons:

◆ Improve the liquidity of its existing shares by using depositary receipts

◆ Increase its share price by overcoming mispricing by a segmented, illiquid home capital market

◆ Support a new equity issue sold in a foreign market

◆ Establish a secondary market for shares used in acquisitions

◆ Increase the firm's visibility and political acceptance to its customers, suppliers, creditors, and host governments

◆ Create a secondary market for shares that will be used to compensate local management and employees in foreign affiliates

Analyze the motivations and goals of a firm issuing new equity shares on foreign equity markets.

◆ If it is to support a new equity issue or to establish a market for share swaps, the target market should also be the listing market.

◆ If it is to increase the firm's commercial and political visibility or to compensate local management and employees, it should be the markets in which the firm has significant operations.

◆ The major liquid stock markets are the NYSE, NASDAQ, London, Euronext, Tokyo, and Deutsche Börse.

◆ The choice among these six markets depends on its size, and the sophistication of its market-making activities, including competitive transaction costs and competent crisis management.

Understand the many barriers to effectively penetrating foreign equity markets through cross-listing and selling equity abroad.

◆ Increased commitment to full disclosure

◆ A continuing investor relations program

Examine the alternative financial instruments that can be used to source equity in the global equity markets.

◆ Lowering cost of capital and increasing liquidity by selling shares to foreign investors in a variety of forms

◆ Sale of a directed share issue to investors in one particular foreign equity market

◆ Sale of a Euroequity share issue to foreign investors simultaneously in more than one market, including both foreign and domestic markets

◆ Private placement under SEC Rule 144A

◆ Sale of shares to private equity funds

◆ Sale of shares to a foreign firm as part of a strategic alliance

Extend the theory of optimal financial structure to the multinational enterprise (MNE).

◆ The domestic theory of optimal financial structures needs to be modified by four variables in order to accommodate the case of the MNE: 1) the availability of capital; 2) diversification of cash flows; 3) foreign exchange risk; and 4) the expectations of international portfolio investors.

◆ A multinational firm's marginal cost of capital is constant for considerable ranges of its capital budget. This statement is not true for most small domestic firms because they do not have access to the national equity or debt markets.

◆ By diversifying cash flows internationally, the MNE may be able to achieve the same kind of reduction in cash flow variability as portfolio investors receive from diversifying their security holdings internationally.

◆ When a firm issues foreign currency-denominated debt, its effective cost equals the after-tax cost of repaying the principal and interest in terms of the firm's own currency. This amount includes the nominal cost of principal and interest in foreign currency terms, adjusted for any foreign exchange gains or losses.

◆ Therefore, regardless of other factors, if a firm wants to raise capital in global markets, it must adopt global norms that are close to the U.S. and U.K. norms. Debt ratios up to 60% appear to be acceptable. Any higher debt ratio is more difficult to sell to international portfolio investors.

Analyze the factors that, in practice, determine the financial structure of foreign subsidiaries within the context of the MNE.

◆ A compromise position is possible between minimizing the global cost of capital and conforming to local capital norms (localization) when determining the financial structure of a foreign subsidiary. Both multinational and domestic firms should try to minimize their overall weighted average cost of capital for a given level of business risk and capital budget, as finance theory suggests.

◆ The debt ratio of a foreign affiliate is in reality only cosmetic, because lenders ultimately look to the parent and its consolidated worldwide cash flow as the source of repayment. In many cases, debt of subsidiaries must be guaranteed by the parent firm.

Evaluate the various internal and external sources of funds available for the financing of foreign subsidiaries.

◆ The international debt markets offer the borrower a variety of different maturities, repayment structures, and currencies of denomination. The markets and their many different instruments vary by source of funding, pricing structure, maturity, and subordination or linkage to other debt and equity instruments.

◆ The three major sources of debt funding on the international markets are *international bank loans and syndicated credits*, the *Euronote market*, and the *international bond market*.

Identify the relevant characteristics of different international debt instruments in financing both the MNE itself, and its various foreign affiliate components.

◆ Eurocurrency markets serve two valuable purposes: 1) Eurocurrency deposits are an efficient and convenient money market device for holding excess corporate liquidity, and 2) the Eurocurrency market is a major source of short-term bank loans to finance corporate working capital needs, including the financing of imports and exports.

◆ Three original factors in the evolution of the Eurobond markets are still of importance: 1) absence of regulatory interference, 2) less stringent disclosure practices, and 3) favorable tax treatment.

Petrobrás of Brazil and the Cost of Capital

Petrobrás stands out in terms of deepwater technology . . . but currently lags in the area of cost of capital. We believe that in the long term, if Petrobrás is to become a competitive player in what looks to be the future in underwater fuel exploration, it would be headed in the right direction by expanding internationally, securing its presence in the Golden Triangle, and lowering its cost of capital.

WACC reduction could be immediate. If Petrobrás were to acquire one of the North American independents —which we estimate on average have a WACC in the range of 6% to 8%—it could raise debt at the acquired company and subsequently lower its WACC in the short term. Petrobrás could even cancel some of its own debt and/or issue new debt through the newly acquired entity. We've seen other savvy Latin companies (i.e., Cemex via its Spanish subsidiary Valenciana) do this successfully in the past.

"Foreign Expansion Makes Sense at the Right Price," Morgan Stanley Equity Research, January 18, 2002, p. 4.

Petróleo Brasileiro S.A. (Petrobrás) was an integrated oil and gas company founded in 1954 by the Brazilian government as the national oil company of Brazil. In 1997, the Brazilian government initiated a number of major privatization efforts, including Petrobrás. The company was listed in São Paulo in 1997, and on the New York Stock Exchange (NYSE: PBR) in 2000. Despite the equity listings, the Brazilian government continued to be the controlling shareholder, with 33% of the total capital and 55% of the voting shares. As the national oil company of Brazil, the company's singular purpose was the reduction of Brazil's dependency on imported oil. A side effect of this focus, however, had been a lack of international diversification. Many of the company's critics argued that being both Brazilian and undiversified internationally resulted in an uncompetitive cost of capital.

Need for Diversification

In 2002, Petrobrás was the largest company in Brazil, and the largest publicly traded oil company in South America. It was not, however, international in its operations. This inherent lack of international diversification was clearly apparent to international investors, who assigned the company the same country risk factors and premiums they did all other Brazilian companies. The result was a cost of capital in 2002, as seen in Exhibit 1, that was 6% higher than

---

EXHIBIT 1   Petrobrás Suffers an Uncompetitive Cost of Capital

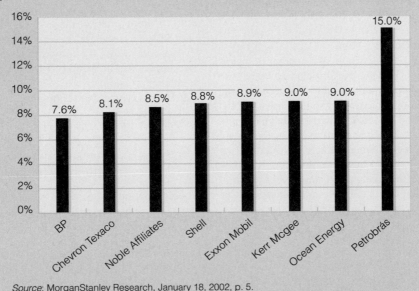

Source: MorganStanley Research, January 18, 2002, p. 5.

all others. The equity strategists and markets considered this a distinct competitive disadvantage.

Petrobrás embarked on a globalization strategy, with several major transactions heading up the process. In December 2001, Repsol-YPF of Argentina and Petrobrás concluded an exchange of operating assets valued at $500 million. In the exchange, Petrobrás received 99% interest in the Eg3 S.A. service station chain, while Repsol-YPF gained a 30% stake in a refinery, a 10% stake in an offshore oil field, and a fuel resale right to 230 service stations in Brazil. The agreement included an eight-year guarantee against currency risks.

In October 2002, Petrobrás purchased Perez Companc (Pecom) of Argentina. Pecom had quickly come into play following the Argentine financial crisis in January 2002. Although Pecom had significant international reserves and production capability, the combined forces of a devalued Argentine peso, a largely dollar-denominated debt portfolio, and a multitude of Argentine government regulations that hindered its ability to hold and leverage hard currency resources, the company had moved quickly to find a buyer to re-fund its financial structure. Petrobrás took advantage of the opportunity. Pecom's ownership had been split between the owning family and foundation, 58.6%, and public flotation of the remaining 41.4%. Petrobrás had purchased the controlling interest, the full 58.6% interest, outright from the family.

In the following three years, Petrobrás focused on restructuring much of its debt (and the debt it had acquired via the Pecom acquisition) and investing in its own growth. But progress in revitalizing its financial structure had come slowly, and by 2005, there was renewed discussion of a new equity issuance to increase its equity capital.[1] But at what cost? What was the company's cost of capital?

Cost of Capital and Country Risk

Exhibit 1 presented the cost of capital of a number of major oil and gas companies across the world, including Petrobrás in 2002. This comparison could occur only if all capital costs were calculated in a common currency, in this case, the U.S. dollar. The global oil and gas markets had long been considered "dollar-denominated," and any company operating in these markets, regardless of where it actually operated in the world, was considered to have the dollar as its functional currency. Once that company listed its shares in a U.S. equity market like the NYSE, the *dollarization* of its capital costs became even more accepted.

But what was the cost of capital—in dollar terms—for a Brazilian business? Brazil has a long history of bouts with high inflation, economic instability, and currency devaluations and depreciations (depending on the regime *de jure*). One of the leading indicators of the global market's opinion of Brazilian country risk was the *sovereign spread*, the additional yield or cost of dollar funds that the Brazilian government had to pay on global markets over and above that which the U.S. Treasury paid to borrow dollar funds. As illustrated in Exhibit 2, the Brazilian sovereign spread had been both high and volatile over the past decade.[2] The spread was sometimes as low as 400 basis points (4.0%), as in recent years, or as high as 2,400 basis points (24%), during the 2002 financial crisis in which the real was first devalued then floated. And that was merely the cost of debt for the government of Brazil. How was this sovereign spread reflected in the cost of debt and equity for a Brazilian company like Petrobrás?

One approach to the estimation of Petrobrás's cost of debt in U.S. dollar terms ($k_d^\$$) was to build it up: the government of Brazil's cost of dollar funds adjusted for a private corporate credit spread.

$$k_d^\$ = \text{U.S. Treasury risk-free rate}$$
$$+ \text{ Brazilian sovereign spread } + \text{ Petrobrás credit spread}$$
$$k_d^\$ = 4.000\% + 4.000\% + 1.000\% = 9.000\%$$

If the U.S. Treasury risk-free rate was estimated using the Treasury 10-year bond rate (yield), a base rate in August 2005 could be 4.0%. The Brazilian sovereign spread, as seen in Exhibit 2, appeared to be 400 basis points, or an additional 4.0%. Even if Petrobrás's credit spread was then only 1.0%, the company's current cost of dollar debt would be 9%. This cost was clearly higher than the cost of debt for most of the world's oil majors who were probably paying only 5% on average for debt in late 2005.

Petrobrás's cost of equity would be similarly affected by the country risk-adjusted risk-free rate of interest. Using a simple expression of the Capital Asset Pricing Model (CAPM) to estimate the company's cost of equity capital in dollar terms ($k_e^\$$):

$$k_e^\$ = \text{risk-free rate}$$
$$+ (\beta_{\text{Petrobrás}} \times \text{market risk premium}) = 8.000\%$$
$$+ (1.10 \times 5.500\%) = 14.05\%$$

This calculation assumed the same risk-free rate as used in the cost of debt previously, with a beta (NYSE basis) of 1.10

---

[1] By 2005, the company's financial strategy was showing significant diversification. Total corporate funding (not debt, in that project finance is nonrecourse to the company after operational start-up) was well-balanced: bonds, $4 billion; BNDES (bonds issued under the auspices of a Brazilian economic development agency), $3 billion; project finance, $5 billion; other, $4 billion.

[2] The measure of sovereign spread presented in Exhibit 2 is that calculated by JPMorgan in its Emerging Market Bond Index Plus (EMBI+) index. This is the most widely used measure of country risk by practitioners.

EXHIBIT 2   The Brazilian Sovereign Spread (December 1997–August 2005)

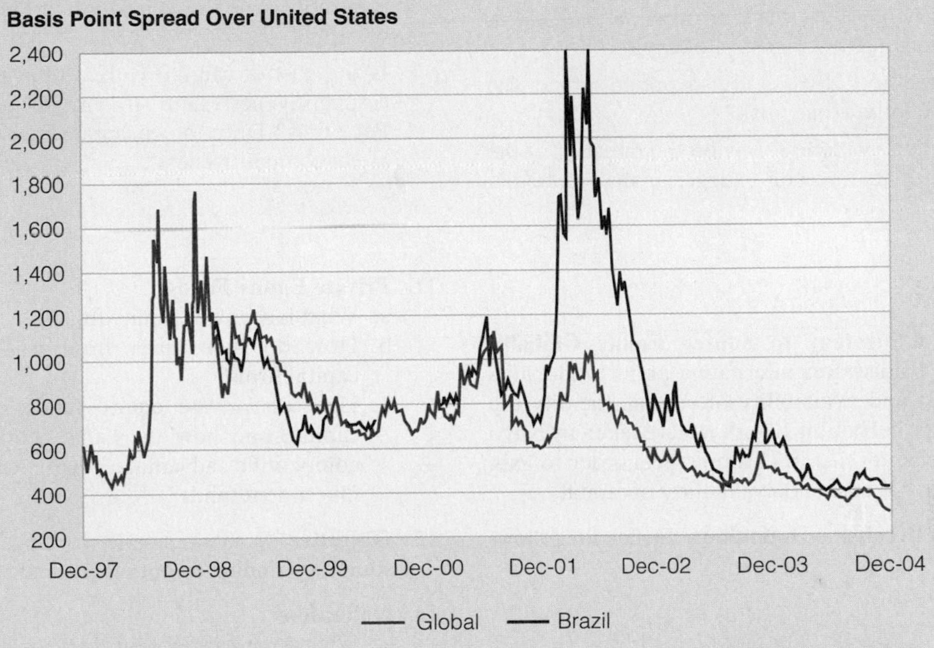

Basis Point Spread Over United States

Source: JPMorgan's EMBI+ Spread, as quoted by Latin Focus, www.latin-focus.com/latinfocus/countries/brazilbisprd.htm, August 2005.

and a market risk premium of 5.500%. Even with these relatively conservative assumptions (many would argue that the company's beta was actually higher or lower, and the market risk premium to be 6.0% or higher), the company's cost of equity was 14%.

Finally, the corporate weighted average cost of capital (WACC) could be calculated:

$$\text{WACC} = (\text{debt/capital} \times k_d^{\$} \times (1 - \text{tax rate})) +$$
$$(\text{equity/capital} \times k_e^{\$})$$

Assuming a long-term target capital structure of one-third debt and two-thirds equity, and an effective corporate tax rate of 28% (after special tax concessions, surcharges, and incentives for the Brazilian oil and gas industry), Petrobrás's WACC was estimated at a little over 11.5%:

$$\text{WACC} = (0.333 \times 9.000\% \times 0.72) +$$
$$(0.667 \times 14.050\%) = 11.529\%$$

So, after all of the efforts to internationally diversify the firm and internationalize its cost of capital, why was Petrobrás's cost of capital still so much higher than its global counterparts? Not only was the company's weighted average cost of capital high compared to other major global players, but this was the same high cost of capital used as

the basic discount rate in evaluating many potential investments and acquisitions.

A number of the investment banking firms that covered Petrobrás noted that the company's share price had shown a very high correlation with the EMBI+ sovereign spread for Brazil (shown in Exhibit 2), hovering around 0.84 for a number of years. Similarly, Petrobrás's share price was also historically correlated—inversely—with the Brazilian reais/U.S. dollar exchange rate. This correlation had averaged−0.88 over the 2000–2004 period. Finally, the question of whether Petrobrás was considered an oil company or a Brazilian company was also somewhat in debate:

Petrobrás's stock performance appears more highly correlated to the Brazilian equity market and credit spreads based on historical trading patterns, suggesting that one's view on the direction of the broad Brazilian market is important in making an investment decision on the company. If the historical trend were to hold, an improvement in Brazilian risk perception should provide a fillip to Petrobrás's share price performance.

—"Petrobrás: A Diamond in the Rough,"
JPMorgan Latin American Equity Research,
June 18, 2004, pp. 26–27.

CASE QUESTIONS

1. Why do you think Petrobrás's cost of capital is so high? Are there better ways, or other ways, of calculating its weighted average cost of capital?

2. Does this method of using the sovereign spread also compensate for currency risk?

3. The final quote on "one's view on the direction of the broad Brazilian market" suggests that potential investors consider the relative attractiveness of Brazil in their investment decision. How does this perception show up in the calculation of the company's cost of capital?

4. Is the cost of capital really a relevant factor in the competitiveness and strategy of a company like Petrobrás? Does the corporate cost of capital really affect competitiveness?

Questions

1. Designing a Strategy to Source Equity Globally. Exhibit 13.1 illustrates alternative paths to globalizing the cost and availability of capital. Identify the specific steps in Exhibit 13.1 that were taken by Novo Industri (Chapter 12) in chronological order to gain an international cost and availability of capital.

2. Depositary Receipts—Definitions. Define the following terms:
a. ADRs
b. GDRs
c. Sponsored depositary receipts
d. Unsponsored depositary receipts

3. ADRs. Distinguish between the three levels of commitment for ADRs traded in the United States.

4. Foreign Equity Listing and Issuance. Give five reasons why a firm might cross-list and sell its shares on a very liquid stock exchange.

5. Cross-Listing Abroad. What are the main reasons causing U.S. firms to cross-list abroad?

6. Barriers to Cross-Listing. What are the main barriers to cross-listing abroad?

7. Alternative Instruments. What are five alternative instruments that can be used to source equity in global markets?

8. Directed Public Share Issue
a. Define what is meant by a "directed public share issue."
b. Why did Novo choose to make a $61 million directed public share issue in the United States in 1981?

9. Euroequity Public Share Issue. Define what is meant by a "euroequity public share issue."

10. Private Placement under SEC Rule 144A.
a. What is SEC Rule 144A?
b. Why might a foreign firm choose to sell its equity in the United States under SEC Rule 144A?

11. Private Equity Funds.
a. What is a private equity fund?
b. How do they differ from traditional venture capital firms?
c. How do private equity funds raise their own capital, and how does this action give them a competitive advantage over local banks and investment funds?

12. Objective. What, in simple wording, is the objective sought by finding an optimal capital structure?

13. Definitions
a. What is the "cost of debt" and how is it determined?
b. What is the "cost of equity" and how is it determined?

14. Varying Debt Proportions. As debt in a firm's capital structure is increased from no debt to a significant proportion of debt (say, 60%), what tends to happen to the cost of debt, to the cost of equity, and to the overall weighted average cost of capital?

15. Availability of Capital. How does the availability of capital influence the theory of optimal capital structure for a multinational enterprise?

16. Marginal Cost. Define "marginal" weighted average cost of capital.

17. Diversified Cash Flows. If a multinational firm is able to diversify its sources of cash inflow so as to receive those flows from several countries and in several currencies, do you think that tends to increase or decrease its weighted average cost of capital?

18. Ex-post Cost of Borrowing. Many firms in many countries borrow at nominal costs that later prove to be very different. For example, Deutsche Bank recently borrowed at a nominal cost of 9.59% per annum, but later that debt was selling to yield 7.24%. At the same time, the Kingdom of Thailand borrowed at a nominal cost of 8.70% but later found the debt was sold in the market at a yield of 11.87%. What caused these changes, and what might management do to benefit (as Deutsche Bank did) rather than suffer (as the Kingdom of Thailand did)?

19. Local Norms. Should foreign subsidiaries of multinational firms conform to the capital structure norms of the host country or to the norms of their parent's country? Discuss.

20. Argentina. In January 2002, the government of Argentina broke away from its currency board system that had tied the peso to the U.S. dollar and devalued the peso from APs1.0000/$ to APs1.40000. This caused some Argentine firms with dollar-denominated debt to go bankrupt. Should a U.S. or European parent in good financial health "rescue" its Argentine subsidiary that would otherwise go bankrupt because of the inept nature of Argentine political and economic management in the four or five years prior to January 2002? Assume the parent has not entered into a formal agreement to guarantee the debt of its Argentine subsidiary.

21. Internal Financing. What is the difference between "internal" financing and "external" financing for a subsidiary? List three types of internal financing and three types of external financing available to a foreign subsidiary.

22. Eurodollar Deposits. Why would anyone, individual or corporation, want to deposit U.S. dollars in a bank outside of the United States when the natural location for such deposits would be a bank within the United States?

23. Euro-Euros.
What, if anything, is a "euro-euro?"

24. International Debt Instruments. Bank borrowing has been the long-time manner by which corporations and governments borrowed funds for short periods of time. What then, is the advantage over bank borrowing for each of the following:
   a. Syndicated loans
   b. Euronotes
   c. Euro-Commercial Paper
   d. Euro-Medium-Term Notes
   e. International bonds

25. Euro versus Foreign Bonds. What is the difference between a "eurobond" and a "foreign bond" and why do two types of international bonds exist?

Problems

1. JPMorgan: Petrobrás's WACC. JPMorgan's Latin American Equity Research department produced the following WACC calculation for Petrobrás of Brazil versus Lukoil of Russia in their June 18, 2004, report. Evaluate the methodology and assumptions used in the calculation. Assume a 28% tax rate for both companies.

	Petrobrás	Lukoil
Risk-free rate	4.8%	4.8%
Sovereign risk	7.0%	3.0%
Equity risk premium	4.5%	5.7%
Market cost of equity	16.3%	13.5%
Beta (relevered)	0.87	1.04
Cost of debt	8.4%	6.8%
Debt/capital ratio	0.333	0.475
WACC	14.7%	12.3%

2. UNIBANCO: Petrobrás's WACC. UNIBANCO estimated the weighted average cost of capital for Petrobrás to be 13.2% in Brazilian reais in August of 2004. Evaluate the methodology and assumptions used in the calculation.

Risk-free rate	4.5%	Cost of debt (after-tax)	5.7%
Beta	0.99	Tax rate	34%
Market premium	6.0%	Debt/total capital	40%
Country risk premium	5.5%	WACC (R$)	13.2%
Cost of equity (US$)	15.9%		

3. Citigroup SmithBarney (Dollar): Petrobrás's WACC. Citigroup regularly performs a U.S. dollar-based discount cash flow (DCF) valuation of Petrobrás in its coverage. That DCF analysis requires the use of a discount rate which they base on the company's weighted average cost of capital. Evaluate the methodology and assumptions used in the 2003 Actual and 2004 Estimates of Petrobrás's WACC below.

Capital Cost Components	July 28, 2005		March 8, 2005	
	2003A	2004E	2003A	2004E
Risk-free rate	9.400%	9.400%	9.000%	9.000%
Levered beta	1.07	1.09	1.08	1.10
Risk premium	5.500%	5.500%	5.500%	5.500%
Cost of equity	15.285%	15.395%	14.940%	15.050%
Cost of debt	8.400%	8.400%	9.000%	9.000%
Tax rate	28.500%	27.100%	28.500%	27.100%
Cost of debt, after-tax	6.006%	6.124%	6.435%	6.561%
Debt/capital ratio	32.700%	32.400%	32.700%	32.400%
Equity/capital ratio	67.300%	67.600%	67.300%	67.600%
WACC	12.20%	12.30%	12.10%	12.30%

4. **Citigroup SmithBarney (Reais).** In a report dated June 17, 2003, Citigroup SmithBarney calculated a WACC for Petrobrás denominated in Brazilian reais (R$). Evaluate the methodology and assumptions used in this cost of capital calculation.

Risk-free rate (Brazilian C-Bond)	9.90%
Petrobrás levered beta (β)	1.40
Market risk premium	5.50%
Cost of equity	17.60%
Cost of debt	10.00%
Brazilian corporate tax rate	34.00%
Long-term debt ratio (% of capital)	50.60%
WACC (R$)	12.00%

5. **BBVA Investment Bank: Petrobrás's WACC.** BBVA utilized a rather innovative approach to dealing with both country and currency risk in their December 20, 2004, report on Petrobrás. Evaluate the methodology and assumptions used in this cost of capital calculation.

Cost of Capital Component	2003 Estimate	2004 Estimate
U.S. 10-year risk-free rate (in US$)	4.10%	4.40%
Country risk premium (in US$)	6.00%	4.00%
Petrobrás premium "adjustment"	−1.00%	−1.00%
Petrobrás risk-free rate (in US$)	9.10%	7.40%
Market risk premium (in US$)	6.00%	6.00%
Petrobrás beta (β)	0.80	0.80
Cost of equity (in US$)	13.90%	12.20%
Projected 10-year currency devaluation	2.50%	2.50%
Cost of equity (in R$)	16.75%	14.44%
Petrobrás cost of debt after-tax (in R$)	5.50%	5.50%
Long-term equity ratio (% of capital)	69%	72%
Long-term debt ratio (% of capital)	31%	28%
WACC (in R$)	13.30%	12.00%

6. **Petrobrás's WACC Comparison.** The various estimates of the cost of capital for Petrobrás of Brazil appear to be very different, but are they? Reorganize your answers to problems, 1 through 5 into those costs of capital which are in U.S. dollars versus Brazilian reais. Use the estimates for 2004 as the basis of comparison.

7. **Copper Mountain Group (USA).** The Copper Mountain Group, a private equity firm headquartered in Boulder, Colorado (U.S.), borrows £5,000,000 for one year at 7.375% interest.
   a. What is the dollar cost of this debt if the pound depreciates from $2.0260/£ to $1.9460/£ over the year?
   b. What is the dollar cost of this debt if the pound appreciates from $2.0260/£ to $2.1640/£ over the year?

8. **McDougan Associates (USA).** McDougan Associates, a U.S.-based investment partnership, borrows €80,000,000 at a time when the exchange rate is $1.3460/€. The entire principal is to be repaid in three years, and interest is 6.250% per annum, paid annually in euros. The euro is expected to depreciate vis à vis the dollar at 3% per annum. What is the effective cost of this loan for McDougan?

9. **Sunrise Manufacturing, Inc.** Sunrise Manufacturing, Inc, a U.S. multinational company, has the following debt components in its consolidated capital section. Sunrise's finance staff estimates their cost of equity to be 20%. Current exchange rates are also listed below. Income taxes are 30% around the world after allowing for credits. Calculate Sunrise's weighted average cost of capital. Are any assumptions implicit in your calculation?

Assumption	Value
Tax rate	30.00%
10-year euro bonds (euros)	€6,000,000
20-year yen bonds (yen)	750,000,000
Spot rate ($/euro)	1.2400
Spot rate ($/pound)	1.8600
Spot rate (yen/$)	109.00

10. **Grupo Modelo S.A.B. de C.V.** Grupo Modelo, a brewery out of Mexico that exports such well-known varieties as Corona, Modelo, and Pacifico, is Mexican by incorporation. However, the company evaluates all business results, including financing costs, in U.S. dollars. The company needs to borrow $10,000,000 or the foreign currency equivalent for four years. For all issues, interest is payable once per year, at the end of the year. Available alternatives are as follows:
   a. Sell Japanese yen bonds at par yielding 3% per annum. The current exchange rate is ¥106/$, and the yen is expected to strengthen against the dollar by 2% per annum.
   b. Sell euro-denominated bonds at par yielding 7% per annum. The current exchange rate is $1.1960/€, and the euro is expected to weaken against the dollar by 2% per annum.
   c. Sell U.S. dollar bonds at par yielding 5% per annum.

Which course of action do you recommend Grupo Modelo take and why?

A-Malaysia (accounts in ringgits)		A-Mexico (accounts in pesos)	
Long-term debt	RM11,400,000	Long-term debt	PS20,000,000
Shareholders' equity	RM15,200,000	Shareholders' equity	PS60,000,000

Adamantine Architectonics
(Noncolsolidated Balance Sheet—Selected Items Only)

Investment in subsidiaries		Parent long-term debt	$12,000,000
In A-Malaysia	$4,000,000	Common stock	5,000,000
In A-Mexico	6,000,000	Retained earnings	20,000,000
Current exchange rates:			
Malaysia	RM3.80/$		
Mexico	PS10/$		

11. **Petrol Ibérico.** Petrol Ibérico, a European gas company, is borrowing US$650,000,000 via a syndicated eurocredit for six years at 80 basis points over LIBOR. LIBOR for the loan will be reset every six months. The funds will be provided by a syndicate of eight leading investment bankers, which will charge up-front fees totaling 1.2% of the principal amount. What is the effective interest cost for the first year if LIBOR is 4.00% for the first six months and 4.20% for the second six months.

12. **Adamantine Architectonics.** Adamantine Architectonics consists of a U.S. parent and wholly owned subsidiaries in Malaysia (A-Malaysia) and Mexico (A-Mexico). Selected portions of their nonconsolidated balance sheets, translated into U.S. dollars, are shown in the table at the top of this page. What are the debt and equity proportions in Adamantine's consolidated balance sheet?

13. **Morning Star Air (China).** Morning Star Air, headquartered in Kunming, China, needs US$25,000,000 for one year to finance working capital. The airline has two alternatives for borrowing:
    a. Borrow US$25,000,000 in Eurodollars in London at 7.250% per annum
    b. Borrow HK$39,000,000 in Hong Kong at 7.00% per annum, and exchange these Hong Kong dollars at the present exchange rate of HK$7.8/US$ for U.S. dollars.

    At what ending exchange rate would Morning Star Air be indifferent between borrowing U.S. dollars and borrowing Hong Kong dollars?

14. **Pantheon Capital, S.A.** If Pantheon Capital, S.A. is raising funds via a euro–medium-term note with the following characteristics, how much in dollars will Pantheon receive for each $1,000 note sold?

Coupon rate: 8.00% payable semiannually on June 30 and December 31

Date of issuance: February 28, 2011

Maturity: August 31, 2011

15. **Westminster Insurance Company.** Westminster Insurance Company plans to sell $2,000,000 of euro-commercial paper with a 60-day maturity and discounted to yield 4.60% per annum. What will be the immediate proceeds to Westminster Insurance?

Internet Exercises

1. **Global Equities.** Bloomberg provides extensive coverage of the global equity markets 24 hours a day. Using the Bloomberg site listed here, note how different the performance indices are on the same equity markets at the same point in time all around the world.

    Bloomberg   www.bloomberg.com/markets/stocks/wei.html

2. **JPMorgan's ADR Tracking.** JPMorgan provides up to the minute performance of American Depositary Receipts in the U.S. marketplace. The site highlights the high-performing equities of the day.

    JP Morgan ADRs   www.adr.com/

3. **Bank of New York Mellon.** The Bank of New York Mellon is the world's largest depositary for both American and global depositary receipts. Use the bank's extensive Web site to complete the following assignment:
    a. Prepare a briefing for senior management in your firm encouraging them to consider internationally diversifying the firm's liquid asset portfolio with ADRs

b. Identify whether the ADR program level (I, II, III, 144A) has any significance to which securities you believe the firm should consider

Bank of New York Mellon   www.adrbny.com/home_dr.jsp

4. London Stock Exchange. The London Stock Exchange (LSE) lists many different global depositary receipts among its active equities. Use the LSE's Internet site to track the performance of the largest GDRs active today.

London Stock Exchange   www.londonstockexchange.com/en-gb/products/membershiptrading/securitytypes/globaldepositaryreceipt.htm

Multinational Tax Management

Over and over again courts have said that there is nothing sinister in so arranging one's affairs as to keep taxes as low as possible. Everybody does so, rich and poor, and all do right, for nobody owes any public duty to pay more than the law demands: taxes are enforced extractions, not voluntary contributions. To demand more in the name of morals is mere cant.

—Judge Learned Hand, Commissioner v. Newman, 159 F.2d 848 (CA-2, 1947).

LEARNING OBJECTIVES

◆ Identify the differences between tax systems employed by government around the globe.

◆ Compare corporate income and withholding tax rates used across countries and the way tax treaties affect MNEs.

◆ Explain how value-added taxes are levied by some countries today.

◆ Explain the use of transfer pricing to manage corporate tax burdens.

◆ Compare tax liabilities of domestic- and foreign-source income for U.S.-based firms.

◆ Demonstrate how U.S.-based multinationals manage their excess foreign tax credits and deficits to minimize their global tax liabilities.

◆ Examine the use of tax-haven subsidiaries and international offshore financial centers.

Tax planning for multinational operations is an extremely complex but vitally important aspect of international business. To plan effectively, MNEs must understand not only the intricacies of their own operations worldwide, but also the different structures and interpretations of tax liabilities across countries. *The primary objective of multinational tax planning is the minimization of the firm's worldwide tax burden.* This objective, however, must not be pursued without full recognition that decision making within the firm must always be based on the economic fundamentals of the firm's line of business, and not on convoluted policies undertaken purely for the reduction of tax liability. As evident from previous chapters, taxes have a major impact on corporate net income and cash flow through their influence on foreign investment decisions, financial structure, determination of the cost of capital, foreign exchange management, working capital management, and financial control.

The purpose of this chapter is to provide an overview of how taxes are applied to MNEs globally; how the United States taxes the global earnings of U.S.-based MNEs; and how U.S.-based multinationals manage their global tax liabilities. We do this in four parts. The first section acquaints the reader with the overall international tax environment. This includes a brief overview of the different tax environments which an MNE is likely to encounter globally, and the basics of most inter-country tax treaties. The second part examines transfer pricing. The third part describes how the United States taxes income of MNEs. Although we use U.S. taxes as illustrations, our intention is not to make this chapter or this book U.S.-centric. Most of the U.S. practices that we describe have close parallels in other countries, albeit modified to fit their specific national overall tax systems. The fourth part of the chapter examines the use of tax-haven subsidiaries and international offshore financial centers. The chapter concludes with a Mini-Case, *The U.S. Corporate Income Tax Conundrum,* which discusses the U.S. corporate tax structure.

Tax Principles

The sections that follow explain the most important aspects of the international tax environments and specific features that affect MNEs. Before we explain the specifics of multinational taxation in practice, however, it is necessary to introduce two areas of fundamental importance: *tax morality* and *tax neutrality*.

Tax Morality

The MNE faces not only a morass of foreign taxes but also an ethical question. In many countries, taxpayers—corporate or individual—do not voluntarily comply with the tax laws. Smaller domestic firms and individuals are the chief violators. The MNE must decide whether to follow a practice of full disclosure to tax authorities or adopt the philosophy of "when in Rome, do as the Romans do." Given the local prominence of most foreign subsidiaries and the political sensitivity of their position, most MNEs follow the full disclosure practice. Some firms, however, believe that their competitive position would be eroded if they did not avoid taxes to the same extent as their domestic competitors. There is obviously no prescriptive answer to the problem, since business ethics are partly a function of cultural heritage and historical development.

Some countries have imposed what seem to be arbitrary punitive tax penalties on MNEs for presumed violations of local tax laws. Property or wealth tax assessments are sometimes perceived by the foreign firm to be excessively large when compared with those levied on locally owned firms. The problem is then how to respond to tax penalties that are punitive or discriminatory.

Tax Neutrality

When a government decides to levy a tax, it must consider not only the potential revenue from the tax, or how efficiently it can be collected, but also the effect the proposed tax can have on private economic behavior. For example, the U.S. government's policy on taxation of foreign-source income does not have as its sole objective the raising of revenue; rather it has multiple objectives, including the following:

◆ Neutralizing tax incentives that might favor (or disfavor) U.S. private investment in developed countries

◆ Providing an incentive for U.S. private investment in developing countries

◆ Improving the U.S. balance of payments by removing the advantages of artificial tax havens and encouraging repatriation of funds

◆ Raising revenue

The ideal tax should not only raise revenue efficiently but also have as few negative effects on economic behavior as possible. Some theorists argue that the ideal tax should be completely *neutral* in its effect on private decisions and completely *equitable* among tax-payers. However, other theorists claim that national policy objectives such as balance of payments or investment in developing countries should be encouraged through an active *tax incentive policy* rather than requiring taxes to be neutral and equitable. Most tax systems compromise between these two viewpoints.

One way to view neutrality is to require that the burden of taxation on each dollar, euro, pound, or yen of profit earned in home country operations by an MNE be equal to the burden of taxation on each currency-equivalent of profit earned by the same firm in its foreign operations. This is called *domestic neutrality*. A second way to view neutrality is to require that the tax burden on each foreign subsidiary of the firm be equal to the tax burden on its competitors in the same country. This is called *foreign neutrality*. The latter interpretation is often supported by MNEs because it focuses more on the competitiveness of the individual firm in individual country-markets.

The issue of *tax equity* is also difficult to define and measure. In theory, an equitable tax is one that imposes the same total tax burden on all taxpayers who are similarly situated and located in the same tax jurisdiction. In the case of foreign investment income, the U. S. Treasury argues that since the United States uses the nationality principle to claim tax jurisdiction, U.S.-owned foreign subsidiaries are in the same tax jurisdiction as U.S. domestic subsidiaries. Therefore, a dollar earned in foreign operations should be taxed at the same rate and paid at the same time as a dollar earned in domestic operations.

National Tax Environments

Despite the fundamental objectives of national tax authorities, it is widely agreed that taxes do affect economic decisions made by MNEs. Tax treaties between nations, and differential tax structures, rates, and practices all result in a less than level playing field for the MNEs competing on world markets.

Exhibit 14.1 provides an overview of corporate tax rates as applicable to the United States, Germany, and Japan. The categorizations of income (e.g., distributed versus undistributed profits), the differences in tax rates, and the discrimination in tax rates applicable to income earned in specific countries serve to introduce the critical dimensions of tax planning for the MNE.

Nations typically structure their tax systems along one of two basic approaches: the *worldwide approach* or the *territorial approach*. Both approaches are attempts to determine which firms, foreign or domestic by incorporation, or which incomes, foreign or domestic in origin, are subject to the taxation of host country tax authorities.

Worldwide Approach. The *worldwide approach*, also referred to as the *residential* or *national approach*, levies taxes on the income earned by firms that are incorporated in the host country, regardless of where the income was earned (domestically or abroad). An MNE earning income both at home and abroad would therefore find its worldwide income taxed by its host-country tax authorities. For example, a country like the United States taxes the income earned by firms based in the United States regardless of whether the income earned by the firm is domestically sourced or foreign sourced. In the case of the United States, ordinary foreign-sourced income is taxed only as remitted to the parent firm. As with all questions of tax, however, numerous conditions and exceptions exist. The primary problem is that this does not address the income earned by foreign firms operating within the United States. Countries like the United States then apply the principle of *territorial taxation* to foreign firms within their legal jurisdiction, taxing all income earned by foreign firms in the United States.

EXHIBIT 14.1	Comparison of Corporate Tax Rates for Japan, Germany, and the United States		

Taxable Income Category	Japan	Germany	United States
Corporate income tax rates	41%	29.5%	40%
Withholding taxes on dividends (portfolio):			
with Japan	—	15%	5%
with Germany	15%	—	5%
with United States	10%	0/5/15%	—
Withholding taxes on dividends (substantial holdings):			
with Japan	—	15%	5%
with Germany	10%	—	5%
with United States	0/5%	0/5/15%	—
Withholding taxes on interest:			
with Japan	—	10%	10%
with Germany	10%	—	0%
with United States	10%	25%	—
Withholding taxes on royalties:			
with Japan	—	10%	0%
with Germany	10%	—	0%
with United States	0%	0%	—

Source: Coporate income tax rates drawn from "KPMG's Corporate and Indirect Tax Rate Survey, 2008," KPMG.com. Tax rates as of April 1, 2008. Withholding tax rates extracted from Price Waterhouse Coopers, Corporate Taxes: A Worldwide Summary, 2009.

Territorial Approach. The *territorial approach*, also termed the *source approach*, focuses on the income earned by firms within the legal jurisdiction of the host country, not on the country of firm incorporation. Countries like Germany, that follow the territorial approach, apply taxes equally to foreign or domestic firms on income earned within the country, but in principle not on income earned outside the country. The territorial approach, like the worldwide approach, results in a major gap in coverage if resident firms earn income outside the country, but are not taxed by the country in which the profits are earned. In this case, tax authorities extend tax coverage to income earned abroad if it is not currently covered by foreign tax jurisdictions. Once again, a mix of the two tax approaches is necessary for full coverage of income.

Tax Deferral. If the worldwide approach to international taxation is followed to the letter, it would end the *tax-deferral* privilege for many MNEs. Foreign subsidiaries of MNEs pay host-country corporate income taxes, but many parent countries defer claiming additional income taxes on that foreign-source income *until it is remitted to the parent firm.* For example, U.S. corporate income taxes on some types of foreign-source income of U.S.-owned subsidiaries incorporated abroad are deferred until the earnings are remitted to the U.S. parent. However, the ability to defer corporate income taxes is highly restricted and has been the subject of many of the tax law changes in the past three decades.

The deferral privilege was challenged once again in the 2004 U.S. presidential campaign by Senator Kerry, the Democratic candidate for President. Senator Kerry claimed that tax deferrals create an incentive for outsourcing abroad—so called *offshoring*—of certain manufacturing and service activities by U.S. firms. The added concern to the potential loss of American jobs was the potential reduction in tax collections in the United States, enlarging the already sizable U.S. government's fiscal deficit.

Tax Treaties

A network of bilateral tax treaties, many of which are modeled after one proposed by the Organization for Economic Cooperation and Development (OECD), provides a means of reducing double taxation. Tax treaties normally define whether taxes are to be imposed on income earned in one country by the nationals of another, and if so, how. Tax treaties are bilateral, with the two signatories specifying what rates are applicable to which types of income between themselves alone. Exhibit 14.1's specification of withholding taxes on dividends, interest, and royalty payments between resident corporations of the United States, Germany, and Japan, is a classic example of the structure of tax treaties. Note that Germany, for example, imposes a 10% withholding tax on royalty payments to Japanese investors, while royalty payments to U.S. investors are withheld at a 0% rate.

The individual bilateral tax jurisdictions as specified through tax treaties are particularly important for firms that are primarily exporting to another country rather than doing business there through a "permanent establishment." The latter would be the case for manufacturing operations. A firm that only exports would not want any of its other worldwide income taxed by the importing country. Tax treaties define what is a "permanent establishment" and what constitutes a limited presence for tax purposes. Tax treaties also typically result in reduced withholding tax rates between the two signatory countries, the negotiation of the treaty itself serving as a forum for opening and expanding business relationships between the two countries.

Tax Types

Taxes are classified on the basis of whether they are applied directly to income, called *direct taxes*, or on the basis of some other measurable performance characteristic of the firm, called *indirect taxes*. Exhibit 14.2 illustrates the wide range of corporate income taxes in the world today.

Income Tax. Many governments rely on income taxes, both personal and corporate, for their primary revenue source. Corporate income taxes are widely used today. Some countries impose different corporate tax rates on distributed income versus undistributed income. Corporate income tax rates vary over a relatively wide range, rising as high as 45% in Guyana and falling as low as 16% in Hong Kong, 15% in the British Virgin Islands, 10% in Cyprus, and effectively 0% in a number of offshore tax havens.

Withholding Tax. Passive income (dividends, interest, royalties) earned by a resident of one country within the tax jurisdiction of a second country are normally subject to a withholding tax in the second country. The reason for the institution of withholding taxes is actually quite simple: governments recognize that most international investors will not file a tax return in each country in which they invest, and the government therefore wishes to assure that a minimum tax payment is received. As the term "withholding" implies, the taxes are withheld by the corporation from the payment made to the investor, and the taxes withheld are then turned over to government authorities. Withholding taxes are a major subject of bilateral tax treaties, and generally range between 0 and 25%.

Value-Added Tax. One type of tax that has achieved great prominence is the *value-added tax*. The *value-added tax* is a type of national sales tax collected at each stage of production or sale of consumption goods in proportion to the value added during that stage. In general,

EXHIBIT 14.2   Corporate Income Tax Rates for Selected Countries

Country	Rate	Country	Rate	Country	Rate
Albania	10%	Gibraltar	22%	Oman	12%
Angola	35%	Greece	24%	Pakistan	35%
Argentina	35%	Guatemala	31%	Panama	27.5%
Armenia	20%	Honduras	25%	Papua New Guinea	30%
Aruba	28%	Hong Kong	16.5%	Paraguay	10%
Australia	30%	Hungary	19%	Peru	30%
Austria	25%	Iceland	18%	Philippines	30%
Bahamas	0%	India	33.99%	Poland	19%
Bahrain	0%	Indonesia	25%	Portugal	25%
Bangladesh	27.5%	Iran	25%	Qatar	10%
Barbados	25%	Ireland	12.5%	Romania	16%
Belarus	24%	Isle of Man	0%	Russia	20%
Belgium	33.99%	Israel	25%	Samoa	27%
Bermuda	0%	Italy	31.4%	Saudi Arabia	20%
Bolivia	25%	Jamaica	33.33%	Serbia	10%
Bosnia and Herzegovina	10%	Japan	40.69%	Singapore	17%
Botswana	25%	Jersey	0%	Slovak Republic	19%
Brazil	34%	Jordan	35%	Slovenia	20%
Bulgaria	10%	Kazakhstan	20%	South Africa	34.55%
Cambodia	20%	Korea, Republic of	24.2%	Spain	30%
Canada	31.0%	Kuwait	15%	Sri Lanka	35%
Cayman Islands	0%	Latvia	15%	Sweden	26.3%
Chile	17%	Libya	40%	Switzerland	21.17%
China	25%	Lithuania	15%	Syria	28%
Colombia	33%	Luxembourg	28.59%	Taiwan	17%
Costa Rica	30%	Macau	12%	Tanzania	30%
Croatia	20%	Macedonia	10%	Thailand	30%
Cyprus	10%	Malaysia	25%	Tunisia	30%
Czech Republic	19%	Malta	35%	Turkey	20%
Denmark	25%	Mauritius	15%	Ukraine	25%
Dominican Republic	25%	Mexico	30%	United Arab Emirates	55%
Ecuador	25%	Montenegro	9%	United Kingdom	28%
Egypt	20%	Mozambique	32%	United States	40%
Estonia	21%	Netherlands	25.5%	Uruguay	25%
Fiji	28%	Netherlands Antilles	34.5%	Venezuela	34%
Finland	26%	New Zealand	30%	Vietnam	25%
France	33.33%	Nigeria	30%	Yemen	35%
Germany	29.41%	Norway	28%	Zambia	35%
				Zimbabwe	25.75%

Source: "KPMG's Corporate and Indirect Tax Rate Survey, 2010," KPMG.com, pp. 12–14.

production goods such as plant and equipment have not been subject to the value-added tax. Certain basic necessities, such as medicines and other health-related expenses, education and religious activities, and the postal service are usually exempt or taxed at lower rates. The value-added tax has been adopted as the main source of revenue from indirect taxation by all members of the European Union, most other countries in Western Europe, a number of Latin American countries, Canada, and scattered other countries. A numerical example of a value-added tax computation is shown in Exhibit 14.3.

Other National Taxes. There are a variety of other national taxes, which vary in importance from country to country. The *turnover tax* (tax on the purchase or sale of securities in some country stock markets) and the *tax on undistributed profits* were mentioned before. *Property* and *inheritance taxes*, also termed *transfer taxes*, are imposed in a variety of ways to achieve intended social redistribution of income and wealth as much as to raise revenue. There are a number of red-tape charges for public services that are in reality user taxes. Sometimes foreign exchange purchases or sales are in effect hidden taxes inasmuch as the government earns revenue rather than just regulates imports and exports for balance of payments reasons.

Foreign Tax Credits. To prevent double taxation of the same income, most countries grant a *foreign tax credit* for income taxes paid to the host country. Countries differ on how they calculate the foreign tax credit and what kinds of limitations they place on the total amount claimed. Normally foreign tax credits are also available for withholding taxes paid to other countries on dividends, royalties, interest, and other income remitted to the parent. The value-added tax and other sales taxes are not eligible for a foreign tax credit but are typically deductible from pretax income as an expense.

EXHIBIT 14.3   **Value-Added Tax Applied to the Sale of a Wooden Fence Post**

This is an example of how a wooden fence post would be assessed for value-added taxes in the course of its production and subsequent sale. A value-added tax of 10% is assumed.

Step 1	The original tree owner sells to the lumber mill, for $0.20, that part of a tree that ultimately becomes the fence post. The grower has added $0.20 in value up to this point by planting and raising the tree. While collecting $0.20 from the lumber mill, the grower must set aside $0.02 to pay the value-added tax to the government.
Step 2	The lumber mill processes the tree into fence posts and sells each post for $0.40 to the lumber wholesaler. The lumber mill has added $0.20 in value ($0.40 less $0.20) through its processing activities. Therefore, the lumber mill owner must set aside $0.02 to pay the mill's value-added tax to the government. In practice, the owner would probably calculate the mill's tax liability as 10% of $0.40, or $0.04, with a tax credit of $0.02 for the value-added tax already paid by the tree owner.
Steps 3 and 4	The lumber wholesaler and retailer also add value to the fence post through their selling and distribution activities. They are assessed $0.01 and $0.03 respectively, making the cumulative value-added tax collected by the government $0.08, or 10% of the final sales price.

Stage of Production	Sales Price	Value Added	Value-Added Tax at 10%	Cumulative Value-Added Tax
Tree owner	$0.20	$0.20	$0.02	$0.02
Lumber mill	$0.40	$0.20	$0.02	$0.04
Lumber wholesaler	$0.50	$0.10	$0.01	$0.05
Lumber retailer	$0.80	$0.30	$0.03	$0.08

EXHIBIT 14.4 Foreign Tax Credits		
	Without foreign tax credits	With foreign tax credits
Before-tax foreign income	$10,000	$10,000
Less foreign tax @ 30%	−3,000	−3,000
Available to parent and paid as dividend	$ 7,000	$ 7,000
Less additional parent-country tax at 35%	−2,450	
Less incremental tax (after credits)	—	−500
Profit after all taxes	$ 4,550	$ 6,500
Total taxes, both jurisdictions	$ 5,450	$ 3,500
Effective overall tax rate (total taxes paid ÷ foreign income)	54.5%	35.0%

A *tax credit* is a direct reduction of taxes that would otherwise be due and payable. It differs from a *deductible expense*, which is an expense used to reduce taxable income before the tax rate is applied. A $100 tax credit reduces taxes payable by the full $100, whereas a $100 deductible expense reduces taxable income by $100 and taxes payable by $100 × t, where t is the tax rate. Tax credits are more valuable on a dollar-for-dollar basis than are deductible expenses.

If there were no credits for foreign taxes paid, sequential taxation by the host government and then by the home government would result in a very high cumulative tax rate. To illustrate, assume the wholly owned foreign subsidiary of an MNE earns $10,000 before local income taxes and pays a dividend equal to all of its after-tax income. The host country income tax rate is 30%, and the home country of the parent tax rate is 35%, assuming no withholding taxes. Total taxation with and without tax credits is shown in Exhibit 14.4.

If tax credits are not allowed, sequential levying of both a 30% host country tax and then a 35% home country tax on the income that remains results in an effective 54.5% tax, a cumulative rate that would render many MNEs uncompetitive with single-country local firms. The effect of allowing tax credits is to limit total taxation on the *original* before-tax income to no more than the highest single rate among jurisdictions. In the case depicted in Exhibit 14.4, the effective overall tax rate of 35% with foreign tax credits is equivalent to the higher tax rate of the home country (and is the tax rate payable if the income had been earned at home).

The $500 of additional home country tax under the tax credit system in Exhibit 14.4 is the amount needed to bring total taxation ($3,000 already paid plus the additional $500) up to but not beyond 35% of the original $10,000 of before-tax foreign income.

Transfer Pricing

The pricing of goods, services, and technology transferred to a foreign subsidiary from an affiliated company, *transfer pricing*, is the first and foremost method of transferring funds out of a foreign subsidiary. These costs enter directly into the cost of goods sold component of the subsidiary's income statement. This is a particularly sensitive problem for MNEs. Even purely domestic firms find it difficult to reach agreement on the best method for setting prices on transactions between related units. In the multinational case, managers must balance conflicting considerations. These include fund positioning and income taxes.

◆ **Fund Positioning Effect.** A parent wishing to transfer funds out of a particular country can charge higher prices on goods sold to its subsidiary in that country—to the degree that government regulations allow. A foreign subsidiary can be financed by the reverse technique, a lowering of transfer prices. Payment by the subsidiary for imports from its parent or sister subsidiary transfers funds out of the subsidiary. A higher transfer price permits funds to be accumulated in the selling country. Transfer pricing may also be used to transfer funds between sister subsidiaries. Multiple sourcing of component parts on a worldwide basis allows switching between suppliers from within the corporate family to function as a device to transfer funds.

◆ **Income Tax Effect.** A major consideration in setting a transfer price is the *income tax effect*. Worldwide corporate profits may be influenced by setting transfer prices to minimize taxable income in a country with a high income tax rate and maximize income in a country with a low income tax rate. A parent wishing to reduce the taxable profits of a subsidiary in a high-tax environment may set transfer prices at a higher rate to increase the costs of the subsidiary thereby reducing taxable income.

The income tax effect is illustrated in Exhibit 14.5. Trident Europe is operating in a relatively high-tax environment (German corporate income taxes are 45%). Trident U.S. is in a significantly lower tax environment (U.S. corporate income tax rates are 35%), motivating Trident to charge Trident Europe a higher transfer price on goods produced in the United States and sold to Trident Europe.

If Trident Corporation adopts a high-markup policy by "selling" its merchandise at an intracompany sales price of $1,700,000, the same $800,000 of pre-tax consolidated income is allocated more heavily to low-tax Trident U.S.A. and less heavily to high-tax Trident Europe. (Note that it is Trident Corporation, the corporate parent, which must adopt a transfer pricing policy which directly alters the profitability of each of the individual subsidiaries.) As a consequence, total taxes drop by $30,000 and consolidated net income increases by $30,000 to $500,000. All while total sales remain constant.

EXHIBIT 14.5	Effect of Low versus High Transfer Price on Trident Europe's Net Income (thousands of U.S. dollars)			
		Trident U.S. (subsidiary)	**Trident Europe (subsidiary)**	**Europe and U.S. Combined**
Low-Markup Policy				
Sales		$1,400	$2,000	$2,000
Less cost of goods sold*		(1,000)	(1,400)	(1,000)
Gross profit		$ 400	$ 600	$1,000
Less operating expenses		(100)	(100)	(200)
Taxable income		$ 300	$ 500	$ 800
Less income taxes	35% (105)	45% (225)	(330)
Net income		$ 195	$ 275	$ 470
High-Markup Policy				
Sales		$1,700	$2,000	$2,000
Less cost of goods sold*		(1,000)	(1,700)	(1,000)
Gross profit		$ 700	$ 300	$1,000
Less operating expenses		(100)	(100)	(200)
Taxable income		$ 600	$ 200	$ 800
Less income taxes	35% (210)	45% (90)	(300)
Net income		$ 390	$ 110	$ 500

*Trident U.S.'s sales price becomes cost of goods sold for Trident Europe.

Trident would naturally prefer the high-markup policy for sales from the United States to Europe (Germany in this case). Needless to say, government tax authorities are aware of the potential income distortion from transfer price manipulation. A variety of regulations and court cases exist on the reasonableness of transfer prices, including fees and royalties as well as prices set for merchandise. If a government taxing authority does not accept a transfer price, taxable income will be deemed larger than was calculated by the firm, and taxes will be increased.

Section 482 of the U.S. Internal Revenue Code is typical of laws circumscribing freedom to set transfer prices. Under this authority the IRS can reallocate gross income, deductions, credits, or allowances between related corporations in order to prevent tax evasion or to reflect more clearly a proper allocation of income. Under these guidelines the burden of proof is on the taxpaying firm to show that the IRS has been arbitrary or unreasonable in reallocating income. This "guilty until proved innocent" approach means that MNEs must keep good documentation of the logic and costs behind their transfer prices. The "correct price" according to the guidelines is the one that reflects an *arm's length price*, that is, a sale of the same goods or service to a comparable unrelated customer.

IRS regulations provide three methods to establish arm's length prices: comparable uncontrolled prices, resale prices, and cost-plus calculations. All three of these methods are recommended for use in member countries by the Organization for Economic Cooperation and Development (OECD) Committee on Fiscal Affairs. In some cases, combinations of these three methods are used.

Managerial Incentives and Evaluation

When a firm is organized with decentralized profit centers, transfer pricing between centers can disrupt evaluation of managerial performance. This problem is not unique to MNEs; it is also a controversial issue in the "centralization versus decentralization" debate in domestic circles. In the domestic case, however, a modicum of coordination at the corporate level can alleviate some of the distortion that occurs when any profit center suboptimizes its profit for the corporate good. Also, in most domestic cases, the company can file a single (for that country) consolidated tax return, so the issue of cost allocation between affiliates is not critical from a tax-payment point of view.

In the multinational case, coordination is often hindered by longer and less efficient channels of communication, the need to consider the unique variables that influence international pricing, and separate taxation. Even with the best of intent, a manager in one country finds it difficult to know what is best for the firm as a whole when buying at a negotiated price from related companies in another country. If corporate headquarters establishes transfer prices and sourcing alternatives, one of the main advantages of a decentralized profit center system disappears: local management loses the incentive to act for its own benefit.

To illustrate, refer to Exhibit 14.5, where an increase in the transfer price led to a worldwide income gain: Trident Corporation's income rose by $195,000 (from $195,000 to $390,000) while Trident Europe's income fell by only $165,000 (from $275,000 to $110,000), for a net gain of $30,000. Should the managers of the European subsidiary lose their bonuses (or their jobs) because of their "sub-par" performance? Bonuses are usually determined by a company-wide formula based in part on the profitability of individual subsidiaries, but in this case, Trident Europe "sacrificed" for the greater good of the whole. Arbitrarily changing transfer prices can create measurement problems.

Specifically, transferring profit from high-tax Trident Europe to low-tax Trident Corporation in the United States changes the following for one or both companies:

◆ Import tariffs paid (importer only) and hence profit levels

◆ Measurements of foreign exchange exposure, such as the amount of net exposed assets, because of changes in amounts of cash and receivables

◆ Liquidity tests, such as the current ratio, receivables turnover, and inventory turnover

◆ Operating efficiency, as measured by the ratio of gross profit to either sales or to total assets

◆ Income tax payments

◆ Profitability, as measured by the ratio of net income to either sales or capital invested

◆ Dividend payout ratio, in that a constant dividend will show as a varied payout ratio as net income changes (alternatively, if the payout ratio is kept constant the amount of dividend is changed by a change in transfer price)

◆ Internal growth rate, as measured by the ratio of retained earnings to existing ownership equity

Effect on Joint-Venture Partners

Joint ventures pose a special problem in transfer pricing, because serving the interest of local stockholders by maximizing local profit may be suboptimal from the overall viewpoint of the MNE. Often, the conflicting interests are irreconcilable. Indeed, the local joint venture partner could be viewed as a potential "Trojan horse" if they complain to local authorities about the MNE's transfer pricing policy.

Tax Management at Trident

Exhibit 14.6 summarizes the key tax management issue for Trident when remitting dividend income back to the United States from Trident Europe and Trident Brazil.

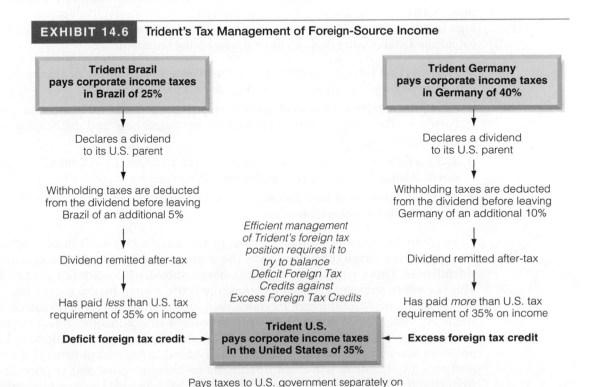

EXHIBIT 14.6   Trident's Tax Management of Foreign-Source Income

◆ Because corporate income tax rates in Germany (40%) are higher than those in the United States (35%), dividends remitted to the U.S. parent result in *excess* foreign tax credits. Any applicable withholding taxes on dividends between Germany and the U.S. only increase the amount of the excess foreign tax credit.

◆ Because corporate income tax rates in Brazil (25%) are lower than those in the United States (35%), dividends remitted to the U.S. parent result in *deficit* foreign tax credits. If there are withholding taxes applied to the dividends by Brazil on remittances to the United States, this will reduce the size of the deficit, but not eliminate it.

Trident's management would like to manage the two dividend remittances in order to match the deficits with the credits. The most straightforward method of doing this would be to adjust the amount of dividend distributed from each foreign subsidiary so that, after all applicable income and withholding taxes have been applied, Trident's excess foreign tax credits from Trident Europe (Germany) exactly match the excess foreign tax deficits from Trident Brazil. There are a number of other methods of managing the global tax liabilities of Trident, so-called *repositioning of funds*, which is examined in detail in Chapter 15.

Tax-Haven Subsidiaries and International Offshore Financial Centers

Many MNEs have foreign subsidiaries that act as tax havens for corporate funds awaiting reinvestment or repatriation. Tax-haven subsidiaries, categorically referred to as International Offshore Financial Centers, are partially a result of tax-deferral features on earned foreign income allowed by some of the parent countries. Tax-haven subsidiaries are typically established in a country that can meet the following requirements:

◆ A low tax on foreign investment or sales income earned by resident corporations and a low dividend withholding tax on dividends paid to the parent firm.

◆ A stable currency to permit easy conversion of funds into and out of the local currency. This requirement can be met by permitting and facilitating the use of Eurocurrencies.

◆ The facilities to support financial services; for example, good communications, professional qualified office workers, and reputable banking services.

◆ A stable government that encourages the establishment of foreign-owned financial and service facilities within its borders.

Exhibit 14.7 provides a map of most of the world's major offshore financial centers. The typical tax-haven subsidiary owns the common stock of its related operating foreign subsidiaries. There might be several tax-haven subsidiaries scattered around the world. The tax-haven subsidiary's equity is typically 100% owned by the parent firm. All transfers of funds might go through the tax-haven subsidiaries, including dividends and equity financing. Thus, the parent country's tax on foreign-source income, which might normally be paid when a dividend is declared by a foreign subsidiary, could continue to be deferred until the tax-haven subsidiary itself pays a dividend to the parent firm. This event can be postponed indefinitely if foreign operations continue to grow and require new internal financing from the tax-haven subsidiary. Thus, MNEs are able to operate a corporate pool

EXHIBIT 14.7   International Offshore Financial Centers

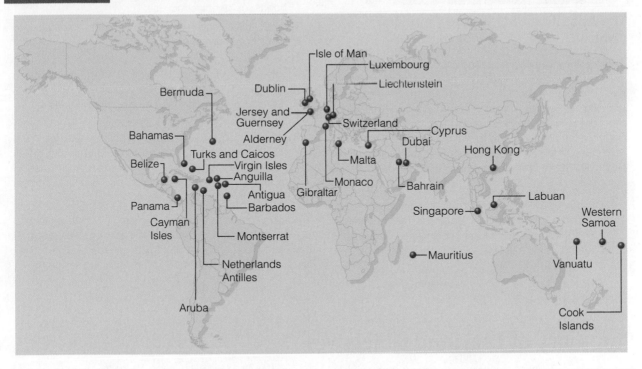

of funds for foreign operations without having to repatriate foreign earnings through the parent country's tax machine.

For U.S. MNEs, the tax-deferral privilege operating through a foreign subsidiary was not originally a tax loophole. On the contrary, it was granted by the U.S. government to allow U.S. firms to expand overseas and place them on a par with foreign competitors, that also enjoy similar types of tax deferral and export subsidies of one type or another.

Unfortunately, some U.S. firms distorted the original intent of tax deferral into tax avoidance. Transfer prices on goods and services bought from or sold to related subsidiaries were artificially rigged to leave all the income from the transaction in the tax-haven subsidiary. This manipulation could be done by routing the legal title to the goods or services through the tax-haven subsidiary, even though physically the goods or services never entered the tax-haven country. This maneuver left no residual tax base for either exporting or importing subsidiaries located outside the tax-haven country. Needless to say, tax authorities of both exporting and importing countries were dismayed by the lack of taxable income in such transactions.

One purpose of the U.S. Internal Revenue Act of 1962 was to eliminate the tax advantages of these "paper" foreign corporations without destroying the tax-deferral privilege for those foreign manufacturing and sales subsidiaries that were established for business and economic motives rather than tax motives. Although the tax motive has been removed, some firms have found these subsidiaries useful as finance control centers for foreign operations. *Global Finance in Practice 14.1* provides a categorization of the primary activities of offshore financial centers.

GLOBAL FINANCE IN PRACTICE   14.1

The Activities of Offshore Financial Centers

Offshore financial centers provide financial management services to foreign users in exchange for foreign exchange earnings. There are several comparative advantages for clients, including very low tax rates, minimal administrative formalities, and confidentiality and discretion. This environment allows wealthy international clients to minimize potential tax liability while protecting income and assets from political, fiscal, and legal risks. There are many vehicles through which offshore financial services can be provided. They include the following:

♦ Offshore banking, which can handle foreign exchange operations for corporations or banks. These operations are not subject to capital, corporate, capital gains, dividend, or interest taxes or to exchange controls.

♦ International business corporations, which are often tax-exempt, limited-liability companies used to operate

businesses or raise capital through issuing shares, bonds, or other instruments.

♦ Offshore insurance companies, which are established to minimize taxes and manage risk.

♦ Asset management and protection, which allows individuals and corporations in countries with fragile banking systems or unstable political regimes to keep assets offshore to protect against the collapse of domestic currencies and banks.

♦ Tax planning, which means multinationals may route transactions through offshore centers to minimize taxes through transfer pricing. Individuals can make use of favorable tax regimes offered by offshore centers through trusts and foundations.

The tax concessions and secrecy offered by offshore financial centers can be used for many legitimate purposes, but they have also been used for illegitimate ends, including money laundering and tax evasion.

Summary of Learning Objectives

Identify the differences between tax systems employed by government around the globe.

♦ Nations typically structure their tax systems along one of two basic approaches: the *worldwide approach* or the *territorial approach*.

♦ Both approaches are attempts to determine which firms, foreign or domestic by incorporation, or which incomes, foreign or domestic in origin, are subject to the taxation of host-country tax authorities.

♦ The *worldwide approach*, also referred to as the *residential* or *national approach*, levies taxes on the income earned by firms that are incorporated in the host country, regardless of where the income was earned (domestically or abroad).

♦ The *territorial approach*, also termed the *source approach*, focuses on the income earned by firms within the legal jurisdiction of the host country, not on the country of firm incorporation.

Compare corporate income and withholding tax rates used across countries and the way tax treaties affect MNEs.

♦ A network of bilateral tax treaties, many of which are modeled after one proposed by the Organization for Economic Cooperation and Development (OECD), provides a means of reducing double taxation.

♦ Tax treaties normally define whether taxes are to be imposed on income earned in one country by the

nationals of another, and if so, how. Tax treaties are bilateral, with the two signatories specifying what rates are applicable to which types of income between themselves alone.

Explain how value-added taxes are levied by some countries today.

♦ The *value-added tax* is a type of national sales tax collected at each stage of production or sale of consumption goods in proportion to the value added during that stage.

Explain the use of transfer pricing to manage corporate tax burdens.

♦ Transfer pricing is the pricing of goods, services, and technology between related companies.

♦ High- or low-transfer prices have an effect on income taxes, fund positioning, managerial incentives and evaluation, and joint venture partners.

♦ To establish an "arm's length" price three methods are typically used: 1) comparable uncontrolled price; 2) resale prices; and 3) cost plus.

Compare tax liabilities of domestic- and foreign-source income of U.S.-based firms.

♦ The United States differentiates foreign source income from domestic source income. Each is taxed separately, and tax deficits/credits in one category may not be used against deficits/credits in the other category.

Demonstrate how U.S.-based multinationals manage their excess foreign tax credits and deficits to minimize their global tax liabilities.

◆ If a U.S.-based MNE receives income from a foreign country that imposes higher corporate income taxes than does the United States (or combined income and withholding tax), total creditable taxes will exceed U.S. taxes on that foreign income. The result is *excess foreign tax credits*.

◆ All firms wish to manage their tax liabilities globally so that they do not end up paying more on foreign-sourced income than they do on domestically sourced income.

Examine the use of tax-haven subsidiaries and international offshore financial centers.

◆ MNEs have foreign subsidiaries that act as tax havens for corporate funds awaiting reinvestment or repatriation.

◆ Tax havens are typically located in countries that have a low corporate tax rate, a stable currency, facilities to support financial services, and a stable government.

MINI-CASE

The U.S. Corporate Income Tax Conundrum[1]

So tonight, I'm asking Democrats and Republicans to simplify the system. Get rid of the loopholes. Level the playing field. And use the savings to lower the corporate tax rate for the first time in 25 years — without adding to our deficit. It can be done.
— President Barack Obama, State of the Union Address, January 25, 2011.

The United States had been debating its corporate income tax rates for years. It was an issue in the 2008 U.S. presidential election, and it continued to be an issue of much debate in the following years. In January 2011, it once again moved into the spotlight of political debate.

But measuring corporate income tax rates and burdens turns out to be quite tricky. The difference lies between *statutory tax rates* and *effective tax rates*. Statutory tax rates are the rates, by law, that companies are required to pay on taxable income. *Effective tax rates* are the actual tax rates paid by companies on all consolidated income — globally, after taking into account differences across countries and all available tax deductions.

Statutory Tax Rates

In 2010, the United States had some of the highest corporate income tax rates in the world. In fact, among the OECD countries — the 31 largest industrialized economies — the U.S. tax rate at 39.2% shown in Exhibit 1 was second highest, only Japan higher at 39.5%. The average of the non-U.S. OECD countries was 25.5%. U.S. corporate

| EXHIBIT 1 | Corporate Combined Tax Rates, OECD Countries, 2010 |

Country	Rate	Country	Rate	Country	Rate
Australia	30.0%	Hungary	19.0%	Poland	19.0%
Austria	25.0%	Iceland	15.0%	Portugal	26.5%
Belgium	34.0%	Ireland	12.5%	Slovak Republic	19.0%
Canada	29.5%	Italy	27.5%	Spain	30.0%
Chile	17.0%	Japan	39.5%	Sweden	26.3%
Czech Republic	19.0%	Korea	24.2%	Switzerland	21.2%
Denmark	25.0%	Luxembourg	28.6%	Turkey	20.0%
Finland	26.0%	Mexico	30.0%	United Kingdom	28.0%
France	34.4%	Netherlands	25.5%	United States	39.2%
Germany	30.2%	New Zealand	30.0%		
Greece	24.0%	Norway	28.0%		

Source: Center for Tax Policy and Administration, OECD.org. Central government corporate income tax rate adjusted for subcentral rates.

income tax rates were now believed to be an increasing impediment to investment in the United States, by both non-U.S. and U.S. corporations.

It had not always been this way. As illustrated by Exhibit 2, the combined federal and state U.S. tax rate had actually been significantly lower than most of the industrial countries for a period during the 1980s. But outside of the 1986 Tax Reform Act in the United States, U.S. rates had largely remained unchanged for 25 years. The rest of the industrial world, however, had continuously cut its combined statutory corporate income tax rate in a continuing effort to attract foreign investment.

Tax Regimes and Tax Deferral

The statutory tax rate, however, is only one element of a country's tax regime. Countries structure their taxation of active corporate earnings on one of two basic approaches, a *territorial system* or a *worldwide system*.[2]

Under a *territorial system*, taxes are paid by a firm only on income where it is earned—by territory or country. For example a company conducting business in Germany owes taxes to the German government only on profits earned within Germany. But under a *worldwide system*, the firm is taxed on its earnings worldwide, regardless of where they are earned. A U.S. company like IBM is subject to worldwide taxation; the United States taxes IBM on the profits it earns everywhere in the world.

As illustrated in Exhibit 3, the United States is only one of five OECD countries that utilizes a worldwide system. The predominance of territorial systems has grown rapidly, as more than half of these same OECD countries used worldwide systems only 10 years ago.[3] In 2009 alone, both Japan and the United Kingdom switched from worldwide to territorial.

What has made the U.S. worldwide tax system tolerable to date (the phrasing used by the Tax Foundation) is that the U.S. does not tax the active earnings from outside the United States until they are repatriated. This is a *tax deferral* on foreign source income. A pure worldwide system would tax all earnings everywhere as earned, regardless of when the profits were repatriated to the home country. This means that U.S. corporations can defer paying U.S. taxes on foreign earnings by not repatriating the profits to the United States.

The relatively high U.S. corporate tax rate, when combined with worldwide taxation, creates a significant problem in principle for the United states today. For example, a U.S. multinational has a subsidiary in Hong Kong. That subsidiary pays corporate income taxes in Hong Kong of 16.5%. But the U.S. company knows that if it repatriates those profits to the United States, it will owe the tax differential, the U.S. effective tax rate less credit for Hong Kong taxes already paid (39.2% − 16.5%). It therefore chooses not to bring the profits back home. In previous years in which the tax differential was not as great, the incentive for

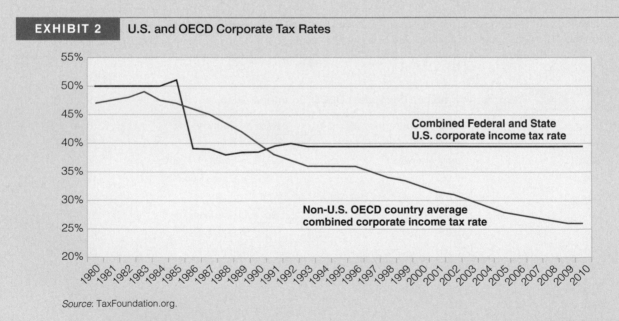

EXHIBIT 2   U.S. and OECD Corporate Tax Rates

Source: TaxFoundation.org.

---

[2]*Active earnings* are profits generated from producing products or providing services. *Passive earnings* are profits derived from the ownership of an asset, business, or technology.

[3]"Special Report: The Importance of Tax Deferral and a Lower Corporate Tax Rate," Tax Foundation, February 2010, No. 174, p. 4.

EXHIBIT 3	OECD: Taxation of Active Foreign Earnings

Territorial Taxation		Worldwide Taxation
Australia	Japan	Ireland
Austria	Luxembourg	Korea
Belgium	Netherlands	Mexico
Canada	New Zealand	Poland
Czech Republic	Norway	United States
Denmark	Portugal	
Finland	Slovak Republic	
France	Spain	
Germany	Sweden	
Greece	Switzerland	
Hungary	Turkey	
Iceland	United Kingdom	
Italy		

Source: "Special Report: The Importance of Tax Deferral and a Lower Corporate Tax Rate," Tax Foundation, February 2010, No. 174, p. 4.

U.S. companies to leave profits abroad was less. It is on this basis that many in the United States argue it is way past time to revise—to lower—the U.S. corporate income tax.

Effective Tax Rates

There are big companies that consider their tax departments to be profit centers.
— National Public Radio, January 29, 2011.

But there is a big difference between statutory rates and what a company actually pays after all tax incentives, deductions, and differences across country tax environments, are taken into account. Because all governments attempt to direct corporate investment and activity toward specific public policy goals, a variety of incentives and deductions are available across the globe. Many multinational companies, for example, General Electric (U.S.), excel at taking advantage of these tax-lowering opportunities to pay a much lower effective tax.

They make money by moving income overseas or in different kinds of activities or adjusting their accounting in such a way that they can pay less taxes than their competitors do.
— Martin Sullivan, tax expert, testimony before the House Ways and Means Committee, January 20, 2011.

Exhibit 4 lists a number of U.S. multinationals which were some of the biggest *winners* and *losers* over recent years in the eyes of one tax expert. In expert testimony

EXHIBIT 4	Effective Tax Rates for Selected U.S. Multinationals

Winners	Effective Rate	Losers	Effective Rate
General Electric	3.6%	CVS Caremark	38.8%
Merck	12.5%	Target	37.2%
Pfizer	17.1%	Disney	36.5%
Medtronic	19.7%	Home Depot	35.4%
Cisco Systems	19.8%	United Health Group	35.4%
Hewlett-Packard	20.0%	Aetna	34.6%
Johnson and Johnson	22.0%	Wal-Mart	33.6%

Source: Testimony of Martin A. Sullivan before the Committee on Ways and Means, U.S. House of Representatives, January 20, 2011. Data is for most recent company annual reports. Tax rates shown here are average of three years presented in most recent report.

before the U.S. Congress, Martin Sullivan listed a few companies like General Electric that had clearly managed to pay a very low effective tax rate over a three-year period (GE paying an average effective tax rate which was only 3.6%). It is interesting to note that none of the biggest losers according to the study had an effective tax rate as high as the statutory rate noted by the OECD.

> ... *I'm asking Congress to eliminate the billions in tax-payer dollars we currently give to oil companies.*
>
> *For example, over the years, a parade of lobbyists has rigged the tax code to benefit particular companies and industries. Those with accountants or lawyers to work the system can end up paying no taxes at all. But all the rest are hit with one of the highest corporate tax rates in the world. It makes no sense, and it has to change.*
>
> —President Barack Obama, excerpts from the State of the Union Address, January 2011.

But Exhibit 4 was an analysis of only U.S.-based multi-nationals. A following exposé, this time by *Business Week*, presented in Exhibit 5, suggested that when you looked at a variety of multinational companies by industry across the globe, the differences were not that significant—at least by country of incorporation. It was clear, however, that global multinationals in specific industries were clearly paying higher rates than in other industry segments.

But it was not the energy or oil companies that were paying the lowest effective tax rates. In fact, they appeared to be paying some of the highest effective tax rates in the world. The lowest rate segment reported was pharmaceuticals, with financial services and some heavy equipment firms also enjoying relatively lower effective rates. Retailers, like the Gap and Home Depot, were also paying relatively higher rates. In fact, of the 30 firms listed in Exhibit 5, the only two firms that were paying at or above the U.S. combined statutory corporate income tax rate of 39.2% were ExxonMobil and Chevron, the two largest American oil companies. (Oil and gas companies like ExxonMobil and Chevron produce their oil and gas in countries all over the world—from Chad to Kazakhstan—and most of those host countries today tax the profits in their countries at rates often above 65%.)

Of course, what was missing from much of the debate and a lot of the tables or exhibits was how much discretion or choice multinational companies have in terms of where they make their taxable profits. A firm, as a result of corporate strategy and history, making more and more of its

---

EXHIBIT 5   Effective Tax Rates for Selected Multinational Firms

Industrial and Heavy Machinery	Rate	Pharmaceuticals	Rate
Siemens, Germany	29.0%	AstraZeneca, Britain	29.5%
United Technologies, U.S.	27.5%	Johnson and Johnson, U.S.	22.8%
Caterpillar, U.S.	24.7%	Bayer, Germany	20.0%
Hyundai Industries, Korea	24.2%	Pfizer, U.S.	18.7%
General Electric, U.S.	11.5%	Sanofi-Aventis, France	18.2%
Technology	**Rate%**	**Financial Services**	**Rate**
SAP, Germany	31.0%	Wells Fargo, U.S.	30.9%
Apple, U.S.	28.5%	Royal Bank of Canada, Canada	24.7%
Microsoft, U.S.	26.7%	Bank of America, U.S.	24.7%
Nokia, Finland	23.9%	Deutsche Bank, Germany	24.2%
Cisco Systems, U.S.	21.6%	HSBC, Britain	20.6%
Retailers	**Rate**	**Energy**	**Rate**
Gap, U.S.	38.6%	Chevron, U.S.	43.9%
Home Depot, U.S.	36.7%	ExxonMobil, U.S.	41.7%
Costco, U.S.	36.3%	BP, Britain	33.8%
Carrefour, France	32.0%	Petrobrás, Brazil	30.2%
Inditex, Spain	23.5%	Petrochina, China	24.7%

Source: "The Multinational Tax Advantage," by Peter Cohn and Mathrew Conniti, *BusinessWeek Magazine,* January 20, 2011. Effective tax rates, in percentages, averaged over 2005–2009.

consolidated profits in a low-tax environment—for example, in Ireland (12.5%), Iceland (15%), or Chile (17%), would have a lower effective tax rate. But companies do not always get to choose where they do business or make profits. If you are a copper mining company, Chile is where you want to be. If, however, you were shopping for a country in which to locate a regional service center for the European Union, Ireland would be a very attractive tax choice.

U.S. Tax Revenues

From the U.S. government's perspective, it's about collecting taxes—and it seems to be collecting fewer and fewer taxes from U.S. multinational companies. Consider the following statistics:

◆ Corporate income taxes in the United States have fallen from 6% of GDP in the 1950s to just 2.1% in 2008.[4]

◆ Corporate income taxes today make up only 12% of all tax revenues collected by the U.S. government.

◆ A 2004 GAO study found that the average effective tax rate on the *domestic income* of large corporations was 25.2%.[5]

◆ That same GAO study found that the average effective tax rate on *foreign-source income* of large corporations was about 4%. This low rate was driven by the fact that the United States only taxes foreign source income (active earnings) upon repatriation, and then it is a residual tax reflecting the credits given on foreign taxes paid on that same income.

In short, U.S. multinationals were not bringing their active foreign earnings back home. They knew if they did they would be paying more taxes. GE, for example, is estimated to have deferred tax on a cumulative $75 billion in foreign active earnings over the past decade by choosing not to bring the profits back home. Given GE's demonstrated track record in paying such low U.S. taxes, it is probably a good thing that GE's Chief Executive Officer Jeffrey Immelt was named by President Barack Obama to lead an economic advisory group on corporate tax reform!

CASE QUESTIONS

1. Do you think the United States needs to cut its corporate income tax rates, change to a territorial system, or both?

2. Do you believe that lower tax rates attract foreign investment?

3. Many public policy experts argue that tax codes should be revised and simplified, so that all firms pay a basic flat rate regardless of who they are or where they do business. What do you think?

[4]"Outsourcing Jobs and Taxes," by Roya Wolverson, CFR.org, February 11, 2011, p. 2.

[5]"U.S. Multinational Corporations: Effective Tax Rates Are Correlated with Where Income Is Reported," General Accounting Office, GAO-08-950, August 2008, p. 3.

Questions

1. **Tax Morality.**
   a. What is meant by the term "tax morality"?
   b. Your company has a subsidiary in Russia, where tax evasion is a fine art. Discuss whether you should comply with Russian tax laws or violate the laws as do your local competitors.

2. **Tax Neutrality.**
   a. Define the term "tax neutrality."
   b. What is the difference between *domestic neutrality* and *foreign neutrality*?
   c. What are a country's objectives when determining tax policy on foreign source income?

3. **Worldwide versus Territorial Approach.** Nations typically structure their tax systems along one of two basic approaches: the *worldwide approach* or the *territorial approach*. Explain these two approaches and how they differ from each other.

4. **Tax Deferral.**
   a. What is meant by the term "tax deferral"?
   b. Why do countries allow tax deferral on foreign source income?

5. **Tax Treaties.**
   a. What is a bilateral tax treaty?
   b. What is the purpose of a bilateral tax treaty?
   c. What policies do most tax treaties cover?

6. **Tax Types.** Taxes are classified on the basis of whether they are applied directly to income, called *direct* taxes, or to some other measurable performance characteristic of the firm, called *indirect* taxes. Identify each of the following as a "direct tax," an "indirect tax," or something else.
   a. Corporate income tax paid by a Japanese subsidiary on its operating income
   b. Royalties paid to Saudi Arabia for oil extracted and shipped to world markets

c. Interest received by a U.S. parent on bank deposits held in London

d. Interest received by a U.S. parent on a loan to a subsidiary in Mexico

e. Principal repayment received by U.S. parent from Belgium on a loan to a wholly owned subsidiary in Belgium

f. Excise tax paid on cigarettes manufactured and sold within the United States

g. Property taxes paid on the corporate headquarters building in Seattle

h. A direct contribution to the International Committee of the Red Cross for refugee relief

i. Deferred income tax, shown as a deduction on the U.S. parent's consolidated income tax

j. Withholding taxes withheld by Germany on dividends paid to a United Kingdom parent corporation

7. Foreign Tax Credit. What is a foreign tax credit? Why do countries give credit for taxes paid on foreign source income?

8. Tax Averaging. How does tax averaging help or hinder a U.S.-based MNE in managing its global tax liabilities?

9. Passive versus Active Income. What is the difference between passive and active income?

10. Value-added tax.

a. What is a value-added tax?

b. What are the advantages and disadvantages of a value-added tax?

c. Although the value-added tax has been proposed numerous times, the United States has never adopted one. Why do you think the United States is so negative on it when the value-added tax is widely used outside the United States?

11. Subpart F Income. The rule that U.S. shareholders do not pay taxes on foreign source income until that income is remitted to the United States (tax deferral) was amended in 1962 by the creation of special *Subpart F income*.

a. Why was this revision adopted?

b. What is defined as being Subpart F income?

c. When is Subpart F income taxed?

12. Transfer Pricing Motivation. What is a transfer price and can a government regulate it? What difficulties and motives does a parent multinational firm face in setting transfer prices?

13. Sister Subsidiaries. Subsidiary Alpha in Country Able faces a 40% income tax rate. Subsidiary Beta in Country Baker faces only a 20% income tax rate. Presently, each subsidiary imports from the other an amount of goods and services exactly equal in monetary value to what each exports to the other. This method of balancing intra-company trade was imposed by a management keen to reduce all costs, including the costs (spread between bid and ask) of foreign exchange transactions. Both subsidiaries are profitable, and both could purchase all components domestically at approximately the same prices as they are paying to their foreign sister subsidiary. Does this seem like an optimal situation?

14. Correct Pricing. Section 482 of the U.S. Internal Revenue Code specifies use of a "correct" transfer price, and the burden of proof that the transfer price is "correct" lies with the company. What guidelines exist for determining the proper transfer price?

15. Branch Income. Branches are often used as the organizational structure for foreign operations that are expected to lose substantial amounts of money in their first years of operation. Why would branches be preferable to wholly owned subsidiaries?

16. Foreign Sales Corporation (FSC). What is a foreign sales corporation? Why are many other countries arguing that the U.S. FSCs are illegal under the World Trade Organization's current rules for the conduct of international trade?

17. Tax-Haven Subsidiary.

a. What is meant by the term "tax haven"?

b. What are the desired characteristics for a country if it expects to be used as a tax haven?

c. Identify five tax havens.

d. What are the advantages leading an MNE to use a tax-haven subsidiary?

e. What are the potential distortions of an MNE's taxable income that are opposed by tax authorities in non–tax-haven countries?

18. Tax Treaties. What do most bilateral tax treaties cover? How do they affect the operations and structure of MNEs?

19. Passive. Why do the U.S. tax authorities tax passive income generated offshore differently from active income?

Problems

1. Avon's Foreign-Source Income. Avon is a U.S.-based direct seller of a wide array of products. Avon markets leading beauty, fashion, and home products in more than 100 countries. As part of the training in its corporate treasury offices, it has its interns build a spreadsheet analysis of the following hypothetical subsidiary earnings/distribution analysis. Use the spreadsheet presented in Exhibit 14.6 for your basic structure.

Baseline Values	Case 1	Case 2
a. Foreign corporate income tax rate	28%	45%
b. U.S. corporate income tax rate	35%	35%
c. Foreign dividend withholding tax rate	15%	0%
d. U.S. ownership in foreign firm	100%	100%
e. Dividend payout rate of foreign firm	100%	100%

a. What is the total tax payment, foreign and domestic combined, for this income?

b. What is the effective tax rate paid on this income by the U.S.-based parent company?

c. What would be the total tax payment and effective tax rate if the foreign corporate tax rate was 45% and there were no withholding taxes on dividends?

d. What would be the total tax payment and effective tax rate if the income was earned by a branch of the U.S. corporation?

2. **Pacific Jewel Airlines (Hong Kong).** Pacific Jewel Airlines is a U.S.-based air freight firm with a wholly owned subsidiary in Hong Kong. The subsidiary, Jewel Hong Kong, has just completed a long-term planning report for the parent company in San Francisco, in which it has estimated the following expected earnings and payout rates for the years 2011–2014.

Jewel Hong Kong Income Items (millions US$)	2011	2012	2013	2014
Earnings before interest and taxes (EBIT)	8,000	10,000	12,000	14,000
Less interest expenses	(800)	(1,000)	(1,200)	(1,400)
Earnings before taxes (EBT)	7,200	9,000	10,800	12,600

The current Hong Kong corporate tax rate on this category of income is 16.5%. Hong Kong imposes no withholding taxes on dividends remitted to U.S. investors (per the Hong Kong-United States bilateral tax treaty). The U.S. corporate income tax rate is 35%. The parent company wants to repatriate 75% of net income as dividends annually.

a. Calculate the net income available for distribution by the Hong Kong subsidiary for the years 2004–2007.

b. What is the amount of the dividend expected to be remitted to the U.S. parent each year?

c. After gross-up for U.S. tax liability purposes, what is the total dividend after tax (all Hong Kong and U.S. taxes) expected each year?

d. What is the effective tax rate on this foreign-sourced income per year?

3. **Kraftstoff of Germany.** Kraftstoff is a German-based company that manufactures electronic fuel-injection carburetor assemblies for several large automobile companies in Germany, including Mercedes, BMW, and Opel. The firm, like many firms in Germany today, is revising its financial policies in line with the increasing degree of disclosure required by firms if they wish to list their shares publicly in or out of Germany.

Kraftstoff's primary problem is that the German corporate income tax code applies a different income tax rate to income depending on whether it is retained (45%) or distributed to stockholders (30%).

a. If Kraftstoff planned to distribute 50% of its net income, what would be its total net income and total corporate tax bills?

b. If Kraftstoff was attempting to choose between a 40% and 60% payout rate to stockholders, what arguments and values would management use in order to convince stockholders which of the two payouts is in everyone's best interest?

Chinglish Dirk

Use the following company case to answer questions 4 through 6. Chinglish Dirk Company (Hong Kong) exports razor blades to its wholly owned parent company, Torrington Edge (Great Britain). Hong Kong tax rates are 16% and British tax rates are 30%. Chinglish calculates its profit per container as follows (all values in British pounds).

Constructing Transfer (Sales) Price per Unit	Chinglish Dirk (British pounds)	Torrington Edge (British pounds)
Direct costs	£10,000	£16,100
Overhead	4,000	1,000
Total costs	£14,000	£17,100
Desired markup	2,100	2,565
Transfer price (sales price)	£16,100	£19,665

Income Statement (prices × volume)

Sales price	£16,100,000	£19,665,000
Less total costs	(14,000,000)	(17,100,000)
Taxable income	£2,100,000	£2,565,000
Less taxes	(336,000)	(769,500)
Profit, after-tax	£1,764,000	£1,795,500

4. **Chinglish Dirk (A).** Corporate management of Torrington Edge is considering repositioning profits within the multinational company. What happens to the profits of Chinglish Dirk and Torrington Edge, and the consolidated results of both, if the markup at Chinglish was increased to 20% and the markup at

Torrington was reduced to 10%? What is the impact of this repositioning on consolidated tax payments?

5. **Chinglish Dirk (B).** Encouraged by the results from the previous problem's analysis, corporate management of Torrington Edge wishes to continue to reposition profit in Hong Kong. It is, however, facing two constraints. First, the final sales price in Great Britain must be £20,000 or less to remain competitive. Secondly, the British tax authorities—in working with Torrington Edge's cost accounting staff—has established a maximum transfer price allowed (from Hong Kong) of £17,800. What combination of markups do you recommend for Torrington Edge to institute? What is the impact of this repositioning on consolidated profits on after-tax and total tax payments?

6. **Chinglish Dirk (C).** Not to leave any potential tax repositioning opportunities unexplored, Torrington Edge wants to combine the components of problem 4 with a redistribution of overhead costs. If overhead costs could be reallocated between the two units, but still total £5,000 per unit, and maintain a minimum of £1,750 per unit in Hong Kong, what is the impact of this repositioning on consolidated profits after-tax and total tax payments?

Internet Exercises

1. **International Taxation and Bulgaria.** The following Web site is a good resource for finding a multitude of global tax and accounting rules, regulations, and rates. Use it to find the specific tax issues facing an MNE that wishes to do business in Bulgaria today.

   Taxsites.com   www.taxsites.com/international
                               .html

2. **Global Taxes.** Sites like TaxWorld provide detailed insights into the conduct of business and the associated tax and accounting requirements of doing business in a variety of countries.

   International Tax Resources   www.taxworld.org/OtherSites/
                                International/international.htm

3. **International Taxpayer.** The United States Internal Revenue Service (IRS) provides detailed support and document requirements for international taxpayers. Use the IRS site to find the legal rules and regulations and definitions for international residents tax liabilities when earning income and profits in the United States.

   U.S. IRS Taxpayer   www.irs.gov/businesses/small/
                               international/index.html

4. **Official Government Tax Authorities.** Tax laws are constantly changing, and an MNE's tax planning and management processes must therefore include a continual updating of tax practices by country. Use the following government tax sites to address specific issues related to those countries:

Hong Kong's ownership change to China	www.gov.hk/en/business/taxes/profittax/
Ireland's international financial services center	www.revenue.ie/
Czech Republic's tax incentives for investment	www.czech.cz/homepage/busin.htm

5. **Tax Practices for International Business.** Many of the major accounting firms provide online information and advisory services for international business activities as related to tax and accounting practices. Use the following Web sites to find current information on tax law changes and practices.

Arthur Andersen	www.arthurandersen.com/
Ernst and Young	www.ey.com/tax/
Deloitte & Touche	www.deloitte.com/view/en_US/us/Services/tax/index.htm
KPMG	www.kpmg.com/
Price Waterhouse Coopers	www.pwc.com/us/en/tax-services/ index.jhtml
Ernst & Young	www.eyi.com/

6. **International Tax Blog.** Follow the latest changes in global tax rules and treaties on the following blog:

   International Tax Blog   blogs.cbh.com/international/

Foreign Investment Decisions

CHAPTER 15

Foreign Direct Investment and Political Risk

CHAPTER 16

Multinational Capital Budgeting
and Cross-Border Acquisitions

15

Foreign Direct Investment and Political Risk

*People don't want a quarter-inch drill. They want a
quarter-inch hole.* —Theodore Levitt, Harvard Business School.

LEARNING OBJECTIVES

◆ Demonstrate how key competitive advantages support MNEs' strategy to originate and sustain direct foreign investment.

◆ Show how the OLI Paradigm provides a theoretical foundation for the globalization process.

◆ Identify factors and forces that must be considered in the determination of where multinational enterprises invest.

◆ Illustrate the managerial and competitive dimensions of the alternative methods for foreign investment.

◆ Identify the strategies used by MNEs originating in developing countries to compete in global markets.

◆ Define and classify foreign political risks.

◆ Analyze firm-specific risks.

◆ Examine country-specific risks.

◆ Identify global-specific risks.

The strategic decision to undertake foreign direct investment (FDI), and thus become an MNE, starts with a self-evaluation. This self-evaluation combines a series of questions including the nature of the firm's competitive advantage, what business form and commensurate risks the firm should use and accept upon entry, and what political risks—both macro and micro in context—the firm will be facing. This chapter explores this sequence of self-evaluation, as well as methods for both measuring and managing the political risks confronting MNEs today in both the established industrial markets and the most promising emerging markets. The Mini-Case at the end of this chapter, *Corporate Competition from the Emerging Markets*, highlights the growing complexity of emerging market competitiveness in the global economy, and how many of tomorrow's most competitive MNEs may be arising from the emerging markets themselves.

Sustaining and Transferring Competitive Advantage

In deciding whether to invest abroad, management must first determine whether the firm has a sustainable competitive advantage that enables it to compete effectively in the home market. The competitive advantage must be firm-specific, transferable, and powerful enough to compensate the firm for the potential disadvantages of operating abroad (foreign exchange risks, political risks, and increased agency costs).

Based on observations of firms that have successfully invested abroad, we can conclude that some of the competitive advantages enjoyed by MNEs are 1) economies of scale and scope arising from their large size; 2) managerial and marketing expertise; 3) superior technology owing to their heavy emphasis on research; 4) financial strength; 5) differentiated products; and sometimes 6) competitiveness of their home markets.

Economies of Scale and Scope

Economies of scale and scope can be developed in production, marketing, finance, research and development, transportation, and purchasing. All of these areas have significant competitive advantages of being large, whether size is due to international or domestic operations. Production economies can come from the use of large-scale automated plant and equipment or from an ability to rationalize production through global specialization.

For example, some automobile manufacturers, such as Ford, rationalize manufacturing by producing engines in one country, transmissions in another, and bodies in another and assembling still elsewhere, with the location often being dictated by comparative advantage. Marketing economies occur when firms are large enough to use the most efficient advertising media to create global brand identification, as well as to establish global distribution, warehousing, and servicing systems. Financial economies derive from access to the full range of financial instruments and sources of funds, such as the Euroequity and Eurobond markets. In-house research and development programs are typically restricted to large firms because of the minimum-size threshold for establishing a laboratory and scientific staff. Transportation economies accrue to firms that can ship in carload or shipload lots. Purchasing economies come from quantity discounts and market power.

Managerial and Marketing Expertise

Managerial expertise includes skill in managing large industrial organizations from both a human and a technical viewpoint. It also encompasses knowledge of modern analytical techniques and their application in functional areas of business. Managerial expertise can be developed through prior experience in foreign markets. In most empirical studies multinational firms have been observed to export to a market before establishing a production facility there. Likewise, they have prior experience sourcing raw materials and human capital in other foreign countries either through imports, licensing, or FDI. In this manner, the MNEs can partially overcome the supposed superior local knowledge of host-country firms.

Advanced Technology

Advanced technology includes both scientific and engineering skills. It is not limited to MNEs, but firms in the most industrialized countries have had an advantage in terms of access to continuing new technology spin-offs from the military and space programs. Empirical studies have supported the importance of technology as a characteristic of MNEs.

Financial Strength

Companies demonstrate financial strength by achieving and maintaining a global cost and availability of capital. This is a critical competitive cost variable that enables them to fund FDI and other foreign activities. MNEs that are resident in liquid and unsegmented capital markets are normally blessed with this attribute. However, MNEs that are resident in small industrial or emerging market countries can still follow a proactive strategy of seeking foreign portfolio and corporate investors.

Small- and medium-size firms often lack the characteristics that attract foreign (and maybe domestic) investors. They are too small or unattractive to achieve a global cost of capital. This limits their ability to fund FDI, and their higher marginal cost of capital reduces the number of foreign projects that can generate the higher required rate of return.

Differentiated Products

Firms create their own firm-specific advantages by producing and marketing differentiated products. Such products originate from research-based innovations or heavy marketing expenditures to gain brand identification. Furthermore, the research and marketing process continues to produce a steady stream of new differentiated products. It is difficult and costly for competitors to copy such products, and they always face a time lag if they try. Having developed differentiated products for the domestic home market, the firm may decide to market them worldwide, a decision consistent with the desire to maximize return on heavy research and marketing expenditures.

Competitiveness of the Home Market

A strongly competitive home market can sharpen a firm's competitive advantage relative to firms located in less competitive home markets. This phenomenon is known as the "competitive advantage of nations," a concept originated by Michael Porter of Harvard. The theory's primary concepts are summarized in Exhibit 15.1.[1]

A firm's success in competing in a particular industry depends partly on the availability of factors of production (land, labor, capital, and technology) appropriate for that industry. Countries that are either naturally endowed with the appropriate factors or able to create them will probably spawn firms that are both competitive at home and potentially so abroad. For example, a well-educated work force in the home market creates a competitive advantage for firms in certain high-tech industries. Firms facing sophisticated and demanding customers in the home market are able to hone their marketing, production, and quality control skills. Japan is such a market.

Firms in industries that are surrounded by a critical mass of related industries and suppliers will be more competitive because of this supporting cast. For example, electronic firms located in centers of excellence, such as in the San Francisco Bay area, are surrounded by efficient, creative suppliers and enjoy access to educational institutions at the forefront of knowledge.

A competitive home market forces firms to fine-tune their operational and control strategies for their specific industry and country environment. Japanese firms learned how to organize to implement their famous just-in-time inventory control system. One key was to use numerous subcontractors and suppliers that were encouraged to locate near the final assembly plants.

In some cases, host-country markets have not been large or competitive, but MNEs located there have nevertheless developed global niche markets served by foreign subsidiaries. Global competition in oligopolistic industries substitutes for domestic competition. For example, a number of MNEs resident in Scandinavia, Switzerland, and the Netherlands fall into this category. They include Novo Nordisk (Denmark), Norske Hydro (Norway), Nokia (Finland), L.M. Ericsson (Sweden), Astra (Sweden), ABB (Sweden/Switzerland), Roche Holding (Switzerland), Royal Dutch Shell (the Netherlands), Unilever (the Netherlands), and Philips (the Netherlands).

Emerging market countries have also spawned aspiring global MNEs in niche markets even though they lack competitive home-country markets. Some of these are traditional exporters in natural resource fields such as oil, agriculture, and minerals, but they are in

[1]Michael Porter, *The Competitive Advantage of Nations*, London: Macmillan Press, 1990.

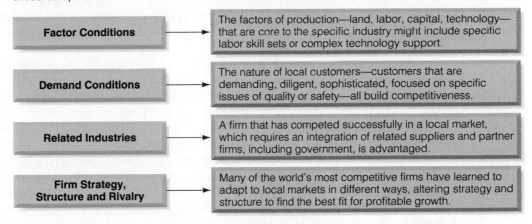

EXHIBIT 15.1   Determinants of National Competitive Advantage

A firm's competitiveness can be significantly strengthened based on its having competed in a highly competitive home market. Home country competitive advantage must be based on at least one of four critical components.

Factor Conditions	The factors of production—land, labor, capital, technology—that are core to the specific industry might include specific labor skill sets or complex technology support.
Demand Conditions	The nature of local customers—customers that are demanding, diligent, sophisticated, focused on specific issues of quality or safety—all build competitiveness.
Related Industries	A firm that has competed successfully in a local market, which requires an integration of related suppliers and partner firms, including government, is advantaged.
Firm Strategy, Structure and Rivalry	Many of the world's most competitive firms have learned to adapt to local markets in different ways, altering strategy and structure to find the best fit for profitable growth.

Source: Based on concepts described by Michael Porter in "The Competitive Advantage of Nations," *Harvard Business Review*, March–April 1990.

transition to becoming MNEs. They typically start with foreign sales subsidiaries, joint ventures, and strategic alliances. Examples are Petrobrás (Brazil), YPF (Argentina), and Cemex (Mexico). Another category is firms that have been recently privatized in the telecommunications industry. Examples are Telefonos de Mexico and Telebrás (Brazil). Still others started as electronic component manufacturers but are making the transition to manufacturing abroad. Examples are Samsung Electronics (Korea) and Acer Computer (Taiwan).

The OLI Paradigm and Internalization

The OLI Paradigm (Buckley and Casson, 1976; Dunning, 1977) is an attempt to create an overall framework to explain why MNEs choose FDI rather than serve foreign markets through alternative modes such as licensing, joint ventures, strategic alliances, management contracts, and exporting.[2]

The OLI Paradigm states that a firm must first have some competitive advantage in its home market—"O" or owner-specific—that can be transferred abroad if the firm is to be successful in foreign direct investment. Second, the firm must be attracted by specific characteristics of the foreign market—"L" or location-specific—that will allow it to exploit its competitive advantages in that market. Third, the firm will maintain its competitive position by attempting to control the entire value chain in its industry—"I" or internalization. This leads it to foreign direct investment rather than licensing or outsourcing.

Definitions. The "O" in OLI stands for owner-specific advantages. As described earlier, a firm must have competitive advantages in its home market. These must be firm-specific, not easily copied, and in a form that allows them to be transferred to foreign subsidiaries. For example, economies of scale and financial strength are not necessarily firm-specific because

[2]Peter J. Buckley and Mark Casson, *The Future of the Multinational Enterprise*, London: Macmillan, 1976; and John H. Dunning, "Trade Location of Economic Activity and the MNE: A Search for an Eclectic Approach," in *The International Allocation of Economic Activity*, Bertil Ohlin, Per-Ove Hesselborn, and Per Magnus Wijkman, eds., New York: Holmes and Meier, 1977, pp. 395–418.

they can be achieved by many other firms. Certain kinds of technology can be purchased, licensed, or copied. Even differentiated products can lose their advantage to slightly altered versions, given enough marketing effort and the right price.

The "L" in OLI stands for location-specific advantages. These factors are typically market imperfections or genuine comparative advantages that attract FDI to particular locations. These factors might include a low-cost but productive labor force, unique sources of raw materials, a large domestic market, defensive investments to counter other competitors, or centers of technological excellence.

The "I" in OLI stands for internalization. According to the theory, the key ingredient for maintaining a firm-specific competitive advantage is possession of proprietary information and control of the human capital that can generate new information through expertise in research. Needless to say, once again, large research-intensive firms are most likely to fit this description.

Minimizing transactions costs is the key factor in determining the success of an internalization strategy. Wholly owned FDI reduces the agency costs that arise from asymmetric information, lack of trust, and the need to monitor foreign partners, suppliers, and financial institutions. Self-financing eliminates the need to observe specific debt covenants on foreign subsidiaries that are financed locally or by joint venture partners. If a multinational firm has a low global cost and high availability of capital, why share it with joint venture partners, distributors, licensees, and local banks, all of which probably have a higher cost of capital?

The Financial Strategy

Financial strategies are directly related to the OLI Paradigm in explaining FDI, as shown in Exhibit 15.2. Proactive financial strategies can be controlled in advance by the MNE's financial managers. These include strategies necessary to gain an advantage from lower

---

EXHIBIT 15.2   Finance-Specific Factors and the OLI Paradigm: "X" Indicates a Connection between FDI and Finance-Specific Strategies

	Ownership Advantages	Location Advantages	Internalization Advantages
Proactive Financial Strategies			
1. Gaining and maintaining a global cost and availability of capital			
a. Competitive sourcing of capital globally	X	X	
b. Strategic preparatory cross-listing	X		
c. Providing accounting and disclosure transparency	X		
d. Maintaining competitive commercial and financial banking relationships	X		
e. Maintaining a competitive credit rating	X	X	X
2. Negotiating financial subsidies and/or reduced taxation to increase free cash flow	X	X	
3. Reducing financial agency cost through FDI			X
4. Reducing operating and transaction exposure through FDI	X		
Reactive Financial Strategies			
1. Exploiting undervalued or overvalued exchange rates		X	
2. Exploiting undervalued or overvalued stock prices		X	
3. Reacting to capital control that prevents the free movement of funds		X	
4. Minimizing taxation		X	X

Source: Lars Oxelheim, Arthur Stonehill, and Trond Randøy, "On the Treatment of Finance Specific Factors Within the OLI Paradigm," *International Business Review* 10 (2001), pp. 381–398.

global cost and greater availability of capital. Other proactive financial strategies are negotiating financial subsidies and/or reduced taxation to increase free cash flows, reducing
financial agency costs through FDI, and reducing operating and transaction exposure
through FDI.

Reactive financial strategies, as illustrated in Exhibit 15.2, depend on discovering market
imperfections. For example, the MNE can exploit misaligned exchange rates and stock prices.
It also needs to react to capital controls that prevent the free movement of funds and react to
opportunities to minimize worldwide taxation.

Deciding Where to Invest

The decision about where to invest abroad is influenced by behavioral factors. The decision
about where to invest abroad for the first time is not the same as the decision about where to
reinvest abroad. A firm learns from its first few investments abroad and what it learns influences subsequent investments.

In theory, a firm should identify its competitive advantages. Then it should search worldwide for market imperfections and comparative advantage until it finds a country where it
expects to enjoy a competitive advantage large enough to generate a risk-adjusted return
above the firm's hurdle rate.

In practice, firms have been observed to follow a sequential search pattern as described
in the behavioral theory of the firm. Human rationality is bounded by one's ability to gather
and process all the information that would be needed to make a perfectly rational decision
based on all the facts. This observation lies behind two behavioral theories of FDI described
next—the *behavioral approach* and *international network theory*.

The Behavioral Approach to FDI

The behavioral approach to analyzing the FDI decision is typified by the so-called Swedish
School of economists.[3] The Swedish School has rather successfully explained not just the
initial decision to invest abroad but also later decisions to reinvest elsewhere and to change
the structure of a firm's international involvement over time. Based on the internationalization process of a sample of Swedish MNEs, the economists observed that these firms
tended to invest first in countries that were not too far distant in psychic terms. *Close psychic distance* defined countries with a cultural, legal, and institutional environment similar
to Sweden's, such as Norway, Denmark, Finland, Germany, and the United Kingdom. The
initial investments were modest in size to minimize the risk of an uncertain foreign environment. As the Swedish firms learned from their initial investments, they became willing
to take greater risks with respect to both the psychic distance of the countries and the size
of the investments.

MNEs in a Network Perspective

As the Swedish MNEs grew and matured, so did the nature of their international involvement. Today, each MNE is perceived as being a member of an international network,
with nodes based in each of the foreign subsidiaries, as well as the parent firm itself.

---

[3]Johansen, John and F. Wiedersheim-Paul, "The Internationalization of the Firm: Four Swedish Case Studies,"
Journal of Management Studies, Vol. 12, No. 3, 1975; and John Johansen and Jan Erik Vahlne, "The Internationaliza-
tion of the Firm: A Model of Knowledge Development and Increasing Foreign Market Commitments," *Journal of
International Business Studies*, Vol. 8, No. 1, 1977.

Centralized (hierarchical) control has given way to decentralized (heterarchical) control. Foreign subsidiaries compete with each other and with the parent for expanded resource commitments, thus influencing the strategy and reinvestment decisions. Many of these MNEs have become political coalitions with competing internal and external networks. Each subsidiary (and the parent) is embedded in its host country's network of suppliers and customers. It is also a member of a worldwide network based on its industry. Finally, it is a member of an organizational network under the nominal control of the parent firm. Complicating matters still further is the possibility that the parent itself may have evolved into a transnational firm, one that is owned by a coalition of investors located in different countries.[4]

Asea Brown Boveri (ABB) is an example of a Swedish-Swiss firm that has passed through the international evolutionary process all the way to being a transnational firm. ABB was formed through a merger of Sweden-based ASEA and Switzerland-based Brown Boveri in 1991. Both firms were already dominant players internationally in the electrotechnical and engineering industries. ABB has literally hundreds of foreign subsidiaries, which are managed on a very decentralized basis. ABB's "flat" organization structure and transnational ownership encourage local initiative, quick response, and decentralized FDI decisions. Although overall strategic direction is the legal responsibility of the parent firm, foreign subsidiaries play a major role in all decision making. Their input in turn is strongly influenced by their own membership in their local and worldwide industry networks. Despite all the planning and analysis that goes with FDI, MNEs are still often confronted with unexpected challenges.

How to Invest Abroad: Modes of Foreign Involvement

The globalization process includes a sequence of decisions regarding where production is to occur, who is to own or control intellectual property, and who is to own the actual production facilities. Exhibit 15.3 provides a road map to explain this FDI sequence.

Exporting versus Production Abroad

There are several advantages to limiting a firm's activities to exports. Exporting has none of the unique risks facing FDI, joint ventures, strategic alliances, and licensing. Political risks are minimal. Agency costs, such as monitoring and evaluating foreign units, are avoided. The amount of front-end investment is typically lower than in other modes of foreign involvement. Foreign exchange risks remain, however. The fact that a significant share of exports (and imports) are executed between MNEs and their foreign subsidiaries and affiliates further reduces the risk of exports compared to other modes of involvement.

There are also disadvantages. A firm is not able to internalize and exploit the results of its research and development as effectively as if it invested directly. The firm also risks losing markets to imitators and global competitors that might be more cost efficient in production abroad and distribution. As these firms capture foreign markets, they might become so strong that they can export back into the domestic exporter's own market. Remember that defensive FDI is often motivated by the need to prevent this kind of predatory behavior as well as to preempt foreign markets before competitors can get started.

---

[4]Forsgren, Mats, *Managing the Internationalization Process: The Swedish Case*, London: Routledge, 1989.

EXHIBIT 15.3   The FDI Sequence: Foreign Presence and Foreign Investment

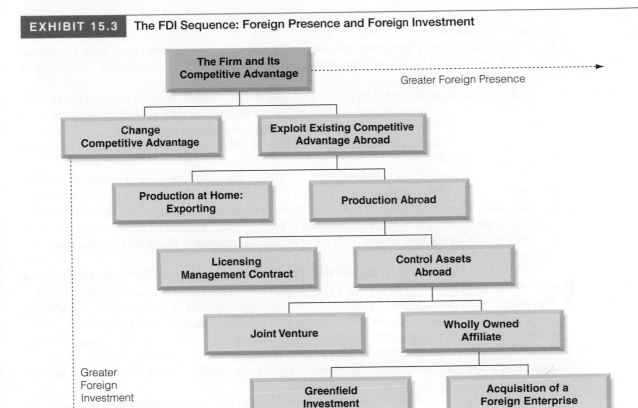

Source: Adapted from Gunter Dufey and R. Mirus, "Foreign Direct Investment: Theory and Strategic Considerations," unpublished, University of Michigan, 1985. Reprinted with permission from the authors. All rights reserved.

Licensing and Management Contracts versus Control of Assets Abroad

Licensing is a popular method for domestic firms to profit from foreign markets without the need to commit sizable funds. Since the foreign producer is typically wholly owned locally, political risk is minimized. In recent years, a number of host countries have demanded that MNEs sell their services in "unbundled form" rather than only through FDI. Such countries would like their local firms to purchase managerial expertise and knowledge of product and factor markets through management contracts, and purchase technology through licensing agreements.

The main disadvantage of licensing is that license fees are likely to be lower than FDI profits, although the return on the marginal investment might be higher. Other disadvantages include the following:

◆ Possible loss of quality control
◆ Establishment of a potential competitor in third-country markets
◆ Possible improvement of the technology by the local licensee, which then enters the firm's home market
◆ Possible loss of opportunity to enter the licensee's market with FDI later
◆ Risk that technology will be stolen
◆ High agency costs

MNEs have not typically used licensing of independent firms. On the contrary, most licensing arrangements have been with their own foreign subsidiaries or joint ventures. License fees are a way to spread the corporate research and development cost among all operating units and a means of repatriating profits in a form more acceptable to some host countries than dividends.

Management contracts are similar to licensing insofar as they provide for some cash flow from a foreign source without significant foreign investment or exposure. Management contracts probably lessen political risk because repatriation of managers is easy. International consulting and engineering firms traditionally conduct their foreign business on the basis of a management contract.

Whether licensing and management contracts are cost effective compared to FDI depends on the price host countries will pay for the unbundled services. If the price were high enough, many firms would prefer to take advantage of market imperfections in an unbundled way, particularly in view of the lower political, foreign exchange, and business risks. Because we observe MNEs continuing to prefer FDI, we must assume that the price for selling unbundled services is still too low.

Why is the price of unbundled services too low? The answer may lie in the synergy created when services are bundled as FDI in the first place. Managerial expertise is often dependent on a delicate mix of organizational support factors that cannot be transferred abroad efficiently. Technology is a continuous process, but licensing usually captures only the technology at a particular point in time. Most important of all, however, economies of scale cannot be sold or transferred in small bundles. By definition they require large-scale operations. A relatively large operation in a small market can hardly achieve the same economies of scale as a large operation in a large market.

Despite the handicaps, some MNEs have successfully sold unbundled services. An example is sales of managerial expertise and technology to the OPEC countries. In this case, however, the OPEC countries are both willing and able to pay a price high enough to approach the returns on FDI (bundled services) while receiving only the lesser benefits of the unbundled services.

Joint Venture versus Wholly Owned Subsidiary

A *joint venture* is here defined as shared ownership in a foreign business. A foreign business unit that is partially owned by the parent company is typically termed a *foreign affiliate*. A foreign business unit that is 50% or more owned (and therefore controlled) by the parent company is typically designated a *foreign subsidiary*. A joint venture would therefore typically fall into the categorization of being a foreign affiliate but not a foreign subsidiary.

A joint venture between an MNE and a host-country partner is a viable strategy if, and only if, the MNE finds the right partner. Some of the obvious advantages of having a compatible local partner are as follows:

◆ The local partner understands the customs, mores, and institutions of the local environment. An MNE might need years to acquire such knowledge on its own with a 100%-owned greenfield subsidiary.

◆ The local partner can provide competent management, not just at the top but also at the middle levels of management.

◆ If the host country requires that foreign firms share ownership with local firms or investors, 100% foreign ownership is not a realistic alternative to a joint venture.

◆ The local partner's contacts and reputation enhance access to the host-country's capital markets.

◆ The local partner may possess technology that is appropriate for the local environment or perhaps can be used worldwide.

◆ The public image of a firm that is partially locally owned may improve its sales possibilities if the purpose of the investment is to serve the local market.

Despite this impressive list of advantages, joint ventures are not as common as 100%-owned foreign subsidiaries because MNEs fear interference by the local partner in certain critical decision areas. Indeed, what is optimal from the viewpoint of the local venture may be suboptimal for the multinational operation as a whole. The most important potential conflicts or difficulties are these:

◆ Political risk is increased rather than reduced if the wrong partner is chosen. The local partner must be credible and ethical or the venture is worse off for being a joint venture.

◆ Local and foreign partners may have divergent views about the need for cash dividends, or about the desirability of growth financed from retained earnings versus new financing.

◆ Transfer pricing on products or components bought from or sold to related companies creates a potential for conflict of interest.

◆ Control of financing is another problem area. An MNE cannot justify its use of cheap or available funds raised in one country to finance joint venture operations in another country.

◆ Ability of a firm to rationalize production on a worldwide basis can be jeopardized if such rationalization would act to the disadvantage of local joint venture partners.

◆ Financial disclosure of local results might be necessary with locally traded shares, whereas if the firm is wholly owned from abroad such disclosure is not needed. Disclosure gives nondisclosing competitors an advantage in setting strategy.

Valuation of equity shares is difficult. How much should the local partner pay for its share? What is the value of contributed technology, or of contributed land in a country where all land is state owned? It is highly unlikely that foreign and host-country partners have similar opportunity costs of capital, expectations about the required rate of return, or similar perceptions of appropriate premiums for business, foreign exchange, and political risks. Insofar as the venture is a component of the portfolio of each investor, its contribution to portfolio return and variance may be quite different for each.

Strategic Alliances

The term *strategic alliance* conveys different meanings to different observers. In one form of cross-border strategic alliance, two firms exchange a share of ownership with one another. A strategic alliance can be a takeover defense if the prime purpose is for a firm to place some of its stock in stable and friendly hands. If that is all that occurs, it is just another form of portfolio investment.

In a more comprehensive strategic alliance, in addition to exchanging stock, the partners establish a separate joint venture to develop and manufacture a product or service. Numerous examples of such strategic alliances can be found in the automotive, electronics, telecommunications, and aircraft industries. Such alliances are particularly suited to high-tech industries where the cost of research and development is high and timely introduction of improvements is important.

A third level of cooperation might include joint marketing and servicing agreements in which each partner represents the other in certain markets. Some observers believe such arrangements begin to resemble the cartels prevalent in the 1920s and 1930s. Because they reduce competition, cartels have been banned by international agreements and many national laws.

Political Risk

In addition to business and foreign exchange risks, foreign direct investment faces political risks. How can multinational firms anticipate government regulations that, from the firm's perspective, are discriminatory or wealth depriving? Normally a twofold approach is utilized.

At the macro level, firms attempt to assess a host country's political stability and attitude toward foreign investors. At the micro level, firms analyze whether their firm-specific activities are likely to conflict with host-country goals as evidenced by existing regulations. The most difficult task, however, is to anticipate changes in host-country goal priorities, new regulations to implement reordered priorities, and the likely impact of such changes on the firm's operations.

Defining and Classifying Political Risk

In order for an MNE to identify, measure, and manage its political risks, it needs to define and classify these risks. Exhibit 15.4 classifies the political risks facing MNEs as being firm-specific, country-specific, or global-specific.

◆ *Firm-specific risks,* also known as *micro risks*, are those risks that affect the MNE at the project or corporate level. *Governance risk* due to goal conflict between an MNE and its host government is the main political firm-specific risk.

◆ *Country-specific-risks*, also known as *macro risks*, are those risks that also affect the MNE at the project or corporate level but originate at the country level. The two main political risk categories at the country level are *transfer risk* and *cultural and institutional risks*. Cultural and institutional risks spring from ownership structure, human resource norms, religious heritage, nepotism and corruption, intellectual property rights, and protectionism.

◆ *Global-specific risks* are those risks that affect the MNE at the project or corporate level but originate at the global level. Examples are terrorism, the antiglobalization movement, environmental concerns, poverty, and cyber attacks.

EXHIBIT 15.4   Classification of Political Risks

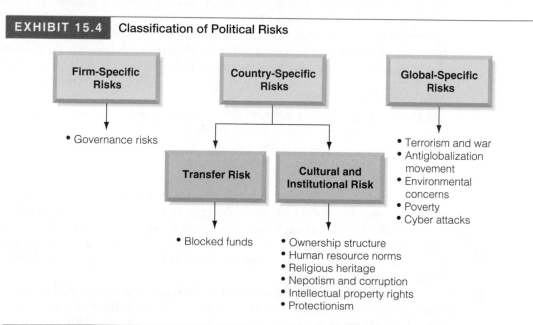

This method of classification differs sharply from the traditional method that classifies risks according to the disciplines of economics, finance, political science, sociology, and law. We prefer our classification system because it is easier to relate the identified political risks to existing and recommended strategies to manage these risks.

Predicting Firm-Specific Risk (Micro Risk)

From the viewpoint of a multinational firm, assessing the political stability of a host country is only the first step, since the real objective is to anticipate the effect of political changes on activities of a specific firm. Indeed, different foreign firms operating within the same country may have very different degrees of vulnerability to changes in host-country policy or regulations. One does not expect a Kentucky Fried Chicken franchise to experience the same risk as a Ford manufacturing plant.

The need for firm-specific analyses of political risk has led to a demand for "tailor-made" studies undertaken in-house by professional political risk analysts. This demand is heightened by the observation that outside professional risk analysts rarely even agree on the degree of macro-political risk which exists in any set of countries.

In-house political risk analysts relate the macro risk attributes of specific countries to the particular characteristics and vulnerabilities of their client firms. Mineral extractive firms, manufacturing firms, multinational banks, private insurance carriers, and worldwide hotel chains are all exposed in fundamentally different ways to politically inspired restrictions. Even with the best possible firm-specific analysis, MNEs cannot be sure that the political or economic situation will not change. Thus, it is necessary to plan protective steps in advance to minimize the risk of damage from unanticipated changes.

Predicting Country-Specific Risk (Macro Risk)

Macro political risk analysis is still an emerging field of study. Political scientists in academia, industry, and government study country risk for the benefit of multinational firms, government foreign policy decision makers, and defense planners.

Political risk studies usually include an analysis of the historical stability of the country in question, evidence of present turmoil or dissatisfaction, indications of economic stability, and trends in cultural and religious activities. Data are usually assembled by reading local newspapers, monitoring radio and television broadcasts, reading publications from diplomatic sources, tapping the knowledge of outstanding expert consultants, contacting other business persons who have had recent experience in the host country, and finally conducting on-site visits.

Despite this impressive list of activities, the prediction track record of business firms, the diplomatic service, and the military has been spotty at best. When one analyzes trends, whether in politics or economics, the tendency is to predict an extension of the same trends into the future. It is a rare forecaster who is able to predict a cataclysmic change in direction. Who predicted the overthrow of Ferdinand Marcos in the Philippines? Indeed, who predicted the collapse of communism in the Soviet Union and the Eastern European satellites? Who predicted the fall of President Suharto in Indonesia in 1998? As illustrated by *Global Finance in Practice 15.1*, the 2011 public protests in Egypt serve as one corporate reminder of risk and the reaction of markets to perceived vulnerability.

Despite the difficulty of predicting country risk, the MNE must still attempt to do so in order to prepare itself for the unknown. A number of institutional services provide updated country risk ratings on a regular basis.

GLOBAL FINANCE IN PRACTICE   **15.1**

Apache Takes a Hit from Egyptian Protests

The January and February 2011 protests in Egypt took billions of dollars of value away from Apache Corporation (NYSE: APA). The U.S.-based oil exploration and production company has significant holdings and operations in Egypt, and the political turmoil that engulfed the country in early 2011 caused the investment public to start dumping Apache's shares. Although actual oil and gas production was not disrupted during this period, Apache did evacuate all expatriate workers from Egypt. Egypt made up roughly 30% of Apache's revenue in 2011, 26% of total production, and 13% of its estimated proved reserves of oil and gas.

Apache Corporation's Share Price (NYSE: APA)

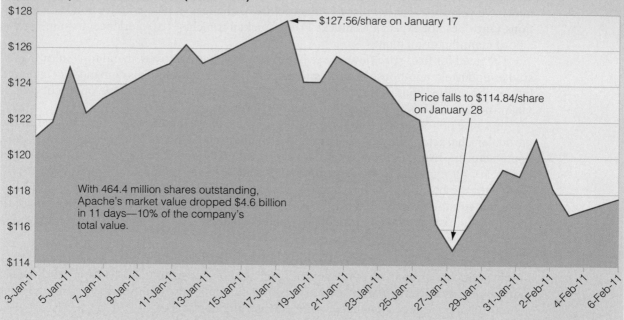

Predicting Global-Specific Risk

Predicting global-specific risk is even more difficult than the other two types of political risk. Nobody predicted the surprise attacks on the World Trade Center and the Pentagon in the United States on September 11, 2001. On the other hand, the aftermath of this attack, that is, the war on global terrorism, increased U.S. homeland security, and the destruction of part of the terrorist network in Afghanistan was predictable. Nevertheless, we have come to expect future surprise terrorist attacks. U.S.-based MNEs are particularly exposed not only to Al-Queda but also to other unpredictable interest groups willing to use terror or mob action to promote such diverse causes as antiglobalization, environmental protection, and even anarchy.

Since there is a great need to predict terrorism, we can expect to see a number of new indices, similar to country-specific indices, but devoted to ranking different types of terrorist threats, their locations, and potential targets.

Firm-Specific Risks

The firm-specific risks which confront MNEs include foreign exchange risks and governance risks. The various business and foreign exchange risks were detailed in Chapters 10 and 11. We focus our discussion here on governance risks.

Governance Risks. *Governance risk* is the ability to exercise effective control over an MNE's operations within a country's legal and political environment. For an MNE, however, governance is a subject similar in structure to consolidated profitability—it must be addressed for the individual business unit and subsidiary, as well as for the MNE as a whole.

The most important type of governance risk for the MNE on the subsidiary level arises from a goal conflict between bona fide objectives of host governments and the private firms operating within their spheres of influence. Governments are normally responsive to a constituency consisting of their citizens. Firms are responsive to a constituency consisting of their owners and other stakeholders. The valid needs of these two separate sets of constituents need not be the same, but governments set the rules. Consequently, governments impose constraints on the activities of private firms as part of their normal administrative and legislative functioning.

Historically, conflicts between objectives of MNEs and host governments have arisen over such issues as the firm's impact on economic development, perceived infringement on national sovereignty, foreign control of key industries, sharing or nonsharing of ownership and control with local interests, impact on a host country's balance of payments, influence on the foreign exchange value of its currency, control over export markets, use of domestic versus foreign executives and workers, and exploitation of national resources. Attitudes about conflicts are often colored by views about free enterprise versus state socialism, the degree of nationalism or internationalism present, or the place of religious views in determining appropriate economic and financial behavior.

The best approach to goal conflict management is to anticipate problems and negotiate understandings ahead of time. Different cultures apply different ethics to the question of honoring prior "contracts," especially when they were negotiated with a previous administration. Nevertheless, prenegotiation of all conceivable areas of conflict provides a better basis for a successful future for both parties than does overlooking the possibility that divergent objectives will evolve over time. Prenegotiation often includes negotiating investment agreements, buying investment insurance and guarantees, and designing risk-reducing operating strategies to be used after the foreign investment decision has been made.

Investment Agreements. An investment agreement spells out specific rights and responsibilities of both the foreign firm and the host government. The presence of MNEs is as often sought by development-seeking host governments as a particular foreign location sought by an MNE. All parties have alternatives and so bargaining is appropriate.

An investment agreement should spell out policies on financial and managerial issues, including the following:

◆ The basis on which fund flows, such as dividends, management fees, royalties, patent fees, and loan repayments, may be remitted

◆ The basis for setting transfer prices

◆ The right to export to third-country markets

◆ Obligations to build, or fund, social and economic overhead projects, such as schools, hospitals, and retirement systems

◆ Methods of taxation, including the rate, the type of taxation, and means by which the rate base is determined

◆ Access to host-country capital markets, particularly for long-term borrowing

◆ Permission for 100% foreign ownership versus required local ownership (joint venture) participation

- Price controls, if any, applicable to sales in the host-country markets
- Requirements for local sourcing versus import of raw materials and components
- Permission to use expatriate managerial and technical personnel, and to bring them and their personal possessions into the country free of exorbitant charges or import duties
- Provision for arbitration of disputes
- Provisions for planned divestment, should such be required, indicating how the going concern will be valued and to whom it will be sold

Investment Insurance and Guarantees: OPIC. MNEs can sometimes transfer political risk to a host-country public agency through an investment insurance and guarantee program. Many developed countries have such programs to protect investments by their nationals in developing countries.

The U.S. investment insurance and guarantee program is managed by the government-owned Overseas Private Investment Corporation (OPIC). OPIC's stated purpose is to mobilize and facilitate the participation of U.S. private capital and skills in the economic and social progress of less-developed friendly countries and areas, thereby complementing the developmental assistance of the United States. OPIC offers insurance coverage for four separate types of political risk, which have their own specific definitions for insurance purposes:

1. *Inconvertibility* is the risk that the investor will not be able to convert profits, royalties, fees, or other income, as well as the original capital invested, into dollars.

2. *Expropriation* is the risk that the host government takes a specific step that for one year prevents the investor or the foreign subsidiary from exercising effective control over use of the property.

3. *War, revolution, insurrection, and civil strife* coverage applies primarily to the damage of physical property of the insured, although in some cases inability of a foreign subsidiary to repay a loan because of a war may be covered.

4. *Business income* coverage provides compensation for loss of business income resulting from events of political violence that directly cause damage to the assets of a foreign enterprise.

Operating Strategies after the FDI Decision. Although an investment agreement creates obligations on the part of both foreign investor and host government, conditions change and agreements are often revised in the light of such changes. The changed conditions may be economic, or they may be the result of political changes within the host government. The firm that sticks rigidly to the legal interpretation of its original agreement may well find that the host government first applies pressure in areas not covered by the agreement and then possibly reinterprets the agreement to conform to the political reality of that country. Most MNEs, in their own self-interest, follow a policy of adapting to changing host-country priorities whenever possible.

The essence of such adaptation is anticipating host-country priorities and making the activities of the firm of continued value to the host country. Such an approach assumes the host government acts rationally in seeking its country's self-interest and is based on the idea that the firm should initiate reductions in goal conflict. Future bargaining position can be enhanced by careful consideration of policies in production, logistics, marketing, finance, organization, and personnel.

Local Sourcing. Host governments may require foreign firms to purchase raw material and components locally as a way to maximize value-added benefits and to increase local employment. From the viewpoint of the foreign firm trying to adapt to host-country goals, local sourcing reduces political risk, albeit at a trade-off with other factors. Local strikes or other turmoil may shut down the operation and such issues as quality control, high local prices because of lack of economies of scale, and unreliable delivery schedules become important. Often, the MNE lowers political risk only by increasing its financial and commercial risk.

Facility Location. Production facilities may be located so as to minimize risk. The natural location of different stages of production may be resource-oriented, footloose, or market-oriented. Oil, for instance, is drilled in and around the Persian Gulf, Russia, Venezuela, and Indonesia. No choice exists for where this activity takes place. Refining is footloose; a refining facility can be moved easily to another location or country. Whenever possible, oil companies have built refineries in politically safe countries, such as Western Europe, or small islands (such as Singapore or Curaçao), even though costs might be reduced by refining nearer the oil fields. They have traded reduced political risk and financial exposure for possibly higher transportation and refining costs.

Control of Transportation. Control of transportation has been an important means to reduce political risk. Oil pipelines that cross national frontiers, oil tankers, ore carriers, refrigerated ships, and railroads have all been controlled at times to influence the bargaining power of both nations and companies.

Control of Technology. Control of key patents and processes is a viable way to reduce political risk. If a host country cannot operate a plant because it does not have technicians capable of running the process, or of keeping up with changing technology, abrogation of an investment agreement with a foreign firm is unlikely. Control of technology works best when the foreign firm is steadily improving its technology.

Control of Markets. Control of markets is a common strategy to enhance a firm's bargaining position. As effective as the OPEC cartel was in raising the price received for crude oil by its member countries in the 1970s, marketing was still controlled by the international oil companies. OPEC's need for the oil companies limited the degree to which its members could dictate terms. In more recent years, OPEC members have established some marketing outlets of their own, such as Kuwait's extensive chain of Q8 gas stations in Europe.

Control of export markets for manufactured goods is also a source of leverage in dealings between MNEs and host governments. The MNE would prefer to serve world markets from sources of its own choosing, basing the decision on considerations of production cost, transportation, tariff barriers, political risk exposure, and competition. The selling pattern that maximizes long-run profits from the viewpoint of the worldwide firm rarely maximizes exports, or value added, from the perspective of the host countries. Some will argue that if the same plants were owned by local nationals and were not part of a worldwide integrated system, more goods would be exported by the host country. The contrary argument is that self-contained local firms might never obtain foreign market share because they lack economies of scale on the production side and are unable to market in foreign countries.

Brand Name and Trademark Control. Control of a brand name or trademark can have an effect almost identical to that of controlling technology. It gives the MNE a monopoly on something that may or may not have substantive value but quite likely represents value in the eyes of consumers. Ability to market under a world brand name is valuable for local firms and thus represents an important bargaining attribute for maintaining an investment position.

Thin Equity Base. Foreign subsidiaries can be financed with a thin equity base and a large proportion of local debt. If the debt is borrowed from locally owned banks, host-government actions that weaken the financial viability of the firm also endanger local creditors.

Multiple-Source Borrowing. If the firm must finance with foreign source debt, it may borrow from banks in a number of countries rather than just from host-country banks. If, for example, debt is owed to banks in Tokyo, Frankfurt, London, and New York, nationals in a number of foreign countries have a vested interest in keeping the borrowing subsidiary financially strong. If the multinational is U.S.-owned, a fallout between the United States and the host government is less likely to cause the local government to move against the firm if it also owes funds to these other countries.

Country-Specific Risks: Transfer Risk

Country-specific risks affect all firms, domestic and foreign, that are resident in a host country. Exhibit 15.5 presents a taxonomy of most of the contemporary political risks that emanate from a specific country location. The main country-specific political risks are *transfer risk*, and *cultural and institutional risks*.

Blocked Funds

Transfer risk is defined as limitations on the MNE's ability to transfer funds into and out of a host country without restrictions. When a government runs short of foreign exchange and cannot obtain additional funds through borrowing or attracting new foreign investment, it usually limits transfers of foreign exchange out of the country, a restriction known as *blocked funds*. In theory, this does not discriminate against foreign-owned firms because it applies to everyone; in practice, foreign firms have more at stake because of their foreign ownership. Depending on the size of a foreign exchange shortage, the host government might simply require approval of all transfers of funds abroad, thus reserving the right to set a priority on

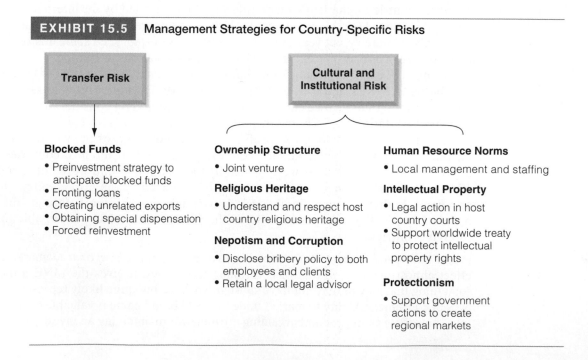

EXHIBIT 15.5   Management Strategies for Country-Specific Risks

the use of scarce foreign exchange in favor of necessities rather than luxuries. In very severe cases, the government might make its currency nonconvertible into other currencies, thereby fully blocking transfers of funds abroad. In between these positions are policies that restrict the size and timing of dividends, debt amortization, royalties, and service fees. MNEs can react to the potential for blocked funds at three stages:

1. Prior to investing a firm can analyze the effect of blocked funds on expected return on investment, the desired local financial structure, and optimal links with subsidiaries.

2. During operations a firm can attempt to move funds through a variety of repositioning techniques.

3. Funds that cannot be moved must be reinvested in the local country in a manner that avoids deterioration in their real value because of inflation or exchange depreciation.

Preinvestment Strategy to Anticipate Blocked Funds. Management can consider blocked funds in their capital budgeting analysis. Temporary blockage of funds normally reduces the expected net present value and internal rate of return on a proposed investment. Whether the investment should nevertheless be undertaken depends on whether the expected rate of return, even with blocked funds, exceeds the required rate of return on investments of the same risk class. Preinvestment analysis also includes the potential to minimize the effect of blocked funds by financing with local borrowing instead of parent equity, swap agreements, and other techniques to reduce local currency exposure and thus the need to repatriate funds. Sourcing and sales links with subsidiaries can be predetermined so as to maximize the potential for moving blocked funds.

Moving Blocked Funds. What can a multinational firm do to transfer funds out of countries having exchange or remittance restrictions? At least six popular strategies are used:

1. Providing alternative conduits for repatriating funds
2. Transfer pricing goods and services between related units of the MNE
3. Leading and lagging payments
4. Signing fronting loans
5. Creating unrelated exports
6. Obtaining special dispensation

Fronting Loans. A *fronting loan* is a parent-to-subsidiary loan channeled through a financial intermediary, usually a large international bank. Fronting loans differ from "parallel" or "back-to-back" loans, discussed in Chapter 11. The latter are offsetting loans between commercial businesses arranged outside the banking system. Fronting loans are sometimes referred to as link financing.

In a direct intracompany loan, a parent or sister subsidiary loans directly to the borrowing subsidiary, and at a later date, the borrowing subsidiary repays the principal and interest. In a fronting loan, by contrast, the "lending" parent or subsidiary deposits funds in, say, a London bank, and that bank loans the same amount to the borrowing subsidiary in the host country. From the London bank's point of view the loan is risk-free, because the bank has 100% collateral in the form of the parent's deposit. In effect, the bank "fronts" for the parent—hence the name. Interest paid by the borrowing subsidiary to the bank is usually slightly higher than the rate paid by the bank to the parent, allowing the bank a margin for expenses and profit.

The bank chosen for the fronting loan is usually in a neutral country, away from both the lender's and the borrower's legal jurisdiction. Use of fronting loans increases the chances for repayment should political turmoil occur between the home and host countries. Government authorities are more likely to allow a local subsidiary to repay a loan to a large international bank in a neutral country than to allow the same subsidiary to repay a loan directly to its parent. To stop payment to the international bank would hurt the international credit image of the country, whereas to stop payment to the parent corporation would have minimal impact on that image and might even provide some domestic political advantage.

Creating Unrelated Exports. Another approach to blocked funds that benefits both the subsidiary and host country is the creation of unrelated exports. Because the main reason for stringent exchange controls is usually a host country's persistent inability to earn hard currencies, anything an MNE can do to create new exports from the host country helps the situation and provides a potential means to transfer funds out.

Some new exports can often be created from present productive capacity with little or no additional investment, especially if they are in product lines related to existing operations. Other new exports may require reinvestment or new funds, although if the funds reinvested consist of those already blocked, little is lost in the way of opportunity costs.

Special Dispensation. If all else fails and the multinational firm is investing in an industry that is important to the economic development of the host country, the firm may bargain for special dispensation to repatriate some portion of the funds that otherwise would be blocked. Firms in "desirable" industries such as telecommunications, semiconductor manufacturing, instrumentation, pharmaceuticals, or other research and high-tech industries may receive preference over firms in mature industries. The amount of preference received depends on bargaining among the informed parties, the government and the business firm, either of which is free to back away from the proposed investment if unsatisfied with the terms.

Self-Fulfilling Prophecies. In seeking "escape routes" for blocked funds—or for that matter in trying to position funds through any of the techniques discussed in this chapter—the MNE may increase political risk and cause a change from partial blockage to full blockage. The possibility of such a self-fulfilling cycle exists any time a firm takes action that, no matter how legal, thwarts the underlying intent of politically motivated controls. In the statehouses of the world, as in the editorial offices of the local press and TV, MNEs and their subsidiaries are always potential scapegoats.

Forced Reinvestment. If funds are indeed blocked from transfer into foreign exchange, they are by definition "reinvested." Under such a situation, the firm must find local opportunities that will maximize the rate of return for a given acceptable level of risk.

If blockage is expected to be temporary, the most obvious alternative is to invest in local money market instruments. Unfortunately, in many countries, such instruments are not available in sufficient quantity or with adequate liquidity. In some cases, government Treasury bills, bank deposits, and other short-term instruments have yields that are kept artificially low relative to local rates of inflation or probable changes in exchange rates. Thus, the firm often loses real value during the period of blockage.

If short- or intermediate-term portfolio investments, such as bonds, bank time deposits, or direct loans to other companies, are not possible, investment in additional production facilities may be the only alternative. Often, this investment is what the host country is seeking by its exchange controls, even if the existence of exchange controls is by itself counterproductive to the idea of additional foreign investment. Examples of forced direct reinvestment can be cited for Peru, where an airline invested in hotels and in maintenance facilities for other airlines; for Turkey, where a fish canning company constructed a plant to manufacture cans needed for packing the catch; and for Argentina, where an automobile company integrated vertically by acquiring a transmission manufacturing plant previously owned by a supplier.

If investment opportunities in additional production facilities are not available, funds may simply be used to acquire other assets expected to increase in value with local inflation. Typical purchases might be land, office buildings, or commodities that are exported to global markets. Even inventory stockpiling might be a reasonable investment, given the low opportunity cost of the blocked funds.

Country-Specific Risks: Cultural and Institutional Risks

When investing in some of the emerging markets, MNEs that are resident in the most industrialized countries face serious risks because of cultural and institutional differences. Many such differences include the following:

◆ Differences in allowable ownership structures
◆ Differences in human resource norms
◆ Differences in religious heritage
◆ Nepotism and corruption in the host country
◆ Protection of intellectual property rights
◆ Protectionism
◆ Legal liabilities

Ownership Structure. Historically, many countries have required that MNEs share ownership of their foreign subsidiaries with local firms or citizens. Thus, joint ventures were the only way an MNE could operate in some host countries. Prominent countries that used to require majority local ownership were Japan, Mexico, China, India, and Korea. This requirement has been eliminated or modified in more recent years by these countries and most others. However, firms in certain industries are still either excluded from ownership completely or must accept being a minority owner. These industries are typically related to national defense, agriculture, banking, or other sectors that are deemed critical for the host nation.

Human Resource Norms. MNEs are often required by host countries to employ a certain proportion of host-country citizens rather than staffing mainly with foreign expatriates. It is often very difficult to fire local employees due to host-country labor laws and union contracts. This lack of flexibility to downsize in response to business cycles affects both MNEs and their local competitors. It also qualifies as a country-specific risk.

Cultural differences can also inhibit an MNE's staffing policies. For example, it is somewhat difficult for a woman manager to be accepted by local employees and managers in many Middle Eastern countries. The most extreme example of discrimination against women has been highlighted in Afghanistan when the Taliban were in power. Since the Taliban's downfall in late 2001, several women have been suggested for important government roles. It is expected that the private sector in Afghanistan will also reintegrate women into the workforce.

Religious Heritage. The current hostile environment for MNEs in some Middle Eastern countries such as Iran, Iraq, and Syria is being fed by some extremist Muslim clerics who are enraged about the continuing violence in Israel and the occupied Arab territories. However, the root cause of these conflicts is a mixture of religious fervor for some and politics for others. Although it is popular to blame the Muslim religion for its part in fomenting the conflict, a number of Middle Eastern countries, such as Egypt, Saudi Arabia, and Jordan, are relatively passive when it comes to Jihads. Jihads are calls for Muslims to attack the infidels (Jews and Christians). Osama Bin Laden's call for Jihad against the United States has not generated any great interest on the part of moderate Muslims. Indeed one Muslim country, Turkey, has had a secular government for many decades. It strongly supported efforts to rid the world of Bin Laden, which was finally accomplished in May 2011.

Despite religious differences, MNEs have operated successfully in emerging markets, especially in extractive and natural resource industries, such as oil, natural gas, minerals, and forest products. The main MNE strategy is to understand and respect the host country's religious traditions.

Nepotism and Corruption. MNEs must deal with endemic nepotism and corruption in a number of important foreign investment locations. Indonesia was famous for nepotism and corruption under the now-deposed Suharto government. Nigeria, Kenya, Uganda, and a number of other African countries have a history of nepotism and corruption after they threw out their colonial governments after World War II. China and Russia have recently launched well-publicized crackdowns on those evils.

Bribery is not limited to emerging markets. It is also a problem in even the most industrialized countries, including the United States and Japan. In fact, the United States has an antibribery law that would imprison any U.S. business executive found guilty of bribing a foreign government official. This law was passed in reaction to an attempt by Lockheed Aircraft to bribe a Japanese Prime Minister.

MNEs are caught in a dilemma. Should they employ bribery if their local competitors use this strategy? There are alternative strategies:

◆ Refuse bribery outright, or else demands will quickly multiply.

◆ Retain a local advisor to diffuse demands by local officials, customs agents, and other business partners.

◆ Do not count on the justice system in many emerging markets, because Western-oriented contract law may not agree with local norms.

◆ Educate both management and local employees about the bribery policy the firm intends to follow.

Intellectual Property Rights. Rogue businesses in some host countries have historically infringed on the *intellectual property rights* of both MNEs and individuals. *Intellectual property rights* grant the exclusive use of patented technology and copyrighted creative materials. Examples of patented technology are unique manufactured products, processing techniques, and prescription pharmaceutical drugs. Examples of copyrighted creative materials are software programs, educational materials (textbooks), and entertainment products (e.g., music, film, art).

MNEs and individuals need to protect their intellectual property rights through the legal process. However, in some countries, courts have historically not done a fair job of protecting intellectual property rights of anyone, much less of foreign MNEs. In those countries, the legal process is costly and subject to bribery.

The agreement on Trade-Related Aspects of Intellectual Property Rights (TRIPS) to protect intellectual property rights has recently been ratified by most major countries. It remains to be seen whether host governments are strong enough to enforce their official efforts to stamp out intellectual piracy. Complicating this task is the thin line that exists between the real item being protected and look-alikes or generic versions of the same item.

Protectionism. *Protectionism* is defined as the attempt by a national government to protect certain of its designated industries from foreign competition. Industries that are protected are usually related to defense, agriculture, and "infant" industries.

Defense. Even though the United States is a vocal proponent of open markets, a foreign firm proposing to buy Lockheed Missile Division or other critical defense suppliers would not be welcome. The same attitude exists in many other countries, such as France, which has always wanted to maintain an independent defense capability.

Agriculture. Agriculture is another sensitive industry. No MNE would be foolish enough as to attempt to buy agricultural properties, such as rice operations, in Japan. Japan has desperately tried to maintain an independent ability to feed its own population. Agriculture is the typical "Mother Earth" industry that most countries want to protect for their own citizens.

Infant Industries. The traditional protectionist argument is that newly emerging, "infant" industries need protection from foreign competition until they can get firmly established. The infant industry argument is usually directed at limiting imports but not necessarily MNEs. In fact, most host countries encourage MNEs to establish operations in new industries that do not presently exist in the host country. Sometimes the host country offers foreign MNEs "infant industry" status for a limited number of years. This status could lead to tax subsidies, construction of infrastructure, employee training, and other aids to help the MNE get started. Host countries are especially interested in attracting MNEs that promise to export, either to their own foreign subsidiaries elsewhere or to unrelated parties.

Tariff Barriers. The traditional methods for countries to implement protectionist barriers were through tariff and non-tariff regulations. Negotiations under the General Agreements on tariffs and Trade (GATT) have greatly reduced the general level of tariffs over the past decades. This process continues today under the auspices of the World Trade Organization (WTO). However, many non-tariff barriers remain.

Non-Tariff Barriers. Non-tariff barriers, which restrict imports by something other than a financial cost, are often difficult to identify because they are promulgated as health, safety, or sanitation requirements. A list of the major types of non-tariff barriers include those shown in Exhibit 15.6.

Strategies to Manage Protectionism. MNEs have only a very limited ability to overcome host country protectionism. However, MNEs do enthusiastically support efforts to reduce protectionism by joining together in regional markets. The best examples of regional markets are the European Union (EU), the North American Free Trade Association (NAFTA), and the Latin American Free Trade Association (MERCOSUR). Among the objectives of

EXHIBIT 15.6   Management Strategies for Global-Specific Risks

Terrorism and War
- Support government efforts to fight terrorism and war
- Crisis planning
- Cross-border supply chain integration

Antiglobalization
- Support government efforts to reduce trade barriers
- Recognize that MNEs are the targets

Environmental Concerns
- Show sensitivity to environmental concerns
- Support government efforts to maintain a level playing field for pollution controls

Poverty
- Provide stable, relatively well-paying jobs
- Establish the strictest of occupational safety standards

Cyber Attacks
- No effective strategy except Internet security efforts
- Support government anticyber attack efforts

*MNE movement toward multiple primary objectives:
Profitability, Sustainable Development, Corporate Social Responsibility*

regional markets are elimination of internal trade barriers, such as tariffs and non-tariff barriers, as well as the free movement of citizens for employment purposes. External trade barriers still exist.

The EU is trying to become a "United States of Europe," with a single internal market without barriers. It is not quite there, although the European Monetary Union and the euro have almost eliminated monetary policy differences. The EU still tolerates differences in fiscal policies, legal systems, and cultural identities. In any case, the movement toward regional markets is very favorable for MNEs serving those markets with foreign subsidiaries.

Legal Liabilities. Despite good intentions, MNEs are often confronted with unexpected legal liabilities. *Global Finance in Practice 15.2* illustrates why Hospira, a U.S.-based pharmaceutical manufacturer, decided to cancel a DFI project in Italy as a result of potential legal and associated financial liabilities.

Global-Specific Risks

Global-specific risks faced by MNEs have come to the forefront in recent years. Exhibit 15.6 summarizes some of these risks, and strategies that can be used to manage them. The most visible recent risk was, of course, the attack by terrorists on the twin towers of the World Trade Center in New York on September 11, 2001. Many MNEs had major operations in the World Trade Center and suffered heavy casualties among their employees. In addition to terrorism, other global-specific risks include the antiglobalization movement, environmental concerns, poverty in emerging markets, and cyber attacks on computer information systems.

GLOBAL FINANCE IN PRACTICE   15.2

Drugs, Public Policy, and the Death Penalty in 2011

Foreign direct investment can be a very tricky thing. Just ask Hospira, a U.S.-based pharmaceutical manufacturer. Hospira, of Lake Forest, Illinois (U.S.), stopped manufacturing of *Pentothal* (sodium thiopental) in North Carolina in the United States in mid-2009. It intended to shift all production to Italy. Hospira's press release read as follows:

Hospira Statement Regarding Pentothal™ (Sodium Thiopental) Market Exit

LAKE FOREST, Ill., Jan. 21, 2011—Hospira announced today it will exit the sodium thiopental market and no longer attempt to resume production of its product, Pentothal™.

Hospira had intended to produce Pentothal at its Italian plant. In the last month, we've had ongoing dialogue with the Italian authorities concerning the use of Pentothal in capital punishment procedures in the United States—a use Hospira has never condoned. Italy's intent is that we control the product all the way to the ultimate end user to prevent use in capital punishment. These discussions and internal deliberation, as well as conversations with wholesalers—the primary

distributors of the product to customers—led us to believe we could not prevent the drug from being diverted to departments of corrections for use in capital punishment procedures.

Based on this understanding, we cannot take the risk that we will be held liable by the Italian authorities if the product is diverted for use in capital punishment. Exposing our employees or facilities to liability is not a risk we are prepared to take.

Given the issues surrounding the product, including the government's requirements and challenges bringing the drug back to market, Hospira has decided to exit the market. We regret that issues outside of our control forced Hospira's decision to exit the market, and that our many hospital customers who use the drug for its well-established medical benefits will not be able to obtain the product from Hospira.

Source: Hospira.com

The news was met with dismay by the medical industry. Pentothal, at one-time a widely used anesthetic, is today only used in a variety of special cases. The drug is preferred in specific cases because it does not cause blood pressure to drop severely, including the care of the elderly, patients with heart disease, or expecting mothers requiring emerging C-sections in which the possibility of low blood pressure is threatening. Second-best solutions would now have to be good enough.

Terrorism and War. Although the World Trade Center attack and its aftermath, the war in Afghanistan, have affected nearly everyone worldwide, many other acts of terrorism have been committed in recent years. More terrorist acts are expected to occur in the future. Particularly exposed are the foreign subsidiaries of MNEs and their employees. As mentioned earlier, foreign subsidiaries are especially exposed to war, ethnic strife, and terrorism because they are symbols of their respective parent countries.

Crisis Planning. No MNE has the tools to avert terrorism. Hedging, diversification, insurance, and the like are not suited to the task. Therefore, MNEs must depend on governments to fight terrorism and protect their foreign subsidiaries (and now even the parent firm). In return, governments expect financial, material, and verbal support from MNEs to support antiterrorist legislation and proactive initiatives to destroy terrorist cells wherever they exist.

MNEs can be subject to damage by being in harm's way. Nearly every year one or more host countries experience some form of ethnic strife, outright war with other countries, or terrorism. It seems that foreign MNEs are often singled out as symbols of "oppression" because they represent their parent country, especially if it is the United States.

Cross-Border Supply Chain Integration. The drive to increase efficiency in manufacturing has driven many MNEs to adopt just-in-time (JIT) near-zero inventory systems. Focusing on so-called *inventory velocity*, the speed at which inventory moves through a manufacturing process, arriving only as needed and not before, has allowed these MNEs to generate increasing profits and cash flows with less capital being bottled-up in the production cycle itself. This finely tuned supply chain system, however, is subject to significant political risk if the supply chain itself extends across borders.

Supply Chain Interruptions. Consider the cases of Dell Computer, Ford Motor Company, Dairy Queen, Apple Computer, Herman Miller, and The Limited in the days following the terrorist attacks of September 11, 2001. An immediate result of the attacks of the morning of September 11 was the grounding of all aircraft into or out of the United States. Similarly, the land (Mexico and Canada) and sea borders of the United States were also shut down and not reopened for several days in some specific sites. Ford Motor Company shut down five of its manufacturing plants in the days following September 11 because of inadequate inventories of critical automotive inputs supplied from Canada. Dairy Queen experienced such significant delays in key confectionary ingredients that many of its stores were also temporarily closed.

Dell Computer, with one of the most highly acclaimed and admired virtually integrated supply chains, depends on computer parts and subassembly suppliers and manufacturers in both Mexico and Canada to fulfill its everyday assembly and sales needs. In recent years, Dell has carried less than three full days sales of total inventory—by cost of goods value. Suppliers are integrated electronically with Dell's order fulfillment system, and deliver required components and subassemblies as sales demands require. But with the closure of borders and grounding of air freight, the company was literally brought to a near standstill because of its supply chain's reliance on the ability to treat business units and suppliers in different countries as if they were all part of a single seamless political unit. Unfortunately, that proved not to be the case with this particular unpredictable catastrophic terrorist event.

As a result of these newly learned lessons, many MNEs are now evaluating the degree of exposure their own supply chains possess in regard to cross-border stoppages or other cross-border political events. These companies are not, however, about to abandon JIT. It is estimated that many U.S. companies alone have saved more than $1 billion a year in inventory carrying costs by using JIT methods over the past decade. This substantial benefit is now being weighed against the costs and risks associated with the post-September 11 supply chain interruptions.

To avoid suffering a similar fate in the future, manufacturers, retailers, and suppliers are now employing a range of tactics:

◆ **Inventory Management.** Manufacturers and assemblers are now considering carrying more buffer inventory in order to hedge against supply and production-line disruptions. Retailers, meanwhile, should think about the timing and frequency of their replenishment. Rather than stocking up across the board, companies are focusing on the most critical parts to the product or service, and those components which are uniquely available from international sources.

◆ **Sourcing.** Manufacturers are now being more selective about where the critical inputs to their products come from. Although sourcing strategies will have to vary by location (those involving Mexico for example will differ dramatically from Canada), firms are attempting to work more closely with existing suppliers to minimize cross-border exposures and reduce the potential costs with future stoppages.

◆ **Transportation.** Retailers and manufacturers alike are reassessing their cross-border shipping arrangements. Although the mode of transportation employed is a function of value, volume, and weight, many firms are now reassessing whether higher costs for faster shipment balance out the more tenuous delivery under airline stoppages from either labor, terrorist, or even bankruptcy disruptions in the future.

Antiglobalization Movement. During the past decade, there has been a growing negative reaction by some groups to reduced trade barriers and efforts to create regional markets, particularly to NAFTA and the European Union. NAFTA has been vigorously opposed by those sectors of the labor movement that could lose jobs to Mexico. Opposition within the European Union centers on loss of cultural identity, dilution of individual national control as new members are admitted, over-centralization of power in a large bureaucracy in Brussels, and most recently, the disappearance of individual national currencies in mid-2002, when the euro became the only currency in 12 of the 15 member nations.

The antiglobalization movement has become more visible following riots in Seattle during the 2001 annual meeting of the World Trade Organization. However, antiglobalization forces were not solely responsible for these riots, or for subsequent riots in Quebec and Prague in 2001. Other disaffected groups, such as environmentalists and even anarchists, joined in to make their causes more visible.

MNEs do not have the tools to combat antiglobalism. Indeed they are blamed for fostering the problem in the first place. Once again, MNEs must rely on governments and crisis planning to manage these risks.

Environmental Concerns. MNEs have been accused of "exporting" their environmental problems to other countries. The accusation is that MNEs frustrated by pollution controls in their home country have relocated these activities to countries with weaker pollution controls. Another accusation is that MNEs contribute to the problem of global warming. However, that accusation applies to all firms in all countries. It is based on the manufacturing methods employed by specific industries and on consumers' desire for certain products such as large automobiles and sport vehicles that are not fuel efficient.

Once again, solving environmental problems is dependent on governments passing legislation and implementing pollution control standards. In 2001, a treaty attempting to reduce global warming was ratified by most nations, with the notable exception of the United States. However, the United States has promised to combat global warming using its own strategies. The United States objected to provisions in the worldwide treaty that allowed emerging nations to follow less restrictive standards, while the economic burden would fall on the most industrialized countries, particularly the United States.

Poverty. MNEs have located foreign subsidiaries in countries plagued by extremely uneven income distribution. At one end of the spectrum is an elite class of well-educated, well-connected, and productive persons. At the other end is a very large class of persons living at or below the poverty level. They lack education, social and economic infrastructure, and political power.

MNEs might be contributing to this disparity by employing the elite class to manage their operations. On the other hand, MNEs are creating relatively stable and well-paying jobs for those who would be otherwise unemployed and living below the poverty level. Despite being accused of supporting "sweat shop" conditions, MNEs usually compare favorably to their local competitors. For example, Nike, one of the targeted MNEs, usually pays better, provides more fringe benefits, maintains higher safety standards, and educates their workforce to allow personnel to advance up the career ladder. Of course, Nike cannot manage a country's poverty problems overall, but it can improve conditions for some persons.

Cyber Attacks. The rapid growth of the Internet has fostered a whole new generation of scam artists and cranks that disrupt the usefulness of the World Wide Web. This is both a domestic and an international problem. MNEs can face costly cyber attacks by disaffected persons with a grudge because of their visibility and the complexity of their internal information systems.

At this time, we know of no uniquely international strategies that MNEs can use to combat cyber attacks. MNEs are using the same strategies to manage foreign cyber attacks as they use for domestic attacks. Once again, they must rely on governments to control cyber attacks.

Summary of Learning Objectives

Demonstrate how key competitive advantages support MNEs' strategy to originate and sustain direct foreign investment.

◆ In order to invest abroad a firm must have a sustainable competitive advantage in the home market. This must be strong enough and transferable enough to overcome the disadvantages of operating abroad.

◆ Competitive advantages stem from economies of scale and scope arising from large size; managerial and marketing expertise; superior technology; financial strength; differentiated products; and competitiveness of the home market.

Show how the OLI Paradigm provides a theoretical foundation for the globalization process.

◆ The OLI Paradigm is an attempt to create an overall framework to explain why MNEs choose FDI rather than serve foreign markets through alternative modes, such as licensing, joint ventures, strategic alliances, management contracts, and exporting.

◆ Finance-specific strategies are directly related to the OLI Paradigm, including both proactive and reactive financial strategies.

Identify factors and forces that must be considered in the determination of where multinational enterprises invest.

◆ The decision about where to invest is influenced by economic and behavioral factors, as well as the stage of a firm's historical development.

◆ Psychic distance plays a role in determining the sequence of FDI and later reinvestment. As firms learn from their early investments they venture further afield and are willing to risk larger commitments.

◆ The most internationalized firms can be viewed from a network perspective. The parent firm and each of the foreign subsidiaries are members of networks. The networks are composed of relationships within a worldwide industry, within the host countries with suppliers and customers, and within the multinational firm itself.

Illustrate the managerial and competitive dimensions of the alternative methods for foreign investment.

◆ Exporting avoids political risk but not foreign exchange risk. It requires the least up-front investment but it might eventually lose markets to imitators and global competitors that might be more cost efficient in production abroad and distribution.

- Alternative (to wholly owned foreign subsidiaries) modes of foreign involvement exist. They include joint venture, strategic alliances, licensing, management contracts, and traditional exporting.
- Licensing enables a firm to profit from foreign markets without a major front-end investment. However, disadvantages include limited returns, possible loss of quality control, and potential of establishing a future competitor.
- The success of a joint venture depends primarily on the right choice of a partner. For this reason and a number of issues related to possible conflicts in decision making between a joint venture and a multinational parent, the 100%-owned foreign subsidiary approach is more common.
- The completion of the European Internal Market at end-of-year 1992 induced a surge in cross-border entry through strategic alliances. Although some forms of strategic alliances share the same characteristics as joint ventures, they often also include an exchange of stock.

Identify the strategies used by MNEs originating in developing countries to compete in global markets.

- There are six major strategies employed by emerging market MNEs: take brands global; engineer to innovation; leverage natural resources; develop an export business model; acquire offshore assets; target a market niche.

Define and classify foreign political risks.

- Political risks can be defined by classifying them on three levels: *firm-specific*, *country-specific*, or *global-specific*.
- *Firm-specific risks*, also known as *micro risks*, affect the MNE at the project or corporate level.
- *Country-specific risks*, also known as *macro risks*, affect the MNE at the project or corporate level but originate at the country level.
- *Global-specific risks* affect the MNE at the project or corporate level but originate at the global level.

Analyze firm-specific risks.

- The main firm-specific risk is *governance risk*, which is the ability to exercise control over the MNE as a whole, globally, and within a specific country's legal and political environment on the individual subsidiary level.
- The most important type of governance risk arises from a goal conflict between bona fide objectives of governments and private firms.
- The main tools used to manage goal conflict are to negotiate an investment agreement; to purchase investment insurance and guarantees; and to modify operating strategies in production, logistics, marketing, finance, organization, and personnel.

Examine country-specific risks.

- The main *country-specific risks* are *transfer risk*, known as *blocked funds*, and certain cultural and institutional risks.
- Blocked funds can be managed by at least five different strategies: 1) considering blocked funds in the original capital budgeting analysis; 2) fronting loans; 3) creating unrelated exports; 4) obtaining special dispensation; and 5) planning on forced reinvestment.
- Cultural and institutional risks emanate from host-country policies with respect to ownership structure, human resource norms, religious heritage, nepotism and corruption, intellectual property rights, protectionism, and legal liabilities.
- Managing cultural and institutional risks requires the MNE to understand the differences, take legal actions in host-country courts, support worldwide treaties to protect intellectual property rights, and support government efforts to create regional markets.

Identify global-specific risks.

- The main global-specific risks are currently caused by terrorism and war, the antiglobalization movement, environmental concerns, poverty, and cyber attacks.
- In order to manage global-specific risks, MNEs should adopt a crisis plan to protect its employees and property. However, the main reliance remains on governments to protect its citizens and firms from these global-specific threats.

MINI-CASE

Corporate Competition from the Emerging Markets

BCG [Boston Consulting Group] argues that this is because they have managed to resolve three trade-offs that are usually associated with corporate growth: of volume against margin; rapid expansion against low leverage (debt); and growth against dividends. On average the challengers have increased their sales three times faster than their established global peers since 2005. Yet they have also reduced their debt-to-equity ratio by three percentage points and achieved a higher ratio of dividends to share price in every year but one.

— "Nipping at Their Heels: Firms from the Developing World Are Rapidly Catching Up with Their Old-World Competitors," *The Economist*, January 22, 2011, p. 80.

Leadership in all companies, public and private, new and old, start-ups and maturing, have all heard the same threat in recent years: the emerging market competitors are coming. But despite the threat, there have been other forces at work which would prevent their advancing—too fast: the ability to raise sufficient capital at a reasonable cost; the ability to reach the larger and more profitable markets; the competition in markets which value name recognition and brand identity; global reach. But a number of market prognosticators—the gurus and consultants—are now contending that these new competitors are already here.

One such analysis was recently published by BCG, the Boston Consulting Group.[1] BCG labels these firms the *global challengers*, companies based in rapidly developing economies that are "shaking up" the established economic order. Their list of 100 global companies, most of which are from Brazil—13, Russia—6, India—20, and China—33 (the so-called BRICs), and Mexico—7, are all innovative and aggressive, but have also proven to be financially fit.

The value created by these firms for their shareholders is very convincing. The total shareholder return (TSR) for the global challengers between 2005 and 2009 was 22%; the same TSR for their *global peers*, public companies in comparable business lines from the industrialized economies, a mere 5%. They have, according to BCG, been able to achieve these results by resolving three classic trade-offs confronting emerging players. These strategic trade-offs turn out to be uniquely financial in character.

The Three Trade-Offs

The three trade-offs could also be characterized as three financial dimensions of competitiveness—the market, the financing, the offered return.

Trade-Off #1: Volume versus Margin. Traditional business thinking assumes that large scale, large market sales, like that of WalMart, requires incredibly low prices which in turn impose low margin returns to the scale competitors. Higher margin products and services are usually reserved for specialty market segments which may be much more expensive to service, but are found justifiable by the higher prices and higher margins they offer.

BCG argues that the *global challengers* have been able to have both volume and margin, relying on exceptionally low direct costs of materials and labor, combined with the latest in technology and execution found in the developed country markets.

Trade-Off #2: Rapid Expansion versus Low Leverage. One of the key advantages always held by the world's largest companies is their preferred access to capital. The advantages afforded companies in large market economies, capitalist economies, is access to plentiful and affordable capital. Companies arising from the emerging markets have often been held back in their expansion efforts, not having the capital to exercise their ambitions. Only after gaining access to the world's largest capital markets, providers of both debt and equity, can these firms pose a serious threat beyond their immediate country market or region. In the past, access meant higher levels of debt and the associated risks and burdens of higher leverage.

But the *global challengers* have again fought off the trade-off, finding ways to increase both equity and debt in proportion, and therefore to grow without taking on a riskier financial structure. The obvious solution has been to gain increasing access to affordable equity, often in London and New York.

Trade-Off #3: Growth versus Dividends. Financial theory has always emphasized the critical distinctions between what opportunities and threats *growth firms* and *value firms* offer investors. *Growth firms* are typically smaller firms, start-ups, companies with unique business models based on new technologies or services. They have enormous upside potential, but need more time, more experience, more breadth, and most importantly, more capital. Investors in these companies know the risks are

[1]"Companies on the Move, Rising Stars from Rapidly Developing Economies Are Reshaping Global Industries," Boston Consulting Group, January 2011.

high, and as a result, accept those risks in focusing on prospective returns from capital gains, not dividend distributions. Investors also know that these firms, often very small firms, will show large share price movements quickly with commensurate business developments. For that, the firm needs to be nimble, quick, and not laden with debt.

Value companies, a polite term for mature or older, larger, well-established global competitors, are of a size in which new business developments, new markets or new technologies, are rarely large enough to move share prices significantly and quickly. Investors in these companies, according to agency theory, do not "trust management" to take sufficient risks to generate returns. So they prefer the firm to bear some artificial financial burdens to assure diligence. Those financial burdens are typically higher levels of debt and growing distributions of profit as dividends. Both elements serve as financial disciplines, requiring management to maintain watchfulness over costs and cash flows to service debt, and generate sufficient profitability over time to supply dividends.

The *global challengers* have arguably thwarted this trade-off as well, paying dividends at growing rates and similar dividend yields to more mature firms with stronger and sustained cash flows. This may actually be the easiest of the three to accomplish given their already substantial sizes and strong profitability.

Continuing Questions

Many still have doubts. If these global challengers can defeat these traditional financial trade-offs, can they overcome the corporate strategic challenges that so many firms from so many markets flailed against before them? As *The Economist* notes, "*All this is impressive, but it seems implausible that these trade-offs have been 'resolved'.*"[2]

Many emerging market or rapidly developing economy analysts argue that these firms not only understand emerging markets, but also they have demonstrated sustained innovation and remained financially healthy. Others argue that these three factors are likely to be more simultaneous than causal. It is clear, however, that most of these new global players are arising from large underdeveloped and underserved markets, markets that are providing large bases for their rapid development.

One strategy being rapidly deployed by many of these firms is the use of strategic partnerships, joint ventures, or share swap agreements.[3] In each of these forms, the companies are gaining a competitive reach, a global partner, and access to technology and markets without major growth on their part.

Not to mention one of the biggest continuing debates, whether they may be able to continue to grow as successfully while being conglomerates—diversified global conglomerates. That is an organizational and strategic structure enjoyed by few in the highly industrialized economies today.

CASE QUESTIONS

1. How are the three trade-offs interconnected according to financial principles?

2. Do you believe these firms have truly resolved or conquered these trade-offs, or have they benefited from some other competitive advantages at this stage of their development?

[2]"Nipping at Their Heels: Firms from the Developing World Are Rapidly Catching Up with Their Old-World Competitors," *The Economist*, January 22, 2011, p. 80.

[3]"Big Emerging Market Mergers Create Global Competitors," by Gordon Platt, *Global Finance*, July/August 2009.

Questions

1. **Evolving into Multinationalism.** As a firm evolves from purely domestic into a true multinational enterprise, it must consider a) its competitive advantages, b) its production location, c) the type of control it wants to have over any foreign operations, and d) how much monetary capital to invest abroad. Explain how each of these considerations is important to the success of foreign operations.

2. **Theory of Comparative Advantage.** What is the essence of the theory of comparative advantage?

3. **Market Imperfections.** MNEs strive to take advantage of market imperfections in national markets for products, factors of production, and financial assets. Large international firms are better able to exploit such imperfections. What are their main competitive advantages?

4. **Strategic Motives for Foreign Direct Investment (FDI).**
   a. Summarize the five main motives that drive the decision to initiate FDI.

b. Match these motives with the following MNEs:
   General Motors (USA)
   Royal Dutch Shell (Netherlands/UK)
   Kentucky Fried Chicken (USA)
   Jardine Matheson (Hong Kong)
   Apple Computer (USA)
   NEC (Japan)

5. **Competitive Advantage.** In deciding whether to invest abroad, management must first determine whether the firm has a sustainable competitive advantage that enables it to compete effectively in the home market. What are the necessary characteristics of this competitive advantage?

6. **Economies of Scale and Scope.** Explain briefly how economies of scale and scope can be developed in production, marketing, finance, research and development, transportation, and purchasing.

7. **Competitiveness of the Home Market.** A strongly competitive home market can sharpen a firm's competitive advantage relative to firms located in less competitive markets. This phenomenon is known as Porter's "diamond of national advantage." Explain what is meant by the "diamond of national advantage."

8. **OLI Paradigm.** The OLI Paradigm is an attempt to create an overall framework to explain why MNEs choose FDI rather than serve foreign markets through alternative modes. Explain what is meant by the O, the L, and the I of the paradigm.

9. **Financial Links to OLI.** Financial strategies are directly related to the OLI Paradigm.
   a. Explain how *proactive* financial strategies are related to OLI.
   b. Explain how *reactive* financial strategies are related to OLI.

10. **Where to Invest.** The decision about where to invest abroad is influenced by behavioral factors.
    a. Explain the *behavioral approach* to FDI
    b. Explain the *international network theory* explanation of FDI.

11. **Exporting versus Producing Abroad.** What are the advantages and disadvantages of limiting a firm's activities to exporting compared to producing abroad?

12. **Licensing and Management Contracts versus Producing Abroad.** What are the advantages and disadvantages of licensing and management contracts compared to producing abroad?

13. **Joint Venture versus Wholly Owned Production Subsidiary.** What are the advantages and disadvantages of forming a joint venture to serve a foreign market compared to serving that market with a wholly owned production subsidiary?

14. **Greenfield Investment versus Acquisition.** What are the advantages and disadvantages of serving a foreign market through a greenfield foreign direct investment compared to an acquisition of a local firm in the target market?

15. **Cross-Border Strategic Alliance.** The term "cross-border strategic alliance" conveys different meanings to different observers. What are the meanings?

16. **Governance Risk.**
    a. Define what is meant by the term "governance risk."
    b. What is the most important type of governance risk?

17. **Investment Agreement.** An *investment agreement* spells out specific rights and responsibilities of both the foreign firm and the host government. What are the main financial policies that should be included in an investment agreement?

18. **Investment Insurance and Guarantees (OPIC).**
    a. What is OPIC?
    b. What types of political risks can OPIC insure against?

19. **Operating Strategies after the FDI Decision.** The following operating strategies, among others, are expected to reduce damage from political risk. Explain each one and how it reduces damage.
    a. Local sourcing
    b. Facility location
    c. Control of technology
    d. Thin equity base
    e. Multiple-source borrowing

20. **Country-Specific Risk.** Define the following terms:
    a. Transfer risk
    b. Blocked funds
    c. Sovereign credit risk

21. **Blocked Funds.** Explain the strategies used by an MNE to counter blocked funds.

22. **Cultural and Institutional Risks.** Identify and explain the main types of cultural and institutional risks, except protectionism.

23. **Strategies to Manage Cultural and Institutional Risks.** Explain the strategies that an MNE can use to manage each of the cultural and institutional risks that you identified in question 22, except protectionism.

24. **Protectionism Defined.**
    a. Define protectionism and identify the industries that are typically protected.
    b. Explain the "infant industry" argument for protectionism.

25. **Managing Protectionism.**
    a. What are the traditional methods for countries to implement protectionism?
    b. What are some typical non-tariff barriers to trade?
    c. How can MNEs overcome host country protectionism?

26. **Global-Specific Risks.** What are the main types of political risks that are global in origin?

27. **Managing Global-Specific Risks.** What are the main strategies used by MNEs to manage the global-specific risks you have identified in question 26?

28. **U.S. Antibribery Law.** The United States has a law prohibiting U.S. firms from bribing foreign officials and business persons, even in countries where bribery is a normal practice. Some U.S. firms claim this places the United States at a disadvantage compared to host-country firms and other foreign firms that are not hampered by such a law. Discuss the ethics and practicality of the U.S. antibribery law.

Internet Exercises

1. **The World Bank.** The World Bank provides a growing set of informational and analytical resources to aid in the assessment and management of risk cross-border. The Risk Management Support Group has a variety of political risk assessment tools which are under constant development. Visit the following site and compose an executive briefing (one page or less) of what the political risk insurance provided by the World Bank will and will not cover.

World Bank Risk Management	www.worldbank.org/business/01risk_manage.html

2. **Global Corruption Report.** Transparency International (TI) is considered by many to be the leading nongovernmental anticorruption organization in the world today. Recently, it has introduced its own annual survey analyzing current developments, identifying ongoing challenges, and offering potential solutions to individuals and organizations. One dimension of this analysis is the Bribe Payers Index. Visit TI's Web site to view the latest edition of the Bribe Payers Index.

Corruption Index	www.transparency.org/policy_research/surveys_indices/cpi

Bribe Payers Index	www.transparency.org/policy_research/surveys_indices/bpi

3. **Sovereign Credit Ratings Criteria.** The evaluation of credit risk and all other relevant risks associated with the multitude of borrowers on world debt markets requires a structured approach to international risk assessment. Use Standard and Poor's criteria, described in depth on their Web page, to differentiate the various risks (local currency risk, default risk, currency risk, transfer risk, etc.) contained in major sovereign ratings worldwide. (You may need to complete a free login for this site.)

Standard and Poor's	www.ratings.com/criteria/sovereigns.index/

4. **Milken Capital Access Index.** The Milken Institute's Capital Access Index (CAI) is one of the most recent informational indices which aids in the evaluation of how accessible world capital markets are to MNEs and governments of many emerging market countries. According to the CAI, which countries have seen the largest deterioration in their access to capital in the last two years?

Milken Institute	www.milken-inst.org/

5. **Overseas Private Investment Corporation.** The Overseas Private Investment Corporation (OPIC) provides long-term political risk insurance and limited recourse project financing aid to U.S.-based firms investing abroad. Using the organization's Web page, answer the following questions:
    a. Exactly what types of risk will OPIC insure against?
    b. What financial limits and restrictions are there on this insurance protection?
    c. How should a project be structured to aid in its approval for OPIC coverage?

Overseas Private Investment Corp	www.opic.gov/

6. **Political Risk and Emerging Markets.** Check the World Bank's political risk insurance blog for current issues and topics in emerging markets.

Political Insurance Blog	blogs.worldbank.org/miga/category/tags/political-risk-insurance

Multinational Capital Budgeting and Cross-Border Acquisitions

C H A P T E R

16

Whales only get harpooned when they come to the surface, and turtles can only move forward when they stick their neck out, but investors face risk no matter what they do. —Charles A. Jaffe.

LEARNING OBJECTIVES

◆ Extend the domestic capital budgeting analysis to evaluate a greenfield foreign project.

◆ Distinguish between the project viewpoint and the parent viewpoint when analyzing a potential foreign investment.

◆ Adjust the capital budgeting analysis of a foreign project for risk.

◆ Introduce the use of real option analysis as a complement to discounted cash flow analysis.

◆ Examine the use of project finance to fund and evaluate large global projects.

◆ Introduce the principles of cross-border mergers and acquisitions.

This chapter describes in detail the issues and principles related to the investment in real productive assets in foreign countries, generally referred to as *multinational capital budgeting*. The chapter first describes the complexities of budgeting for a foreign project. Second, we describe the insights gained by valuing a project from both the project's viewpoint and the parent's viewpoint using a hypothetical investment by Cemex of Mexico in Indonesia. The chapter then discusses both *real option analysis* and the use of *project financing* today. The following section describes the stages involved in affecting cross-border acquisitions. We conclude the chapter with the Mini-Case, ***Yanzhou (China) Bids for Felix Resources (Australia)***.

Although the original decision to undertake an investment in a particular foreign country may be determined by a mix of strategic, behavioral, and economic decisions, the specific project, as well as all reinvestment decisions, should be justified by traditional financial analysis. For example, a production efficiency opportunity may exist for a U.S. firm to invest abroad, but the type of plant, mix of labor and capital, kinds of equipment, method of financing, and other project variables must be analyzed within the traditional financial framework of discounted cash flows. It must also consider the impact of the proposed foreign project on consolidated net earnings, cash flows from subsidiaries in other countries, and on the market value of the parent firm.

Multinational capital budgeting for a foreign project uses the same theoretical framework as domestic capital budgeting—with a few very important differences. The basic steps are as follows:

◆ Identify the initial capital invested or put at risk.

◆ Estimate cash flows to be derived from the project over time, including an estimate of the terminal or salvage value of the investment.

439

◆ Identify the appropriate discount rate for determining the present value of the expected cash flows.

◆ Apply traditional capital budgeting decision criteria such as net present value (NPV) and internal rate of return (IRR) to determine the acceptability of or priority ranking of potential projects.

Complexities of Budgeting for a Foreign Project

Capital budgeting for a foreign project is considerably more complex than the domestic case. Several factors contribute to this greater complexity:

◆ Parent cash flows must be distinguished from project cash flows. Each of these two types of flows contributes to a different view of value.

◆ Parent cash flows often depend on the form of financing. Thus, we cannot clearly separate cash flows from financing decisions, as we can in domestic capital budgeting.

◆ Additional cash flows generated by a new investment in one foreign subsidiary may be in part or in whole taken away from another subsidiary, with the net result that the project is favorable from a single subsidiary's point of view but contributes nothing to worldwide cash flows.

◆ The parent must explicitly recognize remittance of funds because of differing tax systems, legal and political constraints on the movement of funds, local business norms, and differences in the way financial markets and institutions function.

◆ An array of nonfinancial payments can generate cash flows from subsidiaries to the parent, including payment of license fees and payments for imports from the parent.

◆ Managers must anticipate differing rates of national inflation because of their potential to cause changes in competitive position, and thus changes in cash flows over a period of time.

◆ Managers must keep the possibility of unanticipated foreign exchange rate changes in mind because of possible direct effects on the value of local cash flows, as well as indirect effects on the competitive position of the foreign subsidiary.

◆ Use of segmented national capital markets may create an opportunity for financial gains or may lead to additional financial costs.

◆ Use of host-government subsidized loans complicates both capital structure and the parent's ability to determine an appropriate weighted average cost of capital for discounting purposes.

◆ Managers must evaluate political risk because political events can drastically reduce the value or availability of expected cash flows.

◆ Terminal value is more difficult to estimate because potential purchasers from the host, parent, or third countries, or from the private or public sector, may have widely divergent perspectives on the value to them of acquiring the project.

Since the same theoretical capital budgeting framework is used to choose among competing foreign and domestic projects, it is critical that we have a common standard. Thus, all foreign complexities must be quantified as modifications to either expected cash flow or the rate of discount. Although in practice many firms make such modifications arbitrarily, readily available information, theoretical deduction, or just plain common sense can be used to make less arbitrary and more reasonable choices.

Project versus Parent Valuation

A strong theoretical argument exists in favor of analyzing any foreign project from the viewpoint of the parent. Cash flows to the parent are ultimately the basis for dividends to stockholders, reinvestment elsewhere in the world, repayment of corporate-wide debt, and other purposes that affect the firm's many interest groups. However, since most of a project's cash flows to its parent, or to sister subsidiaries, are financial cash flows rather than operating cash flows, the parent viewpoint usually violates a cardinal concept of capital budgeting, namely, that financial cash flows should not be mixed with operating cash flows. Often the difference is not important because the two are almost identical, but in some instances a sharp divergence in these cash flows will exist. For example, funds that are permanently blocked from repatriation, or "forcibly reinvested," are not available for dividends to the stockholders or for repayment of parent corporate debt. Therefore, shareholders will not perceive the blocked earnings as contributing to the value of the firm, and creditors will not count on them in calculating interest coverage ratios and other evidence of ability to service debt.

Evaluation of a project from the local viewpoint serves some useful purposes, but it should be subordinated to evaluation from the parent's viewpoint. In evaluating a foreign project's performance relative to the potential of a competing project in the same host country, we must pay attention to the project's local return. Almost any project should at least be able to earn a cash return equal to the yield available on host government bonds with a maturity the same as the project's economic life, if a free market exists for such bonds. Host-government bonds ordinarily reflect the local risk-free rate of return, including a premium equal to the expected rate of inflation. If a project cannot earn more than such a bond yield, the parent firm should buy host government bonds rather than invest in a riskier project—or, better yet, invest somewhere else!

Multinational firms should invest only if they can earn a risk-adjusted return greater than locally based competitors can earn on the same project. If they are unable to earn superior returns on foreign projects, their stockholders would be better off buying shares in local firms, where possible, and letting those companies carry out the local projects. Apart from these theoretical arguments, surveys over the past 35 years show that in practice multinational firms continue to evaluate foreign investments from both the parent and project viewpoint.

The attention paid to project returns in various surveys probably reflects emphasis on maximizing reported consolidated net earnings per share as a corporate financial goal. As long as foreign earnings are not blocked, they can be consolidated with the earnings of both the remaining subsidiaries and the parent. As mentioned previously, U.S. firms must consolidate foreign subsidiaries that are over 50% owned. If a firm is owned between 20% and 49% by a parent, it is called an *affiliate*. Affiliates are consolidated with the parent owner on a pro rata basis. Subsidiaries less than 20% owned are normally carried as unconsolidated investments. Even in the case of temporarily blocked funds, some of the most mature MNEs do not necessarily eliminate a project from financial consideration. They take a very long-run view of world business opportunities.

If reinvestment opportunities in the country where funds are blocked are at least equal to the parent firm's required rate of return (after adjusting for anticipated exchange rate changes), temporary blockage of transfer may have little practical effect on the capital budgeting outcome, because future project cash flows will be increased by the returns on forced reinvestment. Since large multinationals hold a portfolio of domestic and foreign projects, corporate liquidity is not impaired if a few projects have blocked funds; alternate sources of funds are available to meet all planned uses of funds. Furthermore, a long-run historical perspective on blocked funds does indeed lend support to the belief that funds are almost never permanently blocked. However, waiting for the release of such funds can be frustrating, and sometimes the blocked funds lose value while blocked because of inflation or unexpected exchange rate deterioration, even though they have been reinvested in the host country to protect at least part of their value in real terms.

In conclusion, most firms appear to evaluate foreign projects from both parent and project viewpoints. The parent's viewpoint gives results closer to the traditional meaning of net present value in capital budgeting. Project valuation provides a closer approximation of the effect on consolidated earnings per share, which all surveys indicate is of major concern to practicing managers. To illustrate the foreign complexities of multinational capital budgeting, we analyze a hypothetical market-seeking foreign direct investment by Cemex in Indonesia.

Illustrative Case: Cemex Enters Indonesia[1]

It is early in 1998. Cementos Mexicanos, Cemex, is considering the construction of a cement manufacturing facility on the Indonesian island of Sumatra. The project, Semen Indonesia (the Indonesian word for "cement" is semen), would be a wholly owned greenfield investment with a total installed capacity of 20 million metric tonnes per year (mmt/y). Although that is large by Asian production standards, Cemex believes that its latest cement manufacturing technology would be most efficiently utilized with a production facility of this scale.

Cemex has three driving reasons for the project: 1) the firm wishes to initiate a productive presence of its own in Southeast Asia, a relatively new market for Cemex; 2) the long-term prospects for Asian infrastructure development and growth appear very good over the longer term; and 3) there are positive prospects for Indonesia to act as a produce-for-export site as a result of the depreciation of the Indonesian rupiah (Rp) in 1997.

Cemex, the world's third-largest cement manufacturer, is an MNE headquartered in an emerging market but competing in a global arena. The firm competes in the global marketplace for both market share and capital. The international cement market, like markets in other commodities such as oil, is a dollar-based market. For this reason, and for comparisons against its major competitors in both Germany and Switzerland, Cemex considers the U.S. dollar its functional currency.

Cemex's shares are listed in both Mexico City and New York (OTC: CMXSY). The firm has successfully raised capital—both debt and equity—outside Mexico in U.S. dollars. Its investor base is increasingly global, with the U.S. share turnover rising rapidly as a percentage of total trading. As a result, its cost and availability of capital are internationalized and dominated by U.S. dollar investors. Ultimately, the Semen Indonesia project will be evaluated—in both cash flows and capital cost—in U.S. dollars.

Overview

A road map of the complete multinational capital budgeting analysis for Cemex in Indonesia is illustrated in Exhibit 16.1. The basic principle is that, starting at the top left, the parent company invests U.S. dollar denominated capital, which flows clockwise through the creation and operation of an Indonesian subsidiary, which then generates cash flows that are eventually returned in a variety of forms to the parent company—in U.S. dollars. The first step is to construct a set of pro forma financial statements for Semen Indonesia, all in Indonesian rupiah (Rp). The next step is to create two capital budgets, the *project viewpoint* and *parent viewpoint*.

Semen Indonesia will take only one year to build the plant, with actual operations commencing in year 1. The Indonesian government has only recently deregulated the heavier

[1]Cemex is a real company. However, the greenfield investment described here is hypothetical.

EXHIBIT 16.1   A Road Map to the Construction of Semen Indonesia's Capital Budget

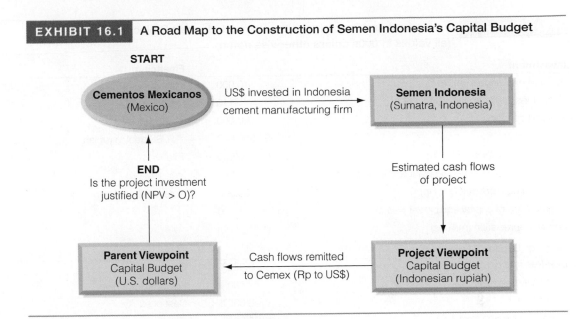

industries to allow foreign ownership. The following analysis is conducted assuming that purchasing power parity (PPP) holds for the Rp/US$ exchange rate for the life of the Indonesian project. This is a standard financial assumption made by Cemex for its foreign investments. The projected inflation rates for Indonesia and the United States are 30% per annum and 3% per annum, respectively.

If we assume an initial spot rate of Rp10,000/US$, and Indonesian and U.S. inflation rates of 30% and 3% per annum, respectively, for the life of the project, forecasted spot exchange rates follow the usual PPP calculation. For example, the forecasted exchange rate for year 1 of the project would be as follows:

$$\text{Spot rate (year 1)} = \text{Rp10,000/US\$} \times \frac{1 + .30}{1 + .03} = \text{Rp12,621/US\$}$$

The following series of financial statements are based on these assumptions.

Capital Investment. Although the cost of building new cement manufacturing capacity anywhere in the industrial countries is now estimated at roughly $150/tonne of installed capacity, Cemex believed that it could build a state-of-the-art production and shipment facility in Sumatra at roughly $110/tonne (see Exhibit 16.2). Assuming a 20 million metric ton per year (mmt/y) capacity, and a year 0 average exchange rate of Rp10,000/$, this cost will constitute an investment of Rp22 trillion ($2.2 billion). This figure includes an investment of Rp17.6 trillion in plant and equipment, giving rise to an annual depreciation charge of Rp1.76 trillion if we assume a 10-year straight-line depreciation schedule. The relatively short depreciation schedule is one of the policies of the Indonesian tax authorities meant to attract foreign investment.

Financing. This massive investment would be financed with 50% equity, all from Cemex, and 50% debt, 75% from Cemex and 25% from a bank consortium arranged by the Indonesian government. Cemex's own U.S. dollar-based weighted average cost of capital (WACC) was currently estimated at 11.98%. The WACC on a local Indonesian level in rupiah terms, for the project itself, was estimated at 33.257%. The details of this calculation are discussed later in this chapter.

EXHIBIT 16.2   Investment and Financing of the Semen Indonesia Project (all values in 000s unless otherwise noted)

Investment

Investment		Financing	
Average exchange rate, Rp/$	10,000	Equity	11,000,000,000
Cost of installed capacity ($/tonne)	$110	Debt:	11,000,000,000
Installed capacity	20,000	Rupiah debt	2,750,000,000
Investment in US$	$2,200,000	US$ debt in rupiah	8,250,000,000
Investment in rupiah	22,000,000,000	Total	22,000,000,000
Percentage of investment in plant and equipment	80%		
Plant and equipment (000s Rp)	17,600,000,000	Note: US$ debt principal	$825,000
Depreciation of capital equipment (years)	10.00		
Annual depreciation (millions)	(1,760,000)		

Costs of Capital: Cemex

Risk-free rate	6.000%	Cemex beta	1.50
Credit premium	2.000%	Equity risk premium	7.000%
Cost of debt	8.000%	Cost of equity	16.500%
Corporate income tax rate	35.000%	Percent equity	60.0%
Cost of debt after-tax	5.200%	WACC	11.980%
Percent debt	40.0%		

Cost of Capital: Semen Indonesia

Risk-free rate	33.000%	Semen Indonesia beta	1.000
Credit premium	2.000%	Equity risk premium	6.000%
Cost of rupiah debt	35.000%	Cost of equity	40.000%
Indonesia corporate income tax rate	30.000%	Percent equity	50.0%
Cost of US$ debt, after-tax	5.200%	WACC	33.257%
Cost of US$ debt, (rupiah equivalent)	38.835%		
Cost of US$ debt, after-tax (rupiah equivalent)	27.184%		
Percent debt	50.0%		

The cost of the US$ loan is stated in rupiah terms assuming purchasing power parity and U.S. dollar and Indonesian inflation rates of 3% and 30% per annum, respectively, throughout the subject period.

The explicit debt structures, including repayment schedules, are presented in Exhibit 16.3. The loan arranged by the Indonesian government, part of the government's economic development incentive program, is an eight-year loan, in rupiah, at 35% annual interest, fully amortizing. The interest payments are fully deductible against corporate tax liabilities.

The majority of the debt, however, is being provided by the parent company, Cemex. After raising the capital from its financing subsidiary, Cemex will relend the capital to Semen Indonesia. The loan is denominated in U.S. dollars, five years maturity, with an annual interest rate of 10%. Because the debt will have to be repaid from the rupiah earnings of the Indonesian enterprise, the pro forma financial statements are constructed so that the expected costs of servicing the dollar debt are included in the firm's pro forma income statement. The dollar loan, if the rupiah follows the purchasing power parity forecast, will have an effective interest expense in rupiah terms of 38.835% before taxes. We find this rate by determining the internal rate of return of repaying the dollar loan in full in rupiah (see Exhibit 16.3).

EXHIBIT 16.3	Semen Indonesia's Debt Service Schedules and Foreign Exchange Gains/Losses					
Spot rate (Rp/$)	10,000	12,621	15,930	20,106	25,376	32,028
Project Year	0	1	2	3	4	5
Indonesian loan @ 35% for eight years (millions of rupiah)						
Loan principal	2,750,000					
Interest payment		(962,500)	(928,921)	(883,590)	(822,393)	(739,777)
Principal payment		(95,939)	(129,518)	(174,849)	(236,046)	(318,662)
Total payment		(1,058,439)	(1,058,439)	(1,058,439)	(1,058,439)	(1,058,439)
Cemex loan @ 10% for five years (millions of U.S. dollars)						
Loan principal	825					
Interest payment		($82.50)	($68.99)	($54.12)	($37.77)	($19.78)
Principal payment		($135.13)	($148.65)	($163.51)	($179.86)	($197.85)
Total payment		($217.63)	($217.63)	($217.63)	($217.63)	($217.63)
Cemex loan converted to Rp at scheduled and current spot rates (millions of Rp):						
Scheduled at Rp10,000/$:						
Interest payment		(825,000)	(689,867)	(541,221)	(377,710)	(197,848)
Principal payment		(1,351,329)	(1,486,462)	(1,635,108)	(1,798,619)	(1,978,481)
Total payment		(2,176,329)	(2,176,329)	(2,176,329)	(2,176,329)	(2,176,329)
Actual (at current spot rate):						
Interest payment		(1,041,262)	(1,098,949)	(1,088,160)	(958,480)	(633,669)
Principal payment		(1,705,561)	(2,367,915)	(3,287,494)	(4,564,190)	(6,336,691)
Total payment		(2,746,823)	(3,466,864)	(4,375,654)	(5,522,670)	(6,970,360)
Cash flows in Rp on Cemex loan (millions of Rp):						
Total actual cash flows	8,250,000	(2,746,823)	(3,466,864)	(4,375,654)	(5,522,670)	(6,970,360)
IRR of cash flows	38.835%					
Foreign exchange gains (losses) on Cemex loan (millions of Rp):						
Foreign exchange gains (losses) on interest		(216,262)	(409,082)	(546,940)	(580,770)	(435,821)
Foreign exchange gains (losses) on principal		(354,232)	(881,453)	(1,652,385)	(2,765,571)	(4,358,210)
Total foreign exchange losses on debt		(570,494)	(1,290,535)	(2,199,325)	(3,346,341)	(4,794,031)

The loan by Cemex to the Indonesian subsidiary is denominated in U.S. dollars. Therefore, the loan will have to be repaid in U.S. dollars, not rupiah. At the time of the loan agreement, the spot exchange rate is Rp10,000/$. This is the assumption used in calculating the "scheduled" repaying of principal and interest in rupiah. The rupiah, however, is expected to depreciate in line with purchasing power parity. As it is repaid, the "actual" exchange rate will therefore give rise to a foreign exchange loss as it takes more and more rupiah to acquire U.S. dollars for debt service, both principal and interest. The foreign exchange losses on this debt service will be recognized on the Indonesian income statement.

Revenues. Given the current existing cement manufacturing in Indonesia, and its currently depressed state as a result of the Asian crisis, all sales are based on export. The 20 mmt/y facility is expected to operate at only 40% capacity (producing 8 million metric tonnes). Cement produced will be sold in the export market at $58/tonne (delivered). Note also that, at least for the conservative baseline analysis, we assume no increase in the price received over time.

Costs. The cash costs of cement manufacturing (labor, materials, power, etc.) are estimated at Rp115,000 per tonne for 1999, rising at about the rate of inflation, 30% per year. Additional production costs of Rp20,000 per tonne for year 1 are also assumed to rise at the rate of inflation. As a result of all production being exported, loading costs of $2.00/tonne and shipping of $10.00/tonne must also be included. Note that these costs are originally stated in U.S. dollars, and for the purposes of Semen Indonesia's income statement, they must be converted to rupiah terms. This is the case because both shiploading and shipping costs are international services governed by contracts denominated in dollars. As a result, they are expected to rise over time only at the U.S. dollar rate of inflation (3%).

Semen Indonesia's pro forma income statement is illustrated in Exhibit 16.4. This is the typical financial statement measurement of the profitability of any business, whether domestic or international. The baseline analysis assumes a capacity utilization rate of only 40%

EXHIBIT 16.4	Semen Indonesia's Pro Forma Income Statement (millions of rupiah)					
Exchange rate (Rp/US$)	10,000	12,621	15,930	20,106	25,376	32,028
Project Year	0	1	2	3	4	5
Sales volume		8.00	10.00	12.00	12.00	12.00
Sales price (US$)		58.00	58.00	58.00	58.00	58.00
Sales price (Rp)		732,039	923,933	1,166,128	1,471,813	1,857,627
Total revenue		5,856,311	9,239,325	13,993,541	17,661,751	22,291,530
Less cash costs		(920,000)	(1,495,000)	(2,332,200)	(3,031,860)	(3,941,418)
Less other production costs		(160,000)	(260,000)	(405,600)	(527,280)	(685,464)
Less loading costs		(201,942)	(328,155)	(511,922)	(665,499)	(865,149)
Less shipping costs		(1,009,709)	(1,640,777)	(2,559,612)	(3,327,495)	(4,325,744)
Total production costs		(2,291,650)	(3,723,932)	(5,809,334)	(7,552,134)	(9,817,774)
Gross profit		3,564,660	5,515,393	8,184,207	10,109,617	12,473,756
Gross margin		*60.9%*	*59.7%*	*58.5%*	*57.2%*	*56.0%*
Less license fees		(117,126)	(184,787)	(279,871)	(353,235)	(445,831)
Less general and administrative		(468,505)	(831,539)	(1,399,354)	(1,942,793)	(2,674,984)
EBITDA		2,979,029	4,499,067	6,504,982	7,813,589	9,352,941
Less depreciation and amortization		(1,760,000)	(1,760,000)	(1,760,000)	(1,760,000)	(1,760,000)
EBIT		1,219,029	2,739,067	4,744,982	6,053,589	7,592,941
Less interest on Cemex debt		(825,000)	(689,867)	(541,221)	(377,710)	(197,848)
Foreign exchange losses on debt		(570,494)	(1,290,535)	(2,199,325)	(3,346,341)	(4,794,031)
Less interest on local debt		(962,500)	(928,921)	(883,590)	(822,393)	(739,777)
EBT		(1,138,965)	(170,256)	1,120,846	1,507,145	1,861,285
Less income taxes (30%)		—	—	—	(395,631)	(558,386)
Net income		(1,138,965)	(170,256)	1,120,846	1,111,514	1,302,900
Net income (millions of US$)		(90)	(11)	56	44	41
Return on sales		*−19.4%*	*−1.8%*	*8.0%*	*6.3%*	*5.8%*
Dividends distributed		—	—	560,423	555,757	651,450
Retained		(1,138,965)	(170,256)	560,423	555,757	651,450

EBITDA = earnings before interest, taxes, depreciation, and amortization; EBIT = earnings before interest and taxes; EBT = earnings before taxes.

Tax credits resulting from current period losses are carried forward toward next year's tax liablities. Dividends are not distributed in the first year of operations as a result of losses, and are distributed at a 50% rate in years 2000–2003.

All calculations are exact, but may appear not to add due to reported decimal places . The tax payment for year 3 is zero, and year 4 is less than 30%, as a result of tax loss carry-forwards from previous years.

(year 1), 50% (year 2), and 60% in the following years. Management believes this is necessary since existing in-country cement manufacturers are averaging only 40% of capacity at this time.

Additional expenses in the pro forma financial analysis include license fees paid by the subsidiary to the parent company of 2.0% of sales, and general and administrative expenses for Indonesian operations of 8.0% per year (and growing an additional 1% per year). Foreign exchange gains and losses are those related to the servicing of the U.S. dollar-denominated debt provided by the parent and are drawn from the bottom of Exhibit 16.3. In summary, the subsidiary operation is expected to begin turning an accounting profit in its fourth year of operations (2000), with profits rising as capacity utilization increases over time.

Project Viewpoint Capital Budget

The capital budget for the Semen Indonesia project from a project viewpoint is shown in Exhibit 16.5. We find the net cash flow, or *free cash flow* as it is often called, by summing EBITDA (earnings before interest, taxes, depreciation, and amortization), recalculated taxes, and changes in net working capital (the sum of the net additions to receivables, inventories, and payables necessary to support sales growth).

Note that EBIT, not EBT, is used in the capital budget, which contains both depreciation and interest expense. Depreciation and amortization are noncash expenses of the firm and therefore contribute positive cash flow. Because the capital budget creates cash flows that will be discounted to present value with a discount rate, and the discount rate includes the cost of debt—interest—we do not wish to subtract interest twice. Therefore, taxes are recalculated on the basis of EBITDA. (This highlights the distinction between an income statement and a capital budget. The project's income statement shows losses the first two years of operations as a result of interest expenses and forecast foreign exchange losses, so it is not expected to pay taxes. But the capital budget, constructed on the basis of EBITDA, before these financing and foreign exchange expenses, calculates a positive tax payment.) The firm's cost of capital used in discounting also includes the deductibility of debt interest in its calculation.

EXHIBIT 16.5	Semen Indonesia Capital Budget: Project Viewpoint (millions of rupiah)					
Exchange rate (Rp/US$)	10,000	12,621	15,930	20,106	25,376	32,028
Project Year	0	1	2	3	4	5
EBIT		1,219,029	2,739,067	4,744,982	6,053,589	7,592,941
Less recalculated taxes @ 30%		(365,709)	(821,720)	(1,423,495)	(1,816,077)	(2,277,882)
Add back depreciation		1,760,000	1,760,000	1,760,000	1,760,000	1,760,000
Net operating cash flow		2,613,320	3,677,347	5,081,487	5,997,512	7,075,059
Less changes to NWC		(240,670)	(139,028)	(436,049)	(289,776)	(626,314)
Initial investment	(22,000,000)					
Terminal value	–	–	–	–	–	21,274,102
Free cash flow (FCF)	(22,000,000)	2,372,650	3,538,319	4,645,438	5,707,736	27,722,847
NPV @ 33.257%	(7,855,886)					
IRR	18.6%					

NWC = net working capital; NPV = net present value. Discount rate is Semen Indonesia's WACC of 33.257%. IRR = internal rate of return, the rate of discount yielding an NPV of exactly zero. Values in exhibit are exact and are rounded to the nearest million.

The initial investment of Rp22 trillion is the total capital invested to support these earnings. Although receivables average 50 to 55 days sales outstanding (DSO) and inventories 65 to 70 DSO, payables and trade credit are also relatively long at 114 DSO in the Indonesian cement industry. Semen Indonesia expects to add approximately 15 net DSO to its investment with sales growth. The remaining elements to complete the project viewpoint's capital budget are the terminal value (discussed below) and the discount rate of 33.257% (the firm's weighted average cost of capital).

Terminal Value. The terminal value (TV) of the project represents the continuing value of the cement manufacturing facility in the years after year 5, the last year of the detailed pro forma financial analysis shown here. This value, like all asset values according to financial theory, is the present value of all future free cash flows that the asset is expected to yield. We calculate the TV as the present value of a perpetual net operating cash flow (NOCF) generated in the fifth year by Semen Indonesia, the growth rate assumed for that net operating cash flow (g), and the firm's weighted average cost of capital (k_{wacc}):

$$\text{Terminal value} = \frac{\text{NOCF}_5\,(1 + g)}{k_{wacc} - g} = \frac{7,075,059\,(1 + 0)}{.33257 - 0} = \text{Rp } 21,274,102$$

or Rp21,274,102 trillion. The assumption that $g = 0$, that is, that net operating cash flows will not grow past year 5 is probably not true, but it is a prudent assumption for Cemex to make when estimating future cash flows.

The results of the capital budget from the project viewpoint indicate a negative net present value (NPV) and an internal rate of return (IRR) of only 18.6% compared to the 33.257% cost of capital. These are the returns the project would yield to a local or Indonesian investor in Indonesian rupiah. The project, from this viewpoint, is not acceptable.

Repatriating Cash Flows to Cemex

Exhibit 16.6 now collects all incremental earnings to Cemex from the prospective investment project in Indonesia. As described in the section preceding the case, a foreign investor's assessment of a project's returns depends on the actual cash flows that are returned to it, in its own currency. For Cemex, this means that the investment must be analyzed in terms of U.S. dollar cash inflows and outflows associated with the investment over the life of the project, after-tax, discounted at its appropriate cost of capital.

We build this *parent viewpoint capital budget* in two steps:

1. First, we isolate the individual cash flows, adjusted for any withholding taxes imposed by the Indonesian government and converted to U.S. dollars. (Statutory withholding taxes on international transfers are set by bilateral tax treaties, but individual firms may negotiate lower rates with governmental tax authorities. In the case of Semen Indonesia, dividends will be charged a 15% withholding tax, 10% on interest payments, and 5% license fees.) Mexico does not tax repatriated earnings since they have already been taxed in Indonesia. (The United States does levy a contingent tax on repatriated earnings of foreign source income, as discussed in Chapter 14.)

2. The second step, the actual *parent viewpoint capital budget*, combines these U.S. dollar after-tax cash flows with the initial investment to determine the net present value of the proposed Semen Indonesia subsidiary in the eyes (and pocketbook) of Cemex. This is illustrated in Exhibit 16.6, which shows all incremental earnings to Cemex from the prospective investment project. A specific peculiarity of this parent viewpoint capital budget is that only the capital invested into the project by Cemex itself, $1,925 million, is

EXHIBIT 16.6	Semen Indonesia's Remittance of Income to Parent Company (millions of rupiah and US$)					
Exchange Rate (Rp/US$)	10,000	12,621	15,930	20,106	25,376	32,028
Project Year	0	1	2	3	4	5
Dividend Remittance						
Dividends paid (Rp)		—	—	560,423	555,757	651,450
Less Indonesian withholding taxes		—	—	(84,063)	(83,364)	(97,717)
Net dividend remitted (Rp)		—	—	476,360	472,393	553,732
Net dividend remitted (US$)		—	—	23.69	18.62	17.29
License Fees Remittance						
License fees remitted (Rmb)		117,126	184,787	279,871	353,235	445,831
Less Indonesian withholding taxes		(5,856)	(9,239)	(13,994)	(17,662)	(22,292)
Net license fees remitted (Rmb)		111,270	175,547	265,877	335,573	423,539
Net license fees remitted (US$)		8.82	11.02	13.22	13.22	13.22
Debt Service Remittance						
Promised interest paid (US$)		82.50	68.99	54.12	37.77	19.78
Less Indonesian withholding tax @ 10%		(8.25)	(6.90)	(5.41)	(3.78)	(1.98)
Net interest remitted (US$)		74.25	62.09	48.71	33.99	17.81
Principal payments remitted (US$)		135.13	148.65	163.51	179.86	197.85
Total principal and interest remitted		$209.38	$210.73	$212.22	$213.86	$215.65
Capital Budget: Parent Viewpoint (millions of U.S. dollars)						
Dividends		—	—	23.7	18.6	17.3
License fees		8.8	11.0	13.2	13.2	13.2
Debt service		209.4	210.7	212.2	213.9	215.7
Total earnings		218.2	221.8	249.1	245.7	246.2
Initial investment	(1,925.0)					
Terminal value	—	—	—	—	—	664.2
Net cash flows	(1,925.0)	218.2	221.8	249.1	245.7	910.4
NPV @ 17.98%	(903.9)					
IRR	−1.12%					

NPV calculated using a company-determined discount rate of WACC + foreign investment premium, or 11.98% + 6.00% = 17.98%.

included in the initial investment (the $1,100 million in equity and the $825 million loan). The Indonesian debt of Rp 2.75 billion ($275 million) is not included in the Cemex parent viewpoint capital budget.

Parent Viewpoint Capital Budget

Finally, all cash flow estimates are now constructed to form the parent viewpoint's capital budget, detailed in the bottom of Exhibit 16.6. The cash flows generated by Semen Indonesia from its Indonesian operations, dividends, license fees, debt service, and terminal value are now valued in U.S. dollar terms after-tax.

In order to evaluate the project's cash flows that are returned to the parent company, Cemex must discount these at the corporate cost of capital. Remembering that Cemex considers its functional currency to be the U.S. dollar, it calculates its cost of capital in U.S.

dollars. As described in Chapter 12, the customary weighted average cost of capital formula is as follows:

$$k_{\text{wacc}} = k_e \frac{E}{V} + k_d (1 - t) \frac{D}{V},$$

k_e = risk-adjusted cost of equity

k_d = before-tax cost of debt

t = marginal tax rate

E = market value of the firm's equity

D = market value of the firm's debt

V = total market value of the firm's securities $(E + D)$

Cemex's cost of equity is calculated using the capital asset pricing model (CAPM):

$$k_e = k_{rf} + (k_m - k_{rf}) \, \beta_{\text{Cemex}} = 6.00\% + (13.00\% - 6.00\%) \, 1.5 = 16.50\%$$

k_e = risk-adjusted cost of equity

k_{rf} = risk-free rate of interest (U.S. Treasury intermediate bond yield)

k_m = expected rate of return in U.S. equity markets (large stock)

β_{Cemex} = measure of Cemex's individual risk relative to the market

The calculation assumes the current risk-free rate is 6.00%, the expected return on U.S. equities is 13.00%, and Cemex's beta is 1.5. The result is a cost of equity—required rate of return on equity investment in Cemex—of 16.50%.

The investment will be funded internally by the parent company, roughly in the same debt/equity proportions as the consolidated firm, 40% debt (D/V) and 60% equity (E/V). The current cost of debt for Cemex is 8.00%, and the effective tax rate is 35%. The cost of equity, when combined with the other components, results in a weighted average cost of capital for Cemex of

$$k_{\text{wacc}} = k_e \frac{E}{V} + k_d (1 - t) \frac{D}{V} = (16.50\%)(.60) + (8.00\%)(1 - .35)(.40) = 11.98\%$$

Cemex customarily uses this weighted average cost of capital of 11.98% to discount prospective investment cash flows for project ranking purposes. The Indonesian investment poses a variety of risks, however, which the typical domestic investment does not.

If Cemex were undertaking an investment of the same relative degree of risk as the firm itself, a simple discount rate of 11.980% might be adequate. Cemex, however, generally requires new investments to yield an additional 3% over the cost of capital for domestic investments, and 6% more for international projects (these are company required spreads, and will differ dramatically across companies). The discount rate for Semen Indonesia's cash flows repatriated to Cemex will therefore be discounted at 11.98% + 6.00%, or 17.98%. The project's baseline analysis indicates a negative NPV with an IRR of −1.12%, which means that it is an unacceptable investment from the parent's viewpoint.

Most corporations require that new investments more than cover the cost of the capital employed in their undertaking. It is therefore not unusual for the firm to require a hurdle rate of 3% to 6% above its cost of capital in order to identify potential investments that will literally add value to stockholder wealth. An NPV of zero means the investment is "acceptable," but NPV values that exceed zero are literally the present value of wealth that is expected to be added to that of the firm and its shareholders. For foreign projects, as discussed previously, we must adjust for agency costs and foreign exchange risks and costs.

Sensitivity Analysis: Project Viewpoint

So far, the project investigation team has used a set of "most likely" assumptions to forecast rates of return. It is now time to subject the most likely outcome to sensitivity analyses. The same probabilistic techniques are available to test the sensitivity of results to political and foreign exchange risks as are used to test sensitivity to business and financial risks. Many decision makers feel more uncomfortable about the necessity to guess probabilities for unfamiliar political and foreign exchange events than they do about guessing their own more familiar business or financial risks. Therefore, it is more common to test sensitivity to political and foreign exchange risk by simulating what would happen to net present value and earnings under a variety of "what if" scenarios.

Political Risk. What if Indonesia should impose controls on the payment of dividends or license fees to Cemex? The impact of blocked funds on the rate of return from Cemex's perspective would depend on when the blockage occurs, what reinvestment opportunities exist for the blocked funds in Indonesia, and when the blocked funds would eventually be released to Cemex. We could simulate various scenarios for blocked funds and rerun the cash flow analysis in Exhibit 16.6 to estimate the effect on Cemex's rate of return.

What if Indonesia should expropriate Semen Indonesia? The effect of expropriation would depend on the following factors:

1. When the expropriation occurs, in terms of number of years after the business began operation
2. How much compensation the Indonesian government will pay, and how long after expropriation the payment will be made
3. How much debt is still outstanding to Indonesian lenders, and whether the parent, Cemex, will have to pay this debt because of its parental guarantee
4. The tax consequences of the expropriation
5. Whether the future cash flows are forgone

Many expropriations eventually result in some form of compensation to the former owners. This compensation can come from a negotiated settlement with the host government or from payment of political risk insurance by the parent government. Negotiating a settlement takes time, and the eventual compensation is sometimes paid in installments over a further period of time. Thus, the present value of the compensation is often much lower than its nominal value. Furthermore, most settlements are based on book value of the firm at the time of expropriation rather than the firm's market value.

The tax consequences of expropriation would depend on the timing and amount of capital loss recognized by Mexico. This loss would usually be based on the uncompensated book value of the Indonesian investment. The problem is that there is often some doubt as to when a write-off is appropriate for tax purposes, particularly if negotiations for a settlement drag on. In some ways, a nice clear expropriation without hope of compensation, such as occurred in Cuba in the early 1960s, is preferred to a slow "bleeding death" in protracted negotiations. The former leads to an earlier use of the tax shield and a one-shot write-off against earnings, whereas the latter tends to depress earnings for years, as legal and other costs continue and no tax shelter is achieved.

Foreign Exchange Risk. The project team assumed that the Indonesian rupiah would depreciate versus the U.S. dollar at the purchasing power parity "rate" (approximately 20.767% per year in the baseline analysis). What if the rate of rupiah depreciation were greater? Although this event would make the assumed cash flows to Cemex worth less in dollars, operating exposure analysis would be necessary to determine whether the cheaper rupiah made Semen Indonesia more competitive. For example, since Semen Indonesia's exports to Taiwan are denominated in U.S. dollars, a weakening of the rupiah versus the dollar could result in greater rupiah earnings from those export sales. This serves to somewhat offset the imported components that Semen Indonesia purchases from the parent company that are also denominated in U.S. dollars. Semen Indonesia is representative of firms today which have both cash inflows and outflows denominated in foreign currencies, providing a partial natural hedge against currency movements.

What if the rupiah should appreciate against the dollar? The same kind of economic exposure analysis is needed. In this particular case, we might guess that the effect would be positive on both local sales in Indonesia and the value in dollars of dividends and license fees paid to Cemex by Semen Indonesia. Note, however, that an appreciation of the rupiah might lead to more competition within Indonesia from firms in other countries with now-lower cost structures, lessening Semen Indonesia's sales.

Other Sensitivity Variables. The project rate of return to Cemex would also be sensitive to a change in the assumed terminal value, the capacity utilization rate, the size of the license fee paid by Semen Indonesia, the size of the initial project cost, the amount of working capital financed locally, and the tax rates in Indonesia and Mexico. Since some of these variables are within control of Cemex, it is still possible that the Semen Indonesia project could be improved in its value to the firm and become acceptable.

Sensitivity Analysis: Parent Viewpoint Measurement

When a foreign project is analyzed from the parent's point of view, the additional risk that stems from its "foreign" location can be measured in at least two ways, *adjusting the discount rates* or *adjusting the cash flows*.

Adjusting Discount Rates. The first method is to treat all foreign risk as a single problem, by adjusting the discount rate applicable to foreign projects relative to the rate used for domestic projects to reflect the greater foreign exchange risk, political risk, agency costs, asymmetric information, and other uncertainties perceived in foreign operations. However, adjusting the discount rate applied to a foreign project's cash flow to reflect these uncertainties does not penalize net present value in proportion either to the actual amount at risk or to possible variations in the nature of that risk over time. Combining all risks into a single discount rate may thus cause us to discard much information about the uncertainties of the future.

In the case of foreign exchange risk, changes in exchange rates have a potential effect on future cash flows because of operating exposure. The direction of the effect, however, can either decrease or increase net cash inflows, depending on where the products are sold and where inputs are sourced. To increase the discount rate applicable to a foreign project, on the assumption that the foreign currency might depreciate more than expected, ignores the possible favorable effect of a foreign currency depreciation on the project's competitive position. Increased sales volume might more than offset a lower value of the local currency. Such an increase in the discount rate also ignores the possibility that the foreign currency may appreciate (two-sided risk).

Adjusting Cash Flows. In the second method, we incorporate foreign risks in adjustments to forecasted cash flows of the project. The discount rate for the foreign project is risk-adjusted only for overall business and financial risk, in the same manner as for domestic projects. Simulation-based assessment utilizes scenario development to estimate cash flows to the parent arising from the project over time under different alternative economic futures.

Certainty regarding the quantity and timing of cash flows in a prospective foreign investment is, to quote Shakespeare, "the stuff that dreams are made of." Due to the complexity of economic forces at work in major investment projects, it is paramount that the analyst realize the subjectivity of the forecast cash flows. Humility in analysis is a valuable trait.

Shortcomings of Each. In many cases, however, neither adjusting the discount rate nor adjusting cash flows is optimal. For example, political uncertainties are a threat to the entire investment, not just the annual cash flows. Potential loss depends partly on the terminal value of the unrecovered parent investment, which will vary depending on how the project was financed, whether political risk insurance was obtained, and what investment horizon is contemplated. Furthermore, if the political climate were expected to be unfavorable in the near future, any investment would probably be unacceptable. Political uncertainty usually relates to possible adverse events that might occur in the more distant future, but that cannot be foreseen at the present. Adjusting the discount rate for political risk thus penalizes early cash flows too heavily while not penalizing distant cash flows enough.

Repercussions to the Investor. Apart from anticipated political and foreign exchange risks, MNEs sometimes worry that taking on foreign projects may increase the firm's overall cost of capital because of investors' perceptions of foreign risk. This worry seemed reasonable if a firm had significant investments in Iraq, Iran, Russia, Serbia, or Afghanistan in the 1990s. However, the argument loses persuasiveness when applied to diversified foreign investments with a heavy balance in the industrial countries of Canada, Western Europe, Australia, Latin America, and Asia where, in fact, the bulk of FDI is located. These countries have a reputation for treating foreign investments by consistent standards, and empirical evidence confirms that a foreign presence in these countries may not increase the cost of capital. In fact, some studies indicate that required returns on foreign projects may even be lower than those for domestic projects.

MNE Practices. Surveys of MNEs over the past 35 years have shown that about half of them adjust the discount rate and half adjust the cash flows. One recent survey indicated a rising use of adjusting discount rates over adjusting cash flows. However, the survey also indicated an increasing use of multifactor methods—discount rate adjustment, cash flow adjustment, real options analysis, and qualitative criteria—in evaluating foreign investments.[2]

Portfolio Risk Measurement

The field of finance has distinguished two different definitions of risk: 1) the risk of the individual security (standard deviation of expected return) and 2) the risk of the individual security as a component of a portfolio (*beta*). A foreign investment undertaken in order to enter a local or regional market—market seeking—will have returns that are more or less correlated with those of the local market. A portfolio-based assessment of the investment's prospects would then seem appropriate. A foreign investment undertaken for *resource-seeking* or *production-seeking* purposes may have returns related to those of the parent company or units located somewhere else in the world and have little to do with local markets. Cemex's proposed investment in Semen Indonesia is both *market seeking* and *production seeking* (for export). The decision about which approach is to be used by the MNE in evaluating prospective foreign investments may be the single most important

---

[2]Tom Keck, Eric Levengood, and Al Longfield, "Using Discounted Cash Flow Analysis in an International Setting: A Survey of Issues in Modeling the Cost of Capital," *Journal of Applied Corporate Finance*, Vol 11, Number 3, Fall 1998, pp. 82–99.

analytical decision it makes. An investment's acceptability may change dramatically from one criteria to the other.

For comparisons within the local host country, we should overlook a project's actual financing or parent-influenced debt capacity, since these would probably be different for local investors than they are for a multinational owner. In addition, the risks of the project to local investors might differ from those perceived by a foreign multinational owner because of the opportunities an MNE has to take advantage of market imperfections. Moreover, the local project may be only one out of an internationally diversified portfolio of projects for the multinational owner; if undertaken by local investors it might have to stand alone without international diversification. Since diversification reduces risk, the MNE can require a lower rate of return than is required by local investors.

Thus, the discount rate used locally must be a hypothetical rate based on a judgment as to what independent local investors would probably demand were they to own the business. Consequently, application of the local discount rate to local cash flows provides only a rough measure of the value of the project as a stand-alone local venture, rather than an absolute valuation.

Real Option Analysis

The discounted cash flow (DCF) approach used in the valuation of Semen Indonesia—and capital budgeting and valuation in general—has long had its critics. Investments that have long lives, cash flow returns in later years, or higher levels of risk than those typical of the firm's current business activities are often rejected by traditional DCF financial analysis. More importantly, when MNEs evaluate competitive projects, traditional discounted cash flow analysis is typically unable to capture the strategic options that an individual investment option may offer. This has led to the development of real option analysis. Real option analysis is the application of option theory to capital budgeting decisions.

Real options is a different way of thinking about investment values. At its core, it is a cross between decision-tree analysis and pure option-based valuation. It is particularly useful when analyzing investment projects that will follow very different value paths at decision points in time where management decisions are made regarding project pursuit. This wide range of potential outcomes is at the heart of real option theory. These wide ranges of value are volatilities, the basic element of option pricing theory described previously.

Real option valuation also allows us to analyze a number of managerial decisions which in practice characterize many major capital investment projects:

◆ The option to defer
◆ The option to abandon
◆ The option to alter capacity
◆ The option to start up or shut down (switching)

Real option analysis treats cash flows in terms of future value in a positive sense, whereas DCF treats future cash flows negatively (on a discounted basis). Real option analysis is a particularly powerful device when addressing potential investment projects with extremely long life spans, or investments that do not commence until future dates. Real option analysis acknowledges the way information is gathered over time to support decision making. Management learns from both active (searching it out) and passive (observing market conditions) knowledge gathering and then uses this knowledge to make better decisions.

Project Financing

One of the hottest topics in international finance today is *project finance*, which refers to the arrangement of financing for long-term capital projects, large in scale, long in life, and generally high in risk. This is a very general definition, however, as there are many different forms and structures which fall under this generic heading.

Project finance is not new. Examples of project finance go back centuries, and include many famous early international businesses such as the Dutch East India Company and the British East India Company. These entrepreneurial importers financed their trade ventures to Asia on a voyage by voyage basis, with each voyage's financing being like venture capital; investors would be repaid when the shipper returned and the fruits of the Asian marketplace were sold at the docks to Mediterranean and European merchants. If all went well, the individual shareholders of the voyage were paid in full.

Project finance is used widely today in the development of large-scale infrastructure projects in China, India, and many other emerging markets. Although each individual project has unique characteristics, most are highly leveraged transactions, with debt making up more than 60% of the total financing. Equity is a small component of project financing for two reasons: first, the simple scale of the investment project often precludes a single investor or even a collection of private investors from being able to fund it; second, many of these projects involve subjects traditionally funded by governments—such as electrical power generation, dam building, highway construction, energy exploration, production, and distribution.

This level of debt, however, places an enormous burden on cash flow for debt service. Therefore, project financing usually requires a number of additional levels of risk reduction. The lenders involved in these investments must feel secure that they will be repaid; bankers are not by nature entrepreneurs, and do not enjoy entrepreneurial returns from project finance. Project finance has a number of basic properties which are critical to its success.

Separability of the Project from Its Investors. The project is established as an individual legal entity, separate from the legal and financial responsibilities of its individual investors. This not only serves to protect the assets of equity investors, but also it provides a controlled platform upon which creditors can evaluate the risks associated with the singular project, the ability of the project's cash flows to service debt, and to rest assured that the debt service payments will be automatically allocated by and from the project itself (and not from a decision by management within an MNE).

Long-Lived and Capital-Intensive Singular Projects. Not only must the individual project be separable and large in proportion to the financial resources of its owners, but also its business line must be singular in its construction, operation, and size (capacity). The size is set at inception, and is seldom, if ever, changed over the project's life.

Cash Flow Predictability from Third Party Commitments. An oil field or electric power plant produces a homogeneous commodity product which can produce predictable cash flows if third party commitments to take and pay can be established. In addition to revenue predictability, nonfinancial costs of production needs to be controlled over time, usually through long-term supplier contracts with price adjustment clauses based on inflation. The predictability of net cash inflows to long-term contracts eliminates much of the individual project's business risk, allowing the financial structure to be heavily debt-financed and still safe from financial distress.

The predictability of the projects revenue stream is essential in securing project financing. Typical contract provisions which are intended to assure adequate cash flow normally include the following clauses: quantity and quality of the project's output; a pricing formula that enhances the predictability of adequate margin to cover operating costs and debt service payments; a clear statement of the circumstances that permits significant changes in the contract such as force majeure or adverse business conditions.

Finite Projects with Finite Lives. Even with a longer-term investment, it is critical that the project have a definite ending point at which all debt and equity has been repaid. Because the project is a stand-alone investment in which its cash flows go directly to the servicing of its capital structure, and not to reinvestment for growth or other investment alternatives, investors of all kinds need assurances that the project's returns will be attained in a finite period. There is no capital appreciation, but only cash flow.

Examples of project finance include some of the largest individual investments undertaken in the past three decades, such as British Petroleum's financing of its interest in the North Sea, and the Trans-Alaska Pipeline. The Trans-Alaska Pipeline was a joint venture between Standard Oil of Ohio, Atlantic Richfield, Exxon, British Petroleum, Mobil Oil, Philips Petroleum, Union Oil, and Amerada Hess. Each of these projects was at or above $1 billion, and represented capital expenditures which no single firm would or could attempt to finance. Yet, through a joint venture arrangement, the higher than normal risk absorbed by the capital employed could be managed.

Cross-Border Mergers and Acquisitions

The drivers of M&A activity, summarized in Exhibit 16.7, are both macro in scope—*the global competitive environment*—and micro in scope—the variety of industry and firm-level forces and actions driving individual firm value. The primary forces of change in the

---

EXHIBIT 16.7   Driving Forces behind Cross Border M & A

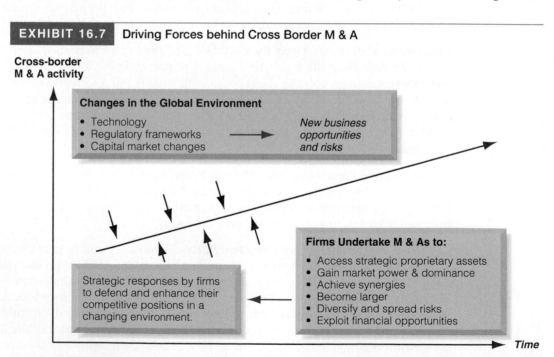

Source: UNCTAD, *World Development Report 2000: Cross-border Mergers and Acquisitions and Development,* figure V.1., p. 154.

global competitive environment—technological change, regulatory change, and capital market change—create new business opportunities for MNEs, which they pursue aggressively.

But the global competitive environment is really just the playing field, the ground upon which the individual players compete. MNEs undertake cross-border mergers and acquisitions for a variety of reasons. As shown in Exhibit 16.7, the drivers are strategic responses by MNEs to defend and enhance their global competitiveness by the following:

◆ Gaining access to strategic proprietary assets

◆ Gaining market power and dominance

◆ Achieving synergies in local/global operations and across different industries

◆ Becoming larger, and then reaping the benefits of size in competition and negotiation

◆ Diversifying and spreading their risks wider

◆ Exploiting financial opportunities they may possess and others desire

As opposed to greenfield investment, a cross-border acquisition has a number of significant advantages. First and foremost, it is quicker. Greenfield investment frequently requires extended periods of physical construction and organizational development. By acquiring an existing firm, the MNE shortens the time required to gain a presence and facilitate competitive entry into the market. Second, acquisition may be a cost-effective way of gaining competitive advantages such as technology, brand names valued in the target market, and logistical and distribution advantages, while simultaneously eliminating a local competitor. Third, specific to cross-border acquisitions, international economic, political, and foreign exchange conditions may result in market imperfections, allowing target firms to be undervalued.

Cross-border acquisitions are not, however, without their pitfalls. As with all acquisitions—domestic or cross-border—there are problems of paying too much or suffering excessive financing costs. Melding corporate cultures can be traumatic. Managing the post-acquisition process is frequently characterized by downsizing to gain economies of scale and scope in overhead functions. This results in nonproductive impacts on the firm as individuals attempt to save their own jobs. Internationally, additional difficulties arise from host governments intervening in pricing, financing, employment guarantees, market segmentation, and general nationalism and favoritism. In fact, the ability to successfully complete cross-border acquisitions may itself be a test of competency of the MNE when entering emerging markets.

The Cross-Border Acquisition Process

Although the field of finance has sometimes viewed acquisition as mainly an issue of valuation, it is a much more complex and rich process than simply determining what price to pay. As depicted in Exhibit 16.8, the process begins with the strategic drivers discussed in the previous section.

The process of acquiring an enterprise anywhere in the world has three common elements: 1) identification and valuation of the target, 2) completion of the ownership change transaction—the *tender*, and 3) management of the post-acquisition transition.

Stage 1: Identification and Valuation

Identification of potential acquisition targets requires a well-defined corporate strategy and focus.

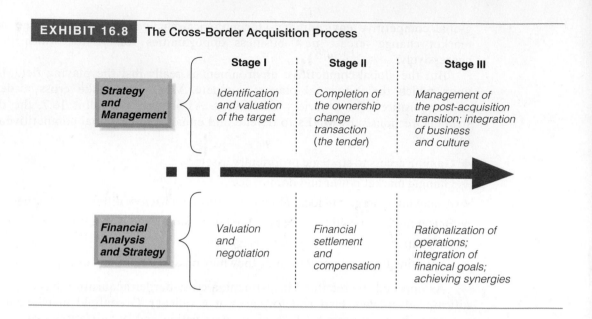

EXHIBIT 16.8   The Cross-Border Acquisition Process

	Stage I	Stage II	Stage III
Strategy and Management	Identification and valuation of the target	Completion of the ownership change transaction (the tender)	Management of the post-acquisition transition; integration of business and culture
Financial Analysis and Strategy	Valuation and negotiation	Financial settlement and compensation	Rationalization of operations; integration of finanical goals; achieving synergies

Identification. The identification of the target market typically precedes the identification of the target firm. Entering a highly developed market offers the widest choice of publicly traded firms with relatively well-defined markets and publicly disclosed financial and operational data. In this case, the tender offer is made publicly, although target company management may openly recommend that its shareholders reject the offer. If enough shareholders take the offer, the acquiring company may gain sufficient ownership influence or control to change management. During this rather confrontational process, it is up to the board of the target company to continue to take actions consistent with protecting the rights of shareholders. The board may need to provide rather strong oversight of management during this process, to ensure that management does not take actions consistent with its own perspective but not with protecting and building shareholder value.

Valuation. Once identification has been completed, the process of valuing the target begins. A variety of valuation techniques are widely used in global business today, each with its relative merits. In addition to the fundamental methodologies of discounted cash flow (DCF) and multiples (earnings and cash flows), there are also a variety of industry-specific measures that focus on the most significant elements of value in business lines. The completion of a variety of alternative valuations for the target firm aids not only in gaining a more complete picture of what price must be paid to complete the transaction, but also in determining whether the price is attractive.

Stage 2: Settlement of the Transaction

The term *settlement* is actually misleading. Once an acquisition target has been identified and valued, the process of gaining approval from management and ownership of the target, getting approvals from government regulatory bodies, and finally determining method of compensation can be time-consuming and complex.

Tender Process. Gaining the approval of the target company has itself been the subject of some of the most historic acquisitions. The critical distinction here is whether the acquisition is supported or not by the target company's management.

Although there is probably no "typical transaction," many acquisitions flow relatively smoothly through a friendly process. The acquiring firm will approach the management of the target company and attempt to convince them of the business logic of the acquisition. (Gaining their support is sometimes difficult, but assuring target company management that it will not be replaced is often quite convincing!) If the target's management is supportive, they may then recommend to stockholders that they accept the offer of the acquiring company. One problem that occasionally surfaces at this stage is that influential shareholders may object to the offer, either in principle or based on price, and therefore feel that management is not taking appropriate steps to protect and build their shareholder value.

The process takes on a very different dynamic when the acquisition is not supported by target company management—the so-called *hostile takeover*. The acquiring company may choose to pursue the acquisition without the target's support and go directly to the target shareholders. In this case, the tender offer is made publicly, although target company management may openly recommend that its shareholders reject the offer. If enough shareholders take the offer, the acquiring company may gain sufficient ownership influence or control to change management. During this rather confrontational process, it is up to the board of the target company to continue to take actions consistent with protecting the rights of shareholders. The board may need to provide rather strong oversight of management during this process, to ensure that management does not take actions consistent with its own perspective but not with protecting and building shareholder value.

Regulatory Approval. An acquisition may be subject to significant regulatory approval if it involves a company in an industry considered fundamental to national security, or if there may be concern over major concentration and anticompetitive results from consolidation.

The proposed acquisition of Honeywell International (itself the result of a merger of Honeywell U.S. and Allied-Signal U.S.) by General Electric (U.S.) in 2001 was something of a watershed event in the field of regulatory approval. General Electric's acquisition of Honeywell had been approved by management, ownership, and U.S. regulatory bodies, when it then sought approval within the European Union. Jack Welch, the charismatic chief executive officer and president of GE did not anticipate the degree of opposition that the merger would face from EU authorities. After a continuing series of demands by the EU that specific businesses within the combined companies be sold off to reduce anticompetitive effects, Welch withdrew the request for acquisition approval, arguing that the liquidations would destroy most of the value-enhancing benefits of the acquisition. The acquisition was canceled. This case may have far-reaching effects on cross-border M&A for years to come, as the power of regulatory authorities within strong economic zones like the EU to block the combination of two MNEs, may foretell a change in regulatory strength and breadth.

Compensation Settlement. The last act within this second stage of cross-border acquisition is the payment to shareholders of the target company. Shareholders of the target company are typically paid either in shares of the acquiring company or in cash. If a share exchange occurs, which exchange may be defined by some ratio of acquiring company shares to target company shares (say, two shares of acquirer in exchange for three shares of target), the stockholder is typically not taxed. The shareholder's shares of ownership have simply been replaced by other shares in a nontaxable transaction.

If cash is paid to the target company shareholder, it is the same as if the shareholder has sold the shares on the open market, resulting in a capital gain or loss (a gain, it is hoped, in the case of an acquisition) with tax liabilities. Because of the tax ramifications, shareholders are typically more receptive to share exchanges so that they may choose whether and when tax liabilities will arise.

A variety of factors go into the determination of type of settlement. The availability of cash, the size of the acquisition, the friendliness of the takeover, and the relative valuations of both acquiring firm and target firm affect the decision. One of the most destructive forces that sometimes arise at this stage is regulatory delay and its impact on the share prices of the two firms. If regulatory body approval drags out over time, the possibility of a drop in share price increases and can change the attractiveness of the share swap.

Stage 3: Post-Acquisition Management

Although the headlines and flash of investment banking activities are typically focused on the valuation and bidding process in an acquisition transaction, post transaction management is probably the most critical of the three stages in determining an acquisition's success or failure. An acquiring firm can pay too little or too much, but if the post transaction is not managed effectively, the entire return on the investment is squandered. Post-acquisition management is the stage in which the motivations for the transaction must be realized. Those reasons, such as more effective management, synergies arising from the new combination, or the injection of capital at a cost and availability previously out of the reach of the acquisition target, must be effectively implemented after the transaction. The biggest problem, however, is nearly always melding corporate cultures.

The clash of corporate cultures and personalities pose both the biggest risk and the biggest potential gain from cross-border mergers and acquisitions. Although not readily measurable like price/earnings ratios or share price premiums, in the end, the value is either gained or lost in the hearts and minds of the stakeholders.

Currency Risks in Cross-Border Acquisitions

The pursuit and execution of a cross-border acquisition poses a number of challenging foreign currency risks and exposures for an MNE. As illustrated by Exhibit 16.9, the nature of the currency exposure related to any specific cross-border acquisition evolves as the bidding

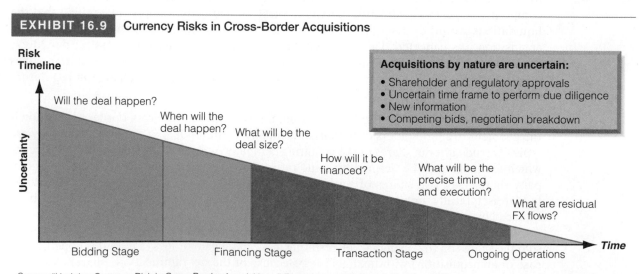

EXHIBIT 16.9   Currency Risks in Cross-Border Acquisitions

Risk Timeline

Uncertainty

Will the deal happen?

When will the deal happen?

What will be the deal size?

How will it be financed?

What will be the precise timing and execution?

What are residual FX flows?

Acquisitions by nature are uncertain:
- Shareholder and regulatory approvals
- Uncertain time frame to perform due diligence
- New information
- Competing bids, negotiation breakdown

Bidding Stage   Financing Stage   Transaction Stage   Ongoing Operations   *Time*

Source: "Hedging Currency Risk in Cross-Border Acquisitions," Eileen Liu and Michael J. Mariano, JPMorgan.

and negotiating process itself evolves across the bidding, financing, transaction (settlement), and operating stages.

The assorted risks, both in the timing and information related to the various stages of a cross-border acquisition, make the management of the currency exposures difficult. As illustrated in Exhibit 16.9, the uncertainty related to the multitude of stages declines over time as stages are completed and contracts and agreements reached.

The initial bid, if denominated in a foreign currency, creates a *contingent foreign currency exposure* for the bidder. This contingent exposure grows in certainty of occurrence over time as negotiations continue, regulatory requests and approvals are gained, and competitive bidders exit. Although a variety of hedging strategies might be employed, the use of a purchased currency call option is the simplest. The option's notional principal would be for the estimated purchase price, but the maturity, for the sake of conservatism, might possibly be significantly longer than probably needed to allow for extended bidding, regulatory, and negotiation delays.

Once the bidder has successfully won the acquisition, the exposure evolves from a contingent exposure to a transaction exposure. Although a variety of uncertainties remain as to the exact timing of the transaction settlement, the certainty over the occurrence of the currency exposure is largely eliminated. Some combination of forward contracts and purchased currency options may then be used to manage the currency risks associated with the completion of the cross-border acquisition.

Once consummated, the currency risks and exposures of the cross-border acquisition, now a property and foreign subsidiary of the MNE, changes from being a transaction-based cash flow exposure to the MNE to part of its multinational structure and therefore part of its operating exposure from that time forward. Time, as is always the case involving currency exposure management in multinational business, is the greatest enemy to the MNE. As illustrated by *Global Finance in Practice 16.1*, however, things do not always work out for the worst.

GLOBAL FINANCE IN PRACTICE   16.1

Statoil of Norway's Acquisition of Esso of Sweden

Statoil's acquisition of Svenska Esso (Exxon's wholly owned subsidiary operating in Sweden) in 1986 was one of the more uniquely challenging cross-border acquisitions ever completed. First, Statoil was the national oil company of Norway, and therefore a government-owned and operated business bidding for a private company in another country. Second, if completed, the acquisition's financing as proposed would increase the financial obligations of Svenska Esso (debt levels and therefore debt-service), reducing the company's tax liabilities to Sweden for many years to come. The proposed cross-border transaction was characterized as a value transfer from the Swedish government to the Norwegian government.

As a result of the extended period of bidding, negotiation, and regulatory approvals, the currency risk of the transaction was both large and extensive. Statoil, being a Norwegian oil company, was a Norwegian kroner (NOK)-based company

with the U.S. dollar as its functional currency as a result of the global oil industry being dollar-denominated. Svenska Esso, although Swedish by incorporation, was the wholly owned subsidiary of a U.S.-based MNE, Exxon, and the final bid and cash settlement on the sale was therefore U.S. dollar-denominated.

On March 26, 1985, Statoil and Exxon agreed upon the sale of Svenska Esso for $260 million, or NOK2.47 billion at the current exchange rate of NOK9.50/$. (This was by all modern standards the weakest the Norwegian krone had ever been against the dollar, and many currency analysts believed the dollar to be significantly overvalued at the time.) The sale could not be consummated without the approval of the Swedish government. That approval process—eventually requiring the approval of Swedish Prime Minister Olaf Palme—took nine months. Because Statoil considered the U.S. dollar as its true operating currency, it chose not to hedge the purchase price currency exposure. At the time of settlement the krone had appreciated to NOK7.65/$, for a final acquisition cost in Norwegian kroner of NOK1.989 billion. Statoil saved nearly 20% on the purchase price, NOK0.481 billion, as a result of not hedging the exposure.

Summary of Learning Objectives

Extend the domestic capital budgeting analysis to evaluate a greenfield foreign project.

◆ The proposed greenfield investment in Indonesia by Cemex was analyzed within the traditional capital budgeting framework (base case).

◆ The foreign complications were introduced to the analysis, including foreign exchange and political risks.

Distinguish between the project viewpoint and the parent viewpoint when analyzing a potential foreign investment.

◆ Parent cash flows must be distinguished from project cash flows. Each of these two types of flows contributes to a different view of value.

◆ Parent cash flows often depend on the form of financing. Thus, cash flows cannot be clearly separated from financing decisions, as is done in domestic capital budgeting.

◆ Remittance of funds to the parent must be explicitly recognized because of differing tax systems, legal and political constraints on the movement of funds, local business norms, and differences in how financial markets and institutions function.

◆ Cash flows from subsidiaries to parent can be generated by an array of nonfinancial payments, including payment of license fees and payments for imports from the parent.

◆ Differing rates of national inflation must be anticipated because of their importance in causing changes in competitive position, and thus in cash flows over a period of time.

Adjust the capital budgeting analysis of a foreign project for risk.

◆ When a foreign project is analyzed from the project's point of view, risk analysis focuses on the use of sensitivities, as well as consideration of foreign exchange and political risks associated with the project's execution over time.

◆ When a foreign project is analyzed from the parent's point of view, the additional risk that stems from its "foreign" location can be measured in at least two ways, *adjusting the discount rates* or *adjusting the cash flows.*

Introduce the use of real option analysis as a complement to discounted cash flow analysis.

◆ Real option analysis is a different way of thinking about investment values. At its core, it is a cross between decision-tree analysis and pure option-based valuation.

◆ Real option valuation allows us to evaluate the option to defer, the option to abandon, the option to alter size or capacity, and the option to start up or shut down a project.

Examine the use of project finance to fund and evaluate large global projects.

◆ Project finance is used widely today in the development of large-scale infrastructure projects in many emerging markets. Although each individual project has unique characteristics, most are highly leveraged transactions, with debt making up more than 60% of the total financing.

◆ Equity is a small component of project financing for two reasons: first, the simple scale of the investment project often precludes a single investor or even a collection of private investors from being able to fund it; second, many of these projects involve subjects traditionally funded by governments—such as electrical power generation, dam building, highway construction, energy exploration, production, and distribution.

Introduce the principles of cross-border mergers and acquisitions.

◆ The process of acquiring an enterprise anywhere in the world has three common elements: 1) identification and valuation of the target; 2) completion of the ownership change transaction (the tender); and 3) the management of the post-acquisition transition.

◆ The settlement stage of a cross-border merger or acquisition requires gaining the approval and cooperation of management, shareholders, and eventually regulatory authorities.

◆ Cross-border mergers, acquisitions, and strategic alliances, all face similar challenges: They must value the target enterprise on the basis of its projected performance in its market. This process of enterprise valuation combines elements of strategy, management, and finance.

MINI-CASE

Yanzhou (China) Bids for Felix Resources (Australia)[1]

On 13 August 2009, the Felix Board announced it had entered into a Scheme Implementation Agreement for an all cash offer by Yanzhou Coal (through its Wholly Owned Subsidiary Austar) to acquire all the issued shares of Felix (the Transaction) to be implemented by way of a scheme of arrangement (the Scheme).

—Felix Resources, *Scheme Booklet*,
30 September 2009, p. 6.

While we continue to believe the emergence of a counter-bidder is likely, the short list has diminished thus reducing the probability of such an outcome. That said, we would not recommend shareholders accept the $18ps offer for now.

—"Felix Resources: A New Year, A New Mine,"
Macquarie Equities, 1 September 2009, p. 1.

To the CEO, Mr Brian Flannery. Dear Brian. The consensus is that the right value is about AUD24 per share. A discrepancy of 33% seems beyond the purported claim of "Fair." As soon as the offer was announced, Yanzhou's share price went up considerably whilst Felix's went down.

—Blog note by Felix shareholder, August 2009.

It was late October 2009, and Quillan and his fellow investors were debating on what to do about their shares in Felix Resources (FLX AU), an Australian coal mining company. Yanzhou Coal Company of China had been courting Felix for nearly a year, and had made a formal offer on August 13 worth AUD18 per share—the *Scheme*, which Felix's Board and management team had endorsed.[2] But many stockholders were not sure the offer was a good one. When Yanzhou had first approached Felix in December 2008, the offer had been AUD20 per share. But a lot had changed since then, including the price of coal, the value of the Australian dollar, and concerns over Chinese acquisitions of Australian mineral producers. Shareholders were now being pressured to accept the *Scheme*.

China, Coal, and Yanzhou Coal Company

The Chinese economy consumed massive quantities of coal. The rapid economic growth of China drove the demand for both thermal or steam coal (for electrical

power production) and coking coal (for steel production) ever skyward. Coal-fired electric power provided roughly 80% of China's electricity, and was expected to stay at that level for a number of years. In 2008 alone, China, accounted for 43% of global coal consumption.

Chinese Coal. China was rich in coal itself, with reserves of its own estimated at 14% of global reserves. Although a global commodity, most of the world's countries consume coal in the country where it is produced, with one large exception—Australia. Australia exports 75% of its production, mostly to Japan, South Korea, and China.

But the Chinese coal market had grown increasingly complex. The Chinese government had imposed a freeze on all new coal exports in February 2008 and increased its export tax to 13% on existing export commitments. At the same time, China had ordered more than 15,000 small coal mines closed in recent years, primarily a result of unsafe working conditions and continued mine accidents. With much of China's coal reserves in the far north and west of the country, far from the coastal markets and not readily accessible, China has been looking more and more to foreign markets to fulfill its growing coal demands.

Thus, Chinese coal companies have been looking to purchase more coal from outside China. Because of its proximity, high level of development and abundant natural resources, Australia had been the target of a number of these Chinese acquisition efforts. One such purchase attempt had generated negative press and strained relationships between the two governments. In June 2009, Australian-based Rio Tinto rejected China's Chinalco's bid to purchase its major mining assets and partnered with rival BHP Billiton in a shocking last-minute effort. Despite the tensions, Chinese companies continued to buy overseas assets.

Coal Prices. As illustrated in Exhibit 1, Australian thermal coal prices had long been relatively flat—at least until 2008. Strong demand from countries such as Japan, South Korea, and China, and limited supply due to inclement weather and under-sized ports in Australia, had induced a price run-up in mid-2008.[3]

But just as quickly as they had gone up, coal prices collapsed. The global recession caused coal demand and prices to fall in late 2008. But they did not stay down for long, as the Chinese and Indian economies recovered relatively

[2]The Australian dollar, depending on the source cited, may be shown as AUD, A$, or $.

[3]Note that Australian coal prices are quoted in U.S. dollars. This is in-line with global practice of pricing coal in U.S. dollars, similar in industry practice to that of oil or other major global commodities.

| EXHIBIT 1 | Australian Thermal Coal Price (January 2001–October 2009) |

USD/metric tonne

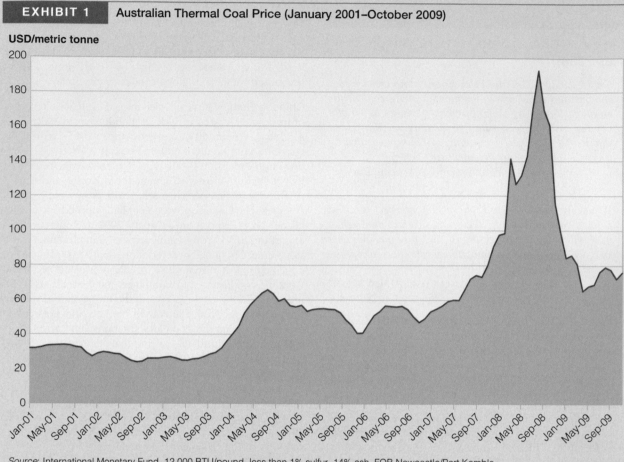

Source: International Monetary Fund. 12,000 BTU/pound, less than 1% sulfur, 14% ash. FOB Newcastle/Port Kembla.

quickly, once again stoking the demand for coal. Yanzhou, as part of its valuation of Felix, believes that coal prices are likely to stay between USD88 and USD104 per tonne for several years.

Yanzhou Coal Company. With expected 2009 revenues and after-tax profits of HKD19 billion and HKD6.1 billion, respectively, Yanzhou Coal Company was China's fourth largest coal producer. The company was also representative of much of China's new industry, as it was both government-controlled but publicly traded. Yanzhou was listed on the Hong Kong Stock Exchange, the New York Stock Exchange, and the Shanghai Stock Exchange. Its total market capitalization was RMB70.1 billion (USD10.3 billion) on September 30, 2009.

Yanzhou had begun its investment in Australian coal in 2004 when it acquired the Austar coal mine. But since that time, Yanzhou had failed to increase production from Austar significantly, the company falling behind its strategic

plan. Additionally, because of stricter safety requirements, production had fallen at six of its mines in Shandong Province, China. Therefore, without the purchase of Felix, Yanzhou's production would plateau and it risked falling behind its competitors.

Felix Resources Limited (Australia). Felix Resources Limited of Australia (FLX.AU) was Australia's 12th largest coal mining firm. Felix was expected to close 2009 with more than AUD260 million in profits on more than AUD680 million in sales. The company owned four underground and open cut mines in New South Wales and Queensland, and was expanding its mining operations at Moolarben in New South Wales. Felix sold the majority of its production to the export market—to South Korea, Japan, and now China.

Felix also owned 15% interest in the Newcastle Coal Infrastructure Group port under construction, and Ultra Clean Coal (UCC), a technology for producing a cleaner coal. Felix's coal was also low in sulphur content, an added feature given China's commitment to both coal-fired electrical power and the simultaneous commitment to reduce carbon emissions by 40% by 2020.

Bids and Negotiations

In July 2008, as coal prices started to rise, Felix reported that a number of companies were interested in acquiring the firm. Felix's share price trended upward. In December 2008, Felix reported that Yanzhou had surpassed all competitive bidders, with an "indicative offer of AUD20/share." At AUD20/share and 196,325,038 shares outstanding, the offer was AUD3,926,500,760. At that same time, the Australian dollar was trading at roughly AUD1.50/USD, making the "indicative offer" worth USD2.62 billion.

The debate over price was in many ways personal. Felix Resources was closely held, with the CEO Brian Flannery holding 15% interest, Chairman Travers Duncan 15%, American Metals and Coal International 19.2%—largely controlled by Hans Mende, and former Felix CFO David Knappick another 7.4%. Four people controlled 56.6% of Felix's shares.

Meetings between the two companies were held in China in February, but little progress was made. By March, the two companies were still negotiating price. The fall in coal prices and coal company share prices had changed the negotiating range.

> Felix surged 37 percent to A$7.43 on Dec. 5, the biggest gain since February 1989, after the Australian Financial Review reported Yanzhou was in talks to buy the company for more than A$3 billion. Since then, Felix has slipped 11 percent. Yanzhou gained 5.4 percent yesterday in Hong Kong, paring the stock's drop this year to 20 percent. Yanzhou may be willing to offer only A$10 to A$12 per share, valuing Felix at up to A$2.35 billion, one of the people said. Felix may want at least A$15 per share, said the other person.
>
> —Yanzhou Coal Talks with Felix Resources Said to Stall on Price," Bloomberg, March 12, 2009.

Yanzhou was now offering only AUD12 per share. Both Felix and Yanzhou were feeling the effects of lower share prices. Because of the scope of the deal, both Chinese and Australian regulatory authorities continued to review the proposed transaction, although the parties appeared to be far apart on price.

The following months saw a number of Chinese acquisitions of Australian mineral producers.

> Yanzhou is the latest in a long line of Chinese suitors to consider buying Australian mining assets—not all of which have been successful. This month, Chinalco's $19.5bn tie-up with Rio Tinto collapsed. However, Oz Minerals shareholders recently accepted an offer from Minmetals to purchase the company's mining assets after the Chinese group raised its offer in a pre-emptive move to head off opposition. Felix indicated on Wednesday that its own discussions with interested parties regarding a takeover deal were ongoing.
>
> —"Linc Energy ends talks with Yanzhou over sale," Financial Times, June 24, 2009.

In August 2009, after intensive discussions, Yanzhou made an all-cash offer totaling AUD18 per share. The offer combined AUD16.95 per share cash, plus an AUD1.00 per share fully franked dividend (AUD0.50 immediately, with another AUD0.50 per share on approval of the acquisition), and an AUD0.05 share distribution of a startup firm, SACC. (A franking credit represents taxes already paid on the dividend. Although the stockholder receives in cash only the dividend, the tax authorities record stockholder income as dividend plus credit, eliminating most of the double taxation for small investors on dividend income.) On August 13, 2009, Felix announced that it had received—and the board had unanimously supported—the offer. As illustrated in Exhibit 2, Felix's share price rose to about AUD17 per share where it had remained.

Valuation Throughout the deal's discussions, Yanzhou, Felix, and a host of analysts used a variety of different methods to value the company, including discounted cash flow (DCF), reserve valuation, and market comparables.

DCF. The most widely used traditional financial valuation technique for firms is discounted cash flow (DCF). DCF first forecasts the firm's net operating cash flows, then discounts them to present value using the firm's cost of capital. Financial technicals aside, the true driver of value for the DCF or any other valuation analysis was still what the price of coal would do in the short-to-medium-term. Forecasting coal prices added up to "sophisticated guesswork" in the words of one analyst.

One DCF valuation of Felix presented in Exhibit 3, indicates a value of AUD10.74 per share (baseline analysis), a much lower value than the current market price and prospective bid price. A variety of sensitivities and scenarios established a range between AUD9 and AUD14 per share.

Control Premium. One feature often overlooked in acquisition valuations is an added "boost" or premium to the offered share price reflecting a change in control of the company. This is additional compensation to investors who had invested by choice, but who would now be removed without their individual approval. This control premium may vary between 5% and 10% in many cases.

EXHIBIT 2   Felix Resources Share Price (January 2008–October 2009)

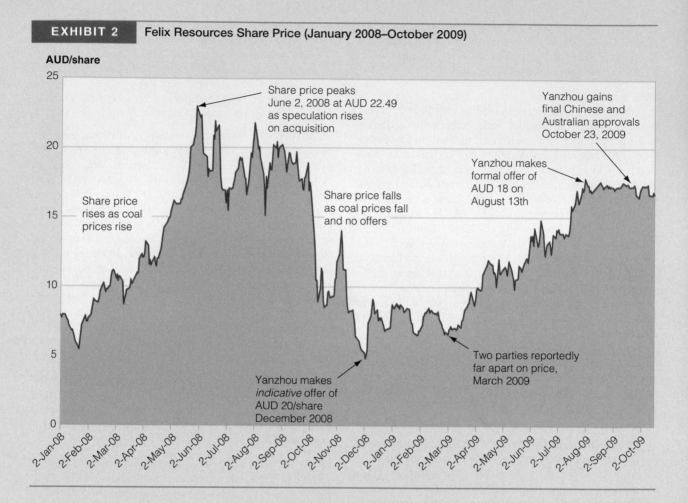

Reserve Valuation. All industries use a variety of industry specific valuation techniques which focus on value drivers in that specific industry. In mining, production today is important, but reserves to support production tomorrow is critical. When buying a coal, copper, or oil company, the buyer is also buying both *proved* and *probable reserves* (often referred to in the minerals industries as *2P*). Exhibit 4 provides one analyst's overview of a reserve-based valuation on Felix.

Comparables. Again, the analysts and interested parties looked at a multitude of other valuation ratios of other regional and Chinese peer companies. Comparables on peers, presented in Exhibit 5, generally showed Felix to be valued on par with other major publicly traded coal companies, if not on the high side.

Contracted Valuation. Felix's management, after announcing their support for the Yanzhou offer, commissioned an independent valuation study by a consultant, Deloitte. On September 30, Felix reported that Deloitte's study concluded that "the proposed scheme is fair," and that the estimated fair market value of Felix Resources was likely between AUD16.70 and AUD18.70 per share.

Currency-Based Valuation. One final valuation note by one consultant had caught Quillan's eye. That analysis, presented in Exhibit 6, argued that once the U.S. dollar-based value of coal was translated into the currency of the investor (Chinese yuan for Yanzhou), and that CNY value used to calculate an Australian dollar (AUD) value, the value of a pound of Australian coal assets had dropped from December 2008 to October 2009. This was, hypothetically, the "cost" of Australian coal assets to a Chinese buyer. This change was a combination of changing coal prices and the appreciation of the Australian dollar against the yuan.

EXHIBIT 3	Discounted Cash Flow Valuation of Felix Resources

Thousands of AUD	Years 09-12	2004	2005	2006	2007	2008	Forecast 2009	2010	2011	2012	2013
Net sales		75,068	117,357	208,536	236,318	420,506	462,557	508,812	559,693	615,663	677,229
Sales growth %	10%		56%	78%	13%	78%					
Cost of goods sold		40,481	47,329	80,685	107,275	57,093	62,908	69,198	76,118	83,730	92,103
% of sales	13.6%	54%	40%	39%	45%	14%					
Gross profit		34,587	70,028	127,851	129,043	363,413	399,649	439,614	483,575	531,933	585,126
Selling, general and admininstrative		31,791	59,213	95,191	114,783	227,503	245,155	269,670	296,638	326,301	358,931
% of sales	53%	42%	50%	46%	49%	54%					
Operating profit (EBITDA)		2,796	10,815	32,660	14,260	135,910	154,494	169,943	186,938	205,631	226,195
Depreciation and amortization		1,547	5,501	11,381	17,469	28,639	31,454	34,599	38,059	41,865	46,052
% of sales	6.8%	2.1%	4.7%	5.5%	7.4%	6.8%					
EBIT		1,249	5,314	21,279	(3,209)	107,271	123,040	135,344	148,878	163,766	180,143
NWC		1,199	10,742	14,277	(2,770)	53,775	46,256	50,881	55,969	61,566	67,723
% of sales	10%	1.6%	9.2%	6.8%	−1.2%	12.8%					

DCF Valuation		2004	2005	2006	2007	2008	2009	2010	2011	2012	2013
EBIT							123,040	135,344	148,878	163,766	180,143
Less taxes	30%						36,912	40,603	44,664	49,130	54,043
EBITDA after tax							159,952	175,947	193,542	212,896	234,186
Add back depreciation and amortization							31,454	34,599	38,059	41,865	46,052
Less ANWC							7,519	(4,626)	(5,088)	(5,597)	(6,157)
Less Capex							(31,454)	(34,599)	(38,059)	(41,865)	(46,052)
Free Cash Flow (FCF)							167,471	171,322	188,454	207,299	228,029
Terminal Value (FCF growth rate, %)	1.0%										2,303,095
FCF including terminal value							167,471	171,322	188,454	207,299	2,531,124
Enterprise value (NPV)	11.00%						2,293,674				
Less debt							188,031				
Market value (AUD)							2,105,643				
Shares outstanding							196,000,000				
Value per share, Felix (AUD)							**10.74**				

Notes: Felix has an estimated weighted average cost of capital of 11.07%, assuming a risk-free rate of 5.44% (10-year Australian government bond), an expected market return of 9.94%, a beta of 1.63, a cost of debt of 8.50%, a corporate income tax rate of 30%, and a financial structure which is 30% debt and 70% equity. Discount rate rounded to 11%.

EXHIBIT 4	Reserve Valuation Analysis				
Coal Company Stock	**Yanzhou Coal**	**Shenhua Energy**	**Bumi Resources**	**Banpu**	**Felix Resources**
Bloomberg Reference	1171 HK	1088 HK	Bumi IJ	BANPU TB	FLX AU
Share price currency	HKD	HKD	IDR	THB	AUD
Share price 13 August 2009	12.40	31.95	3,175.00	422.00	16.95
Spot exchange rate	7.75	7.75	9,950.00	34.06	1.19
	(HKD/USD)	(HKD/USD)	(IDR/USD)	(THB/USD)	(AUD/USD)
Shares outstanding	4,918,000,000	19,900,000,000	19,400,000,000	300,000,000	196,325,000
Total market capitalization	$7,868,800,000	$82,039,354,839	$6,190,452,261	$3,716,970,053	$2,803,461,457
Proved and probable reserves (equity, t)	1,866,000,000	7,320,000,000	1,100,000,000	288,000,000	386,000,000
Market cap/Coal reserve (USD/t)	4.22	11.21	5.63	12.91	7.26

Source: Bloomberg, DBS Vickers. Analysis revised by authors based on "Hong Kong/China Flash Notes: Yanzhou Coal," DBS Group Research Equity, 14 August 2009, p. 2. t = tonne. Proved and probable reserves are on an equity ownership basis.

EXHIBIT 5	Valuation Based on Comparables of Peers						
Company Name	**Code**	**Currency**	**Market Capitalization (million USD)**	**PE**	**P/CF**	**P/Book**	**EV/EBITDA**
Bumi Resources	BUMI IJ	IDR	6,186	13.3	9.7	3.2	6.7
Straits Asia	SAR SP	SGD	1,761	5.5	7.8	3.2	5.6
Banpu	BANPU TB	THB	3,356	9.4	8.7	2.3	7.7
Centennial Coal	CEY AU	AUD	1,083	17.5	8.3	2.1	6.7
Coal and Allied	CAN AU	AUD	6,123	16.4	13.8	5.2	12.0
Arch Coal	ACI US	USD	2,970	53.3	7.5	1.4	10.2
Consol Energy	CNX US	USD	7,476	12.6	7.8	3.7	6.3
Felix Resources	FLX AU	AUD	2,911	12.6	10.6	4.8	8.3
Weighted Average: Regional				16.7	9.7	3.6	8.1
China Shenhua	1088 HK	HKD	14,316	19.1	14.1	3.8	10.8
Yanzhou Coal	1171 HK	HKD	3,133	13.6	11.8	1.9	7.0
China Coal	1898 HK	HKD	5,638	17.1	15.2	1.9	10.0
Hidili Industry	1393 HK	HKD	2,041	24. 2	18.7	2.2	20.5
Weighted Average: H-shares (Hong Kong)				18.4	14.4	3.0	10.9

Source: "Yanzhou Coal," Flash Notes, DBS Group Research, 14 August 2009. PE is price to earnings; P/CF is price to cash flow; P/Book is price to book value; EV/EBITDA is enterprise value to earnings before interest, taxes, depreciation and amortization. Enterprise value is the market value of all debt and equity less cash and cash equivalents. All ratios are for forecasts for 2009.

EXHIBIT 6	The Price of Australian Thermal Coal to a Chinese Buyer				
(1)	(2)	(3)	(4)	(5)	(6)
Date	Price of Coal (USD)	Spot Rate (CNY/USD)	Translated Price of Coal in CNY	Spot Rate (CNY/AUD)	Translated Price of Coal in AUD
Jan 2008	98.30	7.25	712.68	6.25	114.03
July 2008	192.86	6.83	1,317.23	6.67	197.59
Dec 2008	84.27	6.85	577.25	4.55	126.99
March 2009	65.36	6.84	447.06	4.55	98.35
August 2009	77.68	6.83	530.55	5.56	95.50
October 2009	76.15	6.83	520.10	6.25	83.22

Coal is priced globally in USD (column 2). Starting with the market price of Australian thermal coal, the price of coal in USD is translated into Chinese yuan (CNY) at official yuan exchange rate to the dollar (column 3). This value in the eyes of a Chinese investor like Yanzhou is then translated into Australian dollars (AUD) at the current spot rate of exchange (column 5). Column 6 is, in theory, the coal-based cost of acquiring an Australian coal producer.

Government Approval The Assistant Treasurer of the Government of Australia and the Foreign Investment Review Board (FIRB) gave final approval to the deal on October 23. But the government's approval was conditional on all of the following stipulations, which Yanzhou thought acceptable:

◆ Felix's employees and management would be 100% retained

◆ Yancoal Australia, a mine operating company, incorporated and headquartered in Australia would be created

◆ Yancoal would be managed primarily by Australian managers and sales staff

◆ Yancoal's CEO and CFO would maintain their primary residences in Australia

◆ The coal would be marketed on an arm's-length basis consistent with international benchmarks and practices

◆ Yancoal would be listed on the Australian Securities Exchange by the end of 2012 and over 30% of the shares would be available for sale

Although the analysts continued to counsel investors to hold out for a competing bid, the share price had stabilized and no other bidders had come forward. Quillan and his fellow investors wondered if they should tender their shares now or hold out for a higher offer.

CASE QUESTIONS

1. When should stockholders doubt their own company's support of a friendly acquisition?

2. What is your assessment of the stipulations placed on the acquisition by the Australian government?

3. Which of the various valuation techniques do you find the most and least useful?

4. Do you think the offer is a good one? Should Quillan take it?

Questions

1. **Capital Budgeting Theoretical Framework.** Capital budgeting for a foreign project uses the same theoretical framework as domestic capital budgeting. What are the basic steps in domestic capital budgeting?

2. **Foreign Complexities.** Capital budgeting for a foreign project is considerably more complex than the domestic case. What are the factors that add complexity?

3. **Project versus Parent Valuation.**
   a. Why should a foreign project be evaluated both from a project and parent viewpoint?
   b. Which viewpoint, project or parent, gives results closer to the traditional meaning of net present value in capital budgeting?
   c. Which viewpoint gives results closer to the effect on consolidated earnings per share?

4. **Which Cash Flows?** Capital projects provide both operating cash flows and financial cash flows. Why

are operating cash flows preferred for domestic capital budgeting but financial cash flows given major consideration in international projects?

5. **Risk-Adjusted Return.** Should the anticipated internal rate of return (IRR) for a proposed foreign project be compared to a) alternative home country proposals, b) returns earned by local companies in the same industry and/or risk class, or c) both? Justify your answer.

6. **Blocked Cash Flows.** In the context of evaluating foreign investment proposals, how should a multinational firm evaluate cash flows in the host foreign country that are blocked from being repatriated to the firm's home country?

7. **Host Country Inflation.** How should an MNE factor host country inflation into its evaluation of an investment proposal?

8. **Cost of Equity.** A foreign subsidiary does not have an independent cost of capital. However, in order to estimate the discount rate for a comparable host-country firm, the analyst should try to calculate a hypothetical cost of capital. As part of this process, the analyst can estimate the subsidiary's proxy cost of equity by using the traditional equation: $k_e = k_{rf} + (k_m - k_{rf})$. Define each variable in this equation and explain how the variable might be different for a proxy host country firm compared to the parent MNE.

9. **Viewpoints.** What are the differences in the cash flows used in a project point of view analysis and a parent point of view analysis?

10. **Foreign Exchange Risk.** How is foreign exchange risk sensitivity factored into the capital budgeting analysis of a foreign project?

11. **Expropriation Risk.** How is expropriation risk factored into the capital budgeting analysis of a foreign project?

12. **Real Option Analysis.** What is real option analysis? How is it a better method of making investment decisions than traditional capital budgeting analysis?

Problems

1. **Natural Mosaic.** Natural Mosaic Company (U.S.) is considering investing Rs50,000,000 in India to create a wholly owned tile manufacturing plant to export to the European market. After five years, the subsidiary would be sold to Indian investors for Rs100,000,000. A pro forma income statement for the Indian operation predicts the generation of Rs7,000,000 of annual cash flow, is listed in the following table.

Sales revenue	30,000,000
Less cash operating expenses	(17,000,000)
Gross income	13,000,000
Less depreciation expenses	(1,000,000)
Earnings before interest and taxes	12,000,000
Less Indian taxes at 50%	(6,000,000)
Net income	6,000,000
Add back depreciation	1,000,000
Annual cash flow	7,000,000

The initial investment will be made on December 31, 2011, and cash flows will occur on December 31st of each succeeding year. Annual cash dividends to Philadelphia Composite from India will equal 75% of accounting income.

The U.S. corporate tax rate is 40% and the Indian corporate tax rate is 50%. Because the Indian tax rate is greater than the U.S. tax rate, annual dividends paid to Natural Mosaic will not be subject to additional taxes in the United States. There are no capital gains taxes on the final sale. Natural Mosaic uses a weighted average cost of capital of 14% on domestic investments, but will add six percentage points for the Indian investment because of perceived greater risk. Natural Mosaic forecasts the rupee/dollar exchange rate for December 31st on the next six years are listed below.

	R$/$		R$/$
2011	50	2014	62
2012	54	2015	66
2013	58	2016	70

What is the net present value and internal rate of return on this investment

2. **Grenouille Properties.** Grenouille Properties (U.S.) expects to receive cash dividends from a French joint venture over the coming three years. The first dividend, to be paid December 31, 2011, is expected to be € 720,000. The dividend is then expected to grow 10.0% per year over the following two years. The current exchange rate (December 30, 2010) is $1.3603/€. Grenouille's weighted average cost of capital is 12%.
   a. What is the present value of the expected euro dividend stream if the euro is expected to appreciate 4.00% per annum against the dollar?
   b. What is the present value of the expected dividend stream if the euro were to depreciate 3.00% per annum against the dollar?

3. **Carambola de Honduras.** Slinger Wayne, a U.S.-based private equity firm, is trying to determine what it should pay for a tool manufacturing firm in Honduras

named Carambola. Slinger Wayne estimates that Carambola will generate a free cash flow of 13 million Honduran lempiras (Lp) next year (2012), and that this free cash flow will continue to grow at a constant rate of 8.0% per annum indefinitely.

A private equity firm like Slinger Wayne, however, is not interested in owning a company for long, and plans to sell Carambola at the end of three years for approximately 10 times Carambola's free cash flow in that year. The current spot exchange rate is Lp14.80/$, but the Honduran inflation rate is expected to remain at a relatively high rate of 16.0% per annum compared to the U.S. dollar inflation rate of only 2.0% per annum. Slinger Wayne expects to earn at least a 20% annual rate of return on international investments like Carambola.

a. What is Carambola worth if the Honduran lempira were to remain fixed over the three year investment period?

b. What is Carambola worth if the Honduran lempira were to change in value over time according to purchasing power parity?

4. **Finisterra, S.A.** Finisterra, S.A., located in the state of Baja California, Mexico, manufactures frozen Mexican food which enjoys a large following in the U.S. states of California and Arizona to the north. In order to be closer to its U.S. market, Finisterra is considering moving some of its manufacturing operations to southern California. Operations in California would begin in year 1 and have the following attributes.

Assumptions	Value
Sales price per unit, year 1 (US$)	$ 5.00
Sales price increase, per year	3.00%
Initial sales volume, year 1, units	1,000,000
Sales volume increase, per year	10.00%
Production costs per unit, year 1	$ 4.00
Production cost per unit increase, per year	4.00%
General and administrative expenses per year	$100,000
Depreciation expenses per year	$ 80,000
Finisterra's WACC (pesos)	16.00%
Terminal value discount rate	20.00%

The operations in California will pay 80% of its accounting profit to Finisterra as an annual cash dividend. Mexican taxes are calculated on grossed up dividends from foreign countries, with a credit for host-country taxes already paid. What is the maximum U.S. dollar price Finisterra should offer in year 1 for the investment?

5. **Doohicky Devices.** Doohickey Devices, Inc., manufactures design components for personal computers. Until the present, manufacturing has been subcontracted to other companies, but for reasons of quality control Doohicky has decided to manufacture itself in Asia. Analysis has narrowed the choice to two possibilities, Penang, Malaysia, and Manila, the Philippines. At the moment only the summary of expected, after-tax, cash flows displayed at the bottom of this page is available. Although most operating outflows would be in Malaysian ringgit or Philippine pesos, some additional U.S. dollar cash outflows would be necessary, as shown in the table at the top of this page.

The Malaysia ringgit currently trades at RM3.80/$ and the Philippine peso trades at Ps50.00/$. Doohicky expects the Malaysian ringgit to appreciate 2.0% per year against the dollar, and the Philippine peso to depreciate 5.0% per year against the dollar. If the weighted average cost of capital for Doohicky Devices is 14.0%, which project looks most promising?

6. **Wenceslas Refining Company.** Privately owned Wenceslas Refining Company is considering investing in the Czech Republic so as to have a refinery source closer to its European customers. The original investment in Czech korunas would amount to K250 million, or $5,000,000 at the current spot rate of K32.50/$, all in fixed assets, which will be depreciated over 10 years by the straight-line method. An additional K100,000,000 will be needed for working capital.

For capital budgeting purposes, Wenceslas assumes sale as a going concern at the end of the third year at a price, after all taxes, equal to the net book value of fixed assets alone (not including working capital). All free cash flow will be repatriated to the United States as soon as possible. In evaluating the

Doohicky in Penang (after-tax)	2012	2013	2014	2015	2016	2017
Net ringgit cash flows	(26,000)	8,000	6,800	7,400	9,200	10,000
Dollar cash outflows	—	(100)	(120)	(150)	(150)	—
Doohicky in Manila (after-tax)						
Net peso cash flows	(560,000)	190,000	180,000	200,000	210,000	200,000
Dollar cash outflows		(100)	(200)	(300)	(400)	—

Assumptions	0	1	2	3
Original investment (Czech korunas, K)	250,000,000			
Spot exchange rate (K/$)	32.50	30.00	27.50	25.00
Unit demand		700,000	900,000	1,000,000
Unit sales price		$ 10.00	$ 10.30	$ 10.60
Fixed cash operating expenses		$1,000,000	$1,030,000	$1,060,000
Depreciation		$ 500,000	$ 500,000	$ 500,000
Investment in working capital (K)	100,000,000			

venture, the U.S. dollar forecasts are shown in the table above.

Variable manufacturing costs are expected to be 50% of sales. No additional funds need be invested in the U.S. subsidiary during the period under consideration. The Czech Republic imposes no restrictions on repatriation of any funds of any sort. The Czech corporate tax rate is 25% and the United States rate is 40%. Both countries allow a tax credit for taxes paid in other countries. Wenceslas uses 18% as its weighted average cost of capital, and its objective is to maximize present value. Is the investment attractive to Wenceslas Refining?

Hermosa Beach Components (U.S.)

Use the following information and assumptions to answer problems 7–10.

Hermosa Beach Components, Inc., of California exports 24,000 sets of low-density light bulbs per year to Argentina under an import license that expires in five years. In Argentina, the bulbs are sold for the Argentine peso equivalent of $60 per set. Direct manufacturing costs in the United States and shipping together amount to $40 per set. The market for this type of bulb in Argentina is stable, neither growing nor shrinking, and Hermosa holds the major portion of the market.

The Argentine government has invited Hermosa to open a manufacturing plant so imported bulbs can be replaced by local production. If Hermosa makes the investment, it will operate the plant for five years and then sell the building and equipment to Argentine investors at net book value at the time of sale plus the value of any net working capital. (Net working capital is the amount of current assets less any portion financed by local debt.) Hermosa will be allowed to repatriate all net income and depreciation funds to the United States each year. Hermosa traditionally evaluates all foreign investments in U.S. dollar terms.

◆ **Investment.** Hermosa's anticipated cash outlay in U.S. dollars in 2012 would be as follows:

Building and equipment	$1,000,000
Net working capital	1,000,000
Total investment	$2,000,000

All investment outlays will be made in 2012, and all operating cash flows will occur at the end of years 2013 through 2017.

◆ **Depreciation and Investment Recovery.** Building and equipment will be depreciated over five years on a straight-line basis. At the end of the fifth year, the $1,000,000 of net working capital may also be repatriated to the United States, as may the remaining net book value of the plant.

◆ **Sales Price of Bulbs.** Locally manufactured bulbs will be sold for the Argentine peso equivalent of $60 per set.

◆ **Operating Expenses per Set of Bulbs.** Material purchases are as follows:

Materials purchased in Argentina (U.S. dollar equivalent)	$20 per set
Materials imported from Hermosa Beach—USA	10 per set
Total variable costs	$30 per set

◆ **Transfer Prices.** The $10 transfer price per set for raw material sold by the parent consists of $5 of direct and indirect costs incurred in the United States on their manufacture, creating $5 of pre-tax profit to Hermosa Beach.

◆ **Taxes.** The corporate income tax rate is 40% in both Argentina and the United States (combined federal and state/province). There are no capital gains taxes on the future sale of the Argentine subsidiary, either in Argentina or the United States.

◆ **Discount Rate.** Hermosa Components uses a 15% discount rate to evaluate all domestic and foreign projects.

7. **Hermosa Components: Baseline Analysis.** Evaluate the proposed investment in Argentina by Hermosa Components (U.S.). Hermosa's management wishes the baseline analysis to be performed in U.S. dollars (and implicitly also assumes the exchange rate remains fixed throughout the life of the project). Create a project viewpoint capital budget and a parent viewpoint capital budget. What do you conclude from your analysis?

8. **Hermosa Components: Revenue Growth Scenario.** As a result of their analysis in problem 7, Hermosa wishes to explore the implications of being able to grow sales volume by 4% per year. Argentine inflation is expected to average 5% per year, so sales price and material cost increases of 7% and 6% per year, respectively, are thought reasonable. Although material costs in Argentina are expected to rise, U.S.-based costs are not expected to change over the five-year period. Evaluate this scenario for both the project and parent viewpoints. Is the project under this revenue growth scenario acceptable?

9. **Hermosa Components: Revenue Growth and Sales Price Scenario.** In addition to the assumptions employed in problem 8, Hermosa now wishes to evaluate the prospect of being able to sell the Argentine subsidiary at the end of year 5 at a multiple of the business's earnings in that year. Hermosa believes that a multiple of six is a conservative estimate of the market value of the firm at that time. Evaluate the project and parent viewpoint capital budgets.

10. **Hermosa Components: Revenue Growth, Sales Price, and Currency Risk Scenario.** Melinda Deane, a new analyst at Hermosa and a recent MBA graduate, believes that it is a fundamental error to evaluate the Argentine project's prospective earnings and cash flows in dollars, rather than first estimating their Argentine peso (Ps) value and then converting cash flow returns to the United States in dollars. She believes the correct method is to use the end-of-year spot rate in 2012 of Ps3.50/$ and assume it will change in relation to purchasing power. (She is assuming U.S. inflation to be 1% per annum and Argentine inflation to be 5% per annum). She also believes that Hermosa

should use a risk-adjusted discount rate in Argentina which reflects Argentine capital costs (20% is her estimate) and a risk-adjusted discount rate for the parent viewpoint capital budget (18%) on the assumption that international projects in a risky currency environment should require a higher expected return than other lower-risk projects. How do these assumptions and changes alter Hermosa's perspective on the proposed investment?

Internet Exercises

1. **Capital Projects and the EBRD.** The European Bank for Reconstruction and Development (EBRD) was established to foster market-oriented business development in the former Soviet Bloc. Use the EBRD Web site to determine which projects and companies EBRD is currently undertaking.

European Bank for   www.ebrd.org
Reconstruction and
Development

2. **Emerging Markets: China.** Long-term investment projects such as electrical power generation require a thorough understanding of all attributes of doing business in that country. China is currently the focus of investment and market penetration strategies of multinational firms worldwide. Using the Web (you might start with the Web sites listed below), build a database on doing business in China, and prepare an update of many of the factors discussed in this chapter.

Ministry of Foreign Trade   en.trade2cn.com/index.html
and Economic Cooperation,
PRC

China Investment Trust   www.citic.com/wps/portal/
and Investment Corporation encitic

ChinaNet Investment Pages   www.business-china.com/
                            invest

3. **BeyondBrics: The *Financial Times*' Emerging Market Hub.** Check the *FT*'s blog on emerging markets for the latest debates and guest editorials.

Financial Times Blog on   blogs.ft.com/beyond-brics/
Emerging Markets

Answers to Selected End-of-Chapter Problems

Chapter 1: Current Multinational Challenges and the Global Economy

6. a. $14.77
   b. U.S. = 30.5%, Brazil = 27.1%, Germany = 40.1%, China = 2.4%
   c. 69.5%
9. Appreciation case: +13.9%
   Depreciation case: −13.9%

Chapter 2: Financial Goals and Corporate Governance

1. a. 25.000%
   b. 33.333%
   c. Dividend yield = 8.333%, capital gains = 25.00%, total shareholder return = 33.333%
3. a. 64.23%
   b. 4.19%
   c. 71.12%

Chapter 3: The International Monetary System

4. −41.82%
6. 1.1398
11. If 20%, 6.76; if 30%, 6.24

Chapter 4: The Balance of Payments

		2000	2001	2002
1.	Brazil's balance on goods?	−698	2,650	13,121
2.	Brazil's balance on services?	−7,162	−7,759	−4,957
3.	Brazil's balance on goods and services?	−7,860	−5,109	8,164
4.	Brazil's balance on goods, services and income?	−25,746	−24,852	−10,026
5.	Brazil's current account balance?	−24,225	−23,215	−7,637

Chapter 5: Current Multinational Financial Challenges: The Credit Crisis of 2007–2009

1. | | 3-month | 6-month |
   |---|---|---|
   | a. | $6.07 | $23.26 |
   | b. | 0.0607% | 0.2331% |
   | c. | 0.2432% | 0.4668% |

Chapter 6: The Foreign Exchange Market

2. a. 2.71
   b. 1,221,177
9. a. Profit of 26,143.79
   b. Loss of (26,086.96)

Chapter 7: International Parity Conditions

2. a. 1.17
   b. −63.307%
   c. inflation and a balance of payment crisis
4. A CIA profit potential of −0.042% tells Takeshi he should borrow Japanese yen and invest in the higher yielding currency, the U.S. dollar, to earn a CIA profit of 55,000.

Chapter 8: Foreign Currency Derivatives and Swaps

2. a. Sallie should buy a call on Singapore dollars
   b. $0.65046
   c. Gross profit = $0.05000   Net profit = $0.04954
   d. Gross profit = $0.15000   Net profit = $0.14954
4. a. ($49,080.00)
   b. $38,920.00
   c. ($9,080.00)

Chapter 9: Foreign Exchange Rate Determination and Forecasting

1. −7.79%
6. a. 85,000
   b. −32.0% and −15.0%
8. −13.79%

Chapter 10: Transaction and Translation Exposure

2. Foreign exchange loss of $921,400,000
10. Do nothing: Could be anything
    Forward: $216,049.38
    Money market: $212,190.81
    Forward is preferable choice if bank allows an expanded line
17. A net exposure of $U420,000 or $21,000

Chapter 11: Operating Exposure

3. Case 1: Same yuan price: $33,913,043
   Case 2: Same dollar price: $54,000,000 (better)
7. Present value of year-end cash flows of ($605,247)

Chapter 12: The Global Cost and Availability of Capital

1. a. 6.550%
   b. 5.950%

3.

CAPM	ICAPM
a. 9.250%	7.400%
b. 5.460%	5.460%
c. 8.113%	6.8180%

Chapter 13: Sourcing Equity and Debt Globally

2. 13.23%
4. 12.03%

Chapter 14: Multinational Tax Management

1. Case 1: 38.8%
   Case 2: 45.0%
4. Change in consolidated tax payments of −11.17%

Chapter 16: Multinational Capital Budgeting and Cross-Border Acquisitions

5. Penang: NPV = $560
   Manila: NPV = ($266)
6. Project Viewpoint cum cash flow of $265,073
   Parent Viewpoint cum cash flow of ($2,249,812)

Chapter 17: International Portfolio Theory and Diversification

2.

	Expected Return	Expected Risk
a. Equally weighted portfolio	17.30%	20.93%
b. 70% Boeing, 30% Unilever	17.82%	21.08%
c. Min Risk is 55% Boeing, 45% Unilever	17.43%	20.89%

5. Share price appreciation = 6.456%
   Annual return, including dividends = 10.698%

Chapter 18: Working Capital Management

2. a. 19.41%
   b. 1,800,000
6. Dividend Only: Total return, after-tax = $247,500
   License Fee Only: Total return, after-tax = $178,200

Chapter 19: International Trade Finance

3. 11.765%
5. a. 5.128%
   b. $196,000.00

Glossary

A/P. In international trade documentation, an abbreviation for authority to purchase or authority to pay. In accounting, an abbreviation for accounts payable.

Absolute advantage. The ability of an individual party or country to produce more of a product or service with the same inputs as another party. It is therefore possible for a country to have no absolute advantage in any international trade activity. *See also* comparative advantage.

Accounting exposure. Another name for translation exposure. *See* Translation exposure.

Ad valorem duty. A customs duty levied as a percentage of the assessed value of goods entering a country.

ADB. Asian Development Bank.

Adjusted present value. A type of present value analysis in capital budgeting in which operating cash flows are discounted separately from (1) the various tax shields provided by the deductibility of interest and other financial charges, and (2) the benefits of project-specific concessional financing. Each component cash flow is discounted at a rate appropriate for the risk involved.

ADR. *See* American Depositary Receipt.

AfDB. African Development Bank.

Affiliate. A foreign enterprise in which the parent company owns a minority interest.

Agency for International Development (AID). A unit of the U.S. government dealing with foreign aid.

Agency theory. The costs and risks of aligning interests between shareholders of the firm and their agents, management, in the conduct of firm business and strategy.

All-equity discount rate. A discount rate in capital budgeting that would be appropriate for discounting operating cash flows if the project were financed entirely with owners' equity.

Alt-A Mortgage. A mortgage type that, although not prime, is considered a relatively low-risk loan to a creditworthy borrower, but lacks some technical qualifications to be categorized as "conforming."

American Depositary Receipt (ADR). A certificate of ownership, issued by a U.S. bank, representing a claim on underlying foreign securities. ADRs may be traded in lieu of trading in the actual underlying shares.

American option. An option that can be exercised at any time up to and including the expiration date.

American selling price (ASP). For customs purposes, the use of the domestic price of competing merchandise in the United States as a tax base for determining import duties. The ASP is generally higher than the actual foreign price, so its use is a protectionist technique.

American terms. Foreign exchange quotations for the U.S. dollar, expressed as the number of U.S. dollars per unit of non-U.S. currency.

Anticipated exposure. A foreign exchange exposure that is believed by management to have a very high likelihood of occurring, but is not yet contractual, and is therefore not yet certain.

Appreciation. In the context of exchange rate changes, a rise in the foreign exchange value of a currency that is pegged to other currencies or to gold. Also called revaluation.

Arbitrage. A trading strategy based on the purchase of a commodity, including foreign exchange, in one market at one price while simultaneously selling it in another market at a more advantageous price, in order to obtain a risk-free profit on the price differential.

Arbitrageur. An individual or company that practices arbitrage.

Arithmetic return. A calculation in which the mean equals the average of the annual percentage changes in capital appreciation plus dividend distributions.

Arm's-length price. The price at which a willing buyer and a willing unrelated seller freely agree to carry out a transaction. In effect, a free market price. Applied by tax authorities in judging the appropriateness of transfer prices between related companies.

Asian currency unit. A trading department within a Singaporean bank that deals in foreign (non-Singaporean) currency deposits and loans.

Ask price. The price at which a dealer is willing to sell foreign exchange, securities or commodities. Also called offer price.

Asset Backed Security (ABS). A derivative security that typically includes second mortgages and home-equity loans based on mortgages, in addition to credit card receivables and auto loans.

Asset market approach. A strategy that determines whether foreigners are willing to hold claims in monetary form, depending on an extensive set of investment considerations or drivers.

At-the-money (ATM). An option whose exercise price is the same as the spot price of the underlying currency.

Back-to-back loan. A loan in which two companies in separate countries borrow each other's currency for a specific period of time and repay the other's currency at an agreed maturity. Sometimes the two loans are channeled through an intermediate bank. Back-to-back financing is also called link financing.

Backlog exposure. The period of time between contract initiation and fulfillment through delivery of services or shipping of goods.

Balance of payments (BOP). A financial statement summarizing the flow of goods, services, and investment funds between residents of a given country and residents of the rest of the world.

Balance of trade (BOT). An entry in the balance of payments measuring the difference between the monetary value of merchandise exports and merchandise imports.

Balance sheet hedge. An accounting strategy that requires an equal amount of exposed foreign currency assets and liabilities on a firm's consolidated balance sheet.

Bank for International Settlements (BIS). A bank in Basel, Switzerland, that functions as a bank for European central banks.

Bank rate. The interest rate at which central banks for various countries lend to their own monetary institutions.

Bankers' acceptance. An unconditional promise by a bank to make payment on a draft when it matures. This comes in the form of the bank's endorsement (acceptance) of a draft drawn against that bank in accordance with the terms of a letter of credit issued by the bank.

Barter. International trade conducted by the direct exchange of physical goods, rather than by separate purchases and sales at prices and exchange rates set by a free market.

Basic balance. In a country's balance of payments, the net of exports and imports of goods and services, unilateral transfers, and long-term capital flows.

Basis point. One one-hundredth of one percentage point, often used in quotations of spreads between interest rates or to describe changes in yields in securities.

Basis risk. A type of interest rate risk in which the interest rate base is mismatched.

Bearer bond. Corporate or governmental debt in bond form that is not registered to any owner. Possession of the bond implies ownership, and interest is obtained by clipping a coupon attached to the bond. The advantage of the bearer form is easy transfer at the time of a sale, easy use as collateral for a debt, and what some cynics call taxpayer anonymity, meaning that governments find it hard to trace interest payments in order to collect income taxes. Bearer bonds are common in Europe, but are seldom issued any more in the United States. The alternate form to a bearer bond is a registered bond.

Beta. Second letter of the Greek alphabet, used as a statistical measure of risk in the Capital Asset Pricing Model. Beta is the covariance between returns on a given asset and returns on the market portfolio, divided by the variance of returns on the market portfolio.

Bid. The price that a dealer is willing to pay to purchase foreign exchange or a security.

Bid-ask spread. The difference between a bid and an ask quotation.

Big Bang. The October 1986 liberalization of the London capital markets.

Bill of exchange (B/E). A written order requesting one party (such as an importer) to pay a specified amount of money at a specified time to the writer of the bill. Also called a draft. *See* Sight draft.

Bill of lading (B/L). A contract between a common carrier and a shipper to transport goods to a named destination. The bill of lading is also a receipt for the goods. Bills of lading are usually negotiable, meaning they are made to the order of a particular party and can be endorsed to transfer title to another party.

Black market. An illegal foreign exchange market.

Blocked funds. Funds in one country's currency that may not be exchanged freely for foreign currencies because of exchange controls.

Border tax adjustments. The fiscal practice, under the General Agreement on Tariffs and Trade, by which imported goods are subject to some or all of the tax charged in the importing country and re-exported goods are exempt from some or all of the tax charged in the exporting country.

Branch. A foreign operation not incorporated in the host country, in contrast to a subsidiary.

Bretton Woods Conference. An international conference in 1944 that established the international monetary system that was in effect from 1945 to 1971. The conference was held in Bretton Woods, New Hampshire, United States.

Bridge financing. Short-term financing from a bank, used while a borrower obtains medium- or long-term fixed-rate financing from capital markets.

Bulldogs. British pound-denominated bonds issued within the United Kingdom by a foreign borrower.

Cable. The U.S. dollar per British pound cross rate.

CAD. Cash against documents. International trade term.

Call option. The right, but not the obligation, to buy foreign exchange or another financial contract at a specified price within a specified time. *See* Option.

Capex. Capital expenditures.

Capital account. A section of the balance of payments accounts. Under the revised format of the International Monetary Fund, the capital account measures capital transfers and the acquisition and disposal of nonproduced, nonfinancial assets. Under traditional definitions, still used by many countries, the capital account measures public and private international lending and investment. Most of the traditional definition of the capital account is now incorporated into IMF statements as the financial account.

Capital Asset Pricing Model (CAPM). A theoretical model that relates the return on an asset to its risk, where risk is the contribution of the asset to the volatility of a portfolio. Risk and return are presumed to be determined in competitive and efficient financial markets.

Capital budgeting. The analytical approach used to determine whether investment in long-lived assets or projects is viable.

Capital flight. Movement of funds out of a country because of political risk.

Capital markets. The financial markets of various countries in which various types of long-term debt and/or ownership securities, or claims on those securities, are purchased and sold.

Capital mobility. The degree to which private capital moves freely from country to country in search of the most promising investment opportunities.

Carry trade. The strategy of borrowing in a low interest rate currency to fund investing in higher yielding currencies. Also termed *currency carry trade,* the strategy is speculative in that currency risk is present and not managed or hedged.

Cash budgeting. Planning for future receipts and disbursements of cash.

Cash flow return on investment (CFROI). A measure of corporate performance in which the numerator equals profit from continuing operations less cash taxes and depreciation. This is divided by cash investment, which is taken to mean the replacement cost of capital employed.

Certificate of Deposit (CD). A negotiable receipt issued by a bank for funds deposited for a certain period of time. CDs can be purchased or sold prior to their maturity in a secondary market, making them an interest-earning marketable security.

CIF (cost, insurance, and freight). *See* Cost, insurance, and freight.

CKD. Completely knocked down. International trade term for components shipped into a country for assembly there. Often used in the automobile industry.

Clearinghouse. An institution through which financial obligations are cleared by the process of settling the obligations of various members.

Clearinghouse Interbank Payments System (CHIPS). A New York-based computerized clearing system used by banks to settle interbank foreign exchange obligations (mostly U.S. dollars) between members.

Collar option. The simultaneous purchase of a put option and sale of a call option, or vice versa, resulting in a form of hybrid option.

Collateralized Debt Obligation (CDO). A portfolio of debt instruments of varying credit qualities created and packaged for resale as an asset-backed security. The collateral in the CDO is the real estate, aircraft, heavy equipment, or other property the loan was used to purchase.

COMECON. Acronym for Council for Mutual Economic Assistance. An association of the former Soviet Union and Eastern European governments formed to facilitate international trade among European Communist countries. COMECON ceased to exist after the breakup of the Soviet Union.

Commercial risk. In banking, the likelihood that a foreign debtor will be unable to repay its debts because of business events, as distinct from political ones.

Common market. An association through treaty of two or more countries that agree to remove all trade barriers between themselves. The best known is the European Common Market, now called the European Union.

Comparative advantage. A theory that everyone gains if each nation specializes in the production of those goods that it produces relatively most efficiently and imports those goods that other countries produce relatively most efficiently. The theory supports free trade arguments.

Competitive exposure. *See* Operating exposure.

Concession agreement. An understanding or contract between a foreign corporation and a host government defining the rules under which the corporation may operate in that country.

Consolidated financial statement. A corporate financial statement in which accounts of a parent company and its subsidiaries are added together to produce a statement which reports the status of the worldwide enterprise as if it were a single corporation. Internal obligations are eliminated in consolidated statements.

Consolidation. In the context of accounting for multinational corporations, the process of preparing a single reporting currency financial statement, which combines financial statements of subsidiaries that are in fact measured in different currencies.

Contagion. The spread of a crisis in one country to its neighboring countries and other countries with similar characteristics—at least in the eyes of cross-border investors.

Contingent foreign currency exposure. which is not yet certain. The final determination of the exposure is contingent upon another firm's decision, such as a decision to invest or the winning of a business or construction bid.

Controlled foreign corporation (CFC). A foreign corporation in which U.S. shareholders own more than 50% of the combined voting power or total value. Under U.S. tax law, U.S. shareholders may be liable for taxes on undistributed earnings of the controlled foreign corporation.

Convertible bond. A bond or other fixed-income security that may be exchanged for a number of shares of common stock.

Convertible currency. A currency that can be exchanged freely for any other currency without government restrictions.

Corporate governance. The relationship among stakeholders used to determine and control the strategic direction and performance of an organization.

Corporate wealth maximization. The corporate goal of maximizing the total wealth of the corporation rather than just the shareholders' wealth. Wealth is defined to include not just financial wealth but also the technical, marketing and human resources of the corporation.

Correspondent bank. A bank that holds deposits for and provides services to another bank, located in another geographic area, on a reciprocal basis.

Cost and freight (C&F). Price, quoted by an exporter, that includes the cost of transportation to the named port of destination.

Cost, insurance, and freight (CIF). Exporter's quoted price including the cost of packaging, freight or carriage, insurance premium, and other charges paid in respect of the goods from the time of loading in the country of export to their arrival at the named port of destination or place of transshipment.

Counterparty. The opposite party in a double transaction, which involves an exchange of financial instruments or obligations now and a reversal of that same transaction at an agreed-upon later date.

Counterparty risk. The potential exposure any individual firm bears that the second party to any financial contract may be unable to fulfill its obligations under the contract's specifications.

Countertrade. A type of international trade in which parties exchange goods directly rather than for money, a type of barter.

Countervailing duty. An import duty charged to offset an export subsidy by another country.

Country risk. In banking, the likelihood that unexpected events within a host country will influence a client's or a government's ability to repay a loan. Country risk is often divided into sovereign (political) risk and foreign exchange (currency) risk.

Country-specific-risk. Political risks that affect the MNE at the country level, such as transfer risk (blocked funds) and cultural and institutional risks.

Covered interest arbitrage (CIA). The process whereby an investor earns a risk-free profit by (1) borrowing funds in one currency, (2) exchanging those funds in the spot market for a foreign currency, (3) investing the foreign currency at interest rates in a foreign country, (4) selling forward, at the time of original investment, the investment proceeds to be received at maturity, (5) using the proceeds of the forward sale to repay the original loan, and (6) sustaining a remaining profit balance.

Covering. A transaction in the forward foreign exchange market or money market that protects the value of future cash flows. Covering is another term for hedging. *See* Hedge.

Crawling peg. A foreign exchange rate system in which the exchange rate is adjusted very frequently to reflect prevailing rate of inflation.

Credit Default Swap (CDS). A derivative contract that derives its value from the credit quality and performance of any specified asset. The CDS was invented by a team at JPMorgan in 1997, and designed to shift the risk of default to a third party. It is a way to bet whether a specific mortgage or security will either fail to pay on time or fail to pay at all.

Credit enhancement. A process of restructuring or recombining assets of different risk profiles in order to obtain a higher credit rating for the combined product.

Credit risk. The possibility that a borrower's credit worth, at the time of renewing a credit, is reclassified by the lender.

Crisis planning. The process of educating management and other employees about how to react to various scenarios of violence or other disruptive events.

Cross rate. An exchange rate between two currencies derived by dividing each currency's exchange rate with a third currency. Colloquially, it is often used to refer to a specific currency pair such as the euro/yen cross rate, as the yen/dollar and dollar/euro are the more common currency quotations.

Cross-border acquisition. A purchase in which one firm acquires another firm located in a different country.

Cross-currency swap. *See* Currency swap.

Cross-listing. The listing of shares of common stock on two or more stock exchanges.

Cumulative translation adjustment (CTA) account. An entry in a translated balance sheet in which gains and/or losses from translation have been accumulated over a period of years.

Currency basket. The value of a portfolio of specific amounts of individual currencies, used as the basis for setting the market value of another currency. Also called currency cocktail.

Currency board. A currency board exists when a country's central bank commits to back its money supply entirely with foreign reserves at all times.

Currency swap. A transaction in which two counterparties exchange specific amounts of two different currencies at the outset, and then repay over time according to an agreed-upon contract that reflects interest payments and possibly amortization of principal. In a currency swap, the cash flows are similar to those in a spot and forward foreign exchange transaction. *See also* Swap.

Current account. In the balance of payments, the net flow of goods, services, and unilateral transfers (such as gifts) between a country and all foreign countries.

Current rate method. A method of translating the financial statements of foreign subsidiaries into the parent's reporting currency. All assets and liabilities are translated at the current exchange rate.

Current/noncurrent method. A method of translating the financial statements of foreign subsidiaries into the parent's reporting currency. All current assets and current liabilities are translated at the current rate, and all noncurrent accounts at their historical rates.

D/A. Documents against acceptance. International trade term.

D/P. Documents against payment. International trade term.

D/S. Days after sight. International trade term.

Deductible expense. A business expense which is recognized by tax officials as deductible toward the firm's income tax liabilities.

Deemed-paid tax. That portion of taxes paid to a foreign government that is allowed as a credit (reduction) in taxes due to a home government.

Delta. The change in an option's price divided by the change in the price of the underlying instrument. Hedging strategies are based on delta ratios.

Demand deposit. A bank deposit that can be withdrawn or transferred at any time without notice, in contrast to a time deposit where (theoretically) the bank may require a waiting period before the deposit can be withdrawn. Demand deposits may or may not earn interest. A time deposit is the opposite of a demand deposit.

Depositary receipt. *See* American Depositary Receipt.

Depreciate. In the context of foreign exchange rates, a drop in the spot foreign exchange value of a floating currency, i.e., a currency whose value is determined by open market transactions.

Depreciation. A market-driven change in the value of a currency which results in reduced value or purchasing power.

Derivative. An asset which derives all changes in value on a separate underlying asset.

Devaluation. The action of a government or central bank authority to drop the spot foreign exchange value of a currency that is pegged to another currency or to gold.

Direct quote. The price of a unit of foreign exchange expressed in the home country's currency. The term has meaning only when the home country is specified.

Directed public share issue. An issue that is targeted at investors in a single country and underwritten in whole or in part by investment institutions from that country.

Dirty float. A system of floating (i.e., market-determined) exchange rates in which the government intervenes from time to time to influence the foreign exchange value of its currency.

Discount. In the foreign exchange market, the amount by which a currency is cheaper for future delivery than for spot (immediate) delivery. The opposite of discount is premium.

Dividend yield. The current period dividend distribution as a percentage of the beginning of period share price.

Dollarization. The use of the U.S. dollar as the official currency of a country.

Domestic International Sales Corporation (DISC). Under the U.S. tax code, a type of subsidiary formed to reduce taxes on exported U.S.-produced goods. It has been ruled illegal by the World Trade Organization.

Draft. An unconditional written order requesting one party (such as an importer) to pay a specified amount of money at a specified time to the order of the writer of the draft. Also called a bill of exchange. Personal checks are one type of draft.

Dragon bond. A U.S. dollar-denominated bond sold in the so-called Dragon economies of Asia, such as Hong Kong, Taiwan, and Singapore.

Dumping. The practice of offering goods for sale in a foreign market at a price that is lower than that of the same product in the home market or a third country. As used in GATT, a special case of differential pricing.

Economic exposure. Another name for operating exposure. *See* Operating exposure.

Economic Value Added (EVA). A widely used measure of corporate financial performance. It is calculated as the difference between net operating profits after tax for the business and the cost of capital invested (both debt and equity). EVA is a registered trademark of Stern Stewart & Company.

Edge Act and Agreement Corporation. Subsidiary of a U.S. bank incorporated under federal law to engage in various international banking and financing operations, including equity participations that are not allowed to regular domestic banks. The Edge Act subsidiary may be located in a state other than that of the parent bank.

Effective exchange rate. An index measuring the change in value of a foreign currency determined by calculating a weighted average of bilateral exchange rates. The weighting reflects the importance of each foreign country's trade with the home country.

Effective tax rate. Actual taxes paid as a percentage of actual income before tax.

Efficient market. A market in which all relevant information is already reflected in market prices. The term is most frequently applied to foreign exchange markets and securities markets.

EOM. End of month. International trade term.

Equity risk premium. The average annual return of the market expected by investors over and above riskless debt.

Euro. A new currency unit that replaced the individual currencies of 12 European countries that belong to the European Union.

Euro equity public issue. A new equity issue that is underwritten and distributed in multiple foreign equity markets, sometimes simultaneously with distribution in the domestic market.

Euro zone. The countries that officially use the euro as their currency.

Euro-commercial paper (ECP). Short-term notes (30, 60, 90, 120, 180, 270, and 360 days) sold in international money markets.

Eurobank. A bank, or bank department, that bids for time deposits and makes loans in currencies other than that of the country where the bank is located.

Eurobond. A bond originally offered outside the country in whose currency it is denominated. For example, a dollar-denominated bond originally offered for sale to investors outside the United States.

Eurocredit. Bank loans to MNEs, sovereign governments, international institutions, and banks denominated in Eurocurrencies and extended by banks in countries other than the country in whose currency the loan is denominated.

Eurocurrency. A currency deposited in a bank located in a country other than the country issuing the currency.

Eurodollar. A U.S. dollar deposited in a bank outside the United States. A Eurodollar is a type of Eurocurrency.

Euronote. Short- to medium-term debt instruments sold in the Eurocurrency market.

European Central Bank (ECB). Conducts monetary policy of the European Monetary Union. Its goal is to safeguard the stability of the euro and minimize inflation.

European Currency Unit (ECU). A composite currency created by the European Monetary System prior to the euro, which was designed to function as a reserve currency numeraire. The ECU was used as the numeraire for denominating a number of financial instruments and obligations.

European Economic Community (EEC). The European common market composed of Austria, Belgium, Denmark, Finland, France, Germany, Greece, Ireland, Italy, Luxembourg, the Netherlands, Portugal, Spain, and the United Kingdom. Officially renamed the European Union (EU) January 1, 1994.

European Free Trade Association (EFTA). European countries not part of the European Union but having no internal tariffs.

European Monetary System (EMS). A monetary alliance of fifteen European countries (same members as the European Union).

European option. An option that can be exercised only on the day on which it expires.

European terms. Foreign exchange quotations for the U.S. dollar, expressed as the number of non-U.S. currency units per U.S. dollar.

European Union (EU). The official name of the former European Economic Community (EEC) as of January 1, 1994.

Ex dock. Followed by the name of a port of import. International trade term in which seller agrees to pay for the costs (shipping, insurance, customs duties, etc.) of placing the goods on the dock at the named port.

Exchange rate. The price of a unit of one country's currency expressed in terms of the currency of some other country.

Exchange Rate Mechanism (ERM). The means by which members of the EMS formerly maintained their currency exchange rates within an agreed-upon range with respect to the other member currencies.

Exchange rate pass-through. The degree to which the prices of imported and exported goods change as a result of exchange rate changes.

Exercise price. Same as the *strike price*; the agreed upon rate of exchange within an option contract to buy or sell the underlying asset.

Export credit insurance. Provides assurance to the exporter or the exporter's bank that, should the foreign customer default on payment, the insurance company will pay for a major portion of the loss. *See also* Foreign Credit Insurance Association (FCIA).

Export-Import Bank (Eximbank). A U.S. government agency created to finance and otherwise facilitate imports and exports.

Expropriation. Official government seizure of private property, recognized by international law as the right of any sovereign state provided expropriated owners are given prompt compensation and fair market value in convertible currencies.

Factoring. Specialized firms, known as factors, purchase receivables at a discount on either a non-recourse or recourse basis.

FAF. Fly away free. International trade term.

FAQ. Free at quay. International trade term.

FAS (free alongside ship). An international trade term in which the seller's quoted price for goods includes all costs of delivery of the goods alongside a vessel at the port of embarkation.

FASB 8. A regulation of the Financial Accounting Standards Board requiring U.S. companies to translate foreign affiliate financial statements by the temporal method. FASB 8 was in effect from 1976 to 1981. It is still used under specific circumstances.

FASB 52. A regulation of the Financial Accounting Standards Board requiring U.S. companies to translate foreign subsidiary financial statements by the current rate (closing rate) method. FASB 52 became effective in 1981.

FI. Free in. International trade term meaning that all expenses for loading into the hold of a vessel apply to the account of the consignee.

Financial account. A section of the balance of payments accounts. Under the revised format of the International Monetary Fund, the financial account measures long-term financial flows including direct foreign investment, portfolio investments, and other long-term movements. Under the traditional definition, which is still used by many countries, items in the financial account were included in the capital account.

Financial derivative. A financial instrument, such as a futures contract or option, whose value is derived from an underlying asset like a stock or currency.

Financial engineering. Those basic building blocks, such as spot positions, forwards, and options, used to construct positions that provide the user with desired risk and return characteristics.

Firm-specific risks. Political risks that affect the MNE at the project or corporate level. Governance risk due to goal conflict between an MNE and its host government is the main political firm-specific risk.

First in, first out (FIFO). An inventory valuation approach in which the cost of the earliest inventory purchases is charged against current sales. The opposite is LIFO, or last in, first out.

Fisher Effect. A theory that nominal interest rates in two or more countries should be equal to the required real rate of return to investors plus compensation for the expected amount of inflation in each country.

Fixed exchange rates. Foreign exchange rates tied to the currency of a major country (such as the United States), to gold, or to a basket of currencies such as Special Drawing Rights.

Flexible exchange rates. The opposite of fixed exchange rates. The foreign exchange rate is adjusted periodically by the country's monetary authorities in accordance with their judgment and/or an external set of economic indicators.

Floating exchange rates. Foreign exchange rates determined by demand and supply in an open market that is presumably free of government interference.

Floating-rate note (FRN). Medium-term securities with interest rates pegged to LIBOR and adjusted quarterly or semiannually.

FOB. Free on board. International trade term in which exporter's quoted price includes the cost of loading goods into transport vessels at a named point.

Foreign affiliate. A foreign business unit that is less than 50% owned by the parent company.

Foreign bond. A bond issued by a foreign corporation or government for sale in the domestic capital market of another country, and denominated in the currency of that country.

Foreign Corrupt Practices Act of 1977. A U.S. law that punishes companies and their executives if they pay bribes or make other improper payments to foreigners.

Foreign Credit Insurance Association (FCIA). An unincorporated association of private commercial insurance companies, in cooperation with the Export- Import Bank of the United States, that provides export credit insurance to U.S. firms.

Foreign currency intervention. Any activity or policy initiative by a government or central bank with the intent of changing a currency value on the open market. They may include both direct intervention, in which the central bank may buy or sell its own currency, or indirect intervention, in which it may change interest rates in order to change the attractiveness of domestic currency obligations in the eyes of foreign investors.

Foreign currency translation. The process of restating foreign currency accounts of subsidiaries into the reporting currency of the parent company in order to prepare a consolidated financial statement.

Foreign direct investment (FDI). Purchase of physical assets, such as plant and equipment, in a foreign country, to be managed by the parent corporation. FDI is distinguished from foreign portfolio investment.

Foreign exchange broker. An individual or firm that arranges foreign exchange transactions between two parties, but is not itself a principal in the trade. Foreign exchange brokers earn a commission for their efforts.

Foreign exchange dealer (or trader). An individual or firm that buys foreign exchange from one party (at a bid price), and then sells it (at an ask price) to another party. The dealer is a principal in two transactions and profits via the spread between the bid and ask prices.

Foreign exchange rate. The price of one country's currency in terms of another currency, or in terms of a commodity such as gold or silver. *See also* Exchange rate.

Foreign exchange risk. The likelihood that an unexpected change in exchange rates will alter the home currency value of foreign currency cash payments expected from a foreign source. Also, the likelihood that an unexpected change in exchange rates will alter the amount of home currency needed to repay a debt denominated in a foreign currency.

Foreign sales corporation (FSC). Under U.S. tax code, a type of foreign corporation that provides tax-exempt or tax-deferred income for U.S. persons or corporations having export-oriented activities.

Foreign tax credit. The amount by which a domestic firm may reduce (credit) domestic income taxes for income tax payments to a foreign government.

Forfaiting (forfeiting). A technique for arranging nonrecourse medium-term export financing, used most frequently to finance imports into Eastern Europe. A third party, usually a specialized financial institution, guarantees the financing.

Forward contract. An agreement to exchange currencies of different countries at a specified future date and at a specified forward rate.

Forward differential. The difference between spot and forward rates, expressed as an annual percentage.

Forward discount or premium. The same as forward differential.

Forward rate. An exchange rate quoted for settlement at some future date. The rate used in a forward transaction.

Forward rate agreement (FRA). An interbank-traded contract to buy or sell interest rate payments on a notional principal.

Forward transaction. An agreed-upon foreign exchange transaction to be settled at a specified future date, often one, two, or three months after the transaction date.

Free cash flow. Operating cash flow less capital expenditures (capex).

Free-trade zone. An area within a country into which foreign goods may be brought duty free, often for purposes of additional manufacture, inventory storage, or packaging. Such goods are subject to duty only when they leave the duty-free zone to enter other parts of the country.

Freely floating exchange rates. Exchange rates determined in a free market without government interference, in contrast to dirty float.

Fronting loan. A parent-to-subsidiary loan that is channeled through a financial intermediary such as a large international bank in order to reduce political risk. Presumably government authorities are less likely to prevent a foreign subsidiary repaying an established bank than repaying the subsidiary's corporate parent.

Functional currency. In the context of translating financial statements, the currency of the primary economic environment in which a foreign subsidiary operates and in which it generates cash flows.

Futures, or futures contracts. Exchange-traded agreements calling for future delivery of a standard amount of any good, e.g., foreign exchange, at a fixed time, place, and price.

Gamma. A measure of the sensitivity of an option's delta ratio to small unit changes in the price of the underlying security.

Gap risk. A type of interest rate risk in which the timing of maturities is mismatched.

General Agreement on Tariffs and Trade (GATT). A framework of rules for nations to manage their trade policies, negotiate lower international tariff barriers, and settle trade disputes.

Generally Accepted Accounting Principles (GAAP). Approved accounting principles for U.S. firms, defined by the Financial Accounting Standards Board (FASB).

Geometric return. A calculation that uses the beginning and ending returns to calculate the annual average rate of compounded growth, similar to an internal rate of return.

Global depositary receipt (GDR). Similar to American Depositary Receipts (ADRs), it is a bank certificate issued in multiple countries for shares in a foreign company. Actual company shares are held by a foreign branch of an international bank. The shares are traded as domestic shares, but are offered for sale globally by sponsoring banks.

Global registered shares. Similar to ordinary shares, global registered shares have the added benefit of being tradable on equity exchanges around the globe in a variety of currencies.

Global-specific risks. Political risks that originate at the global level, such as terrorism, the anti-globalization movement, environmental concerns, poverty, and cyber attacks.

Gold standard. A monetary system in which currencies are defined in terms of their gold content, and payment imbalances between countries are settled in gold.

Greenfield investment. An initial investment in a new foreign subsidiary with no predecessor operation in that location. This is in contrast to a new subsidiary created by the purchase of an already existing operation. An investment which starts, conceptually if not literally, with an undeveloped "green field."

Gross up. *See* Deemed-paid tax.

Hard currency. A freely convertible currency that is not expected to depreciate in value in the foreseeable future.

Hedge accounting. An accounting procedure that specifies that gains and losses on hedging instruments be recognized in earnings at the same time that the effects of changes in the value of the items being hedged are recognized.

Hedging. Purchasing a contract (including forward foreign exchange) or tangible good that will rise in value and offset a drop in value of another contract or tangible good. Hedges are undertaken to reduce risk by protecting an owner from loss.

Historical exchange rate. In accounting, the exchange rate in effect when an asset or liability was acquired.

Hot money. Money that moves internationally from one currency and/or country to another in response to interest rate differences, and moves away immediately when the interest advantage disappears.

Hybrid foreign currency options. Purchase of a put option and the simultaneous sale of a call (or vice versa) so that the overall cost is less than the cost of a straight option.

Hyperinflation countries. Countries with a very high rate of inflation. Under United States FASB 52, these are defined as countries where the cumulative three-year inflation amounts to 100% or more.

IMM. International Monetary Market. A division of the Chicago Mercantile Exchange.

Impossible Trinity. An ideal currency would have exchange rate stability, full financial integration, and monetary independence.

In-house bank. An internal bank established within an MNE if its needs are either too large or too sophisticated for local banks. The in-house bank is not a separate corporation but performs a set of functions by the existing treasury department. Acting as an independent entity, the in-house bank transacts with various internal business units of the firm on an arm's length basis.

In-the-money (ITM). Circumstance in which an option is profitable, excluding the cost of the premium, if exercised immediately.

Indirect quote. The price of a unit of a home country's currency expressed in terms of a foreign country's currency.

Integrated foreign entity. An entity that operates as an extension of the parent company, with cash flows and general business lines that are highly interrelated with those of the parent.

Intellectual property rights. Legislation that grants the exclusive use of patented technology and copyrighted creative materials. A worldwide treaty to protect intellectual property rights has been ratified by most major countries, including most recently by China.

Interest rate futures. *See* Futures, or futures contracts.

Interest rate parity. A theory that the differences in national interest rates for securities of similar risk and maturity should be equal to but opposite in sign (positive or negative) to the forward exchange rate discount or premium for the foreign currency.

Interest rate risk. The risk to the organization arising from interest bearing debt obligations, either fixed or floating rate obligations. It is typically used to refer to the changing interest rates which a company may incur by borrowing at floating rates of interest.

Interest rate swap. A transaction in which two counterparties exchange interest payment streams of different character (such as floating vs. fixed), based on an underlying notional principal amount.

Internal bank. The use of an internal unit of the corporation to act as a bank for exchanges of capital, currencies, or obligations between various units of the company.

Internal rate of return (IRR). A capital budgeting approach in which a discount rate is found that matches the present value of expected future cash inflows with the present value of outflows.

Internalization. A theory that the key ingredient for maintaining a firm-specific competitive advantage in international competition is the possession of proprietary information and control of human capital that can generate new information through expertise in research, management, marketing, or technology.

International Bank for Reconstruction and Development (IBRD, or World Bank). International development bank owned by member nations that makes development loans to member countries.

International Banking Facility (IBF). A department within a U.S. bank that may accept foreign deposits and make loans to foreign borrowers as if it were a foreign subsidiary. IBFs are free of U.S. reserve requirements, deposit insurance, and interest rate regulations.

International CAPM (ICAPM). A strategy in which the primary distinction in the estimation of the cost of equity for an individual firm using an internationalized version of the domestic capital asset pricing model is the definition of the "market" and a recalculation of the firm's beta for that market.

International Fisher Effect. A theory that the spot exchange rate should change by an amount equal to the difference in interest rates between two countries.

International Monetary Fund (IMF). An international organization created in 1944 to promote exchange rate stability and provide temporary financing for countries experiencing balance of payments difficulties.

International Monetary Market (IMM). A branch of the Chicago Mercantile Exchange that specializes in trading currency and financial futures contracts.

International monetary system. The structure within which foreign exchange rates are determined, international trade and capital flows are accommodated, and balance of payments adjustments made.

Intrinsic value. The financial gain if an option is exercised immediately.

Investment agreement. An agreement that spells out specific rights and responsibilities of both the investing foreign firm and the host government.

Investment grade. A credit rating of BBB- or higher.

J-curve affect. The adjustment path of a country's trade balance following a devaluation or significant depreciation of the country's currency. The path first worsens as a result of existing contracts before improving as a result of more competitive pricing conditions.

Joint venture. A business venture that is owned by two or more entities, often from different countries.

Jumbo loans. Loans of $1 billion or more.

Kangaroo bonds. Australian dollar-denominated bonds issued within Australia by a foreign borrower.

Lag. In the context of leads and lags, payment of a financial obligation later than is expected or required.

Lambda. A measure of the sensitivity of an option premium to a unit change in volatility.

Last in, first out (LIFO). An inventory valuation approach in which the cost of the latest inventory purchases is charged against current sales. The opposite is FIFO, or first in, first out.

Law of one price. The concept that if an identical product or service can be sold in two different markets, and no restrictions exist on the sale or transportation costs of moving the product between markets, the product's price should be the same in both markets.

Lead. In the context of leads and lags, the payment of a financial obligation earlier than is expected or required.

Lender of last resort. The body or institution within an economy which is ultimately capable of preserving the financial survival or viability of individual institutions. Typically the country's central bank.

Letter of credit (L/C). An instrument issued by a bank, in which the bank promises to pay a beneficiary upon presentation of documents specified in the letter.

Link financing. *See* Back-to-back loan or Fronting loan.

Liquid. The ability to exchange an asset for cash at or near its fair market value.

Location-specific advantage. Market imperfections or genuine comparative advantages that attract foreign direct investment to particular locations.

London Interbank Offered Rate (LIBOR). The deposit rate applicable to interbank loans in London. LIBOR is used as the reference rate for many international interest rate transactions.

Long position. A position in which foreign currency assets exceed foreign currency liabilities. The opposite of a long position is a short position.

Maastricht Treaty. A treaty among the 12 European Union countries that specified a plan and timetable for the introduction of a single European currency, to be called the euro.

Macro risk. *See* Country-specific risk.

Macroeconomic uncertainty. Operating exposure's sensitivity to key macroeconomic variables, such as exchange rates, interest rates, and inflation rates.

Managed float. A country allows its currency to trade within a given band of exchange rates.

Margin. A deposit made as security for a financial transaction otherwise financed on credit.

Marked to market. The condition in which the value of a futures contract is assigned to market value daily, and all changes in value are paid in cash daily. The value of the contract is revalued using the closing price for the day. The amount to be paid is called the variation margin.

Market liquidity. The degree to which a firm can issue a new security without depressing the existing market price, as well as the degree to which a change in price of its securities elicits a substantial order flow.

Market segmentation. The divergence within a national market of required rates of return. If all capital markets are fully integrated, securities of comparable expected return and risk should have the same required rate of return in each national market after adjusting for foreign exchange risk and political risk.

Matching currency cash flows. The strategy of offsetting anticipated continuous long exposure to a particular currency by acquiring debt denominated in that currency.

Merchant bank. A bank that specializes in helping corporations and governments finance by any of a variety of market and/or traditional techniques. European merchant banks are sometimes differentiated from clearing banks, which tend to focus on bank deposits and clearing balances for the majority of the population.

Micro risk. *See* Firm-specific risk.

Monetary assets or liabilities. Assets in the form of cash or claims to cash (such as accounts receivable), or liabilities payable in cash. Monetary assets minus monetary liabilities are called net monetary assets.

Monetary/nonmonetary method. A method of translating the financial statements of foreign subsidiaries into the parent's reporting currency. All monetary accounts are translated at the current rate, and all nonmonetary accounts are translated at their historical rates. Sometimes called temporal method in the United States.

Money market hedge. The use of foreign currency borrowing to reduce transaction or accounting foreign exchange exposure.

Money markets. The financial markets in various countries in which various types of short-term debt instruments, including bank loans, are purchased and sold.

Moral hazard. When an individual or organization takes on more risk than it would normally as a result of the existence or support of a secondary insuring or protecting authority or organization.

Mortgage Backed Security (MBS or MBO). A derivative security composed of residential or commercial real estate mortgages.

Most-favored-nation (MFN) treatment. The application by a country of import duties on the same, or most favored, basis to all countries accorded such treatment. Any tariff reduction granted in a bilateral negotiation will be extended to all other nations granted most-favored-nation status.

Multilateral netting. The process of netting intracompany payments in order to reduce the size and frequency of cash and currency exchanges.

Multinational enterprise (MNE). A firm that has operating subsidiaries, branches, or affiliates located in foreign countries.

Natural hedge. The use or existence of an offsetting or matching cash flow from firm operating activities to hedge a currency exposure.

Negotiable instrument. A written draft or promissory note, signed by the maker or drawer, that contains an unconditional promise or order to pay a definite sum of money on demand or at a determinable future date, and is payable to order or to bearer. A holder of a negotiable instrument is entitled to payment despite any personal disagreements between the drawee and maker.

Nepotism. The practice of showing favor to relatives over other qualified persons in conferring such benefits as the awarding of contracts, granting of special prices, promotions to various ranks, etc.

Net present value. A capital budgeting approach in which the present value of expected future cash inflows is subtracted from the present value of outflows.

Net working capital (NWC). Accounts receivable plus inventories less accounts payable.

Netting. The mutual offsetting of sums due between two or more business entities.

Nominal exchange rate. The actual foreign exchange quotation, in contrast to real exchange rate, which is adjusted for changes in purchasing power.

Nondeliverable forward. A forward or futures contract on currencies, settled on the basis of the differential between the contracted forward rate and occurring spot rate, but settled in the currency of the traders. For example, a forward contract on the Chinese yuan that is settled in dollars, not yuan.

Nontariff barrier. Trade restrictive practices other than custom tariffs, such as import quotas, voluntary restrictions, variable levies, and special health regulations.

North American Free Trade Agreement (NAFTA). A treaty allowing free trade and investment between Canada, the United States, and Mexico.

Note issuance facility (NIF). An agreement by which a syndicate of banks indicates a willingness to accept short-term notes from borrowers and resell those notes in the Eurocurrency markets. The discount rate is often tied to LIBOR.

Notional principal. The size of a derivative contract, in total currency value, as used in futures contracts, forward contracts, option contracts, or swap agreements.

NPV. *See* Net present value.

NSF. Not-sufficient funds. Term used by a bank when a draft or check is drawn on an account not having a sufficient credit balance.

O/A. Open account. Arrangement in which the importer (or other buyer) pays for the goods only after the goods are received and inspected. The importer is billed directly after shipment, and payment is not tied to any promissory notes or similar documents.

Offer. The price at which a trader is willing to sell foreign exchange, securities, or commodities. Also called ask.

Official reserves account. Total reserves held by official monetary authorities within the country, such as gold, SDRs, and major currencies.

Offshore finance subsidiary. A foreign financial subsidiary owned by a corporation in another country. Offshore finance subsidiaries are usually located in tax-free or low-tax jurisdictions to enable the parent multinational firm to finance international operations without being subject to home country taxes or regulations.

OLI paradigm. An attempt to create an overall framework to explain why MNEs choose foreign direct investment rather than serve foreign markets through alternative modes such as licensing, joint ventures, strategic alliances, management contracts, and exporting.

On the run. International banks of the highest credit quality that are willing to exchange obligations on a no-name basis.

Operating cash flows. The primary cash flows generated by a business from the conduct of trade, typically composed of earnings, depreciation and amortization, and changes in net working capital.

Operating exposure. The potential for a change in expected cash flows, and thus in value, of a foreign subsidiary as a result of an unexpected change in exchange rates. Also called economic exposure.

Option. In foreign exchange, a contract giving the purchaser the right, but not the obligation, to buy or sell a given amount of foreign exchange at a fixed price per unit for a specified time period. Options to buy are calls and options to sell are puts.

Order bill of lading. A shipping document through which possession and title to the shipment reside with the owner of the bill.

Organization of Petroleum Exporting Countries (OPEC). An alliance of most major crude oil producing countries, formed for the purpose of allocating and controlling production quotas so as to influence the price of crude oil in world markets.

Originate-to-Distribute (OTD). A common practice in the U.S. real estate market during the 2001–2007 real estate boom in which a real estate lender, or originator, makes loans expressly for the purpose of immediate resale.

Out-of-the-money (OTM). An option that would not be profitable, excluding the cost of the premium, if exercised immediately.

Outright quotation. The full price, in one currency, of a unit of another currency. *See* Points quotation.

Outsourcing. *See* Supply chain management.

Over-the-counter market. A market for share of stock, options (including foreign currency options), or other financial contracts conducted via electronic connections between dealers. The over-the-counter market has no physical location or address, and is thus differentiated from organized exchanges that have a physical location where trading takes place.

Overseas Private Investment Corporation (OPIC). A U.S. government-owned insurance company that insures U.S. corporations against various political risks.

Overvalued currency. A currency with a current foreign exchange value (i.e., current price in the foreign exchange market) greater than the worth of that currency. Because "worth" is a subjective concept, overvaluation is a matter of opinion. If the euro has a current market value of $1.20 (i.e., the current exchange rate is $1.20/€) at a time when its "true" value as derived from purchasing power parity or some other method is deemed to be $1.10, the euro is overvalued. The opposite of overvalued is undervalued.

Owner-specific advantage. A firm must have competitive advantages in its home market. These must be firm-specific, not easily copied, and in a form that allows them to be transferred to foreign subsidiaries.

Panda Bond. The issuance of a yuan-denominated bond in the Chinese market by a foreign borrower.

Parallel loan. Another name for a back-to-back loan, in which two companies in separate countries borrow each other's currency for a specific period of time, and repay the other's currency at an agreed maturity.

Parallel market. An unofficial foreign exchange market tolerated by a government but not officially sanctioned. The exact boundary between a parallel market and a black market is not very clear, but official tolerance of what would otherwise be a black market leads to use of the term parallel market.

Parity conditions. In the context of international finance, a set of basic economic relationships that provide for equilibrium between spot and forward foreign exchange rates, interest rates, and inflation rates.

Participating forward. A complex option position which combines a bought put and a sold call option at the same strike price to create a net zero position. Also called zero-cost option and forward participation agreement.

Pass-through period. The period of time it takes for an exchange rate change to be reflected in market prices of products or services.

Phi. The expected change in an option premium caused by a small change in the foreign interest rate (interest rate for the foreign currency).

Plain vanilla swap. An interest rate swap agreement exchange fixed interest payments for floating interest payments, all in the same currency.

Points. The smallest units of price change quoted, given a conventional number of digits in which a quotation is stated.

Points quotation. A forward quotation expressed only as the number of decimal points (usually four decimal points) by which it differs from the spot quotation.

Political risk. The possibility that political events in a particular country will influence the economic well-being of firms in that country. *See also* Sovereign risk.

Portfolio investment. Purchase of foreign stocks and bonds, in contrast to foreign direct investment.

Possessions corporation. A U.S. corporation, the subsidiary of another U.S. corporation located in a U.S. possession such as Puerto Rico, that for tax purposes is treated as if it were a foreign corporation.

Premium. In a foreign exchange market, the amount by which a currency is more expensive for future delivery than for spot (immediate) delivery. The opposite of premium is discount.

Prime mortgage. A mortgage categorized as conforming (also referred to as conventional loans), meaning it would meet the guarantee requirements for resale to Government-Sponsored Enterprises (GSEs) Fannie Mae and Freddie Mac.

Private equity. Assets that are composed of equity shares in companies that are not publicly traded.

Private placement. The sale of a security issue to a small set of qualified institutional buyers.

Profit warning. The public announcement by a publicly traded company that current period earnings will fall significantly either from a previously reported period or investor expectations.

Project financing. Arrangement of financing for long-term capital projects, large in scale, long in life, and generally high in risk.

Protectionism. A political attitude or policy intended to inhibit or prohibit the import of foreign goods and services. The opposite of free trade policies.

Psychic distance. Firms tend to invest first in countries with a similar cultural, legal, and institutional environment.

Purchasing power parity (PPP). A theory that the price of internationally traded commodities should be the same in every country, and hence the exchange rate between the two currencies should be the ratio of prices in the two countries.

Put. An option to sell foreign exchange or financial contracts. *See* Option.

Qualified institutional buyer (QIB). An entity (except a bank or a savings and loan) that owns and invests on a discretionary basis a minimum of $100 million in securities of non-affiliates.

Quota. A limit, mandatory or voluntary, set on the import of a product.

Quotation. In foreign exchange trading, the pair of prices (bid and ask) at which a dealer is willing to buy or sell foreign exchange.

Range forward. A complex option position that combines the purchase of a put option and the sale of a call option with strike prices equidistant from the forward rate. Also called flexible forward, cylinder option, option fence, mini-max, and zero-cost tunnel.

Real exchange rate. An index of foreign exchange adjusted for relative price-level changes from a base point in time, typically a month or a year. Sometimes referred to as real effective exchange rate, it is used to measure purchasing-power-adjusted changes in exchange rates.

Real option analysis. The application of option theory to capital budgeting decisions.

Reference rate. The rate of interest used in a standardized quotation, loan agreement, or financial derivative valuation.

Registered bond. Corporate or governmental debt in a bond form in which the owner's name appears on the bond and in the issuer's records, and interest payments are made to the owner.

Reinvoicing center. A central financial subsidiary used by a multinational firm to reduce transaction exposure by having all home country exports billed in the home currency and then reinvoiced to each operating subsidiary in that subsidiary's local currency.

Relative purchasing power parity. A theory that if the spot exchange rate between two countries starts in equilibrium, any change in the differential rate of inflation between them tends to be offset over the long run by an equal but opposite change in the spot exchange rate.

Renminbi (RMB). The alternative official name (the yuan, CNY) of the currency of the People's Republic of China.

Reporting currency. In the context of translating financial statements, the currency in which a parent firm prepares its own financial statements. Usually this is the parent's home currency.

Repositioning of funds. The movement of funds from one currency or country to another. An MNE faces a variety of political, tax, foreign exchange, and liquidity constraints that limit its ability to move funds easily and without cost.

Representative office. A representative office established by a bank in a foreign country to help clients doing business in that country. It also functions as a geographically convenient location from which to visit correspondent banks in its region rather than sending bankers from the parent bank at greater financial and physical cost.

Repricing risk. The risk of changes in interest rates charged or earned at the time a financial contract's rate is reset.

Restricted stock. Stock shares given to management that are not tradable or transferable before a specified future date (when they vest) or other specified conditions.

Revaluation. A rise in the foreign exchange value of a currency that is pegged to other currencies or to gold. Also called appreciation.

Rho. The expected change in an option premium caused by a small change in the domestic interest rate (interest rate for the home currency).

Risk-sharing agreement. A contractual arrangement in which the buyer and seller agree to share or split currency movement impacts on payments between them.

Risk. The likelihood that an actual outcome will differ from an expected outcome. The actual outcome could be better or worse than expected (two-sided risk), although in common practice risk is more often used only in the context of an adverse outcome (one-sided risk). Risk can exist for any number of uncertain future situations, including future spot rates or the results of political events.

Rules of the Game. The basis of exchange rate determination under the international gold standard during most of the 19th and early 20th centuries. All countries agreed informally to follow the rule of buying and selling their currency at a fixed and predetermined price against gold.

Samurai bonds. Yen-denominated bonds issued within Japan by a foreign borrower.

Sarbanes-Oxley Act. An act passed in 2002 to regulate corporate governance in the United States.

SEC Rule 144A. Permits qualified institutional buyers to trade privately placed securities without requiring SEC registration.

Section 482. The set of U.S. Treasury regulations governing transfer prices.

Securitization. The replacement of nonmarketable loans (such as direct bank loans) with negotiable securities (such as publicly traded marketable notes and bonds), so that the risk can be spread widely among many investors, each of whom can add or subtract the amount of risk carried by buying or selling the marketable security.

Self-sustaining foreign entity. One that operates in the local economic environment independent of the parent company.

Selling short (shorting). The sale of an asset which the seller does not (yet) own. The premise is that the seller believes he will be able to purchase the asset for contract fulfillment at a lower price before sale contract expiration.

Shared services. A charge to compensate the parent for costs incurred in the general management of international operations and for other corporate services provided to foreign subsidiaries that must be recovered by the parent firm.

Shareholder wealth maximization (SWM). The corporate goal of maximizing the total value of the shareholders' investment in the company.

Sharpe measure (SHP). Calculates the average return over and above the risk-free rate of return per unit of portfolio risk. It uses the standard deviation of a portfolio's total return as the measure of risk.

Shogun bonds. Foreign currency-denominated bonds issued within Japan by Japanese corporations.

Short position. *See* Long position.

SIBOR. Singapore interbank offered rate.

Sight draft. A bill of exchange (B/E) that is due on demand; i.e., when presented to the bank. *See also* Bill of exchange.

SIMEX. Singapore International Monetary Exchange.

SIV. Structure Investment Vehicle. The SIV is an off-balance-sheet entity first created by Citigroup in 1988. It was designed to allow a bank to create an investment entity that would invest in long term and higher yielding assets such as speculative grade bonds, mortgage-backed securities (MBSs) and collateralized debt obligations (CDOs), while funding itself through commercial paper (CP) issuances.

Society for Worldwide Interbank Financial Telecommunications (SWIFT). A dedicated computer network providing funds transfer messages between member banks around the world.

Soft currency. A currency expected to drop in value relative to other currencies. Free trading in a currency deemed soft is often restricted by the monetary authorities of the issuing country.

Sovereign risk. The risk that a host government may unilaterally repudiate its foreign obligations or may prevent local firms from honoring their foreign obligations. Sovereign risk is often regarded as a subset of political risk.

Sovereign spread. The credit spread paid by a sovereign borrower on a major foreign currency denominated debt obligation. For example, the credit spread paid by the Venezuelan government to borrow U.S. dollars over and above a similar maturity issuance by the U.S. Treasury.

Special Drawing Right (SDR). An international reserve asset, defined by the International Monetary Fund as the value of a weighted basket of five currencies.

Special purpose vehicle (SPV) or special purpose entity (SPE). An off-balance sheet legal entity, typically a partnership, set up for a very special business purpose that will isolate or limit the partner's financial risks associated with risks associated with the SPV's activities or assets. Similar in function to an SIV.

Speculation. An attempt to make a profit by trading on expectations about future prices.

Speculative grade. A credit quality that is below BBB, below investment grade. The designation implies a possibility of borrower default in the event of unfavorable economic or business conditions.

Spot rate. The price at which foreign exchange can be purchased (its bid) or sold (its ask) in a spot transaction. *See* Spot transaction.

Spot transaction. A foreign exchange transaction to be settled (paid for) on the second following business day.

Spread. The difference between the bid (buying) quote and the ask (selling) quote.

Stakeholder capitalism. Another name for corporate wealth maximization.

Statutory tax rate. The legally imposed tax rate.

Strategic alliance. A formal relationship, short of a merger or acquisition, between two companies, formed for the purpose of gaining synergies because in some aspect the two companies complement each other.

Strike price. The agreed upon rate of exchange within an option contract.

Stripped bonds. Bonds issued by investment bankers against coupons or the maturity (corpus) portion of original bearer bonds, where the original bonds are held in trust by the investment banker. Whereas the original bonds will have coupons promising interest at each interest date (say June and December for each of the next twenty years), a given stripped bond will represent a claim against all interest payments from the entire original issue due on a particular interest date. A stripped bond is in effect a zero coupon bond manufactured by the investment banker.

Subpart F. A type of foreign income, as defined in the U.S. tax code, which under certain conditions is taxed immediately in the United States even though it has not been repatriated to the United States. It is income of a type that is otherwise easily shifted offshore to avoid current taxation.

Subprime (subprime mortgage). Subprime borrowers have a higher perceived risk of default, normally as a result of credit history elements which may include bankruptcy, loan delinquency, default, or simply a borrower with limited experience or history of debt. They are nearly exclusively floating-rate structures, and carry significantly higher interest rate spreads over the floating bases like LIBOR.

Subsidiary. A foreign operation incorporated in the host country and owned 50% or more by a parent corporation. Foreign operations that are not incorporated are called branches.

Supply chain management. A strategy that focuses on cost reduction through imports from less costly foreign locations with lower wages.

Sushi bonds. Eurodollar or other non-yen-denominated bonds issued by a Japanese corporation for sale to Japanese investors.

Swap. This term is used in many contexts. In general it is the simultaneous purchase and sale of foreign exchange or securities, with the purchase executed at once and the sale back to the same party carried out at an agreed-upon price to be completed at a specified future date. Swaps include interest rate swaps, currency swaps, and credit swaps. A swap rate is a forward foreign exchange quotation expressed in terms of the number of points by which the forward rate differs from the spot rate.

SWIFT. *See* Society for Worldwide Interbank Financial Telecommunications.

Syndicated loan. A large loan made by a group of banks to a large multinational firm or government. Syndicated loans allow the participating banks to maintain diversification by not lending too much to a single borrower.

Synthetic forward. A complex option position which combines the purchase of a put option and the sale of a call option, or vice versa, both at the forward rate. Theoretically, the combined position should have a net-zero premium.

Systematic risk. In portfolio theory, the risk of the market itself, i.e., risk that cannot be diversified away.

T/A. Trade acceptance. International trade term.

Tariff. A duty or tax on imports that can be levied as a percentage of cost or as a specific amount per unit of import.

Tax deferral. Foreign subsidiaries of MNEs pay host country corporate income taxes, but many parent countries, including the United States, defer claiming additional taxes on that foreign source income until it is remitted to the parent firm.

Tax exposure. The potential for tax liability on a given income stream or on the value of an asset. Usually used in the context of a multinational firm being able to minimize its tax liabilities by locating some portion of operations in a country where the tax liability is minimized.

Tax haven. A country with either no or very low tax rates that uses its tax structure to attract foreign investment or international financial dealings.

Tax morality. The consideration of conduct by an MNE to decide whether to follow a practice of full disclosure to local tax authorities or adopt the philosophy, "When in Rome, do as the Romans do."

Tax neutrality. In domestic tax, the requirement that the burden of taxation on earnings in home country operations by an MNE be equal to the burden of taxation on each currency equivalent of profit earned by the same firm in its foreign operations. Foreign tax neutrality requires that the tax burden on each foreign subsidiary of the firm be equal to the tax burden on its competitors in the same country.

Tax on undistributed profits. A different income tax applied to retained earnings from that applied to distributed earnings (dividends).

Tax treaties. A network of bilateral treaties that provide a means of reducing double taxation.

Technical analysis. The focus on price and volume data to determine past trends that are expected to continue into the future. Analysts believe that future exchange rates are based on the current exchange rate.

TED Spread. Treasury Eurodollar Spread. The difference, in basis points, between the 3-month interest rate swap index or the 3-month LIBOR interest rate, and the 90-day U.S. Treasury bill rate. It is sometimes used as an indicator of credit crisis or fear over bank credit quality.

Temporal method. In the United States, term for a codification of a translation method essentially similar to the monetary/nonmonetary method.

Tenor. The length of time of a contract or debt obligation; loan repayment period.

Tequila effect. Term used to describe how the Mexican peso crisis of December 1994 quickly spread to other Latin American currency and equity markets through the contagion effect.

Terms of trade. The weighted average exchange ratio between a nation's export prices and its import prices, used to measure gains from trade. Gains from trade refers to increases in total consumption resulting from production specialization and international trade.

Territorial taxation (territorial approach). Taxation of income earned by firms within the legal jurisdiction of the host country, not on the country of the firm's incorporation.

Theta. The expected change in an option premium caused by a small change in the time to expiration.

Time draft. A draft that allows a delay in payment. It is presented to the drawee, who accepts it by writing a notice of acceptance on its face. Once accepted, the time draft becomes a promise to pay by the accepting party. *See also* Bankers' acceptance.

Total Shareholder Return (TSR). A measure of corporate performance based on the sum of share price appreciation and current dividends.

Tranche. An allocation of shares, typically to underwriters that are expected to sell to investors in their designated geographic markets.

Transaction exposure. The potential for a change in the value of outstanding financial obligations entered into prior to a change in exchange rates but not due to be settled until after the exchange rates change.

Transfer pricing. The setting of prices to be charged by one unit (such as a foreign subsidiary) of a multi-unit corporation to another unit (such as the parent corporation) for goods or services sold between such related units.

Translation exposure. The potential for an accounting-derived change in owners' equity resulting from exchange rate changes and the need to restate financial statements of foreign subsidiaries in the single currency of the parent corporation. *See also* Accounting exposure.

Transnational firm. A company owned by a coalition of investors located in different countries.

Transparency. The degree to which an investor can discern the true activities and value drivers of a company from the disclosures and financial results reported.

Treynor measure (TRN). A calculation of the average return over and above the risk-free rate of return per unit of portfolio risk. It uses the portfolio's beta as the measure of risk.

Triangular arbitrage. An arbitrage activity of exchanging currency A for currency B for currency C back to currency A to exploit slight disequilibrium in exchange rates.

Turnover tax. A tax based on turnover or sales, and is similar in structure to a VAT, in which taxes may be assessed on intermediate stages of a good's production.

Unaffiliated. An independent third-party.

Unbiased predictor. A theory that spot prices at some future date will be equal to today's forward rates.

Unbundling. Dividing cash flows from a subsidiary to a parent into their many separate components, such as royalties, lease payments, dividends, etc., so as to increase the likelihood that some fund flows will be allowed during economically difficult times.

Uncovered interest arbitrage (UIA). The process by which investors borrow in countries and currencies exhibiting relatively low interest rates and convert the proceeds into currencies that offer much higher interest rates. The transaction is "uncovered" because the investor does not sell the higher yielding currency proceeds forward.

Undervalued. The status of currency with a current foreign exchange value (i.e., current price in the foreign exchange market) below the worth of that currency. Because "worth" is a subjective concept, undervaluation is a matter of opinion. If the euro has a current market value of $1.20 (i.e., the current exchange rate is $1.20/e) at a time when its "true" value as derived from purchasing power parity or some other method is deemed to be $1.30, the euro is undervalued. The opposite of undervalued is overvalued.

Unsystematic risk. In a portfolio, the amount of risk that can be eliminated by diversification.

Value date. The date when value is given (i.e., funds are deposited) for foreign exchange transactions between banks.

Value today. A spot foreign exchange transaction in which delivery and payment are made on the same day as the contract. Normal delivery is two business days after the contract.

Value tomorrow. A spot foreign exchange transaction in which delivery and payment are made on the next business day after the contract. Normal delivery is two business days after the contract.

Value-added tax. A type of national sales tax collected at each stage of production or sale of consumption goods, and levied in proportion to the value added during that stage.

Volatility. In connection with options, the standard deviation of daily spot price movement.

Weighted average cost of capital (WACC). The sum of the proportionally weighted costs of different sources of capital, used as the minimum acceptable target return on new investments.

Wire transfer. Electronic transfer of funds.

Working capital management. The management of the net working capital requirements (A/R plus inventories less A/P) of the firm.

World Bank. *See* International Bank for Reconstruction and Development.

Worldwide approach to taxes. The principle that taxes are levied on the income earned by firms that are incorporated in a host country, regardless of where the income was earned.

Writer. Seller.

Yankee bonds. Dollar-denominated bonds issued within the United States by a foreign borrower.

Yield to maturity. The rate of interest (discount) that equates future cash flows of a bond, both interest and principal, with the present market price. Yield to maturity is thus the time-adjusted rate of return earned by a bond investor.

Yuan (CNY). The official currency of the People's Republic of China, also termed the renminbi.

Zero coupon bond. A bond that pays no periodic interest, but returns a given amount of principal at a stated maturity date. Zero coupon bonds are sold at a discount from the maturity amount to provide the holder a compound rate of return for the holding period.

Index

A

ABB (Asea Brown Boveri), 414
Absolute advantage, 9–11
Absolute purchasing power parity, 236
ABSs (Asset-backed securities), 118, 126–127
Account payables, managing, 275–277
Accounting
  corporate governance reform, 47
  exposures. see Transaction exposure; Translation exposure
Accounts, balance of payments
  capital and financial, 89–94
  current account, 86–87
  goods trade, 87–88
  major subaccounts, 84–85
ACN (American Chung Nam Incorporated), 19–20
Acquisitions
  cross-border. see Cross-border mergers and acquisitions
  funding with directed share issue, 367
  increasing share swap potential with, 365–366
ADRs. see American depositary receipts (ADRs)
Advanced technology, competitive advantage of MNEs, 409
Aelphia, corporate governance corruption, 42
Affiliates, defined, 441
Agency problem
  family-controlled firms and, 30
  limiting financial globalization, 17
  between ownership and management, 30–31, 48
Agency theory
  corporate governance and, 45–47
  opponents of hedging based on, 266
  overview of, 32
Agriculture industry, cultural and institutional risks of
    MNEs, 429
AIG. see American International Group (AIG)
Alt-A (Alternative-A paper) mortgage loans, 115, 130
American Chung Nam Incorporated (ACN), 19–20
American depositary receipts (ADRs)
  global registered shares vs., 362
  improving liquidity with, 363
  overview of, 360–362
  tracking on JPMorgan Web site, 383
American International Group (AIG)
  bailout through Troubled Asset Recovery Plan, 136–137
  financial fraud and recovery, 134
  Lehman Brothers vs. bailout of, 140–141
  receiving injection from Federal Reserve, 128

American options, 208
American terms, spot market quotes, 158
Americo Industries, 26–27
AMF (Autorité des Marchés Financiers), 50–51
Amortization, project viewpoint capital budget, 447–448
Antiglobalization
  global financial crash and, 130
  as global-specific risk, 418, 432
Apache Corporation, political risk, 420
Arbitragers
  covered interest arbitrage, 185–187
  in foreign exchange market, 150
  uncovered interest arbitrage, 187–188
Argentina
  crisis of 2002, 248–251, 256
  currency board, 69
  problems with nondeliverable forwards, 154
Arithmetic returns, equity risk premiums, 331
Arm's length price, transfer prices, 394
Arnault, Bernard, 49–54
Arthur Andersen, 42, 45
Asea Brown Boveri (ABB), 414
Asian currency crisis of 1997
  causal complexities, 245
  currency collapse, 244–245
  motivation for currency market intervention, 240
  overview of, 243–244
  role of George Soros, 246
  summary, 256
Ask quotations
  foreign exchange rates and, 158–161
  forward, 163–164
Asset allocators, 333
Asset investment, financial account, 90–91
Asset market approach
  to exchange rate determination, 237–238
  to forecasting, 238–240
Asset-backed securities (ABSs), 118, 126–127
Assets
  balance of payments as exchange of, 86
  balance of payments exchanging financial, 86
  of global finance, 4
  mortgages collateralized by value of, 116–117
  securitized, 117–119
  translating at current rate of exchange, 280
  translating with temporal method, 280

I-1

Atlas Copco, 369
At-the-money (ATM) options
    defined, 208
    pricing and valuation, 216
    put option market hedge, 273–274
Auditing
    corporate governance reform, 47
    good corporate governance practices, 43
Auditors, corporate governance structure, 39
Automated trading, foreign exchange market, 147–148
Autorité des Marchés Financiers (AMF), 50–51

B
Backlog exposure, in transaction exposure, 267
Back-to-back loans, in currency hedging, 312–313
Baht, Asian crisis of 1997, 244–245
Bailout
    debate over executive contracts during, 137
    liquidity vs. capital, 137
    Troubled Asset Recovery Plan, 136–137
Balance of payments (BOP)
    accounting, 86
    accounts, 86–89
    capital and financial accounts, 89–91
    capital flight, 103–104
    capital mobility, 102–103
    current and financial account balances, 92–94
    exchange rates and, 98–99, 237
    as flow statement, 85–86
    GDP and, 97–98
    importance of data in, 84
    inflation rates and, 99
    interest rates and, 99
    in international economic transactions, 85
    learning objectives, 83, 104–105
    Mini-Case, 105–108
    review questions, problems, and exercises, 109–112
    in total, 94–97
    trade balances and exchange rates, 99–102
    typical transactions, 84–85
Balance of trade (BOT), 87
Balance sheet
    balance of payments vs., 85
    cross-currency swaps not appearing on, 313–314
    disadvantages of localization, 358
    financial statement for foreign subsidiaries, 35
    localized financial structures for foreign subsidiaries and, 358
    predicting credit crisis of 2007-2009, 129
    SIV as off-balance, 119–121, 139
    translation exposure and, 278–280, 281–284
    translation exposure management. see Balance sheet hedge
    use of securitization and, 118

Balance sheet hedge
    managing translation exposure with, 285–287
    money market hedge acting as, 272
    summary, 287
Banbury Impex (India), 289–292
Bang & Olufsen (B & O) and Philips N.V., 337
Bank for International Settlements (BIS)
    effective exchange rate indices, 171
    ongoing credit crisis analysis, 143
    size of foreign exchange markets, 154–155
Bank loans
    debt funding through international, 370
    Eurocredits as, 370
    fronting loans as, 423–424
Bank of Canada Exchange Rate Index (CERI) Web site, 171
Bank of England
    failure of indirect currency intervention, 242–243
    fallout from credit crisis of 2007, 127
    growth of Eurocurrency market, 8
Bank of New York Mellon Web site, 383–384
Bank-based regimes, comparative corporate governance, 40
Banks
    deregulation, 114–115
    structured investment vehicles, 119–120
Banque Canada Web site, 262
Base currency, 157–158
Basic balance, balance of payments, 94–96
BBA. see British Bankers Association (BBA)
BCG (Boston Consulting Group), 435–436
Bear Stearns
    collapse of hedge funds in 2007, 123, 127
    collaterized debt obligations, 121–122
    Lehman Brothers vs. bailout of, 140
        "Beggar-thy-neighbor," currency market intervention, 240
Behavioral approach, to FDI, 413
Betas
    calculating cost of capital, 328
    global, 330
    ICAPM and, 327, 329
    measuring systematic risk, 326–327
Bid quotations
    foreign exchange rates and, 158–161
    forward, 163–164
"Big Mac Index," 174–176, 198
Bilateral tax treaties, reducing double taxation, 389
Billing exposure, in transaction exposure, 267
Bin Laden, Osama, 427–428
Biotechnology boom, Novo, 344
BIS. see Bank for International Settlements (BIS)
Black market, for bolivars, 167
Blocked funds
    budgeting for foreign project, 441–442

political risk of, 424–427
project viewpoint measurement, 451
Blogs
    Financial Times emerging markets, 473
    international tax, 406
    political insurance, 438
Bloomberg markets Web page, 262, 383
Board of directors
    corporate governance reform, 47
    corporate governance structure, 38
    good corporate governance of, 43
    Sarbanes-Oxley Act requirements, 45
Bolivar, Venezuelan, 166–168
Bonds
    diversifying portfolios using, 333
    international markets for, 372–373
BOP. see Balance of payments (BOP)
Boston Consulting Group (BCG), 435–436
BOT (Balance of trade), 87
Brand name control, reducing political risk via, 423
Brazil
    Petrobrás Mini-Case, 377–380
    Real Plan of, 249
Break-even price
    buyer of call options, 211
    buyer of put options, 213
    money market hedge, 272–273
    option market hedge, 274
    for writer of put option, 213
Bretton Woods, 1944
    capital mobility during era of, 102–103
    summary, 76–77
    U.S. dollar-based international monetary system, 61–62
Bribe Payers Index, TI, 438
Bribery, problem of, 428
BRICs (Brazil, Russia, India, and China), MNEs
    dependent on, 2
British Bankers Association (BBA)
    defining LIBOR, 8
    and LIBOR Web site, 143
    publishing LIBOR Rates, 131–132
British pound
    failure of indirect currency intervention, 242–243
    McDonald's exposure of, 225–226
British Telecom, 368
Bucket shops, 124
Budget rate, transaction exposure, 270
Budgeting. see Multinational capital budgeting
Buffett, Warren, 122
Business risk, optimal financial structure, 353–354
Buyers
    of call options, 210–211
    of put options, 212–213

C
CAI (Capital Access Index), Milken Institute, 438
Calculator, cost of capital, 350
Call options
    buyer of, 210–211
    defined, 207
    options market hedge, 274, 276–277
    writer of, 211–212
Capex (capital expenditure), 24–25
Capital
    global cost of. see Global cost and availability of
        capital
    global sourcing of. see Equity, sourcing globally
Capital Access Index (CAI), Milken Institute, 438
Capital account
    balance of payments in total, 94–96
    defined, 84–85, 87
    migrant remittances reported under, 105
    overview of, 89
Capital asset pricing model (CAPM)
    calculating cost of capital, 327–328
    calculating cost of equity, 326–327
    debate over equity risk premiums, 330–332
    international, 327–329
    parent viewpoint capital budget, 450
Capital budgeting. see Multinational capital budgeting
Capital controls, currency market intervention, 243
Capital flight, balance of payments, 103–104
Capital flows, Asian crisis of 1997 and, 243–246
Capital gains, management not in control of, 34
Capital investment, multinational capital budgeting
        analysis, 443
Capital mobility
    historical patterns of, 102–103
    remedies for global financial crash, 136
Capitalization size, portfolio diversification, 333
CAPM. see Capital asset pricing model (CAPM)
Carry trades, emerging market, 193–194
Case studies. see Mini-Case studies
Cash, capital flight mechanisms, 104
Cash flow statement, 85–86
Cash flows. see also Operating exposure; Transaction
        exposure
    budgeting for foreign project, 440
    consolidated statements of, 278–279
    credit default swaps and, 124–125
    currency swaps and, 223
    diversification of, 355
    global financial crash and, 129–131
    impact of hedging on expected. see Hedging
    interest rate swaps and, 221
    matching currency, 310–311
    parent viewpoint capital budget, 448–450
    parent viewpoint measurement, 452–453

Cash flows. see also Operating exposure; Transaction
    exposure (*continued*)
  in project financing, 455–456
  project viewpoint capital budget, 447–448
  in real option analysis, 454
  risk sharing and, 311–312
  swap agreements and, 221
Cash rates, 163
Casual empiricism, in case studies, 336
CDOs. see Collaterized debt obligations (CDOs)
CDSs (Credit default swaps)
  credit enhancement and, 122–123
  role in credit crisis of 2007–2009, 124–126
Cemex enters Indonesia. see Multinational capital
    budgeting, hypothetical case
Center for Latin American Capital Markets Research
    Web site, 350
Central banks
  direct currency market intervention, 241–242
  in foreign exchange market, 151
  as global financial institutions, 4
CEO. see Chief executive officer (CEO)
CERI (Bank of Canada Exchange Rate Index) Web site,
    171
CFO (Chief financial officer), 38, 45
CFTC (Commodity Futures Trading Commission), 151
Cheung Yan, 19–20
Chicago Board of Trade (CBOT), 219, 364
Chicago Mercantile Exchange (CME)
  foreign currency futures traded on, 205
  foreign currency options traded on, 208–209
  interest rate futures traded on, 219
  merger with CBOT, 364
  Web site, 232
Chief executive officer (CEO)
  board structure, 47
  corporate governance structure, 38
  in family-owned firms, 41
  Sarbanes-Oxley Act requirements, 45
Chief financial officer (CFO), 38, 45
Chief operating officer (COO), 38
Chile, equity issuance, 365
China
  causes of U.S. dollar decline, 75
  credit crisis of 2007–2009 and, 128
  current and financial account balances for, 93
  foreign exchange reserves, 94
  globalization of yuan, 77–80
  trading in foreign exchange market, 156
  trinity/trilemma of international finance, 68
  using Web to understand doing business in, 473
CIA (Covered interest arbitrage), 185–187, 193
Civil strife, OPIC insurance coverage for, 422
Classical gold standard, 60

Clearing House Interbank Payments System (CHIPS), 152
Clearinghouses
  for exchange-traded options, 209
  for foreign currency futures contracts, 206
Client or retail market, foreign exchange, 148–151
Close psychic distance, behavioral approach to FDI, 413
CLS (Continuous Linked Settlement), 151
CME. see Chicago Mercantile Exchange (CME)
CNH, globalization of yuan, 78–80
CNY, globalization of yuan, 80
CNY-NDFs, globalization of yuan, 78–80
Code Napoleon, 41
Codified civil law, 41
Collateral, purchasing foreign currency futures, 206
Collaterized debt obligations (CDOs)
  accountability flaw of, 122–123
  birth of new issues and collapse of, 123
  credit enhancement and, 122–123
  financial fraud and, 134
  ownership flaw of, 122
  role in credit crisis of 2007–2009, 121–122
  structured investment vehicles purchasing, 119–121
Commercial banks
  crisis in corporate lending markets, 129
  Federal Reserve bailouts and, 140
  as global financial institution, 4–5
  results of banking deregulation on, 114
Commercial paper (CP) issuances
  crisis conditions in corporate lending markets, 129
  funding structured investment vehicles, 119–120
  global financial crash and role of, 133
Commodity Futures Modernization Act of 2000, 124, 151
Commodity Futures Trading Commission (CFTC), 151
Comparative advantage
  financial globalization and, 17
  of hedging, 266
  of localized financial structures for MNEs, 358
  overview of, 9–10
  review questions, problems, and exercises, 26
Comparative corporate governance, 39–41
Compensation
  corporate governance of management, 43
  cross-border acquisitions, 459
Competitive advantage of nations, determinants of, 410–411
Competitive advantage, sustaining
  advanced technology, 409
  differentiated products, 410
  economies of scale and scope, 409
  financial strategy, 412–413
  financial strength, 409–410
  home market, 410–411
  managerial and marketing expertise, 409
  OLI Paradigm and internalization, 411–412
  overview of, 409

Competitive exposure. see Operating exposure

Consolidated debt ratio, 358

Consolidated profits, maximizing, 35

Contagion
    of credit crisis of 2007–2009, 129–131
    defined, 238
    driving asset market approach to forecasting, 238–239

Containerboard. see Nine Dragons Paper

Contingent foreign currency exposure, cross-border
    acquisitions, 461

Continuous Linked Settlement (CLS), 151

Contracts
    foreign currency futures, 205–207
    options. see Foreign currency options

Contractual hedges, 269, 288

Control premium, acquisition valuations, 465

Conventional loans, prime mortgages as, 115

Convergence, EMU, 72

COO (Chief operating officer), 38

Coordinated intervention, currency market, 241–242

Corporate governance
    asset market approach to forecasting and, 238–239
    comparative, 39–41
    consensus on good practices, 42–43
    corporate reputation and good, 42–44
    cost of capital and, 337
    failures in, 42
    family ownership and, 41
    goal of, 36–37
    learning objectives, 28, 48–49
    Mini-Case, 49–54
    overview of, 36
    public trading of shares and, 29–30
    reform of, 45–48
    reputation and good, 46
    review questions, problems, and exercises, 54–58
    structure of, 37–39

Corporate responsibility and sustainability, 13

Corporate social responsibility (CSR), 13

Corrugated Duplex containerboard, 20

Corrugated Medium containerboard, 20

Corruption, risks of MNEs, 428

Corruption index, 438

Cost of capital
    corporate governance and, 337
    financing analysis, multinational capital budgeting, 444
    optimal financial structure and, 353–354
    parent viewpoint capital budget, 450
    Petrobrás of Brazil Mini-Case, 378–379
    WACC. see Weighted average cost of capital (WACC)

Cost of Capital calculator, 350

Cost of debt
    calculating, 327–328
    foreign exchange risk and, 355–356

    optimal financial structure and, 353–354

Cost of equity
    calculating international cost of capital, 328
    capital estimation and corporate, 332
    debate over equity risk premiums, 330–332
    measuring using CAPM, 326–327
    for Nestlé of Switzerland, 329–330
    optimal financial structure and, 354
    parent viewpoint capital budget, 450
    Petrobrás of Brazil Mini-Case, 379

Cost of remittances, 107–108

Counterparties, back-to-back loans, 313

Country, portfolio diversification by, 333

Country-specific political risks
    cultural and institutional risks of MNEs, 427–430
    defined, 418
    predicting, 419–420
    summary, 434
    transfer risk with blocked funds, 424–427

Covered hedge, 270

Covered interest arbitrage (CIA), 185–187, 193

Covered transactions, 270

Covering, defined, 270

CP. see Commercial paper (CP) issuances

Crawling pegs, IMF exchange rate, 66

Credit
    international debt markets. see International debt markets
    obtaining in foreign exchange market, 148

Credit (roll-over) risk, 218–219

Credit crisis of 2007–2009
    from collaterized debt obligations, 121–123
    from credit default swaps, 124–126
    from credit enhancement, 126–127
    fallout, global contagion, 129–131
    fallout, LIBOR's role, 131–133
    fallout, overview, 127–129
    financial fraud and recovery example, 134
    future of, 138
    learning objectives, 113, 138–139
    Mini-Case, 139–141
    remedy for, 134–138
    review questions, problems, and exercises, 141–143
    securitization and, 117–119
    from structured investment vehicles, 119–121
    subprime debt as seed of, 114–117

Credit default swaps (CDSs)
    credit enhancement and, 122–123
    financial fraud and, 134
    role in credit crisis of 2007–2009, 124–126

Credit quality
    securitization degrading, 119
    subprime lending and, 115–116

Credit rating firms, marketing CDOs, 121–122

Credit risk management, 15–16

The Crisis of Global Capitalism: Open Society Endangered (Soros), 246
Crisis planning, global-specific risks, 431
Cronyism, Asian crisis of 1997 and, 245
Cross rates
    checking on intermarket arbitrage, 162
    consistency in forecasting, 253–254
    overview of, 161–162
Cross-border foreign direct investment, 235, 238–240
Cross-border mergers and acquisitions
    currency risks in, 460–462
    identification and valuation, 457–458
    learning objectives, 439–440, 462–463
    Mini-Case, 463–469
    overview of, 456
    post-acquisition management, 460
    settlement of transaction, 458–460
Cross-border supply chain integration, 431
Cross-capital budgeting. see Multinational capital budgeting
Cross-currency swaps
    managing foreign exchange risk with, 225–226
    as proactive policies, 313–314
Cross-listing
    barriers to, 366
    effect on share price, 364–365
    issuance of foreign equity, 362–364
    sourcing equity globally, 352–353
    summary, 374
Crude oil, credit crisis of 2007–2009, 128
CSR (corporate social responsibility), 13
Cultural political risks, 418, 426
Culture, impact on business conduct, 46
Currency
    24-hour-a-day global trading in, 147–148
    contemporary regimes, 65–68
    at core of global financial marketplace, 5
    derivatives. see Derivatives; Foreign currency derivatives
    determining exchange rate. see Foreign exchange rate determination and forecasting
    foreign exchange market. see Foreign exchange market
    global financial crash and, 130
    global micromaps of, 27
    market for, 5–7
    substitution theories of exchange rate determination, 237–238
Currency board
    Argentine crisis of 2002, 248–250
    defined, 69
    for emerging markets, 71
Currency contract period, trade balance adjustment, 100–101
Currency futures. see Foreign currency futures
Currency market intervention

capital controls method, 243
    direct, 241–242
    into foreign exchange markets, 240
    indirect, 242
    motivations for, 240–241
    rules of thumb for effective, 242
Currency options. see Foreign currency options
Currency regime choices
    contemporary, 65–68
    of emerging markets, 69–72, 77
Currency risks
    cross-border acquisitions, 460–462
    defined, 265
    fixed exchange rates in emerging markets and, 303
    hedge transaction exposure for, 275
    hedging, 266–267
    management of, 277–278
    Petrobrás of Brazil Mini-Case, 378–379
    symbols, 5
    transaction exposure and, 269–270
Currency swaps
    defined, 221
    McDonald's British pound exposure, 225–226
    overview of, 222–223
    summary, 225
Currency switching, 311
Currency volatilities
    credit crisis of 2007–2009, 278
    Web sites for statistics on, 232, 298
Currency yield curves, forward premium, 183–184
Current account
    balance of payments in total, 94–96
    debate between U.S. and China over yuan, 241
    defined, 84–85
    determining exchange rate, 239
    financial account balances and, 92–94
    GDP and, 97
    goods trade, 87–88
    overview of, 86–87
    service trade, 89
Current rate translation method
    managing translation exposure, 283–284, 286
    overview of, 280
    summary, 288
    U.S. translation procedures using, 281
Current transfers
    in current account, 87
    migrant remittances as, 105
Cyber attacks, 418, 433

D
Daewoo, 287
Daily market commentary Web site, 172
DCF. see Discounted cash flow (DCF)

Debt, 380–384
   credit crisis. see Credit crisis of 2007–2009
   financing analysis, multinational capital budgeting,
      443–445
   financing foreign subsidiary, 358–360
   fixed-rate. see Fixed-rate debt
   interest rate risk and, 217–219
   localized financial structures for MNEs, 357–358
   measuring cost of, 327
   Nine Dragons Paper, 22–25
   securitized, 117–119
   subprime, 114–117
   World Bank's external debt analysis, 27
Debt, sourcing globally. see also International debt markets
   designing strategy for, 352–353
   financial structure and. see Financial structure, foreign
      subsidiaries
   learning objectives, 351, 375–376
   Mini-Case, 377–380
   optimal financial structure, 353–356
   overview of, 351–352
   private placement markets for, 368–369
   review questions, problems, and exercises, 380–384
Defense industry, risks of MNEs, 428
Defensive investments, 14
Deferral privilege, taxes
   overview of, 388
   tax-haven subsidiaries and offshore financial centers,
      396–397
   U.S. conundrum, 400–401
   U.S. tax revenues, 403
Deficit
   complicating global and monetary policies, 3
   implications of BOP, 97
   U.S. goods trade, 88
Demand conditions, home country competitive
      advantage, 411
Demutualization, 363
Denmark. see Novo Industri A/S (Novo)
Depository Institutions Deregulation and Monetary
      Control Act (DIDMCA), 115
Depository receipts (shares), 360–362
Depreciation, project viewpoint capital budget, 447–448
Deregulation
   credit default swaps as result of, 124–126
   crisis in corporate lending markets, 129
   for global financial crash, 135–136
   results of banking, 114
   subprime lending as result of, 115
Derivatives
   as assets of global finance, 7–9
   credit default swaps as, 124–126
   exchanges for global, 364
   foreign currency. see Foreign currency derivatives

remedies for global financial crash, 135
Devaluation, trade and
   overview of, 100
   trade balance adjustment path, 101
DFs. see Domestic firms (DFs)
DIDMCA (Depository Institutions Deregulation and
      Monetary Control Act), 115
Differentiated products, competitive advantage of MNEs,
      410
Dim Sum Bond Market, 80
Direct intervention, currency market, 241–242
Direct investment, financial account, 89–90
Direct quotations, foreign exchange rates, 158
Directed public share issues, 367
Disclosure
   comparative corporate governance and, 40–41
   corporate governance ensuring, 37
   cross-listing and selling equity abroad, 366
   foreign investment via joint venture and, 417
   good corporate governance practices, 43
   less stringent requirements of Eurobonds, 374
   U.S. level of required, 366
Discounted cash flow (DCF)
   cross-border acquisitions, 465–467
   parent viewpoint measurement, 452–453
   real option analysis vs., 454
Disequilibrium
   covered interest arbitrage taking advantage of, 185, 188
   managing operating exposure, 308–309
   measuring operating exposure, 304
   pros of hedging, 266
Disequilibrium, exchange rates in emerging markets, 243
   Argentine crisis of 2002, 248–251
   Asian crisis of 1997, 243–246
   overview of, 243
   Russian crisis of 1998, 246–248
Distributions, translating, 280
Diversification
   operating exposure and, 308–309
   optimal financial structure and, 355
   Petrobrás of Brazil Mini-Case, 377–378
   size and liquidity of market and, 363
Dividends
   advantages of ADRs, 361
   shareholder return objectives of management, 33–34
Dollar rates, spot market quotes, 157–158
Dollarization
   in Ecuador, 70–71
   for emerging markets, 71
   overview of, 69–70
Domestic firms (DFs)
   cost of capital for MNEs vs., 338–341
   defined, 335
   sourcing equity globally, 352–353

Domestic phase, globalization process, 12–15
Domestic portfolio theory, 333–334
Domestic tax neutrality, 387
dot.com bubble, 114
Dumas, Jean-Louis, 52–53
Dynamic operating exposure, 300–301

E

Earnings before interest, taxes, depreciation, and
    amortization (EBITDA), 447–448
EBITDA (earnings before interest, taxes, depreciation,
    and amortization), 447–448
EBRD (European Bank for Reconstruction and
    Development), 473
ECB (European Central Bank), 72–75
Economic channel, of corporate responsibility, 13
Economic exposure, 264
Economies of scale and scope, MNEs, 409
The Economist, "Big Mac Index," 174–176
ECP (Euro-commercial paper), 372
Ecuador, dollar as official currency of, 70–71
Edgar Files, SEC Web site, 321
Effective tax rates
    statutory tax rates vs., 399
    U.S. conundrum, 401–403
Egyptian protests, Apache Corporation, 420
Electronic trading, 364
Eli Lilly and Company Web site, 350
Emerging Era (1971–1997), capital mobility during,
    102–103
Emerging markets
    Argentine crisis of 2002, 248–251
    Asian crisis of 1997, 243–246
    asset market approach to forecasting, 240
    carry trades in, 193–194
    corporate competition from, 435–436
    currency regime choices of, 69–72, 77
    disequilibrium of exchange rates in. see
        Disequilibrium, exchange rates in emerging
        markets
    diversifying portfolio with, 333
    fixed exchange rates and currency risk in, 303
    globalization of securities markets, 336–337, 346
    Internet exercises on, 473
    political risk, 438
    project financing for, 455–456
    Russian crisis of 1998, 246–248
Empirical tests
    of Fisher effect, 182
    of international Fisher effect, 182
    of purchasing power parity, 177–178
Employment
    electronic trading reducing specialist, 364
    growth in GDP leading to higher rates of, 97

privatization expanding sales and, 366, 368
requiring MNEs to maximize use of local, 423
stakeholder capitalism model and, 32, 48
EMS (European Monetary System), 63–65, 72
EMTN (Euro medium-term note), 372
EMU. see European Economic and Monetary Union
    (EMU)
English common law, investor protection, 41
Enron scandal
    failure of corporate governance, 36, 42
    widespread use of special purpose vehicles, 121
Environmental concerns
    as global-specific risk, 418
    political accusations against MNEs, 432
Environmental sustainability, corporate, 13
Equilibrium
    covered interest arbitrage creating, 187
    forecasting exchange rates and, 254
    between interest rates and exchange rates, 188–189
    international parity conditions in, 191–192
    measuring operating exposure for, 303–304
Equitable treatment of shareholders, 37
Equity
    corporate governance structure, 38–39
    financing foreign subsidiaries with thin equity base, 423
    in foreign investments via joint ventures, 417
    seeds of credit crisis of 2007–2009, 114
    swaps, 50–52
    tranches, 122–123
    translating at current rate of exchange, 280
    translating with temporal method, 280
Equity, cost of
    calculating international cost of capital, 328
    debate over equity risk premiums, 330–332
    measuring using CAPM, 326–327
    Nestlé of Switzerland, 329–330
    optimal financial structure and, 354
    Petrobrás of Brazil Mini-Case, 379
Equity, sourcing globally
    cross-listing and selling equity abroad, 364–366
    designing strategy for, 352–353
    directed public share issues vs., 367
    euroequity public issue vs., 367–368
    financial structure of foreign subsidiaries, 356–362
    foreign equity listing and issuance, 362–364
    learning objectives, 351, 375–376
    Mini-Case, 377–380
    optimal financial structure, 353–356
    overview of, 351–352
    private equity funds vs., 369
    private placement markets vs., 368–369
    review questions, problems, and exercises, 380–384
Equity rights index, governance, 44
Equity risk premiums, 330–332

Equity-related issue, Eurobonds, 373
ERM (Exchange Rate Mechanism), European, 242–243
Esso of Sweden, Statoil of Norway's acquisition of, 461
Ethics, corporate governance practices, 41
EUR. see Euro
Euro
    American terms used to quote, 158
    creation of, 72–75, 77
    credit crisis of 2007–2009 and, 278
    emerging market carry trades and, 193–194
    improving market liquidity using, 334
    JPMorgan Chase forecast, 253
    real effective exchange rate of, 179–180
    as rigidly fixed system, 66
    Toyota's European operating exposure, 317–318
Euro medium-term note (EMTN), 372
Eurobanks, 7–8
Eurobond market
    overview of, 372–373
    ratings and other international issues, 374
    sourcing equity globally, 352–353
    unique characteristics of, 373–374
Euro-commercial paper (ECP), 372
Eurocredits, 370–371
Eurocurrencies
    Euronote market for, 371–372
    international debt funding through Eurocredits, 370
    and LIBOR, 8–9
    overview of, 7–8
Eurodollars, 7, 219–220
Euroequity public issue, 367–368
Euroeuros, 7
Euronext, 363–364
Euronote market, 371–372
European Bank for Reconstruction and Development
    (EBRD), 473
European Central Bank (ECB), 72–75
European Economic and Monetary Union (EMU)
    achieving monetary unification, 72
    launch of euro, 73
    Maastricht Treaty, 72
    reasons for monetary unification, 73
European Monetary System (EMS), 63–65, 72
European option, 208
European terms, spot market quotes, 157–158
European Union (EU)
    birth of euro, 72–75
    expansion of euro, 75
    trinity/trilemma of international finance, 68
Eurosterling, 7
Euroyen, 7
Eurozone, 75
Exchange rate, history of
    1876–1913 gold standard, 60

1914–1944 interwar years and World War II, 60
1944 Bretton Woods Agreement, 61
1945–1973 fixed, 62–63
1973–present, 63–65
Exchange Rate Mechanism (ERM), European, 242–243
Exchange rate regimes
    choices of emerging markets, 69–72
    IMF classifications for, 66–68
    trade-offs between, 75–76
Exchange rates
    balance of payments and, 98–99
    capital mobility in historical eras of, 102–103
    currency market intervention, 240–243
    determining and forecasting, Foreign exchange rate
        determination and forecasting
    economic theories and. see International parity
        conditions
    fixed. see Fixed exchange rates
    fixing value of euro, 74
    foreign. see Foreign exchange rates and quotations
    impossible trinity of, 67–68
    interest rates and. see Interest rates, and exchange rates
    large fiscal deficits complicating, 3
    nominal and real indices, 178–180
    official reserves depending on, 92–93
    overview of, 174
    pass-through, 179–181
    purchasing power parity and law of one price, 174–176
    purchasing power parity, empirical tests of, 177–178
    purchasing power parity, relative, 176–177
    quotation conventions, 7
    real effective index for, 178–180
    review questions, problems, and exercises, 80
    terminology, 5–7
    trade balances and, 99–102
Exchange-traded options, 208–209
Exercise (strike) price
    advantage of OTC options, 208–209
    call options, 210–212
    currency option quotations and prices, 209–210
    defined, 208
    put options, 212–214
Exotic currency Web sites, 172
Expected changes in cash flow, 301–302
Exports
    approach to blocked funds, 426
    foreign investment via, 414
    reducing political risk via controlling, 423
Expropriation
    OPIC insurance coverage for, 422
    project viewpoint measurement, 451
External debt, World Bank analysis of, 27
External forces, corporate governance structure, 37–39
External funding of foreign subsidiary, 358–360

F

Factor conditions, home country competitive advantage, 411

Failures, corporate governance, 42

Fair value, 238

Fallout, credit crisis of 2007–2009, 127–129

False invoicing, capital flight mechanism, 104

Family ownership
    corporate governance practices in, 40–41
    LVMH vs. Hermès case, 49–54
    overview of, 28–29
    public/private hybrids of MNE, 35–36
    risk taking in, 34–35
    separation from management, 30–31
    superior performance of, 35–36, 41
    sustainability objective of, 13

Fannie Mae
    government bailout of, 128, 137
    Lehman Brothers vs. bailout of, 140
    selling mortgage loans to, 115

FASB (Financial Accounting Standards Board) Web site, 298

FDI. see Foreign direct investment (FDI)

Federal Deposit Insurance Corporation (FDIC)
    Financial Reform Law of 2010, 137
    insuring deposits in commercial banks, 114
    Lehman Brothers case and, 140–141

Federal Reserve Bank of New York Web site
    currency volatilities, 232, 298
    latest in default rates, 143

Felix Resources, 463–469

FIBOR (Frankfurt Interbank Offered Rate), 8

Fiduciary responsibility, vs. individual profit motives, 134

Financial account
    balance of payments in total, 94–96
    current account balances and, 92–94
    defined, 84–85
    direct investment, 89–90
    overview of, 89

Financial Accounting Standards Board (FASB) Web site, 298

Financial analysis, multinational capital budgeting, 446–447

Financial challenges and global economy
    corporate responsibility and sustainability, 13
    global capital markets entering new era, 3
    global financial management, 12–13
    global financial marketplace, 4–9
    globalization process, 14–17
    learning objectives, 2–3, 18
    market imperfections and rationale for MNEs, 13–14
    Mini-Case, Nine Dragons Paper-2009, 18–25
    overview of, 3

review questions, problems, and exercises, 26–27
    theory of comparative advantage, 9–12

Financial derivatives. see Derivatives; Foreign currency derivatives

Financial globalization and strategy
    cost of capital, 326–328
    equity risk premiums, 330–332
    global betas, 330
    ICAPM, 327–330
    overview of, 324–325

Financial goals
    and corporate governance. see Corporate governance
    learning objectives, 28, 48–49
    of management, 31–36
    Mini-Case, 49–54
    ownership of business, 28–31
    review questions, problems, and exercises, 54–58

Financial hedges, 269

Financial management, global, 12–13

Financial market development, corporate governance, 40

Financial mercantilism, 130

Financial Reform Law of 2010, 137

Financial returns, governance of, 44

Financial strength, competitive advantage of MNEs, 409–410

Financial structure, foreign subsidiaries
    conforming to local debt norms, 357–358
    depository receipts, 360–362
    financing, 358–360
    global registered shares, 362
    optimal, 353–356
    overview of, 356–357

Financial Times, 27, 58, 473

Financing
    analysis in multinational capital budgeting, 443–445
    project, 455–456

Firm strategy, home competitive advantage, 411

Firm-specific political risks
    defined, 418
    predicting, 419
    summary, 434
    types of, 420–424

Fisher effect
    international, 182, 192
    international parity conditions in equilibrium and, 191–192
    overview of, 181–182
    summary, 192

Fixed exchange rates
    balance of payments and, 98
    Bretton Woods and IMF, 1944, 61–62
    and currency risk in emerging markets, 303
    of dollarization, 69–70
    of euro, 74

flexible vs., 67
international monetary system 1945–1973, 62–63
significance of official reserves depending on, 92–93
Fixed-rate debt
  credit vs. repricing risk, 218–219
  currency swap strategies, 222–223
  as foundation of international market, 218
  interest rate swap strategies, 221–222
Fixed-rate regime, 252
Flexible exchange rates, vs. fixed, 67
Floating Era (1971–1997), capital mobility during, 102–103
Floating exchange rate
  Argentine crisis of 2002 and, 250
  balance of payments and, 97–99
  capital mobility during, 102–103
  in emerging markets, 69, 71
  international monetary system dominated by, 2
  long-term movements in currency under, 252
  official reserves depending on, 92–93
Floating-rate debt
  credit vs. repricing risk, 218–219
  currency swap strategies, 222–223
  fixed-rate vs., 218
  interest rate swap strategies, 221–222
Floating-rate note (FRN), Eurobonds, 373
Flow statement, balance of payments as, 85–86
Forced direct reinvestment, from blocked funds, 426
Forecasting foreign exchange rate
  asset market approach to, 238–240
  cross-rate consistency in, 253–254
  making sense of market movements, 255–256
  multinational capital budgeting analysis, 443
  PPP poor at, 236
  in practice, 251–252
  summary of, 256
  technical analysis, 252–253
  thoughts on, 254–255
Foreign affiliates, foreign investment via, 416
Foreign bonds, 373
Foreign currency derivatives
  foreign currency futures contract, 205–207
  interest rate derivatives, 219–223
  interest rate risk, 217–219
  learning objectives, 204, 224–225
  Mini-Case, 225–226
  option pricing and valuation, 215–217
  options. see Foreign currency options
  overview of, 204–205
  prudence in practice, 223–224
  review questions, problems, and exercises, 226–232
Foreign currency futures
  contract specifications, 205–206
  defined, 205

forward contracts vs., 205, 224
long positions strategy, 207
short positions strategy, 206
summary, 224
Foreign currency options
  buyer of call, 210–211
  buyer of put, 212–213
  Internet exercises, 231–232
  markets, 208–209
  New Zealand kiwi and, 214–215
  overview of, 207–208
  pricing and valuation, 215–217, 224, 231
  quotations and prices, 209–210, 224
  review questions, problems and exercises, 226–232
  writer of call, 211–212
  writer of put, 213–214
Foreign currency terms, forward quotations in, 164–165
Foreign direct investment (FDI)
  competitive advantage of. see Competitive advantage, sustaining
  deciding where to invest, 413–414
  learning objectives, 408
  modes of, 414–418
  moving to multinational trade phase, 16
Foreign direct investment (FDI), and political risk
  country-specific risks, 419–420, 424–430
  defining and classifying, 418–419
  firm-specific risks, 419–424
  global-specific risks, 420, 430–433
  learning objectives, 433–434
  Mini-Case, 435–436
  overview of, 418
  review questions, problems, and exercises, 436–438
Foreign direct investment, financial account, 89–90
Foreign exchange
  brokers, 151
  dealers, 149
  exposure, 263–264
Foreign exchange market
  CIA creating equilibrium in, 187
  functions of, 148
  geographical extent of, 147–148
  interest rate parity linking international money markets to, 184–185
  learning objectives, 146, 165
  Mini-Case, 166–168
  participants, 148–151
  rates and quotations. see Foreign exchange rates and quotations
  size of, 154–156
  transactions in interbank market, 151–154
Foreign exchange rate determination and forecasting
  asset market approach to, 237–238
  asset market approach to forecasting, 238–240

Foreign exchange rate determination and forecasting (*continued*)
    balance of payments approach to, 237
    currency market intervention, 240–243
    in emerging markets. see Disequilibrium, exchange rates in emerging markets
    forecasting in practice, 251–256
    infrastructure weaknesses affecting, 235
    learning objectives, 234, 256
    Mini-Case, 257–258
    monetary approach to, 237
    overview of, 234–236
    purchasing power parity approach to, 236
    review questions, problems, and exercises, 259–262
    technical analysis approach to, 238
Foreign exchange rates and quotations
    cross rates, 161–162
    currency symbols, 157
    defined, 156
    forward quotations, 163–164
    forward quotations in percentage terms, 164–165
    intermarket arbitrage, 162
    learning objectives, 146, 165
    Mini-Case, 166–168
    percentage change in spot rates, 163
    review questions, problems, and exercises, 168–172
    spot market quotes, 157–161
Foreign exchange risks
    absorbed by firm in globalization process, 14
    in back-to-back loans, 312–313
    challenges of managing, 315
    cost of debt and, 355–356
    cross currency swaps managing, 225–226, 313–314
    cross-border acquisitions, 460–462
    in exporting, 414
    foreign exchange market minimizing, 147, 153
    in forward market hedge, 270
    hedging, 150
    international financial management and, 12, 18
    International Fisher effect criticisms of, 181
    in international trade, 15
    market segmentation and, 334–335
    of MNEs, 339–341
    Novo example, 344
    parent viewpoint measurement, 452–453
    project viewpoint measurement, 451–452
    in swap transactions, 153
Foreign exchange transactions
    defined, 146
    managing exposure with contractual hedges, 269
    participants in, 148–151
    regulating fraud, 151
Foreign securities. see International portfolio investors
Foreign subsidiaries

    budgeting for foreign project, 440
    financial structure of. see Financial structure, foreign subsidiaries
    foreign investment via joint venture, 416
Foreign tax
    credits, 391–392, 399
    neutrality, 387
Fortune 500 companies
    crisis conditions in corporate lending markets, 129
    global firms in, 58
Forward contracts, 205, 224, 268
Forward market, 151, 152–153
Forward market hedge
    management of account payables, 275, 277
    money market hedge structure vs., 271–272
    overview of, 270–271
    risk management, 278
Forward premium (discount), 164, 183–184
Forward quotations
    foreign exchange rates and, 163–164
    OzForex Web site for, 171
    in percentage terms, 164–165
Forward rate
    option pricing and valuation, 216–217
    overview of, 183–184
    as unbiased predictor of future spot rate, 189–191, 192–193
Forward rate agreement (FRA), 220–221
Forward-forward swaps, 153
FRA (Forward rate agreement), 220–221
Frankfurt Interbank Offered Rate (FIBOR), 8
Franking credits, 465
Fraud
    global credit crisis and, 134
    regulating foreign exchange trading, 151
Freddie Mac
    government bailout of, 128, 137
    Lehman Brothers vs. bailout of, 140
    selling mortgage loans to, 115
Free cash flow, project viewpoint capital budget, 447–448
Free-floating regime, emerging markets, 71–72
FRN (floating-rate note), Eurobonds, 373
Fronting loans, 424–425
Fuld, Richard, Jr., 140
Full financial integration, impossible trinity of, 67–68
Functional currency, of foreign subsidiary, 279, 288
Fund positioning, setting transfer price, 392–393
Fundamental equilibrium path, forecasting exchange rates, 254
Futures. see Foreign currency futures

G
GAAP (generally accepted accounting principles), 39
Gains, from translating, 280–281

Gambler's dilemma, 223
Garman-Kohlhagen options, 231–232
GATT (General Agreements on Tariffs and Trade), 429
GDP. see Gross domestic product (GDP)
General Agreements on Tariffs and Trade (GATT), 429
General Electric, rise of U.S. multinationals, 13
Generally accepted accounting principles (GAAP), 39
Geographical extent, of foreign exchange market, 147–148, 155–156
Geometric returns, equity risk premiums, 331
Glass-Steagall Act, repeal of, 114
Global capital markets
    challenges of, 2–3
    entering new era, 3
    international capital flows, 27
Global challengers, 435–436
Global cost and availability of capital
    dimensions of, 325
    financial globalization and strategy. see Financial globalization and strategy
    financial strength of MNEs due to, 409–410
    international portfolio investors' role. see International portfolio investors
    learning objectives, 324, 342
    Mini-Case, 342–346
    MNEs vs. domestic firms, 338–341
    optimal financial structure, 354–355
    review questions, problems, and exercises, 346–350
Global Crossing, 42
Global depository receipts (GDRs), 360
Global financial marketplace
    assets, 4
    Eurocurrencies and LIBOR, 7–9
    institutions, 4–5
    linkages, 5
    market for currencies, 5–7
    overview of, 4
Global portfolios, 330, 333
Global registered shares (GRSs), 362
Global remittances
    overview of, 105–108
    parent viewpoint capital budget, 449
Global warming, accusations against MNEs, 432
Globalization
    analyses of political risks, 418, 420, 430–433
    changing landscape of economy, 2–3
    credit-induced global recession, 129–131
    domestic to international trade phase of, 14–16
    financial challenge of. see Financial challenges and global economy
    financial management under, 12–13
    financial strategy. see Financial globalization and strategy
    international trade to multinational phase of, 16

limits to financial, 17
    outsourcing as comparative advantage, 11–12
    of securities markets, 336–337, 346
    of yuan, 77–80
GM Asia, 287
GMI (Governance Metrics International), 42–43
Goals
    corporate governance, 36–37
    of corporate sustainability, 13
    financial. see Financial goals
    operational management, 33–36
Godé, Pierre, 52
Gold standard
    capital mobility in era of, 102–103
    as international monetary system 1876–1913, 59–60
    summary, 76
Good news, coinciding intervention with, 242
Goods trade, 86–88
Governance
    corporate. see Corporate governance
    in global economy, 3
    risk, 418, 421
    shopping, 46
Governance Metrics International (GMI), 42–43
Governments
    comparative corporate governance practices, 40
    interfering with comparative advantage, 10
Government-Sponsored Enterprises (GSEs), 115
Gramm-Leach-Bliley Financial Services Modernization Act of 1999, 114
Grantor (seller), options. see Writer (seller) of options
Grassroots movement, effective intervention using, 242
Gross domestic product (GDP)
    Argentine crisis of 2002, 249
    balance of payments and, 97–98
    of global capital markets, 3
Growth, euro and, 75
Growth firms, 435
GRSs (Global registered shares), 362
GSEs (Government-Sponsored Enterprises), 115

H

HealthSouth, 42
Hedging
    Banbury Impex (India) case, 289–292
    contractual hedges, 269, 288
    credit crisis of 2007–2009 impacting, 278
    defined, 265–266
    derivatives for, 204
    foreign exchange transaction exposure, 268, 288
    managing transaction exposure. see also Trident Corporation, transaction exposure, 267–269
    matching, 310–311
    McDonald's British pound exposure and, 225–226

Hedging (*continued*)
   pros and cons of, 266
   unhedgeable, 314–315
   Web site discussions on, 298
Hermès, LVMH vs. Hermès case, 49–54
HKD. see Hong Kong dollar (HKD)
Holder (buyer), options, 207
Home currency terms, forward quotations in, 164–165
Home market, competitive, 410–411
Hong Kong dollar (HKD)
   exchange rates for, 160
   globalization of yuan and, 78, 80
   quotation conventions, 5–7
   surviving currency collapse of 1997, 245
Hong Kong, globalization of yuan, 78
Hospira, 430
Hostile takeovers, cross-border mergers and acquisitions, 459
Housing market. see Credit crisis of 2007–2009
Human resource norms, cultural and institutional risks of MNEs, 427
Hyperinflation countries, translation procedures for, 281

I

IASC (International Accounting Standards Committee), 281
Ibbotson and Associates Web site, 350
ICAPM (international ICAPM), 327–329
ICP Asset Management, and AIG, 134
Ideal currency attributes, 67–68, 77
Identification, cross-border acquisitions, 457–458
Illiquid markets
   effect on firm's securities and cost of capital, 325
   remedies for global financial crash, 136
IMF. see International Monetary Fund (IMF)
IMM (International Monetary Market), foreign currency futures, 205
Impatient capitalism, SWM model, 32
Imperfections in market, rationale for MNEs, 13–14
Implied purchasing power parity rate of exchange, 174–175
"Impossibility trinity," of ideal currency, 67–68, 80
Income
   current account, 87
   privately held firms generating, 34
   translation exposure example, 282–283
Income statement
   capital budget vs., 447
   overview of, 278–280
Income tax, corporate
   overview of, 389–390
   summary, 398
   U.S. conundrum, 399–403
Income tax effect, 393–396

Inconvertibility risk, OPIC insurance, 422
India
   credit crisis of 2007–2009 and, 128
   global outsourcing of software industry to, 11–12
Indication, over-the-counter option, 209
Indirect intervention, of currency market, 242
Indirect quotations, foreign exchange rates, 158
Infant industries, risks of MNEs, 429
Inflation
   balance of payments and, 99
   budgeting for foreign project, 440
   currency market intervention and, 240–243
   Fisher effect and, 181–182
   multinational capital budgeting analysis, 443, 446
   undermining euro, 73–75
Infrastructure
   asset market approach to forecasting and, 238
   effect of weaknesses on foreign exchange rates, 235
Inheritance tax, 391
Initial public offering (IPO)
   in domestic trade phase, 15
   firms going public with, 29–30
   Nine Dragons Paper case study, 22
   venture capital funds, 369
Institutions
   exchange of currencies and, 5
   global financial, 4–5
   political risk of, 418, 426
Insurrection, OPIC insurance for, 422
Integrated foreign entities, 279, 281
Intellectual property rights, risks of MNEs, 428
Interacts, 97
Interbank market
   foreign currency futures contract vs., 206
   in foreign exchange market, 148–151
   global financial crash and role of, 131–133
   outright forward transactions in, 152–153
   spot transactions in, 151–152
   swap transactions in, 153–154
Interest rate derivatives
   currency swaps, 222–223
   forward rate agreements (FRA) based on, 220–221
   interest rate futures, 219–220
   interest rate swaps, 221–222
Interest rate exposure, 219
Interest rate futures, 219–220
Interest rate parity (IRP)
   covered interest arbitrage profit and, 185–187
   in forward-forward swaps, 153
   international parity conditions and, 192
   overview of, 184–185
   summary, 193
Interest rate risk
   credit risk vs. repricing risk, 218–219

overview of, 217–218
  summary, 225
  using forward rate agreements, 220–221
  using futures to manage, 219–220
Interest rate swaps, 221–222, 225
Interest rates
  aiding debt by lowcring, 116–117
  balance of payments and, 99
  carry trades in emerging markets and low, 193–194
  Eurocurrencies, LIBOR and, 8–9
  fiscal deficits complicating, 3
  forecasting using asset market approach, 238–239
  housing sector and mortgage lending, 114–117
  indirect intervention of currency market and, 242
  localized financial structures for MNEs and, 357–358
  managed floats and, 99
  money market vs. forward market hedges and, 271
Interest rates, and exchange rates
  covered interest arbitrage, 185–187
  equilibrium between, 188–189
  in equilibrium with prices, 191–192
  Fisher effect, 181–182
  forward rate, 183–184
  interest rate parity, 184–185
  international Fisher effect, 182
  uncovered interest arbitrage, 187–188
Intermarket arbitrage, 162
Internal forces, corporate governance structure, 37–39
Internal funding of foreign subsidiary, 358
Internal Revenue Service (IRS)
  establishing transfer price, 394
  taxpayer Web site, 406
Internalization, OLI Paradigm, 412
International Accounting Standards Committee (IASC), 281
International Bank for Reconstruction and Development. see World Bank
International bond issue
  international debt funding through, 372–373
  sourcing equity globally, 352–353
International CAPM (ICAPM), 327–329
International Comparison Program, World Bank, 199
International debt markets
  bank loans and syndicated credits, 370–371
  corporate governance structure of, 39
  Eurobond markets, 373–374
  Eurobond ratings and other issues, 374
  Euronote market, 371–372
  international bond market, 372–373
  Islamic finance, 375
  learning objectives, 351, 376
  Mini-Case, 377–380
  optimal financial structure, 353–356
  overview of, 370

  review questions, problems, and exercises, 380–384
International diversification, 349–350
International economic transactions, 85
International financial management, vs. domestic, 12–13
International Fisher effect, 182, 192
International interbank network, 5
International interest rate Web sites, 198–199
International Monetary Fund (IMF)
  Argentine crisis of 2002, 249–250
  avoiding currency manipulation to gain competitive advantages, 241
  exchange rate regime classifications, 66
  fixed exchange rates, 1945-1973, 62–63
  formation of, 61
  nominal exchange rate index of dollar, 63
  Special Drawing Rights (SDRs), 80
  and U.S. dollar-based international monetary system, 62
  Web site, 112
  world economic outlook, 27
International Monetary Market (IMM), foreign currency futures, 205
International monetary system
  birth of euro, 72–75
  contemporary currency regimes, 65–68
  emerging markets and regime choices, 69–72
  future of exchange rate regimes, 75–76
  learning objectives, 59, 76–77
  managed and fixed exchange rates of, 2
  Mini-Case, 77–80
  review questions, problems, and exercises, 80–82
International monetary system, history of
  Bretton Woods and the IMF, 1944, 61–62
  fixed exchange rates, 1945–1973, 62–63
  gold standard, 1876–1913, 59–60
  interwar years and World War II, 1914–1944, 60
  world currency events, 1971–2010, 63–65
International money markets, 184–185, 187
International network theory, FDI, 413–414
International Offshore Financial Centers, 396–397
International parity conditions
  defined, 173
  empirical tests of PPP, 177–178
  exchange rate indices, 178–179
  exchange rate pass-through, 179–181
  forward rate as unbiased predictor of future spot rate, 189–191
  interest rates linked to exchange rates. see Interest rates, and exchange rates
  learning objectives, 173, 192–193
  Mini-Case, 193–194
  PPP and law of one price, 174–176
  prices and exchange rates, 174, 191–192
  relative PPP, 176–177
  review questions, problems, and exercises, 194–198

International payment mechanisms, capital flight, 104
International portfolio investors
    effect of market liquidity and segmentation, 335–336
    expectations of, 356
    globalization of securities markets, 336–337
    improving market liquidity, 333–334
    link between cost and availability of capital, 333
    market segmentation and, 334–335
    overview of, 333
    strategic alliances, 338
International portfolio theory, 330
International Swaps and Derivatives Association (ISDA), 231
International Tax Blog, 406
International trade phase, 14–16
Internationally diversified portfolio. see Global portfolios
Internet exercises
    balance of payments, 112
    credit crisis of 2007–2009, 143
    financial goals and corporate governance, 57–58
    foreign currency derivatives and swaps, 231–232
    foreign exchange market, 171–172
    foreign exchange rate determination and forecasting, 262
    global cost and availability of capital, 349–350
    international monetary system, 80
    international parity conditions, 199
    MNE financial challenges, 26–27
    multinational capital budgeting and cross-border mergers, 473
    multinational tax management, 403–406
    operating exposure, 321
    sourcing equity and debt globally, 383–384
    transaction and translation exposure, 298
Intervention. see Currency market intervention
Interwar years and World War II, 1914–1944
    capital mobility during era of, 102–103
    international monetary system in, 60
    summary, 76
In-the-money (ITM) options, 208, 216
Intrinsic value, options, 215–216
Investment
    agreements, 421–422
    barriers to cross-listing and selling equity abroad, 366
    facilitating transactions using foreign exchange market, 150
    insurance coverage for political risk, 421–422
    legal system protection for investors, 41
Investment banks
    CDOs sold by, 121–123
    collapse of Lehman Brothers, 126, 128
    crisis conditions in corporate lending markets, 129
    deregulation and, 114
    designing capital sourcing strategy, 352–353

    Federal Reserve bailouts and, 140
    SEC regulation for, 114
Investment horizon, SWM model, 32
IPO. see Initial public offering (IPO)
IRP. see Interest rate parity (IRP)
IRS (Internal Revenue Service)
    establishing transfer price, 394
    taxpayer Web site, 406
ISDA (International Swaps and Derivatives Association), 231
Islamic finance, 375
ISO 4217 codes, quotations, 157
ITM (in-the-money) options, 208, 216

J
Japan
    carry trades in, 193
    causes of U.S. dollar decline, 75
    Toyota's European operating exposure, 316–318
    trading in foreign exchange market, 156
    yen intervention of 2010, 257–258
J-curve
    effect, 98–99
    trade balance adjustment path, 100–101
Joint-venture partners
    effect of transfer pricing on, 395
    foreign investment via, 416
JPMorgan Chase (JPMC), forecast of dollar/euro, 253
JPMorgan Web site, ADR tracking, 383
Just-in-time (JIT) near-zero inventory systems, political risk, 431–432

K
Key, Mr. John, 214–215
Kiwi, New Zealand, 214–215
Knowledge seekers, why firms become multinational, 14
Korea Fund, 333
Korean won, Asian crisis of 1997, 245
Krieger, Andrew, 214–215

L
Law of one price
    approach to exchange rate determination, 236
    purchasing power parity and, 174–176
Leaning into the wind, rules for effective intervention, 242
Legal advisers, corporate governance structure, 39
Legal liabilities, of foreign direct investment, 430
Legal systems, and comparative corporate governance practices, 41
Lehman Brothers, 128, 137, 139–141
Lenders, arguments against dollarization, 70
Liabilities
    translating at current rate of exchange, 280
    translating with temporal method, 280

LIBOR. see London Interbank Offer Rate (LIBOR)
Licensing, foreign investment via, 415–416
Life span, transaction exposure, 267
Linerboard, 20
Linkage
    between cost and availability of capital, 333
    in global financial marketplace, 5
Liquidity
    asset market approach to forecasting and, 238
    effect of segmentation and market, 335–336
    Federal Reserve action during credit crisis, 128
    financial globalization and strategy for, 324–325
    improving for foreign equities, 363
    improving market, 333–334
    of interest rate futures, 219–220
    of over-the-counter options, 208–209
    remedies for global financial crash, 137
    securitized, 117–119
Loans
    budgeting for foreign project, 440
    commercial banks competing for mortgage, 114
    currency hedging with back-to-back, 312–313
    debt funding through international bank, 370
    financing analysis, multinational capital budgeting,
        443–445
    fronting, 425–426
    housing sector and mortgage lending, 114–117
    parallel, 312–313
    securitized, 118
Local sourcing, reducing political risk, 423
Localized financial structures, foreign subsidiaries, 357–358
Location-specific advantages, OLI Paradigm, 412
London Interbank Offer Rate (LIBOR)
    British Bankers Association Web site and, 143
    as core of global financial system, 5
    credit vs. repricing risk and, 218
    Eurocurrencies and, 8–9
    expenses for syndicated markets tied to, 371
    global financial crash and role of, 131–133
    interest rate for Eurodollar loans tied to, 370
    pricing and structure of syndicated Eurocredit, 371
    role in credit crisis of 2007–2009, 128
London Stock Exchange (LSE)
    dominance of, 361–362
    electronic trading at, 364
    equity markets and, 38–39
    Novo shares listed on, 342
Long positions, foreign currency futures, 207
Long run, measuring operating exposure, 304
Long-term forecast period, 251–252, 254–255
Long-term maximization, SWM model, 32
Louis Vuitton, LVMH vs. Hermès, 49–54
LSE. see London Stock Exchange (LSE)
LVMH vs. Hermès case, 49–54

M
Maastricht Treaty, 72–75
Macro risks. see Country-specific political risks
Macroeconomic uncertainty, 302
Macroeconomic variables, balance of payments, 97–99
Madrid Interbank Offered Rate (MIBOR), 8
Mahathir, Dr. Mohamad, 245–246
Mahuad, President Jamil, 71
Maintenance margin, foreign currency futures
        contract, 206
Malaysian currency controls, 80
Managed floats, balance of payments and, 99
Management
    account payable, 275–277
    budgeting for foreign project, 440
    comparative corporate governance, 40
    competitive advantage of MNEs, 409
    corporate governance structure, 38
    good corporate governance for compensation of, 43
    operating exposure. see also Proactive management of
        operating exposure, 315
    operational goals of, 33–36
    overview of, 31
    pros and cons of hedging, 266–267
    separation of ownership and, 30–31, 40
    shareholder wealth maximization model of, 31–32
    stakeholder capitalism model of, 32–33
    strategic operating exposure, 308–309
    Toyota's European operating exposure, 317
    transfer pricing incentives for, 394–395
    translation exposure, 285–286, 288
Management contracts, foreign investment via, 416
Mantoloking CDO, 123
Margin, foreign currency futures contract, 206
Marginal cost of capital (MCC), 339–341, 354–355
Marginal return of capital (MRR), 335–336
Marked to market, foreign currency futures contract, 206
Market
    foreign currency options, 5–7, 208–209
    liquidity, 333–336, 342
    movements in exchange rates, 255–256
    rationale for MNEs, 13–14
    reducing political risk by controlling, 423
Market seekers, 14
Market segmentation
    effect of cross-listing on share price, 364–365
    effect of market liquidity and, 335–336
    effect on firm's securities and cost of capital, 324–325
    globalization of securities markets reducing, 346
    Novo, 343–345
    overview of, 334–335
    summary, 342
Market value, exchange rate determination, 238
Market-based regimes, 40

Marketing expertise, competitive advantage of MNEs, 409
Matching
　currency cash flows, 310–311
　hedging repeated transactions as, 271
MBSs. see Mortgage-backed securities (MBSs)
MCC (Marginal cost of capital), 339–341, 354–355
McDonald's
　bond issue in globalization of yuan, 80
　British pound exposure, 225–226
Medium run, measuring operating exposure, 304
Mergers. see Cross-border mergers and acquisitions
Mexico
　equity markets, 39
　government view of remittances across borders, 108
Mezzanine or middle tranches, 122–123
MIBOR (Madrid Interbank Offered Rate), 8
Micro risks. see Firm-specific political risks
Migrant remittances, 105–108
Milken Institute, Capital Access Index, 438
Mini-Case studies
　Banbury Impex (India), 289–292
　carry trades in emerging market, 193–194
　casual empiricism of, 336
　globalization of yuan, 77–80
　Japanese yen intervention of 2010, 257–258
　Lehman Brothers, 139–141
　LVMH vs. Hermès case, 49–54
　McDonald's British pound exposure, 225–226
　migrant remittances, 105–108
　Nine Dragons Paper—2009. see Nine Dragons Paper
　Novo, 342–346
　Petrobrás of Brazil and cost of capital, 377–380
　Toyota's European operating exposure, 316–318
　Venezuelan bolivar, 166–168
　Yanzhou (China) bids for Felix Resources (Australia), 463–469
Minority shareholder rights, 47–48
MNEs (multinational enterprises)
　cost of capital for domestic firms vs., 338–341
　defined, 2
　effect of market liquidity and segmentation, 335–336
　financial challenges of. see Financial challenges and global economy
　global assets/income of, 57
　global financial crash and, 130–131
　globalization of securities markets, 336–337
　improving market liquidity, 333–334
　localized financial structures for foreign subsidiaries, 357–358
　market segmentation, 334–335
　operational financial goals for, 35–36
　optimal financial structure and, 354–355
　tax management for. see Tax management for MNEs

Monetary approach, exchange rate determination, 237
Monetary independence, impossible trinity of, 67–68
Monetary policy, Argentine crisis of 2002, 249–250
Money laundering, capital flight mechanism, 104
Money market hedge
　comparing alternatives to, 274–275
　managing account payable, 275–277
　overview of, 271–273
　risk management with, 278
Money markets, international, 184–185, 187
Montreal Exchange Web site, 232
Moody's Standard and Poor's (S&Ps), 374, 438
Moral channel, of corporate responsibility, 13
Morality tax, for MNEs, 386
Mortgage lending, housing sector and, 115–117
Mortgage-backed securities (MBSs)
　annual issuances of, 118
　credit enhancement for, 126–127
　global financial crash and, 129–131
　structured investment vehicles purchasing, 119
Moving, blocked funds, 425
MRR (Marginal return of capital), 335–336
Multinational capital budgeting
　complexities of, 440
　learning objectives, 439–440, 462–463
　Mini-Case, 463–469
　project financing, 455–456
　project vs. parent valuation, 441–442
　real option analysis, 454
　review questions, problems, and exercises, 469–473
Multinational capital budgeting, hypothetical case
　capital investment, 443
　costs, 446–447
　financing, 443–445
　multinational capital budgeting analysis, 442–443
　overview of, 442
　parent viewpoint, 448–450
　parent viewpoint, sensitivity analysis, 452–453
　portfolio risk measurement, 453–454
　project viewpoint, 447–448
　project viewpoint, sensitivity analysis, 451–452
　revenues, 446
Multinational phase, globalization, 16
Multiple-source borrowing, reducing political risk, 423
Muslims, risks of MNEs, 427
Mutual funds, 349–350

N
Naboa, President Gustavo, 71
NAFTA (North American Free Trade Area)
　antiglobalization movement, 432
　U.S. trade between Mexico and Canada, 15
NASD (National Association of Securities Dealers), 369
National Association of Securities Dealers (NASD), 369

National Bank of Slovakia Web site, 262
National competitive advantage, determinants of, 410–411
National tax environments, 387–389
Natural hedges, 269
NDFs (nondeliverable forwards), interbank market, 153
NDP. see Nine Dragons Paper
Nepotism, risks of MNEs, 428
Nestlé of Switzerland, cost of equity for, 329–330
Net errors and omissions account, BOP, 92, 96
Net portfolio investment, financial account, 90–91
Network approach to FDI, 413–414
Neutrality, tax, 386–387
New York Stock Exchange (NYSE)
    dominance of, 361–362
    electronic trading at, 364
    equity markets and, 38–39
    listing Novo in, 344–345
    merger with Euronext, 362
New York Times Web site, Times Topics, 143
New Zealand kiwi, 214–215
Nike, 433
Nine Dragons Paper
    cash flow concerns, 24–25
    Chinese New Year 2009, 23–24
    expansion, 20–22
    financing expansion, 22–23
    overview of, 18–19
    products, 20
    questions, 24
    the wastepaper queen, 19–20
noise, short-term forecast, 254
Nominal effective exchange rate index, 178
Nondeliverable forwards (NDFs), interbank market, 153
Non-tariff barriers, risks of MNEs, 429
Nonunderwritten facilities, Euronote market, 371–372
North American Free Trade Area (NAFTA)
    antiglobalization movement, 432
    U.S. trade between Mexico and Canada, 15
Notional principal
    foreign currency futures contracts using, 205–206
    forward rate agreements using, 220–221
    McDonald's British pound exposure, 225–226
    OTC options, 208
Novo Industri A/S (Novo)
    asymmetric information, 343
    biotechnology boom, 344
    closing information gap, 344
    directed public share issue, 344–345, 367
    effect on weighted average cost of capital, 345–346
    feasible set of portfolios, 343
    financial, foreign exchange, and political risks, 343–344
    globalization of securities markets, 346
    overview of, 342–343
    road to globalization, 344
    stock market reactions, 345
    taxation, 343
    Web site, 350
Nycomed, 367

O

Obligation, of corporate responsibility, 13
OCI (Other comprehensive income), 226
OECD. see Organization for Economic Cooperation and Development (OECD)
Off-balance-sheet accounting entities, 120–121
Office of Financial Research, Financial Reform Law of 2010, 137
Officers
    corporate governance structure, 38
    Sarbanes-Oxley Act requirements, 45
Official Reserves Account, 92–93
Official settlements balance, 95–96
Offshore financial centers, 396–398
Offshoring, for tax-deferral privileges, 388
Okuda, Hiroshi, 316–318
OLI Paradigm
    competitive advantage of MNEs, 411–412
    financial strategy and, 412–413
    summary, 433
On the Principles of Political Economy and Taxation (Ricardo), 10
Open hedge, 270
Operating cash flows, operating exposure, 301
Operating exposure
    changes in cash flow and, 301–302
    defined, 264
    example, 299–303
    learning objectives, 299, 315
    measuring, 303–308
    Mini-Case, 316–318
    operating and financing cash flows, 301
    proactive management of, 310–315
    review questions, problems, and exercises, 318–321
    static vs. dynamic, 300–301
    strategic management of, 308–309
    translation exposure vs., 288
Operating hedges, 269
Operational financial goals, management, 33–36, 48–49
Operations, diversifying, 309
OPIC (Overseas Private Investment Corporation), 422, 438
Optimal financial structure
    foreign exchange risk and cost of debt, 355–356
    international debt markets and, 353–356
    MNEs and, 354–355
    overview of, 353–354
    summary, 376
Options. see Foreign currency options

Options, real option analysis, 454
Options market hedge
    managing account payable, 276–277
    overview of, 273–274
    risk management with, 277–278
Organization for Economic Cooperation and
        Development (OECD)
    bilateral tax treaties modeled after, 389
    corporate governance practices, 37
    globalization of securities markets, 336, 346
    PPP statistics on Web site, 198
Originate-to-distribute (OTD) model, securitization, 119
OTC (over-the-counter) options, 208–209
OTD (originate-to-distribute) model, securitization, 119
Other comprehensive income (OCI), 226
OTM. see Out-of-the-money (OTM) options
Out-of-the-money (OTM) options
    foreign currency, 208
    pricing and valuation, 216
    writers of put options, 214
Outright forward transactions, interbank market, 152–153
Outsourcing, for tax-deferral privileges, 388
Overall balance, balance of payments, 95–96
Overseas Private Investment Corporation (OPIC), 422,
        438
Overshooting, exchange rates, 255–256
Over-the-counter (OTC) options, 208–209
Ownership of business
    advantages of ADRs, 361
    advantages of, OLI Paradigm, 411–412
    comparative corporate governance practices and, 40
    cultural and institutional risks of MNEs, 427
    financial goals and, 28–30
    in global economy, 3
    percentage owned by affiliates, 441
    public/private hybrids of MNEs, 35–36
    separation of management and, 30–31, 40
    summary, 48
OzForex Foreign Exchange Services Web site
    global currencies, 262
    option pricing, 232

P
Pacific Exchange Rate Service Web site, 172
Panama, dollar as official currency of, 69
Panda Bonds, 80
Parallel loans, 312–313
Parent cash flows, budgeting for foreign project, 440
Parent viewpoint capital budget
    hypothetical case of, 448–450
    roadmap for analysis of, 442–443
    sensitivity analysis of, 451–452
    summary, 462
    vs. project viewpoint, 441–442

Paris Interbank Offered Rate (PIBOR), 8
Parity. see International parity conditions
Parity rate, 93
Parmalat, corporate governance corruption, 42
Passive income, withholding taxes on, 389
Pass-through period
    exchange rate, 179–181
    trade balance adjustment, 101
Patient capitalism, SWM model, 32
Pentothal market exit, 430
People's Republic of China (PRC), globalization of yuan,
        77–80
Percentage change in spot rates, 163
Percentage terms, forward quotations in, 164–165
Perfect hedge, 270
Peso, Argentine crisis of 2002, 69, 248–251
Petrobrás of Brazil and cost of capital, 330, 377–380
Physical currency, capital flight mechanism, 104
PIBOR (Paris Interbank Offered Rate), 8
Pinault, Francois, 50
Pips, quoting forward rates, 163
Plain vanilla swaps, 221
Political acceptance, with equity issuance, 365
Political risk, MNEs
    affect on foreign exchange rates, 235
    budgeting for foreign project, 440
    country-specific, 419–420, 424–430
    defining and classifying, 418–419
    exports and, 414
    firm-specific, 419, 420–424
    foreign investment via joint venture and, 417
    global-specific, 420, 430–433
    learning objectives, 433–434
    Mini-Case, 435–436
    Novo Industri A/S case, 344
    overview of, 418
    project viewpoint measurement, 451
    review questions, problems, and exercises, 436–438
Political safety
    asset market approach to forecasting and, 238–239
    why firms become multinational, 14
Pollution, political accusations against MNEs, 432
PORTAL trading system, 369
Porter, Michael, 411
Portfolio balance approach, exchange rate determination,
        237–238
Portfolio investment
    affect on foreign exchange rates, 235
    international portfolio investors. see International
        portfolio investors
    Novo Industri A/S case, 343
    overview of, 90
    risk measurement in multinational capital budgeting,
        453–454

Portfolio theory, 119–120
Post-acquisition management, 460
Poverty
    as global-specific risk, 418
    political accusations against MNEs for, 433
PPP. see Purchasing power parity (PPP)
PRC (People's Republic of China), globalization of yuan, 77–80
Precious metals, capital flight mechanism, 104
Predictability, for hedging the unhedgeable, 314–315
Preinvestment strategy, blocked funds, 425
Premiums
    for buyer of call option, 210–211
    for buyer of put option, 213
    corporate governance and, 42–43
    equity risk, 330–332
    foreign currency options, 208
    option pricing and valuation, 215–217
    option quotations and prices, 209–210
    for writer of call option, 211–212
    for writer of put option, 213–214
Prenegotiation, governance risk, 421
Price
    break-even. see Break-even price
    effect of cross-listing and equity issuance on share, 364–365
    in equilibrium with interest rates and exchange rates, 191–192
    foreign currency options, 208–210
    law of one, 174–176, 236
    option quotations and premium, 209–210
    option valuation, 215–217
    strike. see Exercise (strike) price
Price elasticity of demand, 99, 180–181
Prime (A-paper) mortgage loans, 115
Private equity funds, 369
Private placement markets, 368
Privately held businesses
    Euroequity public issue and, 368
    overview of, 28–29
    public/private hybrids of MNEs, 35–36
    separation of ownership from management, 30–31
    shareholder return objectives of, 34
Pro forma financial analysis, capital budgeting, 446–447
Proactive investments, 14
Proactive management of operating exposure
    back-to-back loans, 312–313
    cross currency swaps, 313–314
    hedging the unhedgeable, 314–315
    matching currency cash flows, 310–311
    risk sharing for long-term cash flow exposure, 311–312
    summary, 315
Production
    foreign investment in, 414

    locating facilities to reduce risk, 423
    why firms become multinational, 14
Products
    competitive advantage of MNEs, 410
    Nine Dragons Paper case study, 20
Profit warning, Nine Dragons Paper case study, 23
Profitability, corporate responsibility, 13
Project cash flows, budgeting for foreign project, 440
Project financing, 455–456, 462
Project viewpoint capital budget
    hypothetical case of, 447–448
    roadmap for analysis of, 442–443
    sensitivity analysis of, 451–452
    summary, 462
    vs. parent viewpoint, 441–442
Property taxes, 391
Proportional hedging, 278
Protection buyer, credit default swaps, 124–125
Protection seller, credit default swaps, 124–125
Protectionism, 428–430
Public reporting, good corporate governance practices, 43
Publicly traded businesses
    overview of, 28–29
    public/private hybrids of MNEs, 35–36
    separation of ownership from management, 30–31
Purchasing power parity (PPP)
    calculating exchange rate indices, 178–180
    empirical tests of, 177–178
    exchange rate determination, 236
    exchange rate pass-through and, 179–181
    human side of, 175
    international parity conditions in equilibrium, 191
    and law of one price, 174–176
    multinational capital budgeting analysis, 443
    project viewpoint measurement, 451–452
    relative, 176–177
    Web site for, 198
Put options
    buyer of, 212–213
    defined, 207
    market hedge, 273–274
    writer of, 213–214

Q
Qualified institutional buyers (QIBs), 369
Quantity adjustment period, trade balance adjustment, 101
Quotations
    currency exchange rate conventions, 7
    foreign currency option, 209–210
    foreign exchange rates and. see Foreign exchange rates and quotations
    in transaction exposure, 267

R

Ratings, Eurobond, 374
Raw material seekers, 14
Real assets, balance of payments exchanging, 86
Real currency, Brazil, 249
Real effective exchange rate index, 178–180
Real estate. see Credit crisis of 2007–2009
Real option analysis, multinational capital budgeting, 454, 462
Real-Time Gross Settlement (RTGS), 151
Recession, and global capital markets, 3
Reform, corporate governance, 45–48
Regimes
    chosen by emerging markets, 69–72
    comparative corporate governance, 40
    contemporary currency, 65–68
    U.S. tax, 400–401
Region, diversifying portfolios by, 333
Regional markets, 429–430
Regulation
    commercial bank, 114
    corporate governance reform, 45–48
    corporate governance structure, 39
    credit default swaps lacking, 124
    cross-border acquisitions and, 459
    Eurobond market lacking, 373
    foreign exchange trading fraud and, 151
    investment bank and stock brokerage firm, 114
Reinvestment, forced direct, 426
Related industries, home country competitive advantage, 411
Relative advantage in costs, comparative advantage, 11
Relative price of bonds, exchange rate determination, 237–238
Relative purchasing power parity, 176–177, 236
Religious heritage, risks of MNEs, 427
Remittance Prices Worldwide (RPW) database, 107
Remittances. see Global remittances
Renminbi (RMB), Chinese, 77–80
Reporting, good corporate governance for public, 43
Repricing risk, credit risk vs., 218–219
Reputation, in good corporate governance, 42–44
Residential taxation approach, nations, 387–388
Responsibility
    corporate, 13
    individual profit motives vs. fiduciary, 134
Restricted stock, corporate governance reform, 47
Revenues
    multinational capital budgeting analysis, 445
    U.S. corporate tax, 403
Revolution, OPIC insurance coverage, 422
Ricardo, David, 10
Rigidly fixed exchange regimes, 66

Risk
    back-to-back loans and, 313
    credit enhancement reducing, 126–127
    currency. see Currency risks
    derivatives reducing. see Foreign currency derivatives
    equity risk premiums, 330–332
    foreign currency, 210–214
    foreign exchange. see Foreign exchange risks
    global portfolios reducing, 333
    global vs. domestic financial management, 12–13
    hedge transaction exposure and, 275
    interest rate, 217–219
    international credit management, 15–16
    managing financial derivatives, 231
    managing FX, 315
    minimizing foreign exchange market, 148
    of mortgage loan types, 115
    Novo case, 343–344
    in privately held firms, 34–35
    proactive management of operating exposure, 311–312
    shareholder wealth maximization model, 31
    stakeholder capitalism model, 33
    systematic, 31, 326–327
    transfer, 418, 423–427
RMB (renminbi), Chinese, 77–80
Roll-over (credit) risk, 218–219
Round turn, foreign currency futures contract, 206
RPW (Remittance Prices Worldwide) database, 107
RTGS (Real-Time Gross Settlement), 151
Ruble (RUB). see Russian ruble crisis of 1998
Rule 144A, SEC, 369
Rupee, Banbury Impex (India) Mini-Case study, 289–292
Russian ruble crisis of 1998, 245–248, 256

S

S&Ps (Standard and Poor's), 374, 438
Sarbanes-Oxley Act (SOX), 45–46
Scale, competitive advantage of MNEs, 409
SCM (stakeholder capitalism model), 32–33, 48
Scope, competitive advantage of MNEs, 409
Score cord, stakeholder capitalism model, 33
SDRs (Special Drawing Rights), 62, 80
SEC. see Securities and Exchange Commission (SEC)
Securities
    diversifying portfolios according to type of, 333
    globalization of markets, 336–337, 346
    Novo case. see Novo Industri A/S (Novo)
Securities and Exchange Commission (SEC)
    Edgar Files, 321
    Financial Reform Law of 2010, 137
    Novo Industri A/S (Novo) in the U.S., 344–345
    regulating corporate governance, 39
    regulating investment banks and stock brokerage firms, 114

Rule 144A, 369
    shelf registrations for debt issues, 372
Securitization
    remedies for global financial crash, 135
    role in credit crisis of 2007–2009, 117–119
Segmentation. see Market segmentation
Seignorage, arguments against dollarization, 70
Selective hedging, 266
Self-sustaining foreign entity, 279, 281
Seller of options. see Writer (seller) of options
Selling short, 60
Senior tranches, 122–123
September 1985 Plaza Agreement, 241–242
Services trade, current account, 86, 89
Settlement of transaction, cross-border mergers and
    acquisitions, 458–460
Share swaps, 365–366
Shareholder wealth maximization (SWM) model, 31–33,
    48
Shareholders
    compensation settlement in cross-border acquisitions,
        459
    corporate governance goals for, 36–37
    corporate governance reform, 45–48
    management operational goals for, 31, 33–36
    pros and cons of hedging, 266
    rights of minority, 47–48
    in stakeholder capitalism model, 32–33
    world ownership characterized by, 30–31
Shelf registrations, debt issues, 372
Short positions
    bucket shop vs., 124
    foreign currency futures, 206
Short run, measuring operating exposure, 303
Shorting, dollar and euro, 193
Short-term forecast period, 251–252, 254
Short-term maximization, SWM model, 32
Shuhei, Toyoda, 316–318
SIBOR (Singapore Interbank Offered Rate), 8
Siemens (Germany), governance reform, 46–47
Singapore, in foreign exchange market, 156
Singapore Interbank Offered Rate (SIBOR), 8
SIVs (Structured investment vehicles), 119–121
Size, foreign exchange market, 154
Smith, Adam, 9–10
Social repercussions, Argentine crisis of 2002, 250
Social responsibility, corporate, 13
Soros, George, 242–243, 245–246
Source taxation approach, of nations, 388
Sourcing equity and debt globally. see Debt, sourcing
    globally; Equity, sourcing globally
Sovereign credit ratings criteria, S&P, 438
Sovereign wealth funds, U.S. dollar decline and, 75
SOX (Sarbanes-Oxley Act), 45–46

Special dispensation, to release blocked funds, 426
Special Drawing Rights (SDRs), 62, 80
Special purpose vehicles (SPVs), 121–122
Speculation
    affect on foreign exchange rates, 235
    asset market approach to forecasting and, 239
    in foreign exchange market, 150
    purchasing interest rate futures for, 220
    using derivatives for, 204
Sponsored ADRs, 361
Spot exchange rate
    in absolute PPP, 174
    buyer of call options, 210–211
    for buyer of put option, 212–213
    calculating forward rate by adjusting, 183–184
    comparing hedging alternatives, 274–275
    currency option price, 209
    in exchange rate pass-through, 179, 181
    foreign currency options, 208
    forward rate as predictor of future, 189–191, 192–193
    international Fisher effect and, 182
    law of one price and, 174
    management of account payables, 275–277
    measurement of transaction exposure, 267
    money market hedge, 272
    multinational capital budgeting analysis, 443
    option pricing and valuation, 215–217
    in relative PPP, 177
    for writer of call option, 212
    writer of call options, 211–212
    for writer of put option, 214
Spot market
    overview of, 151–152
    quotes, 157–158, 163–164
SPVs (Special purpose vehicles), 121–122
Square hedge, 270
SSFI (Stocks with significant family influence), 36
St. Louis Federal Reserve Web site, 112
Stabilizing expectations, forecasting exchange rates, 255
Stakeholder capitalism model (SCM), 32–33, 48
Standard and Poor's (S&Ps), 374, 438
Static operating exposure, 300–301
Statoil of Norway, acquisition of Esso of Sweden, 461
Statutory tax rates, 399–400
Stock exchanges, liquidity of various, 363–364
Stock markets, global financial crash and, 130
Stockholder wealth maximization (SWM), 48
Stocks, diversifying portfolios with, 333
Stocks with significant family influence (SSFI), 36
Straight fixed-rate issue, Eurobonds, 373
Strategic alliances
    Bang & Olufsen and Philips N.V., 338
    investing abroad using, 417
Strategic exposure. see Operating exposure

Strategic management, of operating exposure, 308–309
Structure, corporate governance, 37–39
Structured investment vehicles (SIVs), 119–121
Subaccounts, balance of payments, 84–85
Subordination, for credit enhancement, 126–127
Subprime debt, 114–117
Subprime differential, 115
Subsidiaries, foreign investment via wholly owned, 416–417
Subsidiary characterization, 279
Supply chain
    cost reduction through imports, 97–98
    outsourcing as comparative advantage, 11–12
    political risks of MNEs, 431–432
Surplus
    in China's current and financial accounts, 93
    implications of BOP, 95
    in U.S services trade income, 87–89
Sustainability, corporate, 13
Swaps
    credit-default, 124–126, 312–313
    cross currency, 225–226, 313–314
    currency. see Currency swaps
    defined, 151, 221
    forward-forward, 153
    interest rate, 221–222
    overview of, 153–154
    plain vanilla, 221
    share, 365–366
Sweat shop conditions, accusations against MNEs, 433
Swedish School of economists, approach to FDI, 413
SWM (shareholder wealth maximization) model, 31–33, 48
Symbols, currency
    euro, 74
    foreign exchange rates and quotations, 157
    understanding, 5
Syndicated credits, 371
Synthetic CDOs, 123
Systematic risk
    cost of capital for MNEs and, 338–339
    measuring. see Betas
    Novo case reducing, 345–346
    shareholder wealth maximization model, 31

T

Taiwan, Asian crisis of 1997, 245
TARGET (Transeuropean Automated Real-time Gross settlement Express Transfer), 72–73
Tariff barriers, risks of MNEs, 429
TARP (Troubled Asset Recovery Plan), 136–137
Tax credits, foreign, 391–392, 399
Tax deferral privilege
    overview of, 388
    tax-haven subsidiaries and offshore financial centers, 396–397

U.S. conundrum, 400–401, 403
Tax management for MNEs
    learning objectives, 385, 398–399
    national tax environments, 387–389
    overview of, 385–386
    review questions, problems, and exercises, 403–406
    tax morality, 386
    tax neutrality, 386–387
    tax treaties, 389
    tax types, 389–392
    tax-haven subsidiaries and international offshore financial centers, 396–398
    transfer pricing, 392–396
    U.S. corporate income tax conundrum, 399–403
Tax Reform Act (TRA) of 1986, 115
Taxation
    equity, 387
    favorable status of Eurobonds, 374
    morality, 386
    national environments, 387–389
    neutrality, 386–387
    Novo Mini-Case, 343
    project viewpoint capital budget, 447–448
    project viewpoint measurement, 451
    treaties, 389
    types of, 389–392
    on undistributed profits, 391
Tax-deferral privileges, MNEs, 388–389, 396–397
Tax-haven subsidiaries, 396–398
Taxsites.com, 406
Technical analysis, forecasting foreign exchange rate, 252–253
Technology control, reducing political risk via, 423
TED Spread, and LIBOR, 132–133
Temporal method of translation
    managing translation exposure, 284–286
    overview of, 280–281
    summary, 288
    U.S. translation procedures using, 281
Tender process, cross-border mergers and acquisitions, 458–459
Tequila effect, Asian crisis of 1997, 244–245
Territorial taxation approach, 398, 400–401
Terrorism
    asset market approach to forecasting and, 239
    effect on foreign exchange rates, 235
    global-specific risk of, 418, 420, 430–431
Thailand's crisis of 1997, 243–246
Theory of comparative advantage. see Comparative advantage
Thomas, Patrick, 49–54
TI (Transparency International) Web site, 438
Time value, options, 215–216
Total value, options, 215–216

Toyota's European operating exposure, 316–318
TRA (Tax Reform Act) of 1986, 115
Trade balances, exchange rates and, 99–102
Trade theory, modern vs. traditional, 10
Trademark control, reducing political risk via, 423
Trade-Related Aspects of Intellectual Property Rights
    (TRIPS), 428
Trading on the run, in interbank market, 131
Tranches, Euroequity public issue, 368
Transaction exposure
    defined, 264
    example. see Trident Corporation, transaction exposure
    foreign exchange, 263–264
    learning objectives, 263, 287–288
    measurement of, 267–269
    Mini-Case, 289–292
    operating exposure vs., 299
    review questions, problems, and exercises, 293–298
Transactions
    balance of payment, 84–85
    interbank market, 151–154
    settlement of in cross-border acquisitions, 458–460
Transeuropean Automated Real-time Gross settlement
    Express Transfer (TARGET), 72–73
Transfer pricing
    defined, 392
    foreign investment via joint venture and, 395, 417
    managerial incentives and evaluation, 394–395
    overview of, 392–393
    summary, 398
    tax management example, 395–396
Transfer risk
    blocked funds, 424–427
    as country-specific political risk, 423
    defined, 418
Transfer taxes, 391
Translation exposure
    current rate method of, 280
    defined, 264
    example, 281–285
    international practices, 281
    learning objectives, 287–288
    managing, 285–286
    Mini-Case, 289–292
    operating exposure vs., 288
    overview of, 278–279
    review questions, problems, and exercises, 293–298
    temporal method of, 280–281
    U.S. procedures for, 281
    using balance sheet hedges, 287
Transparency
    comparative corporate governance and, 40–41
    corporate governance ensuring, 37
    corporate governance reform, 47

Transparency International (TI) Web site, 438
Transportation control, reducing political risk via, 423
Treasuries, in foreign exchange market, 151
Treasury Management Association Web site, 298
Treaties, tax, 389
Triangular arbitrage, 162
Trident Corporation
    calculating cost of capital, 327–328
    cost and availability of capital, 333
    globalization process of, 14–16
    management of translation exposure, 285–286
    measurement of transaction exposure, 267–268
    transfer pricing, 393–396
    translation exposure, 281–285
    used in this book as hypothetical firm, 14
Trident Corporation, operating exposure
    changes in cash flow, 301–302
    measuring operating exposure, 304–308
    operating and financing cash flows, 301
    overview of, 299–303
    static vs. dynamic operating exposure, 300–301
Trident Corporation, transaction exposure
    comparison of alternatives, 274–275
    forward market hedge, 270–271
    management of account payable, 275–277
    money market hedge, 271–273
    options market hedge, 273–274
    overview of, 269–270
    risk management in practice, 277–278
    strategy choice and outcome, 275
    unhedged position, 270
Trilemma of international finance, 67–68
Trinity Elements, of ideal currency, 67–68
triple-bottom line, corporate responsibility, 13
Troubled Asset Recovery Plan (TARP), 136–137
Trust, global credit crisis abusing, 134
Turnover tax, corporations, 391
Tyco, 42

U
UIA (Uncovered interest arbitrage), 187–188, 193–194
Unbiased prediction of future spot exchange rate,
    189–191
Uncovered hedge, 270
Uncovered interest arbitrage (UIA), 187–188, 193–194
Underwriters
    of home equity loan ABSs, 126
    marketing CDOs, 121–122
Underwritten facilities, Euronote market, 371–372
Unexpected changes in cash flow, 302
Unhedged approach
    comparing hedging alternatives, 274
    managing account payables, 275
    transaction exposure example, 270

United Kingdom
   Euroequity public issue in, 368
   indirect currency intervention in, 242–243
   quoting pound sterling in U.S. terms, 158
   trading in foreign exchange market, 156
United Nations Web site, 112
United States
   basic balance deficit, 95–96
   corporate income tax conundrum, 399–403
   current account, 87
   deficit on goods trade, 88
   financial account, 89–91
   high corporate income tax rate of, 399–400
   overall balance surplus, 96
   surplus in service trade, 89
   trading in foreign exchange market, 156
   translation procedures, 281
   trinity/trilemma of international finance, 68
Unsponsored ADRs, 361
Unsystematic risk, SWM model, 31
U.S. Bureau of Economic Analysis Web site, 112
U.S. dollar
   1945–1973 fixed exchange rates and, 62–63
   1973–present, 63–65
   American depositary receipts and, 360–362
   Argentina's currency board and, 69
   asset market approach to forecasting and, 239
   causes of decline in, 75
   collapse of Argentine peso, 251
   credit crisis of 2007–2009 and option volatilities, 278
   dollarization, 69–70
   effective currency interventions, 242
   emerging market carry trades and, 193–194
   euro exchange rate against, 74
   international monetary system based on, 61–62
   JPMorgan Chase forecast of, 253
   real effective exchange rate of, 179–180
   TED Spread, 133
U.S. Federal Reserve
   aiding debt by lowering interest rates, 116–117
   injecting liquidity during credit crisis, 128
   as lender of last resort, 140
   Web site, 171
U.S. Treasury Bond futures, 219

V
Valuation
   cross-border acquisitions, 458, 465–468
   option pricing and, 215–217
Value chain
   Chinese containerboard, 20
   comparative advantage and, 9–12
   global capital markets and, 3
   globalization process, 14–17

   market for currencies, 5–9
   rationale for MNEs, 13–14
   requirements for, 18
Value firms, 435–436
Value-added tax, 389, 391, 398
Variation margin, foreign currency futures contract, 206
Venezuelan bolivar, 154, 166–168
Venture capital funds, 369
Visibility, increasing with equity issuance, 365
Voting shares, 42–43

W
WACC. see Weighted average cost of capital (WACC)
War
   as global-specific risk, 431
   OPIC insurance coverage for, 422
Wastepaper. see Nine Dragons Paper
WDI (World Development Indicators), World Bank, 27
The Wealth of Nations (Smith), 9–10
Weighted average cost of capital (WACC)
   calculating cost of capital, 326
   financing analysis, multinational capital budgeting,
      443–444
   globalization of securities markets, 346
   link between cost and availability of capital, 333
   for MNEs vs. domestic firms, 339–341
   Novo Industri A/S (Novo), 345–346
   optimal financial structure and, 354
   parent viewpoint capital budget, 450
   Petrobrás of Brazil Mini-Case, 377–380
Wholesale market
   eurocurrency market as, 8–9
   in foreign exchange market, 148–151
Wholly owned subsidiaries, foreign investment via,
   416–417
Withholding tax, corporations, 389, 398
WNS Global Services, 46
World Bank
   external debt analysis, 27
   formation of, 61–62
   International Comparison Program, 199
   international economic development, 112
   political insurance blog, 438
   political risk assessment tools, 438
World currency events, 1971–2010, 63–65
World Development Indicators (WDI), World Bank, 27
world economic outlook, IMF, 27
World portfolios, global vs., 330
World Trade Organization (WTO)
   antiglobalization movement and, 432
   tariff barriers, 429
   Web site, 112
World War I, international monetary system in, 60
World War II

international monetary system in, 60
modern Eurocurrency market born after, 7–8
WorldCom, 42
Worldwide taxation approach
overview of, 387–388
summary, 398
U.S. conundrum, 400–401
Writer (seller) of options
calls, 211–212
defined, 207
puts, 213–214

WTO. see World Trade Organization (WTO)

Y
Yanzhou (China) bids for Felix Resources (Australia),
463–469
Yaris, Toyota's European operating exposure, 316–317
Yen
Japanese intervention of 2010, 257–258
real effective exchange rate of, 179–180
Toyota's European operating exposure, 317
Yuan, 241, 243

Currencies of the World

Country	Currency	ISO-4217 Code	Symbol
Afghanistan	Afghan afghani	AFN	
Albania	Albanian lek	ALL	
Algeria	Algerian dinar	DZD	
American Samoa	see United States		
Andorra	see Spain and France		
Angola	Angolan kwanza	AOA	
Anguilla	East Caribbean dollar	XCD	EC$
Antigua and Barbuda	East Caribbean dollar	XCD	EC$
Argentina	Argentine peso	ARS	
Armenia	Armenian dram	AMD	
Aruba	Aruban florin	AWG	ƒ
Australia	Australian dollar	AUD	$
Austria	European euro	EUR	€
Azerbaijan	Azerbaijani manat	AZN	
Bahamas	Bahamian dollar	BSD	B$
Bahrain	Bahraini dinar	BHD	
Bangladesh	Bangladeshi taka	BDT	
Barbados	Barbadian dollar	BBD	Bds$
Belarus	Belarusian ruble	BYR	Br
Belgium	European euro	EUR	€
Belize	Belize dollar	BZD	BZ$
Benin	West African CFA franc	XOF	CFA
Bermuda	Bermudian dollar	BMD	BD$
Bhutan	Bhutanese ngultrum	BTN	Nu.
Bolivia	Bolivian boliviano	BOB	Bs.
Bosnia-Herzegovina	Bosnia and Herzegovina konvertibilna marka	BAM	KM
Botswana	Botswana pula	BWP	P
Brazil	Brazilian real	BRL	R$
British Indian Ocean Territory	see United Kingdom		
Brunei	Brunei dollar	BND	B$
Bulgaria	Bulgarian lev	BGN	
Burkina Faso	West African CFA franc	XOF	CFA
Burma	see Myanmar		
Burundi	Burundi franc	BIF	FBu
Cambodia	Cambodian riel	KHR	
Cameroon	Central African CFA franc	XAF	CFA
Canada	Canadian dollar	CAD	$
Canton and Enderbury Islands	see Kiribati		
Cape Verde	Cape Verdean escudo	CVE	Esc
Cayman Islands	Cayman Islands dollar	KYD	KY$
Central African Republic	Central African CFA franc	XAF	CFA
Chad	Central African CFA franc	XAF	CFA
Chile	Chilean peso	CLP	$

Country	Currency	ISO-4217 Code	Symbol
China	Chinese renminbi	CNY	¥
Christmas Island	see Australia		
Cocos (Keeling) Islands	see Australia		
Colombia	Colombian peso	COP	Col$
Comoros	Comorian franc	KMF	
Congo	Central African CFA franc	XAF	CFA
Congo, Democratic Republic	Congolese franc	CDF	F
Cook Islands	see New Zealand		
Costa Rica	Costa Rican colon	CRC	₡
Côte d'Ivoire	West African CFA franc	XOF	CFA
Croatia	Croatian kuna	HRK	kn
Cuba	Cuban peso	CUC	$
Cyprus	European euro	EUR	€
Czech Republic	Czech koruna	CZK	Kč
Denmark	Danish krone	DKK	Kr
Djibouti	Djiboutian franc	DJF	Fdj
Dominica	East Caribbean dollar	XCD	EC$
Dominican Republic	Dominican peso	DOP	RD$
Dronning Maud Land	see Norway		
East Timor	uses the U.S. Dollar		
Ecuador	uses the U.S. Dollar		
Egypt	Egyptian pound	EGP	£
El Salvador	uses the U.S. Dollar		
Equatorial Guinea	Central African CFA franc	GQE	CFA
Eritrea	Eritrean nakfa	ERN	Nfa
Estonia	Estonian kroon	EEK	KR
Ethiopia	Ethiopian birr	ETB	Br
Faeroe Islands (Føroyar)	see Denmark		
Falkland Islands	Falkland Islands pound	FKP	£
Fiji	Fijian dollar	FJD	F1$
Finland	European euro	EUR	€
France	European euro	EUR	€
French Guiana	see France		
French Polynesia	CFP franc	XPF	F
Gabon	Central African CFA franc	XAF	CFA
Gambia	Gambian dalasi	GMD	D
Georgia	Georgian lari	GEL	
Germany	European euro	EUR	€
Ghana	Ghanaian cedi	GHS	
Gibraltar	Gibraltar pound	GIP	£
Great Britain	see United Kingdom		
Greece	European euro	EUR	€
Greenland	see Denmark		

Country	Currency	ISO-4217 Code	Symbol
Grenada	East Caribbean dollar	XCD	EC$
Guadeloupe	*see* France		
Guam	*see* United States		
Guatemala	Guatemalan quetzal	GTQ	Q
Guernsey	*see* United Kingdom		
Guinea	Guinean franc	GNF	FG
Guinea-Bissau	West African CFA franc	XOF	CFA
Guyana	Guyanese dollar	GYD	GY$
Haiti	Haitian gourde	HTG	G
Heard and McDonald Islands	*see* Australia		
Honduras	Honduran lempira	HNL	L
Hong Kong	Hong Kong dollar	HKD	HK$
Hungary	Hungarian forint	HUF	Ft
Iceland	Icelandic króna	ISK	kr
India	Indian rupee	INR	₹
Indonesia	Indonesian rupiah	IDR	Rp
International Monetary Fund	Special Drawing Rights	XDR	SDR
Iran	Iranian rial	IRR	
Iraq	Iraqi dinar	IQD	
Ireland	European euro	EUR	€
Isle of Man	*see* United Kingdom		
Israel	Israeli new sheqel	ILS	
Italy	European euro	EUR	€
Ivory Coast	*see* Côte d'Ivoire		
Jamaica	Jamaican dollar	JMD	J$
Japan	Japanese yen	JPY	¥
Jersey	*see* United Kingdom		
Johnston Island	*see* United States		
Jordan	Jordanian dinar	JOD	
Kampuchea	*see* Cambodia		
Kazakhstan	Kazakhstani tenge	KZT	T
Kenya	Kenyan shilling	KES	KSh
Kiribati	*see* Australia		
Korea, North	North Korean won	KPW	W
Korea, South	South Korean won	KRW	W
Kuwait	Kuwaiti dinar	KWD	
Kyrgyzstan	Kyrgyzstani som	KGS	
Laos	Lao kip	LAK	KN
Latvia	Latvian lats	LVL	Ls
Lebanon	Lebanese lira	LBP	
Lesotho	Lesotho loti	LSL	M
Liberia	Liberian dollar	LRD	L$
Libya	Libyan dinar	LYD	LD

Country	Currency	ISO-4217 Code	Symbol
Liechtenstein	uses the Swiss Franc		
Lithuania	Lithuanian litas	LTL	Lt
Luxembourg	European euro	EUR	€
Macau	Macanese pataca	MOP	P
Macedonia (Former Yug. Rep.)	Macedonian denar	MKD	
Madagascar	Malagasy ariary	MGA	FMG
Malawi	Malawian kwacha	MWK	MK
Malaysia	Malaysian ringgit	MYR	RM
Maldives	Maldivian rufiyaa	MVR	Rf
Mali	West African CFA franc	XOF	CFA
Malta	European Euro	EUR	€
Martinique	*see* France		
Mauritania	Mauritanian ouguiya	MRO	UM
Mauritius	Mauritian rupee	MUR	Rs
Mayotte	*see* France		
Mexico	Mexican peso	MXN	$
Micronesia	*see* United States		
Midway Islands	*see* United States		
Moldova	Moldovan leu	MDL	
Monaco	*see* France		
Mongolia	Mongolian tugrik	MNT	₮
Montenegro	*see* Italy		
Montserrat	East Caribbean dollar	XCD	EC$
Morocco	Moroccan dirham	MAD	
Mozambique	Mozambican metical	MZM	MTn
Myanmar	Myanma kyat	MMK	K
Nauru	*see* Australia		
Namibia	Namibian dollar	NAD	N$
Nepal	Nepalese rupee	NPR	NRs
Netherlands	European euro	EUR	€
Netherlands Antilles	Netherlands Antillean gulden	ANG	NAf
New Caledonia	CFP franc	XPF	F
New Zealand	New Zealand dollar	NZD	NZ$
Nicaragua	Nicaraguan córdoba	NIO	C$
Niger	West African CFA franc	XOF	CFA
Nigeria	Nigerian naira	NGN	₦
Niue	*see* New Zealand		
Norfolk Island	*see* Australia		
Northern Mariana Islands	*see* United States		
Norway	Norwegian krone	NOK	kr
Oman	Omani rial	OMR	
Pakistan	Pakistani rupee	PKR	Rs.
Palau	*see* United States		

Currencies of the World (continued)

Country	Currency	ISO-4217 Code	Symbol
Panama	Panamanian balboa	PAB	B./
Panama Canal Zone	see United States		
Papua New Guinea	Papua New Guinean kina	PGK	K
Paraguay	Paraguayan guarani	PYG	
Peru	Peruvian nuevo sol	PEN	S/.
Philippines	Philippine peso	PHP	₱
Pitcairn Island	see New Zealand		
Poland	Polish zloty	PLN	
Portugal	European euro	EUR	€
Puerto Rico	see United States		
Qatar	Qatari riyal	QAR	QR
Reunion	see France		
Romania	Romanian leu	RON	L
Russia	Russian ruble	RUB	R
Rwanda	Rwandan franc	RWF	RF
Samoa (Western)	see Western Samoa		
Samoa (America)	see United States		
San Marino	see Italy		
São Tomé and Príncipe	São Tomé and Príncipe dobra	STD	Db
Saudi Arabia	Saudi riyal	SAR	SR
Sénégal	West African CFA franc	XOF	CFA
Serbia	Serbian dinar	RSD	din.
Seychelles	Seychellois rupee	SCR	SR
Sierra Leone	Sierra Leonean leone	SLL	Le
Singapore	Singapore dollar	SGD	S$
Slovakia	European Euro	EUR	€
Slovenia	European euro	EUR	€
Solomon Islands	Solomon Islands dollar	SBD	SI$
Somalia	Somali shilling	SOS	Sh.
South Africa	South African rand	ZAR	R
Spain	European euro	EUR	€
Sri Lanka	Sri Lankan rupee	LKR	Rs
St. Helena	Saint Helena pound	SHP	£
St. Kitts and Nevis	East Caribbean dollar	XCD	EC$
St. Lucia	East Caribbean dollar	XCD	EC$
St. Vincent and the Grenadines	East Caribbean dollar	XCD	EC$
Sudan	Sudanese pound	SDG	
Suriname	Surinamese dollar	SRD	$
Svalbard and Jan Mayen Islands	see Norway		

Country	Currency	ISO-4217 Code	Symbol
Swaziland	Swazi lilangeni	SZL	E
Sweden	Swedish krona	SEK	kr
Switzerland	Swiss franc	CHF	Fr.
Syria	Syrian pound	SYP	
Tahiti	see French Polynesia		
Taiwan	New Taiwan dollar	TWD	NT$
Tajikistan	Tajikistani somoni	TJS	
Tanzania	Tanzanian shilling	TZS	
Thailand	Thai baht	THB	฿
Timor-Leste	uses the U.S. dollar		
Togo	West African CFA franc	XOF	CFA
Trinidad and Tobago	Trinidad and Tobago dollar	TTD	TT$
Tunisia	Tunisian dinar	TND	DT
Turkey	Turkish new lira	TRY	YTL
Turkmenistan	Turkmen manat	TMM	m
Turks and Caicos Islands	see United States		
Tuvalu	see Australia		
Uganda	Ugandan shilling	UGX	USh
Ukraine	Ukrainian hryvnia	UAH	
United Arab Emirates	UAE dirham	AED	
United Kingdom	British pound	GBP	£
United States of America	United States dollar	USD	US$
Upper Volta	see Burkina Faso		
Uruguay	Uruguayan peso	UYU	$U
Uzbekistan	Uzbekistani som	UZS	
Vanuatu	Vanuatu vatu	VUV	VT
Vatican	see Italy		
Venezuela	Venezuelan bolivar	VEB	Bs
Vietnam	Vietnamese dong	VND	đ
Virgin Islands	see United States		
Wake Island	see United States		
Wallis and Futuna Islands	CFP franc	XPF	F
Western Sahara	see Spain, Mauritania, and Morocco		
Western Samoa	Samoan tala	WST	WS$
Yemen	Yemeni rial	YER	
Zaïre	see Congo, Democratic Republic		
Zambia	Zambian kwacha	ZMK	ZK
Zimbabwe	Zimbabwean dollar	ZWD	Z$